KT-556-299

or before

WITHDRAWN

Henley-in-Arden Site

00083407

Sport Promotion and Sales Management

Richard L. Irwin
Director, Bureau of Sport and Leisure Commerce
University of Memphis

William A. Sutton
Vice President Team Marketing
National Basketball Association

Professor
University of Massachusetts at Amherst

Larry M. McCarthy
Associate Professor
Seton Hall University

WARWICKSHIRE COLLEGE
LIBRARY
ROYAL LEAMINGTON SPA & MORETON MORRELL
WARWICK NEW ROAD, LEAMINGTON SPA CV32 5JE
Tel: Leamington Spa 318070

Human Kinetics

Library of Congress Cataloging-in-Publication Data

Irwin, Richard L., 1957-
    Sport promotion and sales management / Richard L. Irwin, William A. Sutton,
Laurence McCarthy.
        p. cm.
    Includes bibliographical references (p.) and index.
    ISBN 0-7360-0320-7
        1. Sports--Public relations. 2. Sports--Marketing. I. Sutton, William Anthony, 1951-
II. McCarthy, Laurence, 1954- III. Title.

    GV714 .I79 2002
    659.2'9796--dc21

                                                                        2001039845

ISBN: 0-7360-0320-7

Copyright © 2002 by Richard Irwin, William Sutton, and Laurence McCarthy

All rights reserved. Except for use in a review, the reproduction or utilization of this work in any form or by any electronic, mechanical, or other means, now known or hereafter invented, including xerography, photocopying, and recording, and in any information storage and retrieval system, is forbidden without the written permission of the publisher.

Acquisitions Editors: Linda Bump, Amy N. Pickering; **Developmental Editor:** Renee T. Thomas; **Assistant Editor:** Amanda S. Ewing; **Copyeditor:** Joyce Sexton; **Proofreader:** Myla D. Smith; **Indexer:** Daniel Connolly; **Permission Managers:** Dalene Reeder and Jaclyn Graham; **Graphic Designer:** Nancy Rasmus; **Graphic Artist:** Denise Lowry; **Photo Manager:** Leslie Woodrum; **Cover Designer:** Jack W. Davis; **Photographer (cover):** Joe Robbins Photography; **Photographers (interior):** William Sutton and Richard Irwin (except where otherwise noted). Photos on pages 65, 141, 158, 184, 286, 388, and 399 by Leslie Woodrum; **Art Managers:** Carl D. Johnson and Craig Newsom; **Illustrator:** Tom Roberts; **Printer:** Edwards

Printed in the United States of America   10   9   8   7   6   5   4   3   2   1

Human Kinetics
Web site: www.humankinetics.com

WARWICKSHIRE COLLEGE LIBRARY

659.29796 Irw

Acc No.
00083407 S

United States: Human Kinetics, P.O. Box 5076, Champaign, IL 61825-5076
800-747-4457
e-mail: humank@hkusa.com

Canada: Human Kinetics, 475 Devonshire Road Unit 100, Windsor, ON N8Y 2L5
800-465-7301 (in Canada only)
e-mail: orders@hkcanada.com

Europe: Human Kinetics, Units C2/C3 Wira Business Park, West Park Ring Road, Leeds LS16 6EB, United Kingdom
+44 (0) 113 278 1708
e-mail: hk@hkeurope.com

Australia: Human Kinetics, 57A Price Avenue, Lower Mitcham, South Australia 5062
08 8277 1555
e-mail: liahka@senet.com.au

New Zealand: Human Kinetics, P.O. Box 105-231, Auckland Central
09-523-3462
e-mail: hkp@ihug.co.nz

*This work is dedicated to
Babe, Buddy, and Bubba.*

CONTENTS

FOREWORD

"Oh, I love marketing. But you won't catch me selling. It's just not something I do."

17,325 failed potential major-minor league executives

At the risk of dating myself, (which is no longer necessary, now that I'm married), may I say that in my quarter-century of sports marketing of (usually unsuccessful) major and minor league baseball teams, I feel a certain twinge of cynicism whenever I hear the above words from a bright, eager interviewee for one of our sales and marketing positions.

But now, after scores of speeches and countless conversations, the venerable Sirs Richard Irwin, William Sutton, and Larry McCarthy have stepped forward from the murky, arcane world of academia and declared to all who would listen, "Methinks we should teach them to sell."

Somewhere along this very same timeline of modern life, *Death of a Salesman* main character Willy Loman has become an American euphemism for a failed life (please forgive me Arthur Miller, but it's true). *Sport Promotion and Sales Management* suggests just the opposite: alongside marketing and promotion, *sales* are to be celebrated, sought after, aspired to—for what good is the greatest idea in the world if no one *buys* it?

We all entered this big, blue marble with the capacity to think terrific ideas— fantastic, stupendous, colossal ideas. But let's face it, the true culmination of *promotion* comes with the knowledge that someone in control of a budget thought that your idea was worthy of spending money on—in short, the ultimate compliment. "You thought; I bought"—one of the most creative and successful human exchanges imaginable.

Let me give you an example of the process in action. In 1978, the Chicago White Sox were attempting to sign centerfielder Chester Lemon. As usual, we were short of cash. But good ol' Comiskey Park had a vacant football pressbox hanging over third base. The box had no plumbing and was accessible only via a dangerous catwalk. Even so, we thought, "Hmmm, we can make this *desirable*." Long story short, we began renting this space to companies (or groups of 40 individuals) for a fee (an *extravagant* fee) and we even threw in a couple cases of beer to boot. It seemed like a great idea. You've heard of "win-win," right? We called it the "Skybox." A little paint, some food, plus a hint of elitism (to my father's chagrin) and voila! It sold out in three days.

What were we most proud of? The idea? No. Ideas come a dime a dozen. The marketing and promotion? Actually, it was somewhat simplistic. The sale? You bet! Good sales *and* marketing—like the Tigris and Euphrates, like ham and eggs, like Heckle and Jeckle—belong in the same breath.

Finally, messieurs Sutton, Irwin, and McCarthy have taken the onus off of selling. One "learns" to hit the slider; one "learns" to play the harpsichord; one also "learns" to sell. Art forms, all.

Let us not, after 25 years in the world's greatest non-business, think we shouldn't read *Sport Promotion and Sales Management*. Our field has accepted the notion that we can teach newcomers promotion and marketing strategies. It is time to embrace that other all-important side of the coin, for the diamonds, courts, tracks, and fields are littered with veterans who "knew it all," who knew how to "market," but preferred not to "sell."

Read this book. Create, go forth, market, promote, and sell, sell, sell!

Michael Veeck

PREFACE

During the past decade, we have observed the emergence of sport as a unique and independent industry within the American economy. With a gross domestic sport product (GDSP) in excess of $150 billion, almost quadruple that reported in 1986, the marketplace for sport-related products and services has become extremely competitive. The competitive nature of the sport industry has resulted in greater attention directed toward the collaborative tasks of promotion and sales. Responding to the developments within the sport marketplace, graduate and undergraduate academic programs worldwide have expanded curriculum offerings to incorporate sales and promotion classes as a means of augmenting existing sport marketing course offerings.

This has created the need for an academic text that addresses the complexity of responsibilities that fall under the responsibility of sales and promotion. However, to date, limited resources have been made available to the instructor or the practitioner. In fact, no concentrated discussion of promotion and sales exists. Instead, the topic is typically given only a few chapters within a text on sport marketing. Moreover, few sport-related texts even tackle the topic of sales. Though it is a challenging subject to teach, quite often sales is a student's initial entryway into the industry, and as such should be a primary aspect of sport marketing curricula.

While many would argue that effective communication with principal constituents is a key characteristic common among sound organizational leaders, the same must be said of organizational leadership with the competitive marketplace: vigorous communication is a must. As with any product or service taken to market, the absence of well-informed, responsive consumers is devastating. Thus, there is a need for marketing communications—a.k.a. promotion and sales. While sport promotion and sales functions comprise an integrated series of communicative and trade functions performed by organizations and businesses (leagues, teams, events, equipment manufacturers, and distributors) that consider the sport industry to be their primary market, it is imperative also to consider the pursuit of promotion and sales through sport. Business, or even municipalities, have used the sport marketplace as a communications vehicle via team and/or event ownership, direct media buys, sponsorship agreements, naming rights deals, or athlete endorsement contracts.

Therefore, an adequate book on the topic of sport promotion and sales must address sport *as well as* its allied, non-sport businesses. For instance, both parties involved in sponsorship negotiations (sponsor and sponsee) should be able to find enlightening and helpful information in such a book. Sport logo licensors, as well as the product manufacturers and retailers seeking a license for logo application, should be able to find material of value to them. Furthermore, such a text should serve as a resource for the community sports commissioner recently awarded the bid to host a multisport international competition, as well as the event's governance board pursuing broadcast rights for the 21st century.

It has been our intent to organize *Sport Promotion and Sales Management* in such a manner. While it has a slight bias toward the decision makers of tomorrow and the academic programs charged with their preparation (by providing chapter objectives, discussion questions, and learning enrichment activities), this book should also appeal to current athletic administrators and coaches; league, team, and event managers as well as their sponsors, advertisers, broadcasters, and licensees; recreation specialists; and staff members constituting municipal sports commissioners, councils, and foundations. Furthermore, it is critically important that a thorough, contemporary discussion of sport promotion and sales address prevailing global issues confronting the sport promoter of the 21st century as well as the profound impact of multi-cultural considerations effecting marketing communication. *Sport Promotion and Sales Management*, in recognition of the emerging multi-cultural and global marketplace, has been organized in a manner which best illustrates these trends. For example, issues addressed within the text range from the design and execution of multi-lingual advertising and sales campaigns to the challenges confronting sport sponsorship managers in Eastern and Central Europe.

It has been our objective within this text not only to provide the theoretical underpinnings of sport promotion and sales, but also to illustrate their application with practical examples and testimonials from the sport marketplace. To this end, many examples have been drawn from several years of professional consultation with a variety of sport enterprises and their allied, non-sport business partners. To provide the reader with insightful cases and analogies for learning enhancement, we have also included perspectives from a variety of field professionals who are challenged on a daily basis by the issues addressed within *Sport Promotion and Sales Management* such as direct and indirect sales techniques, advertising, community relations, and customer service.

As indicated by industry research, the ability to *sell* is the primary characteristic sought by today's sport management professional. Through our own professional experiences, we know only too well how sales and promotion constantly interact. Therefore it is our hope and belief that aspiring—as well as practicing—sport business professionals will find *Sport Promotion and Sales Management* an absolute "must read."

ACKNOWLEDGMENTS

The foundation of this text is revealed in the sources of each chapter, as the terrific work conducted by others has provided us with a basis on which to structure this contribution to the body of literature about sport promotion. However, many others played a significant role in the completion of this enormous task and each warrants our sincere thanks and acknowledgment.

Special thanks go to Jay Gladden and Glenn Wong, both of the University of Massachusetts, for their chapter contributions. Our grateful appreciation is extended to the many professionals who willingly submitted Practitioner Perspectives, sharing their valuable insights into the application of constructs addressed in the text. These are Ray Artigue, Senior Vice President, Marketing Communications, Arizona Diamondbacks; Neal Bendeskey, Game Plan, Inc.; Bruce Bielenberg, Phoenix Coyotes; Ray Borelli, Director of Research, National Basketball Association; Brian Eaton, Media Relations and Marketing Director, U.S. Synchronized Swimming; Richard Ensor, Commissioner, Metro Atlantic Athletic Conference; John L. Johnson, Director, Promotions and Special Events, National Collegiate Athletic Association; Gordon Kaye, Senior Manager, Team Technology, Team Marketing and Business Operations, National Basketball Association; Joe Levy, Phoenix Coyotes; James T. Masteralexis, Esq.; Michael McCullough, Chief Marketing Officer, Miami Heat; Luis Salcedo, Director, Retail Licensing Non-Apparel, PGA TOUR; Michael Schetzel, Director of Sales, Boston Red Sox; Nobuhiro Tanaka, Chief Operating Officer, Axis Marketing; and, Maria Vugrin, Cone, Inc.

Furthermore, a large number of individuals aided us in the acquisition, organization, and development of materials contained in this book, including Nancy Altenburg, FedEx Sport and Event Marketing; Steve Ehrhart, Executive Director, AXA Liberty Bowl; Fred Jones, owner and producer Southern Heritage Classic; Dave Knopp and Angie Womack from the NCAA; Dermot Power, Commercial and Marketing Manager, Gaelic Athletic Association, Dublin, Ireland; Bernie Mullin, Randy Hersh, and Shelby Reed from the NBA; Vic Gregovits, Kathy Guy, and Raimie Zomiskey of the Pittsburgh Pirates; Shawn Hunter from the Phoenix Coyotes; Giorgio Gondolfi from Gigant del Basket (Italy); Rob Cornilles with Game Face Marketing; Steve Swetoha from the Jacksonville Jaguars; Janis Ori at the University of Massachusetts; Lisa and James Masteralexis with DiaMMond Sport Management; Dr. Lori Miller from Wichita State University; and Mike Veeck, of the the Goldklang Group.

We would also like to recognize the editorial team at Human Kinetics for their patience and persistence. Their efforts are greatly appreciated.

Finally, the authors acknowledge the many undergraduate and graduate students, as well as the sport professionals, with whom we have had the fortune to work. You have been our primary source of inspiration throughout this project.

Introduction to Sport Promotion and Sales

chapter objectives

1. Understand the dominant position occupied by promotion and sales within the context of sport marketing

2. Recognize the elements composing the contemporary sport promotion mix

3. Recognize a fully integrated marketing communications operation

4. Understand the basic concept of organizing a sport promotion and sales campaign

Pregame Introductions

A recent study conducted by *Street & Smith's SportsBusiness Journal* revealed that corporations spent approximately $45 billion during 1999 for sport-related promotions in the United States (table 1.1), accounting for 21% of the projected $213 billion sport industry.[1] It is relatively easy to envision how these figures are generated when corporations spend $400 million for an Olympic sponsorship and then several million more to leverage it, while companies advertising during the Super Bowl spend approximately $3 million for a prime 30-second commercial slot. Although many refer to these endeavors as sport marketing, it may be more accurate to refer to them as *sport promotion*.

Table 1.1   1999 Corporate Sport Promotion-Related Expenditures

Promotions	Cost
Broadcast, print, and signage advertising	$28.25 billion
Internet advertising	$295 million
Endorsements	$730 million
Media broadcast rights	$10.57 billion
Sponsorship	$5.09 billion
Total	**$44.935 billion**

Reprinted, by permission, from D. Broughton, J. Lee, and R. Nethery, 1999, "The question: how big is US sports industry?," *Street and Smiths Sports Business Journal* 2 (35):23-29.

Distinguishing Promotion From Marketing

Imperative to the study of promotion and sales is an accurate characterization of the prominent position each occupies within the context of its parent discipline, marketing. Far too often people use the terms marketing and promotion interchangeably, misstating the context of each. For instance, when students are asked to provide a one- or two-word definition of marketing, they often mention advertising, promotion, public relations, and sales. In addition to upsetting the marketing and promotion purist (such as the instructor), this type of misrepresentation dilutes the merits and function of each discipline.

Therefore, it is important to take a moment to distinguish promotion, the core subject of this text, from marketing. As revealed within the following definition, written by noted marketing scholar Philip Kotler, the discipline of marketing embraces a broad context of variables:

Marketing is the analysis, planning, implementing, and controlling of carefully formulated programs designed to bring about voluntary exchanges of values with target markets for the purpose of achieving organizational objectives. It relies heavily on designing the organization's offering in terms of the target markets' needs and desires, and on using effective pricing, communication, and distribution to inform, motivate, and service the markets.[2]

As this definition indicates, the central component of marketing is the organization's programs or offerings, which we typically refer to as the organization's **product offerings.** Also implied by the definition is a complete set of complementary marketing components (price, communication or promotion, and distribution or place) that compose what we commonly refer to as the traditional **marketing mix** (figure 1.1). While ideally all marketing mix components function equally, the product must be a primary concern; for without it the marketer has little to offer and nothing for which to set a price, launch a promotion, or establish a channel of distribution.

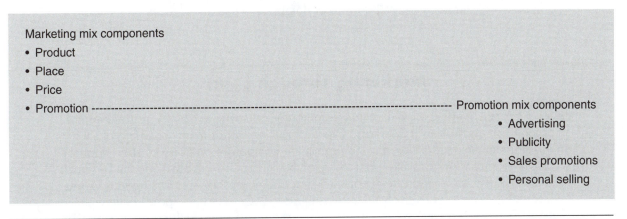

Marketing mix components
- Product
- Place
- Price
- Promotion -- Promotion mix components
  - Advertising
  - Publicity
  - Sales promotions
  - Personal selling

Figure 1.1 Traditional marketing and promotion mix.

However, academics and practitioners alike have struggled to form a consistent definition of sport marketing and, more important, to determine the role of promotion within this discipline. For instance, Mullin, Hardy, and Sutton provide the following definition of sport marketing:

Sport marketing consists of all activities designed to meet the needs and wants of sport consumers through exchange processes. Sport marketing has developed two major thrusts: the marketing of sport products and services directly to consumers of sport, and marketing of other consumer and industrial products or services through the use of sport promotions.[3]

More specifically, the first thrust relates to the broad spectrum of marketing efforts that sport-related businesses employ to fulfill consumer demand via their own products and services. These efforts include product or service development, testing, pricing, distribution, and ultimately communication, which is typically where the sport promotion specialist steps in. The second thrust is the expansive use of sport as a corporate communication platform. While this typically emerges in the form of a fully integrated corporate sport sponsorship involving advertising rights, product sampling, and tickets, a corporation may simply choose to reach consumers through an advertisement run during a broadcast or placed in a commemorative game program.

Often these companies employ one or more sport promotion specialists on staff or contract the services of a professional marketing agency.

Marketing of Sport

If the New York Liberty of the Women's National Basketball Association (WNBA) were interested in increasing attendance among those individuals currently attending fewer than five home games each season, the franchise would draft a marketing plan aimed at achieving this objective. Generally speaking, the plan would include market research to determine the product or products that would have the greatest appeal to this consumer group. If the research revealed that a large volume of the targeted consumer group would be interested in a ticket package consisting of five games, the franchise marketing staff would likely design a prototype of a ticket package containing five attractive home games and field test its marketability by soliciting consumer input. Once the marketing staff was confident that the ticket package (product) appropriately addressed consumer desires, a ticket distribution channel would be established. The final step would be to design the means of communicating or *promoting* the ticket plan's availability to the consuming public. Hopefully, the Liberty obtained names and addresses of all research respondents who initially expressed interest in a five-game ticket package. What a great database to use in a direct mail campaign!

Marketing Through Sport

Federal Express (FedEx), a multinational company primarily engaged in the overnight shipping business, houses a Sport and Event Marketing Department consisting of six full-time staff members responsible for managing the company's portfolio of sport sponsorships. The portfolio includes title sponsorship of the FedEx Orange Bowl and the FedEx St. Jude Golf Classic; series sponsorship of the FedEx Championship Auto Racing Team series; facility naming rights for FedEx Field in Washington, D.C.; a league sponsorship with the National Football League; and various presenting sponsorships with local sport organizations including the Southern Heritage Classic, AXA Liberty Bowl, and Memphis Redbirds of the Pacific Coast League. FedEx has also proposed a cutting-edge team sponsorship deal aimed at luring the National Basketball Association Vancouver Grizzlies to Memphis, Tennessee, home of FedEx's world headquarters. As a result of the deal, the first of its kind in major American professional sport, the team may become the Memphis Express and the players may don uniforms bearing the recognizable FedEx orange and purple colors. FedEx often calls on the services of one or more professional marketing agencies, typically those specializing in the field of sport marketing, for a variety of tasks ranging from market research to media placement. In all cases, FedEx endeavors to use sport as a vehicle for enhancing corporate communications with existing as well as prospective customers (figure 1.2).

Figure 1.2 On-field signage is just one aspect of Federal Express's corporate communications strategy.

A definition from Meenaghan and O'Sullivan echoes the notion that the term "sport marketing" has emerged to represent a diversified range of activities falling into two distinct categories: (1) the application of marketing to the promotion of particular sports, specific sport events, and specific venues; and (2) the very different business of using sport as a marketing tool to create and communicate brand values and associations that companies can use to market their own products and services.[4]

Furthermore, Shaaf defined sport marketing as "any sales or publicity-related activity associated with an organized sporting event, its personalities, or the celebrity lifestyle of its participants,"[5] while Wascovich writes that sport marketing is "the process of selling your product to a company and utilizing their resources to maximize your association."[6] Interestingly, each formulation provides a hint as to the significant role occupied by promotion, or marketing communication, within the context of sport, and more specifically, sport marketing. Sales, sponsorship relations, communication, and publicity are typically considered distinct responsibilities of promotion management. But what is *promotion?*

Kotler refers to promotion as a special form of communication, primarily dedicated to the task of persuasion.[7] Shimp and DeLozier identify promotion as a means of motivating customers to action.[8] According to Mullin and colleagues, promotion involves the vehicles through which the marketer conveys information about the product, place, and price, with concentration on "selling" the product.[9] Therefore, within the context of this text, sport promotion represents the deployment of a fully integrated set of communication exchanges intended to persuade consumers toward a favorable belief or action as a tactical component of the overall marketing campaign.

With this definition as a guide, promotional activity in this text consists of all means available to the sport organization for communicating and persuading defined consumer groups (figure 1.3). It therefore becomes necessary to organize these activities into a promotion mix.

Speeches	Demonstrations	Sponsorship	Autograph sessions
Endorsements	Athlete appearances	Community projects	Ticket brochures
Press conferences	Media guides	Interactive exhibits	Fireworks
Exhibitions	Beanie Babies	Advertisements	Hospitality tents
Web sites	National anthem singers	Films/Videos	
Infomercials	Contests	Sales presentations	

Figure 1.3 Sampling of promotional tools commonly used in sport.

Promotion Mix Composition

A review of several marketing communications or promotions textbooks, as well as those in the area of sport marketing, reveals that most scholars reduce this list of tools into four distinct components ultimately composing the traditional **promotion mix** (see figure 1.1). However, these four categories, as well as the labels (advertising, publicity, sales promotions, and personal selling), do not adequately address characteristics germane to sport and/or the sport industry. For instance, not all promotion activity—recruiting of an athlete by the coach, for example—is intended to result in a transactional sale. Additionally, labels for promotion mix categories such as sales promotion and personal sales fall short of fully describing methods used to attract an athlete to the sport program. Therefore, development of a unique promotion mix for the sport industry appears warranted.

Kotler's nonprofit promotion mix,[10] which consists of advertising, publicity, incentives, personal contact, and atmospherics, serves as a foundation for a sport promotion mix, as the categorical contents and labels more accurately reflect promotional tactics used within the sport industry. We add licensing, community relations, and sponsorship to fully represent a contemporary sport promotion mix that will serve as the topical structure for this text.

Sport Promotion Mix

The following brief description of the proposed sport promotion mix ingredients—advertising, publicity, personal contact, incentives, atmospherics, licensing, and sponsorship—should reveal how all components account for the broad spectrum of sport promotion and sales tactics while operating interdependently with one another to achieve the operational definition just provided.

Advertising

According to one widely accepted definition, advertising is any paid form of nonpersonal presentation of ideas, goods, or services by an identified sponsor. A variety of sources say approximately $15 billion is spent annually on sport-related advertising. This figure accounts for expenditures by sport organizations on advertising as well as expenditures by corporations using sport as an advertising vehicle. The figure includes the current $3 million price tag for a 30-second commercial during the National Football League (NFL) Super Bowl telecast, which annually attracts one of American television's largest viewing audiences.

Billboard advertising enables a sport organization to communicate to a targeted yet broad market.

As a paid form of nonpersonal communication, sport-related advertising may encompass facility signage or naming rights, broadcast commercials, direct mailings, outdoor signage including billboards and bus panels, use of athletes as product endorsers, and what we will refer to as manufactured media. Manufactured media includes all forms of print and electronic media purchased and perhaps produced by the sport organization for the purpose of promoting the core product or products. This may include broadcast advertorials, infomercials, or informational newspaper inserts as well as regular programming formats. While most professional sport leagues and member teams produce a number of print publications, the National Basketball Association (NBA) is the only North American professional sport league that has launched its own television network. In 1999, the NBA established nba.comtv, which provides subscribers with NBA programming (including games, news reports, and supplemental programming) 24 hours a day. Thus the NBA has assumed full responsibility for producing and delivering all content including live game broadcasts, pre- and postgame interviews, up-close-and-personal player profiles, and classic (old!) NBA games. All this makes nba.comtv the epitome of manufactured media.

Within various chapters of this book we discuss a number of key issues related to these advertising tactics, such as how the content can be produced, what should constitute the content, where the advertisement should be placed, and how the advertisement's effect on consumer behavior can be evaluated.

Publicity

Publicity is generally considered to be any nonpersonal stimulation of demand for a product, service, or business unit as a result of supplying commercially significant news to a published medium or obtaining favorable presentation on radio, television, or stage that was not directly paid for by the sponsor. Critical to this definition is the idea that publicity is "not paid for," which often implies that publicity is free or absent any cost.

The limited financial resources of many sport organizations have led to substantial reliance on publicity, often referred to as "free advertising" or "hype." However, generating press coverage, particularly that which is favorable, is far from free of cost. The task of stimulating coverage, known as press agentry, makes up a significant proportion of the job responsibilities of sports information directors or public relations specialists, ranging from supplying media representatives with the materials to build content to manufacturing the content themselves. Individuals occupying these positions within the sport promotion unit must possess specialized skills in orchestrating a sound communications campaign by shaping publicity to interest media decision-makers such as editors, producers, booking agents, beat writers, and even readers, viewers, and listeners. Staging press conferences, producing press releases, and accommodating press member requests (for player interviews, up-to-the-minute statistics, and credentials for the next major event) are but a few of the tasks conducted for the purpose of organizational publicity.

The merits of good publicity (third-party credibility) are revealed in the following three key qualities:

- Publicity appears to be news and not sponsored information, and thus to possess higher truthfulness. Unquestionably, this has led to the explosion of infomercials that are nothing more than carefully scripted advertising messages disguised as third party-produced correspondence.
- Publicity tends to catch off guard a recipient who may otherwise actively avoid advertising. As we will see, consumers are much more inclined to read articles and watch television shows than to read print advertisements and commercials.

- Publicity coming in the guise of a noteworthy event provides high potential for dramatization in that it arouses attention. Narrative content, whether delivered orally or in print, allows for significantly greater elaboration than advertising, which is often limited by time and scope.

Carefully crafted "news items" provide in-depth perspectives on a topic while simultaneously luring recipients' attention and informing them of the merits of consumption.

Perhaps most importantly, publicity carries an illusion of **third-party credibility.** That is, carrying the contents appears to be a choice made by an independent and objective media source based on the relevance or importance of the information to the audience.

Personal Contact

In this text we use the term "personal contact" in place of "personal selling," a common component within the traditional promotion mix. The aim is not to diminish the role of sales (undeniably the ultimate goal of all promotional activity); rather, the concept of personal contact, which incorporates the process of personal selling, better conveys the breadth of promotionally oriented personal interaction that transpires within the sport industry. Here, personal contact refers to any person-to-person communication involving an organizational representative and one or more current or prospective stakeholders that may result in achieving any number of vital promotional objectives, ranging from building organizational goodwill to generating sales.

Personal contact is critical to the success of an effective promotional campaign. Whereas advertising is very public, indiscriminate, and impersonal, personal contact in the form of personal selling can be tailored to the target customer's interests and needs. Perhaps most importantly, personal contact adds a human element to the relationship between the sport organization and the customer, providing a foundation for a two-way dialogue—virtually absent from other forms of marketing communication. As such, personal contact is necessary in order for the sport organization to address the notion of **relationship marketing,** a promotional construct developed and popularized during the 1990s, in response to emerging market conditions and practices.

Relationship marketing has been defined as an integrated effort to identify, maintain, and build a network of individual consumers and to continuously strengthen the network, for the mutual benefit of both sides, through interactive, individualized, and value-added *contacts* over a long period of time.[11] The ultimate objective of relationship marketing is to foster a bond with each customer that leads to three defined levels of patronage loyalty. The lowest level is financial bonding, in which loyalty is pursued through the provision of financial rewards such as frequent-usage programs, or database programs. Relationships developed at this level are weak and are vulnerable to competitor reaction or performance expectations (e.g., winning season).

Level two, social bonding, aims to build reciprocal links between service providers and customers; this demands personalization and customization of the relationship. Elevation to this level of relationship necessitates such actions as friendship-oriented behaviors on the part of the customer and service provider (e.g., addressing one another by name, showing familiarity with personal matters such as children) and expression of a genuine concern for each customer's personal needs.[12]

Progression to level three, or structural bonding, necessitates that each party assume an equal role in the relationship. This level is particularly relevant to sponsor-sponsee relations, as these relationships, based on resource allocation, are likely to be more equitable in the first place. The ascension through each level of relationship marketing (financial, social, and structural) is dependent on the sport organization's willingness to value the customer less as a transactional figure and more as an equal in a long-term relationship with personal interaction as the key form of communication. Research has indicated, we should note, that such relationship marketing tactics have proven to increase purchase as well as the likelihood of repurchase.[13]

According to Shani, relationship marketing contains the following six attributes,[14] each of which we discuss in this text:

- It is relationship driven.
- Communication is one on one.
- Interest is long term (customer lifetime value).
- It uses a large information base (transaction preferences, satisfaction indicators).
- Communication is interactive.
- Emphasis is on making the customer an equal partner.

Thus, *personal contact* embraces a broad set of interpersonal communication tactics that support the overall promotional agenda, including a rich blend of personal selling, customer servicing, and relationship building. In fact, Kotler contends that *personal contact* incorporates three fundamental subcomponents: selling, servicing, and monitoring.[15]

Selling All too frequently the concept of interpersonal promotion is captured under the limited guise of personal selling. However, the concept of personal selling, in its literal context, fails to embrace the full complement of interpersonal communication efforts afforded a sport organization. For instance, an athletic administrator's membership in a service club provides an ideal opportunity for interaction with civic leaders (political as well as corporate), enabling the administrator to "sell" the university athletic program; yet no direct transaction is derived or expected from the personal interaction. Hence, we need to further divide this component of *personal contact* into the subcategories of direct and indirect tactics.

Direct sales tactics range from scheduled sales meetings to suggestive sales procedures employed by the telemarketing team. In each case, the intent of the encounter is to "make the sale" or "close the deal." Indirect sales tactics range from public appearances such as civic group presentations to media interviews. In this case, the intent is to sell or even educate the audience on the merits of the product or service while not actually attempting to close a deal.

A host of organizational representatives regularly engage in personal contact, including administrators, coaches, players, ushers, parking lot attendants, and corporate sales hosts. All of these personnel create distinct stakeholder impressions based on the manner in which they dress, speak, and treat people they come in contact with. These impressions influence the stakeholders' perception of the organization, ultimately determining consumer action.

Servicing Of greatest importance to the promotional merits of personal contact service is the provider-to-patron interaction. Employee-to-customer interfacing represents a pivotal experience capable of building or destroying customer satisfaction and determining future behavioral patterns.[16] In fact, Normann tabbed the employee-customer interaction a "moment of truth."[17] It is speculated that during the course of a sporting event, one spectator may incur between 10 to 20 "moments of truth" (e.g., interaction with parking attendant, ticket seller, ticket taker, usher, souvenir program vendor, merchandise vendor, beverage vendor, food vendor). For many collegiate and professional sport programs this can easily accrue to over 6 million such interactions per season.

Unfortunately, many of the frontline contact personnel employed at sporting events are not under the direct supervision of the sport promoter. For instance, a collegiate basketball team playing in an off-campus arena typically does not oversee event staff members; this responsibility is usually outsourced by arena management. Still, in such cases, in order to maintain good tenant-patron relations, building management should ensure that event staff understand what is appropriate service behavior.

The task of delivering sound customer service does not have to be overwhelming. In fact, research demonstrates that what sport service recipients desire most is simple courtesy. This includes welcoming customers upon their arrival, recognizing and identifying regular customers, providing service without prolonged delay, and thanking the customer after a transaction. Perhaps most importantly, such actions result in sales increases as well as higher customer service ratings.[18]

Martin emphasizes that management must take an active role in the service delivery process, with continuous training for contact personnel. Sport organizations should instill in their *personal contact* personnel the following service-oriented guidelines:[19]

- *Be courteous.* Individuals opting to attend an event or participate in an activity have ultimately responded to a promotional invitation to do so. Thus the service provider assumes the role of host, necessitating that the consumer be treated as a guest. As already noted, the service-oriented personal behaviors that sport consumers most desire are simple acts of cordiality such as a greeting and a thank-you.

- *Be proactive.* Paying customers expect reactive service, but employee-initiated service exceeds typical customer expectations. Therefore, contact personnel should be encouraged to actively seek opportunities to serve customers as a means of providing exceptional service. For instance, an alert stadium usher should be expected to identify novice attendees encountering difficulty locating their seats. Stepping forward to assist provides a welcome service not only to the first-time patron but also to experienced patrons, sparing them delay and discomfort.

- *Establish rapport.* Consumers who can be classified as "regulars" should be known on an individual basis by personnel with whom they most frequently come into contact (e.g., ushers, front desk personnel, sales associates). According to Shani, this is necessary for ascension from relationship marketing level one (financial bonding) to relationship marketing level two (social bonding). To fully embrace advancement to level two, service providers should become familiar with the customer's favorite players and other personal information relevant to ensuring social bonding. Martin found that once rapport is established, customer encounters tend to be positive and criticisms constructive.[20]

- *Plan extra-transactional encounters.* The relationship between sport organization contact personnel, as true service providers, and consumers must not depend solely on transactional encounters, or those actions involving a direct exchange of money or product. All promotional unit employees should be trained and encouraged to initiate nontransactional encounters. An account representative might initiate a friendly conversation with a ticket plan holder, or a media promotions specialist might do so with a sports editor. Sport, in the form of sport-related conversation, has been identified as an important link in relationship marketing: sports talk is a vital element of the interpersonal strategy used to define the relationship. Individuals seeking to develop social and business relationships commonly discuss sport to establish shared values or define patterns of interaction.[21] And sport organization contact personnel have a plentiful supply of ready-made content for an extra-transactional discussion using team, event, facility, and/or player developments as key conversation catalysts.

Of critical importance, the quality of the service has a direct influence on satisfaction and future patronage, and the action of each correspondent (coach, usher, and/or commissioner) molds the organizational impression of each recipient. Consumers do not typically differentiate between service quality of an arena and of its tenant, so habitually bad service encountered at a facility (in the form of rude frontline personnel) that is home to a WNBA franchise, for instance, poses a serious threat to fan satisfaction and repeat attendance in spite of the team's on-court performance.

Monitoring   It is well known that people love to talk about sports. Sport is a common topic of conversation, whether in the form of an endorsement, an expression of admiration, or a complaint.[22] Many believe that of all the elements of the promotion mix, word of mouth is by far the most potent on a one-to-one basis.[23] No amount of advertising can compete with a trusted personal source's recommendation or criticism of a particular product or service. Furthermore, positive word of mouth results in the cost-efficient development of a future customer base. Given the high cost of attracting new customers, positive word of mouth among existing patrons is an extremely cost-efficient means of ensuring the maintenance of the current customer base, as well as development of a future customer base.[24] Therefore, the prudent sport promotion specialist will not only want to *monitor* the tone of public word-of-mouth communication but will also enlist an array of tactics aimed at generating conversation in support of other promotional tools.

Certainly word-of-mouth communication can be stimulated by any number of antics such as launching a controversial ad campaign, signing a high-profile player or coach (e.g., Dennis Rodman), or inviting Roseanne Barr to sing the national anthem. Yet fundamental to an effective positive word-of-mouth campaign is the prudent use of **opinion leaders** who, depending on the situation, may be internal or external to the organization.

Within each industry and marketplace exist target markets of individuals whose comments and actions influence the behavior of others. These individuals generally inherit high levels of *source credibility* based on previous exposure to the product or service (as in the case of an existing ticket plan holder), employment position (as in the case of a retail sales associate), or perceived expert knowledge (as in the case of an industry analyst). Such highly trusted opinion and behavior agents, often referred to as innovators or early adopters, typically seek technical *inside* information, from which they form their influential impressions. While striving to supply opinion agents external to the organization with appropriate forms of information, sport promotion specialists must also seek to proactively engage internal opinion agents in personal contact with the general consuming public. Examples of ways to accomplish this are booster club add-a-friend campaigns and team-style fundraising campaigns.

In an effort to diminish negative conversation regarding the franchise's venue relocation, the NBA's Cleveland Cavs launched a word-of-mouth promotion targeting season ticket holders, who, it was thought, would be the most adversely affected by the perceived inconveniences of the move. Hosting a series of preview parties for this important patron group was intended to alleviate feelings of abandonment; communicate first-hand personal experience of the ease of arena access; and demonstrate the abundance of available parking space, the security of the environment, and the beauty of the facility.[25]

Another effective means of minimizing negative word-of-mouth conversation is to encourage and consequently attempt to resolve customer complaints. Customers aware that management will attempt to resolve unsatisfactory encounters are considerably less inclined to spread negative conversation.

Complaint resolution   The Technical Assistance Research Programs Corporation of Washington, D.C., which publishes statistics on customer complaints, reports that for every customer complaint received, another 26 dissatisfied customers remain silent. Each of the 27 dissatisfied customers will tell 8 to 16 others about their experience, and 10% will tell more than 20 other potential customers. Thus, three complaints may translate into more than 1000 potential customers hearing about the poor service experience.[26] Equally important are the findings that a majority (often between 70% and 95%) of the complaining consumers continue patronizing after they have received a response to their complaint.[27] Therefore, it appears to make good *promotional* sense to actually create a complaint system that encourages patrons to tell organizational representatives about existing as well as potential problems. Martin offers the following recommendations for increasing complaints within the sport environment.[28]

• *Welcome all complaints.* Some complaints may be disguised as requests or suggestions for new products or services that in the long run may be of great benefit to the sport organization. Staff should be trained and encouraged to listen carefully and to view the interaction as an opportunity to improve service delivery.

• *Thank complainants.* Customers who complain obviously care. Their complaint enables the organization to retain the patronage of the complainant and perhaps several other customers while also creating a favorable promotion opportunity.

• *Admit guilt and apologize.* When fielding a complaint, the sport organization's representative should admit responsibility for the problem and offer an immediate apology for the inconvenience. Apologies that are regarded as sincere and specific and that provide clear explanations of all underlying factors have been found to be particularly effective in resolving customer conflict. In fact, listening in an apologetic manner has proven to appropriately pacify complainants.[29]

• *Remedy quickly.* The longer a complaint goes unresolved, the more difficult it becomes to retain the dissatisfied customer.

• *Follow up.* Be sure to communicate personally to the complainant what action has been taken regarding the charge. This necessitates that the complaint recipient collect information on each complainant ranging from phone number to seat location, for example.

As we will discuss throughout the text, it is important for the sport promotion specialist to embrace personal contact as a key component of the promotion mix. Interaction with consumers should serve not only as a means of soliciting and securing a sale but also as a means of stimulating critical two-way dialogue with all existing and potential stakeholders.

© Novastock/The Image Finders

Effective complaint resolution staff are some of the most important employees in any sport organization.

Incentives

Consumers are regularly bombarded with special offers from product and service promoters. These special offers, often referred to as sales promotions, are aimed at influencing buyer behavior and generally come in the form of reduced price deals, premium giveaways, contests, free samples, or any number of other add-ons.[30] However, the term "sales promotion" does not encompass all sporting "consumption experiences," particularly those not involving a direct transactional exchange. For example, the adventure sport athlete is attracted to participation by more intrinsic, self-actualizing features that are not easily categorized as sales promotions. In contrast, any number of special offers including discounted admission, celebrity appearances, and fireworks may be used to attract patrons to a game, while access to real-time statistics and engaging color commentary may serve to lure an electronic broadcast viewer.

Therefore "incentives," which for Kotler represent all emotional, social, psychological, functional, or financial conditions that serve to encourage some overt behavioral response,[31] are more appropriately suited for inclusion as a distinct component in the sport promotion mix. This vital component consists of all activities that act to stimulate quick buyer action.

Obviously, the identification of consumer motives is key to sport behavioral incentivization. Thus the sport promotion specialist inherits the demanding task of becoming acquainted with the fundamental motives, or behavioral incentives, for the full range of organizational stakeholders, from heavily discounted bleacher seat ticket buyers to million-dollar corporate partners.

Researchers have indicated, for example, that a corporation will be more inclined to accept a sponsorship proposal when there is an apparent match between the company's marketing objectives, or desired outcomes, and the sponsee's offerings; this means that sponsorship promoters must familiarize themselves with the potential sponsor's interest.[32] The same response pattern holds for all sport consumers and stakeholder groups; a direct link between desires and product offerings must exist in order for buyer reaction to occur. Therefore, it is imperative that the behavioral incentive (e.g., lower price, added convenience, better accessibility) link with the targeted stakeholder's behavioral motive.

Atmospherics

Atmospherics consist of all efforts initiated to design the place of purchase or consumption so as to create specific cognitive and/or emotional effects in buyers or consumers.[33] This includes all point-of-purchase communications such as displays, posters, signs, and a variety of in-store materials designed to influence choice *at* the point of purchase,[34] as well as venue-based features aimed at influencing choice *of* point of purchase. In other words the *place*, or point of distribution, becomes a key point of promotion. Perhaps nowhere is this more important than in the sport industry, where there is inordinate emphasis on the point of

© Michael Siluk

A point-of-purchase display might coax this consumer to buy some extra wheels for the in-line skates she's purchasing.

production because of the simultaneous production and consumption of the core product or service.[35] For example, during a professional indoor soccer game the core product, the game, is produced on the field at the very same time that it is consumed by the spectator in the seats. During this period of time the sport promotion specialist has little to no control over the consumer's interest in or satisfaction with the core product. Consequently, sport promotion experts such as John Spoelstra recommend that sport promotion specialists direct attention to environmental or atmospheric elements, which they have greater control over and which therefore lead to better assurance of patron satisfaction. Limitless examples exist as new venues spring up, bearing fan-appealing amenities such as retractable roofs, larger seating space, luxury boxes, wait service, hot tubs and swimming pools, picnic areas, and upscale dining facilities, not to mention the ongoing entertainment provided by dance teams, mascots, and spirit groups.

Bands are as much a part of the sport entertainment experience as are the competing teams.

In fact, one could argue that sport has been at the forefront in the creation of what Wolf refers to as the "entertainment economy," a market in which a majority of all consumer decisions are heavily influenced by the infusion of entertainment.[36] As purists continue to account for a smaller and smaller proportion of the typical sporting event audience, organizations have directed significantly more time and effort toward ensuring high patron entertainment value. Few professional, collegiate, or even high school football, basketball, or hockey games take place in the absence of choreographed performances by the dance team, band, cheerleaders, and team mascot, or skits and contests arranged by the sport promotion specialist. In fact, experts strongly recommend that because of the uncontrollable nature of sport's core product, sport promoters direct greater effort toward these controllable ingredients that compose the atmospherics component of the sport promotion mix.

Similar tactics have emerged within the retail and hospitality industries as sporting goods outlets and sports grills have instituted "sport atmospherics," piping in canned crowd noise, providing interactive activities, and installing arena-type lighting in an attempt to attract patrons seeking a sport-style entertainment environment.

Licensing

Licensing, as a part of an organization's branding strategy, has emerged as the fastest-growing component of the contemporary sport promotion mix, with consumer demand for sport-licensed products skyrocketing through the later years of the 20th century and flattening out only in 1999. Similar to a corporate brand, a recognizable symbol for a team, league, or event fosters consumer awareness and identity in the marketplace. These symbols have realized unparalleled commercial value as we find sport logos emblazoned on all sorts of consumer products ranging from caps and T-shirts to the Official Vidalia Onion Sauce of the 1996 Olympic Games.

The *Sporting Goods Manufacturers Association* estimates that sport-licensed product accounted for $11.2 billion in sales in 1998, amounting to more than a 100% increase from 1990.[37] In addition to the significant revenue generated, we need to consider the exposure created through the availability of these products in the marketplace. Bear in mind that when a consumer lays down $50 for a team-logoed sweatshirt, he is paying for the right to be a walking billboard for the franchise! Therefore, revenue production is only one of the benefits of operating an organizational licensing program, among these others:

• *Protection.* The fundamental benefit of an organizational licensing program is the legally defensible right granted to the sport property to exercise control over the use of any name, likeness, symbol, logo, or mark associated with the event, league, team, or athlete. Protection against unauthorized use of these marks, symbols, indicia, or logos—viewed as trademarks of the rights holder—is supplied by the Lanham Act, which carries severe penalties for violators.

• *Profitability.* In the form of a royalty, a fee is charged to a second party (licensee) for the right to use the name, likeness, symbols, logos, or marks of an event, league, team, or athlete. In the neighborhood of 7% to 8% of the wholesale price, these fees can net a professional franchise, national governing body, or major college athletic department more than $1 million annually from retail merchandise licensing alone.

• *Promotion.* Licensing partnerships with the corporate and retail industry have enabled sport promotion specialists to stimulate awareness, interest, and enthusiasm within the consumer marketplace. For example, within one week of being awarded an NFL expansion franchise, the Carolina Panthers sold 1 million pieces of merchandise, thereby establishing a powerful presence throughout the community.[38] While the team had no players, no coach, and no stadium, it had a logo! Furthermore, sport promotion specialists seeking to enhance core property awareness are wise to try to strategically place logoed product in high-density viewing areas such as movies, television shows, mail order catalogs, and fashion shows, as well as assisting with management of the licensed product distribution channel including retail-oriented promotions and operations.

Sponsorship

Sponsorship may be considered the newest entry into the contemporary sport promotion mix. Scholars and practitioners have advocated that sponsorship deserves a spot within the promotion mix because of the integrative promotional benefits yet distinctive features it possesses.[39] In fact, one could argue that a fully integrated sponsorship assumes the role of a totally independent promotion mix containing the following ingredients: arena signage (advertising); event, team, or facility naming rights (publicity); hospitality (personal contact and atmospherics); retail promotional sales (incentives); and event, team, or league co-branding (licensing).

The origins of sport sponsorship may well be traced back to the Roman era, when charioteers adorned themselves in the colors of local merchants in return for operating expenses. The rebirth of the Olympic Games and the subsequent growth in sponsorship of the Games by non-sport companies such as Kodak and Coca-Cola through the 20th century suggested that sport had the potential to speak a universal language and capture the interest of people across all political and cultural boundaries. Corporate marketers, seeking to associate with the values available in the world of sport, viewed sport sponsorship as the appropriate vehicle for developing brand image and capturing the consumer loyalty exhibited among sport fans.[40]

Apparently, corporate marketing decision-makers worldwide agree that sponsorship should occupy a dominant position within the promotion mix, as sponsorship expenditures surpass those for sales promotions and advertising (table 1.2). According to estimates generated by International Events Group, expenditures by corporations for sport sponsorship, which account for approximately two-thirds of all sponsorship spending, grew at an annual rate of 25% during the 1990s.[41] Paralleling the growth has been a shift in anticipated outcomes. Research conducted during the early stages of sport sponsorship revealed that sponsors were more willing to entertain sponsorship as a philanthropic endeavor, with many interested in enhancing the company image and further extending company or brand awareness. More current research has demonstrated that corporate sport sponsors aspire to achieve more measurable outcomes from their sponsorship arrangements in the form of increased sales and market share.[42]

Table 1.2   Sponsorship Growth Compared to Advertising and Sales Promotion

Year	Advertising	Sales promotion	Sponsorship
1999	5.5%	6.7%	12%
1998	7.1%	4.2%	15%
1997	6.6%	3.3%	9%
1996	7.6%	4.6%	15%
1995	7.7%	4.6%	11%

Data from the International Events Group, Inc. (IEG), 1999.

As we discuss later in the text, sport organizations are encouraged to similarly embrace the virtues of sponsorship as a promotional device, as opposed to using sponsorship only as a promotional platform. The limited volume of sponsorship activity among sport organizations, with sport businesses assuming the role of sponsor, appears to closely resemble the roots of corporate sponsorship with philanthropy and image enhancement as the primary charges. For instance, most, if not all, major North American professional sport leagues and member franchises engage in a variety of community relations projects, often donating time, cash, products, and services (to be addressed in chapter 10). As a form of sponsorship these charitable projects serve to involve the league, team, and its players in the franchise community, thereby enhancing the property's image through goodwill gestures.

Integrated Promotional Agendas

"Integrated marketing communication is what clients are looking for," stated Bill Wreaks of KDM International. "Look at ESPN. They have cable TV, a magazine, and restaurants. It's hard for an advertiser who's trying to reach that demographic to ignore them."[43]

The notion of **integrated marketing communication** (IMC), a synergistic approach to preparing and executing organizational promotion schemes, emerged in response to the need for advancing marketing communications beyond advertising and establishing a link between all communication tactics. While debating the roots or the catalyst of IMC is of minimal interest, the application of its basic principles is of critical value given the context of this book, sport promotion and sales.

Adaptation of the process to the sport setting is rather sensible, as this demands that interrelated organizational units such as sales, customer service, and public relations work in harmony to maximize promotional agenda effectiveness. Unfortunately, this occurs rarely, particularly in collegiate athletic departments, where there may be little interaction between the sports information office and the marketing staff.

Duncan and Caywood constructed an IMC framework involving multiple levels of promotional integration. Of considerable significance is the "integrated" nature of this model from both a managerial and a logistical perspective with the greatest emphasis placed on the integration of those involved in the communication process. From a managerial point of view, the integration of specialized units within the organization enables the sport promotion specialist to establish a sound internal communication channel—critical to ensuring support—as well as properly delegated responsibility. The result is a better sense of control over the implementation of the campaign. Logistically, the flow of information, as well as task performance, is controlled systematically from internal to external sources. In fact, while each stage may build on the previous one, several stages can operate independently but simultaneously with one another, enhancing the integrative nature of the process. There are seven stages of promotional integration:[44]

- Awareness
- Image integration
- Functional integration
- Coordinated integration
- Consumer-based integration
- Stakeholder-based integration
- Relationship management integration

• *Awareness.* Serving as the basis of virtually all models of communication as well as consumer or buyer behavior, management justifies the need to generate both internal and external awareness. Once it is determined that a need exists for some type of promotional correspondence, objectives, strategies, and tactics, aimed at enhancing dialogue with existing or potential customers and stakeholders, are set.

• *Image integration.* Stage 2 integration occurs when management recognizes the need for a consistent message theme and style. Consistency in message tone, tag line, logo presentation, and production quality across all media as well as personal contact action is imperative for effective organizational image transfer. This stage of integration sets the tone for building collaborative alliances among internal specialty areas such as marketing, public relations, and sales, as all departments should act to ensure that marketing communication uniformity is achieved.

• *Functional integration.* At this stage, the actual collaborative effort called for in Stage 2 is activated. Within large organizations, a cross-functional team of unit representatives may be assigned to ensure harmonious promotional execution throughout all internal constituencies.

• *Coordinated integration.* Dependent on the objective established in Stage 1, a specialty area (e.g., marketing, public relations, or sales) is assigned to take the project lead. For instance, should the primary objective be to increase business, sales will more than likely assume project leadership, whereas interest in elevating general public awareness would lead to principal responsibility on the part of the public relations or advertising unit.

• *Consumer-based integration.* At this stage, communication is initiated with messages reaching only the fully *targeted* audience. Emphasis is on the tactical execution of the plan, with specific communication media procured, personal interaction maximized, and performance indicators established. A consumer database or profiling system should be formulated to provide management a means of tracking, rewarding, and potentially predicting consumer behavior. This is the time to launch efforts that target customer loyalty.

• *Stakeholder-based integration.* Beyond the direct customer are numerous stakeholder groups that have an interest in or may be affected by the outcome of the firm's success or failure. Sport organization stakeholder groups may include staff, players, the community, government officials, the press, vendors, and suppliers, to name a few. The process demands that stakeholder groups be embraced as well as monitored for reaction to organizational developments.

• *Relationship management integration.* The culmination of a truly effective integrated communications campaign is the emergence of relationships internal and external to the organization. An integrated communications program can assist the company, employees, vendors, customers, and others in meeting the goals of continuous improvement. As previously discussed, it is speculated that a structural relationship is targeted among all members of valued consumer groups.

Planning and Managing the Campaign

The IMC model must be further adapted to fit the context of a sport property promotional campaign. Originating from an analytical process (assessment) that may reveal declining attendance patterns or emerging opportunities in the local marketplace, all steps of the campaign should exhibit the same integration as the IMC model.

Of critical concern is the idea of "promoting the promotion," or a total promotion mix integration whereby all promotional elements are simultaneously activated, producing a consistent, yet broad, sweeping message. Research has demonstrated that integrated promotional campaigns are much more effective for information recall, use, and processing than those relying on single promotion formats (e.g., print advertising).[45]

The emergence of Web-based communication highlights the significance of IMC. Virtually no advertiser today omits the address of its Web site from print or electronic ad copy. Nike's ad for the Air Cross Trainer II featuring American sprinter Marion Jones, which prompted viewers to visit the company's Web site (**whatever.nike.com**) and choose the ad's ending, may best illustrate the value of "hybrid" or "integrated" advertising. The addition of a URL to ad copy creates the opportunity for an organization to lure a prospective consumer to its Web site. The very act of visiting the Web site suggests that the consumer has an interest in the Nike product. Once the consumer is at Nike's well-designed site, the company has the opportunity to present a Pandora's box of opportunity.

Using a template established by Coca-Cola for its sport sponsorship activities, all sport promotions can be organized in the following fashion:[46]

assessment → alignment → design → activation → measurement

Stage 1 is *assessment.* At the outset of any promotional or communication agenda, it is of great value to conduct research to identify key factors that will influence the scope of the project. While a review of the overall corporate marketing plan is warranted, Stage 1 is not intended to resemble in magnitude a marketing plan's situation analysis, in which a variety of environmental conditions are explored in order to reveal how each might affect the company's business operations. Instead, the promotional campaign assessment is geared specifically toward identifying factors that will influence the production and delivery of the property's communications.

This initial step should include both internal and external analyses as well as historical and futuristic assessments.

Internally, an organization must assess such issues as potential budgetary constraints, available resources (in-house production capabilities), the targeted product's unique selling attributes, and the degree of consumer awareness and loyalty. Externally, an assessment should include a review of the competition's promotional activities, the status of existing as well as potential media opportunities, potential legal issues, and emerging marketplace opportunities (open sponsorships).

The historical analysis should include a review of past campaigns to identify successes as well as failures. There is certainly no reason to reinvent the wheel, but there is an opportunity to learn from past mistakes. The futuristic or trend analysis enables the sport promotion unit to identify cutting-edge promotional concepts as well as consumer demands. While Web-based communication, virtual advertising, and naming rights opportunities seem passé today, not so long ago they were classified as "futuristic" promotional platforms.

Stage 2 is *alignment*. Critical to the campaign's success is an appropriate match between the sources involved in disseminating the message. For instance, an appropriate image match should be apparent between the sport and the sponsor, the endorser and the product, and the team and its advertising content. Additionally, Stage 2 mandates alignment of all organizational communication units according to Duncan and Caywood's IMC model. Specific tasks are assigned to units within the communications channel.

Stage 3 is *design*. This stage entails composing a game plan that will provide the campaign with direction, specific objectives, and content considerations. Typically drawn from the assessment conducted in Stage 1, the strategy and subsequent tactics are determined by inputs from a variety of sources, internal as well as external to the organization. At this stage, outside promotional agencies are tapped and their creative abilities used for conceptual development.

Reflecting an IMC philosophy, this stage involves tactical development that necessitates blending all promotional elements together around a central creative component or theme. This is what we call "promoting the promotion." Coca-Cola, for instance, creates communications tactics such as retail promotions and media and interactive activities that enhance the central theme, often a sport sponsorship. Ideally, the promoter can generate supplemental promotional content *from* promotional activity, as a successful promotion should serve as a catalyst for additional communication and thereby maximize cost-effectiveness. For example, each year the creative advertisements that run during the Super Bowl generate significant press coverage on their own. In fact, the week after the game, *USA Today* traditionally runs a section in which these ads are rated. It seems of little or no use to run a great sales promotion, advertisement, or community relations campaign if no one knows about it. Therefore, it is at this stage that the publicity or media relations campaign is prepped.

Stage 4 is *activation*. It's show time! All systems are go. It is finally time to execute the campaign. Proper preparation during Stages 1 through 4 will ensure successful implementation. In order to maintain proper control over the campaign, the sport promotion specialist should consider establishing a timetable and checklist of key campaign milestones such as production deadlines and release dates, and also maintain a list of contacts influential to the campaign. This list may include staff members as well as members of the press, corporate sponsor officials, promotional agency representatives, and others.

Problems are sure to arise, however, particularly in relation to elements that are dependent on resources external to the organization. As in any planning process, it is important to conduct a series of "what ifs" before campaign launch, asking questions such as "What if they don't respond?" Such proactive efforts will minimize challenges as they arise.

Therefore, in addition to the primary campaign game plan, the sport promotion specialist should have a contingency plan, based on the "What ifs," prepared and ready for activation. Before activating a ticket renewal campaign, for example, she should assemble fellow staffers to brainstorm on possible problems that could arise during the course of the campaign. For instance, it is very likely that not all ticket plan holders will respond by the predetermined renewal deadline. Therefore, although it is advisable to mail renewal forms to plan holders as an expedient means of ensuring that they all get the renewal notice, the sales staff should be prepared to telephone all ticket plan holders who do not respond within approximately two weeks after the launch of the campaign. Further follow-up via mail and phone can be planned as necessary. Activation of this type of contingency planning process will help the sport promotion specialist achieve higher levels of promotional effectiveness while also establishing direct interaction with the consumer.

Stage 5 is *measurement*. Often absent from campaigns, this step may be the most important of all. Failure to appropriately assess the performance of each campaign component (formative evaluation), as well as the entire campaign (summative evaluation), generally results in inaccurate conclusions about the effectiveness of various components. Formative evaluation may include recording the number of Web site hits or season ticket brochures mailed, whereas summative performance indicators may include tracking incremental sales generated from accounts of guests entertained at a sponsored event, or conducting consumer surveys to gauge favorable changes in awareness and attitude levels.

A somewhat daunting task, measuring the effectiveness of the campaign and its many components may be best outsourced to an objective, neutral party specializing in promotional assessment. For instance, Joyce Julius & Associates has a long-standing track record in measuring exposure generated through corporate sport sponsorship. Sponsorship managers are well advised to consider utilizing an agency's experience and talent in order to obtain effective and accurate results. It is possible, though, to collect some results via personal correspondence or internally administered surveys that can be quickly tabulated and analyzed by management. An abundance of resources is available to the sport promotion specialist seeking measurement assistance. The results of the measurement process should feed directly into the assessment stage and thereby initiate a new plan. The following Practitioner's Perspective provides insight on how a professional sport franchise organizes as well as executes a promotion and sales campaign.

PRACTITIONER'S PERSPECTIVE

The Arizona Diamondbacks: Set to Strike in the Nation's Most Competitive Sports Marketplace
by Ray Artigue, Senior Vice President, Marketing Communication for the Arizona Diamondbacks

The Promotional Challenge

The primary objective of this first-ever Diamondbacks promotion campaign was to create awareness and sustain excitement for the new franchise for more than two years before the first game would be played. There were a multitude of communication strategies employed in the early promotion effort:

- Sell the excitement of major league baseball, its history, and the superstar athletes.
- Position the Diamondbacks as a young, exciting, and promising MLB team.
- Include the Diamondbacks' front office personnel in appropriate communications so as to build their credibility.
- Utilize a combination of mass and targeted communication channels to reach the target audience.
- Leverage cross-promotional opportunities with corporate sponsors, media partners, community partners, and other local sports teams.

As with any promotion and sales campaign, there were budgetary parameters to respect and adhere to. Finite promotion dollars and a lengthy selling cycle (or product introductory period) suggested that a phased campaign would be most appropriate. Utilizing the aforementioned strategies, the campaign approach was to use communication tactics in a stair-step fashion, beginning with grassroots, less expensive tactics and growing into a more sophisticated campaign.

During the first phase of the campaign, communication tactics focused heavily on cross-promotional opportunities, public relations/publicity, direct marketing, heavy merchandising, and the creation and distribution of sales collateral materials. Paid media were utilized at very base levels and only in a way that expected immediate and measurable results.

Another staple in the early phase of the team's promotional effort was direct mail. Ultimately, hundreds of thousands of letters were sent to pre-qualified customers who had shown themselves in some way to be interested in baseball's coming to the marketplace. Finally, an integral part of phase one of the campaign was the generation of publicity. Although there were no players to publicize, numerous publicity opportunities did exist. And, unlike certain other new product introductions, the media were more than eager to grab at almost any story angle presented to them.

The Sales Strategy

Throughout the first phase of the campaign and leading up to opening day, a hands-on sales approach was initiated. A great deal of effort went into assembling a talented sales staff that possessed baseball knowledge, personality and professionalism, and salesmanship. Keeping in mind that the sales team was responsible for more than just season tickets, an effective sales program was needed to assist them in selling diverse sponsorship packages as well as the 66 luxury suites.

The strategic approach became the creation of a baseball "closing room" that brought some of the look and feel of Bank One Ballpark into being years before its actual completion. This 3000-square-foot area was on the 11th floor of a downtown high-rise building that overlooked the Bank One Ballpark construction site. Inside, the room was adorned with baseball regalia, a mini-ballpark suite, the project model, seating configuration (as well as the actual ballpark seats), and a fan Wall of Fame. The final feature of the room was the motorized undraping of the window that overlooked the ballpark and gave fans a terrific aerial view of the construction process. This unique salesroom and the unique experience it gave customers provided the Diamondbacks' sales staff an enviable platform to sell tickets, sponsorship, television and radio packages, and suites throughout the two years prior to the opening season.

The Advertising Campaign

To generate fan interest, a two-phase advertising campaign was implemented over the two-and-a-half years leading up to opening day. Phase one provided the ongoing awareness in sales support for the franchise while phase two was a louder "love-your-team" excitement generator.

(continued)

(continued)   Print and outdoor mediums were utilized in an attempt to portray the targeted demographic. The creative strategy gave birth to the Two Guys campaign, as a couple of die-hard fans became the representative zealots for real-life baseball fans who just couldn't wait for opening day (figure 1.4). This approach was born out of necessity, as there weren't players or a ballpark to feature in advertising. The positioning line for the campaign was simple yet memorable: It's Gonna Be Big!

Figure 1.4   This advertisement helped to create fan anticipation and create a mentality that nothing could be more exciting than the Diamondbacks' inaugural season.

As the advertising campaign moved from phase one to phase two, it brought radio and television into the media mix and ultimately all media were incorporated to combine for a total market blitz leading up to spring training in 1998 and ultimately to opening day.

Ultimately, the Arizona Diamondbacks spent $850,000 to implement their two-and-a-half year marketing campaign, but received far more in media value due to trade-out agreements with several media outlets. The question as to whether this investment would be prudent would be answered in the final ticket sales results.

Rationale for the Study of Sport Promotion and Sales

As evidenced in the definitions given previously, a critical function of marketing is to provide products that satisfy the inherent needs of the marketplace. Given this, there may appear to be no need for another sport marketing text, as a number of good books on the subject are available in libraries, classrooms, and offices worldwide. While these offerings, virtually nonexistent 10 years ago, have advanced the understanding and application of marketing principles as they relate to sport, the following list of key factors suggests the need for a defined course of study and a supporting text in sport promotion and sales.

- *Communication is the foundation of all buyer behavior.* All buyer/user behavior models begin with, or are heavily influenced by, promotionally oriented variables (e.g., awareness, attention, alternative evaluation). Thus, there is a need for more emphasis on educating future sport promoters about how to communicate with prospective buyers and users.

- *Critical sport marketer duties are promotion or sales related.* The dominant role occupied by promotion within the realm of sport marketing management is evidenced by research revealing that a majority of the key skills demanded of today's sport marketer relate directly to promotionally oriented tasks (figure 1.5). Unfortunately, fewer than 15% of the sport marketing professionals responding to this survey indicated academic preparation as their competency source. On-the-job training and self-study were identified as the most popular means of obtaining competency. Thus, the researchers strongly suggest that in order for the sport marketing academic curricula to be effective it must be expanded, incorporating additional courses in sport promotion that address all 20 competencies listed.[47]

• *Not everyone can (needs to) be a winner.* "Selling sports solely on the win-loss column is very risky. More teams are destined to lose than win. My philosophy has been to sell a night of entertainment. I can control the quality of the concessions, the cleanliness of the arena or stadium and the total ambiance." So said Pat Williams, then the general manager and now senior vice president of the Orlando Magic basketball team.[48] Winning has in fact been found to be a significant predictor of initial ticket, advertising, and sponsorship sales among professional sport teams, while customer interaction through personal contact has been found to better predict renewals.[49] So perhaps we can say that although winning can attract consumers, sound service is required to retain them. And, remember, few teams win on a regular basis, so team promotional platforms must be constructed on factors other than performance. Furthermore, as reported by Gladden and Milne, brand equity contributes more to the decision to purchase National Hockey League (NHL) and Major League Baseball (MLB) team-logoed merchandise than team winning percentage.[50] This highlights the need for team marketing managers to focus more toward brand management tactics that are grounded in promotional practices such as generating awareness, enhancing perception, and strengthening associations.

• *Sales and service are lacking in sport marketing preparation and practice.* Apparently, industry specialists have detected a void in the preparation of sport marketing professionals. Matt Pietsch, vice president of General Sports and Entertainment, offers this insight: "I talk to sports leagues and sports teams all the time and the question I hear most is when are these sports management programs going to teach these students how to sell."[51] Furthermore, according to Alex Martens of RDV Sports, owner of the NBA's Orlando Magic, focus group discussions involving the team's

1. **Establish a positive image of your sporting organization**
2. **Achieve sponsors' promotional goals**
3. **Stimulate ticket sales**
4. **Maximize media exposure for events, athletes, sponsors**
5. **Acquire sponsors through personal contacts**
6. **Maintain good relations with community, authorities, partners**
7. **Acquire sponsors through formal presentation**
8. **Develop special promotions**
9. Improve budget construction of your sport marketing unit
10. **Negotiate promotional contracts**
11. Evaluate sport marketing opportunities and performance
12. Design and coordinate content of events
13. **Coordinate press coverage of events**
14. **Create contracts**
15. **Provide corporate hospitality at events**
16. **Build public image and awareness of athletes**
17. Schedule events and facilities
18. Establish event safety factors
19. **Build rapport with editors, reporters, other media reps**
20. **Buy and resell media rights**

Figure 1.5 Sport marketing competencies deemed most important by sport marketing professionals. Those in bold are considered promotional tasks.

Adapted, by permission, from P. Smolianov and D. Shilbury, 1996, "An Investigation of sport marketing competencies," *Sport Marketing Quarterly* 5 (4):27-36.

promotion staff revealed that a majority of sport management academic program graduates had not had any course work or preparation relating to sales. Unfortunately, sales—a task fundamental to the sport field—is absent from the curriculum of many preparatory programs. Additionally, serious deficiencies appear to exist among professional sports when they are challenged to adopt critical elements of the marketing communications process. In an experiment, letters were sent to 112 major league teams requesting ticket information and team schedules on behalf of respondents planning to relocate to the recipient team's home market. In six weeks, only 58% of the teams had responded to the inquiry—and some had used what the respondents thought appeared to be crayon to label return mailings.[52]

It appears that the rapid emergence of the field has fostered an overemphasis on sport marketing, diluting the essential tasks associated with promotions, communication, and sales. Thus it is with these issues in mind that this book has been prepared. As the need to tailor course work to address this critical industry need emerges, we hope that this text will provide a satisfactory foundation for discussion, comprehension, and application.

Postgame Wrap-Up

This introductory chapter has examined fundamental issues related to sport promotion and sales management, addressing, in particular, the dominant role occupied by promotion within the field of sport. Although promotion is but one component of the marketing mix, we make the case that it dominates marketing-related activity within the broad sport industry as sport businesses actively engage in the promotion of their products and services while non-sport businesses use sport as a viable means of promoting their products and services.

A proposed sport promotion mix, consisting of advertising, publicity, personal contact, incentives, atmospherics, licensing, and sponsorship, provides the framework for the remainder of the text. Although in this book we identify and elaborate on each of these components separately, no component is expected to operate in isolation. Thus we place a major focus on a fully integrated marketing communication campaign that demands coordination among various organizational units and synergistic deployment of various promotion mix ingredients.

In addition, the chapter has presented a five-stage template for organizing the promotion campaign, addressing the key elements of assessment, alignment, design, activation, and measurement. It is important to note that both the first and last stages of the template emphasize the evaluative aspect of effective promotion. It is therefore incumbent on sport promotion specialists to subject promotion campaigns to extensive pre- and postcampaign appraisals in an effort to ensure effectual marketing communication.

Lastly, we have presented the case that the material within this text needs to be more fully incorporated into the preparation of aspiring sport promotion specialists. Although studies involving sport industry professionals have revealed that critical sport management and marketing duties relate primarily to promotion and sales, such content has been absent from the preparatory programs of sport marketing and promotion professionals.

Discussion Items

1. What is meant by promoting the promotion?
2. How does the contemporary sport promotion mix differ from the traditional promotion mix? Why is a unique mix appropriate?

3. What is the difference between marketing and promotion?

4. What marketplace indicators suggest that, within the sport industry, the marketing mix component of promotion occupies an uncustomarily dominant role?

5. How can sport marketer preparatory programs more effectively address the content of promotion and sales management?

Learning Enrichment Activities

1. Conduct interviews with sport promotion specialists representing different sport organizations on the implementation of Duncan and Caywood's IMC model. Specifically ask the respondent questions relating to each stage and to the process that her sport organization employs to ensure promotional integration.

2. Track a promotional campaign launched by a local sport organization. Are there signs of an integrated approach? Do you recognize attempts to emphasize the core promotion? To effectively monitor the campaign, it may be best for you to meet with the sport promotion specialist before the campaign's release. During the meeting, try to ascertain what has been done to integrate all elements of the promotion mix.

Theoretical Foundations for Effective Sport Promotion and Sales

chapter objectives

1. Understand the role of communication in effective sport promotion and sales

2. Identify the elements fundamental to the communication process

3. Describe the role of a promotional agency

4. Become familiar with communication receiver/buyer behavior theory

5. Recognize the fundamental ingredients of an effective sport promotion and sales process

key terms

source power	trustworthiness	boomerang effect	source amnesia
source attractiveness	status-prestige	personal relevance	message placement outlet
source credibility	profile	active discussion	
expertise	event profile	closure	AIDA

Pregame Introductions

Imperative to the design of effective sport promotions and sales campaigns is a sound understanding of the communication process and the key antecedents of consumer reaction. The intent of this chapter is to overview the variables influencing each of these constructs, as well as the means by which the sport promotion specialist may best prepare promotional correspondence with organizational stakeholders. As a later section of the chapter demonstrates, the foundation of most, if not all, consumer/buyer behavior models is awareness. However, the sport promotion specialist is cautioned against simply focusing on generating awareness, as an aware yet "educated" consumer often poses a greater threat to the promotion campaign's effectiveness than an unaware consumer, who has not developed negative perceptions based on limited or incorrect information.

Therefore, we begin by considering how the communication process and its fundamental components—source, message, medium, and receiver—function in harmony. The chapter culminates with a discussion of the unique inducements for, and behavioral patterns of, sport product consumption.

Defining Communication

Communication is a process of transmitting or interchanging information, thoughts, or ideas through speech, writing, images, or signs. Vehicles that are commonly relied on to communicate an organizational message to another party include advertisements, electronic messages, direct mail, newspaper articles, and even human beings. No communication channel is error free, however. For instance, a well-orchestrated communication campaign can be adversely impacted by messages sent by competing organizations, often referred to as communications channel clutter, or noise. Content interpretation can prove problematic if the message or messenger is not well prepared. Therefore it becomes critical to study the underpinnings of the communication process. Typically, the promotional communication process consists of four essential ingredients: the source (or sender), the message, the medium, and the receiver. This section will discuss the source, the message, and the medium; the receiver will be discussed later in the chapter.

The Source

Although people typically think of the source as the originator of the correspondence, consumers might view any one or a combination of the following as a communication source:

- The sport organization (league, governing body, team, event, or agency)
- A hired spokesperson (product endorser, public relations specialist)

- An organization representative (account executive, coach, administrator, player)
- The media vehicle or its staff (newspaper reporter, radio personality, television sportscaster)
- A trade association (National Association of Collegiate Directors of Athletics, Collegiate Sports Information Directors Association)
- A reference group (athletic booster club, alumni association)

© Anthony Neste

Former Dallas Cowboys coach Jimmy Johnson is a representative of his organization when he speaks to the media.

Therefore, the source may assume the role of message producer, deliverer, or both. The ability of any source to effectively communicate with the intended receiver is grounded in the following three basic attributes: (1) **source power,** (2) **source attractiveness,** and (3) **source credibility.**[1]

Source Power

The source's power with respect to communication may relate to direct lines of authority or the source's command of the marketplace, which essentially determines the source's ability to "make people listen." For instance, in order to ensure that players (message receivers) are aware of the league's newly adopted substance abuse policy, the commissioner's office (source) may exercise its power and require all team managers to conduct drug education seminars while issuing warnings that suspensions and/or fines will be levied against any players found in noncompliance. Ultimately, the commissioner's office is employing its power to persuade the players "to get the message."

More commonly, sport organizations rely on, or aspire to obtain, the type of power that enhances delivery of their message to the targeted audience. Marketers might refer to this concept as positioning-based communication *power.* In other words, the better-positioned sport organizations—those with a larger market share such as the most popular professional leagues, some college athletic programs, and mega-events—possess the commercial power to command a greater share of media exposure. For instance, because of the huge market demand for Final Four-licensed products, the National Collegiate Athletic Association (NCAA) exercises its power by requiring all licensees to procure advertising for Final Four-logoed products, thus enhancing not only product communication but also sales. Similarly, when the NBA launched the WNBA, it exercised considerable source-related power over existing business partners in securing the new league corporate sponsorship and media support, thereby enhancing promotional efforts of the WNBA.

As a result, the more resourceful or *powerful* sport organizations will continue to dominate communication channels, perpetuating their commanding market share position. This leaves sport organizations such as minor league sports, small-college athletics, and most women's professional and collegiate sports challenged to acquire communication channel *power*. In essence, the rich continue to get richer. These less visible sport organizations stand little chance of generating substantial media coverage based on social righteousness or fairness alone. Instead, as we explain later in this text (chapter 7), these sport organizations would do well to buy their source power, or *infomercial* their way into the media. Such a source power *development* tactic may necessitate the purchase of media time and space in order to ensure that the targeted public in fact receives the message. As we demonstrate within the text, sport businesses use such a tactic quite often as a means of creating the illusion of source power.

Source Attractiveness

Alternatively, a source may wish to endear itself to the receivers and thereby enhance communication effectiveness. A source is considered attractive if the intended receiver possesses a favorable impression about the source or feels a sense of similarity or familiarity with the source. This is not to imply that the receiver's perception is based purely on physical attractiveness. Attractiveness includes any number of favorable characteristics that a receiver may perceive in a source, such as intelligence, endearing philosophical or personality traits, or cultural understanding.

In many respects, this is the fundamental art of promotion as the source endeavors to attract the consumer's attentiveness through the use of numerous attention-grabbing tactics. For instance, it has been found that individuals ages 25 to 35 (known as Generation X) respond well to sharp images, music, humor, and a dose of satire.[2] This is illustrated by the connection between heavy metal music and snowboarding. Rocking, rollicking heavy metal sounds are an integral part of snowboarding and are an important backdrop to the exploits of athletes such as world champions Tara Dakides and Dresden Howell.

Thus, when receivers perceive a source to be attractive, they are more likely to adopt the attitudes, behaviors, interests, or preferences endorsed by or attributed to the source. In recent years, North American sport franchises attempting to attract the Hispanic market have tailored communication sources to the market's dialect. This effective maneuver has included the use of Spanish-speaking radio and television affiliates; the production of ticket brochures, pocket schedules, and posters in Span-

© J. Selkowitz/Newsport

Snowboarding is part of the X Games competition that is attractive to Generation X.

ish; placement of bilingual directional and informational signage; and use of facility advertisements in Spanish.[3]

As previously mentioned, the source may in fact be considered any organizational representative such as a coach, player, sports information director, or sales staff member who regularly interacts with the general public. Prudent sport managers will assemble a staff that best reflects the values, lifestyle, and personality of the receivers with whom they may come in contact. As a means of generating interest among local market ethnic populations, Major League Soccer assigned players to markets based on cultural links. For instance, Mexican superstar goalkeeper Jorge Campos was assigned to the Los Angeles Galaxy in the drafting of players, while Carlos Valderama of Colombia initially played with the Tampa Bay Mutiny before moving to the Miami Fusion and back to the Mutiny. The Women's United Soccer Association also used this strategy in allocating members from the 1999 World Cup-winning USA squad to teams for the initial season. Brandi Chastain, who starred at Santa Clara, was assigned to the Bay Area Cyber Rays, and San Diego native Julie Foudy was assigned to her hometown Spirit. Similarly, the San Diego Padres, University of Miami, Los Angeles Dodgers, and San Antonio Spurs have all hired sales personnel with ethnic heritages and linguistic skills similar to those of their assigned customer base.

Sport organizations, as well as companies choosing to employ professional athletes as product endorsers, must screen potential candidates on source attractiveness criteria. In fact, a source attractiveness model has been developed for use in appropriately matching products, product consumers, and product endorsers.

Source Credibility

The third attribute influencing the source's effectiveness is credibility, which refers to the tendency for the receiver to believe or trust someone or something such as an organization, group, or individual. One or more of the following criteria typically determine a source's credibility:

- Expertise
- Trustworthiness
- Status-prestige
- Profile

Expertise, of course, refers to the knowledge, experience, or skills possessed by a source as each relates to the communication topic. Today, far too many people consider themselves experts when it comes to the topic of sport, as highlighted by the preponderance of sport talk radio shows and the explosion of fantasy sport leagues. This latter activity encourages participants to play the role of team manager, making personnel decisions on a day-to-day basis and competing globally against other fantasy sport managers perhaps even unknown to the participant. One can become a Virtual GM (general manager) of a professional basketball franchise on the NBA Web site and have player selections evaluated in a season-long competition. Fans of Formula One motor racing can compete against one another by creating dream teams of drivers and following their progress through the Formula One season, with the venerable *Times* of London offering a prize of 20,000 pounds sterling ($30,000) for the winning team at the end of the season. According to national survey research, a majority of respondents believe that given the opportunity they could manage, coach, and/or officiate professional sports as well as, if not better than, the people who are paid to do so.[4]

Fantasy sport management appears to provide just that type of opportunity. With nearly a million participants, organized fantasy sport leagues are available in football, basketball, baseball, hockey, golf, and auto racing. In the presence of a trend of growing uncertainty and waning loyalty, fantasy team management allows fans to control the destiny of their favorite players, decide who coaches the team, and even select team logos and uniforms. As this trend continues upward, hundreds of companies solely devoted to fantasy sport are sprouting up,[5] perpetuating the belief among ardent fans that they could in fact manage the franchise as well as the current administration.

The prevalence of such high levels of personal identification and mediated expertise provides both opportunities and challenges for the sport promotion specialist. Opportunities exist for the sport promotion specialist or designated organizational representative to emerge as an industry expert willing to participate in lectures, interviews, debates, and panel discussions, providing commentary on developments in the field and thereby enhancing the organization's *credibility* within the local as well as the extended marketplace. The challenge will be for the sport promotion specialist to stay ahead of the general public on matters of interest and value to the consuming marketplace. Additionally, sport promotion specialists are challenged to stay abreast of the expert word on the street, searching for, weighing, and preparing reaction to commentary detrimental to the *credibility* of the source—whether it is an owner, player, coach, administrator, mascot, or dance team member.

On the other hand, in an effort to ensure that sales and service representatives possess sound expertise on a product's unique selling attributes, professional sport franchises typically conduct extensive training programs. Under the guise of a sales university or institute, these intensive training sessions educate the sales staff on the organization as well as the merits of the franchise's product offerings. For instance, the Denver Nuggets and Colorado Avalanche offer their sales staff a program that not only accentuates the positive aspects of their product offerings but also advises on strategies for responding to negative responses and gatekeepers. Also common are service training seminars informing game-day personnel of facility layout, important contact numbers, frequently asked questions, and recurring problems. One such program is the FansFirst Plan, launched by the Memphis Redbirds in 1999 (see appendix A), in which all Redbirds' sales and service staff undergo extensive orientation sessions and receive periodical updates on team developments in order to effectively communicate with fans and embrace the FansFirst philosophy. As displayed in appendix A, it is the intent of the program that fans encounter a knowledgeable staff member capable of addressing questions and problems that may arise during the course of attending a game. Consequently, such actions serve to enhance the patron's perception of the service staff member's, and ultimately the team's, *credibility.*

Lastly, initiatives that actively embrace the community's sport "experts" or "opinion leaders," or individuals of great influence, will help to ensure that the sport business is viewed as credible. These actions may include issuing invitations to such people to participate in feedback sessions (focus groups) or to join a distinguished board of advisors, or simply making a personal contact.

Trustworthiness refers to the honesty, integrity, and believability conveyed by a communication source. Attempts to hide the truth or overhype a product or service diminish a source's credibility. For instance, the International Olympic Committee (IOC) vote-buying scandal of 1999, as well as the subsequent denial of any wrongdoing by several IOC delegates, initially damaged the public's trust in and perception of the Olympic movement. And when former University of Memphis basketball coach Tic Price attempted to disguise a player's injury from the media, he was severely ridiculed by the press for what they considered a breach of honesty. Consequently, less than a year later when Coach Price was asked to step down as head coach, not one member of the media offered a counterargument on his behalf. Exaggeration is detrimental to trustworthiness also. Sport promotion specialists are encouraged to avoid using terminology such as "the best" or "the greatest," or any other type of overpromising that can occur when one is hyping a player, team, event, or facility. Too often such labels generate more cynicism than consumerism in the sport industry.

Research among varying sport consumer groups has revealed that elements of trust, typically associated with the sport promotion specialist's ability to evoke trust and instill confidence in consumers as a direct result of her demonstrated knowledge of the task at hand and familiarity with the consumer's needs, are an expected part of the provision of quality service within the sport environment. A study involving collegiate sport media representatives showed such elements to be of the greatest importance,[6] while a similar service-related assessment involving professional-sport spectators revealed that these issues trailed only the tangible features of the service environment (appearance of personnel, venue, and other material products) in terms of importance to the consumer.[7]

Therefore, in their effort to generate a receiver's trust, sources—whether they be organizations or individuals—must endeavor to establish that they are not attempting to be manipulative. By adopting what Ries and Trout refer to as the Law of Candor, a sport organization minimizes the risk of unfulfilled aspirations. This is true particularly when a situation is negative; in these circumstances Ries and Trout recommend admitting and transferring the negative into a positive.[8] Such was the case for the Florida Marlins's 2000 advertising campaign, which included a series of honest ads that featured the team's new slogan: "Every Day. Every Game. All Heart." The campaign successfully played on the team's shortcomings with the hope of winning back fans who had been turned off by the former management's gutting of the 1997 World Series championship team, which was followed by two seasons of poor play. Players, coaches, and executives who echoed the source's message supported the campaign with personal appearances throughout southern Florida.

In general, a source that is perceived to have high **status** or **prestige** is seen by the receiver as possessing more *credibility* and is therefore generally more persuasive. When honoring a speaking engagement request, sport organizations would do well to provide the best-suited, highest-ranking representative available. The audience will derive greater benefit and attribute more *credibility* to the organization if the speaker represents the appropriately perceived level of responsibility in the organization. Similarly, a major college basketball season ticket renewal letter signed by the athletic director will be more convincing and *credible* than one carrying the signature of the ticket manager, head coach, or even the university president. Current as well as prospective season ticket holders know that the coach and president have nothing to do with ticket sales, while they would not find a plea from the ticket manager very persuasive.

Corporations quite frequently seek sport sponsorship opportunities as a means of enhancing the company's status or image.[9] Therefore, it is incumbent on the sport sponsorship promoter to prepare a laundry list of ways in which the sponsorship arrangement will help in achieving any number of the corporation's status-oriented objectives. In fact, research has revealed that companies sponsoring women's sport are more likely to be pursuing corporate status enhancement-type outcomes such as improved image or demonstration of social responsibility.[10] Therefore, a company interested in portraying a global as well as socially conscious image may be interested in sponsoring the Women's Soccer World Cup.

A variety of personal **profile** traits including age, sex, race, dress, mannerisms, and voice inflection have a profound influence on source credibility. This is particularly the case in sales, as consumers subjected to direct personal selling tactics are heavily influenced by characteristics of the seller, quite frequently more so than those of the

Fans at the Women's 2000 Final Four received this information guide, which included a schedule of events, maps of Philadelphia, local restaurants, area hotels, and other information.

"Reprinted with the permission of the NCAA. All rights reserved. 2001."

product. There is little question that a well-mannered, well-dressed, articulate sales representative has the potential to establish more *credibility,* and subsequently buyer responsiveness, with a prospective ticket plan purchaser than does an account executive with a less appealing appearance and manner. In a similar context, an event sporting a successful 25-year history, well-defined target audience, and stable management team—elements that make up the **event profile**—typically has a better chance of establishing source credibility with prospective host communities, media representatives, and corporate sponsors than a yet-to-be-produced event. We could argue that the source's profile is a composite of all other credibility factors and thus carries the greatest influence in determining receiver response.

Should receivers view the source and message to be incompatible, dishonest, or unbelievable, they may find the entire promotional campaign ineffective or counterpersuasive. It is imperative that the receiver interpret the intent of the promotion or communicated message as genuine and also consistent with the perceived reality of the source and its products or services. As an example, the receiver must perceive a sport franchise's community relations initiatives to be a genuine public service designed to give something back to the community. Otherwise, the club risks a receiver **boomerang effect** that occurs when the receiver perceives message and source intent inconsistency. Boomerang effects are antagonistic cognitive responses that are more persuasive than the intended message, with the result that the receiver adopts an attitude counter to that desired by the source. Boomerang effects ultimately lead to negative conversation among and between consumer groups that is detrimental to all sources within the communication channel.

Combined Source Effects

Obviously, the various communication sources cannot operate in total isolation. In reality, the sources' effects combine to influence consumer perceptions. When Tiger Woods launches a community relations effort to support inner-city kids, a number of sources may be actively involved in the campaign, including Woods, his management group (International Management Group), companies that he endorses, the Professional Golf Association Tour, and the campaign beneficiary. Add to this the various communication channels that choose to supply the public with information on the campaign. In fact, in many cases it may prove difficult or unnecessary to define one source to the exclusion of all others. Instead, attractive and credible organizational sources will function harmoniously to present to the viewer a synergistic communication campaign.

Message and Medium

Unquestionably, fundamental to effective communication are the design and delivery of an appropriate message. Should the source fail to produce a communiqué that properly articulates the intended message, leaving the receiver unresponsive or confused, the medium selection is of limited consequence. Likewise, should the source fail to employ the appropriate medium, even the most well-conceived message may go unrecognized. Thus, the two fundamental elements of the communication process operate in synchrony.

Message

In the typical communication network, a message is strategically prepped (coded in an appropriate manner) by the source and sent through the appropriate channel to be decoded by the recipient, who ultimately accepts, rejects, stores, or acts on its contents. The sport promotion specialist's greatest challenge may be in designing and sending a message that will cut through the clutter, noise, or other factors that may distract the targeted receiver or interfere with the proper decoding of the message.

Effective promotional messages typically include three key ingredients: **personal relevance, active discussion,** and **closure.** Each ingredient serves to magnetize the targeted receiver's attention while maximizing comprehension of the message regarding the product or service.

In order for a message to be effective, it must make sense and have meaning or direct personal relevance to the receiver. Misunderstood messages are often ignored or ridiculed by the receiver, leading to negative consumer reaction (boomerang effect). This often occurs when the source attempts to be humorous; frequently the result is not message retention but **source amnesia** as the receiver fails to see the connection between source and content. Meaning can be conveyed to the receiver through modeling or experiential referencing as the message highlights how the source's product or service fulfills needs or wants of the receiver. Perhaps the most important component of effective, long-term learning, message relevance not only enhances the likelihood that the receiver will be interested in the content but also accelerates processing time and strengthens retention.

Stimulation of *discussion* is critical to message retention, particularly long-term content preservation, as discussion helps maintain focus while clarifying sense and meaning (important for sales meetings and public presentations). Research demonstrates that learners, as a type of message receiver, retain and process new information better when the initial exposure to new content is followed by active conversation about the material. This idea has direct application to promotional messaging, where the merits of word-of-mouth communication are well documented. Sport promotion specialists are therefore well advised to create conversation-generating promotional messaging ranging from personal sales calls, to talk show appearances, to trivia contests that spark a sense of dialogue among receivers. Well documented within the sport promotion literature is the late Bill Veeck's ability to effectively stimulate interest and subsequent discussion about his team as a result of gimmickry such as sending a midget to bat during an MLB game.

Interestingly, it is no more important for receivers actually to speak during the discussion than it is for them to feel that they have been included in the conversation simply as observers. This is perhaps best illustrated by the phenomenal growth of the infomercial business. In infomercials, small-group discussions that include participant testimonials provide viewers with the feeling that they are a part of the discussion and privy to inside information. That fitness industry businesses have capitalized on this receiver characteristic is reflected in the volume of television messages promoting products ranging from equipment to nutritional supplements.

The use of closure, whether at the end of a sales presentation or of a television commercial, is crucial to reinforcing *meaning* as well as receiver *retention.* Summarizing the focus at the conclusion of an audible message ensures repetition of the key points within the message while reminding the receiver of the product's or service's fundamental benefits. In fact, at the conclusion of a sales presentation it makes good sense for the source (sales representative) to ask the audience, whether it is a group or a single decision-maker, "What have we discussed (or learned) here today?" It becomes the receiver's responsibility to process and be able to state the most memorable points of the discussion. Such a tactic also enables the sales representative to reinforce vital points omitted from the receiver's recall and to ascertain what knowledge the audience has gained.

Clearly, the sport promotion specialist's fundamental intention is to design messages that extend beyond generating awareness and ultimately to educate the receiver about the promoted product or service merits. While it is important to recognize that awareness is the foundation of most, if not all, consumer behavior models, sport promotion specialists should not design campaigns aimed at simply generating top-of-mind awareness or recognition. Undoubtedly, an aware public represents a potential consuming public; but an ill-informed or uneducated, yet aware, public may be more damaging than an unaware public, as consumers base consumption decisions not only on awareness but also on their perception and understanding of product or brand. It appears that this *acquisition-of-knowledge* component serves to indoctrinate recipients, through text, images, or narration, on key product attributes of genuine interest to them, thereby strengthening their level of familiarity and desire for action.

Devil Rays Believe Smarter Fans = More Fans

When attempting to explain how the Tampa Bay Devil Rays intended to respond to a 36% drop in attendance during the 1999 season, owner Vince Naimoli argued that an educationally oriented awareness campaign was needed to lure fans back to Devil Ray games.[11] Presumably, the educational component was necessary to alert already aware fans to the benefits of game attendance or to inform nonrepeat attendees about attractive new product offerings.

For instance, a study conducted by the University of Memphis Bureau of Sport & Leisure Commerce showed that individuals familiar with the proposed rules of the XFL were significantly more likely to attend or watch televised games than those who were aware of the new professional football league but unfamiliar with its philosophy. Similarly, while studying how to increase horse race attendance among 18- to 28-year-olds, researchers found pre-attendance perceptions primarily to be negative (e.g., "boring"; "for old people"). However, a post-attendance query of the same individuals revealed all positive descriptors such as "exciting" and "fun." Recommendations drawn from this research included designing visual promotional content that better reflected images of these favorable product-experience attributes, enhancing the receiver's knowledge of horse racing.[12]

Furthermore, a strong link has been found between knowledge and sport consumer action. A study of minor league hockey fans revealed a strong correlation between how much the respondent knew about hockey and attendance frequency, thus substantiating the need to create educationally oriented messages, particularly regarding promotional campaigns touting a new product or targeting a new audience. The NFL has realized tremendous success through NFL 101, a promotional campaign designed specifically to inform interested females about the game of football. In fact, the league attributes the recent rise in female patronage to the campaign's effectiveness.

NHL/ESPN Take Viewers to School

On Sunday, January 9, 2000, ESPN2 aired an instructional presentation of NHL rules during its telecast of the Colorado Avalanche-Chicago Blackhawks game. During "NHL Rules!" ESPN2 used audio, video, and real-time features to explain the action as it occurs on the ice. ESPN2 said the presentation was in response to focus group research indicating that viewers want more education and information during game telecasts. National Hockey League Director of Officiating Bryan Lewis explained rules and penalties while one referee and one linesman wore microphones during the telecast. Fifteen cameras were used to capture the action, and ESPN announcers, disregarding the usual format of color commentary and play-by-play, provided detailed insights on the action and responded to viewer questions on ESPN.com.

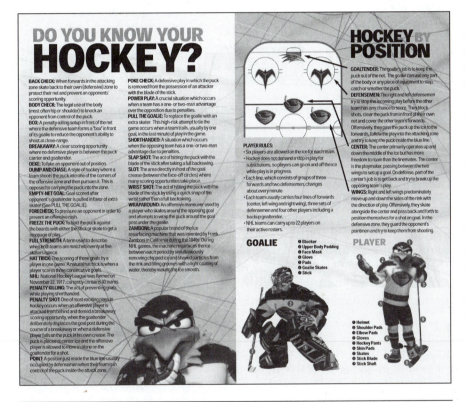

Informational booklets from the Atlanta Thrashers help fans understand the game of hockey.

Reprinted, by permission, from the Atlanta Thrashers Hockey Club.

Although humans use all senses to collect information, about 95% of all information processing occurs through sight, sound, and touch. Receivers favoring one of these three senses are referred to as visual, auditory, and kinesthetic learners, respectively. Comparable to understanding a receiver's motives for consuming, becoming familiar with the targeted receiver group's preferred learning or message-receiving style is of benefit to the sport promotion specialist.

Message elements warranting the greatest level of attention include the basic content ingredients that may range from words to symbols and the message presentation style that addresses such issues as tone and formatting. Errors or omissions within organizational communication seriously jeopardize the source's credibility and hinder the receiver's ability and willingness to respond. Such a situation arose when the advertisement in figure 2.1a appeared in the sport section of the local newspaper on the morning of the women's basketball tournament that was being promoted. The sport promotion specialist submitted the ad copy shown in figure 2.1b, containing all the correct content; but editorial license was granted to the newspaper's advertising department, and the result was major uncorrectable errors. This example illustrates the need not only to thoroughly proofread the properly placed message but also to exercise control over the copy contents. Failure to do so can result in confusion among well-intended, interested consumers.

Figure 2.1 Sport advertisement blunders can confuse your consumers. The add appeared in the paper as *(a)*, but should have been *(b)*—with the consolation and championship games listed.

Whenever possible, it is best for sport promotion specialists to exercise full control over the communication channel, including carefully scripting all forms of verbal communication such as public address announcements, speeches, and interviews while also requesting copies of edited interviews for final review and elimination of items deemed detrimental to the sport organization. To safeguard against print as well as electronic advertising message errors such as the one in figure 2.1*a*, the sport promotion specialist must insist on a review of changes and be prepared to pursue restoration of damages when problems such as this arise. In many cases, such action should be contractually agreed on by both parties.

Medium

Sport promotion specialists are also accountable for determining the appropriate medium or **message placement outlet** to ensure that the carefully crafted promotional material is delivered to the targeted receiver. Organizational marketing strategy has the greatest influence on communication medium decisions, with sound market research providing the most reliable tool for media placement selection. For instance, a racquet club with membership composed of an upscale market will employ a market penetration strategy, opting to place promotion in media popular within this market. However, a golf club that has an existing market of primarily middle-aged, high-volume players and that seeks to increase rounds played by junior golfers (new market development) should place promotion in school publications or on MTV.

Using Strong's classic model of receiver (buyer) responsiveness (**A**wareness-**I**nterest-**D**esire-**A**ction), table 2.1 portrays the general effectiveness of selected communications media at various stages of receiver readiness.[13] This example illustrates a number of key factors for the sport promotion specialist: first, the importance of recognizing the strategic application of various communications tools; second, the importance of recognizing that consumers occupy different stages of receiver (buyer) readiness; and third, the importance of identifying key antecedents (interests and desires) to sport consumer behavior. It should be readily apparent that in order to move a consumer (receiver) beyond the awareness stage, the promotional message must contain stimulants for attracting interest—therefore the source or sender must become familiar with what may trigger the receiver's attention. This figure should also help sport promotion specialists organize a fully integrated marketing communications campaign, as it suggests that no single promotional medium can effectively communicate to a broad spectrum of receivers occupying various stages of buyer readiness.

Table 2.1 Most Effective Communication Tools for Each Stage of Buyer Responsiveness

Stage	Tool
Awareness	Advertising
Interest	Publicity
Desire	Sales promotion (incentives)
Action	Selling

Reprinted, by permission, from P.R. Smith, 1993, *Marketing communications: An integrated approach* (London: Kogan Page Ltd.), 229.

Data reflecting consumer demographic characteristics, as well as reader, listener, or viewership habits, are critical to the ability of sport promotion specialists to place mass media content accurately. The sport organization must generate such information and also request media under placement consideration to provide it. Organizations should be wary before engaging with communication partners unable to provide such fundamental information. Annually, the NBA's Cleveland Cavs collect data from spectators on radio listenership as a means of determining advertisement placement. Similarly, lifestyle activity data collected from patrons attending sporting events at the Pyramid Arena in Memphis, Tennessee, helped management determine that local movie theaters were a sound medium for upcoming event advertising.

Promotional Agency Assistance

The sport promotion specialist may wish to consider using the services of a specialized agency at this stage in order to better understand and reach the targeted receiver. Depending on the availability of internal resources, employment of an external agency may have considerable value for production and placement purposes. For instance, more than 100 colleges and universities, as well as the NCAA, employ the services of Host Communications, Inc. for corporate sponsorship sales and management as well as for designing, producing, and distributing game-day souvenir programs; a similar number have contracted with The Collegiate Licensing Company to assist with institutional licensing matters.

The use of specialty marketing and promotion agencies is not limited to sport organizations. Among the largest sport sponsors, 41% rely on an outside agency for sport sponsorship leveraging expertise, with approximately $100 million annually spent for this type of consulting service.[14] In fact, in an effort to reduce costs after an acquisition of Ameritech, SBC Communications, Inc. chose to streamline its sport marketing staff, outsourcing a majority of the operational duties to an agency.[15]

What are the advantages of using an agency? Table 2.2, adopted from Smith, compares the capabilities of promotional units internal and external to the organization.[16] Sport organizations contemplating outsourcing some or all promotional operations can use this table as a guide in the decision-making process. Organizations adopting a "do-it-yourself" mode of operation stand a good chance of maximizing control as well as management of the project and any sensitive information contained in the campaign, lowering production expenses, and expediting decision-making procedures. Meanwhile, there are several advantages to outsourcing, whether with a full-service agency (whose services should include creative design, market research and planning, and media placement) or with a specialty firm that focuses on one aspect of the promotional campaign (e.g., direct mail vendor). Outsourcing provides the organization with a fresh perspective, sensitivity, and experience in production as well as communications medium placement; and stress levels within the sport organization decrease, allowing direction of focus toward day-to-day operations. Lastly, because of the high volume of advertising inventory it purchases, a full-service agency is typically capable of obtaining discounted rates on mass media advertising placement.[17]

Table 2.2   Capabilities of Promotional Agency Assistance

Aspect	Full-service agency	Specialist	In-house
Project management/coordination	High	Low	High
Control	Moderate	Low	High
Security	High	Low	High
Speed/Response	High	Low	High
Cost	High	Low	High
Media purchasing power	High	Moderate	Low
Fresh views	Yes	Yes	No
Expertise	Yes	Yes	No
Stress	Low	Moderate	High

Agencies have three basic methods for calculating remuneration: commission, fees, and pay-by-results.[18] While a placement commission of 15% is relatively standard within the media-buying industry, creative design and production work agencies—full-service or specialty—are more inclined to charge a fee for services rendered. On a rare occasion, an upstart agency, eager to attract a client base, will offer its services on a pay-by-results basis. In this situation, delineation of the expected outcome (e.g., increased awareness, image transformation, or sales volume), as well as assessment indicators (e.g., market research), is critical to both parties and to the success of the overall campaign.

Agencies Assist All

Agencies can be of assistance to sport organizations of all shapes and sizes. For example, in 1999 the Arena Football League contracted with SFX, a giant sport marketing agency, for the purpose of increasing league sponsorship sales. SFX will retain 15% of the revenues generated from sponsorship sales and licensing and merchandising sales.[19] After a two-year training period, the league fully intends to internalize the sales operations. This type of practice need not be uncommon in sport, as sport promotion specialists can use the period of agency assistance as an apprenticeship in preparation for independent message design and medium placement.

Before selecting an agency, the client should request a set of credentials, which represent current work and previous work completed by the agency. The client should also obtain references, employee profiles, and information on the firm's history. The next step is to forward to qualifying agencies a brief, much like a request for proposal, containing the following: current situation summary, campaign objectives, projected target market, budget, time lines, and campaign performance indicators.[20] Reacting to this brief, interested agencies invest anywhere from a few thousand to hundreds of thousands of dollars to pitch their services to the client through a formalized presentation of the anticipated campaign. The agency selection process may vary, as some organizations use objective assessment tools (e.g., rating scales) for determining the agency that best fits their needs, whereas others make a selection based on the agency's perceived creativity and effort.

The Receiver

Today's consumers, the recipients of a plethora of promotional content, have become rather sophisticated and perhaps somewhat callous. Because consumers have been exposed to a wide array of informational messages since early childhood, it has become increasingly difficult to penetrate their behavioral patterns. What is it that affects the ability of a particular message to cut through the clutter? What motivates a recipient to respond to one communication over another? Identifying what inspires a receiver or consumer to act or not act on promotional stimuli (messages received) has long intrigued practitioners and researchers alike.

Two schools of thought have emerged from the wealth of research addressing the issue of how and why consumers act as they do. The *behavioral school* views consumer actions as somewhat unexplainable events that are believed to result from interaction with prepared stimuli. The *cognitive school* embraces the notion that receiver actions are a by-product of an intellectual thought process.

Essentially, the behavioral theory, commonly referred to as the black box theory, states that all of the promotional elements associated with a product or service are presented to the consumer market with only one recognizable output: an action of some sort. Strangely enough, according to the black box theory, what occurs in the mind of the consumer—that influences the decision to consume or avoid the promoted product or service—is a mystery (figure 2.2).[21]

Meanwhile, the cognitive school attempts to open the lid and look inside that black box constituting the human mind. The cognitive school recognizes that the game-day ticket buyer, recreational soccer player, multinational corporation marketing manager, and global network broadcast producer all have one thing in common: each represents a consumer group of keen interest and great challenge to the sport

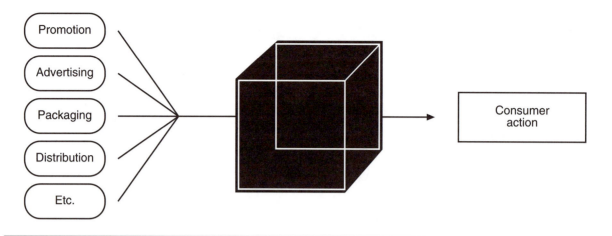

Figure 2.2   Black box theory.

Reprinted, by permission, from D.K. Stotlar, 1993, *Successful sport marketing.*

promotion specialist, each possessing unique consumption interests and desires driven by variables shaped by internal as well as external forces. This more complex consumer behavior model entertains the notion that intervening variables such as perception, motivation, learning, attitudes, beliefs/values, and significant others serve as antecedents to message receiver action.[22] Figure 2.3 presents a similar model developed specifically for the sport industry. This model illustrates the influence of individual as well as environmental factors on sport consumer decisions.[23] The model clearly supports the cognitive school theory that the human mind is exposed to and influenced by myriad interrelated factors ultimately determining behavior patterns, in this case as they relate to sport. As this text will demonstrate throughout, the

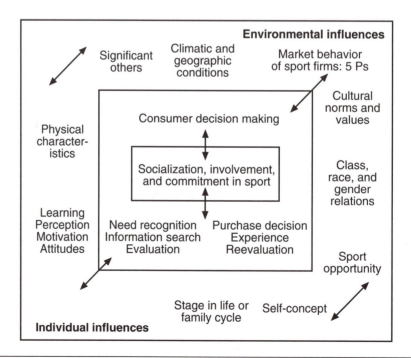

Figure 2.3   Influential sport consumption factors.

Reprinted, by permission, from B.J. Mullin, S. Hardy, and W.A. Sutton, 2000, *Sport marketing*, 2nd ed. (Champaign: Human Kinetics), 58.

resulting behavior as it relates to sport promotion and sales is not limited to individuals.

Many of the influences identified in figure 2.3 similarly affect corporate decisions in relation to such issues as sport sponsorship. For instance, in order not to alienate soccer fans in Glasgow, the media company NTL took the unusual step of sponsoring both Glasgow Scottish Premier League soccer teams. Glasgow Celtic and Glasgow Rangers have a long-standing rivalry, and many of their fans have an animosity for each other that is fueled by a potent mix of religion, politics, class, and soccer. Between them, the two teams have dominated Scottish soccer, and it makes economic sense for a sponsor to engage in a relationship with each rather than alienating a significant portion of its potential market.

Clearly, in order to best stimulate demand among all sport promotion recipients and sport product consumers, it is critical for the sport promotion specialist to become acquainted with the variables affecting consumption decisions among various receivers before transmitting a single message or designing an elaborate promotional campaign. Such familiarity will enable the promoter to customize messages more likely to pique the recipient's attention, thereby stimulating action.

For example, research has shown that companies recognized as actively engaged in sport sponsorship are most interested in using the sponsorship as a means of enhancing the company's position with respect to its competitors, generally by increasing sales or improving market share.[24] Therefore, it is incumbent on all sport promotion specialists involved in designing and selling sponsorship proposals to ensure that sponsorship packages, as well as promotional collateral material, clearly indicate how the arrangement can improve the prospective corporate partner's market position and thereby fulfill fundamental consumption influence variables.

Becoming familiar with all sport consumer motives would be an extremely time-consuming and overwhelming task. However, it is a good idea for sport promotion specialists to take every opportunity, through one-on-one personal correspondence or mass sampling techniques, to unveil the primary consumption incentives among all current as well as prospective stakeholders. Information such as this will then be used as promotional material content ranging from mass advertising campaigns to personal sales calls. Chapter 3 provides a more in-depth discussion of sport consumer motives and recommended incentivization procedures.

Further confounding the communication process is the need to target the appropriate receiver, as frequently sport-related product and service purchasers and end users are not one and the same. In essence, each consumer (receiver) group can be further subdivided into sport product purchasers and users. Consider, as an example, the decision to accept a corporate sponsorship arrangement involving a professional sport franchise in Denver and a national distribution company with an office in Colorado. The agreement may very likely be reviewed and negotiated by a corporate marketing executive at the home office in New York, whereas the *end user* is actually the Denver-based sales force members who make use of the sponsorship by entertaining clients at the team's home games. Similarly, the decision to attend Coach Jones's summer basketball camp typically rests with the parent (purchaser) as opposed to the attending child (end user).

It is a "must" for the sport promotion specialist to actively research the communication network for each product line, ultimately determining the consumption decision-making process of all user groups. It is necessary then to design a communication or promotional campaign with the fundamental intent of capturing the primary decision-maker's attention and properly educating the decision-maker on the benefits of consumption to the end user (who may not be the same person as the decision-maker). In such a case the sport promotion specialist needs to incorporate the end user into the "communication team." Thus the end user must likewise be alerted to the benefits of consumption and encouraged to communicate this information to the consumption decision-maker. That is, using the examples just presented, the Denver-based sales force and the youth basketball player should each be seen as a critical part of the communication or promotional campaign warranting customized communication. For the Denver-based sales force this will involve communicating how the sponsorship will serve as a business-building tool that enhances sales; the aspiring basketball star wants to learn about the fun other kids his age have had at camp. In each case, the end-user receiver's familiarity with and understanding of the product or service, and of the benefit of consumption, will inspire influential correspondence with the consumption decision-making receiver.

The Integrated Marketing Communications Model

To this point the communications models we have considered depict processes that begin when the source encodes and transmits a message through selected promotional channels to the receiver, who in turn decodes the message and evaluates it for use in personal choice or consumption decisions (figure 2.4a). However, critics believe that this process fails to fully describe the dynamic environment of mass as well as personal communication. Criticisms of these linear models include the following:

- The message acts as the starting point, often driven by technology, product improvements, and sender capability.
- The feedback loop is weak and secondary to the message component of the model.
- The receiver is portrayed as an isolated, individual consumer.
- Ultimately the focus of the model is on the message.

In recent years, there is little question that the contemporary communication channel has changed significantly, warranting reconfiguration of models depicting receiver involvement. Today's receiver, armed with an enhanced knowledge of the source, is genuinely more engaged in the communication channel and thus more inclined to provide and seek feedback as well as to assume a role as message transmitter. Today, the communication channel provides opportunity for a seamless stream of dialogue between source and receiver, as communication media like the Internet emerge as prominent means for correspondence.

In response, the integrated marketing communications (IMC) model (figure 2.4b) reflects a stronger interest in how the receiver figures in the communication process. The IMC model is highly interactive—eliminating the weak feedback loop in that there appears to be no specific starting point. Instead, there is constant exchange between receiver and sender. Very appropriate to the sport industry, the model illustrates that the receiver may be any combination of consuming publics. That is, this model recognizes that the receiver may be an individual, another sport enterprise, a consortium of corporate partners, governmental officials, or any one of myriad sport consumer groups—internal or external to the sport promotion specialist.

The Receiver As a Communication Medium

Change is a constant within the sport industry. Whether the change is the creation of a new team (or league, event, or logo), the acquisition of a new sponsor (or player or coach), or a modification (of location, ticket prices, or rules), sport promotion specialists face the challenge of properly communicating the impact of change to a

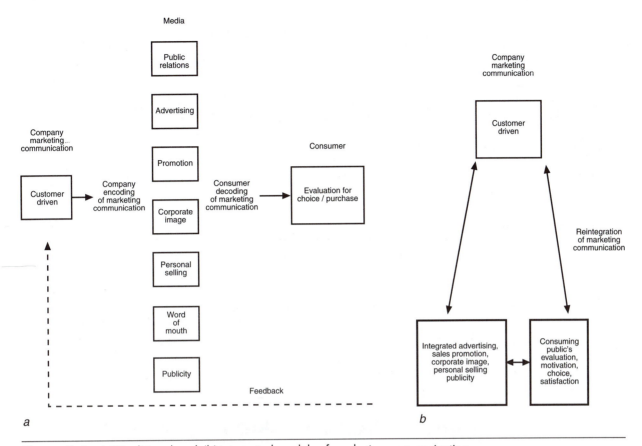

Figure 2.4 *(a)* Traditional and *(b)* integrated models of marketing communication.

Reprinted, by permission, from P.R. Smith, 1993, *Marketing communications: An integrated approach* (London: Kogan Page Ltd.), 53.

plethora of receivers. In order for each of these changes or innovations to be accepted by the consuming public, sport promotion specialists should apply a *diffusion-of-innovation* process. Typically the process involves a multi-step communications network, similar to that shown in figure 2.5. Initial messages target opinion leaders, early adopters, influential individuals, and (perhaps most importantly) existing consumers, who will in turn share this information, via word of mouth, with the next level of receivers—other potential stakeholders.[25]

When embraced as an "inside" stakeholder, the existing customer serves as an extended cog in the communication channel poised to actively promote the product and its ability to fulfill essential needs of other consumers sharing similar characteristics and motives. In fact, industry figures reveal that existing customers refer 70% of new customers—a statistic that dramatically reflects the influence and value of empowered satisfied customers.

The multistep communication process need not be limited to any particular sport consumer group. The power of influential organizations can affect behavior within industrial markets as well. In fact, companies are frequently willing to follow a well-respected and highly successful organization that makes an early decision to act. This type of corporate behavior, called "mimic response," has been found to account for many sponsorship acquisition decisions.[26] For instance, English County Cricket, the top tier of club cricket in the world, had seven financial services companies engaged in national-level sponsorship in 1996 as it appeared that no company wanted to be excluded from the event. Similarly, in the wake of the 1999 Olympic vote bribery scandal, people anticipated that Visa's sponsorship renewal with the IOC would

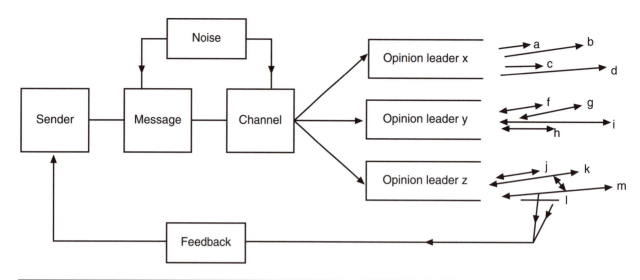

Figure 2.5 Multistep communication model.

Reprinted, by permission, from P.R. Smith, 1993, *Marketing communications: An integrated approach* (London: Kogan Page Ltd.).

favorably influence other sponsors to put the situation behind and renew their sponsorship arrangements. In this case it would be prudent of the IOC, as well as the Salt Lake Olympic Organizing Committee, to provoke positive conversation between Visa and fellow Olympic sponsors contemplating renewal.

Consumer Action and Ongoing Promotion

While traditional communication and/or consumer behavioral models describe buyer/receiver action as a linear, static occurrence, the consumption process—particularly as it relates to sport—is more a dynamic, cyclical experience perhaps best illustrated by O'Sullivan and Spangler's "Three Phases of an Experience" paradigm (figure 2.6).[27] This model accurately depicts not only the ongoing nature of sport consumption but also the need for targeted promotional efforts throughout each experience stage.

The *pre-experience* stage comprises features common to most consumer/buyer behavior models that we have previously discussed, with awareness a key consideration. Therefore, it is the *participation* and *post-experience* stages, or those preceding the initiation of action, that have greatest relevance to the unique nature of the sport consumer action process and that this discussion emphasizes.

Subcomponents of the participation stage provide ample opportunity for promotional exchange with consumers, since promotionally oriented communication does not and should not cease once the sport consumer experience begins. In fact, the process closely resembles that embedded within the aftermarketing philosophy, a concept suggested by Vavra that is aimed at advancing the service-after-the-sale approach and is addressed in chapter 14.

For instance, patrons of professional golf tournaments (Professional Golf Association [PGA] Tour and Ladies Professional Golf Association [LPGA]) frequently ride a shuttle bus from satellite parking facilities to the course entrance on tournament day. As they are engaged in—or, more precisely, captured within—the *anticipation* component of the *experience* stage, an ideal promotional exchange opportunity emerges for event management to distribute relevant information such as pairing sheets, merchandise order forms, and course maps identifying sponsor displays and other points of interest. A shuttle bus "tour director" may also educate patrons by providing up-to-date information on space availability at good viewing areas, leader board positioning, and amazing

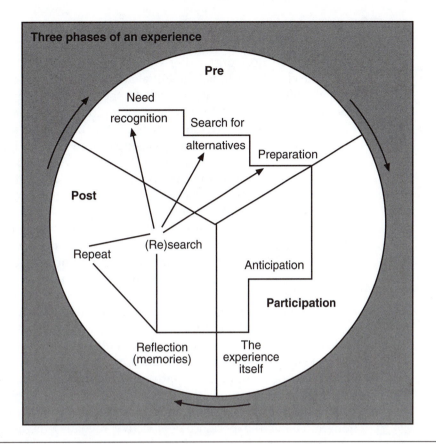

Figure 2.6 Three phases of an experience.

From O'Sullivan, E.J. and Spangler, K.J. (1998), *Experience marketing: Strategies for the new millenium.* State College, PA: Venture Publishing, Inc. Reprinted with permission.

shots of the day while prepping them for their exciting experience by sharing past tournament highlights and stories. Such personal interaction serves to elevate the patron's excitement and anticipation and also becomes a part of the actual experience. To reduce patron anxiety, the director may also address key questions related to shuttle return time or threatening weather conditions; moreover, the director can serve as a customer relations piece by collecting comments to share with event managers.

Once on-site and engaged in the *experience itself* component, event patrons should be provided with feedback aimed at enhancing and validating their experience choice. Messages should emphasize the value of the patrons' action, serving to confirm that the experience fulfills critical patron needs and thereby strengthening the potential for satisfaction and repeat action. Directional signage, scoreboards and message boards, vendors, ushers, and public address announcers are all viewed as sources of *participation* stage communication contributing to the event atmospherics, a promotion mix component we cover in chapter 11. As a promotional vehicle, each of these information sources provides an opportunity for direct or indirect correspondence with the audience, on behalf of the primary communication source, and as such emerges as a key element in the marketing communication process and a major determinant of patron satisfaction.

While engaged in the exhilaration of the *participation* stage, sport experience participants should have an opportunity to ensure repeat action. Messages should alert participants to the next scheduled experience opportunity and the action necessary to reserve participation, as the conversion of positive attitudes into action remains fundamental to effective sport promotion management.

Acting on fan survey information indicating that a large proportion of attendees were interested in attending future championships, the NCAA, in concert with future championship host organizing committees, established sales venues at selected collegiate championships. The initial attempt at this tactic, aimed at capitalizing on the patron's emotional attachment to the attendance experience, was organized during the 1997 NCAA Ice Hockey Championships held in Milwaukee, Wisconsin. During the first day of operation the NCAA realized ticket sales of over $60,000 for the 1998 NCAA Ice Hockey Championships to be held in Boston, Massachusetts! In addition to securing advance ticket sales, the NCAA used this mechanism to build a database of patrons seeking championship information and periodically forwarded this vested group of college hockey patrons updated championship information over the course of the hockey season.

Lastly, it is essential for the source to furnish patrons with messages and tangible mementos for *post-experience* reflection. These items serve to instill the values of participation, foster fond remembrances, and encourage repetitive action. Event-logoed products and sponsor giveaways, common to sporting events, serve as reflection items that stimulate favorable experience recall, not to mention discussion. Sport fantasy camp participants receive photos of themselves posing with star players and friends; when framed and displayed at home, these stand as constant reminders of that great experience and serve as a catalyst for repeat action. Similarly, proactive *post-experience* correspondence, in the form of thank-you notes and e-mail messages, is a vehicle for reminding the patrons of the feeling of that euphoric experience and securing their continued allegiance.

O'Sullivan and Spengler's model more than adequately addresses sport consumption from a micro-experience perspective, revealing the need for tailored marketing communications determined by the participant's position within the experience cycle. However, the frequency escalator for sport attendance and participation (figure 2.7) reflects a relationship between the consumer's magnitude of sport participation and promotion tactical design.[28] For instance, aware nonconsumers tend to be attracted by mass communications and special incentive programs such as product giveaways, price promotions, and celebrity appearances; heavy users, in contrast, or individuals engaged in a high level of consumption such as season ticket holders, are more responsive to personal contact and loyalty reward programs. The application of this type of consumer usage segmentation process enables the sport promotion specialist to customize correspondence based on the degree of consumption exhibited by the consumer, thereby enhancing personal relevance and dramatically improving receptivity to the message.

Postgame Wrap-Up

The promotional communication process consists of four essential ingredients: the source, the message, the medium, and the receiver. The ability of any source to effectively communicate with the targeted receiver is grounded in the source's power, the source's attractiveness, and the source's credibility. In other words, does the source, who may be a player, sales representative, executive, or broadcast partner, command an audience? Does the audience find this source attractive, physically or otherwise? And, does the audience find the source credible? That is, has the source attained some level of expertise, trustworthiness, status, or prestige, and does the source possess profile characteristics of value to the receiver? In the absence of these characteristics, it is quite difficult for appropriately designed messages to reach the receiver.

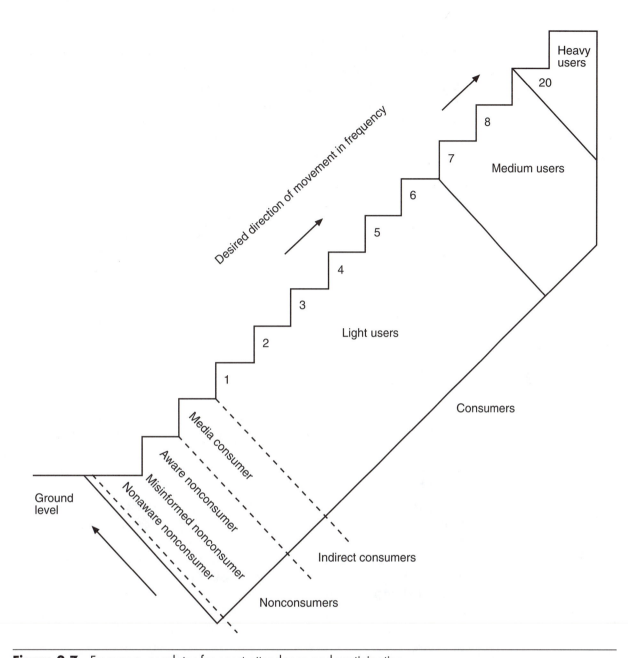

Figure 2.7 Frequency escalator for sport attendance and participation.

Reprinted, by permission, from B.J. Mullin, S. Hardy, and W.A. Sutton, 2000, *Sport marketing*, 2nd ed. (Champaign: Human Kinetics), 36.

As an example, no team would consider sending the high-profile coach alone on a sponsorship sales presentation. As attractive as the coach may be as a sport personality, her lack of expertise or familiarity with the sponsorship sales process makes her a poor choice for the sales call—just as the promising sales account executive has no business calling the team's plays. It is therefore important for the organization to select communication sources that embody a sense of power, attractiveness, and credibility with the receiver.

Once an appropriate source has been selected, it is important that a message be crafted to include personal relevance for the targeted receiver, a stimulant for active discussion, and closure (which may include a review of the main message content)—whether the message is distributed through face-to-face sales calls, public speaking engagements with civic business leaders, or a multimillion-dollar mass media advertising campaign. It is advisable for the sport promotion specialist, when appropriate, to use an arsenal of resources including consumer demographic and psychographic data in determining the most effective promotional message outlets.

At various stages throughout the communication exchange process, the sport promotion specialist may look to a professional promotion agency for assistance with message design and placement. Promotion agencies assist with a multitude of tasks ranging from production to placement to full-scale campaign management efforts. It is important for sport promotion specialists to an agency under consideration to provide a complete set of credentials, including references, employee profiles, and information on the firm's history.

In the end, consumer action—the desired goal of any promotion campaign—results from the meticulous design of an articulate organizational message, diligent selection and preparation of message and its delivery channels (medium), and attention to timing indicative of the recipient's consumption patterns and informational needs. However, the experiential nature of most sport consumption provides the sport promotion specialist with an opportunity to design a seamless channel of communication with the receiver (consumer) and thereby maximize the potential for repeat behavior.

Discussion Items

1. As a consumer, how do you personally assess a source's trustworthiness? How much does this matter to you? How much does this affect your action/reaction?

2. What examples are you aware of in which a source's credibility hindered the effectiveness of a promotion campaign?

3. What is the boomerang effect, and what effect might it have on the success of a promotional campaign? Are you aware of instances in which this has occurred?

4. Over the course of one week, scan advertisements placed in the sport section of the newspaper. Clip and save for discussion any ads that omit critical pieces of information such as those discussed in this chapter.

5. How does the consumer's magnitude of consumption alter promotional design for a sport organization? What impact does this have in the overall campaign?

Learning Enrichment Activities

1. Schedule two interviews, one with a promotional agency representative and one with a sport promotion specialist from a team or event. During each interview, query the representative on the strengths and weaknesses of using the services of an agency.

2. Compare and contrast three campaigns that use product endorsers from the field of sport. Ask at least 10 people (not classmates) how they feel about the match between product and source. What terms do they use to describe this match? Do they feel the source is credible? Trustworthy? Expert?

3. In groups of three or four, attend a local sporting event. While at the event, keep a detailed log of the promotional opportunities that you encounter

during each stage of your attendance experience. Compare your answers with those of other members of your group. Additionally, did you find that the sport organization appropriately capitalized on the opportunities available during each stage of the experience? How would you do things differently?

4. The advertisement in figure 2.1 was produced in-house by the advertiser. What do you find problematic with the ad's contents or message? What would you do as the team's sport promotion specialist to minimize if not eliminate these problems next time?

Incentivizing Sport Consumers

chapter objectives

1. Appreciate an expanded notion of traditional sport promotional sales as a function of a broader scope of tactics, classified as incentives, that are used to induce consumer behavior

2. Become familiar with a menu of sport consumption motives that gives the sport promotion specialist insight into the multitude of consumer incentivization opportunities

3. Become familiar with a structure for strategically launching an effective sport consumer incentivization campaign

key terms

value added	community
promotional giveaways	techtainment
affiliation	

Pregame Introductions

What is it that inspires an individual to attend a sporting event? An opportunity to spend some time with friends? The possibility of receiving a novel collectible item? The chance to see a great athletic performance by one of the best in the game? What is it that motivates a sponsor to accept a sponsorship proposal or a reporter to cover a sporting event? The issue is rather complex, isn't it? Each of the individuals mentioned should be considered a unique sport consumer with an equally unique set of sport consumption motives warranting incentivization.

This chapter explores the fundamental incentives for sport consumption as they relate to the various customer groups affiliated with sport. It also deals with tactics employed by sport organizations to incentivize consumption while providing a basis from which to plan and organize promotional campaigns incorporating these elements. As the basic issue, we focus on what it is that inspires sport consumption and how this can be used within a marketing communication campaign.

Incentives are considered to be *items of perceived value added to an offer to encourage some overt behavioral response.* Incentives are offered to persons or groups who are normally insufficiently motivated, indifferent, or antipathetic with respect to a proposed behavior. Thus incentives alter the perceived price of an offer in an effort to overcome the market's resistance or indifference. Normally considered a function of sales promotions, incentives generally include price deals, premiums, contests, free samples, and a host of other add-ons to encourage the market to try a product or service.[1] Whereas advertising affects the earlier stages of the communication/buying process by generating awareness and interest, incentives tend to affect the later stages, as they often tempt the receiver into action. As a component of the promotion mix, incentives provide the final "push" that moves the receiver (consumer) toward using a particular product or service.[2] Sport-based incentives, as we will explain, comprise a broader range of value-added characteristics, many grounded in basic consumer behavior principles.

Traditional Incentives: Price-Based or Sales Promotions

In this traditional sense, incentives, as defined by Kotler, appear to be a dominant feature within the sport promotion mix.[3] This is particularly true for the sport promotion specialist charged with regularly filling a sport facility or liquidating excess retail inventory; in this situation, items of perceived as well as real financial value are commonly used to induce consumer action. Frequently used *price*-based incentives include discounted pricing, coupon redemption, and free trials.

Although discounting is an effective pricing strategy when the targeted product acts as a loss leader, caution is in order when the sport promotion specialist becomes too reliant on such price-based incentives for the core product. In fact, core product

Fans of all ages enjoy promotion incentives.

price discounting tends to dilute the quality image as well as the selling price of the property or brand.[4] There is also the risk of damaging relations with full-paying customers. For instance, the NHL's Tampa Bay Lightning has eliminated the practice of distributing complimentary tickets. Before changing policy, the Lightning had given away as many as 4000 tickets to each game, angering and seriously endangering relations with season ticket holders.[5]

Sport businesses are therefore encouraged to use price promotions when facing an elastic demand market,[6] and even then on a contingency basis only. A contingency-based price promotion necessitates action on the part of the consumer *prior* to price manipulation. Before receiving a discounted admission or redeeming a coupon, for instance, the consumer may be required to provide personal identification, proof of additional purchase, or responsiveness to an advertising gimmick such as fulfillment of an advance purchase requirement (as instituted by commercial airlines), performance of a prescribed behavior (e.g., shaving the head), or possession of a defined personal characteristic (e.g., for "Ladies Night"). The inclusion of space for name, address, and phone number on the back of each coupon facilitates completion by the customer and initiates development of a critically valuable customer "qualified lead" database.

As research has demonstrated, incentives are an effective promotional tool for attracting infrequent consumers, a market difficult to communicate with. The implementation of incentive-driven database-building tactics provides ample opportunity for capturing key correspondence information with this challenging-to-reach customer group.

A further recommendation is that organizations view a price-based incentive or sales promotion as a means of adding value to the original core product purchase. Price-based value-added incentives include premium giveaways and enhanced entertainment features. Of the 10 most effective incentive programs during the 1998 MLB season, all but one were of the **value-added** type (table 3.1). **Promotional giveaways,** equally popular in the NBA, were considered a high priority among team marketing specialists with respect to their ability to favorably affect attendance (figure 3.1).[7] Spoelstra recommends that giveaway items be meticulously selected based on their ability to add "equity" to the sales price.[8] As the following example indicates, Beanie Babies, the prime giveaway item within professional baseball during the 1998 season, adequately fulfill this recommendation as a collectible with potentially high retention as well as resale value.

Providing the consumer with additional attractions can likewise increase the perceived as well as the real purchase value. Major League Soccer significantly enhanced attendance during the 1999 season by scheduling doubleheaders involving the U.S. Women's World Cup team prior to their competing in the World Cup.[9] Major and minor league American baseball teams have a long history of capitalizing on the enjoyable summer weather by adding postgame fireworks displays to regularly scheduled games. Recently the same teams have added postgame concerts, typically involving bands popular with baby boomers (e.g., Beach Boys), as a means of delivering ticket purchasers a little extra value. Generally, the costs of this type of

Table 3.1 1998 Major League Baseball's Most Effective Promotions

Ranked in terms of percentage attendance increase

Rank	Promotion	% increase	Number of fans
1	Beanie Baby	37.4	9175
2	Beach towel	26.4	7779
3	Umbrella	20.1	5330
4	Coupon	20.0	5249
5	Baseball cap	19.9	5370
6	Fireworks	19.1	3998
7	Hat (not baseball cap)	17.3	4822
8	Bat	15.0	4177
9	Heritage/Family days	14.9	3116
10	Beanbag toy	14.4	4453
11	Schedule magnet	13.8	1079
12	Shirt	13.3	3774
13	Helmet	13.1	3573
14	Fan appreciation	12.1	3535
15	Camera day	11.3	1847
16	Photo	11.1	1985
17	$1 concessions	9.2	1572
18	Businesspeople	8.9	1987
19	Growth chart	8.6	490
20	Backpack	8.0	2468

Note: Increase was calculated by comparing all teams' average attendance with attendance on all promotional dates.

Reprinted, by permission, from B.J. Mullin, S. Hardy, and W.A. Sutton, 2000, *Sport marketing*, 2nd ed. (Champaign: Human Kinetics), 208.

1. Season ticket option
2. Business sponsorships
3. Strategic planning
4. Promotional giveaways
5. Promotional strategies
6. Newspaper advertising
7. Direct mail advertising
8. Good public relations
9. Selected target market
10. Television advertising
11. Home game programs
12. Priority seating/parking
13. Pricing strategies
14. Winning-season incentive
15. Package of options
16. TV games incentive
17. Radio advertising
18. Booster clubs
19. Market research
20. Promoted star player(s)
21. Magazine advertising

Figure 3.1 Priority ranking of marketing techniques for National Basketball Association franchises.

Reprinted, by permission, from L.M. Mawson and E.E. Coan, 1994, "Marketing techniques used by NBA franchises to promote home game attendance," *Sport Marketing Quarterly* 3 (1):40. © Fitness Information Technology.

Beanie Baby Bonanza

In 1998, MLB clubs that gave away Beanie Babies produced by Ty Inc. realized an average attendance increase of 37.4%! According to Lori Tomnitz, a Ty spokesperson, "These promotions work for us because they help us get our product into children's hands, rather than just into the collectibles market. We found that baseball, with its emphasis on families, is where we fit best right now."[10] The next cultural craze of keen interest to youth was Pokemon. In late 1999, the Oakland A's used it as a giveaway and increased attendance by 50% (17,000).[11]

incentive may be shared or absorbed by a sponsor interested in targeting the defined group of consumers.

Again, the sport team promotion specialist must exercise a degree of caution when scheduling price- or non-price-related sales promotion, as the targeted consumers are likely to become "cherry pickers," or patrons who attend games or purchase product only when there is a promotion.[12] When cherry picking occurs, the merits of a sales promotion intended to generate additional full-paying customers are minimized unless the promotion also includes the contingencies discussed earlier.

We might ask at this point how effective traditional sport promotions are. McDonald and Rascher determined that MLB clubs scheduling a traditional sales promotion (e.g., giveaway) realized an average attendance increase of approximately 3893 or 14% per occurrence. The findings further indicated that although a *"watering down"* effect does occur as a consequence of the frequent scheduling of promotional dates in baseball, the impact of this *effect* is marginal (2% of the aforementioned gain appears to be lost). Thus, in baseball it appears that more is better and that it is strategically optimal to have many promotions rather than a few.[13]

Similar research involving professional baseball teams mirrored the findings of McDonald and Rascher and also revealed that promotions held during the week (Monday through Thursday) were considerably more effective at increasing attendance. Thus the researchers recommend that team promotion specialists schedule more promotional events during the weekday games and other anticipated low-attendance events.[14] This recommendation contradicts the intuitively based suggestion from Spoelstra that promotions be scheduled on dates when high attendance is expected, if not almost assured, in order to maximize the total entertainment value of the attendance experience. However, McDonald and Rascher do caution that promotional effectiveness is team specific, warranting careful planning by the sport promotion specialist.

We could argue that within the complex field of sport, and more specifically sport promotion, not all incentives are applied to the product price or are transactional or financial. In fact, all elements of the sport product marketing mix should be scrutinized for incentive adaptation in an effort to stimulate, sustain, or revitalize consumption. For instance, the product itself may be targeted for incentivization; this was the case when the NBA implemented a number of rule changes for the 1999 season with the aim of making the game more fan friendly, by increasing scoring, reducing body bashing, and speeding up the tempo of play. Similarly, when faced with the problem of sophisticated, suffocating defenses and the resulting lack of goals in the early 1990s, the Fédération Internationale de Football Association (FIFA) instituted a simple rule change to alleviate the problem. Instead of two points for a win and one point for a tie (which was the norm in world soccer), the new rule was three points for a win, one point for a tie. This made a significant difference and gave coaches the incentive to play more attractive attacking-style football, with a consequential rise in goal scoring.

Likewise, star players serve as a consumption incentive. According to HBO's Ross Greenberg, John McEnroe provided this incentive to men's tennis during the 1970s and '80s: "He was the reason cab drivers and average sports fans were drawn to tennis."[15] In essence, to maintain a competitive advantage with other sport properties, the sport promotion specialist needs to create and promote unique features associated with the core product.[16]

The sport industry is rich in *place*-based incentives, as a large number of American sport franchises have sought to increase marketing-oriented outcomes such as attendance, naming rights deals, and increased volume of luxury suites through the construction of a new venue. Place-based incentives such as public funding and rent-free lease agreements are now common among municipalities that wish to entice a major league franchise contemplating relocation, while incentives such as interactive video display screens, theme park-type attractions, and on-demand in-seat replay screens act as a means of luring patrons to the venue. In fact, the NFL has signed a five-year deal with ChoiceSeat to install SmartSeat technology in the seating and suites of various stadiums throughout the league. The technology offers the spectator real-time statistics, game analysis, and e-commerce capabilities.

Sport Consumer Behavioral Response Incentives

Sport differs from many other consumer products, particularly those not associated with entertainment, in that it avails itself of a host of *promotion*-based incentives or consumption motives. In fact, one can make the case that within the context of sport, incentives encompass a broad range of behavioral inducements that serve as an ideal framework for a discussion of sport-related sales or, more accurately, consumption-driven promotion. As table 3.2 shows, researchers have compiled no less than 26 fundamental motives for sport consumption.[17]

Table 3.2 Fundamental Motives for Sport Consumption

Motive	Definition
1. Acquisition of knowledge	Learning about the sport, team, or players through media consumption.
2. Aesthetics	The mastery exhibited by athletes/teams during competition. Concerned with the beauty and artistry exhibited in competitive sport.
3. Camaraderie	Derive social identity from a reference group.
4. Catharsis	The reduction of general aggression experienced by an individual after watching a competitive sport event.
5. Compliance	Attending sporting events in order to conform publicly to a reference group's norms.
6. Drama/eustress	Drama: A sports event represents a dramatic construction because it pits a protagonist against

Motive	Definition
	an antagonist in a contest for a scarce resource (i.e., a victory) in a context that is regimented by a fixed structure (i.e., rules) and demarcated by a beginning, middle, and end. The temporal progression of a sports contest unfolds naturally and is comprised of periods of tension, which ultimately lead to an emotional release. Eustress: Concerned with an individual's desire to watch sports in order to fulfill their need to experience stress in socially acceptable, exciting ways.
7. Economic (betting)	Potential for economic gains through sport wagering.
8. Entertainment	Fan's desire to be entertained.
9. Escape	Addresses sport viewing as a means to relieve the "tedium" (i.e., boredom, fatigue) associated with everyday life.
10. Family needs	Wanting to spend quality time with spouse and/or family.
11. Identification with winning	Maintaining the relationship with a winning team.
12. Internalization	The deep personal bond with the sport or team; are true devotees.
13. Mental well-being needs	Motivations that help keep balance in one's life, comprised of the following three categories: • Self-actualization: Desire for self-fulfillment. • Self-esteem: Holding oneself in high regard. • Value development: Building of loyalty, character, and altruism.
14. Nostalgia	Refers to an individual's desire for something in the past. Concerned with the extent to which an individual is drawn to watching sports because of fond or "idealized" memories associated with sports events that took place in the past.
15. Obligation	Characterized by a strong sense of private belonging to the team.
16. Personal needs	A composite of the following: • Skill mastery: An attempt by the viewer to transfer the knowledge obtained through spectating to participation in the activity. • Aesthetics: Beauty, grace, or other artistic characteristics of sport. • Stress reduction: Process of reducing state of anxiety.

(continued)

Table 3.2 *(continued)*

Motive	Definition
17. Personalities	Concerned with an individual's interest in watching a sport event because it features a particular athlete.
18. Physical attractiveness of participants	Concerned with an individual's interest in watching a sport event because of the physical attractiveness or "sex appeal" of an individual athlete or group of athletes.
19. Physical skill of participants	Appreciation of skill excellence.
20. Self-defining experience	Private type of identification with a specific team or what it represents.
21. Self-expression experience	The desire for a unique self-defining experience.
22. Social interaction	Refers to the nonevaluation, noninstrumental, causal, frequently fortuitous social interaction that is freely entered into by two or more parties watching a particular sport event.
23. Social needs	Comprised of the following two categories: • Social facilitation: The social gratification of being with others who enjoy the same activity. • Affiliation: Connecting or associating oneself with the need to interact, socialize with others, and belong.
24. Sport-based needs	Comprised of the following three categories: • Risk taking: Engage in thrill seeking. • Aggression: Entertainment value of aggressive plays in sport. • Competition: The act of entering into a rivalry. • Achievement: Satisfying needs for achievement by identifying with achieving others.
25. Technical aspects	Refers to an individual's preoccupation with monitoring and/or collecting the quantifiable records (e.g., game statistics) resulting from an athlete's/team's performance.
26. Vicarious achievement	Addresses the extent to which spectators are attracted to watching sports because of their need to enhance self-esteem vicariously through the success of an athlete or sport team. This concept represents an indirect tactic of ego-enhancement indirectly when a team/athlete performs well.

Reprinted, by permission, from D. Funk, D. Mahony, J. Gladden , et al., 1999, "Understanding the sport spectator and sport fan: The three A's to allegiance." Used at the Fourteenth Annual North American Society for Sport Management Conference, Vancouver, British Columbia.

Mullin, Hardy, and Sutton have collapsed the primary motives for sport involvement (which undoubtedly serve as the basis for incentivization) into the following broad categories:

- Achievement
- Craft
- Affiliation or community
- Health and/or fitness benefits
- Fun and festival[18]

These motives or incentives for sport involvement, which should serve as the critical underpinnings of any promotional plan, are certainly not limited to personal sport involvement (e.g., participation or spectatorship), as they embody the essence of sport consumption by all sport customer groups. Therein lies yet another challenge for the sport promotion specialist: the breadth of customer groups attracted to the sport product further confounds the issue as sport participants, spectators (attendees and media consumers), media, licensees, and sponsors all warrant specialized incentivization processes.

Although sport consumption incentives may vary from situation to situation, the categories suggested by Mullin et al. appear to capture the scope of incentives for sport consumption across all potential consumer groups. Consider the high school wrestling coach who in an effort to promote team participation offers a variety of incentives—social interaction with fellow team members, the opportunity to perform in front of significant others, team travel, physical fitness, and the potential of being a varsity letter winner. A similar variety of nonmonetary incentives can be used to attract fans to the park, arena, track, or stadium, such as affiliation with friends and family, fun, entertainment, and enhanced self-concept.

In the following sections we provide examples to suggest how each motive or incentive applies to a variety of sport consumer groups and discuss how sport promotion specialists may use this valuable information in formulating an incentive promotional campaign.

Achievement

People may derive a sense of achievement through an intrinsic (internal) or extrinsic (external) reward (incentive) system. For instance, participating on a winning team, running a personal best in a 10K road race, or scaling the face of a mountain provides the participant intrinsic feedback on the perceived accomplishment. These accomplishments may also net the consumer a trophy, medal, or peer recognition—these are all considered extrinsic forms of acknowledgment of the accomplishment.

According to Suggs, a "second running boom" emerged in the 1990s as ordinary runners sought a sense of accomplishment rather than better race times. Such runners are filling marathons and shorter road races across the United States. Road race marketers have modified event parameters, focusing on participation-oriented elements (e.g., by lowering entrance performance standards, extending course completion time to accommodate slower runners and walkers) as opposed to elite racer attractions such as prize money. Such changes attracted more than 9000 participants to the Walt Disney World Marathon, many of whom brought family members and made it a vacation.[19]

A similar focus has enabled the London Marathon to realize strong participation, attracting 33,379 entrants in 2000, while 30,071 finished the race in 2001. While many world-class runners participate, there is also very much a sense of festival and fun

© Barry Bland/Globe Photos, Inc.

Russia's Svetlana Masterkova received both intrinsic and extrinsic rewards winning the 800 meters Olympic gold medal.

about the event. The number of women-only races has increased exponentially, with the Dublin Mini-Marathon attracting 31,000 entrants in 2001. The aim of many of these races is to support research to cure breast cancer.[20]

But achievements in personal sport consumerism are not limited to physical activity. For instance, incentives (of financial value and otherwise) should be offered to spectators who attain perfect season attendance records, and ticket plan holders achieving longevity milestones should be similarly rewarded. Often these incentives do involve a financial reward; however, the unique attributes of the sport product enable the sport promotion specialist to employ creativity and to extend an incentive package so that it might include half-time introductions, coach or player engagements, or behind-the-scene facility tours.

Spectators are often attracted to sport because of a slightly different, but related, motive: their need to enhance self-esteem vicariously through the success of an athlete or team. This concept, referred to as *vicarious achievement,* represents an indirect tactic aimed at ego enhancement. Also referred to as *basking in reflected glory,* this sport consumption motive serves to enhance the sport consumer's self-esteem indirectly by way of a team or athlete's performance. We see this as application rates at American colleges rise immediately after a national championship in football or basketball, and as the sales of logoed merchandise skyrocket after a team claims a world championship. There is also a significant rise in levels of national pride when nations do well in world competition, as Australia did in 1999 in winning the World Rugby Cup, the Cricket World Cup, and the World Netball Championship, or as Nigeria did in winning the 1996 men's Olympic soccer title.

More and more of today's sport fanatics of all ages are driven to acquire as well as demonstrate a sound base of knowledge regarding their favorite player, team, or event. In fact, ESPN themed a majority of the advertising for its NHL and NFL studio shows around the viewer's desire to acquire knowledge as a form of intellectual achievement. The campaigns targeted the die-hard fan craving to amass volumes of information on hockey and football.

On the other hand, sport consumer groups such as corporate sponsors and event host communities are incentivized to achieve a prescribed set of organizational goals as a result of their involvement with sport. Most corporate sponsors of sport seek to achieve increased sales volume or company, brand, and product exposure from their involvement with sport.[21] In contrast, the dominant incentives for hosting sporting events among American municipal sport commissions are to stimulate economic impact, enhance community image, and improve residents' quality of life.[22] In each case, the potential for achievement emerges as a dominant incentive for a particular behavioral response (e.g., accept or reject proposal). Research has revealed that a corporate sport sponsorship decision-maker will be more inclined to accept a sponsorship proposal when an apparent match exists between the company's promotional objectives and the sponsee's offerings.[23] Therefore, it is critical that sport promotion specialists familiarize themselves with the achievement-oriented motives of greatest importance to particular corporate customers or partners and design incentive plans accordingly.

Craft

According to Mullin, Hardy, and Sutton, developing or observing physical skill is a common incentive for personal sport involvement.[24] The quest for enhanced skill therefore becomes a key attraction for sport participants who may range from the "weekend warrior" seeking newfangled training apparatus to budding high school athletes aspiring to attract college scholarship opportunities. In each case the participant engages in sport consumption in order to improve his physical skill or sport craft.

Craft-related incentives are not limited to the participatory-sport consumer, however. For example, the opportunity to observe star players perform their *craft* often ranks as one of the most important factors in attracting attendees and media consumers to professional sport. Additionally, research has demonstrated that a winning record is the highest predicting variable for team sport attendance as well as sponsorship and team advertising sales.[25] The fact that Tiger Woods's amazing 10-stroke victory at the 2000 PGA Championship attracted the largest viewing audience in the event's history proved that most viewers were drawn to the telecast to observe his mastery of the game (or course) as opposed to the drama of a competitive dual. Furthermore, Annika Sörenstam drew huge audiences as she became the first woman to shoot a 59 in professional golf and won four LPGA tournaments in a row in 2001. Her mastery of the competition and her attempt to win five tournaments in a row vaulted women's golf to the front pages and briefly relegated men's professional golf to the "other" category.

However, most believe that the use of anticipated performance outcomes as the basis of team sport consumption incentivization is tenuous at best. In fact, a survey of NBA marketing executives revealed the use of a winning season as an attendance incentive to be a low priority and an infrequent occurrence.[26] Unquestionably the reason is the uncontrollable nature of team performance. Spoelstra recommends occasionally shifting the emphasis to attractive, highly skilled opponents whose infrequent appearance and execution of *craft* will be viewed as a novelty by regularly attending patrons.[27]

Lastly, sport often enables others to perform their professional craft or vocation better. Sport facilitates relationship building among business clients, thus emerging as an incentive that sport promotion specialists can use with prospective clients in corporate sponsorship or hospitality negotiations. The licensing program may include an effort to grant incentives such as royalty waivers, rebates, or deferred payment to licensees who draft unique presentations of the sport property's logo. And finally, many of the tactics discussed in chapter 7, such as sensitivity to deadlines, can stand as incentives for members of the sport media, whose craft depends on the availability and accessibility of newsworthy content.

Affiliation or Community

The desire to be part of or associated with a *recognized* group, whether it is a team, country club, or booster association, represents a motive for sport involvement that transcends sport consumption customer groups. A unique feature of this motivational factor is that the consumer may seek affiliation with more than one source, ranging from the core product (e.g., team) to other patrons (cosponsors). For instance, those seeking affiliation with a team often endeavor to bask in reflected glory, drawing a sense of self-identification from the team's notoriety or success. Hence, fundamentally, affiliation with sport acts as a means of enhancing the consumer's self-concept. The swaying, samba-dancing, bedecked Brazilians who appear wherever Brazil is participating in world-class competition attest to the sense of **affiliation** and **community** generated by national teams.

Consumer-to-Consumer Affiliation

Dependence on social facilitation has been identified as one of the unique features of the sport product, with consumption generally occurring in a public setting and satisfaction greatly influenced by interaction with other people.[28] Interestingly, sport consumption provides a range of affiliation opportunities from casual to intensive. Consider, for example, the casual relationship that emerges between two individuals meeting in the steam room at the fitness center after an exhaustive workout, or the intense relationship that exists between management of a women's professional tennis tournament and representatives from its title sponsor.

Intragroup affiliation   Sport is not often consumed independently, as exemplified by the fact that less than 2% of those attending collegiate and professional sport events in the United States attend by themselves.[29] The recent growth of fan or sport booster clubs among amateur and professional sport teams is also testimony to the fact that sport facilitates social interaction among consumers with similar interests and behavioral patterns. Astute sport promotion specialists will seize opportunities to facilitate intragroup affiliation, or interaction among consumers with a common bond. Manchester United has used this interest wisely in allowing only members of its supporters' clubs access to tickets to their games. Nonseason tickets are distributed only to the official supporters' clubs, which issue the tickets to their members for a game at United's home ground at Old Trafford. It is highly advisable for the sport promotion specialist to take advantage of opportunities to facilitate intragroup affiliation.

Moreover, according to Brindley and Thorogood, social interaction is *the* most influential variable in attracting defined markets to horse racing in the United Kingdom. Because of the group-attendance orientation of this market, the researchers urge the use of group-related incentives to increase attendance—ranging from special services such as party packs and catering facilities to discounted admission.[30] Additionally, print and electronic ad copy should convey a sense of intragroup interaction, or sport involvement among a predetermined set of consumers. For instance, an ad could show a group of individuals representing the targeted audience excitedly cheering for the racehorses as they approach the finish line, or collectively slapping a high five for picking the winning horse. In either case, message recipients see others like themselves enjoying a day at the races.

© Barry Bland/Globe Photos, Inc.

The Olympic Games give sport fans throughout the world the opportunity to feel pride and affiliation with their athletes.

Transgroup affiliation   According to Melnick, sport venues provide the ideal location for casual affiliation among otherwise total strangers or groups of strangers, as patrons are able to use the experience to fulfill a need for noncommittal socialization.[31] While viewing one another as strangers, these consumers or groups of consumers do in fact share one commonality, their interest and possible participation in sport, which therefore acts as an interactive link between one party and another.

Consider, for example, the sociability between two regularly attending stationary bicyclists at the fitness center. The regular encounter, limited to trivial conversation, fills the critical need for human interaction (not to mention passing the time) with someone whom an individual momentarily has something in common with. The situation is similar for spectators at a sporting event. Regardless of the diversity of their everyday lives, display of support for a team forms a common, albeit short-term, bond among fanatics. Diligent efforts on the part of the sport promotion specialist to employ personal contact tactics can serve to crystallize these relationships. Hence, the opportunity for socialization emerges as a fundamental incentive for initial as well as sustained sport involvement and consumption.

Cheering Cubs fans find temporary camaraderie.

This quest for group affiliation extends to the media consumer as well. Mullin, Hardy, and Sutton raise the question, *"Who wants to watch the Super Bowl alone?"* Apparently not many: during the week preceding Super Bowl Sunday, sales of salty chips typically skyrocket to annual records as viewers scramble to prepare for the upcoming party. Meanwhile, millions of other viewers attend functions hosted by sport restaurants and grills. Of course, this behavioral pattern is not limited to the Super Bowl, as consumers of televised sport around the world go to great lengths to develop a viewership *community* in an effort to replicate the social atmosphere of on-site attendance. Capitalizing on this pattern and seizing an opportunity to nurture affiliation with and among consumers, several English Premier soccer clubs operate sports bars within the community where fans congregate to watch televised broadcasts of games.[32] Such a tactic enables club management to effectively package team and fan affiliation and viewership incentives as well as to control the broadcast consumption environment.

Furthermore, Shoham and Kahle contend that unique sport-based communities reach beyond the broadcast medium into publications. In fact, the researchers found that members of the sport communication communities—viewers of televised sport and readers of printed material about sport, as well as sport spectators—all differed significantly on a number of behavioral characteristics. These findings further illustrate that sport behavior can be used to identify and define a unique community of consumers possessing similar personal traits and values.[33]

Intergroup affiliation   As the affiliation intensifies, bonds strengthen between the parties involved (e.g., consumer to consumer; consumer to source). At its highest degree of intensity, affiliation typically results in some type of competition that pits one group (team) representing a "community" of supporters against another group (team) and its "community" of supporters. Sport is rich with rivalries that have existed for years; however, it's a good idea for the sport promotion specialist representing a sport entity that lacks an affiliation incentive of this magnitude to explore creating one for consumption incentivization purposes. Yet, how does one go about "creating" a rivalry? Within-sport rivalries have emerged from a variety of sources including geographical links (state or national boundaries), similar performance records (Yankees vs. Dodgers), and supporter profile characteristics (demographic similarities or dissimilarities). For instance, member institutions of the Big Ten collegiate athletic conference have creatively established football rivalries among themselves that serve as consumption incentives for players and fans alike. Each season the University of Minnesota Golden Gophers battle the University of Wisconsin Badgers for possession of the Golden Ax. Yes, the Golden Ax! Regardless of the respective records entering the contest, an intense struggle ensues not only for custody of the ax but the bragging rights within and across state lines for the next year. Similarly, all other conference universities have at least one rivalry with another institution, giving those who are affiliated intrinsic (bragging rights) and extrinsic (ax, buckets, bells) incentives for involvement. The rivalry's intensity is often maximized by a series of pranks (e.g., mascot capture) and wagers (e.g., governmental officials or institutional administrators staking local cuisine) that the sport promotion specialist can easily orchestrate. Rascher has determined that in MLB, rivalry games raise attendance approximately 25% to 30%.[34]

Such local rivalries are termed "local derbies" in international sport. Teams having geographic proximity, particularly teams that are from the same city or region and that play in the same competition, create the "derbies." These are intense, heated local rivalries, particularly between the two groups of fans, and in many cases are regarded as more important than the competition in which the teams play. Fortitudo Bologna and Virtus Bologna in the Italian Basketball League, Real Madrid and Athletico Madrid in the Spanish Football League, and Glasgow Celtic and Glasgow Rangers in the Scottish Premier Football League are examples of these fanatical local rivalries.

Consumer-to-Organization Affiliation

The aspiration to affiliate is typically predicated on the existence of desirable identification links readily apparent to the consumer, whether an individual purchaser or potential corporate partner. For example, research indicates that minority consumers often have a need to identify with an organization before becoming patrons. Armstrong notes that promoters can enhance this process by helping black consumers find a link or tie to the organization. Affiliation incentives can range from arranging interaction between black employees and the team's coaches, management, and players to amending the core product with culturally salient extensions that appeal to black consumers, which may include offering gospel concerts, involving black performers and entertainers, or creating special programs for black civic organizations and businesses (figure

3.2). According to Armstrong, the NBA has been the leader among American professional sport franchises in appealing to the black consumer. It has positioned itself favorably with the black community through a range of promotional efforts—from community relations programs affecting young urban blacks, to entertainment ventures featuring musical performances by rhythm and blues or rap artists, to culturally appropriate advertisements. Such promotional tactics have provided incentive for the black community to identify and affiliate with professional basketball in numbers far superior to those for any other American professional or amateur sport.[35]

On the other hand, McCarthy indicates that promotional content directed toward

Key findings about black consumers	Strategies for sport promotion specialists
1. The black consumer market is a challenging segment with many cultural nuances that influence individuals' thoughts and behaviors.	Involve individuals with expertise in the black consumer market in the designing of marketing strategies.
2. Black consumers have unique media consumption patterns.	Use black media outlets (particularly black radio) to promote events.
3. Blacks respond more favorably to culturally based approaches to marketing communications.	Advertisements and promotional messages should contain a theme and content that offer a reference point for black audiences.
4. Blacks often seek a means of identifying with organizations as they decide whether or not to support their businesses.	Engage in activities that allow blacks to find a self-reference link to identify with the organization.
5. Black consumers often have an allegiance to black businesses.	Conduct business with black vendors to address organizational needs and involve them as corporate sponsors.
6. Black consumers often seek a cultural experience in their leisure activities.	Amend the product/service with extensions that are culturally salient to black consumers.
7. Black consumers are socially conscious individuals.	Demonstrate a respect for the black community through socially responsible/cause-related marketing.
8. Black consumers may have personal and structural difficulty accessing the existing channels of distribution.	Distribute tickets through outlets that are easily accessible to black consumers. Also, find creative ways of exposing black communities to the product.
9. Sport behaviors are often a result of socialization occurring during childhood.	Invest in programs that include black youths to nurture their involvement.
10. Just as with any other community, the black community has opinion leaders.	Form a support group of black constituents from various realms of the community to serve as staff multipliers.

Figure 3.2 Summary of key findings about black consumers and marketing implications.

Reprinted, by permission, from K.L. Armstrong, 1998, "Ten strategies to employ when marketing sport to black consumers," *Sport Marketing Quarterly* 7 (3):16.

the Hispanic market should emphasize a family or group affiliation. Such messages should convey an incentive to the family rather than the individual through happy images of an extended family at a sporting event. Major League Soccer and MLB have both initiated affiliation incentives targeting Hispanic consumers through community relations programs involving Hispanic players, as well as bilingual advertising and game telecasts.[36]

Sponsorship decisions are likewise based on the potential sponsor's prospects for favorable affiliation benefits. Early research on sponsorship revealed that affiliation-related motives such as image transference (from sponsee to sponsor) were of primary importance, leading many sponsors to seek arrangements based on the anticipated image affiliation benefits. While contemporary research indicates a shift toward a quantifiable-results orientation (sales), image congruence and enhancement remain

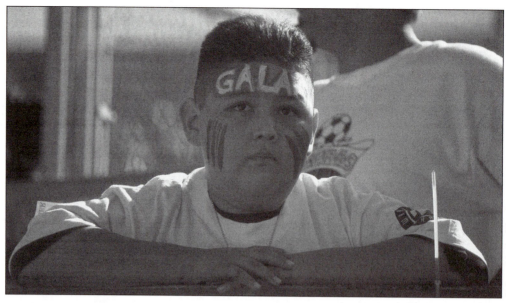

© Jose Marin/The Sporting Image

A young Los Angeles Galaxy fan.

critically valuable to corporate sponsor decision-makers (table 3.3). Certainly this was the case when John Hancock Financial Services threatened not to renew its long-standing relationship with the International Olympic Committee after the vote-bribing scandal of 1999. The firm's concern was that affiliation with the scandal-ridden International Olympic Committee would prove damaging to the company's valuable public image. A renewal of affiliation was struck only after the corporate partner was assured that policies were in place to minimize the possibility of a repeat occurrence of the scandal.

Similarly, the opportunity to affiliate with existing cosponsors frequently emerges as a factor of importance to corporate sport sponsors. The incentive for sponsorship involvement may not be direct affiliation with the sponsee but with members of the sponsee's corporate partner program. Likewise, media outlets may pursue affiliation with high-profile sport properties (e.g., major professional leagues) via execution of a broadcast agreement in an effort to enhance their credibility within the marketplace. Such appeared to be the case when Fox obtained the NFL broadcast rights for what many considered an outlandish fee. In the minds of many critics and viewers, Fox's business affiliation with the NFL significantly enhanced the network's credibility, not to mention overall ratings.

The development of the NFL in Europe was an example of American corporate entities coming together and sponsoring sport as a means of extending their product market. The combination of "the" American beer with the premier American sport helped create an image package for both Budweiser and the NFL that was mutually beneficial.

Sport also often provides corporations the opportunity to affiliate with a special cause. In fact, $300 billion was spent in North America alone in 1998 for the right to associate with various causes, and approximately one-half of these associations were linked via sport.[37] For instance, sponsorship of the PGA TOUR's FedEx St. Jude Golf Classic in Memphis, Tennessee, gives Federal Express an ideal cause-related promotional opportunity as the event has generated millions of dollars for the St. Jude Children's Research Hospital. Furthermore, company-sponsored research showed that existing as well as potential overnight shipping customers value this cause affiliation, which enhances the desire to sustain the sponsorship (figure 3.3).[38]

Table 3.3 Comparative Assessment of North American Corporate Sport Sponsorship Motives

Objective	U.S. rating (n = 151)	Canadian rating (n = 35)
Increase market share/sales	5.99	6.27
Target market awareness	5.92	6.33
Increase public awareness	5.84	6.27
Enhance company image	5.41	5.81
Community involvement	4.45	5.31
Trade relations	4.50	4.35
Trade goodwill	4.47	4.52
Alter public perception	4.09	4.10
Enhance employee relations	3.80	3.47
Block competition	3.67	4.18
Social responsibility	3.10	4.00
Corporate philanthropy	3.08	3.58

A rating of 7 = extremely important. A rating of 1 = extremely unimportant.

Adapted, by permission, from N. Logh, R.L. Irwin, and G. Short, 2000, "Corporate sponsorship motive among North American companies: A contemporary analysis," *International Journal of Sport Management* 1 (4):288. © 2000 American Press, Boston, MA.

Cause-related marketing unites for-profit companies such as FedEx with charitable organizations such as St. Jude Children's Research Hospital in a mutually beneficial manner. With this in mind please indicate your agreement with the following items.

	Strongly disagree				Strongly agree
Cause-related marketing creates a positive company image.	4%	2%	7%	31%	56%
I would be willing to pay more for a service that supports a cause I care about.	2%	5%	23%	33%	35%
FedEx's sponsorship of this golf tournament improves my impression of the company.	3%	3%	15%	31%	47%
Based on its support of this tournament, I will be more likely to use FedEx services.	3%	5%	24%	30%	34%
Based on its support of St. Jude, I will be more likely to use FedEx services.	3%	5%	17%	30%	45%

Figure 3.3 Cause-related consumer research findings.

Mercedes, the official car of the Kroger St. Jude Tennis Classic.

Lastly, the recent nostalgia trend relates to the contemporary sport consumer's desire to affiliate with an idealized past. We see the influence of this consumption motive in sport facility and uniform design, not to mention the prevalent "classic sport" products. This nostalgic perspective concerns the extent to which an individual is drawn to watching sport because of fond memories associated with sporting experiences that took place in the past. For instance, field research conducted in the Cleveland marketplace revealed that preferred team identification was frequently influenced by memorable childhood attendance experiences. Respondents spoke of bonding attendance experiences with relatives (typically fathers) and friends, ultimately inspiring one professional sport franchise to develop a parent-child ticket program aimed at facilitating this nostalgic motive in tomorrow's ticket buyers.

Health and Fitness Benefits

As we might expect, a strong correlation exists between participation in sport and personal physical and mental health characteristics. Recent advertising campaigns from the NCAA and Women's Sport Foundation alert us to the fact that access to sport has had a profound, favorable impact on females. For instance, females who have participated in sport have lower percentages of early pregnancy than other groups, are less likely to be victims of domestic abuse, and possess higher levels of self-esteem. Additionally, recent research involving women from culturally and linguistically diverse backgrounds revealed physical benefits to be the primary motive for sport participation (figure 3.4).[39] Arguments are also often made that sport involvement, in the form of participation as well as spectatorship, contributes to an enhanced mental heath status. For instance, studies have indicated that sport helps to keep balance in one's life and can serve as a catalyst for self-actualization, improved self-esteem, and value development.[40] These findings suggest incentives that can and should be used to inspire active participation in sport, whether in a competitive or a recreational setting.

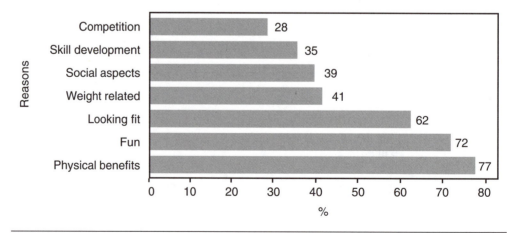

Figure 3.4   Primary motives for female sport participation.

Reprinted, by permission, from T. Taylor and K. Tooney, 1999, "Sport, gender, and cultural diversity: exploring the nexus," *Journal of Sport Management* 13 (1):11.

Additionally, corporations have embraced the notion that healthy employees, engaged in sport and fitness activities, enhance organizational productivity. This has led to the establishment of corporate wellness facilities and corporate-sponsored recreation activities including competitive leagues and tournaments and adventure outings. Occasionally, such activities result in an intracorporate or intercorporate challenge competition that serves as a hybrid incentive program involving health and fitness benefits as well as team-building opportunities (affiliation).

Similarly, corporations often view engagement in sport sponsorship as a means of enhancing employee health and morale. A sponsorship giving employees access to sport and recreation facilities or admission to special events during their leisure time enhances the mental and physical health of company personnel. The inclusion of such information in a sponsorship sales presentation may enhance the appeal for a corporate decision-maker interested in improving the well-being of company personnel.

Fun and Festival

Although typically considered the key incentive for youth sport involvement, the notion of having fun pervades all levels of sport consumption today. You often hear the claim that giveaways and premium items are not just for kids—fun isn't either! In fact, Wolf would argue that fun influences and thus pervades all levels of consumption, as today's consumer possesses an insatiable desire to be entertained.[41] Hansen and Gauthier report that North American (United States and Canadian) professional and collegiate sport promotional specialists believe the delivery of entertainment to be their primary marketing-related objective.[42] This unquestionably implies that consumers of professional and collegiate sport are primarily attracted to the product because of their zeal for good entertainment.

Globetrotters Know How to Have Fun

Under founder Abe Saperstein, the Harlem Globetrotters provided fans with a quality ball team, entertaining stunts, and worldwide goodwill. Clowning, dribbling, and shooting exhibitions were considered product extensions within a highly competitive game. The Globetrotter product offered the fan both high-performance sport and theatrical entertainment.[43]

The shift away from team performance, mentioned earlier in the chapter, has also precipitated a focus on entertainment at sport events. Team sport schedules are now replete with fireworks, concerts, dance team performances, and the like, while sport retail outlets pipe in music and crowd noise and provide minicourts for product trials and games. This philosophy has also spawned a new generation of patrons who possess limited interest in the quality of the core product, primarily seeking the entertainment value resulting from the consumption experience. Although this is readily apparent in team sports, the retail and food and beverage industries are experiencing similar behavioral patterns with the use of sport as the *entertainment* drawing card. Stotlar discovered that the primary motive for attending a sports grill was to have fun.[44]

A sporting event represents a dramatic production, as the potential exists for pitting a protagonist against an antagonist in a contest for a scarce resource (i.e., victory) in a context that is regimented by fixed structure (i.e., rules) and demarcated by a beginning, middle, and end. The sport promotion specialist will find it beneficial to tap the available resources for the event "dramatization" so desired among sport consumers who endeavor to use sport as a primary form of entertainment. We need look no further than the world of professional wrestling to find prime examples of "soap opera"-style entertainment, attractive to a niche market of sport consumers and essentially threatening to the volume for such long-standing sport programming as Monday Night Football.

The infusion of technology has of course enhanced the delivery of entertainment to the sport consumer. The term **techtainment** has emerged to refer to the use of in-arena technology specifically designed to entertain patrons.[45] Similarly, kids and adults alike are lured to sport Web sites by games, puzzles, sweepstakes, and prizes.[46] In fact, chapter 11 is dedicated to the discussion of such consumption environment enhancement under the topic of *atmospherics*.

Who Wants to Be a Hockey Fan?

In an effort to enliven the atmosphere at already sold-out home hockey games, the University of New Hampshire launched "Who Wants to Be a Hockey Fan?" In a format modeled on the successful television show, contestants selected from among the spectators take the ice during intermission and try to answer three questions relating to hockey rules, history, and slang. Participants unsure of the answer may poll the audience as on the TV program. The promotion has proven highly effective in engaging audience as well as sponsor participation.[47]

Implementing the Incentive Plan

In an effort to maximize incentivization campaign efficiencies, it is advisable to adopt a plan similar to the seven-step procedure shown in figure 3.5 for promotional incentive plan implementation.[48] As with all organizational planning efforts, defined procedures offer the sport promotion specialist a valuable guide intended to ensure

1. Specify the objective that makes it necessary or desirable to undertake the use of incentives.

   a. Increase sales by:

      1. rewarding loyal customers.

      2. increasing purchase rates of occasional customers.

      3. generating trials among new customers.

      4. deseasonalize seasonal sales.

   b. Build a database and develop new sales leads.

   c. Move excess stock.

   d. Block a competitor.

   e. Generate organizational goodwill.

2. Determine inclusiveness of the incentive.

3. Specify the recipient of the incentive.

4. Determine the direction of the incentive.

5. Determine the form of the incentive.

6. Determine the amount of the incentive.

7. Determine the time and payment of the incentive.

Figure 3.5   Seven-step approach to incentive promotion plan.

Reprinted, by permission, from P. Kolter, 1975, *Marketing for non-profit organizations* (Englewood Cliffs, NJ: Pearson Education).

incentivization campaign purpose and structure. The proposed incentive campaign is subjected to the same scrutiny as are all other promotional components demanding a focused effort, operational critique, and assessment procedures.

Step 1: Specify the Objective

The incentive promotion should be designed from the start to achieve a specific objective. Objectives may range from increasing sales or usage rates to attempting to block a competitor. Philosophically, it is advisable for the sport promotion specialist to shower existing, loyal customers with incentives before targeting external consumer groups. The goodwill that is established by this *market penetration*-type strategy should lead to invaluable word-of-mouth publicity among existing consumers.

When seeking to attract a new customer base *(new market development)*, the sport promotion specialist should incorporate the promotional incentive in all campaign literature. For instance, the availability of hundreds of thousands of dollars in scholarships appears to be fueling an incredible growth spurt among junior golfers.[49] Junior golf camp administrators and instructors should therefore be sure to include this incentive in all promotional collateral.

Figure 3.6 reveals the effective match between promotional objectives and incentive programs as developed by Cummins. Use of this information will help the sport promotion specialist allow the prescribed objective to dictate the incentive campaign.

Objectives \ Incentive	Immediate free offers	Delayed free offers	Immediate price offers	Delayed price offers	Finance offers	Competitions	Games and draws	Charitable offers	Self-liquidators	Profit-making promotions
Increasing sales volume	9	7	9	7	5	1	3	5	2	1
Increasing product or service trial	9	7	9	2	9	2	7	7	2	1
Increasing repeat purchase	2	9	2	9	5	3	2	7	3	3
Increasing loyalty	1	9	0	7	3	3	1	7	3	3
Widening usage	9	5	5	2	3	1	5	5	1	1
Creating interest	3	3	3	2	2	5	9	8	8	8
Creating awareness	3	3	3	1	1	5	9	8	8	8
Deflecting attention from price	9	7	0	7	7	3	5	5	2	2
Gaining intermediary support	9	5	9	5	9	3	7	5	1	1
Gaining display	9	5	9	5	9	3	7	5	1	1

Each square is filled with a rating from 0 (not well matched) to 10 (very well matched). Use it as a ready reckoner for linking your objectives to the incentive.

Figure 3.6 Linking promotion objective with incentive programs.

Reprinted, by permission, from P.R. Smith, 1993, *Marketing communications: An integrated approach* (London: Kogan Page Ltd.), 61.

Teams Reward Loyalty

No fewer than 12 MLB teams employ fan loyalty programs that track and reward fans for frequent attendance. Attendance prizes may range from free concession items to drawings for World Series tickets. Twenty-five percent of the fans attending San Antonio Spurs games swipe loyalty cards at every home game, providing team management with valuable consumer behavior data.[50]

Step 2: Determine Inclusiveness of the Incentive

Is the incentive for the individual consumer or a group? Typically incentives are offered to individuals for their direct benefit. It is highly recommended that value-added incentives be made available to as many members of the consumer group as possible. For instance, although it is quasi-entertaining to watch someone shoot free throws at half-time of a basketball game for the chance to win valuable prizes, few onlookers feel truly engaged. But if the contestant could win prizes for individuals seated in her row or section, or for all patrons in attendance, there is little question that patron involvement would increase. Pizza Hut and MLB teamed up for just such a contest, with contestants positioned in center field (with a glove) attempting to shag three fly balls launched skyward from a pitching machine. With each catch the *entire* crowd became qualified to receive a list of progressive prizes from Pizza Hut (drink, breadsticks, personal pizza) if they redeemed their game ticket at a local restaurant within 24 hours. In one major league city, so many patrons redeemed tickets after the game that all Pizza Huts within close proximity of the stadium ran out of pizza dough!

If the objective defines a targeted audience, however, the incentive will need to be rather exclusive. Hofacre and Burman suggest that professional sport franchises tailor incentive programs to the senior market (over 65 years of age), as this group of consumers represents a vibrant but challenging market to capture in the coming years. The authors also make the point that giveaways and premiums are not just for kids![51]

Step 3: Specify the Incentive Recipient

Are the incentives going to the sales staff, suppliers, or consumers? Sales force incentives may include bonuses, gifts, and contests. Supplier, or trade, incentives—somewhat similar to those offered consumers—may include buying allowances, discounts, advance purchase premiums, advertising allowances, and sales contests. Within the consumer category, what incentives will be offered to patrons, sponsors, licensees, and the like? A co-op incentive program involving a corporate partner (e.g., product giveaway) engages two recipients as the consumers receive the product giveaway and the sponsor gains desired product exposure.

Step 4: Determine the Direction of the Incentive

The next step is to determine whether the incentive is positive (rewarding) or negative (punishment). Taxing or fining suppliers or retailers for excess inventory would exemplify a negative incentive aimed at promoting action. Similarly, the NBA's $100,000 domestic retail licensing royalty guarantee (necessitating over $1 million in sales) serves as an incentive for league licensees.

Step 5: Determine the Form of the Incentive

Will the incentive consist of monetary or nonmonetary value? The merits of each have been a frequent topic of debate. The sport promotion specialist must determine which form of incentive provides the greatest appeal to one or more consumer groups.

Step 6: Determine the Amount of the Incentive

An overly small incentive is ineffective, particularly if targeted to members of higher income brackets, whereas an overly large incentive is wasteful. This has led to interest in graduated incentives whereby the amount offered varies with the consumer's economic circumstances. For instance, members of a booster club accumulate benefits according to how much they contribute (which typically correlates with annual household income). Similarly, providing a percentage of the total sales purchase as opposed to a standardized fee may inspire the consumer to purchase more product (applicable in retail, sponsorship packaging, etc.). Therefore, the paying consumer is provided a means of controlling the incentive process.

Step 7: Determine the Time of Payment of the Incentive

Most incentives are paid immediately when the consumer takes the intended action. However, delayed or mail-in rebates, as well as flexible or deferred payment plans, not only serve as purchase incentives but are common within the sport industry. Most important, however, is clear articulation of when the incentive is to be made available to the recipient. Upon entry to the stadium? At the game's conclusion? In the mail? And, most importantly, the consumer needs to know, "Must I be present to win?"

Recently Kent State University conducted a contest in which the winner would receive an all-expense-paid trip to Hawaii. When the winner was not in attendance at the drawing, which took place during a home football game, the athletic department—claiming that it was necessary for the winner to have been present—declared no one a winner. Unfortunately for the athletic department, its failure to accurately communicate this critical piece of information enabled the winner to take a trip to Hawaii the next year. Details such as this cannot be overlooked!

Customer Lifetime Value

While no figures have been generated in sport, General Motors estimates that each lifetime customer is worth $276,000. General Motors is credited with initiating the "value ladder," whereby a specific line of cars is offered to customers at each stage of life.[52] Sport organizations have the opportunity to follow suit if product offerings and incentives are appropriately packaged.

Application of the seven-step approach should give the sport promotion specialist a framework for developing effective consumer incentivization campaigns. In order to employ this procedure, the sport promotion specialist faces the challenge of proactively assessing the purpose, design, and delivery of the anticipated incentive and also defining the intended recipients and their anticipated responsiveness. A checks-and-balances system such as this subjects the campaign to an exhaustive evaluative process. Incentive campaigns that do not include these critical ingredients tend to yield less-than-satisfactory results. Micheal Schetzel, director of sales for the

Boston Red Sox, provides the following Practitioner's Perspective illustrating how the club applies the incentive planning process.

PRACTITIONER'S PERSPECTIVE

Ticket Incentives for the Boston Red Sox
by Michael Schetzel, Director of Sales for the Boston Red Sox

To paraphrase a line from a popular baseball movie, if you give it away, they will come. In most cases, the giveaway is used as an incentive to increase game attendance. Over the last couple of years in Boston, with attendance-breaking records and most games sold out, the giveaway has been used more as a value-added incentive, especially as the ticket prices increase.

During the 100th anniversary celebration season, this philosophy toward the giveaway was especially apparent. Coming off a season with 68 of 81 games sold out and a season attendance record set, and with many games sold out before the season even started, the giveaway wasn't going to be a tool to increase attendance. It would, however, add value to the game experience for the fans. The Red Sox used three separate giveaways. The first was a series of collectable lapel pins sponsored by Coca-Cola, each depicting a moment in Red Sox history. The second was a series of pennants commemorating the 100 seasons of the Red Sox, and the third was a series of "Wally the Green Monster" beanbag buddies in different uniforms worn throughout Red Sox history.

Each of these items were quality collectible items that added value to the game-day experience. The dates for these promotions were selected to be in conjunction with both special dates in Red Sox history and other games so that the promotions were spread out over the entire season. When possible, they were for games where it was thought ticket sales could be increased, but that was not the main factor in deciding the dates for the promotions.

The Red Sox do offer incentives to increase attendance of games that are traditionally tougher to sell out. These incentives are centered around ticket discounts. Weeknight games in April, May, and September are generally the toughest dates to sell out at Fenway Park. The unpredictable New England weather in spring and fall is the main reason for games not selling out. Of the 13 non-sellout games in 2000, all were in April and May and all but one was a weeknight.

In deciding what discounts might be offered for the 2001 season, it was necessary to review the discounts offered during 2000. In 2000, the Red Sox offered discounts for 22 games. All the remaining games were full price under all circumstances. Of the 22 games, 12 were considered "Family Games" and the others were "Group Games." On a family game day, tickets could be purchased at half price for selected sections of the stadium, including infield grandstand seats. On group game days, tickets were discounted on an increasing scale depending on group size. To receive a discount, the group had to be a minimum of 40 people.

After reviewing this process, it was discovered that 6 of the 13 non-sellout games were when the discount was restricted to groups only and not open to everyone, as it is on family game days. In an attempt to increase sellouts in 2001, 23 dates in May, April, and September were selected as discount days. On each of these dates, the discount was 50% and available to any size party. The difference between 2000 and 2001 was that the discount in 2001 was restricted to the outfield section of the park and did not extend into the infield grandstand as in 2000. The discount in 2001 was less restrictive than in 2000 with respect to dates available and size of group, but it was limited in seat selection. What this did, though, was to offer a discount on more days and to make it available to more people.

When selecting dates and deciding on what type of discount to offer, you need to be careful that you don't discount games or seats that you would sell at regular prices under the same conditions. It can be a delicate balancing act between what will help sell out that game and whether you could have sold those tickets at regular price. That is why no discounts are offered for games in June, July, and August. Games on the weekends and after school is out for the summer have traditionally sold out, so there is no need to offer discounts (though two weekends early in the season do have discounts), but giveaways are still a way to give fans added value during those months.

After making the change in discount structure from 2000 to 2001, the Red Sox have seen all but three games sell out. These were the fourth, fifth, and sixth games of the season, which were midweek night games in April, and even then the lowest attendance was 26,000+, or about 78% capacity. The changes seem to have been successful.

Incentives, whether they are in the form of a giveaway or a discount, play an important role in cultivating your fan base. Even in the case of the Red Sox, where it appears on the surface that all you have to do is open the gates and Fenway Park will be filled, incentives are needed to keep fans coming to game after game. Each promotion that is put in place has a specific purpose. For the Red Sox, the giveaway is used to reward fans that come out game after game, and the ticket discount is used to attract fans to less desirable games. Both have worked well over the past few years.

In order to properly implement an incentive planning process as suggested by Michael Schetzel, it is recommended that the sport promotions specialist develop a comprehensive list of key issues or checklist of critical elements, such as the checklist described next.

Incentive Plan Checklist

Figure 3.7 presents a 10-item operational checklist.[53] The list comprises key issues that management must address before, during, and after implementing the incentive. Perhaps most frequently overlooked is the means by which the incentive promotion will be evaluated (item 10). Prior to implementation, the sport promotion specialist should establish the parameters for evaluating the promotion's effectiveness. Clear delineation of the promotion objective, as suggested by Kotler, is the element that most facilitates assessment of the outcome. The sport promotion specialist need

---

1. Does the promotion exploit key strengths and unique selling attributes?

2. Is it a franchise building incentive? Does it carry a selling message or at least a subtle reminder? Unrelated premiums, contests, refunds, or price discounts do not reinforce brands or enhance organizational values.

3. What can go wrong? Contingency planning, crisis management, risk assessment, and insurance are worth considering (see chapter 13).

4. Will the incentive yield temporary or permanent gain? Is a continuance plan built into the program?

5. What support is needed from other promotion mix components?

6. Does the incentive program yield opportunity for publicity or word-of-mouth promotion? Is it newsworthy?

7. What is the administrative burden created by the program? Will personnel need to judge contests, generate coupons, choose winners, dispatch gifts, and the like?

8. What kind of time frame is necessary for consumer response and the communication plan?

9. What kind of budget is necessary?

10. How will the plan be assessed?

Figure 3.7 Incentive plan checklist.

Reprinted, by permission, from P.R. Smith, 1993, *Marketing communications: An integrated approach* (London: Kogan Page Ltd.), 53.

simply refer to the original plan objective to determine whether the anticipated outcome was actually met.

Additionally, in order to minimize risk, the sport business should pursue some type of insurance. Although a sponsor may support a premium giveaway or fireworks display, promotional incentives involving contests, sweepstakes, and raffles should be underwritten by a third-party insurer. Using formulas that include such criteria as number of participants, frequency of trials, and degree of difficulty, insurers will agree to cover the potential loss should one or more winners emerge. For instance, Hole In One International, based in Reno, Nevada, provides coverage for hole-in-one contests, a common element in charity golf scrambles. In fact, for as little as $175, Hole In One International will underwrite a $1 million hole-in-one competition. You can bet it has to be one tough hole!

So, remember, when you see that "lucky audience member" shooting a basketball from half-court or kicking a football from midfield for lots of money, the event and its promotional partner are actually cheering for the individual to win the prize. Otherwise, it's a waste of an insurance premium and of a great publicity opportunity!

Sport Promotion Gone Awry?

Brandsmart, a Kansas City electronics store, ran a promotion promising that if the Chiefs shut out their upcoming opponent (San Diego), sales of all items exceeding $399 would be free. The Chargers had advanced the ball to the Chiefs' 1-yard line, but the noise (from the hopeful contest winners) was so loud on the ensuing play that quarterback Jim Harbaugh fumbled the ball, with Kansas City recovering and preserving a shutout victory. Fortunately for Brandsmart, approximately 90% of the promotion was covered by insurance.

Postgame Wrap-Up

Most sport marketing and promotion textbooks capture the notion of incentives under the umbrella of sales promotion. Unfortunately, this fails to accurately embrace the full breadth of sport consumption incentives that are not entirely sales or transaction oriented. In addition to sales-based promotion, incentives for sport consumption include achievement, craft, affiliation, health and fitness, and fun. The sport promotion specialist may use each one of these criteria independently, as well as collectively, to incentivize involvement among any of the sport consumer groups. The incentive promotion should reflect the same level of strategic planning that is typically reserved for other elements of the promotion mix, such as objective specification and outcome assessment.

Discussion Items

1. What measures can be used to assess the effectiveness of an incentive promotion?

2. For the following sport businesses, what incentives would you develop that relate to the five motives for sport consumption provided by Mullin, Hardy, and Sutton?

    a. Professional soccer team

    b. Suburban community recreation center

    c. Urban fitness center

3. How would you go about implementing a discounted admission promotion that would not alienate full-paying customers?

4. How would you approach a sponsor regarding assistance with a premium giveaway item?

Learning Enrichment Activities

1. Compare and contrast the promotional campaigns of two competing sport organizations (e.g., two golf courses). Document the incentivization tactics each employs. How do the tactics differ? How are the incentives communicated to the consumer? What is the ratio between price-based and non-price-based incentives?

2. Arrange an interview with a sport promotion specialist at a local sport business. Ask how the business determines the incentives provided to its consumers. Check to see if the business employs an incentivization plan similar to that presented in this chapter. If so, how closely does the plan resemble the one discussed here? What steps have been omitted? If this business doesn't use a similar plan, why not?

4

Indirect Promotion and Sales Strategies

chapter objectives

1. Understand the concept of positioning

2. Comprehend the role of brand image as it relates to organizational credibility and appeal

3. Become familiar with indirect selling techniques such as endorsements and testimonials

4. Begin to formulate a strategy that integrates indirect selling techniques into the overall sales and promotional game plan

5. Appreciate the role and importance of customer service as a sales strategy

6. Understand that not all selling activities involve directly asking the prospect to buy

Pregame Introductions

While most people view sales as someone's asking them to buy a product or service, that is not an all-encompassing view of the sales process. The sales process begins in the mind of the consumer when they begin to think that they have a need or a want for a particular product or service. In many ways, the sales process begins in an indirect fashion—no one's asking for the sale to be consummated. In this chapter we will focus on what we will define as indirect promotional and sales strategies. These indirect promotional and sales strategies, which include positioning, testimonials, endorsements, and creating impressions, have been documented to be very effective tools in setting the stage for the actual direct selling process, which will be discussed in chapter 5.

Indirect Promotion and Selling

Indirect promotion and selling refer to all the ways and means that the sender—an individual or organization—can create, convey, and place impressions and messages in the mind of the receiver, the prospective consumer. This practice is commonly referred to as **positioning,** and has been defined by consultants and authors Ries and Trout as "what happens to the mind of the prospective consumer."[1] Coca-Cola has positioned itself as the *real thing,* implying that its competitors are just copies of the original, while Nike has used the slogan *Just Do It!* to convey the impression that its footwear and active gear are appropriate for any activity the consumer may choose. In a strategy sense, then, the mind is a battlefield, with countless encounters designed to gain the attention and ultimately the interest of the mind. As we live in an age of overcommunication, it may be interesting to examine how much communication we are exposed to as the new millennium begins. Trout and Rifkin found the following:[2]

- More information has been produced in the last 30 years than in the previous 5000 years.
- The total of all printed knowledge doubles every four or five years.
- One weekday edition of the *New York Times* contains more information than the average person was likely to come across in a lifetime in 17th-century England.
- More than 4000 books are published globally every day.
- The English language contains about half a million usable words.
- It can take someone almost 18 hours, at a rate of 500 words per minute, to read every word of the Sunday edition of the *New York Times.*
- There are more than 8000 electronic databases.

What does this overload of information (print, electronic and spoken words, images, sounds, and impressions) mean to a promoter? It means that a promoter must be concise and clear in designing a message and creative and interesting in order to win space on the "battlefield."

There are four basic motives for these types of indirect selling and promotional strategies:

- Positioning the product (as just discussed)
- Enhancing the brand and building brand equity
- Providing credibility
- Using image transfer and association

Since we have just considered positioning, the remaining three motives bear examination before we proceed to the specific implementation strategies.

- *Enhancing the brand and building brand equity.* **Brand** represents the positive or negative associations with a particular product's name and its related images and marks. Brand equity, then, is the set of assets such as name awareness, customer loyalty, perceived quality, and associations that are linked to the brand, its name and symbol, that add to or subtract from the value provided by the product or service.[3] The success of Michael Jordan on the court was a critical factor in enhancing the brand of Nike (and his other endorsements) and in building brand equity by enlarging Nike's customer base, developing brand preference and loyalty, and creating world-wide recognition for the symbol of the Nike brand, the "swoosh."

- *Providing credibility.* Before a customer makes a decision to buy, she must believe in the product or service and in the company providing that product or service. This belief must relate to the usefulness, prestige, durability, attractiveness, or other perceived attributes of the product or service. Customers also want a product that is accepted[4]—preferred or recognized by others who purchase the same products or services. When professional athletes such as Michael Jordan lace up a pair of Nike athletic shoes, or when Tiger Woods plays a Nike golf ball, the product gains instant credibility. Why? These are athletes playing at the very highest level of competition, so their choice of a particular product implies that they have faith in that product and believe it to be the best. These athletes also have access to, and the resources to choose, any product that they wish—so when they do select and utilize a product, their exploits and reputations give the product credibility in the eyes and minds of the prospective consumers.

- *Using image transfer and association.* Although similar to credibility, image transfer and association extend the power and strength of the position that the product or service occupies in the mind of the consumer. Belief in the product and its properties becomes internalized in that after purchasing it the consumer feels that he has "acquired" the properties of the product. To return to the examples of Michael Jordan and Tiger Woods, the consumer associates with these athletes through selecting "their" basketball shoes or golf balls. These associations may also lead to some image transfer, with the consumer thinking "If that's what Tiger Woods chooses, it should help me play better golf." Whether the consumer's performance improves or not is irrelevant: the key is that the person believes in the image and in the benefits of such an association.

These strategies become messages and can take the form of advertising, branding activities (both of which are discussed in detail in chapter 6), spokespersons, infomercials, endorsements, word-of-mouth referrals, and so forth. Note that none of

© William R. Sallaz/Newsport

Tiger Woods, sporting the Nike swoosh, enhances Nike's brand credibility.

the activities mentioned occur at the point of purchase; all occur at some point during what can be described as the data-gathering or information collection stage of the purchasing process. These activities can also affect consumers who may not even be consciously gathering information or data. How much of the message gets through depends in large part on the product or service that is the subject of the message.[5] As sport and sport-related products and services are in general a topic of significant interest to the majority of the population,[6] sport-related messages have a much better chance than many others of being received by the intended audience.

Indirect promotion and selling activities usually act to increase awareness of the product or service but can also serve to increase interest in or comprehension or appreciation of the product or service. The Pepsi Challenge, which urges consumers to "taste" the difference between Coke and Pepsi, is an excellent example of indirect selling activities. In the Pepsi Challenge, consumers get an *opportunity* to compare the taste of their preferred product with that of the competitor. In other words, a Coke drinker gets a no-risk opportunity to sample Pepsi. The consumer is given the product and merely asked to try it. This is an excellent promotion in that frequently it attracts consumers who may be firmly entrenched in their purchasing behavior. But because no direct selling is involved (the interaction is with the product not with a salesperson), people view the opportunity to try a new product as educational. There is also no guarantee that activities such as the Pepsi Challenge will be successful in the way they are intended to be. Pepsi originated the Pepsi Challenge in the 1980s to attract trial users to their product. The Challenge was so successful that it caused Coke to panic and change its formula to introduce what has become known as New Coke. Coke then introduced its own taste tests, and 200,000 taste tests proved that New Coke tasted better than Pepsi, which tasted better than the original Coke formula (now called Coca-Cola Classic). The result? Coca-Cola Classic effectively became the number one-selling cola worldwide; Pepsi remained number two with its taste test approach damaged in the eyes of the consumer; and New Coke, after securing attention and additional space shelf and displays, was withdrawn in order to position Coke as responsive to the wishes and desires of its loyal purchasers.[7]

In a sport context, Reebok employed a similar strategy by using vans at sporting events to offer consumers an opportunity to feel the comfort and fit of their DMX running or cross-training shoe. The vans contained a display of the entire DMX line as well as a full selection of sizes (figure 4.1). The Reebok staff members who accompanied the van were not sales personnel but instead individuals trained to answer questions regarding the technology and design of the shoe. Once again, the opportunity to try the product without follow-up pressure to purchase provided consumers with a pressure-free, no-risk opportunity to try something new.

Figure 4.1 Marketing efforts such as the Reebok van are designed to provide interaction between the product and the consumer in a non-retail, no-pressure environment.

The Power of Personalities and Recommendations: Testimonials and Endorsements

Testimonials, endorsements, referrals, impressions, and other general types of word-of-mouth discussions are powerful forms of promotion. Although testimonials are not directly involved in the sales process, these forms of promotion can contribute greatly to positioning the product in prospects' minds, improving their perception, arousing their curiosity, and possibly initiating some type of action or response. While the majority of these strategies are controllable by the organization to at least some degree (word of mouth being a notable exception), there is always a risk attached and a possibility that a well-intended promotional campaign or activity could produce less than the desired results.

Testimonials

With regard to indirect selling and promotional activities, the most common format is the use of third parties to convey worth or value messages to prospective consumers about the product or service being promoted. **Testimonials** are a common medium for accomplishing this form of promotion. Testimonials comprise the words and experiences of past users of the product or service being promoted. They can appear in written form, as part of an advertising message, and within electronic formats such as videos and e-mail messages. P.T. Barnum felt that testimonials provided credibility, and he collected testimonials about his products that were specific and convincing.[8] In sport, testimonials are often used to demonstrate the benefits of attending a sporting event. Video spots showing fans enjoying themselves at a sporting event, and on-camera interviews of fans in which they explain the benefits of attendance in their own words, are common practices in sport. Minor league baseball's Durham Bulls produced a year-end highlight film to be used in the off-season that documented a fan's experience from the time the gates opened until they closed. A demographically varied group of fans were asked on camera what they liked about attending Bulls games. These responses were edited and mixed with other video clips to form the final video. Bulls personnel then used this video when speaking to civic, church, and other groups about the Bulls. The testimonials of Bulls fans, sharing their experiences and recommending the experience of attending, were a powerful promotional tool. A testimonial of this type can be highly effective because it comes to prospective fans from another fan ("one of their own"); there is an implied element of trust in that the testimonial is being offered by a "raving fan" of his own free will and without compensation.

Most testimonials that you will use, whether in the form of a letter, brochure, or video or in some other format, should explain some or all of the following elements:

- The nature of the problem or challenge that the testimony is documenting
- The way the problem or challenge was resolved
- The happy feelings that the individual providing the testimonial has about working with you
- The fact that it is easy and pleasant to work with you
- The quality of your customer service and aftercare
- Present or future plans for continued involvement with you and your organization
- Your ongoing interest in the individual and your concern for her future satisfaction[9]

While usually aimed at the mass market, testimonials can also be used to target specific individuals or groups. The person providing the testimonial can be asked to provide referrals, which we consider next.

Referrals

Referrals represent one of the largest areas for potential sales and one of the most desired outcomes for indirect promotional activities. As described in chapter 14, satisfied customers who become "raving fans" are among the most valued assets an organization can possess. Conversely, dissatisfied customers who are vocal and vehement about their dissatisfaction can be detrimental to the organization. As raving fans profess their loyalty to the organization to potential customers, they create what are commonly called referrals. Referrals are actually endorsements by friends, neighbors, and other everyday people. While these individuals may lack the "star quality" associated with celebrities and athletes, they may also possess higher recognition and impact because they are people with whom the prospect has some type of relationship.

According to Bill Cates, author and expert on building sales through referrals, two types of referrals are commonly used in sales—explicit and implicit. In explicit referrals, the referral source contacts the prospect on behalf of the salesperson for the purpose of introduction and endorsement. In implicit referrals, when contacting the prospect, the salesperson uses the name of the individual who made the referral.[10]

Securing referrals is an essential part of the promotional process. The salesperson must be comfortable in asking clients for the names and addresses of friends who might have a similar interest in or need for the product. In sport organizations that use telemarketing (chapter 5), salespersons are taught to close the phone call by asking for a referral regardless of whether or not there has been a sale. The most common referral request involves asking the consumer for help, and the assistance is to provide the names and telephone numbers of three friends or relatives who might be interested in Gotham Bats ticket plans or whatever the telemarketing department is selling. Experts suggest a variety of ways[11] in which as a salesperson you can cultivate and secure referrals:

- *Give thank-you gifts that get people talking about you.* Give something affordable and personal to let customers know you appreciate their business and their help in getting referrals. An autographed ball, seat upgrades, something for the customer's children, and a player appearance at a school or business are examples of items or gestures that have meaning and will create conversation.

- *Create a special gift certificate.* Create a gift certificate for your products or services to give to your satisfied customers, asking them to pass it on to a new potential customer. This should provide a benefit to the current customer as well. Gift certificates may be for meals at special in-arena restaurants, invitations to press conferences, and so forth. The benefit to the new customer should include product trials such as tickets or a free golf lesson or tee time.

- *Host an educational event.* Invite customers and referral alliances to an educational program and ask them to bring a guest or two for free. The Cleveland Cavs hosted a sport marketing seminar designed to teach potential sponsors how the Cavs could help them achieve their business objectives. Dinner and a Cavs game in a luxury suite followed the seminar.[12]

One of the more unique applications of the referral is the party concept that has been successful in the WNBA. The WNBA's Cleveland Rockers expanded their sales force by almost 3000 persons for the 2000 season. Instead of relying on traditional methods to reach prospective ticket buyers, the Rockers used a personal touch while getting a little help from some of the team's closest friends—current ticket plan holders. Existing plan holders were invited to host a Rockers Caravan Party. The Caravan hosts provided the Rockers sales staff with an invitation list of friends and family who the hosts thought would be interested in attending. The team did the rest. The Caravan, composed of a traveling group of players, coaches, and sales personnel, arrived at the home of the host with party favors and refreshments, as well as materials about the team. The players and coaches discussed team and league issues with guests while the sales staff put on a brief sales presentation and distributed ticket plan materials. Contests and trivia games went on throughout the party, which lasted approximately 90 minutes. The Caravan program was promoted via word of mouth among current ticket plan holders. Each host received a gift from the Rockers and additional incentives based on the number of guests who purchased Rockers tickets.[13]

Endorsements

Endorsements are another effective indirect selling and promotional device. **Endorsements** involve enlisting a high-profile individual, usually a celebrity or an athlete, to use his fame or position to assist a company in promoting or selling a product or to enhance the image of that product.[14] There are several different endorsement styles:

- Explicit mode—The message is "I endorse this product."
- Implicit mode—The message is "I use this product."
- Imperative mode—The message is "You should use this product."
- Co-present mode—The endorser appears in some setting with the product.[15]

© Jim Baron/The Image Finders

Pittsburgh Pirate Honus Wagner endorsed the Louisville Slugger.

The utilization of endorsements in sport began in 1905 when Pittsburgh Pirate baseball star (later to be admitted into the first class of the Baseball Hall of Fame) Honus Wagner accepted a payment of $75 from the J.F. Hillerich & Son Company.[16] The Hillerich Company produced Louisville Slugger baseball bats, and who would have more credibility as an endorser for baseball bats than a batting champion?

The continued popularity of professional athletes has led to the proliferation of the sport celebrity. Fans have demonstrated that they can identify with the sponsor as well as the sport and its athletes. The success of Michael Jordan as a promotional vehicle for both Nike and the NBA is an excellent case in point. Fans demonstrated that they wanted to *"Be like Mike"* and to that end purchased underwear, fast food, cologne, and batteries as well as athletic footwear.

Aiming the message at the want (or in some cases more precisely a need) to be like Mike employs the **following the herd**[17] mentality. This approach is one of the reasons for using an endorser: the hope that people will want to be part of the herd—not to stand out but instead to fit in and emulate the leader's (or endorser's) behavior. The *following the herd* philosophy states that we will make fewer mistakes by acting in accord with social evidence than by acting contrary to it. In other words, the idea is that usually when many people are doing something, it is the right thing to do. In the 1980s and early 1990s, athletic shoes were a "fashion statement" (as was sport-licensed apparel), purchased for reasons other than their intended purpose because they were in style. Being fashionable and being like Mike were the "herd" thing to do until the brown shoe craze hit in the late 1990s. The 2000 advertising campaigns conducted by the GAP while this book is in preparation are an excellent example of the herd mentality.

The influence of Michael Jordan is evidenced by his total endorsement value in excess of $40 million and growing. One example of Jordan's value as an endorser is his multimillion-dollar contract with Rayovac (batteries). According to *Sports Marketing Letter,* Rayovac believes that using Jordan could reduce to nearly zero the time it will take to educate consumers—especially single-use battery purchasers—on the advantages of its new product. Rayovac's product is the only rechargeable alkaline battery on the market. As opposed to one long-life use for a regular disposable alkaline battery, the Rayovac product gives as many as 11 long-life uses. So why does Rayovac need Jordan? Jordan, the company believes, will grab instant attention and recognition for the battery. Also, the imagery is a tight fit. Rayovac created advertising themed on Jordan and the product as "the best of their kind," "the greatest ever," and the like. And who is a better choice to endorse a renewable battery than a superstar whose basketball career proved to be renewable?[18] Table 4.1 illustrates the value of Jordan as an endorser along with other top athlete endorsers.

How does a corporation select an athlete or celebrity to serve as an endorser or spokesperson? Some athletes are selected for their accomplishments, others for their personalities, and still others because they convey an image that the corporation

Table 4.1   2001 Top Product Endorsers From Sports

1. Tiger Woods	6. Marion Jones
2. Michael Jordan	7. Andre Agassi
3. Lance Armstrong	8. Muhammad Ali
4. Anna Kournikova	9. Kobe Bryant
5. Mia Hamm	10. Wayne Gretzky

Adapted by permission from Burns Sports & Celebrities, Inc., 2001, "Burns Sports & Celebrities, Inc. 2001 Top Product Endorsers from Sports."

wishes to associate with its products or services. Canon, a manufacturer of cameras, elected to use tennis player Andre Agassi as an endorser because of his nonconforming behavior in order to promote its Rebel model. Wrestler Randy Savage serves as the spokesperson for spicy snack food Slim Jim, and recently Pete Rose began a series of television ads for Maaco, an auto body and painting company. Rose, who during the commercial speaks about the importance of being a member of a good team, sets the stage for Maaco to describe its team and why its members are valuable to prospective consumers.

You could argue that Agassi, Savage, and Rose all have their detractors and thus might not appeal to a broad enough audience. Marketing Evaluations/TvQ is a company that specializes in rating celebrities and sport figures according to their popularity. Through use of a 55,000-household "People Panel," Marketing Evaluations/TvQ collects data regarding preferences about and "likeability" of athletes. The data are converted to a "Q-Score," and that information is sold to corporations and other interested parties who then have a basis to identify celebrities and sport figures to consider for endorsement purposes. Members of the People Panel receive a list of sport figures, both currently playing and retired, and rate them on a scale from favorite to poor, with a category of "N" if the respondent has never heard of that particular athlete.[19]

Obviously when using anyone as an endorser to discuss the attributes of your products or services, you incur an element of risk. The media have extended significant time and coverage to recent unsavory escapades involving Bobby Knight, Latrell Sprewell, Bruce Grobbelar, Hansi Cronje, Tonya Harding, and Ray Lewis, just to mention a few. In fact, Bob McGee of *Sporting Goods Intelligence* has confirmed that there is consumer backlash against the products that athletes represent when they behave inappropriately.[20]

One of the more highly publicized endorsement contracts that proved to be embarrassing for the sponsor was the case of NBA slam dunk champion and Toronto Raptors star Vince Carter and footwear manufacturer Puma. Carter attempted to break his contract with Puma by declaring that the shoes hurt his feet, and he refused to continue wearing the shoes—violating his endorsement contract with Puma. Events turned out to be even more embarrassing for Puma when on national and international television broadcasts Carter won the 2000 NBA Slam Dunk Championship wearing the footwear of a competitor. Although Puma sued Carter and won a breach of contract judgment, the damage had been done.[21]

The possibility of injury poses another risk. Rebecca Lobo of the WNBA's New York Liberty was highly visible as an endorser during the league's initial season. Because of injuries, however, she did not appear on the court during the next two years, saw limited action this past season, and was absent from the national endorsement scene as well. Cubs phenom and fastball specialist Kerry Wood, injured and out for the entire 1999 season, retained some of his endorsements but lost others because of the lack of visibility caused by the injury[22]—fulfilling the old axiom, *out of sight, out of mind.*

Issues such as these, combined with the high cost of securing celebrity endorsers, have caused companies to limit the number of celebrities they use and to show more and more everyday people utilizing and enjoying the products, a trend that has grown in popularity in recent years. For example, Reebok's marketing efforts are primarily focused on Philadelphia 76er Alan Iverson, when at one time Reebok employed more than a dozen celebrity endorsers.

One way to lessen the risk in using celebrity athletes as endorsers is to tie their compensation into product sales by offering them stock options. Dan Marino has an equity share in LaRussa Italian foods; Michael Jordan and Cal Ripken have equity relationships with Oakley sunglasses; and Tiger Woods received stock for his involvement in the official All-Star Café.[23] In a more unconventional approach, some clever marketers have hit on another solution to control the behavior, and hence the image of their endorsers—using celebrities who are deceased. Advances in computer imaging and animation and video technology have permitted companies like Dirt Devil, Mercedes-Benz, and Coors to "resurrect" such cinema and television stars as Fred Astaire, Frank Sinatra, and John Wayne. Why use dead celebrities? There are several reasons. First, "Dead celebrities allow advertisers to tap into feelings of nostalgia about times spent gathered around the television watching classic shows—an emotion that reverberates with baby boomers in particular." Second, with dead celebrities, who can no longer offend consumers through the media by getting arrested or performing other embarrassing behaviors, advertisers know what they are getting. "With dead celebrities, their qualities are known," said Tom Cordner, creative director of Team One Advertising. "They can't get into trouble—they're a safe bet."[24]

Sport marketers have embraced this tactic as well. ESPN's flattering film clips of Ty Cobb were used heavily to promote ESPN's coverage of the 1998 baseball season. Jackie Robinson appeared on Wheaties boxes and commemorative Coca-Cola bottles; he was thanked by current athletes in a Nike commercial; and his estate was projected to receive millions of dollars in endorsement fees—all after he had been dead for 25 years.[25]

What does the future hold with regard to endorsements? As sport marketers and sponsorship experts nationwide work furiously to find new avenues for reaching the preferred demographics common in sport fans, almost any idea merits contemplation. According to Eric Fisher of the *Washington Times,* we may someday see athletes bearing implied endorsements via tattoos or other visible signs of association. While at the moment the idea is mere speculation, perhaps even farfetched, there may come a day when Shaquille O'Neal sports a Pepsi tattoo as a complement to his famous Superman tattoo.[26]

Impressions

Brand identity and association have become a primary reason why corporations choose to link their products to sport and to allocate promotional resources and funds to sport celebrities or leagues and events. Endorsements are a common avenue, but another way to create an association between the product and the sport entity in the mind of the consumer is to use impressions. **Impressions,** sometimes termed exposures, refer to the ability of the sport entity, through some type of media interaction, to create an impression of the association between the product and sport for the viewer, reader, or listener.

This strategy has proven to be very beneficial to NASCAR. The cars, which along with the drivers and sponsors are an integral part of the NASCAR experience, have been called "rolling billboards." These rolling billboards, painted in the colors of the sponsors and featuring their logos and names, are a creative way to make an impression on the television viewer. In fact, a NASCAR car is often referred to as "the Kellogg car," for example—creating an opportunity for additional on-air impressions resulting from the racing activity. Other impressions are created by logo placement on the uniforms and apparel, including caps, that the driver and the pit crew wear. While these impressions in and of themselves are beneficial forms of association and promotion for the sponsor via the media exposure they generate, they are also important because of their impact on the media and the live consumer (attendee). According to Robert Hagstrom, author of *The NASCAR Way,* the real value of stock car racing comes not from the impressions of additional exposures, but from the emotions that the impressions generate.[27] The issue, then, is what is the impact of these emotions, and do they influence factors such as corporate image, brand perception, product purchasing, and brand loyalty? According to a 1994 research study, *RaceStat,* conducted by Performance Research, NASCAR fans are very aware of who sponsors their sport, and these fans also have a strong tendency to purchase the products of sponsoring companies. The study also indicated that survey respondents were able to identify, unaided, more than 200 companies or brands connected to the sport, and that three out of four racing fans purchase products of NASCAR sponsors.[28] These findings are significant in that they point out the success of NASCAR's promotional strategy of indirectly selling the sport while at the same time pleasing its sponsors. According to Lesa Ukman, cofounder of *IEG Sponsorship Report,* NASCAR has done an extraordinary job of educating its fans regarding the sponsor's importance to the sport.[29] This example also speaks to the ability of the corporate community to select an effective product and communication medium through activities designed to promote itself, and indirectly to sell.

The term *impression* within the context of promotion can also carry its traditional meaning, namely to create feeling or emotional association. That was the goal of the Phoenix Coyotes when they decided to put pictures of their fans on their 1999-2000 season tickets. Bruce Bielenberg and Joe Levy of the Coyotes in the following Practitioner's Perspective discuss this activity.

© Anthony Neste

NASCAR rolling billboards.

PRACTITIONER'S PERSPECTIVE

Fans As Marketing Collateral
by Bruce Bielenberg and Joe Levy, Phoenix Coyotes

Each year the Phoenix Coyotes have tried to come up with a unique idea for the design of our season ticket stock. Some teams might not consider this an important promotional stream, but in reality it is. Like many other teams, we have thought about using favorite players on our tickets. However, the uncertainties of trades, injuries, holdouts, and performance usually mean that some of your tickets may not reflect the current state of the team on the date they are intended for use.

For the 1999-2000 season, the Coyotes' marketing slogan was *"Real Sport, Real Fans."* To prove that we really did have real fans, we asked our season ticket holders to mail us photos of themselves showing why they were Real Fans. We received more than 400 photos, ranging from pictures of fans who were married in Coyotes jerseys to photos of animals attired in Coyote apparel. Our staff then selected the best 44 photos to use on our season ticket stock for the season (figure 4.2).

Figure 4.2   Combining real Coyotes fans and tickets was a logical match, and it made the fans feel like a part of the organization.

Reprinted, by permission, from The Phoenix Coyotes.

The response and the promotional impact were tremendous. The media picked up on the idea and interviewed many of the ticket holders who were featured on the tickets. Some fans were even asked to autograph their tickets at the games. The bottom line is that we recognized and promoted our fans, which in turn created awareness in the Phoenix market about the value of our fans and the regard we have for them, who in marketing terms are our most significant assets. We continued to receive photos throughout the season and made the decision to let the fans be the "stars" on the tickets again for the 2000-2001 season.

Not only is the ticket used at every home game by all of the season ticket holders and their guests, it also becomes a collector's item after the game is played. Perhaps of even greater importance with regard to this particular promotional activity is the message sent to the fans: you are important to and valued by the Phoenix Coyotes, and we are honoring that relationship by placing your likeness on our tickets. This is an impression that has staying power, more so than messages sent through other promotional activities or advertising expenditures.

Indirect Personal Selling

In chapter 5, we will discuss personal selling as a direct sales or promotional tool, but personal selling can also function as an indirect promotional sales tool. While each organization employs a specialized staff for the sole purpose of selling, each sport organization includes a large number of other people (administrators, coaches, players) who by the nature of their position or popularity, or both, become involved in the sales process, albeit indirectly. The following are opportunities for indirect personal selling available to sport organizations of various sizes and missions.

Memberships and Affiliations

In an effort to facilitate personal interaction with members of the local as well as extended marketplace, representatives of sport organizations often become members of civic, social, and professional associations. While membership in a local civic club may lead to valuable political and corporate contacts, membership in national or international organizations may produce contacts that can help the sport organization obtain tips on promotional opportunities, market research practices, and luxury seating and hospitality information or secure sites for exhibition contests. Such memberships, whether the association is local, regional, national, or international, are likely to set the stage for establishing personal networks as well as organizational goodwill.

Furthermore, in an effort to expand personal interaction with key members of the community, a sport organization may wish to form an association warranting board member appointment. Collegiate athletic programs engage in this type of practice annually when they launch a booster club drive and designate a major donor or local dignitary as chairperson. Similarly, many professional sport organizations through community initiatives have named prominent local citizens to their advisory boards and boards of directors.

Another type of effort that uses membership is exemplified by an initiative developed by Reebok. In a cross-functional effort between sales and customer service, designed to strengthen personal relationships with specialty retailers, Reebok developed the Quarterly Retail Advisory Summit. This initiative enabled Reebok to personally interact with affiliating retailers who in turn provided valuable input on product and retail opportunities.[30]

Public Speaking

Because of the general public's keen interest in sport, representatives of sport organizations have many opportunities to participate in a wide array of public speaking engagements. In fact, most major professional sport franchises have established speakers' bureaus for the sole purpose of generating personal contact opportunities via an established schedule of organizationally planned speaking engagements. It's a good idea for the sport promotion specialist to proactively arrange speaking engagements with targeted audiences well in advance in order to adequately prepare the speaker and adequately promote the event. A speaking engagement affords the organizational representative a valuable opportunity for personal interaction with a relatively large group of key opinion leaders and potential consumers.

Personal Appearances

As a means of facilitating direct, personal interaction with consumers, sport organizations stage personal or public appearances involving players (current and retired), mascots, dance teams, and so forth. Often arranged in conjunction with a media tour, community relations project, sponsorship agreement, or product endorsement campaign, public appearances also add a lively human element to an otherwise impersonal promotional campaign.

It is advisable for sport organizations to examine the community calendar and ensure personal involvement in promotionally oriented community activities such as festivals, parades, and other mass gatherings. In fact, the sport organization can originate and produce these community-oriented activities as a means of elevating public recognition and interaction, as happens each year in the case of most collegiate football bowl games. In an effort to generate fan interest and familiarity, the NHL's Nashville Predators scheduled a series (nine days, nine stops) of youth hockey clinics featuring players providing instruction and signing autographs as well as distributing schedules, promotional materials, and goodwill.

Popular sport figures are frequently available for appearances at both public and private functions for a fee. For instance, team mascots are generally available on this basis for appearances at events ranging from company meetings to birthday parties. All collective bargaining agreements for professional sport leagues provide for a certain number of free appearances per player. The free appearances are used at the discretion of the team personnel, and once players have made the free appearances they receive compensation for subsequent ones.

Personal appearances can also be part of the core activity. Each year, the FedEx St. Jude Classic golf tournament hosts the Coca-Cola Youth Clinic during tournament week. The clinic attracts several hundred participants eager to interact personally with a PGA TOUR player.[31] Similarly, NASCAR events encourage fans to visit the pit areas and "adopt" drivers, meet their crews, and become more involved with the sport. The success of NASCAR is predicated on pre- and post-race interaction among drivers, pit crews, sponsors, and fans.[32]

Activities such as these involving personal contact with athletes are perceived by spectators and fans in general as a form of gift reciprocation. Similar to any other exchange experience, reciprocated generosity is fundamental to sustained gift provision. That is, fans supply the gift of admiration and the athlete has the opportunity to reciprocate through the gift of personal interaction.[33] In this way the parties appear to

© The Sporting Image

Cynthia Cooper signs autographs and interacts with fans.

be establishing a relationship involving an element of equality potentially advancing to a stage of structural bonding. Activities such as pre- or postgame meet-and-greet sessions or autograph sessions can contribute significantly to maximizing the degree of fan-to-sport organization relationships. As discussed in this chapter and in chapters 3 and 14 also, relationships are the key to successful selling and creating lifetime value.

Interactive Product Sampling and Exposure

As a means of facilitating personal contact between product and consumer, many sport organizations have found the scheduling of interactive product-sampling opportunities very effective. This practice of "taking the product to the consumer" was utilized by Time, Inc., which organized a 16-market bus tour to celebrate the 10th anniversary of *Sports Illustrated for Kids*. The bus, which stopped at grocery stores, retail outlets, and county fairs, contained a variety of sport-related products, as well as various interactive games, and attracted approximately 300,000 kids.[34]

Sport provides a platform for companies in other industries to conduct interactive product sampling and to gain exposure. Product-sampling derivatives (interactive and otherwise) are usually of keen interest as part of a sponsorship program. While corporate sponsors may endeavor to supply mass product sampling to some, if not all, event patrons, sport also provides a pleasant environment for indirect personal selling. This is illustrated by the dominance of corporately owned tickets (and premium seating options such as suites and skyboxes) to American sporting events and the prevalence of corporate hospitality activities at these events. According to Kahle and Elton, the sport setting facilitates a corporate blend of sport talk and business talk, allowing for the development of role and stylistic interaction before the parties get down to business transactions with important consequences.[35]

Customer Service As a Form of Indirect Sales Promotion

Customer service is the focus of chapter 14 but merits consideration here as a form of indirect sales promotion. Study after study reveals that customer service is one of the most important issues facing the sport manager today. Research by Martin illustrates that the merits of customer service are accentuated in the sport environment for several reasons:[36]

- *In the sport environment, customer service is experiential and social.* Spectators, as well as participants, often engage in sport consumption to satisfy a desire for enjoyment. When you enter a fitness center, encountering a disgruntled front desk or counter attendant diminishes your enjoyment of the experience.

- *Service is inseparable from product.* In many cases, the service provider must interact with the spectator or participant in order to produce the product. Aerobics course enrollees may find it difficult to separate the merits of the course from the actions of the instructor.

- *Services in sport are intangible.* Because sport services cannot be literally touched, tasted, or seen, consumers rely on cues within the service environment to mold their perceptions. The actions and appearance of the service providers often influence the service assessment.

- *In the sport environment, service is discretionary and substitutable.* Consumers are less likely to accept the discourteous behavior of a service provider at a sporting event than discourteous service provided by a public utility company employee.

Friendly customer service is vital to sales promotion.

As noted in chapter 1, the task of delivering sound customer service does not have to be overwhelming. Acts of simple courtesy such as offering a welcome upon arrival, recognizing and identifying regular customers, providing service without prolonged delay, and offering a thank-you after a transaction are what sport service recipients desire most. In fact, such actions result in sales increases as well as higher customer service ratings.[37]

Postgame Wrap-Up

Promotional activities that serve as forms of indirect selling are essential to overall sales efforts and customer retention for all sport organizations. In a competitive marketing environment characterized by numerous sport and entertainment options, the consumer must have multiple platforms from which to connect to the sport organization. These multiple platforms must serve not only to connect the consumer to the organization but also to validate the commitment of resources (time as well as money) that the consumer has allocated toward the commitment to the organization.

Some of the most convincing types of indirect selling involve word-of-mouth activities. Testimonials, endorsements, referrals, and activities that emphasize personal contact with the organization are among the most convincing and effective forms of indirect promotion and selling. These activities position the sport organization as an effective producer and supplier of quality sport and entertainment experiences, worthy of investment. Human nature seeks a comfort level with new experiences, and testimonials and referrals from people who have actually purchased the product and enjoyed the experience are effective in creating awareness, stimulating interest, and ultimately initiating action.

Discussion Items

1. Discuss the use of indirect selling activities as outlined in this chapter in relation to the sales process. Generate a list of situational examples that illustrate the effectiveness of such techniques.

2. After selecting a sport-related product or service you are interested in, generate a list of possible celebrity endorsers for the sport product or service. Would celebrity endorsers be the most effective way to promote the product or service? Why or why not?

3. Identify the sport product or service brand that you think conveys the best image of each of the following characteristics: dependability, performance, fashion, value, edginess, and technology.

Learning Enrichment Activities

1. Visit a local middle school or junior high school and secure permission from the principal to interview three to five students about their view of endorsers. From the interviews, what did you learn about the impact of endorsers as it relates to the audience for whom their message is intended? What did these students have in common with regard to endorsers?

2. Select a female and a male athlete who endorse similar products. Are their messages gender specific, or are they aimed at both male and female audiences? Are both messages free from gender bias and portrayal?

3. Create a positioning statement for your university athletic program or a professional sport team in your area. How can this positioning statement be used as an indirect sales tool?

4. Watch a professional auto racing event (preferably NASCAR, but Championship Auto Racing Team or Indy cars will work also) on television. Select one car and driver, and focus your attention on that tandem exclusively. Pay attention to the announcers and the way they describe the cars. At the conclusion of the race, watch the activity and appearance of the winning driver. Do you perceive all of these corporate sponsor impressions to be effective forms of indirect selling? Why or why not?

5. Imagine that you are working for the Gotham Bats, a professional sport franchise in your area. Your supervisor has recently read about the Cool Coyotes Field Trip (chapter 10) and is eager to create some type of event in your marketplace that can affect consumers and initiate an effective grassroots promotional campaign. What type of event would you create and why?

Effective Direct Sales Techniques for Sport Organizations

chapter objectives

1. Understand the steps involved in the sales process and the components of a sale

2. Differentiate between product-focused selling and customer-focused selling

3. Appreciate the qualities and characteristics of successful salespersons

4. Comprehend the strengths and weaknesses of the various sales strategies and methods, and be able to determine the most appropriate method for particular sales situations

5. Define and create sales plans and tactics for the sport-specific inventory unique to the sport industry

key terms	eduselling	full-menu marketing	personal seat license (PSL)
	salable product	permission marketing	marketing partnership
	frequency escalator	telemarketing	outsourcing
	butterfly customer	buyer's market	

Pregame Introductions

Sales are the lifeblood of any sport organization. Whether of tickets, media rights, sponsorships, signage, advertising, luxury suites, or any of the sport products, sales accounts for most, if not all, of the revenue.[1] According to Sergio Zyman, former marketing innovator at Coca-Cola, "marketing is supposed to sell stuff."[2] What we sell and how we sell it will vary from organization to organization, but the bottom line is how effectively we will sell it—effectiveness usually translates into volume. How many tickets, how many advertising segments, how large a sign, how many units?—volume is the measuring stick for sales effectiveness.

This chapter examines the components of a sale, the attributes of successful salespersons, the sales process, and effective and innovative sales techniques employed in the sport industry. Figure 5.1 depicts the critical relationship among the media, sponsors, and fans. This relationship is essentially symbiotic, because the three elements feed off each other to create the types of conditions that stimulate sales and attract additional fans.

Fans are the catalyst in this relationship. Fans and their level of support are used by the sport organization to attract sponsors. The numbers of these fans, and their demographic and psychographic characteristics, are used to attract sponsors in certain product categories who wish to "interact" on some level with these fans. The

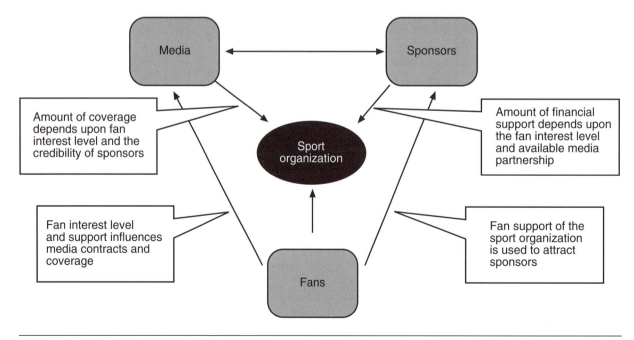

Figure 5.1 Symbiotic relationship of fans, media, and sponsors.

Reprinted, by permission, from B.J. Mullin, S. Hardy, and W.A. Sutton, 2000, *Sport marketing*, 2nd ed. (Champaign: Human Kinetics), 223.

media are critical to this relationship in two ways. First, the media provide coverage of the sport organization according to the interest accorded to the sport by the fans. Secondly, the media, through selling commercial time, provide the vehicle for the sponsor—through the sport organization—to reach the fans. This commercial time is sold to sponsors, who provide financial support for the sport organization by purchasing not only media time, but also signage, promotional activities, luxury seating, and tickets. The support of the fans is used to attract sponsors who then create media demand and sales opportunities. What is being sold? Fans are buying tickets, concessions, merchandise, and hopefully the sponsor products. Sponsors are buying media time and products especially designed for the corporate market (this will be discussed later in the chapter). The media are paying a rights fee to the sport organization for the opportunity to provide television, radio, webcasts, and so forth.[3]

Dr. Bernie Mullin, senior vice president for Team Marketing and Business Operations for the NBA, compares this relationship to a water tower as illustrated in figure 5.2. When a water tower is full, there is pressure on the flow of water, and the water flows freely and rapidly. As the level of the water decreases, pressure declines and the water flows much more slowly. As the water pressure continues to decline, the flow can decrease to a trickle. According to Dr. Mullin, the same is true for a professional sport venue. If the arena is full, there is pressure—pressure on purchasers to buy tickets while they are available. This translates into high attendance, which places pressure on the media to provide coverage; this in turn places pressure on sponsors to purchase sponsorships because of the impact on both the live audience and the televi-sion/radio audience. However, if the arena is less than half full, particularly if the prime seating locations (lower bowl in a basketball arena) are not filled, there is no pressure to attend, provide coverage, or purchase sponsorship.

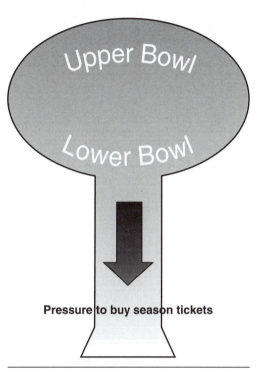

Figure 5.2 Water tower model of sport sales.
Courtesy of Dr. Bernie Mullin.

Defining Sales

The primary role of sales is to sell existing products and services at a level of price, quality, and performance acceptable to customers.[4] Sales can also include selling new products and services, repackaging and positioning existing products and services, and other modifications. In any case, sales is the revenue-producing element of the marketing process. According to IMG (International Management Group) Founder and Chairman Mark McCormack, selling consists of the following elements:

- The process of identifying customers
- Getting through to them (communicating to them and reaching them)

- Increasing their awareness of, and interest in, your product or service
- Persuading them to act on that interest[5]

In breaking down McCormack's components, we find the following:

- Selling involves creating, maintaining, and utilizing an effective, up-to-date database.
- Sending the message is only part of the equation: the organization must select communication methods that actually reach the consumer—that cut through the clutter and secure attention.
- The message should inform, educate, and persuade.
- The sales process must culminate in an action to establish or extend a relationship between the receiver of the message (the "customer" or purchaser) and the sender (the sport organization).

We can also view sales as customer performance—when a customer purchases a product or service, she performs the act of buying.[6] In sport, five main factors cause customers to perform or fail to perform:

- *Quality:* How well is the product or service performing? The win-loss record of the 1999-2000 Los Angeles Lakers, the WNBA dynasty of the Houston Comets, Tiger Woods's participation at a PGA event are all examples of products that have performed well.
- *Quantity:* In what number is the product sold—for example 1 unit, 10 units, 25 units? An individual might purchase a mini-plan for the NHL's Edmonton Oilers that includes 10 games rather than a full-season ticket plan that could include more than 41 games.
- *Time:* Does the consumer have time to utilize the product in a way that is effective for that person? For example, family obligations, work schedules, and the demands of everyday life might dictate that he does not. To make the purchase of a golf membership costing $1000 worthwhile if the daily cost (nonmember cost) of playing golf at that particular venue is $50, the purchaser would need to play a minimum of 20 times.
- *Cost:* Cost not only relates to the overall cost, but also includes such aspects as payment options and value received for the purchase price. Being able to pay $40 per month for a fitness club membership may be more attractive to some consumers than paying $480 upon joining.[7]
- *Fit:* Fit refers to the degree to which all of these elements, when viewed in their totality, fit the lifestyle of the prospective purchaser.

Sales falls primarily into two philosophical styles: product/service focused and customer focused. Product- or service-focused activities emphasize the product, its benefits, features, quality, and reputation. Product or service focus can also be on the provider—the organization supplying the product or service. Customer-focused selling stresses the needs and requirements of the customer, and may involve determining how the product or service benefits or adds perceived value in the mind of the customer.[8] This chapter deals primarily with customer-focused selling, which has become the mantra for sales activities because of the ever changing and unique nature of consumers and their lifestyles in the new millennium.

Customer-Focused Selling

In customer-focused selling, the salesperson should view herself as an inside consultant, helping prospects with the tools available (products or services) to find a solution that helps them achieve their objectives.[9] Table 5.1 examines a number of concepts that are central to the customer-focused selling approach, as well as their relevance to the sport industry.

Table 5.1   Concepts in the Customer-Focused Selling Approach

Concept	Rationale
Every customer is unique.	Every customer is an individual with particular needs and wants, as well as a lifestyle that is unique to that individual. Making the customer fit into what you have to sell is not an effective strategy. Tailor the product to fit the individual—sell the person what he wants, not what you want.
Seek to establish a relationship through rapport and building trust.	Listen to what the customer has to say and appreciate her feelings and logic. State the facts as they are. Don't put yourself in a position where you overpromise and underdeliver.
Ask questions to assess the true needs of the customer.	Ask questions to determine the true needs and wants of the customer. Determine the best products and the best options that "fit" the customer. Asking questions demonstrates that you are interested in the customer's satisfaction with the proposed purchase.
Listen to the customers and hear what they are trying to convey.	If you listen effectively, the customers will convey to you what they are interested in buying and also identify reservations about making a purchase. You must hear what the customer has to say if you are to reach a resolution that is mutually beneficial to both parties.
View the potential customer not only as an individual, but also as an asset to the organization with a lifetime value.	If the intent of the interaction is to build a long-term relationship with the customer, then view the relationship in terms of repeat purchasing and the value of that relationship over a 10- or 20-year period. If you view the relationship as a long-term asset, you are more likely to listen effectively and work to satisfy the expressed needs of the customer.
Customize and personalize your presentation to the audience.	Remember that you are speaking to a specific individual or group. People's attention is focused on you and what you are saying, and therefore your presentation should focus on them and their needs. Technology and "techtainment"-type approaches are encouraged, but the message should be personal and tailored to the audience.
Put yourself in the customer's position.	Think of past unpleasant sales experiences you have had and work not to replicate them for your customers. Remember how you felt and reacted, and demonstrate that same empathy for your own customers.
Help lead your customer to a solution and reach a mutually beneficial agreement.	Closing a sale is something you do for somebody; finding a solution and gaining an agreement are things you do with somebody.
You will be judged by what happens after the sale.	Once the agreement has been reached, how you act as a salesperson will make all the difference regarding future business with this customer and referrals from this customer. Communicate regularly and provide any assistance that you can—good sales are built upon quality and attentive service.

Reprinted, by permission, from *Streetwise Customer Focused Selling* by Nancy J. Stevens. Copyright © 1998 by Adams Media Corporation. Used by permission. All rights reserved.

Remember that customer-focused selling does not help you sell "ice to the Eskimos," nor would you want it to. The basic premise of customer-focused selling is that you are a partner with your customers and that you are helping them find a solution, not trying to convince them to buy something they may not want or need.

Eduselling: Customer-Focused Selling in Sport

Eduselling is an evolutionary form of selling that combines needs assessment, relationship building, customer education, and aftermarketing in a process that originates at the prospect-targeting stage and progresses to an ongoing partnership agreement. Not only does eduselling initiate the communication exchange process, but this communication, which can be initiated by either party at any time, also continues throughout the course of the agreement. Traditional customer education programs educate consumers before they have made the purchase, and some such programs continue for a short duration (via a consumer warranty) to ensure that the customer is satisfied with the purchase and knows how to utilize the purchase. Eduselling goes further, however, by monitoring consumer utilization and satisfaction through regular communication. If the consumer is not utilizing the product or has not been satisfied with the results, eduselling, as an ongoing process that depends on customer utilization and satisfaction, provides logical intervention on the part of the seller because of the partnering aspects of the agreement. The partnering aspect of eduselling is not implied as in the case of most products and services, but is an expressed part of the agreement—a pledge of assistance to help the purchaser realize her business goals through the purchase of the product. Along with this is an understanding on the part of sellers that if they help customers utilize the product so as to achieve corporate objectives, renewal of the sale or expansion of the original agreement is a logical outcome. Eduselling virtually ensures that both parties, if they live up to their commitments, will benefit from the purchase in both the short and the long term.[10]

Among eduselling activities are assisting the purchaser in developing promotional activities involving the tickets or other elements of the corporate purchase. For example, in an eduselling agreement, the owner of Gotham City Motors could expect the sales personnel of the Gotham City Bats to help in developing a test-drive promotion that would deliver two tickets to a Bats game to anyone taking a test drive in the month of July. The Bats' staff could provide assistance in developing the ad, placing the ad, providing player appearances at the dealership, and so forth—any and all activities that would help Gotham City Motors utilize what it has purchased and achieve the corporate objectives.

Components of a Sale

There are four components of a sale:

Salable product

Attitude

Leads

Equity (value)

Salable product is product for which there is an awareness, an interest, a need, and possibly a demand. At this writing, Los Angeles Lakers basketball tickets are a very salable product, while Vancouver Grizzlies tickets are much less salable. Why is this the case? The Lakers have won a championship and by all indications have the capability to compete for a championship again. Tickets have been scarce and are more in demand than in previous years. The Lakers are the premier sport team and entertainment option in Los Angeles and Southern California in general. While Vancouver Grizzlies tickets have been sold, there is doubt regarding their long-term viability and stability in the Vancouver market. The Grizzlies have not been successful in the past, and have little chance of competing for the championship in the upcoming season. (Note: As of July, 2001, the Vancouver Grizzlies have been approved, pending application by the NBA Board of Governors, to relocate to Memphis, Tennessee.)

When we use the term "salable product" we are also referring to the inventory of products for sale. Sport organizations have the ability to offer tickets, memberships, and equipment in a broad array of pricing and quantity packages. Table 5.2 depicts the typical inventory of products that a salesperson in the sport industry may have to sell.

Table 5.2 Inventories—What Do I Have to Sell?

Naming rights	Electronic inventory	Signage inventory	Print inventory

Arena/Stadium
Practice facility
Team
	Television
	Radio
	Web page
		Dasher, score, matrix,
		  and message boards
		Marquees
		Floor/Field/Ice
		Medallions
		Concourse
		Blimps
		Turnstiles
			Game program
			Media guide
			Newsletters
			Ticket backs
			Ticket envelopes
			Scorecards/Roster
			  sheets
			Faxes

Tickets and hospitality inventory	**Promotions inventory**	**Community programs**	**Miscellaneous inventory**

VIP parking
Stadium/Arena clubs
Season tickets
Club seats, suites,
  permanent seat
  licenses
Group tickets
Parties/Special events
	Premium items
	On-floor promotions
	Diamond Vision
	  (or similar brand)
	Contents
	Pre-/Postgame
	  entertainment
		School assemblies
		Camps, clinics
		Awards banquets
		Kickoff luncheons/
		Dinners
		Golf tournaments
			Fantasy camps
			Off-season cruises,
			  trips with players
			Road trips

Reprinted, by permission, from B.J. Mullin, S. Hardy, and W.A. Sutton, 2000, *Sport Marketing*, 2nd ed. (Champaign: Human Kinetics), 229.

Attitude refers to the approach and philosophy of the salesperson. Is the salesperson a good listener? Does she believe in the product? Is the person just attempting to sell inventory or is she working with the customer to reach a solution and a beneficially rewarding agreement? Is the salesperson trying to sell a full set of expensive golf clubs to a parent for his child, or perhaps encouraging the parent to purchase a set of starter clubs for the child to determine whether the child enjoys and will continue with the game?

Leads refers to the ability of the salesperson to identify prospects who can become customers. Productive leads have usually been segmented based on demographic characteristics or classified into groups with special interests, affinities, or attributes.[11] Often leads are generated from past purchasers of the product who may be encouraged to return or to increase their frequency of product or service use. The most common sources of leads in sport are ticket purchases (including online and telephone sales from vendors such as Ticketmaster), contest cards, coupon/rebate redemption, and general inquiries to the organization. Leads can also take the form of referrals from current customers. Sport organizations that employ data-based marketing techniques are successful in generating their own leads and sometimes augment these leads by buying lists of prospective customers who fit the profile of the purchasers of the product or service. For instance, if a customer database indicates

ORCHARDS
GOLF   CLUB
1922
MOUNT HOLYOKE COLLEGE

Earn $500 Cash For New Member Referral

Dear Orchards Member:

The Orchards Staff wants to take this opportunity to thank you for choosing us as your private home away from home. We hope you have been enjoying your summer and that you have had many memorable experiences. With the clubhouse completion quickly approaching (July 28th) the rest of the summer is sure to be amazing!

As we continue to grow our Club through your many referrals, we'd like to take this opportunity to make a very exciting limited-time offer.

For each new Local Member you refer that joins between July 18th and July 28th you will receive $500 cash. For any Regional or National member that joins within this time frame you'll receive $250.

For each new Local Member you refer that joins between July 29th and August 8th you will receive $250 cash. For any Regional or National member that joins within this time frame you'll receive $125.

Additionally, you will also be eligible to win our (3) month carry-over skin which is <u>10 months of complimentary dues</u> and <u>a new set of Titleist DCI irons.</u>

A beautiful clubhouse, exciting member events and, of course, fantastic golf. What better time to refer your friends, family or business associates to become members of your esteemed Club?

If you would like to learn more about our "Referral Skins Game" or have anyone in mind to join The Orchards Golf Club please feel free to stop in or call us in the Membership Office at 534-3806.

Sincerely,

Steve Ballard
Membership Director

Gail Williams
Sales & Activity Director

P.S. This one time opportunity ends on August 8th so refer hard and have some fun!

18 Silverwood Terrace • South Hadley, MA 01075 • p. (413) 535-CLUB f. (413) 534-7336 • www.orchardsgolf.com

Example of a new member referral program.

Reprinted, by permission, from Palmer Golf Management Company.

that a significant number of attorneys have purchased the product or service, then the roster of the local or regional bar association may prove to be a fruitful source of leads.

Equity (value) implies the need for both parties to be vested in and to benefit from the outcome of the sales agreement. If the goal is an agreement, both parties have to have an investment equity of some sort. In the purchase of a Boston Red Sox season ticket, the Boston Red Sox organization receives payment for 81 games per seat purchased. The purchaser receives the right to attend those 81 games in a guaranteed seat location. If the equity is perceived to be one-sided or nonexistent, chances for renewal of the sale and a continued long-term relationship between the purchaser and the Red Sox is greatly diminished.

Equity implies a win-win situation. Not only do both parties receive something from the agreement, but also both are satisfied with the agreement and feel that they have benefited from the agreement.

What Makes an Effective Salesperson?

People have debated for centuries whether salespersons are born or made. In the opinion of experts, the naturally born salesperson is a myth: salespersons are made, not born.[12] Effective salespersons are confident communicators with an aggressive nature, are self-starters, and are motivated to succeed. These traits are developed through training, modeling, and experience. Mark McCormack of IMG looks for the following in his sales staff:

- Belief in the product
- Belief in oneself
- Sales call volume—seeing a lot of people
- Good timing
- Willingness to listen to the customer
- A sense of humor
- Willingness to knock on old doors
- Willingness to ask everyone to buy
- Willingness to follow up after the sale with the same aggressiveness as demonstrated before the sale
- Common sense[13]

The majority of the traits McCormack lists can be classified as communication skills. Communication, both externally with customers and internally with coworkers and other support personnel, is the core of the sales process. You must be able to communicate what you have to sell, why it should be purchased, how it benefits and fits the consumer, and so forth. Figure 5.3 describes the communication skills essential in the sales process.

Before examining the types of sales approaches commonly used in the sport industry, we should consider customers and their role in the sales process.

Zig Ziglar has spent a lifetime studying the nuances of selling and helping people become successful salespeople. The following are the traits of successful salespeople, according to Ziglar and other experts on selling:[14]

- The ability to establish and maintain trust
- Empathy
- Persistence, follow-through, and competitiveness
- Accountability and responsibility

C all on other sales personnel for support.

O ffer assistance and encouragement to your coworkers.

M ake an effort to understand your customers.

M odify the sales process on an ongoing basis to make sure it works.

U nderstand the time constraints and demands in the purchasing decision.

N ever let personal feelings interfere with communicating.

I nitiate dialogue and discussions to keep everyone informed.

C ontact customers regularly—not just for sales and renewals.

A ssess what you hear and what you don't hear.

T alk honestly and openly.

E xchange ideas and possibilities as well as information.

Figure 5.3   Essential skills for salespersons.

- Integrity
- Genuine optimism
- An understanding of the company mission
- An understanding of the prospects
- The willingness to watch and learn from other successful salespeople
- The ability to ask open-ended questions and listen to the prospect
- Knowledge of benefits of the product
- The ability to illustrate for prospects how the product will meet their needs
- The ability to persuade prospects to agree on the major benefits of the product
- The ability to ask for the sale
- The ability to reinforce the sale
- The ability to overcome rejection
- The ability to make prospects feel as though they are buying and not being sold

While it would be unrealistic to think that every successful salesperson possesses all of these traits, it would be realistic to assume that the more of these traits an individual possesses, or can acquire, the more successful that person is likely to be in selling.

The Customer or Prospect As a Participant in the Sales Process

A customer or prospect can be defined as a targeted individual or group with the potential (interest; need or want; and time/money resources) to purchase or utilize your products or services. An organization usually has current customers, past customers, and potential customers, perhaps including customers of its competitors.[15]

Current customers are the most valuable, as this group is demonstrating a current and active behavior that includes purchasing and product utilization. Current or loyal customers are vital organizational assets. Research shows that loyal customers spend more, refer new customers, and cost less to do business with than new customers do.[16] This segment of customers can be further divided into light, moderate, and heavy users. As these consumers are currently active in purchasing your products and services, they represent the most cost-efficient way to increase sales—by increasing their frequency and level of consumption. The **frequency escalator** depicted in figure 2.7[17] (on page 49) shows the types of consumers most common in a sport organization. The goal of the organization is to move customers up the escalator. A professional basketball franchise, for example, might have more than 100,000 people annually attending one game per year. If each of those individuals could be motivated to purchase tickets to one additional game, at an average ticket price of $25, the organizational gross receipts would increase by $2.5 million. Other activities would include changing light users to moderate users through ticket plans and changing moderate users to heavy users. In relation to the escalator, the first objective is to retain the current customer base. The second objective is to increase the frequency of those same consumers. Only after these two objectives have been achieved is an aggressive effort made to expand the base—which is much more costly to do.

Consider the following example of customer frequency. In 1865 the population of the United States was around 35 million people. During P.T. Barnum's management of his museum over this same time period, over 38 million tickets were sold. Obviously Barnum's present customers were repeat customers and also served in a word-of-mouth sales capacity to recommend the museum to their friends and relatives.[18]

Past customers are another group with a connection to the organization. If the organization is able to determine why this group is no longer active with the organization, it can develop and enact strategies to get them to "return." Getting the people in this group reconnected to the organization is a sound strategy because they have demonstrated an interest and have purchased the product or service in the past. If they are unwilling to return, then the organization can at least identify reasons why these customers defected, and can take steps in an effort to retain current customers and keep them from defecting.

Potential customers are individuals or groups who have the potential to become current customers but may never be converted into actual customers. The reasons for failure to convert may relate to

- lack of interest in the product or service,
- lack of comprehension regarding the product or service,
- lack of accessibility to the product or service,
- inadequate resources—time or money—to utilize the product or service, and
- loyalty to and satisfaction with another product or service.

Because of the low conversion rate of potential customers and the high cost related to generating awareness and interest among this group, sport organizations, particularly those that depend on attendance for profit margins, concentrate on current consumers and attempt to increase their level of involvement with the organization.

Competitors' customers are a subset of potential customers because these customers have the ability to switch brands and become your customers. Promotional activities such as the Pepsi Challenge are designed to provide a forum for potential customers who currently use the competitor's product to try a different product and ideally switch.

It has been said that today's customers have limited loyalty—that they are prepared to switch for a better deal even though they are satisfied with the current provider. In recent years we have seen customers switch credit card companies on the basis of lower initial interest rates, switch phone companies on the basis of the cost per minute for long-distance service, and so forth. This phenomenon has created a customer known as the "butterfly customer."

The Butterfly Customer

The **butterfly customer** is a creature more in motion than at rest: flitting from store to store, from bank to bank, from credit card to credit card, and from service to service. The first instinct of butterfly customers is to try something new, something better, and something different, and their last instinct is to stay loyal.[19] Butterfly customers are transient visitors to your business who have replaced the loyal customers of the past.

The unique nature of sport, which is subjective, unpredictable, and inconsistent,[20] contributes to the presence of butterfly customers in sport organizations. Having a product that is unpredictable and inconsistent and that is viewed subjectively would be detrimental to a traditional product or service, yet the sport organization depends on these qualities. These factors result in customers' purchasing the product based on expectations that may be purely personal with no foundation in fact. If the sport product fails to meet expectations, current customers may assume the role of butterfly customers and do their sport or leisure spending elsewhere. Professional sport organizations in their first year of operation, those signing a new and heralded player, and those hosting a premier special event such as the All-Star Game all experience spikes in sales during the given time period. Often these same franchises see a downward spiral the following year as the butterflies who were caught up in the earlier excitement have moved on to something else. Often these butterflies switch without telling anyone why or even attempting to improve their level of satisfaction; this is a far cry from the "vigilante" customers of the early 1990s who were very vocal in telling the organization what they wanted and who expected organizational changes to fit their needs.[21] If our customers today behave as butterflies, our salespersons need a variety of "flowers and scents" to attract them—not just "nets" to catch them.

The Sales Process

Thus far this chapter has addressed the concept of sales; a sport sales philosophy, namely, the customer-focused sales approach; what customers want; and the types of customers we encounter in the sport industry. It is time to focus on initiating the sales process and selecting the sales approach that best fits our products or services—one that is effective in communicating to our customers.

Preparation is a key element in the sales process. While salespersons must be confident self-starters and good communicators, it is essential that they know their products or services and can convey to the customer that they are knowledgeable and trustworthy. Preparation includes having the answers to the following core questions:

- Who are our customers? Who are they, where are they, what do they look like (demographically), and how do they live and act (psychographics and lifestyle)?

- Who are our competitors? Who sells and provides similar products and services? What are these competitors' strengths and weaknesses?

- Why do customers want what we are selling? What is our solution? What is the market's perspective on our products or services?

- What would make customers prefer to buy these products or services from our organization? What is the unique selling proposition (USP) we are perceived to provide? Quality? Customer service? Reliability?

- Why might customers prefer to buy from our competitors? How have our competitors positioned themselves and their products or services? Better service? Better price? More options?

- What incentives or added values do our salespersons have to offer that will be attractive to our customers? In addition to our USP, what do we need to include in the offer? What is the competition offering?[22]

Knowing who our customers are is a critical element of being prepared. Ray Borelli, director of research for the NBA, examines the role of research in the sales process in his Practitioner's Perspective.

PRACTITIONER'S PERSPECTIVE

Utilizing Research in the Sales Process
by Ray Borelli, Director of Research for the National Basketball Association

Research is an integral part of the sales process at the NBA, both at the league level and among the individual teams. Virtually everything that is presented to a potential sponsor, from the size and dynamics of the NBA fan base to the latest consumer trends, is rooted in research. The NBA market research department is intimately involved in the sales process at all stages, from positioning the brand to prospective sponsors to evaluating the effectiveness of an existing sponsorship.

The NBA relies more heavily on syndicated consumer research studies, such as Simmons, MRI, and Scarborough Research, to support sponsorship sales than on custom, proprietary research. We do this for several reasons. First, the syndicated studies measure the entire marketplace, which allows us to compare the NBA fan base to the fan bases of other sports or to the general population. Our proprietary research is usually much more focused on the NBA fan. Second, since the syndicated studies are conducted by an independent third party, they tend to hold more credibility with marketers and advertising agencies than research conducted internally by the NBA.

In addition to demographic information, these syndicated studies collect massive amounts of data on consumers' behavior, such as where they shop, what they buy, what they watch on television, and what sports they follow. This allows us to compare the NBA fan against those people who purchase a particular product or shop at a particular store. For example, we know from Simmons data that NBA fans are more likely than the average American to use their personal computers to purchase stocks. Obviously, those data are included in any sponsorship presentations we make to online brokerage firms.

We also utilize syndicated sports polls such as the ESPN Sports Poll, Nielsen's Sports Quest, and the Harris Interactive Sports Poll. While these polls also measure consumer behavior, they focus more on the sport fan, with detailed trending information on fan avidity, game attendance, viewing, sponsorship awareness, licensed merchandise purchases, and sport/recreation participation. For example, we know from these sources that basketball is the favorite sport to play among kids and teens—information that is valuable to potential NBA sponsors looking to reach a younger demographic.

(continued)

(continued)   We are more likely to use customized research to evaluate a sponsorship after an agreement has been reached and a marketing plan has been developed and activated. For instance, we can conduct a random telephone poll of NBA fans to determine their awareness of an existing sponsorship. We can also elect to commission a research study to measure the equivalent media value of a promotional sponsor generated through on-air product mentions or logo exposure. AT&T, for example, sponsored the AT&T 3-Point Shootout during NBA All-Star Weekend. After the event was over, we commissioned research to evaluate the incremental media value AT&T received from, among other things, television exposure of courtside signage during TNT's coverage of the event. Newspaper articles and television news stories from around the world that mentioned the AT&T Shootout were also included in the evaluation.

In the course of our business, it is critical for us to demonstrate that the NBA is reaching a vibrant audience through our television broadcasts and Internet site. This is the largest segment of our fan base, as only 20% of our fans actually attend our games. Therefore, many sponsors allocate the majority of their marketing dollars to these media channels. We rely on the Nielsen Television Index to position our television viewers and on Media Matrix to position our NBA.com users to both potential and existing sponsors.

It is the responsibility of our department to ensure that anyone involved in the sales process at the NBA understands the product and, more importantly, knows and understands its customer base. We expect our marketing and sales staff to be able to utilize that knowledge to further the promotional and sales objectives of the NBA and the WNBA.

Knowing our customers means more than just knowing who they are, where they are, and what they look like; it also means understanding them and why they buy our products or services. For example, consider the video recorder marketplace in the early 1980s. Sony had developed the technically superior Betamax video recorders to compete with Matsushita Electric Co.'s VHS format and JVC, a leading VHS video recorder brand. Sony, figuring that consumers would be attracted to, and would purchase, the smaller and better-quality Beta format, relied on technological superiority and development rather than marketing. Sony didn't know what customers really wanted—namely to bring the cinema experience home and have a broad selection of movies to choose from for their home entertainment. Sensing this, JVC wisely concentrated on ensuring that a wider range of movies in the VHS format were available in video rental shops, which ultimately sold many more VCRs than Sony.[23]

In some cases, organizations must rely on a vision and their "gut" feeling for what the customer wants, even if it doesn't exist. Consider the case of Bill Rasmussen, the founder of ESPN. Rasmussen, a public relations director, had recently been fired by the Hartford Whalers hockey team and was searching for a job. While sitting in traffic with his son, Scott, the two talked about the sport boom that was going on in 1970s America. Considering the available satellite technology, they envisioned a cable television station featuring sports—just sports—on a 24-hour basis, 365 days a year. Conventional wisdom decried the idea that people wanted sports 24 hours every day of the year. Rasmussen launched his idea 14 months later, investing $8000 borrowed on his credit card. Since its launch in September of 1979, ESPN has evolved into cable television's largest network, reaching more than 62 million U.S. homes and delivered in 11 languages to 120 countries.[24] It has also created its own programming and offers ESPN2, ESPN News, and ESPN Classic networks.

In sport, why people buy and what they buy is subject not only to the economy, trends, and fads, but also to performance, emotional attachment and identification, social interaction,[25] and the "star factor"—the opportunity to watch a superstar athlete such as former Chicago Bull and NBA star Michael Jordan. The opportunity to watch and even "Be like Mike" was an economic juggernaut in the 1980s and 1990s not only in the United States, but also globally. In an article titled "The Jordan Effect," the global impact of Michael Jordan as of the 1998 release of the article was estimated to have been approximately $10 billion.[26] This figure would include ticket sales, movie tickets, athletic apparel, equipment and footwear, cologne, video sales, book sales, sunglasses, cereal and other food products, and so forth.

Why did we want to be like Mike? For a variety of reasons. One reason is fan identification, a personal commitment and emotional involvement that a fan has with a team or a particular player. Another reason is social interaction, the opportunity to socialize and interact with others who have the same feelings and identification. A third reason is not to be left out, to be part of a "community," to be part of a trend.[27]

Figure 5.4, on the hierarchy of sport purchasing rationale, examines the progression in rationale accompanied by an increase in expenditures as the customer's reason to buy changes. The lower stages of the hierarchy relate to individual motivations, such as fan identification and personal enjoyment. The next stages relate to more social and community rationale. The final stages concern business-related reasons culminating in a partnership arrangement. Understanding where the consumer is on this hierarchy allows for sales efforts to be more strategically planned and focused on the consumer and the possible rationale the consumer has for purchasing the product.

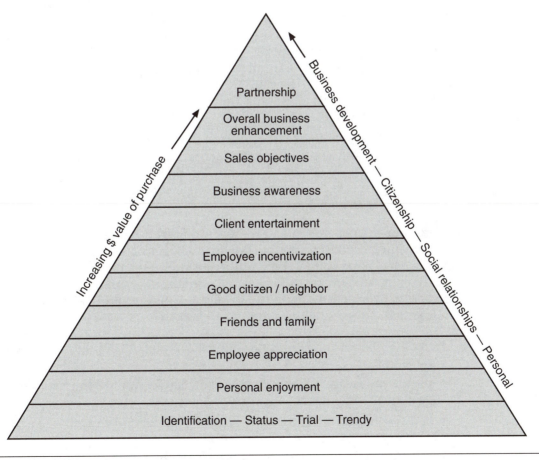

Figure 5.4 Hierarchy of sport purchasing rationale.

The Sales Presentation

While not all selling activities involve an actual presentation, the term presentation in this section refers to the material and information to be shared with the audience. This audience, which can be one or more persons, can be encountered directly via face-to-face selling, telemarketing, and formal sales activities involving an audience or indirectly, through direct mail, cyberselling or online selling, and so on. In each case, the salesperson must have prepared informative materials and presented them to the audience for their consideration. This is the advice Aristotle gave presenters:

- Tell your audience what you are going to tell them (opening).
- Tell them.
- Tell them what you have told them (summary).[28]

The actual form of the presentation should be tailored to the audience. Will it be a one-on-one meeting? Is the sales presentation to a group of executives? Is the purpose of the presentation to provide information that will be analyzed and discussed at a later meeting? The following steps will help the salesperson prepare and collect the information for the initial sales contact with the prospect or customer:

- *Determine what the audience expects to gain from the information.* No matter what the format (brochure, open house telemarketing, direct mail, etc., topics we consider later in the chapter), there is an expectation on the part of the audience that the message will provide some degree of new information. This new information can include details that fill in the blanks, introduce new products or services, or provide some clarification regarding perceptions the audience may have. For example, an audience attending an open house or receiving a direct mail piece may have the perception that season tickets are an expensive proposition. They may be pleasantly surprised or have their perceptions altered when they receive a 2000-2001 ticket brochure from the NBA's Minnesota Timberwolves introducing a season ticket that begins at $9 per game.[29]

- *Determine the one thing you want the audience to remember.* When you design a mailing piece or prepare a telemarketing script, a PowerPoint presentation, or a face-to-face sales call, there is a risk of overwhelming the prospect with information or choices. Being overwhelmed may confuse prospects to the point that they are unlikely to take action on the offer.

For example, a common philosophy in sales is **full-menu marketing.** Full-menu marketing involves the creation of variations of the product that have different price points or entail other options. With full-menu marketing, the salesperson is attempting to have an option for everyone regardless of demographic or lifestyle segmentation characteristics. For example, full-menu marketing in professional baseball might involve offering the following seat-related products:

- Luxury suites (usually 12 seats for every game within a suite for entertainment purposes)
- Club seats (seats for every game that feature waitperson services, charge privileges, and other amenities in a preferred seating location)
- Full-season tickets (seats for every game with limited amenities in a preferred location)
- Half-season ticket plans (tickets for one-half of the games; location similar to that for full-season ticket holders if available)

- Partial plans (tickets for usually up to one-fourth of the games; next best available location after that for half-season ticket plan holders)
- Flex books (coupons—not tickets—that can be redeemed for any game on the schedule; admission and location dependent on availability)

Obviously, offering these options to every prospect could be confusing and overwhelming. What would the prospect remember—price, location, or amenities? Which of those facets is the focal point of the message? The salesperson must plan for the outcome, what the audience will take away from the interaction.

- *Determine the materials necessary to best convey the information and create the impressions you would like to impart to the audience.* The age of information technology in which we live and conduct our business has greatly enhanced the ability of salespersons to convey information and create unique and memorable impressions. CD-ROM sales presentations enable salespersons to add video elements to traditional PowerPoint decks, bringing them to life. These presentations can be easily customized depending on the audience and intent of the communication. Laptop computers give salespeople the opportunity to tie into ticket offices and display ticket locations and seating views to prospective purchasers. Even virtual reality is becoming a sales tool. The Pittsburgh Pirates, in promoting the sale of luxury suites at their new home, PNC Park, utilized virtual reality when selling their luxury suites. Luxury suites usually cost more than $150,000 annually, so the prospective audience for the product may be small and will expect a certain level of treatment, as well as uniqueness in the sales presentation. The Pirates fulfilled this expectation by building a luxury suite in an office building adjacent to the PNC park construction site, appointed exactly as the suites in the new park would be. Adding to the experience during the presentation was the provision of food and beverage by the caterer for the new park. The Pirates offered a view of the construction site, showed a video depicting the rich history of the Pirates, and provided written materials in a brochure that summarized presentation key points. They were able to show the exact view from each luxury suite available for purchase through the use of virtual reality, which created the way the playing field would look from each of the 60-plus suites up for sale.[30] The Pirates sold all of the luxury suites in record time.

Sales Strategies and Methods

Being prepared and having an informative presentation are just two elements of an effective sales program. Choosing the right delivery system is a key element in effectively conveying the organizational message and positioning the product or services under consideration. Although virtual reality was effective for the Pittsburgh Pirates, it would prove inappropriate, not to mention extremely costly, in other situations with a less expensive product or service under consideration. The following examination of delivery systems provides an analysis of the strengths, weaknesses, and appropriateness of the various delivery systems.

Direct Mail

When prospects are contacted through the mail, they are dealing with printed information and order forms rather than a salesperson.[31] Thus the organization has no opportunity to explain the program or the offer, or any opportunity to counter objections or even answer questions.[32] This necessitates that the direct mail material be self-explanatory, clear, and focused in its message and that it contain clear instructions for the reader on what to do and how to do it. Direct mail offers a number of advantages and distinct characteristics:

- *Direct mail is targeted.* The appeal is to certain groups of consumers that are measurable, reachable, and sizable enough to ensure meaningful sales volume. Typically a good response on a direct mail offer is 2%, so the overall targeted market segment must make the cost and effort worthwhile.

- *It is personal.* The message can be personalized not only according to the name of the recipient but also according to other lifestyle characteristics such as Pittsburgh Steelers fan, Oklahoma State University alumnus, and so forth. Given the sophistication of data-based marketing and mail-merge programs, correspondence that begins "Dear Season Ticket Holder" is not only rude; it demonstrates a lack of recognition and appreciation of that individual on the part of the organization.

- *It is measurable.* Because each message calls for some type of action or response, the organization mailing the message is able to measure the return on investment on the mailing.

- *It is testable.* Because the effectiveness is measurable, sales personnel can devise accurate head-to-head tests of offers, formats, prices, terms, and so on.

- *It is flexible.* Direct mail presents few constraints (other than cost); the organization can select almost any size, color, timing, shape, and format for the mailing. Before the beginning of the 1999-2000 NBA season, the Chicago Bulls sent a unique mailing piece to everyone who was on the Bulls' waiting list for season tickets: a cardboard model of the United Center containing a videotape and information on how to acquire season tickets. Although this piece cost a little more and required a delivery service, it was effective in selling new season tickets.

The Appearance of the Mailing Piece

Not every organization can replicate the efforts just mentioned of the Chicago Bulls, but then again there may not be a need to do so. However, because of the volume of junk mail that appears to fill our mailboxes every day, the mailing piece should be unusual and intriguing enough to capture attention and encourage the recipient to open it. In the case of professional sport teams or collegiate athletic departments, the team logo on the envelope is usually enough to distinguish the piece from other mail and motivate the addressee to open it.

In 1998, the NHL's Phoenix Coyotes conducted one of the more unusual direct mail campaigns in professional sport. The Coyotes embarked on a business-to-business mail campaign that proceeded in two stages and actually led to a telemarketing call and meeting. The first stage involved mailing a letter in Russian, ostensibly written by Coyote goalie Nikolai Khabibulin (figure 5.5a), that closed by saying "in the event you don't read Russian, watch your mail for a video." The follow-up letter, in English (figure 5.5b), arrived several days later, along with the promised video, and a mention that recipients should expect a phone call to set up a meeting to discuss how the Coyotes might assist them in reaching their marketing objectives. The campaign involved purchasing a list of 10,000 names (sizable) that fit the demographics of current season ticket holders (targeted) and mailing those materials in waves of 2000 per week. After the mailing of the video, summer sales associates called each recipient and attempted to close a sale over the phone if it appeared interest was high. If the prospect was interested but not willing to commit over the telephone, a meeting was scheduled to assess the business needs of the prospect and explain the Coyotes' ticket program.[33]

Ticket-sales materials are among the most common types of mailing materials used in sport. As with the Coyotes example, these materials should be tailored to specific groups based on knowledge of the organization's customer base and the databases that the organization can access. As this may entail creating a number of different mailing pieces, each piece should have its own identity while still conveying a "branded image" consistent with the organization. A mailing piece should be attractive and colorful and possibly contain photos, seating charts, benefit tables, and other information while at the same time sending the message that this is a desirable activity and that the mailing merits a response.

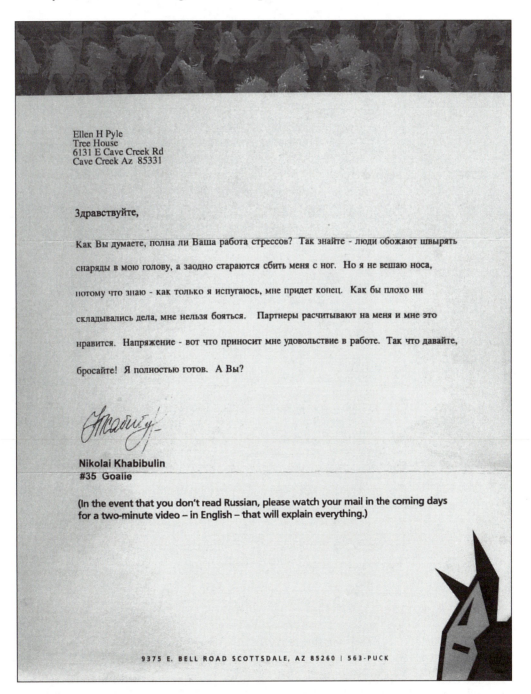

Figure 5.5a Phoenix Coyotes letter campaign: letter in Russian.

Reprinted, by permission, from The Phoenix Coyotes.

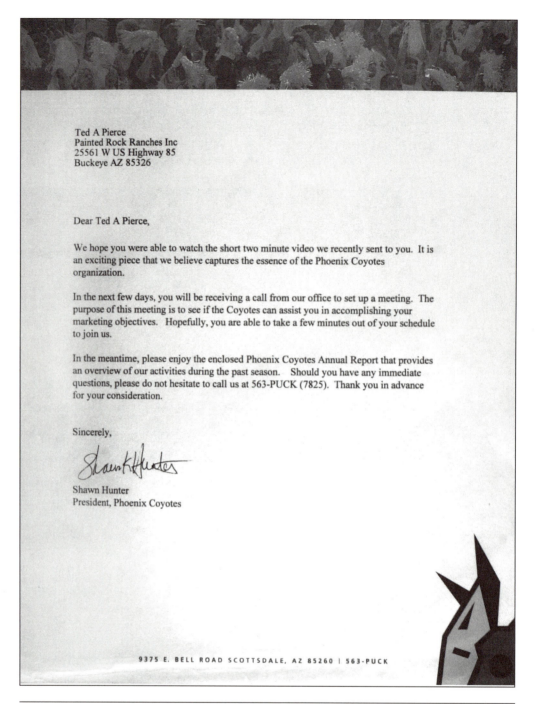

Ted A Pierce
Painted Rock Ranches Inc
25561 W US Highway 85
Buckeye AZ 85326

Dear Ted A Pierce,

We hope you were able to watch the short two minute video we recently sent to you. It is an exciting piece that we believe captures the essence of the Phoenix Coyotes organization.

In the next few days, you will be receiving a call from our office to set up a meeting. The purpose of this meeting is to see if the Coyotes can assist you in accomplishing your marketing objectives. Hopefully, you are able to take a few minutes out of your schedule to join us.

In the meantime, please enjoy the enclosed Phoenix Coyotes Annual Report that provides an overview of our activities during the past season. Should you have any immediate questions, please do not hesitate to call us at 563-PUCK (7825). Thank you in advance for your consideration.

Sincerely,

Shawn Hunter
President, Phoenix Coyotes

9375 E. BELL ROAD SCOTTSDALE, AZ 85260 | 563-PUCK

Figure 5.5b   Phoenix Coyotes letter campaign: letter in English.
Reprinted, by permission, from The Phoenix Coyotes.

The following are among the mailing pieces that sport organizations commonly employ:

• *Full-season ticket brochure.* This type of brochure explains the locations of seats and the costs, levels, and benefits (or advantages) of holding a full-season ticket. The brochure should also include follow-up and contact information and an order/response form.

• *Partial ticket plan brochure.* This is similar to the full-season brochure but must not confuse the reader with too many options. It must also distinguish the partial plan from the full-season plan. The brochure should include follow-up and contact information and an order/response form.

• *Group brochure.* The group brochure lists available dates for group nights, discounts, promotional nights (giveaways, special events, and price promotions), fund-raising options, and the benefits of attending as a group. As a number of groups travel to the sport venue from outside the immediate market area, it should also include information on buses and hotels and area attractions. Photos of people enjoying themselves are essential, and the brochure should also include follow-up and contact information and an order/response form.

• *Pocket schedule.* Pocket schedules of all events and promotional activities include diagrams of the venue, directions, and price listing; additionally they should include follow-up and contact information and an order/response form. These schedules are usually mailed to light attenders—those who purchased less than a partial ticket plan, walked up and purchased tickets with a credit card, purchased by telephone, and so forth.

• *Poster.* Posters can be used in lieu of or in addition to pocket schedules. They contain the same information but are usually mailed to businesses (taverns, restaurants, fitness centers, student union buildings, and the like). They can have tear-off response cards and are usually posted in high-traffic areas.

• *Appeal letter.* Letters of appeal are used primarily by organizations such as collegiate athletic departments and not-for-profit recreational centers (YMCA, etc.). These letters clearly state what the sender is asking for and why. They may also be supplemented with other communication materials such as brochures.[34]

The e-mail message can also be viewed as a form of direct mail. Sport organizations often use e-mail attachments to send the materials listed to customers in their databases. Privacy regulations require that organizations get the permission of addressees before transmitting solicitation efforts. This **permission marketing** (discussed in chapter 12) can take the form of a broadcast message (the same message sent to multiple addresses) about a special offer related to a particular game or product, or may be an invitation from a player or coach for the consumer to become a ticket plan owner.

Another recent trend in the use of direct mail is the annual report. Much as it functions for shareholders, the annual report informs ticket holders or other stakeholders about developments within the sport organization during the past year. Some teams produce an annual report in a brochure format; others compile and mail a video report. According to marketing consultant and author Jon Spoelstra, the annual report provides all the information that interests a particular sponsor and details how the sponsor has benefited.[35] This type of documentation and information should not go only to sponsors, however. Since vested individuals such as ticket plan holders also have a stake in how the organization has performed and an interest in how the organization is doing on the playing field and in the community, an annual report for these stakeholders is equally important.

Phoenix Coyotes President and CEO Shawn K. Hunter and his staff prepare an annual report that is mailed to the Coyotes' "stakeholders" at the end of every season. This report, with a mission of updating the stakeholders on the state of the franchise, contains the following elements:

• A letter from the ownership of the Coyotes
• An overview of the season and suggestions about what to look forward to next season (may include construction updates, information about new programs, etc.)
• A synopsis of charitable activities—Coyotes' Goals for Kids Foundation

- Past season attendance, percentage of capacity
- An explanation and listing of the benefits (advantages) of being a season ticket holder
- Thank-you quotes and notes from the players to the fans
- A photograph montage of last season's highlights and activities[36]

Telemarketing

Telemarketing can be defined as a marketing approach that "utilizes telecommunications technology as part of a well-planned, organized and managed marketing program that prominently features the use of personal selling, using non-face-to-face contacts."[37] Telemarketing efforts are characterized as inbound (the organization receives a phone call from a customer who wishes to place an order) and outbound (the organization, from a "phone room," calls identified leads to solicit sales). Telemarketing used to handle incoming calls is viewed as one-dimensional, with its purpose typically that of fielding inquiries or orders from customers who are responding to advertising messages or other promotional activities. The outbound approach is usually characterized as two-dimensional because the phone room personnel can also respond to incoming calls. Outbound telemarketing provides the opportunity to prospect for customers, follow up leads, or solicit existing customers for repeat or expanded business volume.[38] Ticketmaster is the world leader in both inbound and outbound telemarketing of tickets in the sport and entertainment industry.

Telemarketing via its telephone links, which can be on-site, in the same city as the organization, or even in another region, can be used to complement, support, or substitute for an in-house or direct sales force. Telemarketing offers considerable possibilities for enhancing the productivity of the sales force by permitting more specialization by account type and better focus on high-yield accounts. Telemarketing is also valuable in terms of supporting sales, scheduling sales calls and deliveries, conducting surveys, and checking customer order status and providing customer service.[39] The Boston Red Sox have taken such an approach in their telemarketing efforts. Utilizing software licensed through Advantix and maintained and programmed by Next Ticketing, the Red Sox have implemented a system that can handle up to 90,000 incoming orders in one hour, that operates 24 hours a day, seven days a week, and that generates a database.[40]

The telemarketing sales process[41]   Telemarketing involves training the sales personnel to follow a script, become effective listeners, identify the objections to the sale (if any), and complete the sales process by countering the objection and selling the original offer or modifying the offer (by up-selling or down-selling) to better fit the needs of the consumer. In some cases, the telemarketing supervisor may elect to permit slight modifications in the script in order to make the telemarketer more comfortable and make the "pitch" more personal. The process looks like this:

1. **Precall planning**
   Review client information
   Plan the objective for the call
   "Psych up"—get in the proper mental frame for the call
2. **Approach/positioning**
   Identify who you are and where you're from
   Identify the purpose of the call
   Make interest-creating statement

Build rapport

Get through the gatekeeper (secretary or receptionist) and to the decision-maker

3. **Data gathering**

Gain general understanding of the client or the client's business

Move from general to specific types of questions

Identify a personal or business need

4. **Solution generation**

Tailor communication to the specific client need

Ask in-depth questions to test the feasibility of the solution

Gather data for cost-benefit analysis

Prepare client for the recommendation

5. **Solution presentation**

Get client agreement to area of need

Present recommendation clearly and concisely

Describe use benefits

6. **Close**

Decide on timing—when to close

Listen for buying signals

Handle objections

Use closing techniques

7. **Wrap-up**

Discuss implementation issues

Thank client for the sale

Confirm client commitment

Position next call

Applying the telemarketing process[42]   To see how this process works, let's imagine the following scenario. Jane Micelli is a telemarketer employed by the Detroit Red Wings. Jane has been given a list of leads derived from people who used their credit cards to purchase tickets to one or more games during the past season. Jane's goal is to sell half-season plans (20 games), but she also has the opportunity to up-sell to full-season tickets (41 games) or down-sell to "6-packs"—a new product just being introduced.

1. *Precall planning.* Jane reviews the file on Mary Stuart, an attorney who purchased individual tickets to four games during the past season. Jane notices that Ms. Stuart purchased two tickets for each of the four games she attended, and attended once per month in January, February, March, and April. Jane reviews her script and places the call.

2. *Approach/positioning.* "Hello. This is Jane Micelli of the Detroit Red Wings. May I please speak to Ms. Mary Stuart? Good evening, Ms. Stuart. As I stated, I'm calling from the Detroit Red Wings and we want to thank you for your support of the team during the past season. I'm sure that you were pleased with the performance and effort of the team and I'd like to talk to you about the upcoming season. We anticipate tickets being very difficult to come by next season and we would like to provide loyal fans such as you the opportunity to purchase tickets before they go on sale to the general public. Do you have a few minutes?"

3. *Data gathering.* "According to our records, you purchased tickets to see the Avalanche, Rangers, Penguins, and Stars last season; is that correct? Did you attend any other games? How do you select the games that you attend?"

4. *Solution generation.* "We have designed a ticket plan for people such as you that like to attend the *big* games against name opponents or teams with high-profile players. We also realize that these same games are great opportunities for businesspersons such as you to entertain clients. Would you be interested in a ticket plan that lets you see the best teams in the NHL yet requires a commitment of only six games?"

5. *Solution presentation.* "The Detroit Red Wings have designed a new ticket plan called the *Big Game Plan.* This plan lets you see the Avalanche, Stars, Penguins, Rangers, Devils, and Blackhawks. It also guarantees the same seat for all six games, and the opportunity to purchase tickets for *some* of the playoff games."

6. *Close.* "I'm sure that the *Big Game Plan* will meet your needs and be much more convenient than your current ticket-purchasing options. Can I reserve two *Big Game Plans* for you?"

7. *Wrap-up.* "I'm sure that you will be happy with your ticket plans. I will call you monthly in case you would like to purchase tickets that might be available and are not part of your ticket plan."

New variations are modifying the telemarketing industry and expanding its scope of services. The Washington Capitals Fan Call system, for instance, offers fans the following options: results and recap of the most recent game; messages from the Coaches' Corner or from a player of the caller's choosing; ticket and merchandise information and ordering procedures; news from the minor league affiliates; schedule and fan club information; and a message describing sponsor Pizza Hut's specials—including the option to order pizza directly through the Fan Call line. The latter option generated $500,000 in sales for Pizza Hut on direct-line transfers during the hockey season.[43] Obviously Web pages can be similarly structured, but this is an excellent example of technology helping to revolutionize existing capabilities.

Personal Selling

Personal selling, or face-to-face selling, "is the art of convincing, the use of learnable techniques to close a transaction and the application of basic rules to show a prospect or customer that you have something he needs."[44] Personal selling involves the integration of data-based marketing, relationship marketing (discussed in chapter 14), and benefit selling to effectively communicate to consumers. One of the greatest advantages of personal selling is the opportunity to ask and answer questions and offer rebuttals to consumer objections or misperceptions. Here we look at each of these areas and consider their contribution and importance to the personal selling process.

Data-based marketing Basic data for effective marketing decision-making are essential to any sport organization, regardless of size or scope, because of the rapidly changing fan and participant trends and patterns. Those who market sport products need to gather information systematically and continuously. Rather than taking a reactive approach to communicating with their target markets, sport marketers must be proactive. The ability to collect data is greater than ever, as is the ability to manipulate and segment the database into smaller, more targeted sub-databases. This ability to collect and segment data provides better forums for communication because messages can be better targeted, more relevant, and more personal; recipients can perceive such communications to be more important because they have focus. Figure 5.6 illustrates some questions that marketers should ask to enable them to construct

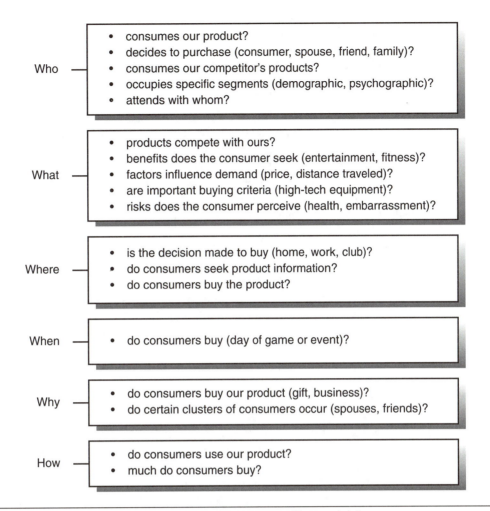

Who
- consumes our product?
- decides to purchase (consumer, spouse, friend, family)?
- consumes our competitor's products?
- occupies specific segments (demographic, psychographic)?
- attends with whom?

What
- products compete with ours?
- benefits does the consumer seek (entertainment, fitness)?
- factors influence demand (price, distance traveled)?
- are important buying criteria (high-tech equipment)?
- risks does the consumer perceive (health, embarrassment)?

Where
- is the decision made to buy (home, work, club)?
- do consumers seek product information?
- do consumers buy the product?

When
- do consumers buy (day of game or event)?

Why
- do consumers buy our product (gift, business)?
- do certain clusters of consumers occur (spouses, friends)?

How
- do consumers use our product?
- much do consumers buy?

Figure 5.6 Issues to be resolved in constructing an effective database.

Reprinted, by permission, from B.J. Mullin, S. Hardy, and W.A. Sutton, 2000, *Sport Marketing*, 2nd ed. (Champaign: Human Kinetics), 81.

effective databases. The time to ask these questions is during design of the database because the answers dictate how the data will be used.

Relationship marketing   Relationship marketing implies finding a way to integrate the customer into the company and to create and sustain a relationship between the company and the customer.[45] Gronroos identifies three main conditions under which relationship marketing is successful and productive:

- The customer has an ongoing desire for service.
- The customer controls selection of the provider.
- There are alternative suppliers (competitors).[46]

These conditions are present in the sport marketplace and even more critical in some markets with multiple providers of the same product or service (e.g., Chicago, New York, Los Angeles). In general, people who consume sport are highly involved consumers who have expressed or implied a desire for long-term association with a sport team or branded product. As there are multiple providers in the sport marketplace, some even in the same sport, we can state that in most cases this marketplace is a **"buyer's market."** That is, competition for the entertainment dollar, which encompasses the sport industry dollar, is so intense that sport organizations must build relationships with their customers that are sustainable and long lasting.

Benefit selling   Benefit selling involves the promotion and creation of new benefits or the promotion and enhancement of existing benefits to offset existing perceptions or assumed negatives related to the sport product or service.[47] Benefits must be identified and publicized and must be judged by the consumer to have worth or value. Sport organizations should conduct research by such means as consumer focus groups to determine the reasons why consumers defect and also the benefits that consumers find attractive and that constitute for consumers a reason to consider making a purchase.

For example, many consumers who are solicited to purchase a ticket plan state that they cannot commit to a ticket plan because of the number of games or because of an inability to guarantee that they will be free to attend games scheduled six or more months in the future. For these individuals, benefit selling may provide the answer. The concept of benefit selling has been responsible for the creation of new products in the sport industry such as the flex book.[48] The flex book, or fan flex as it is sometimes called, was developed in response to the frequent buying objection of potential consumers who could not commit to a certain number of games on specific dates as contained in traditional ticket plans. The flex book (figure 5.7) contains coupons for a specified number of games, usually between 10 and 13. The cost may be discounted and based on a lower figure—13 coupons for the price of 12—as an incentive to purchase. However, the USP is that the coupons have no date and are redeemable (exchangeable for a ticket) either in advance or on game day; the choice is up to the purchaser, who decides when to attend. Purchasers can also use the tickets in any combination that they choose—all at once, in multiples of two, or one ticket for each game. Consumers benefit in that they are not restricted to particular games or specific dates. The incentives for the organization? Flex books extend the concept of full-menu marketing and provide an informal ticket plan that pre-sells tickets, minimizing the impact of team performance, player injuries, and weather. The only limitation is that the coupon is not a ticket and does not guarantee admission; redemption is based on availability. If the game is sold out when the consumer arrives to exchange the coupon for a ticket, he must use that ticket for another game. Thus for very attractive games, such as opening day or key promotional dates featuring fireworks or special giveaways, flex book purchasers need to decide and redeem the coupons as soon as possible to guarantee admission. Teams with less demand and large capacity, as well as new teams or leagues such as the WNBA, WUSA, and arena football's AFL, are more likely than others to employ benefit selling tactics such as the flex book.

Personal selling can be even more effective in the sport industry when it is combined with concepts such as product sampling, trial membership usage promotions, and open houses. These concepts are designed to put the product in the hands of consumers with the intent of letting them "experience" it. Personal selling complements the "experience" by educating consumers about what they have experienced and the benefits of the experience.[49] Consumers can also raise questions and receive answers or clarification that might remove obstacles to the sale. The fitness industry, for example, is a proponent of trial memberships and visits. In these "trial experiences" a potential member gets a guided tour of the facility and an opportunity to work out with professional instruction and attention. A sales presentation in the form of an interview between the salesperson and the consumer usually follows the workout.

Professional sport teams, such as MLB's Pittsburgh Pirates, sometimes conduct open houses in conjunction with their personal selling efforts. The open house, which may occur in the off-season in conjunction with a player draft or in the preseason, can consist of stadium tours, autograph sessions, clinics, roving entertainment such as mascots and other entertainers—and also the opportunity for potential customers to sit in the seats available for sale. Once customers take their seats (an indication of at least some level of interest), sales personnel introduce themselves and initiate the

Figure 5.7 An example of a flex plan, which conforms to the lifestyle of today's consumer.

"The WNBA and WNBA team identifications are trademarks and copyrighted designs, and/or other forms of intellectual property, that are the exclusive property of WNBA Enterprises, LLC. © 2002 WNBA Enterprises, LLC. All rights reserved."

personal selling process. Figure 5.8 describes the activities at the Pittsburgh Pirates' Open House 2000.

One common misperception about personal selling is that it is nothing more than verbal interaction between parties. Remember the axiom: "Actions speak louder than words." The consumer often interprets the actions taken by an organization—or for that matter those not taken—as evidence of what to expect in the future. Thus hospitality management, staff interaction, and the way informational inquiries are handled are all key elements of the personal selling process. To paraphrase the Disney principle, an organization should take the approach *"It's not doing one thing 100% better, it's doing 100 things 1% better."* Disney's involvement in the management of the Anaheim Angels resulted in several changes: a name change, to give the consumer a sense of ownership; a logo change, to give the consumer a sense of identity; changes in the structure of the ballpark, to provide a parklike atmosphere that communicated

Open House 2000

Your final chance for a behind-the-scenes look at the Bucs.
Saturday, March 18, 1:00 - 5:00 p.m.

Take a walking tour of Three Rivers Stadium this Saturday, March 18, from 1:00 - 5:00 p.m. After you check out the Pirates dugout, clubhouse and playing field,* you can personally select the best available seats for a 20-Game, Half-Season or Full-Season Ticket Plan for our last summer at Three Rivers Stadium. And by getting season tickets this year, you'll get priority for seating at PNC Park in 2001.

Enjoy all the fun and activities we've planned for your family, including:
• Kids Fun Zone, with our 80 ft. obstacle course, clowns, face painting, puppets and more
• Pirates Alumni player autographs at Headwaters River Pub, 1:30 - 3:30 p.m.
• See the Press Box, Scoreboard Room and Music/Public address booth

You could also win the chance to sing the National Anthem before a Pirates game. Listen to "Sportstalk with Thor Tolo" weeknights from 6:00-9:00 p.m. on KDKA-AM 1020 for your shot at winning an audition on the field.

Admission and parking for the Open House at Three Rivers Stadium is free. Just pull in to Lot 4 or 5 and enter through Gate B. Visit www.pirateball.com or call 1-800-BUY-BUCS.
*Weather permitting

Figure 5.8 A flyer for the Pirates' Open House 2000.

Reprinted, by permission, from the Pittsburgh Pirates.

a theme park image; and changes in service, to make the customer feel wanted, appreciated, and comfortable. All of this set the stage for the "formalized" personal selling efforts that would follow.[50]

Table 5.3 depicts some rules for personal selling that all sport and entertainment organizations should follow and integrate into their sales philosophy.

Table 5.3 Rules for Effective Personal Selling

Rule	Rationale
Utilize data-based marketing	Generate leads with a high likelihood of interest and ability to purchase
Communicate to the customer as you would with a friend[51]	You have something in common—some level of interest in the product
Follow the UBK rule—let it be known that you are in sales and what you are selling[52]	Be proud and enthusiastic about what you do and what you are selling
Overcome objections and perceived barriers to the sale	Be familiar with the most common objections or barriers to the sale, and modify the product or provide examples showing that people with the same objections have enjoyed the product
Manage the conversation by being an effective listener as well as making your points	Consumers want to be heard—they want a reaction to what they perceive to be concerns
Try to develop a relationship as a consultant rather than just a salesperson[53]	In reality, you are consulting by proposing possible solutions to the various needs and wants of the consumer
Match the consumer with the appropriate product	A good sale "fits" the budget and lifestyle of the consumer

Reprinted, by permission, from B.J. Mullin, S. Hardy, and W.A. Sutton, 2000, *Sport Marketing*, 2nd ed. (Champaign: Human Kinetics), 241.

Selling Products Unique to the Sport Industry

There are products and related services that are unique to the sport industry. Some of these products, discussed in this section, can be highly segmented and targeted to a small audience, while others are mass marketed because of their potential appeal to broader audiences. The selling techniques related to such products or services may also be unique and will vary accordingly. Since we have already covered ticket plans as part of full-menu marketing and utilized these plans as examples throughout the chapter, they are not included in this section.

Luxury Suites

Luxury suites can best be described as exclusive premium seating and entertaining facilities (figure 5.9). Luxury suites contain 12 or more seats—for every event (sport and non-sport)—in the venue. In addition to the seating, a suite contains a wet bar/mini-kitchen, living room, and private restroom. Luxury suites in professional (major league) sport venues usually cost upward of $125,000 annually and are sold on leases of five or more years. As discussed earlier with regard to PNC Park, selling luxury suites involves personal selling to a highly targeted corporate clientele. The personal selling techniques will include trial sampling and an open house, and will be heavily dependent on the experience provided in conjunction with the sales presentation.

Figure 5.9   Luxury suites are essential sales inventory in today's sport marketplace.
Courtesy of the Pittsburgh Steelers.

While luxury suites are a staple in arenas and stadiums in professional sport, they are only a recent phenomenon in collegiate sport. Success of suites at the Value City Arena at Schottenstein Center on the campus of The Ohio State University may lead to more widespread development and redevelopment of venues containing suites. In fact, one estimate is that colleges and universities will invest at least $800 million, probably closer to $1 billion, in new athletic facilities, including skyboxes, stadiums, and club seating between now and 2005.[54]

The **PSL** (permanent or personal seat license) has become a fixture in stadium and arena financing and governmental funding agreements. The NFL's Carolina Panthers, using a strategy developed by Max Muhlman for the Charlotte Hornets of the NBA, generated $90 million toward their stadium cost of $248 million through PSLs. Permanent seat licenses are rights purchased by a fan that allows her to buy permanent season tickets for a particular seat or set of seats in an arena or stadium. The purchase of a seat license guarantees the fan a particular seat for the duration of time she holds the license.[55] Permanent seat licenses have been associated primarily with new construction and are utilized to assist in financing plans. They may be limited to prime seating locations, or they can be spread throughout the venue. Selling PSLs in a new venue is usually tied to demand and seating availability. As demand in new venues can be very high, PSLs are often accepted by the purchaser as a reasonable cost. Payment for a PSL, which can range from $500 to several thousand dollars, can also be financed or can be remitted in installments. Selling PSLs involves the creation of printed materials that explain the rationale and exact costs. These materials can be used in personal selling, direct mail, or telemarketing.

Club Seats

Club seats are premium seating locations with special services or amenities that are not available to fans in other seating locations (with the exception of luxury suite holders). Services can include a personally assigned customer service representative, in-seat service of food and beverage, charge account privileges, special lounge areas, VIP parking and private entrance to the venue, and access to purchasing tickets to other venue events. Other services or amenities may include special restaurant privileges and courtesy memberships in golf courses or other venues. Club seats have been primarily a corporate product—an alternative for smaller businesses that cannot afford or are not interested in luxury suites. Sales techniques are similar to those employed in the sale of luxury suites.

Group Sales

Group sales is the term usually employed to refer to the sale of an opportunity for a group of 25 people or more to attend a game or other event. Group ticket sales, particularly in minor league baseball, can have a significant impact on the profitability of the organization. Group seats can be positioned to corporations as an Employee Night, and food and other hospitality elements can be added to the package. Many sport organizations have created picnic or tailgating areas to better accommodate and facilitate the group experience. Social interaction and facilitation are the key drivers in a group night promotion and sale. Sales materials and scripts should contain photographs and testimonials from groups and group leaders regarding their enjoyment and experiences in the past. The key element in a successful group sale is identifying an individual within the targeted group to serve as the group leader. Incentives such as shirts, tickets to another game, and other forms of recognition are usually effective recruitment devices. Group nights can be sold through telemarketing, direct mail, and personnel selling, or a combination of these techniques.

Sponsorships

Sponsorships are the most complex of the sport products because of the subjectivity they involve, and in some cases intangible benefits and difficulty in measuring ROI (return on investment). Sponsorship has been defined as the "acquisition of rights to affiliate or directly associate with a product or event for the purpose of deriving benefits related to that affiliation or association."[56] Although the term *sponsorship* is still the one that is most often used, this arrangement is being referred to more and more frequently as a **marketing partnership,** emphasizing that both parties benefit from the agreement. We use the two terms interchangeably here. In purchasing a sponsorship, a corporation or other organization wishing an association or affiliation is usually purchasing one or more of the following rights:

- *The right to use a logo, name, trademark or graphic representation signifying the purchaser's connection with the product or event.* As companies are more concerned with sales results, a shopper's choice of one brand over another because of a sport logo on the packaging is seen as indicative of a successful sponsorship, and an inducement to purchase.[57]

- *The right to an exclusive association within a product or service category.* Gatorade is a marketing partner of the WNBA. The terms of the agreement provide that Gatorade receives national and local exclusivity across the sport drink category. Thus the agreement means that no WNBA team can create a sponsorship agreement with

Allsport or any other competitor in the sport drink category because those rights are exclusively guaranteed to Gatorade.[58] Similarly, Visa's Olympic sponsorship agreement provides that the Games will not accept the American Express card as a form of payment.[59]

- *The right of entitlement to an event or facility.* In 1995, the Coors Brewing Company paid $15 million to the Colorado Rockies for the right to name their new ballpark Coors Field. The hope was that the entitlement of the field would provide an additional forum for publicity, garner exposure for Coors products, and increase brand awareness.[60] In addition to events and facilities, entitlement can refer to other sport marketing assets such as cars, racehorses, or, in some cases, teams. General Mills became the title sponsor of Petty racing's No. 43 car driven by John Andretti—in this case the car and the personnel form the General Mills team.[61]

- *The right to use various designations or phrases in connection with the product, event, or facility, such as "official sponsor," "official supplier," "official product," and "presented by."* USG Corporation, the world's largest maker of gypsum wallboard and suspended ceiling suspension grids and ceiling tiles, is the official building products supplier of the National Association for Stock Car Auto Racing (NASCAR).[62]

- *The right of service (use of the product or exclusive use of the product) or the right to use the purchaser's product or service in conjunction with the event or facility.* Through its Olympic sponsorship, Kodak built and operated a state-of-the-art 21,000-square-foot imaging center was used by more than 1000 photojournalists. There an estimated 175,000 rolls of film were to be developed and converted into digital images that could be sent to newsrooms around the world.[63] Another example worth noting is that the Coors sponsorship of Coors Field, aside from entitlement, also provides for Coors to maintain and operate the SandLot Brewery at Coors Field, where it is projected that 10% of Coors's sales at the ballpark will be transacted.[64]

- *The right to conduct certain promotional activities, such as contests, advertising campaigns, or sales-driven activities, in conjunction with the sponsorship agreement.* Visa, official credit card of the NFL, has created a unique promotion in conjunction with the Pro Football Hall of Fame in Canton, Ohio. Fans are asked to write a two-page essay on why they should be inducted into the permanent fans' exhibit at the Hall. One winner is selected from each team and flown to Canton with a guest for the occasion.[65]

Research has identified some of the major sponsorship objectives of corporations. Awareness and understanding of these objectives should help salespersons position the sales opportunities connected to sponsorships. These are the top five sponsorship objectives identified through research:[66]

- Increase sales/market share
- Increase target market awareness
- Enhance general market awareness
- Enhance general company image
- Enhance trade relations

It is apparent that sponsorships are designed in tandem by the prospective sponsor (target market) and the salesperson representing the sport property (the object of the association or affiliation). Personal selling plays *the* critical role in the selling of sponsorships. The personal selling techniques involve fact-finding meetings enabling the parties to get to know one another, presentations, hospitality, and in most cases, site visits to view the property and look at its potential and suitability firsthand.

For example, a prospective sponsor of the Olympics (rights fee: $40 million) would probably be a VIP guest at the Olympic events immediately preceding the Games for which the sponsorship is being solicited. Given the cost and complexity, not to mention possibilities, selling a sponsorship takes time and patience on the part of the salesperson. This is true worldwide—the following Practitioner's Perspective explains the processing of selling a sponsorship in Japan.

PRACTITIONER'S PERSPECTIVE

Selling Sponsorships in Japan
by Nobuhiro Tanaka, COO of Axis Marketing

In Japan, advertising agencies are responsible for sport sponsorship sales. These agencies have their own sports business divisions, and these divisions create sponsorships for sport properties. These divisions are similar to sport marketing agencies in the United States. Agencies create sponsorship proposals and present them to the sport property. The divisions provide marketing expertise in marketing, strategic planning, creative advertising, public relations, and promotional activities. Once the sport property has approved the sponsorship concept, the agencies begin to contact their client bases to identify corporations that may have an interest in the proposed sponsorship. The two largest agencies, Dentsu, Inc. and Hakuhodo, Inc., dominate the sport sponsorship market. Most major sport sponsorships are sold through these two agencies.

A good case to examine is that of the J-League, the professional soccer league of Japan. The J-League has 10 official sponsors and several official suppliers. The J-League was involved in the creation of these sponsor packages with the help of advertising agencies and has sold them through those same agencies. When these sponsorships were first presented for consideration, prospective clients needed to think about whether or not the proposed sponsorships would help them achieve their corporate objectives, particularly in the areas of branding and generating media exposure. The sponsorship proposals were carefully analyzed and evaluated by the prospective sponsors. Benefit calculations of possible media value and estimates of overall ROI were an integral part of the analysis. Another aspect of the proposal that was carefully analyzed was the possibility of recouping some of the sponsorship costs through increased sale of products and services by means of the sponsorship activities.

Once the analysis has been completed, it is up to the general manager of marketing (in some cases also including communications and promotions) to approve or reject the sponsorship proposals. If the proposal is approved at that level, it is sent to the board of directors and sometimes the CEO, where the ultimate decision is made. This stage of the approval process usually takes several months to complete.

Official sponsors of the J-League pay rights fees of $3 million or more annually. Official supplier costs are in the low- to mid-six-figure range. The agreed-on sponsorship or suppliership fee is paid (with commissions) directly to the advertising agency, which is responsible for making payment to the sport property, in this case, the J-League. It is the responsibility of the advertising agency to ensure that the agreed-on sponsorship rights and benefits are being provided to the sponsor by the J-League.

Regarding sponsorship packages containing media time, advertising opportunities are the most common form of sport sponsorship found in Japan. The advertising agency expertise afforded by those individuals who help design and subsequently sell the sponsorship packages may account for the popularity of media time in sponsorship agreements.

While this perspective focused on Japan, many of the activities and practices described are commonplace globally. In the United States, however, the importance of the media element is dependent on the objectives of the sponsor; and in many cases, sales objectives and brand enhancement activities are taking precedence over media exposure and impressions.

Putting It All Together: The Sales Department

In sport, sales departments have a variety of structures, and each structure has been successful in its own way. For example, some sport organizations have sales and service in one department, while others prefer to create separate units to house those functions. This section presents a perspective that would allow the department to be more effectively sales oriented, emphasizing the sales process and ensuring that the situation is optimal for the salespersons.

What Is a Good Sales-Oriented Organizational Structure?

The organizational structure and style of the organization form a key element in determining the overall success and impact of the sales department's efforts. Organizational structure and style considerations include the following:[67]

* *The reporting structure.* Whom you report to, how often, and in what manner are key elements in accountability, autonomy, trust, and relationship building.

* *Relationships between departments with overlapping responsibilities.* In structuring any department with a selling focus, the demands, requirements, and capabilities of departments involved in service delivery and customer satisfaction must be taken into account. For example, a ticket sales department must have an excellent working relationship with the box office since that department functions as the delivery system.

* *Organizational philosophy regarding resource allocation and utilization.* What is the organizational policy with regard to utilizing other internal departments (creative services, printing, accounting) when available? Are these charge-backs to the sales department? Is there a policy on outside consultants and vendors?

* *Sales hierarchy and development process within the department.* Most sales departments start their salespeople out in entry level-type sales—sales with lower potential dollar amounts. In sport, a common practice is for all salespeople to begin as telemarketers and then to move into other positions based on development and productivity. The typical sales development progression begins with telemarketing, moves next to group sales, then on to season ticket sales, and finally to corporate sales, which often involves premium seating, sponsorships, and other products targeted toward the corporate purchaser. According to sport sales consultant Jack Mielke, "organizations should establish separate and distinct departments for ticket and sponsorship sales and divide ticket sales into season, group, corporate and telemarketing."[68]

* *The placement of servicing versus selling.* Similar to the debate between tickets and sponsorships is a much greater debate—where does service best fit? There are two schools of thought, the first advocating distinct sales and customer service depart-

ments, the second favoring combining the functions in one department. Compensation is an issue that clouds this location decision. What is a fair value to pay someone for servicing and renewing an account—maintaining an asset as opposed to identifying and securing an agreement with a new party (creating an asset)? Until this issue is resolved, debate will continue on the division of responsibilities and the ideal situation.

• *Determination of the composition of the sales force and the compensation mix for sales staff.* This decision involves the use of outside sales agencies in lieu of in-house sales departments, using outside agencies in conjunction with an in-house department, or relying solely on in-house expertise. Outside agencies, primarily telemarketing companies, are often engaged to complement the sales activities of an in-house sales department. This operation is viewed as third-party contractual and often has limited inventory to sell. As just noted, there has been a traditional gap in the compensation between those who sell and those who deal with service and retention. Similarly, there has been a gap in the compensation between those who sell tickets and those who sell sponsorships. In order for sales departments to become truly effective, there must be some movement in closing these gaps and reaching an organizational philosophy that recognizes the importance of retention and renewal. As has been suggested throughout this chapter, viewing the customer as an asset with a lifetime value to the organization could be the philosophical change necessary to close this gap.

Organizations that focus on these issues will be leaders in attracting and retaining a qualified, well-motivated, and productive sales force.

Ten Steps for Developing an Effective Sales Staff

One of the main challenges for any sport organization is that of developing an effective sales staff, which in turn obviously contributes to an effective sales department. Miller and colleagues[69] have identified the following 10 steps. We list them here because of their value to individuals looking to enter the sales force and become the sales leaders of tomorrow.

• *Define the task.* What we do we want to accomplish? What are the sales goals? Ensure that each task is related to the goal and that it is timely, attainable, measurable, specific, and ethical.

• *Establish a plan.* How do we reach these goals? What is our "road map"? What are the resources necessary to achieve the goal?

• *Budget.* Plan to secure the resources needed to accomplish the goal and allocate them effectively.

• *Hire.* Determine the appropriate staff size and structure. Determine the balance between in-house and outsourced sales activities.

• *Train.* Create an effective orientation and ongoing training program for the department and, whenever practical, a staff development plan for each member of the sales staff.

• *Motivate.* Continually work to identify varied and effective methods of motivating the sales staff—prizes, bonuses, recognition, trips, and the like have all been used effectively as motivational devices. But while these external tactics are effective, the ideal salesperson will be a self-motivator.

- *Measure.* Communicate results on a regular basis. This ensures that intervention and additional training are available where needed. Posting results is a motivator and positive reinforcement vehicle to maintain and increase productivity.

- *Communicate.* The sales manager should meet individually with all sales staff on a regular basis. This ensures privacy in the exchange of certain information and also provides a vehicle for encouragement, praise, and other reinforcement on a one-to-one basis. Additionally, regular communication serves to ensure that all staff are informed and in the loop.

- *Celebrate.* Celebratory activities send a message of approval to the sales representative and other staff in attendance. It also promotes a contagious environment—success and celebration lead to additional success and more celebration. Finally, a positive attitude on the part of the salesperson is usually conveyed in that person's interaction with the next client.

- *Analyze.* Step back and examine how things have worked and why. What has been effective and what has not been effective? What improvements can be made? What should be altered and what should be retained? Gather feedback from the sales staff and conduct exit interviews with every employee; be open and honest about why you want the feedback—you want to improve.

The Role of a Sales Force

The are numerous views on the role of a sales force. To remain consistent with the theme of customer-focused selling as espoused in this chapter, however, we could state that *"the role of the sales force is to communicate the value of your offerings to the customer."*[70] This is true irrespective of the sales methodology employed. These are the activities through which the sales force represents the organization:

- Communicating the value of the organization's products/services to its customers and its prospects
- Listening attentively to the needs and thoughts expressed by the customer
- Presenting those ideas and thoughts to management
- Assisting in the development of concepts and packages that provide fit and value to today's consumer
- Working continually to build and maintain long-term and valued relationships between the consumers and the organization

Failing to expand the role of the sales force in accordance with this vision would be symptomatic of the marketing myopia[71]—lack of foresight in marketing ventures—first described by Levitt in the 1960s. An organization, particularly one competing for the entertainment dollar, must differentiate itself and create a positioning in the mind of the consumer[72] that reflects value and concern for the customer and the desire for a relationship with long-term value and sustaining power. The sales process in this decade, more than ever before, needs to encompass an understanding that sport and entertainment purchases involve two types of resources: money and time. In the present era of a generally booming consumer economy, money is only part of the equation, and for a number of consumers it is less important than the resource of time. Time is more critical as people decide how to spend resources because it cannot be replenished, and a purchaser's unwise expenditure of time may be a source of regret and a long-term memory for the purchaser.[73] The sales force must understand this about the products and services that they are selling and also with regard to the process being employed to make the sale.

Outsourcing: A Staffing Alternative

Outsourcing is the use of a commercial entity to identify, solicit, secure, and manage revenue streams and marketing tasks previously managed by an internal sales or marketing department. Outsourcing some or all marketing and broadcasting responsibilities has become a trend in collegiate athletics. Many athletic departments initiated outsourcing efforts for the purpose of selling their broadcasting rights and other media-related activities such as coaches' shows. The University of Tennessee has used outsourcing for men's and women's basketball broadcasts, football broadcasts, venue signage, and game-day programs.[74]

Why do sport organizations such as collegiate athletic departments choose to partner with an outside company? Scott Zuffelato, formerly with Host Communications, one of the largest and most successful outsourcers, has identified several reasons:[75]

- To secure additional revenue streams to complement existing sources
- To secure the services of an organization that has experience in selling collegiate sports
- To eliminate expenditure of funds to generate revenue
- To save on salaries and the time expended in searching for and recruiting personnel
- To engage in a no-risk partnership
- To obtain appropriate expertise not possessed by staff

As stated earlier, outsourcing of certain types of activities, most notably telemarketing, has become commonplace. Outsourcing of specialized activities will continue to be a trend because there is no need to budget for the expertise (it is usually hired on a performance basis), and the specialization of expertise permits both parties to be focused on what they do best.

Postgame Wrap-Up

As we said earlier, sales is the lifeblood of the organization, crucial for survival. Sales interactions need to be not only *inbound*, reacting and responding to customers' needs and inquiries; they also need to be *outbound*, proactively seeking customers and selling additional quantities to existing customers.

An organization can employ a variety of strategies and methodologies to sell its products and services—and must find the style that best fits its organizational philosophy and marketing situation. Finding this style, which at times changes according to the fortunes of the sport organization, is an ongoing process and will involve resources within and outside of the organization. Outsourcing some of the sales activities is a common approach, particularly in the area of telemarketing, but also has found a place in collegiate athletics for a broader range of activities.

Two of the more challenging aspects of selling are recruiting and training a qualified sales force and auditing and identifying all salable inventory. Salespeople are constantly in demand, and organizations that produce successful sales personnel are continually raided by other organizations seeking to emulate that success. While salespersons are not necessarily just born, the process of making them is complex and relies on the philosophies of super-salespersons such as Zig Ziglar and IMG founder Mark McCormack. Ziglar and McCormack understand not only the products and services they are selling, but also the individuals, groups, and businesses that are purchasing them.

The second aspect, identifying a salable inventory, is essential to success in these competitive times in the sport marketplace. As revenue from ticket sales can fluctuate greatly and broadcast contracts are finite, creating and capitalizing on new revenue streams are essential. Personal seat licenses, virtual advertising, luxury suites, club seats, on-ice advertising, Web advertising and promotions, blimps, and buses are all examples of creating new inventory that is then sold to provide significant revenue streams.

How sport organizations grow and develop in the new millennium will depend to a great degree on the creativity, vision, and approach of its salespersons. Much of the inventory salespeople will be selling will be the same products they currently sell, but the Internet continues to grow and develop and new products and services will emerge that fit the times and the changing lifestyles and demands of the sport consumer.

Discussion Items

1. Explain why fans are viewed as the catalyst for sponsorship and broadcast sales.

2. Define and explain the concept of eduselling. Is eduselling an appropriate sales strategy for sport? Provide an illustration to justify your position.

3. Explain via an example or mini-case study how market research can assist the salesperson in focusing resources and efforts.

4. What is meant by the term, permission marketing? How is permission marketing utilized in today's sales activities?

5. List and explain three reasons why corporations and other business entities would choose to become involved in sport through sponsorship activities.

6. Compare and contrast the benefits/limitations of a direct mail campaign versus that of a telemarketing campaign. If you were director of ticket sales for the Gotham Bats, which would be your preferred strategy and why?

Learning Enrichment Activities

1. Interview a salesperson involved in selling sport-related products or services. You should determine through the interview how the salesperson began her career, how the individual stays up to date on sales techniques, and what the individual thinks are the biggest challenges and rewards associated with being a salesperson.

2. Visit the basketball arena or football stadium on campus. Conduct an audit of all inventory currently being sold; identify this inventory by category, seating category, on-field signage, concourse signage, and so forth. After completing this portion of the inventory, conduct an audit of potential salable inventory. Share this inventory with athletic department personnel to determine the feasibility of the inventory you have identified—that is, is it salable? Is there a market for it?

3. Write a position paper that explains the benefits of each of the following organizational sales structures: a joint sales and service department, distinct sales and service departments. If you were making a recommendation to a professional sport franchise, which structure would you choose and why?

4. In this chapter and also in chapter 2, we discussed the frequency escalator. Using a sport setting of your own choosing, identify three promotional tactics that can be used to move consumers up the escalator by increasing their frequency of purchase. Identify two promotional strategies for moving a consumer onto the escalator.

5. Explain the philosophy of customer-focused selling. Through research using both primary and secondary sources, provide three distinct examples of customer-focused selling.

6

The Role of Advertising in Strategic Brand Communications

Jay Gladden, Assistant Professor, Department of Sport Management, University of Massachusetts at Amherst

chapter objectives

1. Define advertising and identify the various forms of media that are at the disposal of the sport manager

2. Understand the importance of maintaining a strategic and consistent focus with respect to the messages being created about a sport brand

3. Identify and describe the six steps of the strategic brand communications process

4. Appreciate the importance of triggering brand associations with advertising messages

5. Understand the importance of evaluating the effectiveness of any brand communications campaign

key terms

brand associations   situational analysis

strategic brand communications   segmentation strategy

brand

Pregame Introductions

Thus far, we have introduced you to the concept of sales and described a number of strategies that can be used to sell the sport product. These sales efforts should be supported by other marketing activities within the sport organization. In addition to enhancing or reinforcing an image of the sport organization in the minds of consumers, advertising can serve to support the sales effort. As you may already be aware, there are many ways in which an organization can advertise its product to consumers. The trick is to maximize the efficiency of the advertising efforts.

In this chapter, we look at a variety of advertising media that can be used to communicate with consumers and prospective consumers. However, before the sport organization considers where it will advertise, it must consider how it will advertise. That is, the organization must first determine what images or associations it wants to create or reinforce. With respect to making this decision, this chapter highlights the importance of maintaining a strategic focus toward creating positive feelings or capitalizing on positive feelings that a consumer has about a particular sport organization. These positive feelings are also referred to as **brand associations.** Once the organization decides what its message will be, it must be consistent in communicating that message throughout the many different media through which it can advertise— this is commonly referred to as **strategic brand communications.**

Take the sidebar on page 141 as an example. This case illustrates the importance of creating consistent advertising messages that effectively communicate with both current and potential consumers. This case also illustrates the need for the advertising message to encourage consumption of the sport product. However, most importantly, this case illustrates the need to create advertising messages that communicate points of differentiation about the sport brand. Both the NBA and Nike were extremely successful with their advertising in the 1990s because they communicated the core benefits offered by their products. However, as the sidebar also demonstrates, time can dramatically change the sport product. Thus the advertising efforts for the product must adapt as well. But most importantly, these efforts should be undertaken all within the context of building a successful brand. That is, the advertising efforts should seek to communicate reasons why consumers should spend their money on the sport product over the long term.

Advertising in the context of strategic brand communications is the focus of this chapter. The first section defines the practice of advertising, explains the process, and addresses the effects of advertising. The next section presents a strategic view of advertising, that of strategic brand communications. The third section deals with the process of creating advertisements. Once the messages have been crafted, modes to communicate the message are needed. Therefore, the fourth section of this chapter explores the various modes available for advertisements. The chapter concludes by taking a very important look at how the advertising process should be managed.

The Brand Communication Challenges Facing Two Market Leaders

Studded with superstars such as Magic Johnson, Larry Bird, and most recently Michael Jordan, the NBA has experienced dramatic growth since the 1980s. Under the tag line "I Love This Game," the NBA very effectively communicated its ability to provide an entertaining product that appealed to young and old, male and female. In "I Love This Game," the NBA created a positioning statement that allowed it to be different things to different people, ultimately making the task of selling the product to consumers, sponsors, and media entities even easier. In 1997 and continuing into 1998, the complexion of the NBA changed. First, it experienced a prolonged work stoppage that led to an abbreviated 1998 season. Before the 1998 season, Michael Jordan, arguably the greatest basketball player of all time, decided to retire. In an effort to remind fans of the entertainment provided by the NBA, the 1999 advertising theme was "I Still Love This Game."[1] However, attendance and media ratings suggest that such a statement no longer resonated.[2] This raises several important questions for the NBA. As it moves forward in the wake of a string of marketable superstars, what should the NBA advertising say? How can the NBA use advertising to help sell more tickets?

In a different realm, the athletic footwear and apparel industry, another market leader is struggling to define its advertising after a decade of prolonged success.[3] Nike, the athletic shoe and apparel giant, rode its "Just Do It" advertising slogan to market dominance in the 1990s. "Just Do It" appealed to consumers on the basis of its ability to say, "It doesn't matter what someone thinks, just be your best." This iconoclastic reasoning was the embodiment of what Nike stood for as a brand. Founder Phil Knight created Nike in the late 1960s as an alternative to Adidas, the market leader at the time. Where Adidas was entrenched with the track and field establishment as a sponsor, Nike positioned itself

Nike Town in Chicago.

(continued)

(continued)

as *against* the establishment and *for* the individual runner. As Nike expanded, "Just Do It" came to embody this spirit for athletes in a wide variety of sports. Today, though, Nike is the establishment and its competitors are the upstarts. As a result, Nike discontinued—and then reintroduced—the "Just Do It" advertising campaign. Nike is ultimately facing the problem of deciding how to follow one of the most successful advertising campaigns of all time. Should the company continue to use "Just Do It"? Or does that message no longer represent who Nike is? Or perhaps more importantly, does it accurately represent what Nike wants consumers to think of it as a company?

Advertising

According to authors Mullin, Hardy, and Sutton, advertising is "any paid, nonpersonal (not directed to individuals), clearly sponsored message conveyed through the media."[4] When the NHL promotes professional hockey as the "Coolest Game on Earth" on national television, this is advertising. Similarly, when the Pittsburgh Pirates purchase advertising in the *Pittsburgh Post-Gazette* to spur ticket sales under the "You Gotta See 'Em" tag line, this is advertising. However, when we think about advertising, we need to consider the term "media" from a broad perspective. It includes common mass media sources such as television, radio, newspapers, and magazines. It also includes outdoor advertising (billboards and transit vehicles), direct mail, and of ever-increasing importance, the Internet.[5] Thus, when the University of Massachusetts sends a season ticket brochure for its football team to a database of people who have supported UMass athletics in the past, this is advertising. We will explore the advantages and disadvantages of each of these methods later in this chapter. For now, remember that the "media" through which advertising messages are communicated are more than just the typical forms of mass media.

Advertisers are those organizations (private or public sector) that invest resources in purchasing time or space in the various forms of media just mentioned.[6] For example, when you see the NFL players promoting the cause of the United Way during an NFL telecast, the NFL is advertising its long-standing involvement with the United Way charity. The NFL-United Way advertising campaign is arguably the most successful sport-charity relationship. Part of its success is a result of the NFL's consistency in partnering with the United Way *and* actively communicating the partnership on a yearly basis. In fact, the NFL–United Way tie-in is an excellent example of successful advertising management. Defined, advertising management is "heavily focused on the analysis, planning, control, and decision-making activities of . . . the advertiser."[7] Among other things, advertising management requires a situational analysis, performance-driven objectives, and a clear picture of the market targeted for an advertisement, all *before* a campaign is created.

Making an Impact

Advertising is communication from the advertiser targeted to the consumer. First, the advertiser (or sender) creates a message that is sent through a medium toward the consumer (receiver). However, before that message reaches the receiver, it usually encounters "noise." Noise (also referred to as "clutter") is anything that competes with an advertising message for the receiver's attention. Did you realize that in an average day, you are exposed to 3000 advertising messages?[8] This is clutter. The challenge for the advertiser is to have its message pass through the clutter and be received by the consumer. Only then can the receiver be affected by the message.

Ultimately, the sender of an advertising message is typically trying to achieve six broad objectives.[9] These relate to awareness, attributes, image, association, group norms, and behavior.

- *Awareness.* First, the advertiser may be trying to create awareness about its product. With the advent and growth of the Internet, a number of Internet start-ups have attempted to use sport as a vehicle to create awareness for their sites. For example, Computer.com decided to spend more than $1 million for a 30-second advertisement during the 2000 Super Bowl. Although this may seem like a great deal of money, consider the fact that the traffic to the company's Web site increased over 2000% after the ad ran.[10] The Super Bowl offered Computer.com an effective tool for creating awareness.

- *Attributes.* Secondly, the advertiser may be trying to communicate information about the attributes or benefits offered by a product. Perhaps you remember the ESPN advertising campaign promoting the 2000 WNBA season. Under the tag line "They're better than you," the series of advertisements attempted to promote the high skill level of WNBA players by depicting them in situations versus male recreational players. This series of advertisements was consistent with the WNBA's overall advertising theme "We Got Next," which suggests the serious and competitive nature of women's basketball (figure 6.1).

Figure 6.1 The "We Got Next" ad campaign communicated competition and drive in the WNBA.

"The WNBA and WNBA team identification are trademarks and copyrighted designs, and/or other forms of intellectual property, that are the exclusive property of WNBA Enterprises, LLC. © 2002 WNBA Enterprises, LLC. All rights reserved."

- *Image.* A third focus of advertisers is to develop or change an image or personality. During the late 1990s, sagging attendance led the Chicago White Sox to revamp the makeup of its team from a team with some grumpy superstars (for example, Albert Belle) to a team full of young talent.[11] Accordingly, the White Sox changed their advertising to say "These Kids Can Play," thus suggesting even though the team was young, the players were still going to work hard, hustle, and never quit.[12]

- *Association.* Sponsorship is the perfect example of the fourth goal of advertising: to associate a brand with feelings and emotions. For example, cosmetics giant Avon created the "Avon Running Global Women's Circuit," a series of running races aimed at linking its product with the self-esteem enhancement that comes from running.[13] Similarly, as depicted in figure 6.2, New Balance Athletic Shoe, Inc. attempted to connect the importance of leading a balanced life to the New Balance athletic shoe under the tag line "Achieve New Balance."

- *Group norms.* A fifth goal of advertisers is to create group norms. Through Nike's marketing of the swoosh logo in conjunction with the "Just Do It" advertising, apparel with the swoosh on it became very popular during the mid-1990s.

- *Behavior.* Finally, advertisers seek to alter or affect behavior. Most specifically, this refers to causing someone to purchase a sport-related product. For example, teams have taken to advertising Beanie Babies as a means of convincing people to purchase baseball tickets.[14]

The sixth goal of advertising, to precipitate behavior, reinforces the most often overlooked element of the advertising

Figure 6.2   This New Balance ad connects emotions to running, creating a sense of association. Courtesy of New Balance Athletic Shoe, Inc.

process, feedback. It is important to recognize that advertising is not one-way communication. Rather, it is a two-way communication process in which the receiver provides feedback to the sender. To use one of our earlier examples, if the team advertising a Beanie Baby giveaway at a particular game sells out that game, its consumers have responded with positive feedback. By comparison, if a Web site were to run an ad during a sporting event and not experience increased traffic to its site, the consumers would be saying that either they did not receive the message or they were not motivated to visit the Web site.

This notion of two-way communication in the advertising process is important from two perspectives. First, it suggests that sport advertisers should expend resources to solicit communication from consumers regarding the effectiveness of their ads. In fact, a later section of this chapter looks in depth at evaluation of advertising. In addition, if we assume that advertising is two-way communication, it becomes extremely important also to solicit information from consumers about their tastes, preferences, and interests so that the advertising messages will have a better chance of making it through noise and reaching the consumer.

The Importance of a Strategic Focus

Breaking through the noise is becoming increasingly difficult. As a result, more than ever, a strategic approach to advertising, which communicates with consumers on a number of different levels, is necessary. Technology has broadened the 21st-century consumer's access to a wide variety of goods, thus creating more noise.[15] A fan of professional soccer in the United States is not limited to Major League Soccer (MLS) games to satisfy the desire for professional soccer. In the summer of 2001 the Women's United Soccer Association began play, featuring the best women's soccer players from around the world. Similarly, instead of attending or watching an MLS game, the fan of professional soccer can listen to (or now watch!) the games of his favorite English Premier League team through the Internet. This access to technology will only increase in the future. Experts predict that marketing organizations, channels, media, and consumers will all ultimately create ongoing dialogue.[16] Already this is happening with Internet advertisements. For example, the next time you visit your favorite sport Internet site, an ad may pop up as you enter, asking if you want more information about a particular product. While the consumer has the option to decline, some communication is nevertheless required, not only from the advertiser to the consumer, but also from the consumer to the advertiser.

Because it is increasingly possible to create dialogue with consumers, a major focus of advertising will be to forge an ongoing relationship with consumers. In fact, a strategic advertising program can provide the basis for creating such a relationship. Dan Weiden of Weiden & Kennedy (the advertising agency that has developed popular ad campaigns for Nike and ESPN among others) suggests the following:

> Advertising creates the environment for the relationship. To me, it takes the place of the human contact we once had as consumers. In the beginning, people had relationships with the shopkeeper, and any advertising simply supplemented that relationship. Today things are so complex that advertising needs to embody that relationship by making contact in more than a superficial way.[17]

Thus, while the highly cluttered marketplace has led to a multitude of offerings and depersonalized the personal contact between the producer and the consumer, advertising can provide the means through which to foster interplay between the advertiser and the consumer. In order to be successful in such an endeavor, strategic brand communications is increasingly needed.

On-field signage can be effective, but it can also get lost in the clutter.

Strategic Brand Communications

Many teams develop a new advertising strategy every year. Think about your favorite team: Can you remember an advertisement it has utilized over the past five years? If you can, that means the message made it through the noise and reached you. Certainly, a number of teams have created successful advertising campaigns. For example, for the 2000 season, when the Chicago White Sox were expecting their young but now experienced team to have a winning record, they maintained their advertising slogan, "These Kids Can Play." This simple statement captured much of what the White Sox continued to build toward after alienating a number of fans with a midseason trade in 1997. It communicated, "Yes, we are young, but we will compete with the best." If, on the other hand, you cannot remember one of your favorite team's ads, these ads are not making it through the clutter. So what makes a successful advertising campaign? What kind of campaign makes it through the clutter?

Ultimately it boils down to viewing advertising not as advertising, but as strategic brand communications. Before defining strategic brand communications, it is important to establish what "brand" means in the sport setting. A **brand** is a name, symbol, or term that serves to differentiate one product from another.[18] In the sport setting, Notre Dame represents a brand name that is clearly differentiated from other college sport brands. Similarly, the Brazilian national soccer team represents a brand. The goal of any brand is to develop strong, unique, and favorable associations in consumers' minds with brand names. Think about it for a minute—why is Notre Dame such a strong brand name? It's simple, isn't it? When we think of Notre Dame, we think of great football teams, the Golden Dome, players such as Joe Montana and the Four Horsemen, and coaches such as Ara Parseghian. Do you think it is any coincidence that the College Football Hall of Fame is located in South Bend, Indiana, the home of Notre Dame? More recently, fans of U.S. college basketball may think of women's basketball when they think of Notre Dame, given the team's successes in the NCAA tournament (they won the championship in 2001).

Such positive and favorable associations are created by communication.[19] Of course, many of Notre Dame's associations were created through media reporting and not advertising. However, advertising is one form of communication that *can* help create such associations. Take the San Jose Sharks, for example. The team has yet to win the NHL's Stanley Cup championship, nor has it achieved a winning record.[20] Yet the Sharks have a loyal fan base that ardently supports and follows the team. Why is this? Much of it has to do with strategic brand communications. After being awarded a franchise, the new San Jose franchise undertook extensive market research to construct its visual identity (its logo and family of marks). Through a series of focus groups (60- to 90-minute discussions with 8 to 12 people), the San Jose franchise determined that Sharks was a nickname that would appeal to people. Further, personnel created and went through multiple iterations[21] of a logo so that they were certain that they had created something visually appealing with the potential to garner attention. And that is just what the Sharks did. They built their marketing program around the logo and the nickname "Sharks." For example, the merchandise store is called the "Shark Shoppe"; the fan club is called the "Sharks FanAtical" fan club; and an educational program for kids is called the "Think Tank."[22] Such tie-ins make for both integrated and easy-to-recall advertisements.

In fact, the San Jose Sharks provide an excellent example of strategic brand communications. From the sport consumer's perspective, a team is a bundle of attributes (such as the players and the promotions) and benefits (such as providing people with a source of identification and pride). The team sport manager must never forget this—it is her role to manage the sport entity accordingly. A very important component in such management is the communications that the team emits to the public. If you cannot remember the advertising of your favorite team, it is more than likely that your favorite team has not practiced strategic brand communications. Because there are so many different facets to the sport brand (players, stadium, tradition, the ability to provide family connections, even the owner in many cases), an effective advertising campaign will identify which elements of the sport brand are important to the sport consumer and emphasize them throughout all of its marketing communications. Further, these communications will have some consistency over time. Why were the White Sox ads so effective? The reason was that there was a relationship between the messages that they were communicating from year to year. This is strategic brand communications.

Strategic brand communications is important for several reasons. First, strategic brand communications considers all customer groups (and potential customer groups) that the brand is attempting to serve. Strategic brand communications places the consumer first and the entire organization adapts to focus on supporting the brand communications to reach the consumer.[23] With such a focus, the messages are more cohesive, consistent, and strategically driven than they would be otherwise. In assuming a position with the NHL, President Richie Woodworth was quoted as saying, "We've got to be more consistent about what the brand message is, what the core values of the NHL are and make that more league wide."[24] Second, strategic brand communications account for the fact that brands change over time. Think about the examples of Nike and the NBA presented at the beginning of the chapter. Those two companies were faced with revamping their brand communications as a result of changes in who they were as sport brands. According to Disney CEO Michael Eisner, "a brand is a living entity, and it is enriched or undermined cumulatively over time, the product of a thousand small gestures."[25] A sport brand can experience a sense of change much more acute than the typical consumer brand. The San Diego Padres played in the 1998 World Series, then finished the next two years with a losing record. How much more different could the product be in a very short period of time? Similarly, when a new stadium is built, the sport brand is significantly affected. Think about how the attending experience improved for Cleveland fans when the Indians moved from cavernous Cleveland Stadium to cozy Jacobs Field. Thus, adopting a strategic brand communications view of advertising helps account for the unpredictability and experiential nature of sport.[26]

Finally, strategic brand communications is important because it is crucial to maintain the same voice in advertising messages over time. Because the sport product is attempting to create meaningful associations over time, it only makes sense for the advertising about the brand to consistently emphasize and attempt to promote and foster those key associations.[27] This consistent communication is often referred to as "one-voice communications."[28] Returning to the example of the Chicago White Sox, "These Kids Can Play" was successful because it consistently communicated that while the team was choosing to field young players, they were talented and could compete for league titles. David Hersh, president of the Tennessee Diamond Jaxx, accurately summarized this sentiment when he said, "...you have to think long-term, because your bonds aren't for five years, they're for 20 or 30 years."[29] While it may not be advisable to stay with the same campaign for 20 years, it could make sense to stress some of the key benefits for 20 years.

Before the 2000-2001 NBA season, the Miami Heat undertook a strategic brand communications process to devise their advertising campaign. The following Practitioner's Perspective is Chief Marketing Officer Michael McCullough's description of how the campaign was designed. Additionally, Michael McCullough's perspective sheds light on how important it is to garner organization-wide support for your strategic branding efforts.

PRACTITIONER'S PERSPECTIVE

Developing a Strategic Brand Communication Campaign: The Case of the Miami Heat
by Michael McCullough, Chief Marketing Officer, Miami Heat

Prior to the 2000-2001 NBA season we focused on creating an integrated branding communications campaign that would be versatile, flexible, and effective. Before we could begin considering our advertising, we first needed to make some subtle changes in our logo. Some of the color gradations in our logo were very difficult for our retail licensees to reproduce. As a result, there was little consistency in the way our logo looked across different retailers. With some slight modifications in the colors of the logo, we now had a mark that could be used consistently throughout our licensing and advertising efforts.

In order to ensure that the logo was used in a consistent manner throughout the organization, we set up a new unit, the Creative Services Department, which served as a clearinghouse for all internally produced materials. This department was responsible for developing the look of all items produced by the Heat that bore our logo, which included producing publications and creating names and identities for various team programs, events, and characters.

The next step in our integrated branding process was to hire an outside design firm, named Alonso and Company, to serve as our graphic design group. This relationship gave us access to a number of talented designers who quickly became familiar with our needs and standards. Through extensive communication, Alonso and Company essentially became an extension of our company, but at a fraction of the cost it would have taken to add full-time designers to our staff.

With Alonso and Company in place, we set about branding/theming/positioning all of the activities that the organization undertakes. The goal was to create an identity and association for the various activities and programs offered by the Heat. We began with an all-staff meeting, in which we educated our entire company about the branding strategy and the role that each person within the organization played in creating the brand. Next, we wrote a positioning statement, "Can You Feel the HEAT?" This statement offered a number of benefits. First, it could be used over multiple seasons; because the statement was not based on the success of the team or a star player, there was no need to create a new slogan each year. Second, the positioning statement allowed for creative communications. For example, a local music group wrote a series of songs (in both Spanish and English)—centered on "Can You Feel the Heat?"—that have become quite popular in the Miami area. Finally, the statement allowed for the creation of related statements that could be used throughout our advertising. "Are you feelin' it?" and "Can you feel it?" are shortened variations that we have used in our marketing efforts.

With the positioning in place, we set out to devise a specific advertising campaign for the 2000-2001 season. Entering the season we faced a number of challenges. For example, we were coming off our third consecutive play-off loss on our home floor to our arch-rivals, the New York Knicks, which left the community despondent and looking for changes in our player personnel. Additionally, our star player, Alonzo Mourning, was diagnosed with a kidney disease and would miss most of the season. Fortunately, we completed a huge off-season trade and picked up another key player through free agency. Given all of the new faces, our challenge was to answer the questions: "Who are these guys and why should I be excited about them?" To complicate matters further, we had no footage of any of the new players in Heat uniforms.

Given these constraints, we decided to go with a bold and colorful look that emphasized the team colors. This enabled us to create a sense of unity for a team that had yet to play together. Additionally, it gave us some flexibility. Each execution of the ad campaign was designed to feature the personality of a new player through pace and music. We even had a fictitious disk jockey, named "Big Red," talk about the players and deliver the sales message. Through this execution, we were able to generate awareness of the players' likenesses and names, as well as convey important messages about their unique personalities. The use of colors, player likenesses, and music (where applicable) permeated all of our advertising campaigns.

The Strategic Brand Communications Process

Now that you understand why advertising must ultimately be viewed as strategic brand communications, we will spend the rest of this chapter examining the process of strategic brand communications. As depicted in figure 6.3, the strategic brand communications process entails six steps:

1. Conducting a situational analysis
2. Setting the objectives for the advertising efforts
3. Selecting the target markets for the advertisements
4. Crafting the advertising message
5. Selecting the media through which to transmit the advertising message
6. Evaluating the effectiveness of the advertising

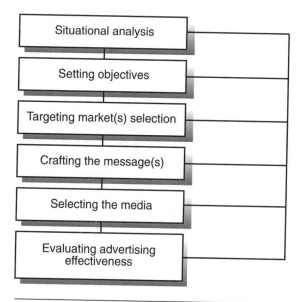

Figure 6.3 The strategic brand communication process.

Reprinted, by permission, from D.E. Schultz and B.E. Barnes, 1999, *Strategic brand communication campaigns* (Lincolnwood, IL: NTC Business Books), 68.

These six steps are integral to the successful implementation of strategic brand communications. In addition, this process does not just happen once; it happens repeatedly over time, driven by the sixth step, evaluation. As figure 6.3 depicts, on the basis of the feedback from the advertisement, any of the previous five steps can be altered or managed. Thus, rather than being a linear process that happens only once, the strategic brand communications campaign is a cyclical process that relies on evaluation. If we remember that advertising is really two-way communication between the sender and the receiver, then it is intuitive that the process of managing advertising should include regular evaluation and analysis, perhaps causing alterations.

A perfect illustration of the strategic brand communications process is the 1980s Coca-Cola advertisement featuring "Mean" Joe Greene of the Pittsburgh Steelers, tossing his jersey to a kid who gave him a Coke after a game. This ad was immensely popular, but was discontinued by Coke's head of marketing, Sergio Zyman. When asked why he discontinued such a popular ad, Zyman replies:

"A lot of people thought that it was a big waste of time to kill an expensive ad so quickly, but I did it because I had a strategic goal—which was to get people to buy more Coke. What would have been a big waste of money is to have kept buying airtime for something that was not doing that."[30]

Zyman is saying that even though people liked the ad, upon evaluation the advertisement was not meeting the objectives set forth.

Step 1: Conducting a Situational Analysis

The Boston Red Sox are positioning Fenway Park as "Friendly Fenway." Their advertisements make a plea to potential consumers to visit Fenway Park because the experience will be a friendly one. With this campaign, the Red Sox are attempting to associate a personality characteristic with Fenway Park. Fenway Park is one of the two oldest MLB stadiums (the other being Wrigley Field). No matter how the Red Sox perform on the field, they are able to leverage the history, tradition, and unique features of Fenway (for example, the high left field wall called the "Green Monster") to regularly draw near-capacity crowds. However, through a variety of incidents (for example, the harsh treatment of first baseman Bill Buckner after he made an error that cost the Red Sox the World Series in 1986), the park and its fans have developed a reputation of being unfriendly. The Friendly Fenway campaign seems to be at least partially designed to soften the image of the Red Sox and its fans. Thus, the campaign may have been based on a situational analysis suggesting that people thought attending games at Fenway was not an especially agreeable social experience.

Before you think about what your ad will say, or where you want to advertise, the very first task of the strategic brand communications process is to conduct a **situational analysis.**[31] Ideally, there are four elements to any thorough situational analysis.[31] The situational analysis should start with an *analysis of both existing and potential consumers of your sport product.* Because the goal of advertising should be to communicate messages to consumers, knowing who the targeted consumers are and what their preferences are will enhance your ability to create successful communications about the sport brand. A wide variety of resources are available to research who sport consumers are and what their preferences are. Table 6.1 lists some of these resources. The organization must also *assess the strength and weaknesses of a product.* The Friendly Fenway ads, as already noted, could have been an outcome of the Red Sox's analyzing their organization and learning that people did not find the environment hospitable or inviting. Thus, as already noted, the new ad campaign could be an attempt to counteract this image. Third, the situational analysis should *review past advertising campaigns.* If the goal is for communications to be consistent, it makes sense to consider the history of advertising around the sport brand as part of the planning for a new strategic brand communications campaign. Finally, the situational analysis needs to include an *analysis of the competition.* This entails determining your product's place in the marketplace. Are you the preferred entertainment offering, as is the case with the Nebraska Cornhusker football team in Lincoln, Nebraska? Or conversely, are

Table 6.1   Consumer Research Resources

Source	Information provided
ESPN Chilton Research	Data on sport consumer interest and consumption
Claritas	Segmentation of consumers into clusters based on geographic and psychographic data
U.S. Census	Demographic data
Database America (**databaseamerica.com**)	Compilation of consumer data from a variety of sources
Simmons Market Research Bureau	Demographic and psychographic information about consumers based on area of residence

Data from D.E. Schultz and B.E. Barnes, 1999.

you one of the least-preferred options, as is the case with the Los Angeles Clippers in their home market?

Step 2: Setting Objectives

Returning to the Friendly Fenway message, what do you think the Red Sox are trying to achieve more specifically? Are they attempting to attract more families to Fenway Park? Or are they attempting to make people feel even better about their experience when attending Fenway Park? (Arguably, the ads are not intended to increase attendance. The Red Sox regularly sell a large portion of their tickets throughout the season.) Whatever the reason, objectives are the driver of successful strategic brand communications campaigns. As with all business objectives, the objectives set for advertising efforts should provide (1) criteria on which to make specific strategic decisions and (2) standards against which results can be compared.[32]

Once objectives are set, all strategic decisions should be made with an eye to achieving objectives. In the case of the Friendly Fenway campaign, strategic decisions tied to achieving objectives would be creating family sections and working with stadium personnel to be more hospitable. Creating standards to evaluate the effectiveness of an ad campaign is more difficult. Because factors other than advertising affect the customer's perception and consumption of the product, it is very hard to isolate the effects of advertising. For example, how do the Red Sox assess the effectiveness of the campaign? What happens if the Red Sox compete to go to the World Series, as they did in 1999? Can the increased enthusiasm and attendance associated with the team be linked to the Friendly Fenway campaign? In order to accurately measure the effect of the campaign, the Red Sox would have to measure people's perceptions of Fenway Park both before and after the campaign.

There are a variety of objectives that a sport advertiser can set. As noted by former Coke executive Zyman, increasingly the success of advertising campaigns is measured by the affect on sales. In the case of the Mean Joe Greene ad, the sport theme may have made people feel warm inside, but it did not help sell Coke. A second objective of advertising might be to attract new customers to purchase your brand. For example, a number of sport entities have created advertising attempting to communicate with and impact attendance by Hispanic people. Among the entities reaching out to Hispanics are the Dallas Burn of MLS and the Texas Rangers and San Diego Padres of MLB.[33] Similarly, given the high proportion of Spanish-speaking people in the Miami area, the WNBA's Miami Sol might want to utilize their advertising to reach the Hispanic market.

Another goal of an advertising program is to increase consumption of the sport product by existing consumers. The Pittsburgh Pirates' ad campaign "You Gotta See 'Em" was an attempt to entice people who might have followed the Pirates casually (through television, the Internet, or the newspaper) to actually attend a game at Three Rivers Stadium. A fourth common objective of an advertising campaign is to create brand awareness for the sport brand. In 1997, New Balance Athletic Shoe sought to increase the awareness of its athletic shoes by advertising during network prime time for the first time ever. Further, this campaign, "Achieve New Balance," was attempting to create more awareness of the New Balance product in the minds of consumers aged 25 to 44 (see figure 6.2). In relation to the objectives, New Balance was successful. Between 1997 and 1999, awareness of the New Balance brand increased from 53% to 72%.[34]

A fifth and final common objective of strategic brand communications is to enhance the image of the sport brand. This is clearly what the Boston Red Sox were attempting to do with their Friendly Fenway campaign. Similarly, with "These Kids Can Play," the Chicago White Sox were trying to alter the pervading perception among fans that the White Sox were more worried about reducing their payroll than about winning baseball games.

___

Step 3: Selecting the Target Market

Before the 1996-1997 season, the Winnipeg Jets relocated and became the Phoenix Coyotes. The NHL was going to the desert. How could this work? A variety of factors seemed stacked against the Coyotes. First, Phoenix, given its warm weather climate, does not possess strong grassroots interest in hockey. Second, the Jets were not one of the better teams in the NHL before moving to Phoenix, so the new management could not market the team based on its prospects for success. Finally, the Coyotes signed a lease to play in America West Arena, the home of the Phoenix Suns. The only problem with this plan was that the arena was not designed with hockey in mind. Therefore, the upper deck of one side of the arena actually hung over the goal, limiting the view of the people seated there to the ice area past the first blue line. Given such a lack of vested hockey fans, one might have expected the relocation to fail. Yet it did not. Part of the Coyotes' success lay in their ability to accurately define target markets for their communication messages.

Three pieces are central to the crafting of any **segmentation strategy**.[35] Segmentation typically entails the identification of a group of consumers that is not served well by your competitors and thus might use your product. The Coyotes identified two markets. First, among the Phoenix population were a large number of people from the "rust belt" cities of Chicago and Detroit, as well as a significant population from Minneapolis. All three of these cities possessed traditions of professional hockey. Further, other than the Dallas Stars, there was no professional hockey in the Southwest. And, other than the Colorado Avalanche, there was no professional hockey in the mountain time zone. Thus there was an established market of people who knew hockey but were not being served. Secondly, the Coyotes turned the obstructed-view seating into a positive by offering those seats for a significant discount, thus attracting people who wanted to attend professional sporting events but could not afford to attend a Suns game in the winter.

A second key to segmentation efforts is to ensure that the identified segment is either large enough or growing in size. With respect to both of the markets identified by the Coyotes, both conditions were satisfied. An increasing number of northerners were moving to Phoenix. Similarly, NBA ticket prices rose at an alarming rate throughout the 1990s, thus increasingly pricing the "common fan" out of the market for tickets. A final condition of a segmentation strategy is that the segment represent a group that is very likely to respond to the benefits offered by the product. In the case of the northern transplants, the Coyotes were reasonably certain that this group would be eager to consume professional hockey.

Ultimately, there are a number of ways to develop a segmentation strategy. Perhaps the most common method is to segment a group based on demographic variables such as age, gender, ethnicity, income level, or number of children in the household. This is what New Balance did with its Achieve New Balance ad campaign. The company attempted to create a message that would resonate with a new market it was targeting, men and women aged 25 to 44.[36] Markets can also be segmented based on geographic data, or where people live and/or work. For example, the Colorado Rockies have been so successful because they have been able to communicate with fans far beyond the Denver metropolitan area. A third way in which markets can be segmented is based on psychographic or lifestyle information such as hobbies, computer usage, or causes supported. ESPN and a number of other sport programmers are increasingly attempting to create two-way dialogue by promoting features on their Web sites during telecasts of sporting events. Fourth, consumers can be segmented by usage. An excellent example of a tool to segment consumers based on usage is the frequency escalator created by Mullin, Hardy, and Sutton that categorizes people as heavy, medium, and light users, as well as aware and unaware.[37] People can also be segmented based on the benefits a product provides. One of the benefits that spectator sport provides is entertainment, created by the way the sport product is delivered; this benefit is often stressed in advertising campaigns. For example, the 2001 advertising campaign for MLB's Los Angeles Dodgers centered on the theme "Being here is everything." The theme suggests that a number of entertainment benefits are provided by a Los Angeles Dodgers baseball game.[38]

Step 4: Crafting the Message

As we documented at the beginning of the chapter, Nike's "Just Do It" slogan accurately represented the image conveyed by the Nike brand. This image came to represent what it meant to wear Nike shoes and apparel. That is, in the mid-1990s, people who wore Nike could be seen as people who would not accept conventional wisdom. In essence, the slogan cemented Nike's brand image as a rebel, which carried with it brand associations of performance, the ability to ignore critics, and a commitment to self. The crafting of the "Just Do It" message represents one of the most successful creative efforts to reach targeted segments with a meaningful communication message. Its success is an excellent example of how important it can be to cultivate key brand associations. Thus, at the core of crafting a successful message is the ability to trigger, create, or reinforce positive brand associations with the sport product. Therefore the remainder of this section is devoted to explaining brand associations and explaining some of the key brand associations that can be triggered in the sport setting.

Brand Associations: Consumer Memories and Perceptions

According to David Aaker, brand associations are anything in a consumer's memory linked to a specific brand.[39] The sport consumer forms a wide variety of brand associations based on the consumption experience. For example, a person attending a Chicago Bulls game during the championship years will probably forever associate Michael Jordan with the Chicago Bulls brand. In fact, this example highlights the advertising challenges faced by teams that lose superstars. People come to expect certain players to be playing for their favorite team. If those players retire, or are traded, or leave as free agents, this dramatically limits the ability of a team to emphasize unique brand associations. Another vivid example of a brand association is Camden Yards as a brand association with the Baltimore Orioles. Camden Yards represented a revolution in stadium construction because it was the first major effort to build a sense of the past into a sporting venue. As such, Camden Yards has brand associations of its own. For example, for some it may represent a comfortable and fun place (by virtue of the food court in the outfield) to watch a game. For others, its location near the old B&O railroad may conjure up fond nostalgic memories of the history of Baltimore.

It is crucial that the people working on strategic brand communications campaigns recognize the importance of creating and nurturing brand associations with their advertising efforts. Ultimately, the creation and maintenance of strong brand associations can lead to four positive outcomes:[40]

Good memories

Differentiation

Motivation

Good feelings

- *Good memories.* First, brand associations help consumers process and retrieve information. For example, if a person has enjoyed attending a Lansing Lugnuts minor league baseball game because of the nice stadium and the family atmosphere, an advertisement featuring kids and a family section in the grassy outfield will trigger those fond memories and perhaps motivate the receiver to purchase tickets to a Lugnuts game.

- *Differentiation.* A second way in which brand associations create value is by providing a point of differentiation from other products. For sport teams competing in the ever-expanding entertainment marketplace, this is increasingly crucial. The point is important, because a sporting event is much different from other entertainment offerings—for example, the outcome of a sporting event is unknown, and the experience is much more social. People often attend a minor league baseball game in groups of five or more. Regular pauses between pitches and between innings leave a significant amount of time for conversation. Compare this to attending a movie—although people may attend in groups, there is no social interaction during the movie. Therefore, pictures and video clips emphasizing the social nature of attending a sporting event can be useful in advertising campaigns.

- *Motivation.* Brand associations can also provide consumers with a reason to purchase the product. For example, one of the keys to the success of the NBA "I Love This Game" was its ability to piece exciting dunks together with pictures of the faces of various recognizable people having a great time at NBA games. In this way the NBA developed and nurtured an association that its brand was "fun." Because the experience was enjoyable, the ad suggested, everyone should purchase a ticket and become part of the action.

- *Good feelings.* Finally, brand associations can create positive attitudes and feelings. Under the tag line "Hey, We Can Play," the LPGA ran a series of advertisements demonstrating that LPGA golfers were excellent golfers and excellent people. One ad chronicles the exploits of Nancy Lopez and concludes by reminding people that she is a mother of three children.

Given the importance of brand associations, we suggest that the major thrust of advertising is to create brand associations that will endure, assisting in the creation of an overarching brand image. Ultimately, these brand associations will provide the "reason why" the product is purchased repeatedly over time.[41] Unfortunately, brand associations can also provide a reason why a product is not consumed. In 1999, the ATP Tour (men's professional tennis) announced that it was creating a series of 10 events that would represent the premiere men's professional tennis events in the world (outside of Wimbledon, the U.S. Open, the French Open, and the Australian Open). However, the ATP Tour made two mistakes in crafting messages for the new series. First, the series was named the "Tennis Masters Series." Can you see what the problem with the name is? When you think of the word "masters" in association with sport, what comes to mind? Yes, certainly golf's Masters Tournament is one association. But you probably also think of international sport for the elderly, often referred to as "Masters" events. Thus, the ATP Tour chose a name for the series that already had key associations with other endeavors. As to the other mistake, the advertising message for the Tennis Masters Series was "Welcome to 21st Century Tennis." What associations does that message convey? Does it tell you anything unique about the new series of events?

The Tennis Masters Series also illustrates the "tag line trap," or the notion that the brand associations for a sport brand should be created in a matter of a few words.[42] In "Welcome to 21st Century Tennis," the intended perception appears to be that professional tennis is changing. But how is it changing? What will be different? These questions are left unanswered. This example also illustrates the challenges associated with devising tag lines and advertising messages. We know that the advertising environment is very cluttered. As a result, a long drawn-out message will probably not make it through the noise and reach the receiver. However, as the example illustrates, those tag lines that fail to say anything significant about the brand are also doomed not to succeed.

Using Key Brand Associations to Craft a Message

Since you now understand the importance of creating or reinforcing brand associations in advertising messages, it is time to turn to the art of actually crafting the messages to create, reinforce, or trigger brand associations. To craft messages that will appeal to sport consumers, one needs a deeper understanding of brand associations. Two common sources of brand association are attributes and benefits. Attributes are the features of a particular brand.[43] For example, a person in Philadelphia may decide to purchase a ticket package of five games because the Phillies signed a free agent. In this case, the player represents an attribute. Benefits, on the other hand, represent the meaning and value consumers attach to the product.[44] When a Boston Red Sox fan purchases a Red Sox hat outside Fenway Park, this fan is purchasing the hat as a means of demonstrating his affiliation with the Red Sox. The ability of the team to provide a basis for identification represents a benefit offered by the particular team.

With an understanding that both attributes and benefits help contribute to the formation of brand associations, it is time to turn to some tangible guidelines on how to create and foster these key associations in sport. Research has indicated that there are eight attributes and five benefits that contribute to the formation of brand associations in the sport setting.[45] These are listed in table 6.2. In the remainder of this section, we examine how each of the 13 brand association dimensions can be used to create positive brand associations with sport consumers. We begin with the attributes.

Table 6.2 Types of Brand Associations in Sport: Attributes and Benefits

Attributes	Benefits
Success	Fan identification
Head coach	Escape
Star players	Nostalgia
Stadium/Arena	Pride in place
Logo design	Peer group acceptance
Product delivery	
Tradition	
Management	

Reprinted, by permission, from J.M. Gladden and D.C. Funk, 2001, "Developing an understanding of brand associations in team sport: Empirical evidence from consumers of professional sport," *Journal of Sport Management* 16 (1).

Success

Perhaps the easiest way for a sport advertiser to motivate people to consume a product would be to promise that the sport team or individual will be successful. People love to affiliate with winning teams. In addition, a wealth of academic research has documented the benefits a team derives from winning. Most notably, ticket sales typically increase when a team is successful.[46] Capitalizing on the potential for success is exactly what the University of Massachusetts football program was attempting to do in promoting its 2000 season as "A Championship Tradition."

While a successful team can definitely create positive brand associations, the strategy can also be very risky. Remember, one of the truly unique facets of the sport product is its unpredictability.[47] Think about it: Before the 1999 NFL season, who predicted that the St. Louis Rams would win the Super Bowl? Certainly if the Rams had promoted the idea that they were going to have a great year and followed up with one, a key brand association could have been established. But it is not that easy. Before the 1999-2000 season, the Minnesota Timberwolves promoted their upcoming season as "How the West was Won," referring to their hopes of winning the Western Conference championship. The narrative for the ad included the following promise based on success: "Forget the past. Believe in the Present. The Wolves are Coming."[48] While the text does not absolutely suggest that the Timberwolves would win the Western Conference, it certainly implied that the Timberwolves were ready to put their history of losing behind them. Unfortunately, the Timberwolves did not win the Western Conference in 1999-2000. Thus, the promise from the Timberwolves brand was broken. Conceivably, this could have damaged the Timberwolves' relationship with their customers.

Star Player

Think back to the way NBC promoted NBA games 5 or 10 years ago. Do you remember hearing "Watch Michael and the Bulls take on Larry and the Celtics"? The players were the primary reason NBC was suggesting that people should watch the NBA. Research has documented that the presence of star players on a particular team can contribute to its overall attractiveness.[49] As a result, advertising programs built around players are very popular today. Witness a recent advertising campaign by the Charlotte Hornets featuring star player Eddie Jones under the tag line "This guy is quick."[50] Similarly, in an attempt to reach the Hispanic community in the Miami area, the Florida Marlins featured Cuban American pitcher Alex Fernandez and Cuban defector Livan Hernandez in a series of billboard ads next to the word *emocion*, Spanish for "excitement." [51]

Although ad campaigns based on star players have proven to be very successful, there are some potential drawbacks. Today's professional athlete is more nomadic than ever. Be it through trade or free agency, players—even star players—move from team to team on a regular basis. Players can also be injured, sometimes missing an entire season. Take the Hornets and Marlins ads we just considered. When the 2000 season started for each club, neither Eddie Jones nor Livan Hernandez played for the respective team. In addition, Alex Fernandez continued to be plagued by arm trouble. So the question is, when should a team build a brand communication campaign around a player or players? We can conclude that the marketer adopting a strategic brand communications approach must proceed with caution when marketing a sport product based on players.

Head Coach

Can you remember the last time your favorite team changed coaches and hired someone whom you were truly excited about? Chances are that the team featured that coach in its marketing as a way of providing hope for the future. As is the case with star players, the head coach is often a central component in advertising programs. For example, given Coach Pat Summit's record of success over a number of years, the University of Tennessee can prominently promote her as a means of reinforcing a key brand association with Tennessee women's basketball. It is easy to document how the arrival of a new head coach has stirred interest among fans—an example is Mike Holmgren and the Seattle Seahawks. The Seahawks' hiring of Holmgren before the 1999 season led to 1700 ticket requests within two-and-a-half days.[52] Because head coaches can be featured so prominently, they often become a centerpiece of the advertising program. To return to the case of the Hornets, in addition to the Eddie Jones ad the Hornets ran a humorous ad in which Head Coach Paul Silas was teaching a dog how to dribble and dunk. The ad closed by saying "This Guy Can Coach."[53] But basing an advertising campaign on a coach can be risky. What if the coach does not improve the team? What if the coach does not deliver the championship he promised when taking over the team? A marketing campaign centered on a new coach can be effective in the short term, but may not be the most effective type of long-term strategic brand communications campaign.

Management

Although the management or ownership is rarely a thrust of advertising campaigns, we suggest that it should be a part of the strategic brand communications effort. Research has demonstrated that a consumer's trust in an organization is helpful with respect to creating a long-term relationship and loyal consumer.[54] If a sport consumer were given a reason not to trust a particular organization, the brand associations with that organization would be negative. For example, one could argue that the Oakland Raiders' problems selling tickets in the renovated Oakland-Alameda Coliseum could be related in large part to the ongoing disputes between owner Al Davis (who has already moved the team twice) and the city of Oakland. This is a perfect example of how advertising used to convince a city to pay for a new stadium can end up producing more negative associations than positive ones. Similarly, think back to the gift-giving scandal associated with the Salt Lake City Olympics in 1998. Critics suggested that this scandal caused significant damage to the Olympic brand.[55] In response to the perceived damage to the brand, the International Olympic Committee unveiled an advertising campaign in 2000 that stressed the Olympic ideals of excellent competition in the spirit of peace among countries. Therefore, while management is not a factor in many advertising campaigns, its consistency and perceived importance may provide cause for strategic brand communications campaigns to center on owners. For example, popular owners like Jerry Colangelo (Phoenix Suns, Phoenix Mercury, and Arizona Diamondbacks) could be a key brand association stressed in conjunction with these teams.

Logo Design

Corporations can bring about and strengthen associations through their visual identity.[56] The San Jose Sharks revolutionized the way team marks were used to create associations. San Jose, by involving the community in coming up with its nickname and logo, as well as developing a visual identity that many marketing programs could be built around, became a "marketing phenomenon" before ever playing a game.[57] Another great example of use of a logo as the centerpiece of a strategic brand communications campaign is the Cleveland Browns' use of their logo (albeit plain) to remind fans that football was returning to Cleveland. Soon after being awarded an expansion franchise, the Browns marketed their merchandise, and it quickly outsold that of a number of other NFL teams.[58] The merchandise sold so quickly because it conjured up the positive brand associations from the rich history of the Cleveland Browns. At the college level, schools such as New Mexico, Xavier, and Villanova have completely reshaped their logos in an attempt to improve the marketing associated with their brands.[59]

Thus, we suggest that sport brands take control of their visual identification. Ultimately this form of identification may represent an opportunity for retooling the strategic brand communications of a losing team. Minor league baseball presents an excellent example of the use of logos to reshape people's associations with teams. Throughout the 1990s, minor league baseball teams created new nicknames and accompanying logos as a means of generating more interest and revenue for their respective clubs. Why don't more major professional sport teams do this? Would there be an uproar if the Los Angeles Clippers changed their nickname? Our point is that some teams could greatly benefit from a nickname change because through the new logo they could produce a whole new set of associations.

Stadium

With the outbreak of new stadium development throughout the 1990s and into this decade, the stadium experience has become increasingly important to creating and fostering positive associations with the team brand. In the case of a team that is performing poorly, a brand communications campaign could theoretically succeed. An attractive or unique stadium, such as Wrigley Field, Fenway Park, Jacobs Field, or Conseco Fieldhouse, could serve to create positive associations regardless of the presence of other factors (e.g., success, star players, a marquee head coach) that are easier to market. In fact, one might argue that the stadium could be the centerpiece of a successful strategic brand communications campaign. Anyone who has attended a game at Wrigley Field knows that it is one of the few places where the outcome of the contest is of secondary importance (figure 6.4). The Cubs could promote this fact

Figure 6.4   Wrigley Field can attract fans whether the Cubs are winning or not.

through their branding campaign. For example, the slogan could be "Make a day of it at Wrigley." As they moved into a new stadium for the 2001 season, MLB's Pittsburgh Pirates attempted to communicate the unique architecture of PNC Park through the tag line "Built for Baseball."[60]

Product Delivery

A seventh theme that teams can stress in their strategic brand communications campaigns is the entertainment value offered by the sport product. Many people develop positive brand associations based on the ability of the sport brand to provide entertainment. Certainly, the outcome is one part of the entertainment provided. However, other elements exist. For example, promotions, player-fan interactions, and entertaining broadcasters (remember that the product is also delivered through the media) can all help positive brand associations and thus enhance the delivery of the product. Many "Olympic sports" (sports that do not generate revenue but are a part of the Olympic Games) at colleges and universities advertise autograph signings after games as a means of increasing youth attendance. Another good example of a campaign that emphasized product delivery was the Golden State Warriors' use of "It's a Great Time Out" to promote the team. The advertisements for the team featured players singing a song and presented visual images of everything that accompanies attendance at a Warriors game (mascot, food and beverage, interaction with other fans).[61]

The ability of fans to interact with the athletes can have a major impact on the delivery of the sport product. For example, after the strike, MLB began to promote the fact that the players were ready to accommodate autograph requests before and after games. By making the players more accessible, MLB was attempting to resurrect some of the goodwill that had been lost when the 1997 World Series was canceled due to a work stoppage. Teams have also been somewhat successful in promoting the youth and energy of teams that may not be ready to compete for championships. In addition to the White Sox slogan "These Kids Can Play," the Reds' 2000 campaign was "It's a Whole New Ballgame" and the campaign stressed the courage, heart, and exuberance of the Reds' young team.[62]

Tradition

The tradition associated with a sport brand can be a very important source for stimulating and nurturing positive brand associations. People tend to think of "tradition" in terms of winning. However, that definition is too narrow; it needs to be broadened to include any significant aspect of a team's history. For example, the Boston Red Sox and Chicago Cubs have two traditions in common. For one, they play in the oldest ballparks in the country. Secondly, both teams have histories of not winning championships yet still having loyal followings. Couldn't this loyalty become the centerpiece of a brand communications campaign? Certainly, though, the ability to win games and championships is important and makes crafting the message based on tradition easier. Witness one of the Chicago Bulls' campaigns for the 1999-2000 season, the second year after Michael Jordan's retirement. A television ad for season tickets began by stating that the Bulls were the most dominant team of the 1990s. It then stressed the trademarks of those Bulls teams: "Hustle. Defense. Exciting Team Play. Fierce Determination." The ad next presented the claim that the revamped team possessed many of the same qualities and suggested that with some tickets available, this was "The Chance You've Been Waiting For."[63] Thus, the communication featured qualities that a championship team and a last-place team have in common, promoting the opportunity to grow with a young team.

Escape

Research has demonstrated how sport can provide people an important escape from their daily routines.[64] Following sport can serve as a coping strategy through which people can find fulfillment and contentment. Can you remember a time when you have procrastinated by researching the statistics of your favorite team's players or spending an extra 15 minutes reading about your team on the Web when you should have been studying? Most people can recall this type of experience. Escape is a viable brand association that sport advertising can cultivate. Interestingly, we do not know of any sport advertising that directly promotes escape, but such a strategy should definitely be considered in the future. For example, a minor league baseball team could promote its family-friendly atmosphere as the "The Perfect Diversion From Your Family's Crazy Life" or as a way to escape pressure and enjoy "Family Fun."

Fan Identification

Sport consumer identification is one of the more widely studied brand association dimensions in sport.[65] Ultimately, identification with a team or sport brand fulfills a sport consumer's need to affiliate with something successful and desirable. One way in which sport brands have sought to foster such identification in the past is by making the athletes seem more approachable, thus encouraging a connection to the sport. For example, in the LPGA "Hey, We Can Play" advertisements mentioned earlier, the thrust was to have people not only respect the excellence of LPGA golfers but also relate to them on a personal level. Similarly, the Phoenix Suns' "Let Yourself Go" campaign featured various Suns players answering questions from children in school classrooms. The presentation of the questions and answers make the Suns players seem more human than they might in their professional setting. For example, guard Penny Hardaway admits that he has cried after losses, and forward Rodney Rogers describes how he likes to drive his dump truck in the off-season. In this sense, both sport brands are presenting successful athletes and aiming to give consumers a reason to identify with their fortunes.

Peer Group Acceptance

Sport events attract groups of friends.

Acceptance from a group of peers is another benefit that team sport can provide consumers. It has been suggested that the products a consumer chooses offer important social signals to peers.[66] If sport consumers feel that friends and family approve of their following a particular team, they will view all elements of the consumption experience more favorably.[67] Again, this is a benefit that not much sport advertising has focused on. However, given the research on this area, it seems reasonable to suggest that a brand association around peer group acceptance could be formed through a strategic brand communications campaign. In fact, this is a peripheral element in many sport-related ads today. For example, the "I Love This Game" ad campaign featured a number of people celebrating a great play together. When the high fives are shown, a secondary message

© Jim Baron/The Image Finders

that the ad conveys is that this is something done in groups. Nowhere is the influence of peer group acceptance more pervasive than on college campuses. Think about the reasons you went to a recent sporting event in which your school participated. For most students, the fact that friends are also attending is a very important factor. Thus, fostering the brand association of peer group acceptance may be particularly useful in the case of stimulating student attendance.

Nostalgia

Sport as a product has the unique ability to satisfy people's need to remember enjoyable experiences of the past. Defined, nostalgia is anything that conjures up a longing for the past or positive feelings associated with experiences that happened in the past.[68] Think about your favorite team for a minute again. Why are you so fond of that team? Chances are that part of the answer lies in certain experiences that immediately come to mind. Some people may recall the experience of watching with friends as their favorite football team competed in the playoffs one year. For others, the affiliation to a favorite team may be the result of a family tradition. Perhaps following a sport team is something that binds friends and family together, so that when that team plays, following them includes upholding a tradition, or being able to continue to share in the experience with the same people. The Chicago Bulls' advertising campaign mentioned earlier is also an excellent example of a campaign that attempts to provide the nostalgia benefit to consumers. The ad begins by reminding consumers of the championship years, something that served as a rallying point throughout the Chicagoland area. Then it suggests that the values are the same—hustle, defense, team play—and that these values will always represent the Bulls franchise. The ad concludes by suggesting that people have a unique opportunity to share in the experience of the future, thus implying that by purchasing season tickets people will be able to create a whole new set of positive memories. Although brand associations such as nostalgia may seem intangible, thorough market research can demonstrate how important this association is to fans of sport brands.

Pride in Place

The final brand association that we recommend focusing communications toward is pride in place. Can you remember the "Saturday Night Live" skits featuring guys talking about "Da Bears?" These skits poke fun at Bears fans. Rather than offending Bears fans, the skits made Bears fans feel special, and even more proud of where they were from. This sentiment is often termed *pride in place*. We suggest that brand communications campaigns can be successful through stimulating brand associations related to people's affiliation with their hometown team. "It's definitely a baseball town" was the advertising slogan for the St. Louis Cardinals' 2001 season.[69] This statement was meant to remind people that several different publications, including *Sports Illustrated*, had described St. Louis as the best baseball town in the United States. Therefore, it seems that the Cardinals' ad campaign was meant to reinforce St. Louisans' pride in receiving such recognition.

In some instances a sport team provides a rallying point for the community. In a broader context, think about how Olympic teams instill pride in being from a particular country. This is pride in place on a broader level. Marketers have yet to fully leverage the importance of this brand association in their advertising campaigns. However, there are examples emerging. Rather than focusing on success or a few star players, for instance, the Utah Jazz's 1999-2000 campaign featured the tag line "It's Our Team."[70] While short and simple, this statement also served to stimulate brand associations tied to the fact that the Jazz are Utah's only professional team. In the case of a new team,

Syracuse fans cheer for their team.

marketing communication campaigns can also be particularly effective if they focus on pride in place. One of the first initiatives undertaken by the expansion Minnesota Wild of the NHL was to immerse itself in the Twin Cities community. One marketing initiative, entitled "Wild About Youth," focused on reminding the 17 million Minnesotans visiting skating rinks of how special the Minnesota hockey culture is.[71]

Although this discussion has highlighted 13 brand associations that can be stimulated through strategic brand communications campaigns, it is also important to think about why strategic brand communications campaigns fail. *Campaigns are not successful if they do not stimulate brand associations.* Think about the last sport-related advertisement that you did not like. What was it about that advertisement that made you dislike it? Why didn't it resonate with you?

In all likelihood, it did not mean anything to you. Probing deeper, you might find that it failed to create or magnify any important brand associations. Unfortunately, examples abound of strategic brand communications campaigns that fail to give rise to associations. For example, past Vancouver Grizzlies advertising campaigns featured a number of scenarios in which people were talking about the Grizzlies. Each ad concluded with the phrase "Believe It Baby."[72] Believe what? The ads did not offer any promises of winning, star players, or other meaningful associations.

Step 5: Selecting the Media for Your Message

Once you have crafted your strategic brand communications campaign message, it is time to formulate your plan for communicating it through the various forms of media. Before turning to a discussion of the various forms of media, it is important to highlight two factors that should guide this decision-making process: a focus on integration and the budget. First, it is important at this juncture to remember one of the key differences between an advertising campaign and a strategic brand communications campaign. An advertising campaign can exist by itself, and different campaigns can be created for different facets of the business. In contrast, one of the key tenets behind a strategic brand communications campaign is that the various advertisements run by an organization all strive to communicate the same message. Using such a strategy, the sport organization offers repeated exposures promoting the same brand association, thus increasing the chances of creating or triggering that brand association in the consumer.

One factor that affects and often inhibits the effective integration of advertisements across all media platforms is an organization's advertising budget. Experts suggest that careful analysis is important in the setting of advertising budgets.[73] Typical methods of analysis include the following:[74]

- Marginal analysis: Grounded in economic theory, this method suggests that a company should add to the advertising for a brand as long as the revenues it produces justify the expenditures.
- Percentage of sales: A fixed percentage of sales is devoted to advertising.
- All that can be afforded: Money available after all other expenses are covered is used for advertising.
- Competitive parity: Advertising is adjusted so that it is competitive with what the competition is doing.

Several of these methods are very prevalent in the sport setting. In particular, the methods of "percentage of sales" and "all that can be afforded" are often employed. The problem with both of these methods is that neither is strategic. Remembering our focus on the strategic nature of advertising, we suggest that budgeting should at the very least consider the goals of the brand communications program. For example, New Balance more than tripled its advertising budget in 1998 to include network advertisements for the first time. The justification for tripling the ad budget was related to the need to increase brand awareness among new consumer groups. We recommend that wherever possible, advertising budgeting start with the strategic objectives for the brand communications campaign. However, as we turn toward a discussion of the available media for advertisements, you should also remember that if the budget is predetermined, you need to make every attempt to maximize the impact of your ads. This includes not only the number of people the ad is reaching, but also the effectiveness with which the ad is reaching them.

Modes of Advertising

There are essentially two forms of advertising that the sport marketer can directly control: mass media advertising and direct marketing. A third form of advertising, word of mouth, is vitally important to the success of any brand, but it is more difficult to control in that the advertising actually happens after a consumer has been affected by the sport brand. The best strategies for creating word-of-mouth advertising are to undertake strategic brand communications and to ensure that the consumer has a favorable experience in all of her interactions with your sport brand. The remainder of this section addresses the various methods of mass media advertising. Direct marketing is discussed briefly, but is covered in greater detail elsewhere in this text (see chapter 5).

Mass Media Advertising

"Mass media advertising" typically refers to advertising through those media that reach a mass audience. Generally, this means television, radio, newspaper, magazine, and outdoor advertisements. There are advantages and disadvantages to mass media advertising. Mass media advertising has proven to be effective at retaining brand-loyal consumers in a cost-effective manner.[75] For example, if a team wanted to use either person-to-person contact or television to thank all the people who supported the team, it would be more effective to create an ad that said "thank you for your support" than it would be to identify and contact every one of those fans. Mass media advertising is also effective at increasing purchasing among light users of the product.[76] For example, we have noted that Beanie Baby Days are a particularly popular promotion that often appeals to people who infrequently attend games. An advertisement during the broadcast of a game about the upcoming Beanie Baby promotion would be the most cost-effective way of communicating the ad and perhaps motivating someone to purchase a ticket for Beanie Baby Day. However, mass media advertising has its disadvantages as well. First, the mass media are cluttered with advertisements, and cutting through the clutter can be particularly difficult.[77] Secondly, mass media advertising can be expensive and less effective than other forms of advertising that are able to reach out to a set of target consumers cost-effectively. For example, a billboard advertisement for tickets near a downtown stadium may be more effective than an advertisement placed with the various cable television stations throughout the area. The remainder of our discussion of mass media advertising focuses on the various forms of mass media advertising and presents the advantages and disadvantages of each.

Television

There are several different modes through which to purchase advertising time for the sport brand. First, the company can purchase time directly from the network. This is what New Balance did when it unveiled its national television advertising campaign. It purchased time on a number of popular network sitcoms such as "Friends" and "Frasier" on NBC. Another approach is to purchase advertising time from the individual cable companies in an area. Every area has a cable television company service. Do you know which company is the cable television company in your area? Cable television companies also have an inventory of advertisements that need to be sold during the different cable TV shows. For example, if you worked for the Boston Celtics, you could contact AT&T, which is your cable television provider, and purchase ads promoting the Celtics on broadcasts of ESPN's "SportsCenter" and MTV's "Real World" at the same time.

Television is a particularly powerful medium because it carries both sight and sound.[78] As a result, it can be particularly effective for products that have to be seen to be understood. For example, the "I Love This Game" NBA brand communications campaign would not have been nearly as successful on radio or in the newspaper. It relied heavily on the ability of television to capture the excitement of attending an NBA game. Television can also be particularly effective in creating an image for a product. Think about the numerous Nike ads featuring Michael Jordan. The ability of television to capture the many dynamic moves Jordan made throughout his career was central to Nike's being able to reinforce its image as a company that produced high-quality athletic footwear.

On the other hand, television ads have two major disadvantages. The last time you watched television, did you use the remote control to "surf" during advertisements? Most people surf. In fact, the phenomenon of surfing is an outcome of the clutter that arises because of the sheer volume of television advertisements. Secondly, for sport organizations, television advertisements can be very expensive. As mentioned earlier, sport brands often use a what-can-be-afforded approach to advertising. Consequently, if the sport marketer chose television as an advertising medium, she would likely end up spending the majority of the advertising budget just on television advertisements.

Radio

Radio is obviously more limited than television in that it delivers only an audio message. In addition, it is not particularly effective at reaching a national audience because most radio is local. However, radio advertising does have some potential up sides for sport brands. For example, radio stations typically attract a specific audience that can be described in terms of segments. If a team has a good idea of the specific audience (in terms of age, gender, etc.), it may be appropriate to advertise an upcoming game on radio because of its cost-effectiveness. A second major advantage of radio is that it can reach consumers when they are outside of the home.[79] Therefore, a brand communication on the radio has the opportunity to reach consumers at home, in their cars, and even at work. A final advantage of radio advertisements, particularly for team brands, is that advertising is typically negotiated into rights fees paid to broadcast the team's games. That is, teams do not have to pay for advertising with the stations that broadcast their games, so the advertisements are much more cost-effective.

Newspapers

Newspapers are a very popular form of local media advertising for several reasons. Similar to what occurs with radio, team brands are often effective at striking sponsorship agreements with newspapers that include advertising space. In addition, the short closing dates of newspapers make them ideal for sport advertisers attempting to convey timely information such as the promotion associated with an upcoming game or the appearance of a star from an opposing team.[80] However, newspapers will face a tremendous challenge to maintaining their readership in the future. Readership may suffer as a consequence of the Internet's ability to deliver up-to-the-minute news and information.

Magazines

Magazines are a form of mass media that team brands do not employ very often. Although magazines can deliver audiences largely defined by their lifestyle,[81] the weekly publication and national-audience reach of magazines lead to a situation that makes them cost prohibitive and less efficient to use than other media, particularly when compared to local television, radio, and newspapers. By contrast, magazine advertisements can be particularly effective for sport brands that sell products nationally. For example, before its first-ever national television campaign, New Balance had risen to prominence by advertising primarily in magazines for runners. This allowed the company to reach a national audience with a specific lifestyle pursuit—running. The superior quality of magazine advertisements is also helpful when the situation is that of a company trying to build a perception of quality for its brand.

Outdoor Advertising

Billboards and mass transit vehicles are also commonly used as advertising media. Typically, these media should be used to reinforce the messages being conveyed through other local advertising vehicles, such as newspapers and television. Given their prominence and visibility to people who are driving or riding by, outdoor ads can be highly effective. In essence, often they are communicating the same message at the same time every day.[82] Think about the person who drives from the suburbs of Atlanta to downtown Atlanta every day. That person will be exposed to the same ad for tickets to Atlanta Thrasher games every day. A particular characteristic of outdoor ads is that they can be very creative in their design. Outdoor advertising does have its inherent drawbacks. For example, the audiences for outdoor ads, other than being called "commuters," are very difficult to segment, so you do not know exactly who is reached with an outdoor advertisement. Similarly, these ads reach only the segment of the population that travels a particular route. In the case of the Thrasher ad, the

Thrashers would have to purchase billboards on all the major highways entering Atlanta if they hoped to reach all the commuters entering the city.

Direct Marketing

Advertising is categorized as direct marketing if

- it is designed to generate a response from the receiver; and/or
- it is designed to generate a request for further information; and/or
- it is designed to generate traffic for the sport brand.[83]

Direct marketing is experiencing a dramatic increase in popularity as compared to the more traditional forms of advertising. This is largely a consequence of advances in technology. The ease with which databases are developed and the sophistication with which they can segment consumers has allowed marketers to become more cost-effective with their advertising expenditures because they know they are reaching a targeted audience.[84] The last time you went to the grocery store, did you present your frequent shopper card to receive a discount on the items that were on sale? If you did, that card served not only to earn you discounts, but also to tell manufacturers how often you're purchasing products in their product category and how much of these products you're purchasing. Sport teams are beginning to capitalize on the availability of databases and the cost-efficiency of building databases full of potential consumers. For example, the fan loyalty cards that are implemented at stadiums and arenas around the country are providing teams with valuable information about anyone who attends a game and chooses to use the card.

Direct marketing typically occurs in three forms—mail, telephone, and Internet. Each of these forms of advertising is addressed elsewhere in the text. Direct mail and direct marketing through the telephone (telemarketing) are discussed in chapter 5. Chapter 12 is a thorough discussion of the use of the Internet as an advertising and marketing medium.

Making the Final Decision

Now that we have discussed the various forms of media available to the sport marketer, the question becomes, how do we choose the best combination of media to communicate our message? Several guidelines are typically employed. First, advertising decisions are often made based on the potential *reach* of the medium. For example, if the Detroit Shock are marketing season tickets at the Palace at Auburn Hills, Michigan, they will be targeting both corporations and families. If you were working for the Shock and were concerned about the reach of the various media, you would try to determine what percentage of your target market each medium reaches. Obviously, you would like to reach 100% of your target market, but that is rarely possible. Frequency often goes hand in hand with reach;[85] for, in addition to what percentage of potential Shock season ticket holders you are reaching, you must think about how often you are communicating with them. Similarly, the time the advertisement is run is important. The Shock would not want their ads for season tickets to be broadcast on the radio during work hours. Instead, they would prefer to have the advertisements broadcast during the rush hour or evening hours so as to optimally communicate with their target audience. In the end, the most effective strategic brand communications campaign will integrate the various forms of media so as to achieve optimal reach and frequency. The final factor that will undoubtedly influence the decision-making process is the advertising budget. Very often, the strategic brand communications plan will have to be modified because the sport brand does not have enough money for the ideal implementation. This is where frequency and reach become particularly important as decision rules for placing advertisements.

Step 6: Evaluating Advertising Effectiveness

As we stated in outlining Step 2, "Setting Objectives," an effective objective can be evaluated. For the sixth and most important phase, it is essential to have objectives that can be assessed, because this sixth step provides important information about the effectiveness of the advertising efforts. But first, we need a reliable method of evaluation. As an example, think about the NFL "Feel the Power" advertising campaign. On the basis of the tag line, we can assume that the NFL is attempting to build a brand association around the delivery of the product by highlighting the force and power involved in professional football. This certainly differentiates football from other sports as well as from other entertainment offerings. How would the NFL go about assessing the effectiveness of this advertisement?

Three general methods are used to evaluate the effectiveness of advertising. The first method is to evaluate the impact of the advertising on sales. In the case of the "Feel the Power" campaign, the NFL could look at game attendance, television ratings, and merchandise purchases as a means of measuring whether sales of the NFL product had increased. This method has some problems, though. First, there may be other factors that led to an increase in sales. For example, the NFL could experience a season in which several of its teams open new stadiums and change head coaches. In this case, it would be hard to separate out the impact of stadium and coaching changes. Therefore, we need to exercise caution using sales as a means of measuring advertising effectiveness. A second method to evaluate the effectiveness of an advertising campaign is to assess the increase in awareness. As discussed earlier, this was the method New Balance used. The third and general measure of advertising effectiveness is attitudes or changes in attitudes. In the case of the "Feel the Power" campaign, the NFL would be interested in determining whether it was successful at creating and triggering the brand association of a powerful game related to product delivery.

This sixth step speaks to the need for market research to understand the effectiveness of the advertising campaign, because we can use this information to affect each step in the advertising process. For example, the NFL might find out that people perceive the NHL to be more "powerful," something not anticipated in the situational analysis (Step 1). This might cause the NFL to reevaluate its positioning to determine whether such a campaign should continue. Alternatively, the NFL might find out that viewership increased significantly, so much so that it is necessary to amend the objectives (Step 2) to include a projection of an even more significant ratings jump. These examples suggest how the evaluation of the advertising campaign can affect each of the five steps in the strategic brand communications process.

Managing the Process: The Advertising Agency

Although some sport brands create their own advertising and choose the venues for dissemination of the advertising message, most sport brands rely heavily on advertising agencies. So, what is the best approach? To make such a decision, it is important to review the role of the advertising agency as well as the advantages and disadvantages of hiring an advertising agency.

An advertising agency typically performs three functions. First, it assesses the needs, desires, and objectives of the client and "pitches" a creative advertising program that will help achieve the objectives. In selecting an agency, organizations should be sure that the agency is one that adopts a strategic brand communications perspective. For example, advertising agency Weiden & Kennedy created the "Just Do It" advertising campaign for Nike. Secondly, the advertising agency often provides recommendations about what media to use to implement the brand communications campaign. Weiden & Kennedy suggested and then purchased time on national television and in magazines to communicate the "Just Do It" positioning. The third function that advertising agencies often perform is to provide marketing research, particularly when making decisions regarding where to place advertisements. Advertising agencies typically have access to, and base their decisions on, media research that helps illuminate the best ways to reach a particular target market.

There are several advantages to using an advertising agency. Most importantly, these agencies possess a wealth of experience in creating and placing advertisements. You probably don't think it's a coincidence that ESPN hired Weiden & Kennedy to create a new advertising campaign for them in the late 1990s. Undoubtedly ESPN decision-makers chose Weiden & Kennedy on the basis of the agency's experience and proven track record. A second advantage of using an advertising agency is that advertising agencies have many more advertising resources that can be utilized in creating an advertising campaign, such as creative *divisions*. This means that it will not be the responsibility of only one person to figure out the best way to deliver the message; rather, the responsibility will be assumed by a group of people assigned to the account. It is much cheaper for a sport organization to hire an advertising agency than to hire an entire group of people to work on creating an advertising campaign. Thus, the third advantage of using an advertising agency is cost-effectiveness. A final advantage is that an advertising agency provides a perspective from outside of the organization. As consultants, the agency personnel operate as separate from the sport brand and can highlight problems or challenges.

However, there are also several disadvantages to using an advertising agency. First and foremost, an advertising agency may not possess the necessary knowledge of the sport industry to construct ads that will appeal to sport consumers.[86] Remember, the sport product is different from the traditional mainstream consumer product. The 13 brand associations that can be triggered by the sport product exemplify this fact perfectly. Thus, it is important that the advertising agency understand what the sport product is and how it differs from products in other industries for which the agency has worked in the past. A second drawback of using an advertising agency relates to the way advertising agencies typically make money. The most popular form of compensation for advertising agencies is the fixed-commission method. Under this method, the agency receives a commission (usually 15%) from the media in which advertisements are placed. In addition, advertising agencies usually mark up the media cost when billing clients.[87] Given this structure, it behooves the advertising agency to place ads in the most expensive medium, which is invariably television. Thus, a significant drawback with an agency may be a proclivity to use television above all other media in an effort to generate more revenue for the agency.

Postgame Wrap-Up

Advertising should be used to support the sales activities of the sport organization. However, given the number of advertising messages that the average person is exposed to daily, it is a challenge to create an effective advertising campaign. Ultimately, the advertising campaign must break through the clutter to reach and communicate with the consumer. In order to realize success in advertising, sport marketers must always remember that advertising is really a two-way process. That is, the organization is sending messages to the consumer or prospective consumer, who then—if the campaign is effective—receives and returns the message in some form (increased awareness, enhanced image, increased purchasing, etc.).

To optimize the effectiveness of an advertising campaign, sport marketers should view the campaign in terms of strategic brand communications. They must recognize all of the various ways in which the organization communicates with target markets and strive to accomplish several objectives. The organization should strive to be consistent, both across communication media and over time, in order to fully realize the benefits of advertising. In addition, the advertising message must be crafted to evoke positive associations with the sport brand being marketed.

In order to achieve these objectives, sport marketers need to attend to a six-step cyclical process for developing strategic brand communications campaigns. The process begins with a situational analysis that leads to the setting of objectives for the campaign. Once the objectives are set, the markets to be targeted are selected and the advertising message is crafted. Most importantly, the message is designed to evoke, create, or reinforce positive mental associations about the sport organization in the minds of consumers. Next, the media for communicating the message are selected. The final step, evaluation, is often overlooked because it takes both time and money and because there is no easy way to measure how much impact a branding campaign has on consumers. Therefore, organizations should invest energy in evaluation and should employ a variety of methods in an ongoing process to evaluate the effectiveness of any strategic brand communications campaign.

Discussion Items

1. In what ways does a sport organization attempt to affect consumers through advertising?
2. Why is it so important for an advertising campaign to be strategic?
3. What is the difference between strategic brand communications and advertising? Why is strategic brand communications recommended?
4. What is a brand association? Why are brand associations important to advertising?
5. What are some brand associations that can be triggered by sport advertising?
6. Identify and describe the six steps to a strategic brand communications campaign.
7. What are the pros and cons of hiring an advertising agency?

Learning Enrichment Activities

1. Watch a sporting event on television over the next few days. During that sporting event, determine whether one or both teams have an advertising tag line. If they have tag lines (or if one of them does), answer the following questions:
   a. Does it evoke a positive brand association with the event?
   b. Does the message appear to be durable over time, or does it seem to be specific to this particular year or season?
   c. Discuss how you might go about evaluating the effectiveness of the advertising campaign.

2. Visit the Web sites of the NBA, NHL, MLB and NFL. Answer the following questions:

   a. What messages are being communicated on each Web site?

   b. Do the Web sites communicate different brand associations about each league?

3. Call the offices of your favorite team or event and request that the organization send you a media guide, ticket brochure, and magnet schedule. When you receive the pieces in the mail, answer the following questions:

   a. Are the messages being communicated among the various pieces consistent with one another?

   b. Are the visual images (color, font, slogans) consistent across the three different pieces?

Supplying and Manufacturing Media Content

chapter objectives

1. Understand and appreciate the sport promotion specialist's role as a supplier of media content and a manufacturer of media content

2. Understand the servicing needs of the two distinct media customer groups: media decision-makers and media consumers

3. Gain an understanding of how to construct a media plan incorporating tactics that target media decision-makers and media consumers

4. Distinguish between a media-rights buy and a media-time buy

5. Understand and apply creativity within the pursuit of publicity

key terms

supply-side media promotion	media
manufactured media	communication channel
media decision-makers	content supplier
media consumers	press agentry

Pregame Introductions

The traditional idea of media promotions, most frequently referred to as media relations, has generally involved providing members of the media supply chain with the basic ingredients from which to manufacture content. Such **supply-side media promotion** endeavors have generally facilitated the production of special-interest feature stories on star athletes, statistical updates for television or radio broadcast crews, or interesting quotes from a coach to supplement a postgame interview.

However, the dynamics of sport-related media promotions have changed dramatically of late. For instance, in 2000, the NBA and USA Networks formed a broad media, e-commerce, and services partnership that will be delivered through USA's Electronic Commerce and Services unit, NBA.com, NBA.com TV, and other USA and NBA divisions. The multichannel, multiyear integrated media agreement provides cross-marketing, commerce, and service initiatives centered on the NBA Store at NBA.com. Aspects of the agreement include airing of NBA programs and specials by Home Shopping Network, delivery of services for NBA customers by Home Shopping Network Fulfillment, and integration of merchandise sales and ticket purchases by Ticketmaster. USA Network television stations in Miami, Dallas, and Atlanta also broadcast local NBA games, while USA Films' home entertainment division will be the exclusive distributor of NBA videos.[1]

As this example reveals, not only has the volume of communication media available for content placement significantly expanded within the past decade to include specialty print publications, cable television, and a plethora of Internet sources, but so also have the methods that sport organizations use to pursue medium procurement. In addition to *supplying* media outlets with basic contents such as press releases, fact sheets, and game notes from which media content is produced, sport organizations of all dimensions, seeking to ensure and manipulate exposure in print as well as electronic media, have chosen to assume responsibility for **manufactured media** through the dissemination of self-produced content. Thus, the bulk of this chapter addresses these two fundamental components of media promotion. Additionally, the sport organization possessing media content of significant commercial value may pursue media retailing, or the selling of media content to print as well as electronic media.

Unfortunately, the complexity of media promotions does not end here. It is a challenge for the sport promotion specialist, as a member of the organizational promotion team, to deal effectively with two different customer groups, **media decision-makers** and **media consumers,** whose attention and subsequent consumption are critical to the effectiveness of a promotion plan. The media decision-makers are individuals who ultimately determine what content is included in the media. Members of this powerful group include any and all of the following: beat reporters, assignment editors, sports directors, producers, and media outlet executives and owners. The media consumer group consists of people who are likely to read, view, or listen to the sport organization's media content. The sport promotion specialist should not limit the design of a media plan to media decision-makers but also incorporate tactics for attracting and maintaining the attention of media consumers.

In this chapter, **media** (plural for *medium*) refers to *a channel or system of communication, information, or entertainment in which content decisions are controlled by the* **communication channel** *or system.* We use this definition primarily to distinguish the media discussed in this chapter from the Internet, which is addressed in chapter 12. The Internet is an increasingly valuable promotional medium and a communication source whose content decisions are not exclusively governed by a controlling body (e.g., producers) external to the **content supplier.**

Media Suppliers: The Traditional Media Promotion Specialty

The fundamental intent of supply-side media promotion is to generate organizational publicity. Publicity is considered to be any nonpersonal stimulation of demand for a product, service, or business unit as a result of supplying commercially significant news to a published medium or obtaining favorable presentation on radio, television, or stage that was not directly paid for by the supplier. Critical to this definition is the element that publicity is "not paid for," which often implies that publicity is free or absent any cost, as opposed to advertising, which is typically considered to be a paid form of presentation of ideas, goods, or services.

As a form of promotion, publicity offers a number of distinct advantages over companion promotion mix components. Promotional information appearing in publicity (news article) format tends to stimulate higher levels of attention and retention of message content than advertising does for two reasons: people reading or hearing an engaging story are much less likely to be distracted or interrupted, and exposure is more likely to be intentional as opposed to incidental. Publicity provides the source an opportunity to tell a story that may include full details of product or service features and benefits, whereas these may not be adequately addressed in an advertisement. Furthermore, research has shown that publicity is generally perceived by consumers as having higher credibility than advertising as it involves the "neutral" opinions of a third-party source.

Another advantage is that consumers generally attribute advertising claims to an external factor, whereas consumers are less likely to question the source's motives from a publicity segment. Lastly, true publicity carries a relatively low cost, as eliminating production and placement costs reduces total cost significantly.[2] Sport teams get "free" daily promotions in a variety of media outlets. In fact, it has been reported that the University of Tennessee at Chattanooga received exposure valued at approximately $22 million from its appearance in the 1997 Sweet Sixteen.[3] We should bear in mind, though, that with the reduction in expense a considerable amount of control is sacrificed.

Unfortunately, the odds of placement are low—only about 10% of all information supplied to media outlets by sport promotion specialists ever gets used.[4] Therefore, Lord and Putrevu recommend that the same degree of promotional creativity be channeled into publicity as is usually reserved for advertising and other more expensive promotional components.[5]

To be effective suppliers of media content, sport promotion specialists need to familiarize themselves with other members of the media supply chain. These include reporters, producers, directors, editors, and webmasters, as well as listeners, readers, viewers, and "surfers." In particular it is important for the sport promotion specialist to be aware of media supply chain members' characteristics and needs. Becoming familiar with the personal characteristics of key supply chain members will necessitate a little research. A database of all primary media contacts should be regularly updated with correct title, surname, spelling, postal and e-mail address, telephone and fax number, and office hours and deadlines, as well as any other information that may enhance the media supplier-manufacturer relationship.

Knowledge about a key member of the supply chain, the media manufacturer's audience, can prove to be powerful. For example, NASCAR significantly increased coverage in *USA Today* by demonstrating that race fan demographic characteristics matched those of the publication's readers. Once the newspaper's editorial staff recognized this link, coverage expanded from a Monday wrap-up of the weekend's races to daily articles and a special Thursday motor sports section mainly about NASCAR racing.[6]

As a sport promotion specialist, you will find it beneficial to have additional information on emerging viewer, listener, or reader behavior patterns and preferences when you approach the media with content or a proposal for a story, series, program, or new format. In fact, "NHL Rules!"—initially aired on ESPN2 in January 2000, using audio, video, and real-time features to explain the action as it occurred on the ice—was created in response to NHL research indicating that viewers wanted more education and information during game telecasts.

The Basic Need of Media Suppliers

The basic need of every media supply chain member is appealing or newsworthy *content*. This means that as a sport promotion specialist you will need to capitalize on the primary incentive of all media supply chain members—enhanced job performance—which results from the availability of quality material. Thus, as already mentioned, you will need to channel the same creative energy into publicity that is often directed toward advertising in order to provide content that media supply chain recipients judge to be valuable. This practice of brokering content is commonly referred to as **press agentry.**

Figure 7.1 lists 20 techniques that sport organizations can use to supply media decision-makers with interesting, newsworthy content.[7] It is important to note that no two techniques are mutually exclusive. In fact, invoking multiple techniques stands a much better chance of sparking content receptivity on the part of media

1. The rivalry (matchup)	11. Controversies
2. New products	12. Speeches
3. Special events	13. Utilizing celebrities
4. Major holidays	14. Ordinary event participation by unusual people
5. Anniversary celebrations	15. Extraordinary events by ordinary people
6. Statistical milestones	16. The stunt
7. Providing advice	17. The roundup
8. Issuing a statement	18. Creating stars
9. Polls and forecasts	19. Contests and elections
10. Announcing an award	20. Current news event tie-ins

Figure 7.1 Twenty techniques for creating news.

"The Dream Job: Sports Publicity, Promotion, and Marketing" Melvin Helitzer, 1999 (Athens, OH: University Sports Press).

personnel and in turn maximizing press coverage. To illustrate this point, figure 7.2 displays a number of examples of the NFL's use of multiple techniques to generate an abundance of media coverage for Super Bowl XXXIV, held in Atlanta, Georgia, on January 30, 2000. An example such as this also illustrates the merits of integrated marketing communication, as collaborative efforts among various units within the NFL provided a seamless flow of interesting information to, and through, the media supply chain.

To attempt to maximize media coverage, sport promotion specialists should conduct a thorough assessment of the potential content generators that exist within the organization. This assessment should involve all elements from which a story could be built as listed in figure 7.1. Equally important is uncovering content that is

Technique	Super Bowl XXXIV: St. Louis Rams vs. Tennessee Titans
1. The rivalry	A rematch: The game pits two teams who met during regular season
2. New products	By virtue of franchise relocation, neither team had appeared in the Super Bowl representing its current home market (the Titans, formerly the Houston Oilers were in fact making their first Super Bowl appearance)
3. Special events	NFL Experience segments appeared on CNN; national anthem singer Faith Hill is a die-hard Titans fan (*USA Today*); pregame performer Tina Turner, born in Tennessee, resides in St. Louis
4. Major holidays	The Super Bowl has emerged as a holiday! One of the highest-volume days for beer and snack food consumption
5. Anniversary celebrations	Former participating players, coaches participate in coin toss
6. Statistical milestones	Several records set, including passing yardage (Kurt Warner)
7. Providing advice	ABC's four-hour pregame show
8. Issuing a statement	Daily interview sessions with players and coaches
9. Polls and forecasts	NFL.com, winning team predictions, office pools
10. Announcing an award	Chris Carter of Minnesota named NFL Man of the Year, Hall of Fame inductees
11. Controversies	The cost of a Super Bowl ad on ABC, the weather
12. Speeches	Commissioner's State of the Game Address
13. Utilizing celebrities	See #3
14. Ordinary event participation by unusual people	There is no ordinary event here
15. Extraordinary events by ordinary people	Former stock boy Kurt Warner earns MVP honors
16. The stunt	No need at this stage
17. The roundup	Sunday night and the Monday after
18. Creating stars	Daily profiles and interviews with formerly unknown players
19. Contests and elections	Hershey's Million Dollar Kick; NFL Hall of Fame election results released with several former Super Bowl heroes inducted, including Joe Montana
20. Current news event tie-ins	Major ice storm cripples Atlanta, drawing attention from all media sources

Figure 7.2 Application of the 20 techniques for creating news applied to Super Bowl XXXIV.

not limited to the sport section, as sport can provide human-interest, business, and entertainment content. A story about the local professional sport franchise's community relations project, for example, provides content for the Metro or Neighbors section of the newspaper, as when the Washington Freedom players (Women's United Soccer Association) served as fashion models at a fund-raiser for multiple sclerosis. An executive profile or new customer service campaign may provide content for the Business section. Likewise, a novel promotional incentive may fit into the Entertainment section, as when the Phoenix Mercury players (WNBA) waited on tables at a local restaurant for a fund-raising spaghetti night to aid the Mercury charities. Although a large proportion of sport content is perishable, the activities just described have an extended shelf life, giving the media some flexibility in placement. The sky virtually is the limit for brokering media content.

Fulfilling Supply-Side Needs

The sport promotion specialist has two basic responsibilities associated with fulfilling the needs of supply-side media representatives. As previously mentioned, the first responsibility is to garner the interest of the media through the provision of attractive, newsworthy content. Secondly, it is imperative for the sport promotion specialist to ensure that members of the press corps are provided quality service.

Typically, as a sport promotion specialist you can use any combination of the following media supply methods to attract media attention and facilitate content distribution:

Direct contact

Press release, fact sheet

Press conference

Statistical or results management

Photography

Interviews

Product placement

Event-site broadcast remotes

Direct Contact

In anticipation of the event being promoted, the sport promotion specialist will schedule a number of initiatives aimed at facilitating direct contact with members of the press.

Personal Contact

Research conducted among urban newspaper, television, and radio sports editors and directors revealed that their preference is to receive content ideas from organizations through personal contact. The respondents viewed face-to-face interaction as helpful, but believed that a phone call was often just as effective if an organization wished to plant a story idea. Newspaper representatives indicated that consistent interaction with a beat reporter or assignment editor two to three times a week would maximize the potential for weekly press coverage. Content most desirable among television and radio sports directors related to athlete, not team, accomplishments.[8] As a sport promotion specialist you may find it most useful to develop a schedule for establishing regular contact dates and times with members of the press corps.

Media Day

Prior to the start of a season, series, game, or event, the hosting organization should stage a session in which members of the media can interact with participants. This session enables the media to collect all pre-event, preseason organizationally supplied resources for content production as well as gathering participant quotes and photographs. Unquestionably the flagship of all media days is that hosted by the NFL during Super Bowl week. With participating players from both teams required to be available for comment, these sessions typically become a media frenzy resulting in trivial, even silly, interview questions. In order to facilitate a more meaningful interview, the sport promotion specialist may wish to provide media representatives a short list of relevant questions to ask the athletes. The supplied quotes and photos tend to dominate sports press coverage for the entire week leading up to the event, generating valuable public exposure, enhancing public attention, and ultimately drawing millions of viewers and listeners to the game broadcast.

Media Tours

Frequently, professional and major college sport teams that draw a regional audience schedule preseason media tours with designated stops in prime media markets. These sessions are generally open to the public and include interviews with coaches, players, and management. Media from these satellite markets are able to compile content supplies to use throughout the season.

Press Releases and Fact Sheets

The electronic age appears to have changed many of the rules that previously governed press relations. The online access to information facilitates the ability of the media to manufacture content at a pace unheard of in the days before the computer. However, notification of a newsworthy event or occurrence has retained its old format. While in many instances the press release has given way to the fact sheet, this is a change in format only; the essential contents remain the same. The press release contains the basic information associated with the promoted activity. The difference is that the press release (figure 7.3) presents the contents in narrative fashion whereas the fact sheet presents only the key points, allowing recipients to construct the material that will tell the story and put the facts in context.

Press releases, of greatest value to understaffed media recipients, typically comprise three brief double-spaced paragraphs written in an "inverted pyramid" format, with the most important information in the lead paragraph (including who, what, when, where, and why). A fact sheet typically consists of a series of bullet points communicating the same information. Each should appear on content supplier letterhead, with 2-inch margins top and bottom, identification of a supplier contact person, and end sign (###) indicating the conclusion of the message (figur e 7.4).[9] We encourage readers who wish to see additional examples to visit **ottawasenators.com** to review all the club press releases, which are archived by date of distribution.

Obviously, it is of greatest importance that all content be complete and accurate. Frequently the release is the initial contact the organization has with the media regarding a particular event or is an invitation to additional activities (e.g., press conference). As such, a press release is of little value if it becomes necessary to issue a second release because of errors or omissions in the first draft, while also damaging the content supplier's credibility. A thorough proofread of all material is absolutely necessary.

PHILADELPHIA WOMEN'S BASKETBALL

FOR IMMEDIATE RELEASE:

2000 NCAA WOMEN'S FINAL FOUR TO GENERATE $25 MILLION FOR CITY OF PHILADELPHIA

PHILADELPHIA (March 27, 2000) - The 2000 NCAA Women's Final Four Championship, to be held Friday, March 31 and Sunday, April 2, at the First Union Center in Philadelphia, is expected to draw over 40,000 participants, coaches and fans, producing a projected $25 million economic impact for the host city.

The Philadelphia Sports Congress released an estimated economic impact of $25 million for the 2000 NCAA Women's Final Four. The $25 million figure includes expenditures by an anticipated 40,000 fans and Women's Basketball Coaches Association members while in Philadelphia during the 2000 NCAA Women's Final Four Championship Week March 27-April 2, 2000. Expenditures represent spending on hotels (15,000 total room nights), restaurants, entertainment and shopping.

"This major collegiate sporting event has the power to electrify the region and elevate the sport to unprecedented levels. Philadelphia is an exceptional host city and residents and tourists will enjoy the Final Four and the citywide Championship Week events and activities," said Cathy Andruzzi, executive director, PWB 2000, the local organizing committee for the 2000 NCAA Women's Final Four.

Championship Week events, celebrations designed to expand and extend the excitement of the NCAA Women's Final Four throughout the community, include Hoop City, an NCAA fan event at the Pennsylvania Convention Center; a free Open Practice and autograph session at the First Union Center; the NCAA YES (Youth Education through Sports) Clinics at five area locations; and PWB Fan Fare 2000, a free fan festival at the Grand Hall of the Pennsylvania Convention Center, with activities, programs and entertainment for sports fans of all ages. PWB Fan Fare 2000 will feature an inspiring exhibit honoring local legends in women's basketball.

Beyond the thousands of national visitors the event will bring to Philadelphia, the city will receive national media exposure via ESPN. In 1999, the NCAA Women's Final Four Championship game received a 4.3 rating, an ESPN record for a women's basketball game. The game was watched by an average of 3.2 million homes, the second biggest audience for an ESPN college basketball game - men's or women's - ever.

"We are working with Philadelphia Women's Basketball 2000 to see that Final Four fans have a great time while they are here and want to come back," said Larry Needle, executive director of the Philadelphia Sports Congress. "Philadelphia has become a tremendous destination for major sporting events and we expect that the Women's Final Four will continue that legacy."

The NCAA Women's Final Four is a highly coveted event, as cities compete for the opportunity to host the nationally-recognized championship. Philadelphia was awarded the 2000 NCAA Women's Final Four in 1995. The 2000 NCAA Women's Final Four will mark the first time the Women's Final Four will be hosted by a city in the northeast United States. San Jose hosted last year's event.

Philadelphia Women's Basketball 2000, a non-profit organization, was created in 1998 to ensure the successful planning and implementation of the 2000 NCAA Women's Final Four in the City of Philadelphia, and to celebrate Philadelphia as the hosting site. The 2000 NCAA Women's Final Four Championship Week, March 27-April 2, culminates with the semifinal games on Friday, March 31 and the championship game on Sunday, April 2.

PWB 2000 is co-chaired by Rosemarie B. Greco, principal, GRECOventures; and G. Fred DiBona, Jr., president-ceo, Independence Blue Cross. The NCAA Women's Final Four will serve as a platform for PWB 2000 to enhance athletic opportunities for girls; to grow women's sports in the region; and to expand the growing reputation of Philadelphia as an exceptional sponsoring city.

For more information on PWB 2000 and the 2000 NCAA Women's Final Four, call the information hotline at (215) 985-6500 or visit our website at www.pwb2000.org.

#PWB2000#

CONTACT: Laura Loro / PWB 2000
             (215) 985-7550 / lauraloro@aol.com

             Danielle Cohn / PCVB
             (215) 636-3320 / danic@pcvb.org

Figure 7.3 This press release for Philadelphia Women's Basketball provides information about an upcoming event, as well as contact information.

"Reprinted with the permission of the NCAA. All rights reserved. 2001."

1. Double-space content on 8.5-by-11-inch paper using only one side of each sheet.
2. Side margins should be 1 inch and top and bottom 2 inches.
3. The supplier's name, address, and contact information should appear on the release.
4. A supplier contact person should be identified.
5. "For Immediate Release" should appear at the top unless the release is describing future events or quotes.
6. Arrange the material in descending order of importance (inverted pyramid) in order to facilitate editorial decisions while still presenting critical information.
7. Include the 5 Ws (who, what, when, where, and why) within the first paragraph.
8. Utilize quotes from key personalities whenever possible.
9. Brevity is key; sentences should not exceed 17 words, and paragraphs should be 2-3 sentences.
10. Number all pages at the top, with the word "More" appearing at the bottom of any incomplete page.
11. Mark the release's conclusion with a series of circled "###" or "End."

Figure 7.4 Standard press release criteria.

Reprinted, by permission, from B.G. Pitts and D.K. Stotlar, 1996, *Fundamentals of sport marketing* (Morgantown, WV: Fitness Information Technology).

Press Conference

A press conference is an ideal forum for disseminating content to a large number of media supply chain members in one step. But if you put on a press conference without the proper forethought and preparation, the promotional value of a press conference can rapidly decrease.

Typically, you will distribute media representative invitations via a press release, allowing all outlets equal access and privileges. The invitation should capture the essence of the press conference without providing all the details and thus reducing the need for people to come. Figure 7.5 presents a press conference checklist that the sport promotion specialist can use as a guide for adequately preparing for and later assessing press conferences.[10]

We caution sport promotion specialists against scheduling press conferences that are not really necessary. Figure 7.6 contains a list of the acceptable reasons for calling a press conference.[11] Unnecessarily organizing a press conference tends to stress the relations with members of the press media supply chain and may result in a boomerang effect for the media content supplier.

From a promotional perspective, it is critical that the atmosphere at a press conference present the appropriate image of the content supplier. The facility, and most importantly podium front and backdrop, should prominently display the media content supplier's logo, facilitating significant media exposure. When appropriate, speakers should also wear content supplier-logoed apparel, preferably a cap or lapel pin for head-shot exposure. They should be well prepared with respect to their comments and answers to potential questions. In fact, all comments, and where possible questions, should be scripted, if not rehearsed. Much like a political speech writer, the sport promotion specialist may wish to draft all information to be delivered by the speaker and then schedule a briefing with the speaker shortly before the press conference. Bear in mind that the press seeks usable, brief, sound bites that do not always represent the entire content supplied.

A "master of ceremonies" should be appointed to manage the conference; this is typically the media relations specialist, who should be familiar with all parties representing the content supplier and all attending members of the press corps. It is critical for this person to monitor the session from start to finish, introducing the speakers and fielding questions from the audience. To enhance the question-and-answer session, it is highly advisable for a "spotter" carrying a wireless microphone to circulate through the audience. This will enable the speaker, as well as audience members, to hear the questions better.

Press corps as well as general public (if the press conference is open to the public) check-in procedures should be established. Sport promotion staff assisting with the check-in should obtain proper identification from all parties and collect names and addresses in order to build a database of interested media and consumers.

This press conference announcing the (now defunct) Memphis XFL franchise prominently displays the XFL logo.

Press Conference Checklist

Value

—— Is the story important?

—— Can the story be released in any better fashion?

—— Are all releases, bios, and backgrounds double-checked for accuracy?

—— Do you have budget authorization?

Timing

—— Will the principals in the story be available?

—— Before setting a date, did you check calendars for possible conflict?

—— Is the time most convenient to most important media?

Site

—— Is it convenient to media? To participants?

—— Does room have the following facilities?

❑ Space size	❑ Electrical outlets
❑ Lighting	❑ Sound equipment
❑ Parking	❑ Furniture
❑ Attractive walls	❑ Refreshment area
❑ No outside noise	❑ Temperature control
❑ Reasonable costs	❑ Security
❑ Projection room	❑ Fire exits
❑ Telephones	❑ Service personnel
❑ Computers	❑ Paper supplies

Setting up facilities (one hour in advance)

—— Podium height and lighting

—— PA system: microphone and speaker

—— Blackboard, easel, screen, and projectors

—— Lectern brackets for press microphones

—— Organization logo displayed

—— Posters, graphics, and artwork

—— Chairs and table for principals

—— Water, glasses for speakers

—— Sufficient chairs for reporters

—— Designated place for video cameras

—— House photographer and assignments

—— Outside directional signs for room location

—— Floor microphones for questions if large room

—— Registration desk or book

—— Press kit or handouts at registration desk

—— Full staff at entry door to greet individuals

—— Technical service operator for all equipment

Invitations

____ Were media lists reviewed and updated?

____ Were editors queried by telephone, mail, or fax?

____ If invitations by mail, were reminder calls made 4-6 hours in advance?

____ Directions to site; parking arrangements

Spokespersons

____ Approval of agenda

____ Rehearsal of anticipated Q & A session

____ Availability of exhibits and marking equipment

____ Advance agreement on participants' order and time

____ Agreement on master of ceremonies opening and closing

____ Table signs with names of participants

____ Lapel badges, if necessary

____ Staff briefing

____ Backup spokespersons

____ Availability of sports information director and staff

Review of operation

____ Did conference start promptly?

____ Did it drag on too long?

____ Were all questions answered?

____ What promises were made for follow-up details?

Follow-up

____ Was post conference review conducted with staff?

____ Were press requests for additional information or material fulfilled?

____ Were you available in person and by phone for last-minute questions and requests?

____ Were thank-you notes sent to specific reporters?

____ Were copies of all clips and tapes sent to management?

Figure 7.5 This checklist is a good tool to use to determine if you're ready for a press conference.

"The Dream Job: Sports Publicity, Promotion, and Marketing" Melvin Helitzer, 1999 (Athens, OH: University Sports Press).

1. A major change in personnel including players, coach, owners, or management
2. Scheduling of an important event such as a title bout, championship game, or interstate rivalry
3. A change in facility location or name
4. Introduction of a new or revised product such as new uniforms or logo
5. Presentation or display of award
6. Announcement of a new rule or policy
7. Announcement of a major sponsor/partnership agreement
8. Announcement of an infraction or rule violation

Figure 7.6 Valid reasons for calling a press conference.

"The Dream Job: Sports Publicity, Promotion, and Marketing" Melvin Helitzer, 1999 (Athens, OH: University Sports Press).

Members of the press should be issued proper credentials as well as a packet of materials. A variety of materials should be made available to the media for use in content production. Often members of the media attending a press conference receive elaborate press kits that include a press release or fact sheet along with biographies, photographs, and canned quotes from each of the speakers.

Immediately following the press conference, key individuals should be available for photo opportunities and one-on-one interviews with attending press corps members. If the press conference is scheduled during midday or early evening hours, it is appropriate to provide a meal for the attendees. However, scheduling at other times reduces or eliminates the need to have food available.

Statistics and Results Management and Distribution

Most content in sport, as a statistically rich industry, has sound results management as its foundation. Statistics ranging from current season batting averages to greens hit in regulation not only are vitally important to athletes and coaches but also are of keen interest to sport consumers, therefore serving as ideal content supply for a number of sport media sources. Moreover, statistical results, in the form of box scores, may serve as the primary source of press coverage among high school, small-college, and other less publicized sports, elevating the need for accurate and timely reporting of game or event statistics.

Where possible, all statistical records should be managed electronically, preferably in a format that appropriate media sources can easily access and use. In fact, the electronic age has enabled sport organizations to provide appropriately credentialed press with real-time game or event statistics, thereby increasing content supply chain speed through the communication channel to the end user (the audience). While a multitude of statistical management software packages have been tailored to the demands of each sport, the most popular, Davis found, include StatMan, Hoop Stat, Grid Stat, and Base/Soft Stat.[12]

A press pass identifies members of the media at a press conference.

Reprinted, by permission, from The Southern Conference. © The Southern Conference.

Photography

According to Davis, a media promotions office cannot exist without quality photography.[13] Often included in a press kit, photographs have emerged as a stand-alone content generator. Within print media, pictures are proven attention-engaging devices, attracting the eye more readily than printed text. In fact, Lechner claims that 95% of newspaper readers look at every photo within the selected reading section, with 75% opting to read the photo headline and 50% reading the full photo caption.[14] Perhaps most importantly from a promotional perspective, the combination of a photograph and text has been shown to favorably enhance recall of the message's content.[15] Therefore, wise use of photography in publicity acts as a reinforcement of text content information while adding an element of perceived attractiveness to the message and its source.

Similar to the way statistics are warehoused, photographs of all organizational personnel, facilities, contestants, product lines, and other related entities should be stored in an easily accessed electronic filing system. The files should include a majority of staged or posed photographs, as these types of pictures among print media in publicity formats outnumber action photos almost five to one. Media outlets file these photos for years to use at their own discretion.[16]

Occasionally, the photo may become the story—witness U.S. Women's Soccer World Cup star Brandi Chastain's provocative appearance in *Gear* magazine. The pose caught the attention of the media and launched a media whirl that drew vast attention to Brandi and her teammates. Stories debating the merits of such photos ran in many publications, drawing more attention to the team and its highly skilled performers. As they were the dominant and successful "home" team, the soccer team members were booked before and after the Cup finals for talk shows including David Letterman's Late Show, speaking engagements, and celebrity appearances and were on the covers of several popular press publications.

As a result of the publicity, the women's soccer team took on a unique personality of genuine interest to the consuming public. The media attention sparked interest in soccer among young people, particularly females. In fact, U.S. Youth Soccer, which helps to organize youth leagues across the country, reported a surge in phone inquiries and Web site hits from people requesting information on how to get started playing soccer. Similarly, the Women's Soccer Federation was overwhelmed by the amount of interest directed its way.[17] The campaign successfully attracted a record number of viewers to ABC's telecast of the Cup final, surpassing television audience ratings for the 1999 NBA finals and the World Series.

Interviews

To maximize player, team, event, or product promotion, sport promotion specialists may wish to schedule personal interviews of organizational representatives with print as well as electronic media. While sport lends itself to the spontaneous interview format (as discussed later in relation to the postgame interview), sport promotion specialists arrange most interviews, whether the interviewee is from the team, the event, or the athlete's personal representation agency.

The topic will dictate whether the interview should involve a player, coach, or someone from management; however, a number of basic principles apply whenever you are scheduling and preparing for an interview. Sport promotion specialists have essentially the following five fundamental responsibilities with respect to arranging interviews:[18]

Setting the interview details

Preparing the spokesperson

Aiding the interviewee when necessary

Recording the interview

Honoring requests for additional information

• *Setting the interview details.* The sport promotion specialist is responsible for booking the interview, ensuring the availability of all involved parties, and determining the parameters of discussion. Quite often celebrity publicists and athlete representatives book an interview for their clients but designate certain topics off-limits.

• *Preparing the spokesperson.* The rules shown in figure 7.7 provide an excellent guide to preparing the spokesperson for the interview. It is not unusual for sport organizations to use a media coach to prepare an organizational representative for an interview. This has become quite common among professional sport teams and major college athletic programs as reflected by MLB's three-day off-season career development program, which includes dealing with the media as one of the major issues.[19] In fact, several major colleges in the United States offer athletes course work on dealing with the media. The interviewee should be reminded that the purpose of the interview is to enhance the player, team, or event profile, not damage it. Required reading among all novice interviewees should be Atlanta Braves pitcher John Rocker's interview with *Sports Illustrated* in which

1. Familiarize the spokesperson with the interview format.

2. Rehearse questions anticipated of the interviewer.

3. Look for opportunities to make a point.

4. No "off-the-record" quotes or comments.

5. Dress conservatively.

6. Project enthusiasm.

7. Avoid non-sport issues.

8. Never lie.

Figure 7.7 Rules for interviewee preparation.

"The Dream Job: Sports Publicity, Promotion, and Marketing" Melvin Helitzer, 1999 (Athens, OH: University Sports Press).

Rocker expressed his opinions on a number of topics including New York fans. Rocker's inability to follow rule 7 led to punishment by the press as well as by MLB.

• *Aiding the interviewee when necessary.* From time to time the sport promotion specialist may need to interpret questions or provide additional background information for spokespeople. The globalization of North American professional sport, and for that matter collegiate sport, has increased the need on the part of athletes for assistance during an interview. In fact, it is often necessary for athletes who speak English as a second language to be accompanied by an interpreter. It is also advisable for sport promotion specialists to be prepared with additional information such as statistics and historical data that may support the spokesperson's position when necessary. For instance, in an interview of a local sport commission executive director about the economic impact of a recent women's soccer tournament, the interviewee, who may be most familiar with such figures as the number of out-of-town visitors attracted to the tournament and the total amount of money brought into the community, may depend on the sport promotion specialist for specific information on such issues as data collection and calculation methods.

• *Recording the interview.* For much the same evaluative purpose as videotaping an athletic performance, an interview can be recorded and analyzed at a later date. This enables the interviewee and sport promotion specialist to critique the interview in preparation for future bookings. In fact, the recorded interview may be shelved and used at a later date.

• *Honoring requests for additional information.* Should the interviewer ask for additional content that is not readily available, the sport promotion specialist should respond as quickly as possible to facilitate completion of the interview. Such content may include historical facts and figures; supplementary quotes from coaches, teammates, or management; or possibly an archived photograph or news clip.

Accommodating Media Decision-Makers

Once you know that members of the press will be covering an event, it is time to turn attention toward providing services to those planning to be there. Members of the press deserve the same level of quality service that any other group of patrons does. In fact, one might argue that they deserve better. We look now at several key service-oriented tasks.

Access and Issuance of Press Credentials

Without established protocol, issuing press credentials can easily turn into a nightmare for the sport promotion specialist, as anyone with a pencil or camera is likely to consider herself a member of the press. Depending on demand, a recommended procedure is for the hosting organization to ask that requests for press credentials be made in writing via an application that includes the requester's name, media affiliation, and the assigned press member's event-related responsibilities (reporter, photographer). If it appears that demand will exceed supply, the hosting organization must establish selection criteria. This may include admission based on the determination of preferential status (national vs. local, daily vs. weekly) or seniority. Otherwise, the distribution of credentials may be based on a first-come, first-serve basis. As illustrated in appendix B, the NCAA has clearly defined its policy and screening procedures for those parties requesting credentials for the Women's Final Four. Although it may appear easier to forward a packet of materials to requesting members of the press well in advance of an event, this practice is strongly discouraged. On-site distribution reduces the possibility of loss or misuse of press credentials.

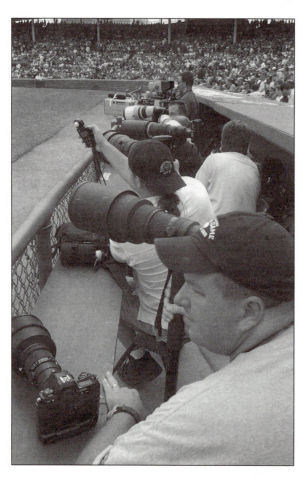

Sport organizations need to exercise control over the distribution of press credentials.

Press Box and Press Row

As determined by the event venue, the press will be supplied appropriate space for simultaneous viewing and reporting of action (figure 7.8). In a process similar to that for credentialing, guidelines need to be established for press box/row seat assignments. Name place cards are commonly used to identify seat assignments (figure 7.9). Prepared resources such as game notes, media guides, and announcements are usually made available in the press box, whereas venues utilizing a press row typically have a pressroom for circulation of additional materials. Statistical updates are circulated through the press box/row as they are prepared. Following significant developments in the action (e.g., scoring, injuries),

Figure 7.8 Press boxes should accommodate members of the media so they can best view and report on the action.

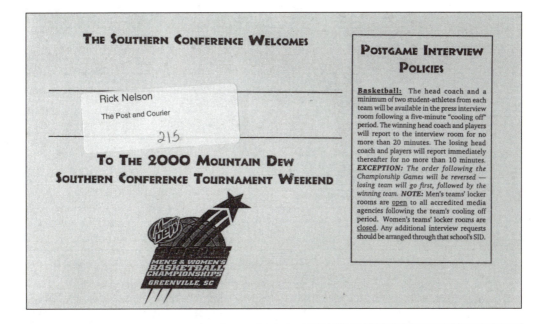

Figure 7.9 Name place cards are a good way to organize a pressroom or press box.
Reprinted, by permission, from The Southern Conference. © The Southern Conference.

oral announcements should be made over a press box loudspeaker and repeated at least once to ensure that the information is recorded accurately.

Pressroom

Occasionally a workroom is made available to the press covering the event. This is common at indoor events where there needs to be a quiet work space with access to a bank of phone lines away from crowd noise. The size of the pressroom varies according to the magnitude of the event. For most events the pressroom resembles a modest-sized office; for major events, expanded structures are typically constructed within conference rooms or ballrooms to accommodate the volume of media representatives. In addition to providing a comfortable work space, including online access, the pressroom serves as a point of distribution for announcements (postgame press conference appearances) and other pertinent materials (e.g., media guides, game notes). Depending on the duration of the event, food may also be sent into the pressroom. Adjacent to the pressroom, or at least within close proximity, an area should be available for conducting postgame interviews.

The Northern European Basketball League media guide is a 60-page booklet chock full of league information for the press.

Reprinted, by permission, from the Northern European Basketball League, *2000 Media guide.*

Game Notes

Before, during, and immediately after an event, members of the press usually seek content supplies, generally referred to as game notes, that help them reconstruct the action. While a significant amount of effort is directed toward pregame supplies, the task is actually never ending, as press covering the event will need periodic updates describing the action as it unfolds.

Pregame highlights typically consist of detailed statistics on participating athletes, starting lineups, roster changes, and injury reports (if applicable), event officials, anticipated weather conditions, potential milestones, and other late-breaking information that may be of keen interest to the media. Pregame notes may be made available in the pressroom, may be included in a press packet, or may be distributed to assigned seats in the press box or press row.

At periodic time points such as following a score, a major injury, the conclusion of each time period, or predetermined stoppage of action, the media should receive updated information including performance statistics. This is of particular interest to members of the broadcast media, who will in turn share the results with the audience. As soon as the event is over, the media should be given a summary of all pertinent information including detailed statistics, scoring summaries, injury reports, and the like. Copies should be available in the pressroom, at the postgame press conference (if applicable), or, for those with tight deadlines, electronically.

Postgame Interviews

Generally speaking, what the media are most interested in are the quotes provided via the postgame interview.[20] After a "cooling-off" period, members of the press should get the opportunity to interview selected event participants at a staged press conference or one-on-one in a predetermined site near the press workroom and locker room. However, in an effort to fully accommodate urgent deadlines and to maximize customer service, most professional sport teams open the locker room to properly credentialed press after the cooling-off period. In preparation for the postgame interview, sport promotion specialists should poll the press to find out which athlete or coaches are in greatest demand. Sending this type of advance notification to the selected parties will serve to expedite the postgame interview process and also allow interviewees to gather their thoughts before meeting with the media.

Product Placement

In the interest of generating exposure, sport organizations often supply *product* (a unique form of content) for inclusion in a variety of visual media sources that need props and personalities. In this case the term "product" refers to any physical object such as apparel or equipment, as well as recognizable personalities such as athletes and coaches. Athletes such as Michael Jordan, Joe Montana, Wayne Gretzky, and Charles Barkley have hosted NBC's "Saturday Night Live." Although their agents typically arrange such appearances, the resulting exposure and favorable audience reaction affect not only the athletes' personal popularity but also that of their team, league, and sport.

More easily controlled by sport promotion specialists is the inclusion of products bearing the logo of a team, event, or league. It is not unusual to see actors in prime-time sitcoms and blockbuster movies wearing sport-logoed apparel. While consumer product companies may be charged hundreds of thousands of dollars for strategic media product placement, sport promotion specialists may be able to secure the same level of exposure through diligent efforts to uncover the favorite team, sport, or event of an actor, director, or producer. Tim Allen's loyalty to the Detroit Lions resulted in significant exposure for the team and for professional football in general during many an episode of ABC's highly rated "Home Improvement," while Bill Cosby's allegiance to his alma mater, Temple, has garnered the institution considerable airtime via product exposure and on-air commentary. Likewise, a sport promotion specialist's familiarity with script or prop requirements may lead to the inclusion of organizationally logoed items, which is highly valuable. Helen Hunt, who starred as Jamie on the NBC hit "Mad About You," often wore Adidas clothing. The well-known three-stripe Adidas logo was visible on much of the leisure clothing she wore throughout the series. While the use of product, or more specifically logos, usually necessitates completion of a licensing agreement between the parties (chapter 9), sport promotion specialists can proactively pursue product placement opportunities that are sure to yield high return on investment.

Event-Site Broadcast Remotes

Frequently, broadcast media personnel, typically those from radio, are open to conducting remote transmissions from the event site. The sport promotion specialist should forward a direct invitation to the sport producer for a pregame or pre-event remote transmission. Remote transmissions may also be secured through a trade agreement with the media source or included in an advertising package purchased by the sport organization or one of its sponsors. An on-site remote may involve a brief interview with an organizational representative or the transmission of a complete show, incorporating the on-air personalities, from the event site. In either case, the sport promotion specialist must anticipate the needs of the technical crew as well as correspondents. These needs may range from generator hookups to food preferences.

Traditionally, the responsibilities of the content supply-side media promotions specialist have included preparing and distributing press releases, fact sheets, game notes, media guides, souvenir game programs (figure 7.10), and media credentials; staging press conferences and interviews; pitching feature story ideas; and managing statistical records and databases. However, as revealed by the listing at the beginning of this section, the role has expanded to include a much broader scope of tasks, placing greater demand on those who work in sport promotion as well as other sport media relations staff members.

Figure 7.10 Souvenir programs provide fans with critical information.

Retailing Media Content: Rights Fee Agreement

For a negotiated fee, a number of major professional, collegiate, and amateur sport organizations supply electronic media networks with broadcast programming content—what is typically referred to as a "media buy." Recently, broadcasters have paid about $30 billion for broadcast rights to major sport properties: $18 billion to the NFL, $6 billion to the NCAA, $2.6 billion to the NBA, $2.4 billion to NASCAR, 1.7 billion to MLB, and $600 million to the NHL.

Decisions about obtaining the rights to broadcast sport programming content are most frequently made on the basis of the size and composition of the anticipated viewing audience. The content supply of the sport organizations just mentioned can attract atypical viewing audiences, generally larger and more diverse than the audiences of non-sport programming; and each of these audiences has considerable appeal to corporate advertisers. Thus, sport programming often provides the media-rights buyer with potential revenue-generating content.

With the exception of NASCAR, major American sport programming has experienced declining ratings over the past few years, and it's unlikely that broadcasters will see a profit in the foreseeable future. However, major sport programming can provide the media-rights buyer with more than just advertising revenue. This is perhaps best illustrated by Fox's decision to purchase NFL broadcast rights in 1994; the network's intent and potential results have implications for both buyers and sellers of media-rights fees. Although it is not known whether Fox, a relatively new entrant into the American television broadcast industry, has generated or will generate a profit from this media-rights buy, it is certain that the purchase gave the network instant credibility and cross-promotional opportunities. The network's initial, albeit expensive, foray into major sport broadcasting sent an immediate message to consumers and competitors alike that Fox was a legitimate player in the American broadcast arena. Additionally, Fox can use the sport content for self-promotion purposes as the supplied sport content becomes a vehicle for attracting and informing the sport content audience of regularly scheduled Fox programming, thereby potentially raising the network's total viewership.

Sport promotion specialists who wish to secure a media-rights agreement will find it imperative to generate existing or potential viewership information, including current or projected broadcast ratings and audience profiling data. Such information is typically assessed periodically by local and/or national rating services. The rating represents the percentage of television households within a selected market that are tuned in to a particular program. For instance, Super Bowl XXXIV garnered a rating of 43, which indicates that 43% of all surveyed U.S. households were tuned in to watch the game (table 7.1).[21] Each rating point represents 1% of the nation's households or approximately 1,008,000 homes. Another figure that is important to the broadcasting industry is a program's share, which is the percentage of household television sets in operation that are tuned in to a particular program. The share for Super Bowl XXXIV was reported to be 62; this meant that 62% of all television sets in use during the Super Bowl were tuned in to the game. The rating service can further stratify the data to reveal viewing habits among audiences with various demographic characteristics such as age, sex, income, gender, and geographic location.[22]

Another recommendation is that sport promotion specialists harboring appealing broadcast content inform the media-rights purchaser of the cumulative benefits to be derived from the partnership. The rapidly evolving electronic broadcast industry may yield future opportunity for a media-rights buyer demonstrating a strong interest in building a business relationship with a sport organization. For example, in an unprecedented move, NBC acquired the rights to the Olympic Games through 2008, enabling the network to block competitors from Olympic content supply, strategically plan content production, and assemble global broadcast partnerships with cable and Internet providers.

Additionally, the supply of media contents via the fulfillment of a rights fee agreement does not relieve the rights holder's sport promotion specialist of his responsibility to provide proper service. The provision of service-related materials

Treat the Media As Any Other Customer

Kevin Paul Dupont of the *Boston Globe* has written that NHL ratings will not increase until there is a monumental cultural shift among owners and players aimed at making the athletes more accessible to the media during their showcase event, the Stanley Cup. If the league and the players don't do their best to market the sport but instead continue to equate media coverage with a root canal, even the low ratings will atrophy and the major news outlets, print and electronic, ultimately will ignore the sport.[23]

Table 7.1   National and Cable Nielsen Ratings for Selected Sport Events Super Bowl Weekend, 2000

Event	Date	Net	Time	Rating/Share
NCAA men's basketball (KY-MIA)	1/29	CBS	1:00-3:00 pm	1.5/4
PGA: Phoenix Open—3rd round	1/29	CBS	3:00-6:00 pm	1.7/4
T & F: Golden Spike Tour	1/29	NBC	2:30-3:30 pm	1.3/3
"NBA Showtime"	1/29	NBC	3:30-4:00 pm	1.5/4
"NBA on NBC" (regional)	1/29	NBC	4:00-6:30 pm	3.0/7
"NBA on NBC" (regional)	1/29	NBC	6:30-9:00 pm	3.1/6
Super Bowl Pregame	1/30	ABC	2:00-5:00 pm	7.2/15
Super Bowl Kickoff	1/30	ABC	5:00-6:26 pm	21.3/38
Super Bowl XXXIV	1/30	ABC	6:26-10:15 pm	43.3/63
NCAA men's basketball (regional)	1/30	CBS	1:00-3:00 pm	1.5/4
PGA: Phoenix Open—4th round	1/30	CBS	3:00-6:00 pm	2.9/6
College football All-Star	1/30	Fox	noon-1:00 pm	1.8/5
All-Madden team	1/30	Fox	1:00-2:00 pm	2.8/7
NBA (Kings-Knicks)	1/30	NBC	noon-2:30 pm	3.1/8
NBA (Lakers-Rockets)	1/30	NBC	2:30-5:00 pm	4.2/9
Northface Expeditions	1/30	NBC	5:00-6:00 pm	2.2/4

Reprinted, by permission, from The Sports Business Daily, February 4, 2000. © The Sports Business Daily.

such as media guides, press kits, and game notes is equally important when one is working with media-rights holders. This was apparent during a lopsided preseason Monday Night Football telecast when color analyst Dan Fouts told play-by-play man Al Michaels, "It's amazing what information you can find in this team media guide when looking for something to talk about at a time like this."

Unfortunately, not all sport organizations share the attractiveness of Olympic or NFL programming and thus are not actively pursued by media-rights buyers for content supply. Similarly, not all sport organizations are the beneficiaries of regular press coverage, and those that are not likewise experience limited acceptance of content supplied to media decision-makers. Furthermore, broadcasters and sport organizations alike have found effective alternatives to the typical media-rights buy arrangements. Hence, the notion of content manufacturing has emerged as a means of fulfilling the interests of each party in the media supply chain.

Sport Content Manufacturing

While the intent in supplying media decision-makers is to provide the basis for potential media exposure, the purpose of content manufacturing is to ensure media exposure. Although media companies, particularly broadcast networks, have paid dearly for the entitlement to carry supplied sport content, it has become more and more usual for the media companies to assume the role of rights holder and thus take on the role of a manufacturer through sport property ownership.

Ownership

The presence of companies with media interests within the ranks of professional sport franchise ownership has recently become commonplace. America Online's recent corporate acquisition of Time Warner, whose assets include Atlanta's Braves (MLB), Hawks (NBA), and Thrashers (NHL), assures the Internet provider/communications company of the availability of sport content. Similarly, Fox's purchase of the Los Angeles Dodgers and Disney's ownership of Anaheim's Angels (MLB) and Mighty Ducks (NHL), as well as the equity position held by cable company Comcast with several Philadelphia sport franchises, reflect the new order of owners within team sport ownership. That sport content is a key asset in today's broadcast network portfolio is evidenced by the attempt on the part of News Corp. (owner of Fox Sports) to purchase Manchester United for $1 billion; by Turner Broadcasting Company's Goodwill Games, an Olympic-style event, originating in the 1980s for the purpose of establishing goodwill between the United States and Soviet Union; and by ESPN's X Games, an extreme sports event targeting 18- to 24-year-olds, countered by NBC's Gravity Games. In most of these situations, however, the media decision-maker as content owner assumes greater if not total control over supply as well as production, to become what we refer to as a *content manufacturer.*

Although not necessarily the pioneer of broadcaster sport content manufacturing, Atlanta Braves owner Ted Turner used the team as the primary source of content supply for his cable Superstation, TBS, during the early 1980s. In return, exposure on TBS, a staple within most American cable television packages, allowed the Braves to label themselves "America's Team," generating a fan following across the continent, particularly in markets void of an MLB franchise. It should come as no surprise that paralleling the team's rise in popularity was a distinct rise in performance as the Braves appeared in the World Series more often than any other franchise during the 1990s. Acting as both media content decision-maker and team owner, Turner was able to control vital components of the content production process, thus ensuring the team nationwide exposure and ensuring the audience an entertaining product.

However, not all sport organizations have the luxury of media interest ownership. Thus, media exposure insurance is rather tenuous, particularly if the sport promotion specialist assumes a reactive as opposed to proactive position. Those whose job it is to promote sport need to explore additional opportunities for manufactured media exposure, as we discuss next.

Broadcast Content Manufacturing

In an effort to ensure broadcast time, sport promotion specialists have a number of options available. These include subscriber-based broadcasting, self-production, and time buys.

Subscription-Based Broadcasting

Subscriber-driven broadcasting is nothing new to the sport industry. Generally speaking, subscriber-driven broadcasting, particularly in the sport of boxing, has been viewed as an alternative source of revenue production rather than an exposure-generating tactic. Recently, a majority of the major North American professional leagues launched a subscriber-based content delivery system in order to elevate exposure and grant fans a broader selection of programming options. These arrangements typically involve a rights fee agreement with the rights holder simply supplying the media-rights buyer with content, thereby relinquishing control and intrapromotional opportunities.

However, in November 1999, the NBA launched one of the most ambitious broadcast content manufacturing efforts to date—nba.com TV. The first league-owned television network, nba.com TV, at first available only in select markets, is transmitted via satellite and digital cable.[24] A subscriber gains access to all NBA game broadcasts as well as real-time statistics and supplemental information. Retaining complete control of all programming production and placement decisions, the NBA is using the channel as a means of saturating the vested subscriber with NBA-branded content. In addition to the regular schedule of league games and events, supplemental NBA programming featuring league personalities maintains the viewer's interest around the clock on the 24-hour channel. It would appear that this trend-setting venture, patterned after the broadcast channel made available by Manchester United of the English Premier League, signals a dramatic shift in the way sport will be broadcast in the 21st century. Major sport organizations endeavoring to exercise greater control over content delivery and availability will be acting less as simply content suppliers and more as content manufacturers, with a complete distribution system owned and operated by the broadcast-rights holders.

Time Buy

Two key factors have led sport organizations to the purchase of broadcast airtime, commonly referred to as a *time buy*. Sport businesses generally consider executing a time buy when no viable media-rights buy is available or when it appears that the sport organization may be able to generate more revenue by retaining the right to sell broadcast advertising spots. Time buys are not uncommon in sport, as sport organizations of all shapes and sizes have used this tactic as a means of guaranteeing media exposure.

Additionally, many amateur sport organizations and professional teams produce their own broadcasts, purchasing or renting necessary equipment and hiring personnel including on-air talent. The cost of producing a broadcast is difficult to estimate because it involves variables such as location, transmission fees, and the cost of assembling the equipment and crew. However, Ashwell reports that a 2-hour telecast could be professionally produced and delivered complete to a local broadcast station for as little as $10,000.[25] A college athletic department can trim costs even further by using on-campus resources such as audiovisual or distance-learning staff and equipment, as well as broadcast journalism faculty and students. Proper use of the exposure generated during this 2-hour time slot, now controlled by the sport organization (within Federal Communications Commission regulations), may well produce more than the estimated $10,000 fee.

From Media Trade to a Time Buy

Prior to 2000, the NBA's Charlotte Hornets had a trade agreement with WBT-AM in which WBT gave the Hornets airtime in exchange for publicity. When the contract expired, however, Hornets management agreed to pay the station to broadcast the games, retaining all revenue from advertising sales.

Conversely, some sport organizations, including many small-market professional sport franchises, have found that retaining broadcast rights, thereby exercising a time buy on a local station and selling advertising time, yields better exposure and revenue production results. This media manufacturing strategy enables the rights holder to control content supply and production, using available airtime for enhanced self-promotion as well as plugging broadcast and organization sponsors. As part of a three-year agreement, the NBA's Houston Rockets and WNBA's Houston Comets will purchase airtime from KTBU-IND, a local independent television station. Under the agreement, KTBU will sell airtime to the teams, which will in turn accept responsibility for producing the telecasts. The teams also plan to develop ancillary programming, such as shows hosted by players and coaches.

Selling broadcast advertising time will once again necessitate research on the existing or anticipated audience. Using the broadcast rating (total audience) and the cost per advertisement solicited, advertisers will calculate the ad's cost per thousand (CPM) in order to assess the efficiency of an advertising rate. An advertisement's CPM ("M" symbolizes 1000 in Roman numerals), expressed as the advertising expense per 1000 audience members, provides advertisers with a standard for evaluating the merits of media advertising proposals. The CPM for Super Bowl XXXIV was roughly $14 ($3 million for a 30-second commercial and a viewing audience of approximately 43 million).

A Time Buy Allows for Content Control

In 1998, the Philadelphia Phillies decided to retain the rights to their radio broadcasts and make significant changes to the broadcast format. Research indicated that a small portion of the audience comprised children. With the aim of increasing listenership among children and growing an audience for the future, a number of kid-friendly features were included in live remote broadcasts by a younger reporter from various parts of the stadium, like the dugout and bullpen.[26]

Electronic Audiovisual Content Manufacturing

Sport promotion specialists are well advised to pursue a variety of electronic audiovisual content sources as platforms for promotional material. For instance, at the conclusion of each season, college and professional teams often produce a highlight video for fans and boosters to remind them of the exciting moments of the past season. In fact, a number of companies like Host Communications have established specific departments to produce highlight videos for client institutions.

As a means of self-promotion, both the NBA's Phoenix Suns and MLB's Toronto Blue Jays have used video production to tap another market and thereby enhance awareness and image via this promotional tactic. The Suns have produced a series of videos that explain the team's marketing and promotional efforts. Viewers gain insight into topics ranging from how to draft and implement a team marketing plan to producing the game presentation. These videos are available for use in sport management courses worldwide, extending the brand name and identity of the "content manufacturer" while favorably influencing the image of team marketing and promotion management.

Print Content Manufacturing

As a sport promotion specialist you will have a number of options available for manufacturing print media. Alternatives may range from media guides distributed on-site to members of the attending press corps to souvenir game-day programs and other property-related publications including books, calendars, magazines, and newsletters.

Media Guides

Typically developed as a preseason or pre-event content *supply* tool, the media guide contains the ingredients necessary for eventual content *production*. For instance, a team media guide includes basic profiles and photographs of each player, coach, and selected members of the administration while featuring one or two key members of the team. A media guide for a professional golf event may include biographical profiles of all participating players in addition to profiles of event management and board members, details of the course, and scoring and purse history. While player profiles can include such riveting information as favorite food, rock band, or holiday, of greatest interest to the media are the basic facts such as height, weight, age, and past performance highlights. Additional information of interest to the media includes a schedule, historical highlights such as team and individual performance statistics, and attendance figures.

Usually team media guides are mailed to members of the media list approximately two to four weeks in advance of the season; they are also made available in the press area throughout the event or season. Event media guides are frequently not available any sooner because of last-minute qualifying or selection procedures.

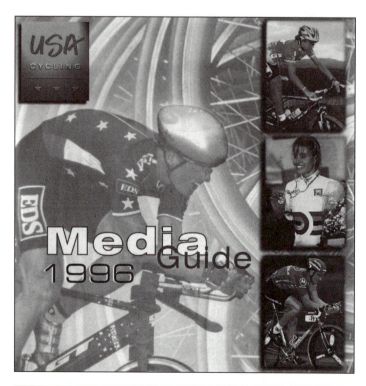

Most governing bodies dictate media guide production standards. For instance, the standard size among most North American professional sport leagues is 4.25 inches by 9 inches. On the other hand, the NCAA, governing body for most North American collegiate athletic programs, mandates that regardless of the size, all media publications must be printed in one color, except on the front and back covers.[27] Electronic media guides, such as that of the United States Cycling Federation, will undoubtedly continue to gain in popularity as organizations wish to expedite content transfer as well as reduce costs (figure 7.11).

However, the utility of the media guide can be expanded beyond the traditional supply chain through distribution among corporate sponsors, as well as attendees. Many sport organizations have effectively bundled the media guide with advance ticket or sponsorship purchasing incentives and thus enhanced the purchaser's benefits without incurring significant organizational costs.

Figure 7.11 Media guides available on CD are an emerging trend.

Courtesy of USA Cycling.

Souvenirs and Commemorative Game Programs

Although souvenir program production may be outsourced for the purpose of cost containment, sport promotion specialists typically retain control over production runs and editorial copy. In contrast to the situation with supply-side media, the sport promotion specialist is typically responsible for copyediting of the program. Even when production is outsourced to a company such as Host Communications or Professional Sports Publications, much of the text is printed without additional copyediting, as these production houses generally focus on generating material and selling advertising space nationally.

This self-produced medium is generally offered to attendees but can also be supplied to the media for the purpose of updating facts and figures. While typically consumers pay for programs, this content medium would appear too valuable to have its circulation limited to those wishing to pay for it. This is the philosophy of the NHL's Ottawa Senators, who decided to supply their program, *Score*, to game attendees for free. The tactic enabled the Senators to substantially increase circulation, thereby enhancing communication with their customers. Another consequence was that the club could increase souvenir program advertising revenues threefold.[28]

The souvenir program contents often reflect those of the preseason media guide, with a roster of participating athletes; feature stories on athletes, administration, and selected dignitaries; future schedules; and team or event records and milestones. Too often, organizations do not view or use the souvenir program as the key communication device it can be. Programs should include a facility layout guide highlighting points of interest to attendees, including restrooms, lost and found, merchandise and concession stands, and sponsor promotional displays and fan interactive booths; a complete time schedule and description of game-related activities including special performances and half-time contests; and any educational content needed to help the novice attendee learn about special cheers or fan action. Bear in mind that the more useful the program's content, the greater the likelihood that demand will increase.

External Market Publications

Sport organizations have historically produced a variety of promotional print publications. These sources of information afford the sport organization a means of establishing or maintaining communication with a variety of market segments. Research has revealed that readers of sport publications exhibit different characteristics from those who attend events and watch sport on television, thus allowing publication manufacturers to penetrate new, untapped consumer markets.[29]

The prevalence of desktop publishing enables a sport property of just about any size to enter the realm of print publication manufacturing and distribution. Besides the media guides and game programs, this resource allows sport organizations to self-produce a variety of print publications in-house. Whether a sport organization enters the publication business or chooses to outsource the production process, it makes sense to employ a centralized system. In such a system, one office, and conceivably one supervisor, assumes responsibility for all printing and publishing issues. This allows adequate control and scrutiny of content and image presentation[30] as required within the integrated marketing communication model discussed in chapter 1. Table 7.2 lists various NBA franchise publications ranging from yearbooks to electronic messages. Note the limited number of teams that now use a newsletter format to communicate with fans in comparison to the number that utilize an e-news format.

The San Jose Sports Authority produces a quarterly annual report that is distributed to a broad mailing list nationwide. The publication addresses the Authority's agenda of past as well as scheduled events and also presents a review of its budgetary status.

Table 7.2 NBA 1999-2000 Team Publications

Team	Yearbook	Magazine	Game program	Newsletter	E-news notifier
Atlanta Hawks	Atlanta Hawks Yearbook	Hawk Talk	Hawks Game Time	None	Nothinbutnetmail
Boston Celtics	Official Celtics Yearbook	Celtics Insider	Celtics Tonight	Game Day Fax	Celticsmail
Charlotte Hornets	1999-2000 Hornets Yearbook	Inside the Hive	The Buzz	None	Bee-Mail
Chicago Bulls	Official Yearbook of the Chicago Bulls	BasketBull	Bullpen	None	Mybulls
Cleveland Cavaliers	30th Anniversary Commemorative Yearbook	TipOff Magazine	TipOff Tonight	None	Cavs-Insider
Dallas Mavericks	Dallas Mavericks Yearbook	None	HOOP Magazine	Teamworks	Fastbreak
Denver Nuggets	None	None	HOOP Magazine	Hard Wood	None
Detroit Pistons	None	None	HOOP Magazine	None	None
Golden State Warriors	Golden State Warriors 1999-2000 Official Yearbook	Warriors Magazine	TipOff	None	None
Houston Rockets	1999-2000 Rockets Blastoff Yearbook	None	Blastoff Express	None	eblastoff
Indiana Pacers	None	None	HOOP Magazine	Fifth Quarter	None
Los Angeles Clippers	None	Clipboard	HOOP Magazine	None	Oneonone
Los Angeles Lakers	Lakers Yearbook	None	HOOP Magazine	None	None
Miami Heat	None	Miami HEAT Magazine	TipOff	None	None
Milwaukee Bucks	None	Full Court Press	HOOP Magazine	None	Fastbreak
Minnesota Timberwolves	None	Wolf Tracks	Timberwolves Tonight	None	None
New Jersey Nets	New Jersey Nets Yearbook	InnerNets	Playball	None	NetsNews
New York Knicks	New York Knicks Yearbook	None	HOOP Magazine	None	NYKMail
Orlando Magic	RDV Sports 2000	Magic Magazine	None	None	Emagic Insider
Philadelphia 76ers	76ers Yearbook	None	HangTimes	BaseLines	None
Phoenix Suns	Phoenix Suns Yearbook	Fastbreak	Free Throw	None	Suns.com
Portland Trail Blazers	None	Rip City Magazine	HOOP Magazine	None	Blazersfastbreak
Sacramento Kings	None	FanFare	Gametime	None	None
San Antonio Spurs	1999-2000 Official Yearbook	SCORE	Gametime	None	None
Seattle SuperSonics	Official Sonics Yearbook	None	PlayBall	None	Sonics SuperNet
Toronto Raptors	Official 2000 Toronto Raptors Yearbook	None	Raptors Tonight	None	Raptorsinsider
Utah Jazz	None	HomeCourt	HOOP Magazine	None	Jazzbeat
Vancouver Grizzlies	Grizzlies Yearbook	Grizzlies Magazine	Grizzlies Program	None	None
Washington Wizards	Wizards Yearbook	None	Wizards Game Time	None	Wizards e-ball

A yearbook is commonly available to fans so they can relish in the season's highlights. Recently, the Yankees took the team yearbook to a high-tech level with a CD-ROM version. It sells for about $20 and includes printed statistics as well as video clips of the Yankees' 25 World Series championships. Users also gain access to the Yankees' server and can download updated statistics for the current season.[31]

Advertorials and Infomercials

Research has demonstrated that advertorials—advertising copy masked as editorial copy and often referred to as infomercials in the broadcast industry—have greater impact on the receiver than a direct advertising message does. This would certainly substantiate the preponderance of late-night paid programming that pitches the newest contraption for toning the abdominal muscles. Studies have demonstrated that advertorials yield such favorable effects as enhanced recall of promoted product, higher levels of influence on buying behavior, higher source credibility, and more favorable impressions of products contained in the message.[32]

It is a mystery, though, why more sport organizations, particularly those that don't get regular media attention, do not incorporate advertorials or infomercials into their promotional agenda. Using data generated from an attendee database showing that a significant proportion of fans lived in surrounding secondary markets, the Ottawa Senators decided to exploit the merits of this form of promotion and developed the *Sens Extra* (figure 7.12). Similar to a team newsletter, the *Sens Extra* was supplied on a monthly basis to the newspapers servicing the defined market; it contained a template of up to eight pages of game highlights, special interest stories, and photographs. Each newspaper is allowed to sell advertising space in the special section and keep all proceeds. The advertising tool, masked as publicity, which has generated approximately 335,000 new customers, represents club-controlled media manufacturing at its best.[33]

Too often the merits of such secondary-tier communication sources, including weekly print publications and local-access cable channels, are grossly underestimated. New Federal Communications Commission regulations will allow radio stations with only a 3.5-mile radius to broadcast in U.S. markets. Ironically, these are the sources that are starved for content and will more than happily run content appealing to their audience with little or no editorial modification. Perhaps most importantly, many of these secondary sources can target a specific audience such as a particular geographical sector of a community, as in the example of the Ottawa Senators.

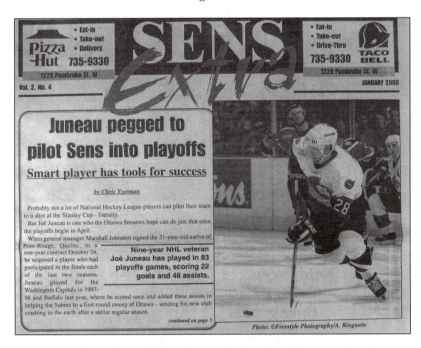

Figure 7.12 The *Sens Extra* allows the club to advertise and gain new customers.

Reprinted, by permission, from the Ottawa Senators and Corel Centre.

Another effective yet rarely utilized form of advertorial is a theme song. Come to think of it, when was the last time Disney released a movie without an accompanying

Top 40 hit or complete sound track? Or, what about the Olympics and its associated song titles? The same should be true of each new season for a professional sport franchise. Catchy tunes commissioned by the sport organization, appearing regularly on the local radio broadcast partner, would function like an infomercial, establishing a top-of-mind presence for the consumer. Furthermore, a theme song provides the possibility of generating publicity as a result of the selection of the singer and the theme, as well as from the fact that proceeds from sales may be donated to charity (so that the song acts as a community service platform).

Bridging the Gap: Media Trade Agreements

When selling or buying media exposure is not a viable option, most if not all sport organizations have the opportunity to formulate a trade agreement with the media as a means of securing a presence. This tactic, often packaged as a sponsorship arrangement, serves as a bridge between content supply and content manufacturing. Most media trades involve an agreed-on volume of exposure by each party. For instance, the sport organization will agree to supply a broadcast partner with facility signage, public address announcements, and souvenir program ad space in return for complementary air space/airtime. A number of sport organizations attempt to further ease the broadcast partner's financial burden by underwriting production or travel expenses.[34]

This is the case for the AXA Liberty Bowl. Officials have annually secured an agreement with the local Fox affiliate to broadcast the AXA Liberty Bowl Parade and have sought sponsor support to offset the parade broadcast production costs. Local businesses sponsoring the parade broadcast (mostly businesses located along the parade route) are essentially purchasing advertisements during the telecast, in turn relieving the affiliate's sales staff of this task.

Sport promotion specialists also need to explore the opportunity for publicity-type exposure based on the merits of this promotion mix component. Therefore, in lieu of excessive advertising placement, trade agreements should include regularly scheduled personal interviews, remote transmissions, or insert distribution (print media). For example, as part of its sponsorship of the 1996 Olympic Games, Time Warner agreed to feature a series of Olympic-themed articles and advertorials (storytelling ads, to be discussed shortly) in *Sports Illustrated*.

Similarly, a media trade agreement may target the acquisition of complementary advertising slots. For instance, it is common for the institution hosting an NCAA championship to secure airtime or print space from local media outlets (as a goodwill gesture or part of the regular-season trade agreement) for running advertisements regarding the upcoming championship. All ads are produced and distributed by the NCAA and forwarded to the host institution for inclusion in the championship media campaign.

The NHL Has GAS

Nickelodeon's digital network—Games and Sports for Kids (GAS)—has formed a programming development partnership with the NHL. Nick's GAS and the NHL will develop original programming based on NHL outreach programs. A half-hour game show based on NHL Breakout, the league's hockey tournament and festival, will be developed. The partnership will also give GAS access to NHL game footage and behind-the-scenes access to NHL events.[35]

Targeting and Nurturing Media Consumers

After having successfully procured media placement, the sport promotion specialist needs to direct attention toward generating readership, listenership, and/or viewership of the supplied, retailed, or manufactured content. As we noted previously, the media plan must address attracting readers to the printed copy, listeners to the radio interview, and viewers to the event telecast/webcast. Unfortunately, the media consumer is one who garners little respect or attention other than as a commodity in rights fee negotiations. However, failure to properly attract and service this key customer group will undoubtedly make it more difficult to secure future media exposure.

If we reflect back on the "Frequency Escalator" discussed in chapter 2, we see that the media consumer occupies an important position in bridging the gap between aware nonconsumers and infrequently attending consumers. From this perspective, sport promotion specialists should view media consumption as the pathway to direct transactional forms of on-site consumption. The live broadcast of home games should be considered an organizational advertorial. Thus the broadcast or print copy should act as a catalyst for on-site consumption, providing cues or incentives for the consumer reaction. The consumer's interpretation of these cues should be that the on-site consumption experience is more meaningful and fulfilling to be at a game than it is to listen at home.

Contrary to popular belief in many sport markets, broadcasting games locally has little or no unfavorable impact on paid attendance. In 2000, attendance at MLB's Tampa Bay Devil Ray home games was approximately 2000 higher when local games were broadcast on local television.[36] It is easy to see that sport promotion specialists need to view the televised and live consumption experiences as two separate product offerings of appeal to unique consumer markets.

This task is not only challenging, but in some respects also counterproductive, when the mediated consumer ardently supports the sport organization but is not able to go to games or events and therefore is possibly left to feel unappreciated. For example, following the 1997 season, the University of Memphis, which had contracted with a local independent station to broadcast most home games in the local market for several years, chose to discontinue doing so in hopes of reversing a declining trend in paid attendance. The Tiger media faithful were forced to attend games at the Pyramid Arena. After three frustrating seasons of continued descending attendance, the university negotiated a new television contract that included broadcasting of home games in the local market. This example illustrates that the absence of a televised product minimized the team's presence in the local media market, besides disenfranchising a critical market of media consumers who did not wish to consume in any other fashion or did not possess the means to do so.

One of the greatest challenges for sport promotion specialists is establishing a means of direct communication with this "satellite" market of media consumers who diligently follow the team or event on the airwaves, in the newspaper, or over the Internet. Organizations should employ interactive programs or contests necessitating two-way communication between content provider and content receiver to facilitate the development of a media market database.

Another option the sport promotion specialist has is to develop a series of trivia contests and have the answers placed in the media on a regular basis. During live game broadcasts, as an example, a team may give television viewers and radio broadcast listeners answers on air to a team trivia contest for which a form has been published that day in the sports section of the local newspaper. Submitted contest forms will provide contact information for people who affiliate with the team via the media, classified as team media consumers. Once such a mechanism is in place, the organization can make direct offers to stimulate increased media product consumption (e.g., ordering publications) and potential "escalation" to infrequent game attendance.

Operational Organization

According to Davis it is critically important that the media relations office be located near all other organizational personnel, particularly those in demand among the media (e.g., coaches and players). Staff sizes may vary considerably from one sport organization to another. While major college sports information offices may employ up to six full-time staff members as well as several graduate assistants or interns because of the number of men's and women's athletic teams warranting press coverage, many small-college teams, minor league teams, hallmark events, and governing bodies employ a streamlined staff of one full-time sport promotion specialist, hiring additional seasonal staff as needed.[37] Brian Eaton, media relations and marketing director for U.S. Synchronized Swimming, offers a Practitioner's Perspective on organizing and operating media promotion.

PRACTITIONER'S PERSPECTIVE

Tools of the Trade
by Brian Eaton, Media Relations and Marketing Director for U.S. Synchronized Swimming

The sport media promotion world is a grab bag of "other duties as assigned"—at best. If you think you're going to go to work every day to write releases and talk to media on the phone, then plan on hiring a staff of 20 to perform all your other tasks.

However, you can carve out a place of stature and significance for yourself in your organization and in the league by making your position and department a model of excellence and professionalism. Essentially, you must create your own importance and make yourself indispensable. Nobody is going to assign you a level of importance in your organization. You are going to have to carve it out of granite with a butter knife. The respect of your constituents will determine your eventual level of success.

Here are a number of suggestions intended to make life as a sport promotion specialist just a little bit easier:

• *Get involved in all aspects of the organization.* You can't be an expert on your team and organization . . . without actually *being* an expert on your team and organization. Take the time to listen and to understand the processes and daily struggles of your colleagues. Don't just be the "media person," or that's the category you'll stay in for the rest of your career. Help with marketing strategies and event planning, brainstorm ideas for sponsors to increase exposure during events, toss out ideas for fund-raising or membership drives, and so on. Be the idea person.

• *Educate your organization.* Simply put, keep the lines of communication open with your constituents—staff, membership, board of directors, sponsors, and the others. Copy them on press releases, time lines and deadlines for events, foreseen problems, incoming clippings, and upcoming appearances. Keep your athletes in the loop, too. They hate last-minute surprises and obligations more than you do, especially when they're juggling an already time-consuming training regimen.

• *Anticipate the needs of the media.* The key to getting all your responsibilities taken care of is to anticipate the needs of the media so that they in turn can take care of their

(continued)

(continued) responsibilities. This includes everything from the in-depth planning of press kits to media and athlete flow patterns, work spaces, photo positions, results distribution, interview rooms, parking, and hospitality.

• *Stay wired.* Someone on your staff at some time will be faced with a question or concern you didn't plan for. Keep your cell phone handy and two-way radio on, and be visible. There's nothing worse than the answer man playing hide-and-go-seek when the media need an answer.

• *Get help.* The sport promotion specialist who tries to do it all will burn out faster than a pack of clove Kools at a frat party. Train, and then trust your worker bees to manage their areas. Also consider that at a vast majority of your larger events, 90% of your staff is volunteer. The quality and training of volunteers can make or break your on-site operation. Educate and empower them to make decisions, then accept the fact that not all of those decisions will be the same decision you would make.

• *Set guidelines.* Guidelines should be established for both your staff and the media. Let everyone know up front what to expect, whether it's workroom hours, credential-control areas, equipment rate cards, or staff liaisons for various areas of the operation.

• *Take a stand.* As the eyes and ears of the organization, you'll hear "it" first, many times before it hits the fan, and most times, you'll be the first asked to comment. Anticipate the negative and help define your organization's position. To be a team in the office and out, you have to present a unified front, sans clichés.

• *Wear the team colors.* The sport promotion specialist is like E.F. Hutton. No matter what you say on or off the record, people are listening (and possibly quoting). So wear your team colors and put on your game face—don't step on the toes of anyone in your organization, sponsors, or affiliates. If you do, you will end up in print, not only that day, but the next day as well, listed in the page 16 agate under "Transactions."

• *Have a crisis management plan.* If you knew exactly when it was going to hit, it wouldn't be called a crisis. Crises range from the death of an athlete on the field, to a positive drug test, to an outspoken athlete hammering your organization, to bombing out at a major event. Hey, Scout—be prepared. Plan who will be involved in the response and the appropriate chain of command for pointed inquiries, practice the scenario on smaller crises, and be confident that your plan of attack will help your organization emerge unscathed.

• *Have a success plan.* When your underdogs suddenly become the top dog, you'll be in the doghouse without the "dream." The "dream" is your media promotion attack plan to manage your team's success. It includes oodles of appearances and media opportunities you've just been dying to attempt. Massage that plan on a regular basis. The window of opportunity to capitalize on success is very narrow, even narrower for unknown personalities. Be proactive in marketing your athletes. Lay the groundwork for your plan in advance by making contacts and developing media pitch materials; have your "spokes-athletes" selected, formally train them to deal with the media, and prepare to sell your athletes to targeted big-name shows and magazines. When *SI* is on the phone, and "Letterman" and "Extra" are on hold, it's too late to begin evaluating which opportunities will best serve your organization. The success of the media promotion operation is not sudden; it's managed. Your team may be 1-23 now, but when they win the conference tournament, you'll be sorry you spent so much time planning your spring break trip to Cancun.

In essence, it appears that Brian Eaton thinks the keys to organizational effectiveness are to be involved and to be prepared. In order to assess the media promotion campaign's overall effectiveness, the sport promotion specialist will employ appropriate evaluative measures similar to those used to assess other components of the integrated marketing communication plan.

Media Promotion Evaluation

With diligent planning and careful organization, you can effectively manage the sport media supply chain. As with any element of the promotional campaign, critical to effectiveness is the establishment of well-defined goals and objectives. The fundamental objective is of course increased exposure or presence in the media, while other typical desired outcomes may include increased press conference attendance, increased requests for content including interview bookings, or increased broadcast ratings.

Several of these objectives can be quantifiably measured quite easily. For instance, exposure may be quantified by the volume of column inches recorded in print media over a period of time, as can broadcast airtime in an analogous fashion. Similarly, Arbitron ratings may be sought from the media-rights holder to determine radio ratings for a show or broadcast.

But you may also interact with or survey the press corps to determine whether and how well their needs have been met. Such an assessment was undertaken at the Conference USA men's basketball tournament in 1997. The analysis, conducted by survey among credentialed media representatives, revealed weaknesses in media parking arrangements, maintenance of the media hospitality area, and the procedures for distributing media credentials. Earning high marks from the visiting media were survey items that addressed the media promotion staff's information distribution system, management of the postgame interview room, and maintenance of the media workroom. Such analyses will enable you to monitor operations and seek ways to enhance service provided to the media.[38]

Postgame Wrap-Up

The complexity of tasks demanded of the sport promotion specialist has dramatically expanded within the past few years. While the need still exists to supply media with the information from which to build a story, more and more of today's sport organizations commonly act as manufacturers and retailers of media content.

Sport promotion specialists may use a number of supply-side methods for media content distribution, including direct correspondence with media decision-makers, delivery of a press release or fact sheet, and staging of a press conference or personal interview. In each case the method may be used to announce details of an upcoming or recent development deemed to be of value to media decision-makers and their audiences. On the other hand, content-building devices available to sport promotion specialists include game, event, or athlete statistics and photographs. Sport promotion specialists are well advised to explore the use of strategic product placement, as well as live remote broadcasts, as creative means for generating media exposure and attracting media consumer attention.

Those sport programs seeking to secure a greater volume of media exposure have derived considerable benefit from taking a more active role in the media distribution chain. Tactics ranging from the execution of broadcast media-time buys to producing print advertorials act essentially as a means of ensuring proper message placement and delivery.

Those considering the role of media manufacturer are strongly advised to assess the costs and benefits of this ambitious endeavor. For instance, will the exposure generate enough interest among potential paying customers, or will the time buy yield advertising sales that exceed the cost of the time slot? These are questions sport promotion specialists must ask before embarking on media manufacturing.

Fundamental to effective sport media promotion management are the identification and servicing of parties consisting of media-oriented customer groups that range from media placement decision-makers to content readers, viewers, and listeners. While members of the press seek services associated with access to participants and information, similar interests exist among the media-consuming public. Essentially, the more information made available to each media consumer group, the higher the levels of satisfaction.

Many have argued that the success of any league, team, or event is determined by the volume of exposure garnered in or by the media. Therefore those who work to promote sport must be creative in exploring the possibility of engaging in the variety of methods addressed within this chapter for securing mass as well as targeted media placement.

Discussion Items

1. What appears to be the most cost-effective method for generating media exposure? Within your response, be sure to discuss and compare the merits of media supply versus media manufacture.

2. What is the best method to prepare for an interview?

3. How would you determine whether or not a media-time buy was a good option?

4. What is your personal reaction to advertorials and infomercials?

5. Within the next quarter-century, what do you think will change with respect to the supplying and manufacturing of sport media content?

Learning Enrichment Activities

1. Attend a press conference with a classmate. While in attendance, each of you should collect all the materials distributed, analyze the environment, and carefully take notes on the question-and-answer session. After the press conference, assess the media coverage. Was important information omitted from the media? If you had been conducting the press conference, would you be pleased with the media coverage?

2. Arrange two interviews. Schedule the first interview with the sport promotion specialist from a local team or event that has a difficult time gaining a presence in the media. Discuss with the individual the tactics she employs to attain media coverage, the challenges she encounters, and what the person would be willing to do in order to increase media exposure. The second interview should be scheduled with a member of the local media. Discuss with this person the challenges she encounters in providing increased coverage for that particular team or event and what is needed in order for the team or event to obtain increased exposure.

The Promotional Role of Sport Sponsorship

chapter objectives

1. Become familiar with a basis from which to incorporate sponsorship into the overall promotional strategy of sport and non-sport businesses

2. Become familiar with a menu of sport sponsorship motives sought by active sponsors of sport

3. Gain a sound understanding of the sponsorship management process, focusing on proper methods for proposal selection and evaluation

4. Become familiar with sport sponsorship proposal design and the criteria commonly desired among active corporate sponsors

key terms		
	trade	corporate partnership
	in-kind	exchange
	sponsee	aided recognition
	exclusivity	unaided recall

Pregame Introductions

Corporate support has played a significant role in the development of sport. Corporate involvement in sport can be traced back to the Roman Circus Maximus when gladiators and chariot drivers dressed in the colors of their supporting merchants. The Jockey Club, based in Newmarket, England, sponsored thoroughbred races for horses owned by the English nobility in the 17th and 18th centuries. Prior to the organization of the Jockey Club around 1750, racehorses had been organized and supported by the aristocracy since the early Middle Ages. More recently, sponsorship from a New England railroad company served as the catalyst for the first American intercollegiate athletic event, a rowing contest between Harvard and Yale in 1852,[1] while the assembling of a sponsor cluster that included Coca-Cola, Bull Durham Tobacco, Gillette, and Chalmers Motor Car Company in 1910 provided a sound financial foundation for MLB.[2]

It would appear that the 1984 Summer Olympic Games, hosted by the city of Los Angeles, served as the catalyst for the recent phenomenal growth in American sport sponsorship. Before the 1984 Games, financing had primarily come from government funding, lotteries, and donations. However, as a result of the economic conditions of the State of California, the fact that lotteries were illegal, and the inability of organizations and charities to make significant monetary contributions, an alternative funding structure, corporate sponsorship, warranted investigation.[3] The corporate sponsorship programs initiated for the 1984 Games enabled the Los Angeles Olympic Organizing Committee to realize a profit of approximately $215 million. As a result of the success achieved by the event and its sponsors, corporate sponsorship of the Olympic Games specifically, and sport in general, has flourished so that few sport events take place today without some type of corporate support.

In 1999, sponsorship spending was expected to surpass $19 billion worldwide, with slightly more than two-thirds (67%) dedicated to sponsoring sport. This represented a 12% annual increase in sponsorship spending around the world. In addition to North America's $7.6 billion, it was estimated that European companies would spend $5.6 billion, Pacific Rim companies $3.4 billion, Central and South American businesses $1.5 billion, and all other countries approximately $1.1 billion. Although these growth rates are commendable, they appear to pale in comparison to those reported for sponsorship of women's sport, which has realized an increase of 100% in just the past five years.[4]

Philip Morris and Anheuser Busch continue to rank at the top of sponsorship spending. Each company spent over $140 million worldwide on sponsorship during 2000 while General Motors, Coca-Cola, and PepsiCo hovered around the $100 million mark. The number of companies engaging in sponsorship increased from approximately 1600 in 1985 to more than 5000 in 1998.[5]

Howard and Crompton cite the following major changes that have contributed to the sustained growth of sport sponsorship in the past two decades:[6]

- Rapid increases in the volume of television channels, radio stations, and magazines, resulting in communication clutter
- The continuing increase in the cost of network television advertising along with a decrease in the viewing audience as a result of cable television
- The fact that sport receives substantially more television exposure than any other potential sponsorship vehicle
- Circumvention of governmental policy by tobacco companies
- The acceptance of sport commercialization
- The success of the 1984 Olympic Games
- Increased efforts at target marketing
- The availability of personal selling and relationship-building opportunities
- The financial difficulties encountered by publicly funded sport agencies

The broad appeal of sport to a diverse array of consumer groups attracts interest among advertisers that in turn triggers the interest of the media, which seeks content and advertising revenue. American sports that have inherent periods of time segmentation such as time-outs or natural breaks in events, along with low production costs and appeal to an identifiable audience, have flourished with respect to attracting media and corporate sponsors. In contrast, soccer, a sport with relatively low production costs and mass audience appeal, continues to find it challenging to obtain airtime in the United States because the game's continuous flow of play restricts a broadcaster's ability to air the event sponsor's advertisements on a timely basis.

Governmental restrictions placed on the tobacco industry during the 1970s that prohibited television advertising in the United States were frequently circumvented by strategic signage placement in sport venues, not to mention the proliferation of corporate logos adorning auto racing. Many scoreboards in stadiums housing professional sport teams carried signage of tobacco companies, guaranteeing the advertisement considerable airtime on national television. However, legislation passed by the Clinton administration prohibiting this practice has eliminated it in American sport venues while posing a serious threat to the American automobile racing industry. Similar restrictions are being proposed by governments in the European Union and will likely go into effect in 2006. The impact of such restrictions will be felt most keenly by Formula One motor racing teams, who have had a long mutually beneficial relationship with the tobacco industry.

Paralleling the phenomenal growth in sport sponsorship has been consumer receptivity to commercialism in sport. As displayed in figure 8.1, a survey of spectators at a series of 2000-2001 NCAA championships ranging from the Women's College Cup (soccer) to the College World Series (baseball), showed that a majority of respondents felt that the championships were not too commercialized and in some

Please indicate which of the following responses best describes your opinion regarding the commercialization (corporate advertising) of the NCAA championship.	
Not enough	58.7%
Appropriate amount	36.4%
Too much	5.0%

Figure 8.1 NCAA championship patron responses to sport commercialization.

cases indicated that more commercialization was acceptable. Just as interestingly, many respondents indicated that they considered corporate advertising including banners, signage, announcements, giveaways, and the like a welcome addition to the sporting event atmosphere.

The inability of public funding to keep pace with the skyrocketing cost of sport, as well as an unwillingness of taxpayers to increase public funds for sport, has challenged sport promotion specialists to seek alternative means of generating revenue for sports ranging from those based in schools to those associated with the Olympic movement. Consequently, corporate sponsorship has emerged as one of the primary sources of income as well as a means of reducing expenses. In fact, sponsorship accounts for nearly half of all revenue generated by major college athletic programs within the United States.

Corporate sport sponsorship has continued to thrive on the basis of a sponsorship's ability to serve as a platform for a specific type of brand extension, cut through the clutter of traditional media advertising, and provide a cost-effective business-building technique. Corporations freely spend thousands, if not millions, to nurture relationships with current as well as prospective clients at sporting events. In fact, data collected from customers entertained by Federal Express during the 2001 Bowl Championship Series revealed that the opportunity to interact with the sales host significantly improved personal relations with the company, thereby solidifying customers' willingness to continue shipping with Federal Express.[7]

Sport Sponsorship Platforms

The platform for sport sponsorship extends beyond events to include governing bodies, teams, athletes, media channels, facilities, and specific sports. Although sponsorship may be built upon each independent platform, opportunities exist within many sport businesses for platform integration. For example, the NBA's Cleveland Cavs and WNBA's Cleveland Rockers are able to offer corporate sponsors team as well as facility sponsorship entitlements, as the team and building owners are one and the same.

A corporate partnership with the NCAA enables General Motors to display its Buick Rendezvous at various NCAA championships.

Governing Body Sponsorship

Governing bodies ranging from the International Olympic Committee (IOC) to local adult recreation leagues have secured sponsorship from corporate partners. Unfortunately, governing body sponsorship can become rather complex, as Kmart discovered in the early 1990s, when as a sponsor of USA Wrestling, the company believed it was entitled to use of the Olympic rings. Following a protracted legal dispute with the United States Olympic Committee, Kmart was informed that the sponsorship provided entitlement to use of only those symbols associated specifically with the wrestling governing body. Similarly, corporate partnership with the NCAA (figure 8.2) provides a company the opportunity to affiliate with any or all men's and women's national championships administered by the NCAA but renders no entitlement to affiliation with member institutions. Meanwhile, sponsorship of the NBA and WNBA can allow for use of all league and individual team logos in national advertising campaigns.

Figure 8.2 Corporate partnerships with the NCAA are beneficial both to the Association and to the individual corporations. Partnerships allow for name exposure to large numbers of people.

March 17, 2000 NCAA Corporate Partners banner. "Reprinted with the Permission of the NCAA. All Rights Reserved. 2001."

Team Sponsorship

Depending on the limitations imposed by a governing body, sponsorships may be offered in noncompetitive product categories or to local corporations. For instance, NFL teams are precluded from arranging sponsorships with direct competitors of sponsors of the league. Therefore, when Dallas Cowboys' owner Jerry Jones signed an agreement with Pepsi, the sponsorship was assigned to Texas Stadium, where the Cowboys play their home games, in order to conform to league policy because the leaguewide NFL sponsor is Coca-Cola.

Athlete Sponsorship

A sponsor may choose to develop a sponsorship based on support of an individual athlete. Such arrangements typically involve some type of endorsement of the sponsor's product by the sponsored athlete. Athletes in individual sports (e.g., golf, tennis, motor racing, skiing) tend to attract more sponsor interest, often because they are able to generate a greater number of visible, well-focused sponsor impressions on television. This accounts for the location of sponsor logos on the head and shoulders of most golf and tennis players and the need for all downhill skiers to appear on the post-race interview with goggles on backward and tips of dismounted skis facing the camera.

Yet the impressions these athletes make pale in comparison to the audible and visible impressions generated by auto racers. NASCAR champions such as Jeff Gordon pose in Victory Lane drinking Pepsi *and* milk while wearing the appropriate sponsor-logoed cap during the post-race victory photograph sessions. As the winning driver is photographed wearing the team sponsor's hat, the sponsor gets a chance to have its product endorsed as contributing to the driver's victory—an excellent way to service a sponsorship relationship.

Media Channel Sponsorship

Often recognized as broadcast sponsors, media channel sponsors represent companies purchasing advertising space during sport-related media transmission. These "sponsors" typically have no affiliation or entitlement to the sponsored or mediated entity other than the delivery of commercial ad space. Many argue that such a tactic, referred to as ambush marketing, is intended to distort the media consumer's understanding of the sport content provider's existing corporate sponsors. For instance, Charles Schwab and Conseco purchased significant amounts of broadcast advertising time during the 2000 Men's Final Four, but Phoenix Insurance is in fact the financial services corporate partner for the NCAA. And annually PepsiCo purchases the largest amount of advertising time during the Super Bowl compared to that spent by any other company; however, Coke has purchased the rights to be recognized as the official soft drink of the NFL. In an effort to protect their sponsors from the ambush marketing practices of "parasite" companies, the IOC required NBC to initially offer 1996 Summer Olympic broadcast advertising to members of The Olympic Program (TOP). As mentioned in chapter 7, media manufacturing sport businesses afford themselves the opportunity to construct a sponsorship package that includes media channel exposure.

Facility Sponsorship

As sport facility management sought alternative means of financing, the notion of embedding a corporation's name into the facility's name emerged. Although not a new concept, corporate facility naming rights flourished in the 1990s. Virtually every sport structure built in the United States and Canada since 1995 to house or attract a major league sport franchise bears a corporate moniker. Examples of facility sponsorships, often called naming rights agreements, have included Coors Field in Denver, home of the Colorado Rockies; Salt Lake City's Delta Center, home of the WNBA's Utah Staarz; and Adelphia Stadium in Nashville, home of the NFL's Tennessee Titans.

Event Sponsorship

To some, sponsorship is a term synonymous with event marketing, as events account for a significant proportion of all sponsorship activity. Within the realm of sport sponsorship, it is the event atmosphere that appears to be most appealing and thus attractive to sponsors. This contention is supported by Brian Kelly, director of event marketing for Sears Merchandise Group, who stated that sponsorship of an event "can extend and reach consumers, while passive elements of the marketing mix such as advertising cannot. You can bring the excitement of an event to the store."[8] American college football bowl games, including the Tostitos Fiesta Bowl, FedEx Orange Bowl, and AXA Liberty Bowl, perhaps best illustrate enthusiasm for event sponsorship in that all but one (the Rose Bowl) have secured a title sponsor.[9] The situation is similar with events such as Murphy's Irish Open (European PGA event); the Australian Open tennis championship, sponsored by Ford Motor Company; and the 1999 Rugby World Cup, sponsored by Guinness.

Sport-Specific Sponsorship

Directing sponsorship efforts toward a specific sport may also appeal to a corporation. This type of sponsorship is particularly common among sporting goods manufacturers endeavoring to generate brand identity and targeted consumer affinity. Such a strategic penetration is quite difficult to achieve without at least athlete, governing body, or media channel sponsorship.

Brine's association with soccer gear allows it to sponsor soccer-specific events.
Courtesy of Dr. Richard Irwin.

Ambush Marketing

While we have already mentioned the procurement of broadcast advertising during a sporting event as one way a company can engage in ambush marketing, a company can employ several other tactics to confuse the consumer regarding its affiliation status with a sporting event. One is to put on a contest or sweepstakes associated with the event, such as when nonsponsor Pepsi conducted the Pro Hockey Playoff Pool during the NHL's Stanley Cup. Another is to sponsor participating athletes or teams rather than the event, a practice frequently used by Wendy's during the Olympic Games to ambush the status of McDonald's as official sponsor. Still another tactic involves conducting advertising or promotional activities at or near the event, as Nike did by creating a temporary Nike Town in Atlanta at the 1996 Olympic Games and in Paris at the 1998 Men's Soccer World Cup.[10]

Unfortunately, continued acceptance of these ambush marketing practices degrades the merits of corporate sport sponsorship and threatens such sponsorship as a source of funding. Companies can employ a number of tactics to defend against ambush marketing efforts (figure 8.3). Suggested actions range from creating specific logos to be used by affiliating sponsors only (thus distinguishing sponsors from potential ambushers) to conducting event extensions, those activities that function to complement the main event while also acting as a promotional platform for affiliating sponsors. Annually, many major American sport organizations such as the LPGA,

1. Create unique logos, trademarks, or service marks for use among official sponsors only.

2. Include broadcast advertisement segments in official sponsorship (if applicable).

3. Develop an official sponsors advertising campaign.

4. Form a sponsor protection committee.

5. Reevaluate sponsorship categories.

6. Create event extensions for official sponsors.

Figure 8.3   Ambush marketing defense tactics.

Reprinted, by permission, from A. McCauley and W.A. Sutton, 1999, "In search of a new defender: The threat of ambush marketing in thee global sport arena," *International Journal of Sports Marketing and Sponsorship*, 1 (1):64-86. © Winthrop Publications Limited.

which conducts the LPGA Fan Village, stage interactive areas in conjunction with their main activity. Additionally, sport promotion specialists seeking to properly service sponsors are well advised to execute an aggressive media campaign recognizing affiliating corporate partners, while also assembling a team of representatives from existing sponsors to review all sponsorship and broadcast agreements in order to protect against potential ambushing or other questionable marketing practices.[11] In essence, each tactic serves to protect the interests of those companies rightfully associating with a sport property while protecting the integrity of the property's overall corporate sponsorship program.

Sponsorship Levels

An Oakland A's Visa card, which fans can sign up for at A's games, prominently displays the team logo.

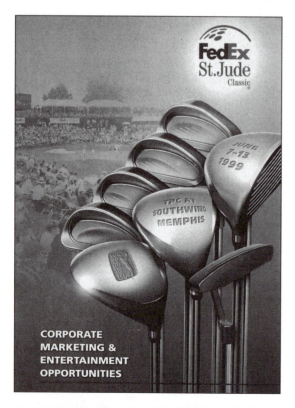

Figure 8.4 The FedEx St. Jude Classic is a good example of title sponsorship.

Typically, sponsors should receive a menu of options for expressing the magnitude of their sport sponsorship affiliation. In fact, the levels of sponsorship offered by the sport organization are limited only by the sport promotion specialist's creativity. Various elements within an event serve as sponsorship opportunities. For instance, within a college postseason bowl game, title sponsorship may be attached to any number of the surrounding festivities such as the parade, various social functions, and pep rallies, in addition to the actual game. Even within the game itself, elements such as pregame, half-time, timeouts, and touchdowns lend themselves to serving as sponsorship platforms.

Typically we would divide sponsors into the following categories: title sponsor, major or presenting sponsor, cosponsor, and **trade** or **in-kind** sponsor (an in-kind sponsorship is an arrangement typically resulting from the provision of product or services by the sponsoring company in lieu of cash payments). One would anticipate that each level or type of sponsorship would yield proportionate benefits for the sponsoring agency. Title sponsorship of an entire event certainly carries a greater cost and subsequently renders greater benefit to the sponsoring company. Federal Express's title sponsorship of the FedEx St. Jude Golf Classic, an annual stop on the PGA TOUR, provides the company event broadcast advertising slots, extensive on-course signage, a corporate hospitality pavilion on the fairway of the 18th hole, print media advertising including pairing sheets and souvenir tournament guide, and a variety of admission passes (figure 8.4). Depending on the prospective sponsor's budgetary considerations and desired outcome, a cosponsorship arrangement may be most appealing. This type of sponsorship, in which two or more corporate partners may split the sponsorship fee and subsequent benefits package, is common among retailers and suppliers. Automobile manufacturers often partner with their local area dealers, for instance, in sponsoring events, and soft drink manufacturers will partner with the regional bottlers of their product.

Sport Sponsorship Management

The evolution of sport sponsorship has forced corporations to integrate strategic market planning tactics into the sport sponsorship identification, selection, implementation, and evaluation process. As with any marketing communications tool, sport sponsorship decisions are guided by the corporate marketing plan and the broad set of corporate-based marketing and communications objectives it contains. Once the company determines that sport sponsorship is a viable option for attaining these corporate-level goals, corporate marketing decision-makers generally prescribe a similar set of specific objectives related to the potential sponsorship. This set of anticipated outcomes serves to steer the screening and eventual selection process. After the decision has been made to engage in a particular sport sponsorship, the sponsor as well as the sponsee is charged with successfully implementing the program and effectively leveraging the arrangement. It is incumbent on both parties to conduct a post-sponsorship assessment referring to the set of anticipated outcomes identified early in the process. A universal approach to this process, depicted in figure 8.5, will serve as a framework for the remainder of this chapter.[12]

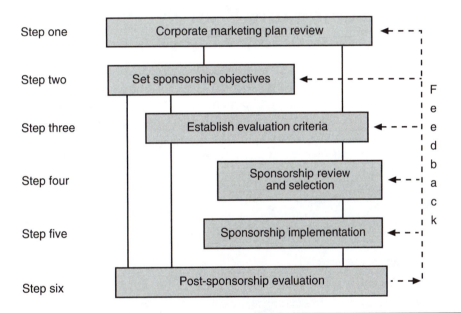

Figure 8.5 Six-step approach to sport sponsorship management.

Reprinted, by permission, from R.L. Irwin and M.K. Assimakopoulos, 1992, "An approach to the evaluation and selection of sport sponsorship proposals," *Sport Marketing Quarterly* 1 (2):43-51. © Fitness Information Technology.

Marketing Plan Review

Corporate sponsorship has continued to thrive primarily because of its diverse abilities to serve as a platform for a specific type of brand extension, cut through the clutter of traditional media advertising, and provide a cost-effective business-building technique.[13] Defined as an investment "to support overall corporate objectives and/or marketing objectives,"[14] sponsorship has become such a successful communications vehicle that it has emerged as a distinct element of many organizations' promotion mix. It appears that corporations use sport sponsorship as a means of supplementing rather than replacing traditional marketing communications.

This is not to suggest that it is not appropriate for sport businesses themselves to integrate sponsorship-type activities into their organizational marketing plans. In fact, many would strongly recommend that a sport organization's marketing should include sponsorship in a key role. This may occur in one of two ways: a sport property can be a **sponsee,** in which case it exploits support garnered from sponsors to achieve its promotional objectives; or it can be a sponsor, in which case the sport organization assumes a supportive role for an external business or organization. Up to now, most sport businesses have relied far too heavily on the first alternative, failing to fully maximize the advantages of the second sponsorship alternative.

Whether sport assumes the role of sponsor or serves as the sponsorship platform, however, it is necessary for the organization to determine that sponsorship makes good business sense and is compatible with its overall marketing strategy. Far too many parties have entered the sponsorship arena for the wrong reasons, such as decision-maker personal interests or hobbies, thus wasting valuable organizational resources and hampering the two parties' relationship.[15] Critical to the effective management of a sport sponsorship is determining what it is the sponsor desires to achieve as a result of the partnership. It therefore behooves corporate sponsorship decision-makers to prepare a list of desired outcomes before entering into the sponsorship.

Setting and Prioritizing Sponsorship Objectives

Once the organization has decided that sponsorship makes sense, the next step is to establish a set of clearly defined objectives for engagement, as is usual with all promotion mix components. The corporate marketing and communication plan is typically the driving force behind any determination of specific sport sponsorship objectives. These sponsorship objectives are in turn used to guide the sponsorship proposal screening. As shown in figure 8.6, corporations engage in the sponsorship of sport for diverse purposes, ranging from demonstrating "good corporate citizenship" through support of civic events to achieving product- or brand-related outcomes such as direct communication with a specific target market through leisure or lifestyle activities.

A. Corporation-related objectives

1. Increase public awareness of the company and its services
2. Enhance company image
3. Alter public perception
4. Become involved with the community
5. Build business/trade relations and goodwill
6. Enhance staff/employee relations and motivation

B. Product- or brand-related objectives

1. Increase target market awareness
2. Identify/Build image within target market (positioning)
3. Block/Preempt the competition
4. Increase sales and market share

Figure 8.6　Common sport sponsorship objectives.

Corporation-Related Sport Sponsorship Objectives

Companies use a sport sponsorship to achieve a broad range of objectives. Several of these objectives relate to the company engaging in the sponsorship.

Increase public awareness of the company and its services　Sport has proven to be highly effective as a communication medium for increasing public awareness. When Philips, an electronics company, sponsored the Soccer World Cup (event sponsorship), it had as one of its objectives the improvement of public awareness for both the company and its products. To achieve this objective, Philips leveraged the sponsorship by using an integrative marketing communications plan, which along with the international coverage of the World Cup was implemented to generate international name recognition for Philips.

Enhance company image Each company strives to attain a particular image with customers, stockholders, and the general public. Sport is associated with a healthy lifestyle; this association can be good for the sponsor and was the rationale that led Campbell Soup Company to sponsor the physical fitness testing programs in American schools. Companies may also want to enhance their geographical image. For example, companies often become involved with major international sporting events such as the Olympic Games in order to enhance their global image.

Alter public perception A long-term commitment is required in order to effectively alter public perception and build a strong corporate image through a sport sponsorship, as it takes longer to change an already established public perception than to maintain an existing one. Nike's attempt to portray itself as a soccer company is an excellent example of an attempt by an organization to alter its public perception. Having established itself as a very strong force in many major sports, particularly in North America, Nike viewed soccer as the one sport where it could grow its market substantially. Because soccer is the most popular sport in the world, Nike reasoned that becoming established in soccer would enlarge its opportunity to create a global brand. The company entered into a sponsorship arrangement with the Brazilian Football Federation. Brazil at the time held the Men's Soccer World Cup and was also the most successful team ever in the competition, having won on three occasions. Nike was attempting to convince a skeptical global market that its soccer product was good enough to be worn and used by the most successful and famous soccer nation on earth. Nike was attempting to change the soccer market's perception.

Involvement with the community It is often part of a company's "good-citizenship" effort to contribute to the local and the surrounding community. Studies have shown this to be especially the case for telephone companies, utilities, banks, real estate agencies, supermarkets, and retail outlets. Regional, state, and local championships, involving teams within a targeted geographical drawing radius, provide an excellent opportunity to enhance a company's involvement and recognition within a community. Such was the case for Farm Bureau Insurance when it became the exclusive sponsor of the Indiana State High School Athletic Association. Many recent facility sponsorships, such as PacBell's sponsorship of PacBell Park in San Francisco, have resulted from a company's response to a challenge from the community to retain a professional sport franchise that is threatening relocation and demanding an improved facility.

Build business and trade relations and goodwill Sport offers an opportunity for building relationships with businesses, affiliates, and trade customers beyond the daily business operations. The opportunity for potential customers to be present, as well as the provision of guest hospitality accommodations such as choice reserved or skybox seating, special receptions, and corporate hospitality tents, is unique to sport sponsorship programs and has become a priority.

Enhance staff and employee relations and motivation Sport sponsorship can help increase staff motivation and corporate pride. For instance, Piedmont Airlines—sponsoring an entry in car races—found that employees were inspired to follow and support the company's car and thus that the sponsorship enhanced employee motivation and pride in the company. Another desirable sponsorship feature is the ability to use the hospitality accommodations at a sponsored event for employees and staff.

Product and Brand-Related Sport Sponsorship Objectives

Sport sponsorship often serves as a platform for promoting a specific brand or product. Objectives that may be achieved range from increasing awareness within a defined market segment to increasing sales and market share of a particular product.

Increase target market awareness   The selection of a sport that provides exposure to the company's target market is crucial for realizing product brand-related objectives. Thus, the demographics of the participants or spectators, size of the immediate (spectators) and extended (media) audience, and the strength of the audience's association with the sport are important evaluation criteria for companies seeking to increase awareness within a specific market. Volvo recognized a consumer demographic match with tennis fans and chose to sponsor a variety of amateur and professional tennis tournaments. Sponsoring established teams or events, or having the name of the brand in the title of the team or event, can quickly produce high awareness levels.

Sharp achieved such recognition when it entered into a shirt sponsorship with Manchester United. It is quite common, outside of North America, to have sponsors' names displayed in "the heart of the action," that is, on the field of play or on the players themselves. By having its name on the front of the Manchester United shirts, Sharp achieved market awareness virtually overnight. In contrast, FedEx's attempt to use the word "Express" in association with the NBA's Vancouver Grizzlies' move to Memphis was blocked by the league office.

Identify and build image within the target market (positioning)   Sport sponsorship is a valuable tool for creating or altering the image of a product. For instance, Bud Light sponsored the Ironman Triathlon in Hawaii, a combination of swimming, cycling, and running, as an effective means of promoting a healthy, low-calorie image for the product.

Increase sales or market share   Although an increase in sales is the desirable outcome of any communication campaign, it is very difficult to attribute that increase exclusively to any individual promotion mix element, in particular a sport sponsorship. Contrary to this theoretical argument, sport sponsors persistently evaluate sponsorship programs exclusively on the achievement of sales objectives. It is therefore necessary for the sponsorship promoter to develop a sponsorship incorporating sales enhancement opportunities. Companies often do this using on-site product sales opportunities (a tactic frequently employed by soft drink vendors), in-store promotions, sponsorship-linked coupon campaigns, or customer entertainment opportunities such as on-site corporate hospitality or auxiliary social functions. These provide sales executives a forum for interacting with invited business guests and often discussing, if not negotiating, deals on behalf of the host firm.

Block or preempt competition   Frequently companies can use sport sponsorship as a means of fighting the competition. Categorical **exclusivity** is extremely crucial for achieving this objective because this strategy prevents the competition from entering into a particular sport whose exposure is large and whose demographics fit the industry's target market. The continued support of the IOC's TOP program by credit card company Visa keeps American Express, Visa's arch-rival, from achieving any connection with the largest multisport event in the world. This is an association American Express craves, judging by its continued attempts at ambushing Visa's involvement with the Olympic Games.

Table 8.1   North American Corporate Sport Sponsorship Objective Dimensions

Dimension	Objective
1: Position enhancement	Increase general public awareness Increase market share/sales Block competition Display community involvement
2: Status enhancement	Alter public perception Enhance corporate image
3: Trade networking	Enhance trade relations Enhance trade goodwill
4: Public service	Corporate philanthropy Social responsibility Employee relations

Researchers have found that the most common objectives of corporations actively involved in sport sponsorship fit into one of four sport sponsorship dimensions as revealed in table 8.1.[16] However, while data gathered from corporate sponsorship decision-makers around the world have consistently indicated that position enhancement objectives (such as increasing sales or market share and increasing target market awareness) are of the greatest importance, the purpose for sponsorship involvement varies depending on the sponsorship's level of "maturity."[17] As with any marketable commodity, it appears that sport sponsorship experiences a product life cycle with defined periods of introduction, growth, maturity, and potential decline. Recent research indicates that as a sponsorship matures during its life cycle, a sponsor's purpose or objective for engagement changes in its orientation from public service to position enhancement (figure 8.7). Factors influencing the sponsorship's stage of maturity appear to be demographic (age, sex, geographical location, and income) in nature. For instance, corporations engaging in relatively newer or less mature forms of sport sponsorship (e.g., American women's sport, Special Olympics, and sport facility naming rights) typically were most interested in achieving public service-oriented objectives. Meanwhile, corporations involved in relatively mature forms of sport sponsorship (e.g., NFL, NBA, MLB) expressed significantly greater interest in position enhancement-type objectives. According

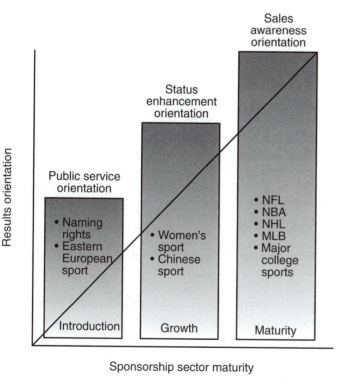

Figure 8.7 Sponsorship product growth life cycle.

to these results, experienced sport sponsorship decision-makers acknowledge that the product warrants a qualitative incubation period before measurable outcome expectations are established.

Sponsorship expectations that are incongruent with sponsorship product maturity lead to dissatisfaction and counterproductive action as evidenced in central Europe, where corporate decision-makers, familiar with sport sponsorship success stories from western Europe and North America, initially established unrealistic position enhancement-type expectations from a very youthful form of sport sponsorship.[18] Sponsors mistakenly entered many agreements with the aspiration of immediately realizing increased sales among team patrons. Lack of sponsorship familiarity among team marketing representatives hindered the effectiveness of those arrangements. Similar mistakes are not limited to regions of emerging economies but can be common for maturing sport sponsorships.

In any case, the selected objectives should be prioritized prior to the sponsorship screening, selection, or implementation process. The predetermined sponsorship objectives then act as a guide for all subsequent decisions and actions. Statements of the selected objectives should be specific; specificity will help the organization not only establish selection criteria and but also perform a successful post-sponsorship evaluation.

Setting Sponsee Objectives

As in the case of the prospective sponsor, the sponsee must establish a defined set of objectives or benefits to be achieved as a result of the anticipated partnership. In fact, it is highly advisable for sponsees to share these objectives with prospective sponsors and include them in submitted proposals. Generally speaking, the sponsorship promoter seeks to achieve one or more of the following from a **corporate partnership:**[19]

The provision of financial resources

The provision of media exposure

The provision of in-kind product or services

It is important to note that a majority of sponsorships are noncash **exchanges.** Even the $40 million sponsorships solicited for the 1996 Olympic Games in Atlanta were commonly partial cash and in-kind. Therefore the sport sponsorship promoter needs to use sponsorship as a means of maximizing the communication strategy of the sport organization. Many sponsorship promoters believe that securing in-kind mass media trade (as discussed in chapter 7) is a primary consideration. This type of arrangement enables the sport promoter to build a cost-effective foundation for all other promotional vehicles, including attracting and servicing other sponsors seeking similar media benefits.

Obviously, the pursuit of such an objective is dependent on the nature of the sport business, since a community recreation program or high school athletic program will not be seeking or servicing sponsors with mass media trade. Instead, these sport businesses can design in-kind sponsorship packages aimed at reducing operational expenses through the procurement of products or services used on a regular basis. In these arrangements, commonly referred to as *trade agreements,* the contracting parties (sponsor and sponsee) essentially assist one another in achieving critical promotional and operational objectives. Trade agreements are typically more attractive than cash agreements in that they enable a sponsor to partner with a sport organization without significant capital outlay yet provide the sponsor a real cost-saving tactic. For instance, Nike gives the AXA Liberty Bowl a significant supply of athletic apparel that the bowl uses as gifts for participating players, coaches, institutional administrators, and other sponsors as trade for event tickets and advertising. The relationship enables the bowl to save thousands of dollars in gift purchases while allowing Nike to receive comparable sponsor benefits.

Sport Sponsorship Proposal Criteria and Entitlements

Corporations generally prepare a "laundry list" of desired sponsorship-related criteria before becoming involved in a specific sponsorship program. It is important that sport sponsorship promoters learn what proposal criteria and entitlements are of greatest interest to those reviewing and selecting sponsorship programs. Research involving corporate sport sponsorship decision-makers has revealed that the most highly desired sponsorship inventory criteria can be classified as those relating to image projection, audience profile, and media exposure (figure 8.8).[20] As in the case of sponsorship motives, the importance and application of proposal criteria may vary from one sponsorship to another depending on the sponsorship's stage in the product life cycle. Figure 8.9 presents a comprehensive list of 42 possible sport sponsorship proposal criteria; the discussion here focuses on the criteria that are most important to key sponsorship decision-makers.

Objective	Mean rating
Image related	
Fit of product or service with sport image	6.3
Product category exclusivity	6.1
Consumer related	
Demographic profile of immediate audience	6.0
Demographic profile of extended audience	6.0
Media related	
Signage opportunities	5.9
Media coverage guarantees	5.8

Figure 8.8 Mean ratings of corporate sport sponsorship criteria.

Reprinted, from Irwin, Assimakopoulos, and Sutton, 1994, *Journal of Promotion Management*, Vol.2 (3) (Binghamton, New York: Haworth Press, Inc.), 53-69.

Image Projection

Although image enhancement no longer ranks as the primary motive for general or "mature" sport sponsorship involvement, image-related issues become critically important in the proposal analysis process. Corporate sport sponsorship decision-makers remain genuinely interested in having the proposal reflect the sponsee's image, an objective that is far more easily stated than met. Representing a sport business's image within the context of a written proposal demands a significant amount of imagination and attention to detail.

For instance, should the proposal target a multinational, industry-leading computer services company, it may be necessary to project an upscale image using high-resolution photography and imported graphics, if not a computerized virtual demonstration program. On the other hand, a sponsee attempting to portray an image of

Criteria	Wt	-4	-3	-2	-1	0	+1	+2	+3	+4	Total
Budget considerations											
Affordability											
Cost-effectiveness											
Management issues											
Event profile											
Organizing committee status											
Media guarantees											
Legal status											
Regulatory policy											
Athlete cooperation											
Governing body status											
Marketing agency profile											
Positioning image											
Product-sport image fit											
Product utility fit											
Image-target market fit											
Targeting of market											
Immediate audience											
Demographic fit											
Size											
Fan association strength											
Extended media coverage											
National coverage											
Local coverage											
Extended audience profile											
Demographics fit											
Size											
Public relations											
Hospitality accommodation											
Community leader presence											
Customers' presence											
Staff sport knowledge											
Event sales/recall tie-in											
New account opportunities											
Promotional opportunities											
Promotional licensing											
Complimentary advertising											
Signage opportunities											
Competition consideration											
Competition's interest											
Ambush market avoidance											
Sponsorship status											
Title sponsor											
Major sponsor											
Exclusivity											
Established											
Long-term involvement											
Alternative sponsorship											
Cosponsor											
In-kind supplier											
Sponsorship type											
Team											
League/championship											
Event											
Facility											
Grand total											

Figure 8.9 Sport sponsorship proposal evaluation model.

Reprinted, from Irwin, Assimakopoulos, and Sutton, 1994, *Journal of Promotion Management*, Vol. 2 (3/4) (Binghamton, New York: Haworth Press, Inc.), 67.

need, seeking support from businesses in a blue-collar community, may find that a proposal with a less sophisticated look is more readily accepted. According to a director of athletics at a small American college, "Our proposal is intended to look a little cheap so that the prospective sponsor is not offended, and clearly understands that we need their help. If I designed a fancy, slick proposal, prospective as well as existing sponsors would undoubtedly perceive that as wasteful as well as beyond their means."

Then, how can a firm successfully identify which sport or event will contribute to, or match up with, the firm's current or desired image? Perceptual mapping, as used by Martin, is one means a sponsor or sponsorship promoter can use to assess the market's image of each party. The results of Martin's analysis (figure 8.10) indicate that a firm seeking to project an image of speed would explore sponsorship opportunities in basketball or football, whereas one seeking to project an image of precision would pursue golf.[21] This type of image-matching process contributed to FedEx's decision to secure the Championship Auto Racing Team series title sponsorship in 1998. Follow-up research with customers has validated the sponsor-sponsee image match for such attributes as speed, timing, and technology.[22]

An image-related criterion of keen interest to sponsorship decision-makers is that of category exclusivity, reportedly the proposal criterion of greatest importance to Canadian sport sponsors.[23] Recognition as the "official" or exclusive sponsor or supplier within the defined product or service class should represent a position of distinction and a measure of renown. Furthermore, such a distinction should suggest that the sponsor plays a critical role in the sponsee's operational status.

Additionally, as previously mentioned, the criterion of exclusivity serves to achieve a strategic block against competition that might wish to associate with the sponsee. Visa often touts a sport sponsorship by indicating that the event does not accept American Express. Therefore, Visa's sponsorship in essence blocks American Express, or any other credit card for that matter, from doing business with the sponsee. Similar arrangements occur when a soft drink supplier, usually Coca-Cola or Pepsi, enters into a sponsorship with a sport venue. For instance, PepsiCo products are poured at the concession stand in Denver's Pepsi Arena, home of the NBA's Denver Nuggets and NHL's Colorado Avalanche, while the alcohol beverages available at Coors Field in Denver are undoubtedly Coors products.

Audience Profile

According to one sponsorship decision-maker, "The quickest means to rejection is omitting audience characteristics from the proposal." Information of greatest interest to prospective sponsors is a demographic description of the audience, immediate (those in attendance) as well as extended (those consuming through the media), where appropriate. Additionally, partnering corporations will be interested in receiving information pertaining to audience lifestyle characteristics as well as sponsorship impact data. Tables 8.2, 8.3, and 8.4 display event patron information collected annually by the NCAA and used to maintain as well as to solicit sponsors. A prospective sponsor can review the information and assess the potential consumer "fit" for its particular market.

A recent poll revealed that corporate executives considered NASCAR the best sport sponsorship opportunity primarily because of the sponsor brand loyalty exhibited by NASCAR consumers. Performance Research reports that NASCAR fans have a higher level of trust toward sponsors' products than other fan groups do—approximately 60% of NASCAR fans compared to only 30% for football fans. More importantly, more than 40% of NASCAR fans purposely switched brands when a manufacturer became a NASCAR sponsor.[24]

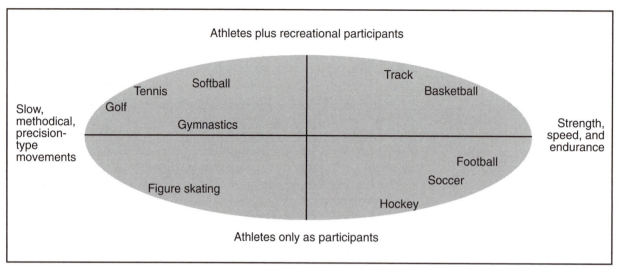

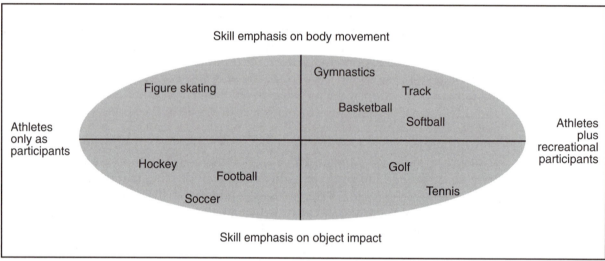

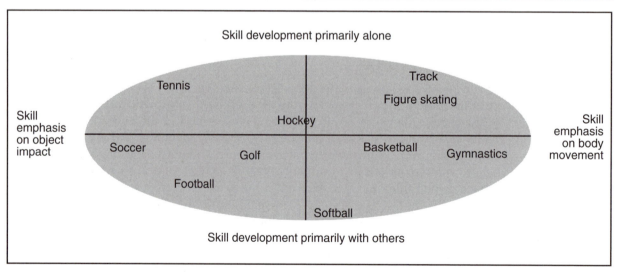

Figure 8.10 Perceptual mapping for sports.

Reprinted, by permission, from J.H. Martin, PhD, 1994, "Using a perceptual map of the consumer's sport schema to help make sponsorship decisions," *Sport Marketing Quarterly* 3 (3):32. © Fitness Information Technology.

Table 8.2 NCAA Corporate Partner Research

NCAA corporate partner	Is this a brand you prefer or use often?	Does this partnership improve your impression of this company?	Based on its support of the NCAA, would you consider usage of this brand?	Before today, were you aware of this company's NCAA partnership?
American Express	30%	48.9%	38.4%	18.6%
Aquafina	32.6%	46.1%	48.7%	20.2%
Champion International	21.2%	42.9%	39.7%	12.4%
Compaq	29.6%	45.3%	40.9%	14.4%
Continental Airlines	17.4%	44.8%	38.8%	11.9%
GM	33.6%	45.7%	39.6%	19.6%
GTE	35.7%	44.8%	41.1%	18.3%
Gillette	56.2%	49.1%	46.8%	16%
Hershey's	69.3%	50.6%	53.3%	22.5%
KFC	37.4%	43.9%	43.6%	14%
Kraft	58.4%	47.2%	45.9%	13.8%
Marriott	55%	50%	47.5%	13.4%
Nabisco	63.9%	51.5%	49.2%	12.7%
Ocean Spray	55.1%	52.8%	50.4%	15.3%
Pepsi	60.9%	51.2%	46.1%	26.2%
Phoenix Insurance	3%	37.3%	24.2%	5.3%
Pizza Hut	42.6%	47.6%	42.9%	26.5%
Rawlings	24.8%	45.5%	40%	12.8%
Sears	48.2%	49.2%	45.5%	19.3%
Taco Bell	61.8%	49%	46.8%	18.3%

Only favorable responses are reported. The data reflects the degree of association among the NCAA, its corporate partners, and the championship patrons.

Reprinted, by permission, from R.L. Irwin and W.A. Sutton, 1994, "Sport sponsorship objectives: An analysis of their relative importance for major corporate sponsors," *European Journal for Sport Management* 1 (12):93-101.

Table 8.3 — NCAA Championship Patron Analysis Assessing Consumer Behavior Patterns

Question	% consumer response
Dine at fast food restaurant 3 times a week (average bill $[1])	36.8
Have food (pizza) delivered once a week	19.7
Have two or more credit cards (average balance $[2])	47.3
Own my home or residence	74.8
Use a cellular/mobile phone (average bill $[3])	53.6
Travel out of town for business at least once a month	31.0
Travel out of town for pleasure at least twice a year	42.3
Use a professional financial planning service	28.4
Have at least one home computer (home Internet access[4])	77.4
Consume at least one 12-oz. can of soda daily	43.6
Consume at least one 12-oz. bottle of water daily	62.5
Spend at least $25 on sporting goods equipment monthly	61.2
Plan to purchase/lease a new vehicle in the next year (anticipated model)	21.4

[1]Average bill was $13.38.
[2]Average balance was $1103.00.
[3]Average bill was $66.25.
[4]46% have Internet access.
Note: Only affirmative responses reported.

Media Opportunities

An integrated sport sponsorship proposal will give the sponsor guaranteed as well as non-guaranteed media exposure opportunities. Guaranteed sponsorship-linked media opportunities are those under the control of the sponsorship promoter, such as public address announcements, facility signage, print and media advertising, and on-air broadcast mentions. The most popular media opportunities provided by American collegiate athletic programs are found in table 8.5.[25] In-venue signage garners significant interest because it draws immediate as well as extended audience recognition if appropriately placed. For instance, placing corporate signage in high-visibility areas such as the scoreboard, scorer's table, or dasher boards will generate the greatest volume of media impressions for the sponsor. However, as a means of protection against unforeseen circumstances, the sponsee may wish to include a clause in the sponsorship agreement indicating that sponsor signage exposure during event telecasts is not controlled by the sponsee and therefore not guaranteed. The advent of virtual advertising, enabling the broadcaster to project images (typically in the form of advertisements) on background venue signage may make the inclusion of this clause more common in sport sponsorship agreements.

Table 8.4 NCAA Championship Patron Analysis Constructing Consumer Demographic Profile

Age[1]	% of consumers
<25	7
25-34	19
35-44	26
45-54	39
55 or more	9
Annual household income	**% of consumers**
Less than $25,000	4.3
$25,000-$49,999	12.8
$50,000-$74,999	17.9
$75,000-$99,999	22.2
$100,000-$124,999	10.6
$125,000 or more	32.2

[1]The average age was 42.7.

Table 8.5 Frequency of Guaranteed Media Opportunities Within Collegiate Athletic Program Sponsorship Packages

Media opportunities	% of frequency
Public address announcements	95
Facility signage	94
Souvenir program advertising	82
Ticket back advertising	82
On-air broadcast mentions	68

Reprinted, by permission, from D. Irwin, 1993, "In search of sponsors," *Athletic Management* 5 (3:May):10-16. © Momentum Media. Reprinted from *Athletic Management* magazine.

Matching Objectives and Proposal Ingredients

A sponsorship arrangement is more likely to be consummated when there is a close correspondence between what the corporation seeks to achieve from the sponsorship (sponsorship objective) and what the sponsee has to offer, or the criteria contained within a sport sponsorship proposal. Therefore, early on, sponsorship promoters should familiarize themselves with a prospective sponsor's sponsorship objectives to learn about the company's desired outcome. Once familiar with the prospect's objectives, the sponsorship organizer has a paradigm for customizing sponsorship packages and incorporating criteria most desired by corporate sponsorship decision-makers.[26]

Research has revealed that the desirability of sport sponsorship criteria is to some extent predictable. Table 8.6 presents the individual and collective criteria that may be expected to match a prospective sponsor's desired objectives.[27] Corporations interested in achieving position enhancement as well as status enhancement via sport sponsorship seek diversified, integrated sponsorship proposals. For example, when ShasCo, Inc., makers of Shasta beverages, sought to expand their market west of the Mississippi, the company elected to become involved with the Women's Tennis Association Tour in Los Angeles, the Los Angeles Marathon, the Freedom Bowl, and a number of fairs and festivals in Arizona, California, and Hawaii. The rationale for downplaying traditional advertising and media and emphasizing sporting events was based on the multidimensional ways in which these events provide for cost-effective position enhancement opportunities with large, captive audiences.

Table 8.6 Sport Sponsorship Inventory Criteria Predicted by Corporate Sponsorship Objective Dimension

	Trade networking	Public service	Status enhancement	Position enforcement
Hospitality accommodations			X	
Community leader presence		X		
Current customers' presence	X			X
Staff sport knowledge		X		
Event sales/retail tie-in				X
New account opportunities				X
Promotional licensing provisions			X	
Complimentary advertising provisions				X
Signage opportunities				X
Competition's interest in proposal			X	X
Ambush market avoidance				X
Title sponsorship			X	
Major sponsorship				X
Exclusivity			X	X
Established sponsorship			X	
Long-term agreement			X	
Cosponsorship opportunity	X			

	Trade networking	**Public service**	**Status enhancement**	**Position enforcement**
In-kind supplier				X
Team sponsorship			X	
Series/league sponsorship		X	X	
Event sponsorship			X	
Facility sponsorship		X		X
Affordability			X	X
Cost-effectiveness			X	X
Sponsoree profile				X
Status of sponsoree management	X			
Media guarantees				X
Governing body regulatory policy			X	X
Participating athlete cooperation	X			
Governing body status			X	
Marketing agency profile			X	
Product-sport image fit			X	X
Image-target market fit			X	X
Immediate audience demographic fit				X
Immediate audience size				X
Fan association strength (loyalty)			X	
National media coverage opportunities				X
Local media coverage opportunities				X
Extended audience demographic fit			X	X
Extended audience size				X

Reprinted, by permission, from R.L. Irwin and W.A. Sutton, 1995, "Creating the ideal sponsorship arrangement," *Proceedings from the Bi-annual World Marketing Congress*, Melbourne, Australia. © Academy of Marketing Science.

On the other hand, the limited number of sponsorship inventory criteria that match up with the sponsorship dimensions of public service and trade networking appears to indicate the specificity with which proposal elements are desired for fulfillment of these infrequently demanded, narrowly defined sponsorship objectives. According to senior marketing decision-makers, Texaco entered into an Olympic sponsorship relationship for the purpose of enhancing trade relations with a leading supplier of Texaco Food Marts and event cosponsor, Coca-Cola. In fact, trade networking has been found to be the most important sport sponsorship objective dimension for food and beverage companies.[28] Therefore, it would appear that cosponsorship opportunities, as well as other matching criteria, would be desirable inventory criteria for proposals targeted to prospective sponsors in this industry category.

Adherence to this "tailored" packaging approach will lead to symbiotic sponsee-sponsor relationships, thereby significantly enhancing the rates of receptivity to sport sponsorship proposals. Furthermore, undertaking this process permits sport organizations to prepare proposals more efficiently and in all probability to reduce the number of proposals they need to prepare and submit. This will help maximize the resources (personnel, time, and money) allocated to the sponsorship recruitment process, and the potential savings will enable the sport organization to redirect energies to other organizational initiatives.

Additionally, sponsorship promoters may allow for enhanced pricing scales if a proposal accurately matches what the potential sponsor is seeking. Proposals "engineered" to fit corporate shopping lists could warrant more serious consideration and receive funding at a higher level than proposals designed without the benefit of this process. It is imperative that the sponsee establish a means (e.g., personal contact, questionnaire) of appraising a potential sponsor's objectives and determining how these indicators affect the chances for successful solicitation.

For sport sponsorship promoters unable to design sponsorship programs tailored to the specific interests of each prospective sponsor, table 8.6 provides some information on appropriate "packaging" of generic proposals. As we know that the dimension of position enhancement includes a majority of the sport sponsorship objectives that are most important to key corporate sponsorship decision-makers, it follows that proposals including specific criteria matching up with this dimension rate higher in the decision-making process. Such proposals are the most likely to simultaneously meet multiple critical interests of the corporate sponsor. Proposals addressing position enhancement should therefore have wider appeal and acceptance within the departmental negotiations that characterize decision-making processes for agendas like sponsorship proposals, advertising allocations, and promotional spending, even when the screening audiences are diverse.

All sponsorship proposals contain numerous strengths and potential advantages, each hopefully minimizing risk and effectively reaching the targeted market with the intended message. Integrated proposals designed with criteria that will work separately or together minimize the prospective sponsor's risk by providing a number of possible ways to achieve a defined objective. Thus the proposal that presents a diverse, multidimensional approach to achieving the corporation's objectives should merit the highest degree of consideration.

Sport Sponsorship Selection

Although most corporations appear to be selecting sport sponsorships on the basis of objective criteria that originate from within the sponsoring organization, Berrett and Slack have identified a number of subjective factors external to the firm, and outside its control, that influence the sponsorship selection process. In particular, they found that social networks in the form of personal friendships of high-ranking officials and interlocking directorships, thought to have been outdated, influenced a number of sponsorship selection decisions. Unfortunately, it appeared that this frequently led to irrational decisions, warranting the use of objective screening and selection processes.[29]

A Sponsorship Proposal Screening Tool

The sport sponsorship proposal evaluation model (SSPEM) was developed in an effort to address the need for a screening tool.[30] The instrument, shown in figure 8.9, consists of 42 potential sport sponsorship criteria, positioned within 11 sponsorship management dimensions. It allows the evaluator to weight or prioritize preferable criteria on a scale of 1 (low priority) to 10 (high priority) depending on the corporation's predefined sport sponsorship objectives. On the horizontal axis, submitted proposals are rated (–4 to +4) on their perceived ability to fulfill the weighted criteria. These features give the evaluator the opportunity to analyze and compare strengths and weaknesses of various proposals, which should make possible a more objective selection of the most appropriate sponsorship arrangement. Using the SSPEM enables the sponsorship management team to position the funding decision as a quantifiable decision on the basis of a formula using key criteria that the management team has agreed on. This is especially important given the emotional nature of decisions often associated with consumption of the sport product and the need for accountability in decision-making in today's marketplace.

Arthur, Scott, and Woods conceptualized a sport sponsorship acquisition model as depicted in figure 8.11. The process, which may include the use of an objective screening instrument, also incorporates a buying grid (table 8.7). This illustrates to some degree the influence of the sponsorship's maturity on the volume of information that key sponsorship decision-makers typically want. The model also depicts the role of a "buying center"

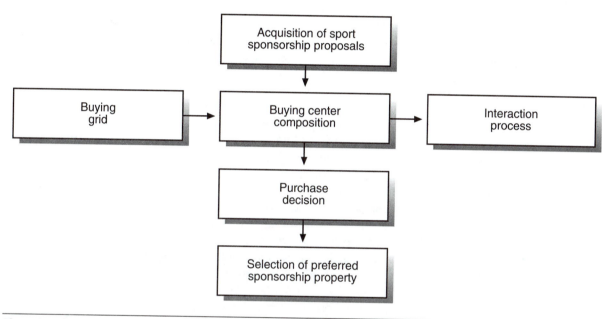

Figure 8.11   Sport sponsorship acquisition model.

Reprinted, by permission, from D. Arthur, D. Scott, and T. Woods, 1997, "A conceptual model of the corporate decision-making process of sport sponsorship acquisition," *Journal of Sport Management* 11 (3):223-233.

Table 8.7   Sponsorship Buying Decision Grid

The sponsorship buying situation	Newness of the problem	Information requirements	Consideration of new alternatives
New sponsorship	High	Maximum	Important
Modified sponsorship rebuy	Medium	Moderate	Limited
Straight sponsorship rebuy	Low	Minimal	None

Reprinted with permission from the *Journal of Marketing,* published by the American Marketing Association, E. Anderson, W. Chu, and B. Weitz, July 1987, 51: 71-86.

that may comprise representatives, internal as well as external, to the potential sponsor. For instance, a corporation may employ the services of a sport marketing agency to assist with or conduct the review of proposed sport sponsorship agreements. Interaction among these constituencies ultimately leads to a purchase decision.[31]

Once approval is given for a sponsorship program, it is vitally important that the terms and conditions be set out in the form of a written, legally binding sponsorship agreement. It is critical that the obligations of each party be specified as well as remuneration, nonperformance, and early-termination provisions.

Implementation and Execution

Before, during, and after the sponsorship review and selection process, discussion must focus on the concept of sponsorship linking. According to Cornwell, sponsorship linking is based on self-evident links as well as strategic links.[32] Self-evident links are those that are logically sanctioned, for example when a product is used within the context of the activity. This type of linkage is common among sporting equipment manufacturers and suppliers as well as ergogenic aid distributors who sponsor sport. On the other hand, strategic links most often relate to sponsee-based characteristics such as the audience profile. In certain companies this means that it is necessary to make a critical decision regarding the sponsor's targeted unit. To achieve the prescribed marketing or sponsorship objectives, a sponsor may chose to link a sponsorship with the company, a product line, or a specific brand. General Motors (GM), the official corporate partner of the NCAA, has chosen to link different car models with preselected NCAA championships depending on the audience profile and host community characteristics. For instance, GM chose to target Buick at the 2000 Women's Final Four while opting to target Pontiac at the 1999 Women's Soccer Championship. In a similar situation, Time-Warner chose to target *Sports Illustrated* for its sponsorship of the 1996 Olympics held in Atlanta.

The type of sponsorship link relates to the sponsor's level of participation in the sponsored activity. Nonparticipatory sponsorship linking more closely resembles corporate philanthropy in that the sponsor does not maintain an ongoing presence in the sponsored event, activity, or organization. However, research indicates that although sponsorship is an effective communication strategy it is also rather ineffective as a stand-alone technique.[33] For that reason, some level of participation, whether it be fully active or arms-length participation, is strongly encouraged among sponsorship managers. Participatory arms-length sponsorship involves delegation of responsibility to a third party, most likely an advertising agency, that executes the sponsorship on behalf of the corporation, thus minimizing the involvement of company resources, human and otherwise. In participatory sponsorship, management and staff from the sponsoring group are actively involved. Such personal participation affords the sponsor the best opportunity to achieve personal contact as discussed in chapter 5.

Participatory sponsorship also gives the sponsoring corporation a means of leveraging the initial sponsorship investment. In fact, on average, for every dollar spent on sport sponsorship, a sponsor spends another five on sponsorship-linked marketing efforts including television, radio, and print advertising; hospitality; and other forms of corporate promotion.[34] The most popular supplemental sponsorship activities are listed in table 8.8.[35]

Companies tracking sponsor awareness have found that significant growth occurs within the first three years of the sponsorship.[36] Perhaps these data have influenced sponsorship negotiations, as most sponsorship contractual obligations apply for a period of approximately three to five years.[37] This varies in the case of facility naming rights agreements, which commonly extend for 10 to 20 years. So that the sponsor has the security of knowing that the agreement will remain in place only as long as it is

Table 8.8 Frequency of Supplemental Sponsorship Activities

Activities	% of supplementation
Advertising	89
Public relations activities	78
Consumer promotions	67
Trade promotions	53
Sales force promotions	52

Reprinted, by permission, from R. Copeland, W. Frisby, and R. McCarville, 1996, "Understanding the sport sponsorship process," *Journal of Sport Management* 10 (1):32-48.

beneficial to both parties, termination clauses should be adopted for sponsors with legitimate claims of limited or no return on investment. This leads to the need for both the sponsor and sponsee to perform evaluations to determine the effectiveness of the relationship.

Sponsorship Evaluation

As sponsorship has evolved from its philanthropic roots to its contemporary commercial orientation, so too has the need for sophisticated post-sponsorship evaluation measures. As with all other elements of an organization's promotion mix, sponsorship should be subjected to heavy analytical protocol. Of course the actual methods of evaluation will depend to a great extent on the level of the sponsorship: those involving larger allocations of resources attract far more rigorous and complex evaluation that those involving less expenditure.[38]

The most popular means of postevent assessment are shown in table 8.9.[39] From this table we can hypothesize that the evaluation measure closely corresponds with the established sponsorship objective. Likewise, table 8.10 presents the most common

Table 8.9 Common Sport Sponsorship Evaluation Methods

Measure	% of sponsors that use measure
1. Awareness, exposure, media coverage	61.5
2. Sales	46.2
3. Dealer/trade feedback	26.2
4. Attendance at event	15.4
5. Targeted	13.8
6. Involvement of field	10.8
7. Corporate image	10.8
8. Market share	10.8

Reprinted, by permission, from R. Copeland, W. Frisby, and R. McCarville, 1996, "Understanding the sport sponsorship process," *Journal of Sport Management* 10 (1):32-48.

grounds for discontinuing sponsorships.[40] In each case it appears that the established sponsorship objectives play a dominant role in determining a sponsor's level of satisfaction, strengthening the case that sponsorship promoters should become familiar with the prospective sponsor's motives for seeking a sponsorship before the agreement is made.

Table 8.10   Sport Sponsorship Discontinuance Rational

Reason	% of non-renewing sponsors
1. Little value/return on investment	36.5
2. Not achieving objectives	27.0
3. Different corporate direction/strategy	20.6
4. Budget cutbacks	20.6
5. Poor execution/performance of event organizer	19.0
6. Increased sponsorship cost	12.7
7. Conflict with organizer	9.5

Reprinted, by permission, from R. Copeland, W. Frisby, and R. McCarville, 1996, "Understanding the sport sponsorship process," *Journal of Sport Management* 10 (1):32-48.

Sponsorship promoters should prepare a summary report that documents the entitlements provided and impressions generated for each sponsor. The Cleveland Cavs of the NBA give team sponsors a detailed year-end evaluation including a listing of all contractual elements and verification and description of fulfillment. Figure 8.12 presents a generic sample. When necessary, sponsors receive videotape or photograph verification for game-related promotions. Any value-added features (such as extra radio, television, or public address spots), tickets, or a promotion that extends beyond the contractual obligation of the club is documented as well. While this documentation is typically provided in summary format, frequent status reports are shared with sponsors.[41]

Organizations can generate supportive evidence on sponsor awareness, recognition, and recall through consumer surveys. Respondents may be asked to identify participating sponsors from a list (**aided recognition**) or requested to supply the names of companies they believe sponsored a particular activity or organization (**unaided recall**). Figure 8.13 (page 235) and table 8.11 (page 236) display the results of aided-recognition and unaided-recall studies. The right-hand column of table 8.11 shows the results of a weighting system applied to the data contained in the left-hand column with the goal of determining a sponsor's quality or "top-of-mind" recall among consumers. The first sponsor cited by the respondent was awarded a 19 (the number of event sponsors), the company listed second received a score of 18, and so on.[42]

Additional types of research can be conducted to service the sponsee-sponsor relations and demonstrate an audience's responsiveness to a supportive party. For instance, data collected on behalf of the Gay Games, an event second only to the Olympics in terms of participant volume, revealed that 97% of the participants believed that the event organizers should actively solicit sponsors; the data also showed that an astounding 92% of the participants would be likely to purchase products of event sponsors.[43] Such data should prove enticing for existing as well as potential event supporters.

Team Evaluation

	Source	Impressions	Audience	Location	Number	Size	Sample Y/N	Value
Client:			Date:			Event:		
Initial P.R.								
Trade								
General print								
Television								
Radio								
Integrated signage								
Exterior building ID								
Electronic marquee								
Parking lot								
Concession cups								
Concession napkins								
Concourse displays								
On-ice or on-floor								
Flip-ins								
Scoreboard								
Highway directional signs								
Event tickets								
Parking tickets								
Visitor passes								
Ticket envelopes								
Electronic media								
Four scoreboard screens								
Parapet matrix boards								
Concourse TVs								
Suite TVs								
Coming event boards								
Ticket window message board								
Information booth								
Service desk								
Group sales								
Event brochures								
Event mailings								
Ticket order forms								
Advertising								
Game programs								

(continued)

Figure 8.12 Sponsorship affidavit form.

	Source	Impressions	Audience	Location	Number	Size	Sample Y/N	Value
Advertising *(continued)*								
Print ads								
TV								
Radio								
Billboards								
Bus shelters								
Buses								
Transit platforms								
Mass transit TV monitors								
Ticketmaster event guide								
Collateral								
Posters								
Giveaways								
Heralds								
Discount coupons								
Premiums								
Priority mailers								
Promotion								
Retail stores								
Manufacturers								
Fast-food restaurants								
Shopping malls								
Supermarkets								
Convenience stores								
Gas stations								
Ticketmaster outlet								
Ongoing P.R.								
Trade print								
General print								
TV								
Radio								
Customized marketing								
Season tickets								
Media								
Printed materials								
Programs								

Figure 8.12 *(continued)*

Reprinted, by permission, from L. Komoroski and H. Biemond, 1996, *Sport Marketing Quarterly* 5 (2):35-39. © Fitness Information Technology.

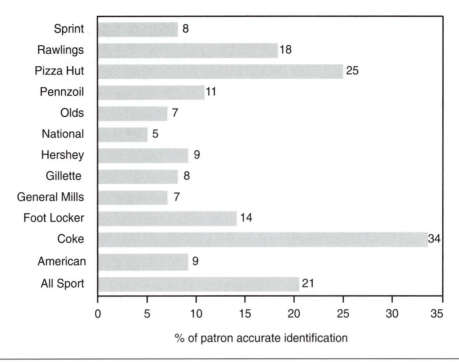

Figure 8.13　NCAA patron corporate partner recognition.

Reprinted, by permission, from A.B. White and R.L. Irwin, 1996, "Assessing a corporate partner program: A key to success," *Sport Marketing Quarterly* 5 (2):24. © Fitness Information Technology.

Evaluate With Research

The NBA's Toronto Raptors have developed an innovative approach to evaluate sponsorship effectiveness. The team offered all of its sponsors the opportunity to participate in a survey designed to track consumer recall of, and reaction to, Raptors' sponsorship programs. Although initial survey results have indicated less-than-flattering statistics regarding fans' recognition of the Raptors' sponsors, team corporate representatives remain optimistic.[44]

Sport promotional specialists may also discover useful sponsorship program benchmarking data in the academic literature. For instance, according to research conducted by Stotlar, a ranking of the North American sponsorship programs that are considered the most sponsor friendly supported the notion that NASCAR leads the industry in sponsor servicing; MLB, on the other hand, appears to be in dire need of help, according to the respondents (table 8.12, page 237).[45] Such results are of great value to the organizations investigated, as they reveal perceptions and expectations of national-level sponsors while also assessing a sport property's servicing position relative to those of similar sport agencies seeking national sponsorship agreements.

Because a sponsorship program is a complex promotional strategy, assessments may be more effective if they involve a comprehensive analysis by highly trained, third-party professional agencies that can be called on for specialized services. For an assessment of its Corporate Partner Program, the NCAA commissioned services of the International Events Group to undertake a total program critique. The purpose of the evaluation was to analyze the current program relative to other available sport sponsorship opportunities, develop specific objectives for the NCAA and its corporate partners, and develop strategies and tactical plans aimed at achieving these

Table 8.11 Top-of-Mind Sponsorship Recall[1]

	% of patrons recalling sponsor	Weighted recall[2]
FedEx	57.5	2430
Auto Zone	54.0	2208
Coca-Cola	46.0	1822
Nike	28.0	1112
Piggly Wiggly	16.7	668
Coors/Coors Light	15.0	591
Grand Casino	12.8	474
Bell South	12.4	498
Channel 5/WMC	11.0	415
AllState	8.0	341
Bank of America	8.0	312
MedPlus	4.0	299
Nokia	3.0	133
Jimmy Dean Foods	2.0	74
U-Tech	1.0	51
Ford	1.0	39
Texaco	1.0	34
O'Charley's	1.0	17
Applebee's	1.0	13

[1]During the late stages of the game through postgame, 233 patrons were asked to recite all companies they believed were sponsors of the Southern Heritage Classic. Approximately 25 patrons (10%) were unable to think of any company associated with the event and thus were not included in the analysis.

[2]Responses were weighted based on hierarchy of recall. For instance, similar to college football polling, a score of 19 was assigned to any company recited first by each respondent (since a list of 19 sponsors was provided); a score of 18 was assigned to a company recited second; and so on.

Table 8.12 Sports Rated Most Effective in Marketing and Promotion by Corporate Sponsor Decision-Makers

Sport	Ranked by sponsor	% of respondents
NASCAR	1	43.5
NBA	2	21.7
Golf	3	17.4
NHL	4	8.7
NFL	4	4.3
WNBA	6	8.7
College basketball	7	4.3
College football	8	0
MLB	8	0

objectives.[46] As a result of the assessment there have been numerous changes in the Corporate Partner Program, most notably moving sponsorship servicing and fulfillment in-house.

Preparing the Proposal

Although there is no standard format for a sport sponsorship proposal, the following information should be provided by the sales staff to sponsor prospects.

Objectives of the sponsorship program

Profile/background of the sponsee

Sponsorship criteria/entitlements available

Levels of involvement available

Fee structure

Evaluation methodology

Bear in mind that sponsorship decision-makers receive hundreds of sponsorship proposals annually and that the initial stage of proposal evaluation may consist of a brief content review. In such cases, the proposal must begin with an executive summary containing a brief description of the six elements just listed. Where necessary, a second component of the proposal provides details for each element as found in figure 8.14.[47]

Unfortunately, there is no magic formula for pricing a sport sponsorship. More than likely, a competitive pricing strategy will be used. In this case, it is helpful to

1. Profile of the sport organization
   - Brief description of the activity or event
   - Brief history
   - Mission goals and objectives of the sport organization

2. Description of the event
   - Date, day, time, location
   - Past attendance figures and target audience description
   - Content, theme
   - Organization's capabilities and experience in presenting the event

3. Compatibility with potential sponsor's image and target market
   - How is the event compatible with the sponsor's image?
   - Why would the sponsor be willing to associate with the event?

4. Sponsorship benefits
   - Clearly outline all sponsor opportunities and benefits. Try to provide information on exactly what the sponsor could derive from the partnership, for example:
     - Public awareness of this similar sponsorship reached x percent, compared to only y percent for z.
     - The event would have a television audience of x million viewers, of whom about y percent are in your target market.
     - In terms of interest, x ranks above every other sport in the country among your target markets.
     - Each year, thousands of people come to the team's games and we had x hundred column inches in the local paper, whose circulation is x thousand.
   - List the opportunities for exposure of the sponsor's involvement.

5. Media and promotion plan
   - State proposed (or approved) media coverage.
   - Explain how the event will be promoted.

6. Sponsorship investments
   - List the range of opportunities for investment and their magnitude.

7. Impact measurement
   - Explain how the sponsor's benefits will be measured and evaluated.

8. Addenda support materials
   - Newspaper clippings, photos, letters from satisfied sponsors at previous events
   - Past event programs or brochures
   - Video material

Figure 8.14 Elements to include in a proposal.

Reprinted, by permission, from D. Howard and J. Crompton, 1995, *Financing sport management*, 324. © Fitness Information Technology.

know the prevailing cost of similar advertising or hospitality arrangements within the sponsee's geographical area. By contacting media sales representatives, the sponsorship promoter can obtain an advertising rate card as well as the cost per thousand (CPM) advertising fee. This figure refers to what it costs an advertiser to generate 1000 impressions or exposures of its message. If the going rate for advertising CPM in the sponsee's market is approximately $20, the proposal should also reflect that figure. The difficulty with spectator sport is determining the number of impressions generated by on-site visual media. For instance, how many times does a spectator view scoreboard signage during the course of a ball game? In this case the sponsorship promoter should compare costs among outdoor advertising media such as billboards, banners, and bus panels.

Uncovering Sponsorship Candidates

Likely candidates for sponsorship involvement may come from several sources. Initially, the sponsorship promoter should target companies that have a target market or other business interests in common with the sport organization. This prospecting tactic requires the sport promoter to do presolicitation research to generate data on his consumer base as well as that of the prospective partner. Second, the sport sponsorship promoter must be knowledgeable about active sport sponsors in the marketplace. Prior behavior is often a predictor of future behavior. Therefore, companies demonstrating a propensity for sport sponsorship are well worth soliciting. Lastly, it is advisable to pursue establishing a sponsorship with an existing or potential business partner. As indicated earlier, current suppliers may emerge as likely candidates and ultimately reduce organizational operational costs if they become sponsors.

Postgame Wrap-Up

As a result of issues ranging from the increased demand for television content to the financial challenges experienced by publicly funded sport programs, sponsorship has emerged as one of the most popular yet complex promotion mix components. However, the truly integrated sport sponsorship incorporates many, if not all, of the other promotion mix elements, thus differentiating itself from advertising.

Whether soliciting firms to become sponsors or seeking sponsorship opportunities for organizational promotion, sport promotion specialists are advised to employ the sponsorship management process discussed in this chapter. In essence, this includes determining whether sponsorship is a promotion vehicle compatible with the organization's overall marketing agenda; setting clearly defined sponsorship outcomes; establishing a systematic sponsorship screening and selection process; actively implementing and leveraging the sponsorship program; and systematically evaluating the sponsorship.

Sponsors have found that they can make effective sponsorship arrangements with teams, individual athletes, an event, a particular sport, a sport facility, a governing body, or a media channel. Organizations typically determine the appropriate sponsorship platform according to the preestablished sponsorship objective as well as selecting the vehicle most capable of cost-effectively reaching the target audience. The sponsorship platform decision is also influenced by existing sponsors, existing organizational sponsorship arrangements, and budgetary constraints.

Sport promotion specialists charged with designing sponsorships need to prepare proposals that specify the fundamental purpose or objective of the sponsorship program; present a profile of the sponsee; delineate available entitlements and benefits, possible levels of involvement, and the corresponding fee structure; and any means that may be used to accurately assess the sponsorship's effectiveness for both parties involved in the partnership.

An effective sponsorship should render benefit to the sponsor and sponsee. In other words, a sponsorship viewed as a win-win situation has a promising future.

Discussion Items

1. How can sponsorship serve as the focal point of all promotional efforts? Should sponsorship serve in this capacity? Why or why not?

2. How does sponsorship differ from advertising?

3. Describe the following terms: leveraging a sponsorship, in-kind sponsorship, and arms-length sponsorship participation.

4. Discuss where the following sports would fit in Martin's perceptual map: snowboarding, Arena football, and beach volleyball.

5. If you were a sponsorship decision-maker, what pre- and post-sponsorship information would you like to see provided by your sponsee?

Learning Enrichment Activities

1. Immediately following a major national or international sporting event, poll approximately 20 people to find out if they are aware of who sponsored the event. For each correctly identified company, ask the respondents how they were made aware of the company's sponsorship of the event.

2. Make plans to attend an upcoming sporting event that you know has sponsor support. While in attendance, take detailed notes on the signage, scoreboard messaging, public address announcements, and other event-related consumer impression opportunities. Based on your observations, prepare a rank order of sponsors according to the exposure that each received during your attendance at the event. Schedule a meeting with the event sport promotion specialist to share your findings. Are your findings congruent with each sponsor's level of sponsorship? What does the sport promotion specialist think of your research?

3. Conduct the same assessment as in the previous activity, but this time use a televised sporting event.

The Promotional Merits of Licensing

chapter objectives

1. Understand the fundamental benefits of licensing with particular emphasis on the promotional merits

2. Understand the importance of licensee and retailer relations programs

3. Understand the various issues related to revenue (royalty) management

4. Understand the importance of promoting the licensing program

5. Understand how to thoroughly assess available licensable property existing within a sport business

key terms

intellectual property   exclusivity

joint-use agreements   royalty rate

fan shops   counterfeiters

shops in shops

Pregame Introductions

This chapter addresses issues related to the management of a sport licensing program. While a licensing program provides three fundamental benefits to the licensor, namely promotional exposure, profit from license application, and protection against unauthorized logo usage, the emphasis in this textbook is on the promotional value derived from such programs.

Licensed Products Are for the Birds

You live in Denver, Colorado, and need a 2001 Baltimore Ravens world championship sweatshirt? No problem. How about a matching T-shirt and cap? Piece of cake. How about a book bag or book cover for the kids? Easy. How about a birdhouse for the backyard? Yeah, a Ravens-logoed birdhouse for the backyard. All these products are available as a result of license agreements executed between the league (NFL), or licensor, and the manufacturer, which is referred to as the licensee.

Licensing, the act of granting a second party permission to use a mark, name, symbol, or likeness, once tabbed as the fastest-growing marketing strategy,[1] may have hit its peak in the mid-1990s within the sport industry, when retail sales of sport-logoed merchandise doubled from $5.3 billion (in 1990) to $10.6 billion (in 1994) according to the Sporting Goods Manufacturers Association (table 9.1). However, don't tell that to the various properties divisions in the major league headquarters in the United States where these programs are managed. At NBA Properties, the marketing arm of the NBA, which manages license agreements for the league and its 30 franchises, programs continue to expand—with the league aiding 140 licensees worldwide to produce and distribute NBA-branded products ranging from youth apparel to home furnishings.[2]

As a component of the organization's branding strategy, licensing still affords the sport promotion specialist a series of significant benefits unavailable through more traditional channels of marketing communication. For instance, as a promotional vehicle, licensing a second party the right to produce and distribute goods bearing a logo or design, otherwise referred to as **"intellectual property,"** has enabled many a sport organization to generate consumer awareness and interest with little or no capital outlay and minimal risk. In fact, licensing has provided more than one new sport franchise the opportunity to generate significant marketplace presence before the team even played its first game. Within one week of being awarded an NFL franchise, the Carolina Panthers sold over 1 million items featuring the team's new logo.[3] Furthermore, due in part to the global expansion of sport broadcasting, the market for sport-logoed merchandise, once limited to on-site distribution, has exploded with skyrocketing global demand for both domestic and international merchandise.

Table 9.1　Sales Figures for NBA, NFL, MLB, NHL, and Major Colleges

Year	Sales (in billions of dollars)
1990	$5.35
1991	$6.73
1992	$8.24
1993	$9.95
1994	$10.6
1995	$10.35
1996	$10.8
1997	$11.03
1998	$10.6
1999	$10.95

Data from the Sporting Goods Manufacturers Association (SGMA).

Consequently, sport organizations have found licensing to be a healthy auxiliary revenue source as manufacturers are assessed a variety of licensing fees for the right to produce merchandise bearing the logos, marks, and insignias of sport businesses. Basil DeVito, president of the upstart XFL, indicated that revenues generated from the league's licensing program would trail only broadcast- and sponsorship-rights fees. DeVito estimated that within the first year of operation the league would generate $8 million in licensing revenue.[4] This prediction was made four months before the league identified team markets, drafted any players, or played its first game!

Why is licensing so profitable? The primary reason is the consumer's desire to demonstrate her affiliation and devotion to a sport property, whether that be a team, event, or athlete. Furthermore, the ability to buy, display, or wear a product aimed at capturing or rekindling a sport experience is an alluring prospect for highly vested sport consumers.[5] Research conducted by ESPN and Chilton revealed that 51% of all "sports fans" purchased a sport-licensed apparel item within the three-month period prior to the poll.[6] Amazingly, one-third of all surveyed fans attest to owning at least one piece of apparel bearing an NFL logo,[7] while a study conducted by *Sports Illustrated for Kids* revealed that 60% of the boys and 37% of the girls who live in the United States claim to possess NBA-branded apparel.[8]

However, critical to achieving the promotional and profit benefits of sport licensing is the application of sound protective measures afforded the sport licensing specialist via trademark law. The proper enforcement of such regulations greatly enhances the sport licensing program's opportunity for generating valuable exposure and revenue on behalf of the sport organization.

Therefore, a properly administered licensing program gives a sport business the opportunity to

- establish a presence in the marketplace (promotion),
- establish an alternative means of revenue production (profit), and
- establish the power to legally defend itself against defamatory or unauthorized logo usage (trademark protection).

Licensing As a Promotion Tool

In an effort to enhance consumer affinity and expand market penetration, the NFL in 1963 launched the first sport licensing program under the visionary direction of then-commissioner Pete Rozelle.[9] Subsequently, all other American professional sport leagues followed suit, internalizing licensing operation under the guise of the league properties division. Professional and amateur sport organizations around the world have similarly exercised their right to promote, protect, and profit from the marks identified with their organization.

As an element of the sport promotion mix, licensing provides an opportunity for stimulating year-round marketplace presence. In fact, one of NFL Properties' primary goals for 1999 was to give fans different ways of experiencing NFL merchandise—apparel ranging from high-end embroidered parkas to T-shirts, to wear not only on game Sundays but also year-round.[10]

While licensing is considered a key component of the promotion mix, it is also promotion *of* the licensing program that ultimately determines the program's effectiveness. Consequently, the material in this section is divided into promotion *through* licensing and promotion *of* the sport organization's licensing program.

Goal!!!!!! = Money!!!!!!

Imagine documenting every time you heard that familiar exclamation of "Goal!!!" Well, if some of the world's top football players have their way, someone will have to. English football's top stars are pursuing the registration of spectacular strikes as their own intellectual property, which would result in the Premier League's paying them every time the goal is replayed on television by their club or by the broadcaster for promotional purposes.[11] A favorable ruling would unquestionably alter the ways in which many professional teams design electronic as well as print promotional campaigns. However, it most likely would eliminate what some consider the biggest taboo in sport promotion—overemphasizing a star player.

Promotion Through Licensing

In the mind of the sport licensing specialist, licensed material is itself promotional content. For example, NBA Entertainment grants electronic licensees the use of taped footage for television, movies, and the Internet.[12] Likewise, licensed merchandise is often made available in auctions, at trade shows, and in store windows. The availability of licensed products in the marketplace generates valuable exposure, establishing a presence and familiarity in the mind of the consumer. Therefore, marketplace product placement is key to promotional effectiveness, affording each party (licensor and licensee) an opportunity for product and/or brand exposure in mass as well as targeted markets. The tactics we discuss in this section represent ways in which the sport promotion specialist may pursue several key promotional objectives by establishing an organizational licensing program.

Creating Brand Awareness and Appeal

In securing a license agreement with a major professional sport organization, a licensee stands to realize not only significant revenue production but also enhanced brand exposure and credibility. In fact, a highly demanded licensor such as one of the

A birdhouse with The Ohio State University logo is a unique example of a licensed product.

Reprinted, by permission, from Ohio State University and Bird U™, Inc.

major professional leagues may be viewed as a *source* capable of transferring some element of source credibility to the licensed product's manufacturer (licensee).

An argument can be made that this form of source (licensor) credibility influences consumer brand affinity, thereby affecting purchase decisions of licensee-produced goods not bearing the licensor's marks. For instance, in an effort to compete against name-brand products such as Tommy Hilfiger, Nautica, or Ralph Lauren, sport-licensed apparel manufacturers seek to use licensing as a means of developing brand affinity, much the way an automobile manufacturer endeavors to use sport sponsorship as a means to influence future consumer purchase decisions. Likewise, the sport licensor must seek to execute agreements with licensees who themselves will foster goodwill associated with the organization's brand (logo) and enhance demand for the licensor's brand through the distribution of high-quality products.

In fact, such a case may have influenced the four American professional leagues' decision not to renew Starter's licenses after the company's reorganization in 1999. Everyone believed that the company's products would be mass marketed through discount merchants, thereby damaging the leagues' reputations and seriously affecting the sales of higher-priced goods available at department stores and sporting goods outlets.[13]

Of course a well-recognized licensee brand will also supply source credibility to the licensed product. According to the Sporting Goods Manufacturers Association, the addition of Adidas to the list of NFL licensees added considerable strength to an already elite group of licensed product manufacturers.[14] Essentially, the co-branded merchandise will trigger top-of-mind high-quality impressions in the marketplace.

Penetrating New Markets

Likewise, licensing products can serve as a means of accessing a new market through the availability of branded product. For instance, in 1998, in an effort to capture the market's attention, the NBA introduced its first line of licensed apparel designed specifically for women. The female-oriented line featured high-quality fabrics, subdued graphics, and logo placement dictated by a combination of fashion, team shades, and neutrals.[15] Soon thereafter the NBA recorded its highest ever ratings among female fans.

In an effort to cultivate the youth market, MLB teamed up with Hasbro to produce action figures and with Mattel to provide "Major League Baseball Barbie," and the WNBA has launched an extensive line of children's apparel.[16] Of keen interest to those pursuing the youth market is knowledge that individuals as young as six months of age begin to form mental images of and affinity with logos.[17] Similarly, NASCAR has successfully used its licensing program, involving outlet stores, restaurants, and speed parks, to reach new, non-race markets.[18]

The 1992 initiative that reduced European trade barriers created a new market of 300 million consumers. The internationalization of American collegiate and professional sport also provides many new opportunities for product demand, as fan bases following a particular player will seek means of associating with the local hero's team. This has been particularly true for the NHL, where European-born players account for almost one-fourth of all those in uniform. The NHL has aggressively pursued opportunities in the home countries of these players. The NHL has also expanded awareness through licensed product availability in Japan, where its domestic retail partner, JSV, operates 12 NHL Japan Shops. In fact, JSV boasts of offering the widest selection of NHL product found anywhere in the world.

Explore New Licensed Product Categories

Sport licensors and licensees have collectively found great opportunity in the use of licensing as a means of extending the brand through the penetration of new product categories. In an interesting twist, Rawlings Sporting Goods, typically an MLB licensee, granted Lombardo Ltd. an exclusive license to use the company's rich leather, typically reserved for Rawlings baseball gloves, to manufacture other products such as luggage, backpacks, daily planners, and checkbook cases.[19] Now the Rawlings brand name and familiar intoxicating leather scent are available to consumers in a series of non-sport products.

The NFL tapped a variety of new product categories in an effort to rejuvenate market demand. With sales from traditional product categories such as T-shirts and caps flattening out, the NFL at-home merchandise, which ranges from items used for tailgating to bedroom sets, grew 30% in 1998 and 1999. Creatively exploring opportunities such as this enabled the NFL to extend its brand presence in the marketplace and significantly increase royalty production during what was otherwise viewed as a lean period in sport-related licensing.[20]

Joint-Use Agreements

Sport licensors of all sizes have actively pursued **joint-use agreements,** in which two or more rights holders allow their marks to appear together on merchandise or other items of commercial value. Annually the NCAA enters into joint-use agreements with the universities qualifying for the association's national championships. Similarly, two rival teams or a sport property along with any number of character licensors may execute a joint-use arrangement with royalties proportionally split between the parties. Disney, Warner Brothers, and other popular non-sport cartoon characters provide ideal co-branding opportunities, often allowing the sport licensor to establish a presence in an untapped market.

Promotional License Agreements

The execution of a promotional license permits a licensee to use the sport property's symbols or logos in a promotional campaign. For instance, when a quick-service restaurant gives away a 32-ounce glass bearing the name and logo of the community's professional soccer franchise with a $20 purchase, the company more than likely has entered into a promotional license agreement with the sport property licensor. Such an agreement provides the licensee with an *incentivization* opportunity capitalizing on the licensor's goodwill and demand within the marketplace, while the licensor seizes the opportunity for brand extension and awareness as well as revenue generation. Unlike merchandise license agreements, promotional licenses are typically executed on a flat fee (royalty) basis, similar to the way corporate sponsorship arrangements are handled.

Promotion of the Licensing Program

The success of any licensing program boils down to licensee and retailer profitability. If licensees and retailers succeed, the licensor succeeds. Therefore, it is imperative that any licensing program promotional plan incorporate direct interaction with

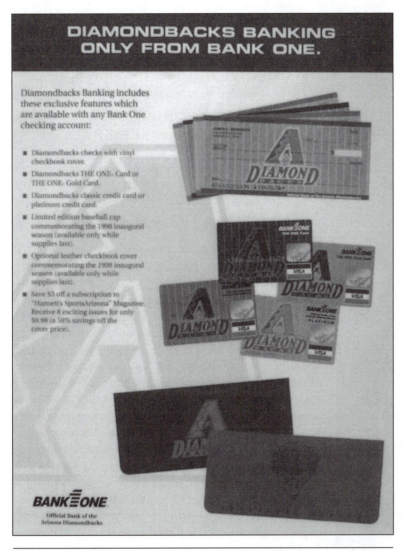

DIAMONDBACKS BANKING
ONLY FROM BANK ONE.

Diamondbacks Banking includes these exclusive features which are available with any Bank One checking account:

■ Diamondbacks checks with vinyl checkbook cover.

■ Diamondbacks THE ONE® Card or THE ONE® Gold Card.

■ Diamondbacks classic credit card or platinum credit card.

■ Limited edition baseball cap commemorating the 1998 inaugural season (available only while supplies last).

■ Optional leather checkbook cover commemorating the 1998 inaugural season (available only while supplies last).

■ Save $3 off a subscription to "Harnett's SportsArizona" Magazine. Receive 8 exciting issues for only $9.98 (a 58% savings off the cover price).

BANK≡ONE
Official Bank of the
Arizona Diamondbacks

An example of a sponsor tie-in involving promotional licensing is shown in the various items offered by Bank One bearing the name and logo of the Arizona Diamondbacks.

Reprinted, by permission, from Bank One.

existing organizational licensees and retailers.

Licensee Management

Of primary concern is the recruitment and selection of licensees, which is considered the foundation of any effective licensing program, as a program is built on the acquisition of properly motivated and cooperative licensees.[21] Unproductive and unresponsive licensed product manufacturers tend to stifle a licensor's opportunity for market growth, damaging brand image and the opportunity for achieving promotional and revenue production objectives.

Similar to the way any prospective business partner would be evaluated, a potential licensee should be required to submit a list of references, samples of previous work, and business/distribution plan for the targeted product category. This type of information gives the licensor a means of determining whether or not to issue the license on the basis of the prospect's previous performance record as well as intent to perform the plan. It is important to make every effort to ensure that correspondence is with prospective licensees that have a proven record within the industry.

Licensee Recruitment

The most popular methods of recruiting licensees have included the circulation of program literature and trade show networking.[22]

• *Licensing program literature.* As with information for any consumer group, materials must properly articulate the benefits of involvement. Brochures and other printed materials highlighting such program features as historical sales volume, existing licensees/retailers, and cooperative promotional programs, as well as licensee/retailer testimonials, should be available for distribution and review.

• *Trade show networking.* The annual *Super Show* is an ideal opportunity for sport licensors and licensees to meet and review each other's wares.

Maximizing Licensee Relations

It is imperative that the licensor spend time with the licensees to define the product and to work on creative applications of current and potential licensable property. Such interaction helps create the right product for the consumer, one that is meaningful, fashionable, relevant, and fresh, as licensees are typically more in tune with market demands than licensors.

Those working with licensees to identify new product offerings or logo applications should employ the following three-step process, as suggested by Mazzeo, Cuneen, and Claussen:[23]

- Conduct a *market analysis* to identify present and potential consumer markets, distribution channels, promotional plans, and past and present demands for similar product offerings.
- Conduct a *technical analysis* to determine production channels such as the technology needed to create the product, production equipment, schedules, and labor needs.
- Conduct a *financial analysis* to estimate product and distribution costs, as well as profitability.

Interchange with a licensee may also result in an adapted or new logo that may enable the licensor to broaden its merchandising campaign. When the Chicago White

Uniforms and logos give fans a sense of allegiance and should not be changed without careful thought and consideration.

Sox originally changed their uniforms to a predominantly black color scheme, sales of team-logoed products skyrocketed. In fact, they led sales in all of MLB the following year.[24] However, teams should consider implementing logo changes only when their team is winning, as this conveys a positive brand image in the marketplace. Too often, teams change logos when losing—only to find that fans associate the new logo with a loser. Therefore, sport managers should wait until the team begins to show improvement before considering logo modifications.[25] In fact, uniform design changes have become so prevalent in merchandising that professional sport leagues have placed restrictions on the practice. Parents' organizations in England have criticized Manchester United for the timing and regularity with which they change their playing strip (uniform design). The new strip usually debuts at the start of the new season in early August. This is a time when parents are facing the high cost of a new school year, and many see the high cost of the new kit as an unnecessary added burden.

The Value of a Good Name

The Rancho Cucamonga Class A minor league baseball team, located in the Southern California desert, found that a little creativity in team and facility name could be quite profitable. After the renaming of the team to the Quakes and of the stadium to the Epicenter, sales of team-licensed products hit $500,000.[26]

Licensee Exclusivity

According to Schlossberg, limiting the number of licensees enhances licensor-licensee relations, thereby creating a family-type promotional partnership.[27] This "less is more" philosophy also minimizes the possibility of diluting the licensee base. Furthermore, by restricting the number of licensees in a particular product category (e.g., head wear), "in-demand" licensors afford themselves the opportunity to deliver greater value and return on investment to the "exclusive" licensed product manufacturer. However, the licensor does run the risk of limiting the product availability, service, and creativity that often result from competitive business practices.

Licensee Preparation and Responsiveness

The sport licensor must develop a close working relationship with licensees in order to accurately prepare for and capitalize on peak demand periods or "hot markets." The ability to put merchandise on the streets as soon as humanly possible is critical to taking advantage of the winning moment associated with a particular team or event. Such was the case for Pro Player, an NBA licensee, which had its production people on alert at machines ready to produce merchandise bearing the New York Knicks logo immediately following the Knicks' upset victory in the 1999 NBA Eastern Conference finals. Crazed fans wishing to demonstrate their team allegiance grabbed all available product within hours of the victory.

Retailer Programs

You may find it difficult to comprehend that until the early 1990s, almost the only way to purchase a sport-logoed T-shirt, cap, or mug was to attend a sporting event or visit the campus bookstore. In fact, it wasn't until the mid-1990s that hundreds of **"fan shops"** were built to supply new products, through retail, to the consumer.

Eventually, distribution spread through other channels, such as sporting goods stores, mass merchants, and even cable television. In order to compete, most of the major sporting goods chains and many department stores developed separate areas devoted exclusively to sport-licensed products. In 1999 alone, MLB developed licensing retail programs for JCPenney, Sears, Wal-Mart, Kmart, Champs, Lids, Sports Authority, Foot Locker, Modell's, and a number of major regional sport specialty outlets.[28]

In fact, Schlossberg contends that one of the keys to licensing program success is a strong relationship with the retailers that sell the logoed products.[29] According to a number of licensees, failure to exercise a sound retailer promotional program prior to the 1999 Women's World Cup limited licensed product sales to game venues and undoubtedly hindered the total sales volume.[30] In order for other sport businesses to learn from this type of mistake and maximize licensed product merchandising opportunities, it is imperative for them to implement a comprehensive retailer promotion program, ranging from education about the licensor's event to recognition of participating outlets. Next we discuss a few of the retailer initiatives that sport licensors have launched.

Sporting events are no longer the only places to purchase logoed merchandise, but they still provide a good market for sales.

Pitching the Program

Even while generating $50 million in retail sales, which resulted in licensing royalties of approximately

$2.5 million for event organizers,[31] the Women's World Cup did not effectively promote itself to the retailers prior to the event, according to Rick Chastain, Adidas USA's director of event marketing. Similar to what occurs with any other consumer group, an educational awareness campaign, targeting prospective retailers, should have been initiated well in advance of the buying season. For instance, as a means of generating awareness and interest among Final Four host community retailers, the NCAA gives an annual luncheon approximately six months prior to the event in order to showcase the event's licensed products and allow the association's licensees to take orders from interested buyers.

Licensors who won't be seeing the demand of an event such as the NCAA's Final Four would be wise to at least supply retailers with a list of current licensees and to pursue a face-to-face meeting with retail decision-makers, much as a sponsorship promoter would in order to pitch a corporate sponsorship package. In fact, valuable shelf space should be a key component of a sponsorship arrangement entered into with any retail chain.

Retailer Recognition Program

There are two ways to implement a retailer recognition program. Initially, participating retailers can be provided storefront identification material such as a window decal or banner showing that the place of business is an "Official Licensed Product Retail Outlet." The licensor then needs to "drive foot traffic" by aggressively encouraging loyal licensed product consumers to patronize only those outlets bearing such identification. The licensor can use a variety of advertising and publicity tactics to inform the licensed product consumer about retailers carrying appropriately licensed merchandise. For instance, the licensor can recognize all "Official Licensed Product Retail Outlets" in a print ad campaign or via athletic event public address announcements promoting the availability of product as well as the merchant.

Secondly, as part of the retailer recognition program the licensor can honor the outlets through various forms of public identification such as awards, banquets, and even a well-orchestrated publicity campaign. The recognition program should clearly indicate that being a licensed product retailer has a multitude of benefits.[32] Furthermore, utilizing the talents of the media relations staff, the licensor can get occasional stories into print and the electronic media alerting consumers to shop only for "authentic" licensed products, at the same time addressing the damage caused by illegal behavior of unlicensed vendors.

Retail Concept Shops

In an effort to service retailers as well as to standardize the licensed retail sales environment, several professional sport licensors have developed a series of retail concept shops, which are stores within a store. For instance, in 1998, the NFL opened Play Football Endzone in two Florida FAO Schwarz stores. The concept blends NFL branding and entertainment with the retail shopping experience. The NFL supported the concept with in-store events involving current and former players. That same year, the Sports Authority opened 72 NHL concept shops within outlets in Dallas, New York, New Jersey, North Carolina, Philadelphia, and Florida under the theme "Coolest Game on Earth."

Soon afterward, in 1999, the NBA launched an aggressive retail initiative known as the Global Retail Environment Program (GREP), which offers retailers varying sizes of **"shops in shops"** (the NBA Shop, 350-600 square feet; the NBA Court, 200-350 square feet; or the NBA Zone, 50-200 square feet). Each setup utilizes a number of atmospheric components such as design elements, fixtures, and display pieces that incorporate maple wood, metal fencing, rotating-content graphics, and basketball accents, as well as interactive attractions similar to those found in the NBA Store on Fifth Avenue in New York City. Retailers who carry GREP gain access to exclusive proprietary products from the NBA Store such as personalized jerseys or the "Logoman" collection (trademarked basketball player silhouette); a line of NBA-branded sportswear targeted to an older, sophisticated consumer; and promotional support from the league that includes player appearances.

However, licensors with well-established and consistent levels of brand equity are encouraged to consider owning and operating merchandise distribution channels such as retail outlets, catalog sales centers, and cyberstores.[33] Today, 26 NBA franchises own and operate their own "fan shops," with the Utah Jazz independently managing 28 licensed product outlets in the Salt Lake area. Likewise, NASCAR manages approximately 20 NASCAR Thunder Stores around the United States.[34]

Retail Partnerships

Licensors should explore opportunities that enable them to link a retail program with a corporate partnership, thereby not only expanding retail traffic but also increasing the overall promotional value of the sponsorship campaign. Licensed rights should in fact become a standard part of most sponsorship agreements, with the sponsor getting the opportunity to exploit use of the sponsee's licensable property where contractually deemed appropriate.

As an example, in 1999, MLB implemented a series of multipartner programs with Toys R Us (Pepsi, Cracker Jack, and Upper Deck), Foot Locker (MasterCard, New Era, and Majestic Athletic), Blockbuster (Fox), and Wal-Mart (Pepsi). Similarly, an NBA co-op initiative partnered the league with Sears and *Nickelodeon,* a popular children's magazine. A series of youth basketball-related stories appeared in the magazine, as did an advertisement for NBA-logoed youth apparel available only at Sears.[35]

On the other hand, the NFL formed an advisory group comprising licensees and retailers to develop a cross-merchandising program of home products. The Home Advisory Group worked to develop a program for distributing home products in home stores as well as sporting goods outlets nationwide.[36]

Outlet Exclusivity

Retailers can benefit from the same type of **exclusivity** that is occasionally granted licensees. In an outlet that is the "only place to shop" for highly demanded items, stock can disappear fast. As the exclusive outlet for the NHL's North American All-Star team jersey, Foot Locker reported a near 100% sell-through during the league's All-Star Weekend in 1999. In addition to producing record sales on licensed merchandise, the availability of such items allows retailers to ring up incremental sales on nonlicensed goods as well. Typically, such arrangements are structured similarly to corporate sponsorships, entitling a retailer to licensed product merchandising opportunities in return for a rights fee. Retail agreements enable the licensor to simultaneously capitalize on demand and exercise control over the entire licensed product distribution channel.

Web Promotions

Several sport properties have capitalized on the licensed product retail opportunities provided prospective consumers via the Internet. The Internet affords licensed product consumers the chance to find information, preview merchandise, and purchase online. For instance, the NHL.com Virtual Product Showroom informs visitors about NHL licensees while offering an opportunity to view officially licensed league merchandise. Each page in the showroom features product photos, promotional copy, and links to the participating licensee's Web site. Similarly, the NFL launched NFLretailbuzz.com, a Web site updated each week that allows retailers and licensees to obtain news on NFL products, markets, and leaguewide promotional platforms. A photo of each newly licensed item is accompanied by a description of the vendor, product, and targeted fan.

Consumer (End-User) Relations

Communication with the end user cannot begin until licensees and retailers (or at least points of distribution) have been put into place. However, once the production and distribution process has been established, it is important that the sport licensing specialist set up integrated consumer promotions. As with all other forms of integrated marketing communication, the consumer should recognize a clear, consistent message across all advertising, retail promotion, and all means of brand identification. Sport licensing specialists can use a number of methods to promote the licensing program to the end user, which we look at next.

Media Advertising

Consumer advertising campaigns are one way to promote the availability of sport-licensed products, with costs often shared by several parties involved in the licensed product distribution chain. In support of its video game category, for instance, MLB launched a three-tiered promotional strategy consisting of a comprehensive advertising and public relations campaign, in-stadium sampling, and targeted retail promotions.

Meanwhile, NBA Properties deployed a consumer advertising campaign under the theme of "Product Test" with print ads targeting teens and young adults that appeared in issues of *Blaze, ESPN Magazine, Rolling Stone, Slam, Spin, The Source,* and *Vibe.* Television spots aired during NBA programming on NBC, TNT, and ESPN.[37] Likewise, to accelerate female fan growth and demand for female-oriented licensed products, the NFL placed advertisements in *People, TV Guide,* and *Entertainment Weekly.*[38]

As demonstrated by the NBA, sport organizations can make good use of broadcast opportunities to place advertising messages on television and radio. The University of Iowa exploits this type of advertising opportunity available in conjunction with the broadcasting of all Hawkeye football and basketball games.

Standard criteria requested in most major sport league licensee screening materials is a plan for a consumer, trade, and point-of-purchase promotional campaign for the proposed licensed product.

Additionally, the license agreement often includes a clause that requires the licensee to ensure product advertising.[39] For instance, a licensee of the NCAA agrees to expend no less than 3% of gross sales during the contract year for promotion. In fact, the licensee must submit a record to the NCAA of all promotional expenditures made within the term of the agreement.[40]

Similarly, retailers are often willing to co-op if not fully absorb licensed product advertising costs in return for recognition as an "Official Licensed Outlet" or the ability to display "hot market" licensed products prominently within store advertising.

Collegiate licensing programs typically pursue the use of several on-campus publicity sources including athletic event public address announcements, souvenir programs, and the school newspaper. Flyers can also be inserted in season ticket brochures and other mailings sent to students, faculty, boosters, and donors.[41]

Personal Contact

Personal appearances by players and celebrities have proven to maximize consumer interest while also servicing retailers. The NHL's "Cup Crazy" Caravan

Tour runs from April to May annually in the league's four conference finalist markets. Stanley Cup player appearances are rare, but the Stanley Cup itself is on display at participating retail outlets, allowing fans a glimpse of the mammoth trophy. The NFL New York Shop at Macy's, which includes merchandise from the Jets and Giants, is supported by four "Touchdown Tuesdays" during the fall season with in-store events involving personal appearances of current and former players.

A Licensed Product Catalog

At a minimum, all licensors should compile and distribute a product catalog. MLB Properties sent its 1999 product catalog, "Manny's Baseball Land," to over 4 million homes, showcasing traditional products as well as the hard-to-find collector items and autographed products.[42] "Hot Off The Ice," the NHL's official merchandise catalog, has a circulation of 1.2 million.[43] The NBA's licensed product catalog, "Nothin' But Hoops," started in 1998, features an array of NBA as well as WNBA products.[44]

It is not uncommon for sport licensors to share, if not secure, catalog production and distribution costs from licensees whose merchandise is prominently displayed within the catalog. Either party can initiate such cooperative ventures.

Publicity

Sport licensors rely heavily on various forms of publicity in order to correspond with consumers about the licensing program. Licensing programs, not unlike other components of the sport promotion campaign, are challenged to stimulate appealing, newsworthy content. Such content may originate from topics associated with the program management such as the royalty distribution policy. For instance, approximately two-thirds of the licensing royalties generated by many colleges are used to provide scholarships to the general student population. Public communication of this information is likely to be considered newsworthy content by a number of media sources.

Secondly, the NCAA has used publicity extensively as the foundation of a Final Four licensing program public awareness campaign. Starting several months in advance and continuing through the week of the event, local news media outlets of all sizes receive press releases for widespread distribution; the purpose is to communicate to the general public the association's intent to actively "police" the marketplace for unauthorized product and its willingness to prosecute offenders. The resulting absence of counterfeit product identified during the event has generally been attributed to this aggressive communications campaign (figure 9.1).[45]

Under Federal Communications Commission licenses, television and radio stations must provide public service programming to local not-for-profit organizations. As nonprofit organizations, sport governing bodies, many college bowl games, and collegiate athletic departments have the opportunity to utilize public address announcements to promote the licensing program. When the context is similar to that for the NCAA campaign, it is advisable for the message to demonstrate willingness to protect the organization against unauthorized manufacturers and distributors.

In order to manage an effective retail licensing program, there are obviously a number of key issues that should be considered. The following Practitioner's Perspective highlights some of these key issues.

Figure 9.1   The NCAA works hard to make sure only officially licensed merchandise is sold at its Final Four tournaments.

Retail Licensing Insights
by Luis Salcedo, PGA TOUR Director of Retail Licensing, Non-Apparel

Anyone working in the retail licensing business automatically will become well versed in a wide variety of consumer products and businesses such as home furnishings, electronics, interactive games, collectibles, artwork, memorabilia, and novelties. Individuals in this field must be diversified as well, as you will be part salesperson, contract lawyer, marketing manager, problem solver, product manager, public relations manager, bill collector, quality control supervisor, juggler, advertising agent, and logo cop. As someone working in the licensing industry, I offer the following insights on the business.

Know Your Brand and Your Audience

In licensing, you're really selling, promoting, and protecting your brand or brand position. Therefore, it is important that you are able to clearly identify and understand what your brand is and what it means to your targeted audience. Similar to a business mission statement, once you have a clear understanding of your brand, most of your everyday and long-term decision-making becomes easier. Spend a great deal of time understanding your brand.

Know Your Consumers

Remember that you are not the consumer. You learn this quickly once you begin to see consumer trends for products you would never buy for yourself. For example, you may never wear brown plaid pants or $190 silk golf shirts or buy a $200 putter. However, there are consumers that do—and a lot of them. In short, as a licensor you try to identify, develop, and license products for targeted consumers, not for your personal use.

Assess Your Licensee

The quickest and surest way to assess a potential licensee is to visit their offices and manufacturing facility. This will enable you to see the size of their facility, their equipment, technology, number of employees, and how workers interact on the production floor. While visiting, be sure to ask a lot of basic questions, even when you already know the answers. You will be surprised at what other additional and useful information is revealed. Also, see what other types of products are being produced by the manufacturer. Is it busy or slow? How well maintained is the facility?

Develop New Products

While it is great when you can develop a new product idea or promotion, new licensed product ideas usually involve adapting someone else's existing product or concept while adding a little twist. For example, rather than offer home furnishings similar to traditional furniture, we collaborated with our licensees and created golf-themed home furniture. These furnishings carry a very subtle golf theme, including our TOUR logo, popular golf images, or even a golf course landscape image. We position this collection to golfers, particularly those who live the golf lifestyle.

Learn to Say No

In the licensing business, you are often approached by a large number of individuals who are trying to sell you their newest and greatest branded product idea. It is best to stick to a set list of criteria for rejecting proposed licensed products. Also, existing license agreements, exclusive or not, do factor into decision-making. Additionally, make sure you do not over-saturate the market with an abundance of similar products.

Form Good Relationships With Your Retailers

To be an effective licensing manager, you need to develop and maintain a good relationship with your retail partners. Not only do these retailers sell your licensed products but they are also very aware of consumer and market trends. Therefore, they should be viewed as a great resource in developing as well as promoting your products. It is also important to get to know the retail operations of your competitors. Walk through shopping centers, strip malls, grocery stores, and so on in your spare time or on the weekends. You will be surprised at how much you can learn from other retailers.

Be Informed

While trying to juggle all your commitments, meetings, and projects, you must also stay informed. This can be done by reading such publications as the *Licensing Letter, License Magazine, Street & Smith Sports Business, Furniture Today, Sports Business Daily, Sporting Goods Business, The Wall Street Journal,* and so on. Moreover, don't forget to stay on top of technological trends. New products will open up new avenues and potential opportunities for your licensing business.

Attend Trade Shows

Anyone in the licensing business needs to attend as many relevant industry trade shows as possible, as they provide the opportunity to see what is taking place in the industry. At trade shows you usually will see your licensees, retailers, and competitors, as well as prospective clients. Trade shows are also great places to see industry trends and get the latest industry news.

In addition to the standard event seminars, look for the new product displays, daily fashion shows, media events, and the international pavilions in an effort to find the hot trends or products. Do not neglect after-hours functions. Business often takes place after the show ends.

(continued)

(continued)   It is good to sponsor an event for key clients or business partners, as well as attending events given by other major companies or competitors.

Plan for the Unexpected

No two days in this industry are alike. No matter what you have planned for the day, something unexpected usually comes along. Therefore, always have a long-term promotion plan worked out in advance to revert back to following those unexpected interruptions.

Cowboys Plan to Go Solo

The Dallas Cowboys were the first NFL team to become the private wholesaler, distributor, and retailer of the team's logoed apparel. In spite of the league's new 10-year, $250 million exclusive apparel agreement with Reebok, the Cowboys exercised a new option allowing teams to privately manage their own logoed product distribution channel. Owner Jerry Jones stated, "I can market and sell the Dallas Cowboys better than anyone else." Jones had lobbied for years for the right of teams to manage their own licensing, merchandising, and retailing programs. Whereas in the past, teams received an equal share of the collective licensing royalties generated, the new option allows teams to retain revenues generated by their independent merchandising operations. This type of policy, similar to that existing in the NHL and MLB, may similarly lead to the revenue stream imbalance experienced by franchises in each of these other leagues.

Profitability

According to the Sporting Goods Manufacturers Association, the sales of sport-licensed merchandise exceeded $11 billion in 1997 (see table 9.1). In fact, sport properties of all shapes and sizes have gotten into the licensing business, ranging from the four major American professional leagues, which collectively account for over $8 billion in annual retail sales;[46] the World Cup, which realized $1.5 billion in licensed product sales worldwide;[47] NASCAR, where licensed sales have been reported to surpass $1 billion annually;[48] the 1996 Olympics, with approximately $1 billion in annual retail sales;[49] collegiate athletic programs, which generate approximately $2.5 billion annually;[50] and even minor league baseball, where $32 million in licensed products sales are generated each year.[51] Sport-licensed products include a wide variety of goods, such as novelties, sport memorabilia, trading cards, and apparel. While apparel accounts for almost 60% of all sport-licensed product sales, demand has declined in recent years.[52] However, huge gains in video game sales have offset much of the recent revenue loss experienced in the apparel industry.[53]

But the sport organizations, whose logos adorn this merchandise, realize a surprisingly small proportion of these sales figures. The sport property, or licensor, derives its earnings in the form of a royalty, which is charged to the licensed manufacturer, otherwise known as the licensee. Interestingly, royalty fees have not changed much since the NFL instituted a 5% royalty in 1963.[54] Today, **royalty rates** generally range from 6% to 10% of the product's wholesale price (the price a retailer pays the licensee, not the price paid by the end user). It is highly recommended that the fee be assessed on the *gross* wholesale price, prior to the application of wholesaler- or retailer-driven discounts. Such a measure standardizes the royalty calculation process and thus eliminates problems that may result from licensee-established distribution incentives.

The royalty fee imposed by product manufacturers appears rather modest when you consider that the unlabeled product has little or no value without the sport-

The NBA sells many licensed products, such as the hats and shirts shown here.

"The NBA and individual NBA member team identifications are trademarks and copyrighted designs, and/or other forms of intellectual property, that are the exclusive property of NBA Properties, Inc. and the respective NBA member teams. © 2002 NBA Properties, Inc. All rights reserved."

related logo. In fact, in a study measuring consumer opinion, 80% of those surveyed believed that a product bearing an NBA logo has a higher perceived value than one without, while a whopping 98% of the respondents indicated a willingness to pay more for a product bearing the NBA brand identification.[55] A similar study involving college students showed that the students were willing to pay more for goods bearing the institution's logo, with the university assured a small fee from the sale.[56]

However, in securing a license to produce products bearing logos of a sport property, the licensee agrees to assume a significant amount of risk with respect to production and overhead costs, unpredictable demand and excess inventory, and promotion expenditures. Although the assessment of licensing royalties may appear to be a rather simple task, this is far from the case, as sport licensing administrators face a number of royalty management issues.

Basic Royalty Management Procedures

In addition to requesting that licensees pay a royalty on product sold, the sport licensing program administrator will need to consider implementing additional royalty management procedures including the assessment of advance royalty fees, establishment of royalty performance guarantees, submission of royalty reports, execution of royalty computation audits, and royalty exemption allowances.

Advance royalty fees, typically due at license agreement execution, are a form of earnest money that acts as an incentive for the licensee to generate a particular volume of sales of the licensor's product. As the term implies, advance royalty payments are almost always applied toward future royalties owed (figure 9.2). However, some sport licensees do require a flat rate advance payment that is not applicable to future royalties. In such cases the licensee is basically paying a license agreement activation fee.

Sport licensors offering exclusive licenses appear to be more likely to negotiate royalty advance payments as well as royalty rates. In highly competitive product

MICHIGAN STATE UNIVERSITY

S A M P L E

Quarterly Royalty Report
(Report must be filed even if no royalties are due)

Licensee:

Licensee, Inc.

123 4th St.

Anytown, USA 00000

July 7, 2001

Date of Report

June 30, 2001 (Apr. - June)

(for quarter ending)

Royalty checks payable to:

Michigan State University

University Licensing Programs
Michigan State University
MSU Union
East Lansing, MI 48824-1029

(517) 355-3434

(Date of shipment may be used in lieu of Invoice date when appropriate)

Product sold to	Invoice date	Invoice number	Product description/style no.	Quantity	Price per unit	Gross sales for licensed products
MSU Bookstore	5/15/01	0001	T-shirt 001/a	72	$5.95	$428.40
SBS East Lansing	4/24/01	0002	SS Sweatshirt 002/b	108	6.39	690.12
JCPenney Grand Rapids	6/1/01	0003	T-shirt 001/a	144	5.95	856.80
JCPenney Okemos	5/15/01	0004	T-shirt 001/a	96	5.95	571.20
KMart	4/15/01	0005	LS sweatshirt 003/c	108	7.95	858.60
Returns						
JCPenney	5/15/01	0004	T-shirt 001/a	48	5.95	285.60

Prepared by:

I.M. Wright

Title:

Bookkeeper

Total Gross Sales of Licensed Products:	$ 3,405.12
Less: returns and/or transportation charges on returns:	− 285.60
Total "Net" Gross Sales of Licensed Products subject to royalties:	3,119.52
Royalty Percentage:	× 6.5%
Subtotal:	$ 202.77
Less: advance royalty balance:	− 100.00
Royalties Due for This Quarter: (and payment enclosed with report)	$ 102.77

Complete and return within thirty (30) days after each calendar quarter. Thank you.

LATE CHARGES WILL BE ASSESSED 1/2 PERCENT SURCHARGE

Figure 9.2 Royalty report form.

categories or distribution regions, licensors appear to benefit significantly by granting the "highest bidder" categorical exclusivity.[57]

Royalty guarantees, an additional business-generating incentive, are minimum royalty production thresholds established by the licensor and typically contained within the basic license agreement for the duration of the contract. For example, NFL Properties requires an annual payment of between $50,000 and $100,000 depending on the product category.[58] Should the licensee fail to produce, distribute, or sell enough licensed product to achieve the royalty guarantee threshold, the obligation must be fulfilled in cash payment and the opportunity for agreement renewal is jeopardized. In fact, lack of performance (e.g., failure to achieve royalty minimums) have been found to be one of the most prevalent criteria for nonrenewal or revocation of agreements.

On a regular basis, typically four times a year, all licensees must supply a royalty report. A royalty report summarizes all sales activity for the defined period of time and includes any payment due. As illustrated in figure 9.2, advance royalty payments are deducted from the amount due when applicable.

While royalty reports and payments are typically submitted on a quarterly basis, sport licensing program administrators typically need to verify the accuracy of royalty-reporting procedures. Such audits, considered standard practice among licensors and licensees, can be performed as part of a comprehensive compliance review and often reveal unintentional errors in accounting practice. In fact, according to one auditing specialist, approximately one-half of all royalty reviews reveal some type of underpayment, and errors as high as $100,000 are not uncommon.[59] In a typical year, sport licensing programs audit one-quarter of their licensees.[60] League

No Need to Show the Money

Figure 9.3 Window decals identify stores as official outfitters of Western State College.

Courtesy of Western State College of Colorado.

In a move specifically aimed at maximizing protection against unauthorized use of institutional trademarks, achieving promotionally oriented licensing objectives, and enhancing the availability of institutionally logoed merchandise in the marketplace, Western State College, an NCAA Division II athletic powerhouse, implemented a royalty-exempt licensing program. In addition to eliminating any perception of a royalty-driven *surcharge*, the program allowed participating retailers to co-op merchandise orders with the campus bookstore. This lowered start-up costs and excess inventory volume while facilitating program acceptance, product placement, and institutional awareness. Additionally, participating retailers received window decals identifying the outlet as an official Western State College Mountaineer Outfitter (figure 9.3) and were offered attractive in-store product display units at a limited cost.

or association officials often perform these tasks, but programs occasionally use outside specialists or licensing agency representatives for auditing.

Licensors may, for various reasons and at their own discretion, opt to exempt a manufacturer from royalty payment. Exemptions are typically for products that are internally consumed (e.g., team apparel, office supplies), but licensors have also granted exemptions to manufacturers that were producing merchandise bearing the licensor's logo prior to the establishment of a formal licensing program, or for products to be used by corporate sponsors or nonprofit organizations.

Royalty exemptions are frequently a basis for royalty miscalculation and tend to be more problematic for the licensee. It can be challenging for the licensee to determine the exempt parties. As a result, some sport organizations have instituted a royalty rebate system for sources deemed exempt from royalty payment. In such cases the exempt party may seek a refund from the licensor upon submitting evidence of a royalty charge (licensee invoice), thereby allowing the licensee to maintain consistency in royalty assessment and license accountancy.

Royalty Distribution

Michigan

Notre Dame

Ohio State

Penn State

Kentucky

North Carolina

Figure 9.4 Top-selling college brands in 1998.

Data from the Association of Collegiate Licensing Administrators (ACLA).

Before organizations amass licensing program revenues, they must make decisions about where the proceeds are to be directed. The major American professional sport leagues split the royalties in some fashion among the teams, the league office (or properties division), the players' union, and even the players themselves.[61] In the NFL, all royalties are divided up equally among the teams, whereas the NHL allows each team to retain all the royalties from the sale of merchandise within a 75-mile radius of that team's market.[62]

However, the NFL's existing revenue-sharing plan, involving the equal sharing of licensing royalties, is due to expire in 2003. Sources indicate that a significant proportion of the team owners believe they can do more with their own licensable property than the league does, thus jeopardizing maintenance of this plan.[63]

Collegiate licensing programs often deposit a portion of the royalties in the athletic fund, as the institution's athletic success is often closely linked to the school's royalty production. Therefore it's easy to see why the universities listed in figure 9.4 are year in and year out the leaders in collegiate licensing royalty production. Ohio State University, for example, directs approximately 25% of the institution's $1.5 million in licensing revenue to the athletic department.[64]

Protection

Although in this chapter we have underscored the promotion and profit opportunities that proper execution of a licensing program affords a sport organization, the fundamental benefit realized by administrators of such programs is protection against unauthorized use of associated names, marks, logos, and symbols. Absent the rights and enforcement procedures granted by trademark law, the licensing program has little merit or grounds for success. Therefore, it is critical that sport promotion specialists exercise these rights (as outlined in chapter 13) in order to maximize the triad of available program benefits. There are several procedures that the sport promotion specialist can follow in order to maximize the promotional benefits available as a result of comprehensive licensing program management.

Identification of All Licensable Property

Sport organizations from the Olympic Games to the NCAA have hired brand specialists in an effort to properly depict the organizational image as well as to develop a commercially appealing logo. While it is critical for most sport organizations to seek to establish an identifiable brand, it is also essential to take inventory of all available licensable material. To this end, in collaboration with promotional staff, sport promotion specialists should properly identify all property that could be claimed by the sport organization as licensable. This entails essentially two steps: creating a portfolio of all marks and symbols claimed to be trademarks of the organization, and then creating a means for properly identifying items bearing these marks in the marketplace.

A licensed property portfolio is a list of all potentially appealing marks associated with the organization, in addition to team or event names, symbols, and logos. Most likely this will include facility names and designs, mascot nicknames and character references, and even any catchy slogans originating from advertisements or characteristics associated with the organization. In 1999, soon after a Tennessee Titans season ticket holder coined the phrase "Flame Pit" for a seating section in Adelphia Stadium, the NFL requested that Pro Player, an official league licensee, begin manufacturing T-shirts bearing the term along with "Member 1999" in time for the season opener. Much to the fan's chagrin, failure to use or register the term allowed the NFL to initiate use without seeking permission. In fact, the NFL, following use of the term for commercial purposes, can now exercise its rights and claim the term as a league trademark.[65]

Similarly, the NFL successfully defended its claim to the use of "Dirty Bird" as a league trademark. After "Dirty Bird" was popularized by the Atlanta Falcons during their Super Bowl season of 1998, the NFL quickly secured the rights to the term in order to block fraudulent usage by **counterfeiters.** Although challenges have been brought by various Atlanta business owners, the league's claim has been successfully defended in the courts.

An interesting case also arose recently when Pinehurst, Inc. owners and operators of Pinehurst Country Club claimed the term "Pinehurst" as a registered trademark of the company and requested that local businesses as well as the *city* of Pinehust, North Carolina discontinue use of the word due to trademark infringement. Pinehurst, Inc. contends that name or mark usage is limited to the golf course and resort. Businesses that had previously included "Pinehurst" in their company names responded by changing their names instead of facing costly litigation.[66]

Although most sport organizations have registered their names, symbols, and slogans as trademarks at the state or federal level (typically determined by breadth of distribution), registration is not required in order for rights to be granted under trademark law. Several cases involving unregistered marks have been successfully litigated. What appears to be critical in the mind of the court is that the mark is in fact used by, and closely associated with, the sport licensor.[67]

Accentuate the Positive; Control the Negative

Western State College in Gunnison, Colorado, has chosen to exercise its trademark rights as a means to stifle use of a derogatory institutional nickname. Designated by *Playboy* in the mid-1970s as the top party school in the United States, this quaint campus of 2500 nestled at the basin of Crested Butte, Colorado, has had a difficult time living down the reputation associated with this national distinction. In fact, the institution was subsequently nicknamed Wasted State, a term familiar to any one growing up in Colorado. After more than 25 years of ridicule, campus administrators finally realized that an institutional licensing program might allow them to put an end to the availability of Wasted State merchandise. Having claimed and registered the term as a trademark of the institution with the state Office of Trademarks and Patents, the school has the clout to either (1) prosecute individuals using the term without institutional authorization or (2) derive profits from the sale of merchandise bearing the term. You've got to wonder who's having the last laugh!

Change Logos Cautiously

Too often teams rush to change their logo when merchandise sales are down. Unfortunately, research has shown that sales are generally down as a result of poor team performance. In fact, table 9.2 demonstrates what a winning season can do for licensed merchandise sales, as the leader in licensed product sales in each American major professional sport league was the one that had captured the league's championship during the most recent season. Changing a logo during a lean performance period only causes fans to associate the new logo with a losing team. Therefore teams should change their logo when they are winning, as this projects a positive brand image in the marketplace.[68]

Table 9.2   **Top 10 American Professional Team Licensed Product Retail Sales (1999)**

Teams	% of sales	Teams	% of sales
NFL		**NBA**	
Broncos	14	Bulls	20
Cowboys	11	Knicks	15
Browns	8	Spurs	14
49ers	8	Lakers	8
Vikings	8	Pacers	7
Packers	8	Jazz	4
Steelers	5	Kings	4
Falcons	4	Celtics	3
Raiders	4	Sonics	3
Jets	4	T'Wolves	3
MLB		**NHL**	
Yankees	25	Stars	12
Indians	11	Red Wings	11
Braves	7	Rangers	9
Cubs	6	Bruins	7
Mariners	5	Sabres	7
Red Sox	4	Blackhawks	6
Giants	4	Flyers	5
Cardinals	4	Avalanche	5
Orioles	3	Devils	4
Mets	2.5	Blue Jackets	4

Data from Sports Business Daily, January 24, 2000.

The second step in identifying licensable property is marketplace identification. You are probably familiar with the hangtags, such as the one displayed in figure 9.5. These recognizable tags, commonly affixed to all licensable property of the American professional sport leagues, help the consumer identify authentic licensed merchandise. Similarly, the sticker displayed in figure 9.3 was designed for consumers to recognize licensed products for Western State College. In each case, product that doesn't have this hangtag or sticker is very likely to be counterfeit; this is the message that must be communicated to consumers in the public awareness campaign mentioned earlier. The hangtag also enables sport licensors who are actively policing the marketplace to recognize authorized and unauthorized merchandise.

Figure 9.5 Hangtags identify authentic licensed merchandise.

The NBA and individual NBA member team identifications are trademarks and copyrights designs, and/or other forms of intellectual property, that are the exclusive property of NBA Properties, Inc. and the respective NBA member team, © 2002 NBA Properties, Inc. All rights reserved.

Counterfeit Detection Program

In order to maintain licensing program integrity with consumers, licensees, and retailers, an aggressive market surveillance program is necessary to deter and detect unauthorized use of organizational symbols and confiscate products bearing them. While the regular presence of program staff is often enough to discourage counterfeiters, program representatives should police the marketplace regularly, confiscating detected counterfeit goods. The lack of such a program severely jeopardizes relations between licensor and licensees, who are paying for such protection, while endangering the value of properly licensed merchandise in the mind of the consumer.

Licensing Program Leadership

A trend appears to have emerged for the internalization of licensing operations. Although a healthy proportion of collegiate licensing programs, including the NCAA's, rely on the services of a professional licensing agency, all professional sport organizations have brought the licensing program in-house, typically under the management of their properties division.

Unfortunately, no one operation model is applicable to the administration of sport licensing programs. Although limited information is available, one investigation of the cost-effectiveness of licensing administration models revealed that the percentage of royalty revenue expended for annual operating costs for agency-assisted programs was nearly 2.5 times that for independently administered licensing programs. Likewise, for all licensing programs analyzed, a 3 to 1 return on investment was reported.[69] Whether the program is administered with professional agency assistance or independently, the program's efficacy is greatly influenced by the organizational commitment through the allocation of tangible resources (budget, personnel) or organizational philosophy (emphasis on the protection and promotional benefits).[70] Proper prioritization will undoubtedly lead to higher returns.

Postgame Wrap-Up

As a key component of the marketing communications mix, licensing renders a variety of benefits of value to the sport promotion specialist. Fundamentally, the purpose of a trademark licensing program is to protect the sport organization against unauthorized use of and profit from the organization's brand goodwill and demand. The importance of this critical function cannot be minimized as programs are being planned and implemented.

However, this chapter has elaborated on the promotional benefits, as an effective licensing program affords a sport business the opportunity to aggressively penetrate the marketplace, generating brand exposure and awareness while also providing an alternative stream of revenues. Sport promotion specialists can use a number of tactics in order to fully maximize licensing program potential in these particular areas.

To realize the full potential of the promotional benefits, the sport promotion specialist will initially want to launch a promotion campaign targeting licensees and retailers, as well as consumers. The licensor should develop an extensive plan for soliciting and screening potential licensees, companies manufacturing products bearing the licensor's logos. To ensure quality control, licensors should request a formal application as well as a list of references and product samples from a prospective licensee. Prospective licensees may be recruited through the circulation of licensing program literature as well as through trade show networking.

Since the licensing agreement is a vehicle for a business partnership between licensor and licensee, the licensor needs to engage actively in promoting the licensee's products to potential licensed product buyers. These promotional efforts may target retailers with whom the licensor has established relations or has recently secured a sponsorship arrangement. Several sport licensors—in particular, a number of professional sport franchises—have experienced considerable success in assuming responsibility for the retail operations.

Lastly, the licensor must communicate licensed product availability to the general consuming public. Using tactics common to all promotional efforts (advertising, publicity, personal contact, etc.), the sport promotion specialist can alert consumers interested in logoed products to the availability of new and existing logo product lines.

Fees generated from licensing, typically referred to as royalties, provide a valuable source of revenue to the licensor. Royalty rates may vary between 5% and 10% of the product's *wholesale* cost, less any discounts, and are paid directly by the licensee to the licensor. Licensors do have the option of offering a royalty-exempt license to any licensee; this allows licensors to maintain a sense of control over the use and distribution of items bearing their marks without seeking financial compensation. Whether a royalty is charged or not, the licensor should request a quarterly report from each licensee that describes sales and distribution activity.

Remember, it is because of sport licensing programs that consumers worldwide are able to establish links with leagues, teams, and events by collecting novelty items bearing those entities' logos, names, marks, and indicia. So, the next time you see someone wearing a sweatshirt of the NFL Europe franchise Berlin Thunder, there is no need to ask how he got it. You know better than to think he went to Germany!

Discussion Items

1. What do you see as the greatest challenge confronting the sport licensing specialist?

2. How can the licensing program be best utilized within the sport marketing communication mix? How does this vary for smaller events and teams?

3. As the director of licensor relations, what would you do to embrace all 140 licensees if you were in charge of licensing for the NBA?

4. When do you think it is appropriate to offer a royalty-exempt agreement? How do you think licensees required to pay a royalty would react?

5. How would you plan to use a telecast of your team or event to stimulate awareness of new licensed apparel available in the market?

Learning Enrichment Activities

1. Develop a multipartner program involving a sponsor, a retail outlet, and a licensee. Be sure to set up the appropriate distribution and communication channels.

2. Construct a plan that will properly address market surveillance. Be sure to include all internal and external parties in your plan. Within your plan, indicate how you will deal with identified counterfeiters.

The Role of Community Relations in Promoting and Selling the Sport Product

chapter objectives

1. Understand the role that community relations can play in the marketing and sales process

2. Become familiar with the community relations programs and activities of professional sport leagues and teams as well as corporate and foundation entities

3. Recognize the rationale involved in utilizing community relations programming

4. Comprehend the term "community" as used in a social context for communication

5. Appreciate the role of cause marketing as it relates to community relations activities and image enhancement

key terms

CPR	cause marketing	impact community
MPR	site community	cyber community
public relations	employee community	common-interest community
PSA	fenceline community	cause branding

Pregame Introductions

In its most common form, the role of community relations in sport has been derived from the classical corporate public relations **(CPR)** model, a program encompassing all non-sales-oriented public relations activities designed to reach their target audiences. For the most part, these activities were described as "giving something back," "being a good citizen," "taking pride in the community," and so forth. Today's activities in the corporate sector can best be described as a combination of CPR and **MPR**, or marketing public relations. Marketing public relations can best be described as integrating the sales and marketing efforts of the corporation with an awareness of the social, political, and economic environment that affects consumers and opinion makers who in turn influence attitudes toward companies and their products. According to Sue Bohle, president of the Los Angeles-based Bohle Company, 80% of all dollars spent for public relations services in the United States today are allocated to marketing support activities.[1]

This chapter examines the role of community relations in sport employing an integrated CPR + MPR approach. We will focus on governing body, league, and conference initiatives; team and school programs; individual player or athlete activities; and foundation-based efforts designed to affect public perception, enlist support, and increase market awareness of and involvement with the sport product.

Real-Life Public Community Relations Efforts

As defined by Mullin, Hardy, and Sutton, in sport marketing,

> **public relations** is an interactive marketing communications strategy that seeks to create a variety of mediums designed to convey the organizational philosophies, goals, and objectives to an identified group of publics for the purpose of establishing a relationship built on comprehension, interest, and support. This communication strategy, which may take the form of activities as well as formal communication, may also involve players, media personnel, staff, mascots and other product extensions, sponsors, and other key components of the organization.[2]

This communication strategy is the practice we refer to as community relations—the process of interaction and "connection" between the sport organization and its assets on the one hand and the community or service market and the target population within that community on the other hand.

Sport-based community relations programs are, for the most part, activity based. Being activity based, they depend on athletes and professionals from the organization for visibility, newsworthiness, desirability, buy-in, effectiveness, and longevity. Community relations programs usually are implemented in one of three ways—they are league initiated, team initiated, or player initiated. Players (athletes) are an integral part of all three types of initiatives, because it is the presence of the players and their involvement that attract funding to the program via sponsorship, garner media interest and coverage, and attract an audience of participants and observers to the programs.[3]

An examination of the NBA Community Relations Programs will illustrate how league initiatives translate into team and player programs.

CASE STUDY

The National Basketball Association and Community Relations Initiatives

Like the Phoenix Suns, other teams in the NBA have taken the initiative to help local youths.

Reprinted, by permission, from the Phoenix Suns. © Phoenix Suns, 1999.

The NBA, its teams, and its players are committed to programs that improve the quality of life for all people. For years the NBA has created and implemented programs to address important social issues, with special emphasis on helping youth. The NBA and its 29 teams continue to make a difference in North America through donations to various charities and community outreach initiatives, and in the production and airing of public service announcements **(PSAs)**. This section describes several of these initiatives.

NBA TeamUp Program

This leaguewide community outreach initiative debuted at the beginning of the 1996-1997 season. Continuing the league's long-standing commitment to youth and education, the program's primary goals are to encourage youth to volunteer to improve their communities, and to help youths recognize that one of the best ways to help yourself is by helping others. Program components include motivational visits by NBA players and representatives; the NBA TeamUp Award, which honors youth service; a public service campaign; and the NBA TeamUp Celebration, a television special saluting youth volunteers held during NBA All-Star Weekend. Hall of Famer and eight-time NBA All-Star Bob Lanier serves as the program's chairman, while former NBA players Rolando Blackman, Lafayette "Fat" Lever, and John Shumate are program spokesmen.

NBA/WNBA Sportsmanship Initiative

This initiative, composed of the NBA/WNBA Student-Athlete Sportsmanship program and the NBA and WNBA Sportsmanship Awards, focuses on fostering the ideals of sportsmanship in amateur and professional basketball players. The NBA/WNBA Student-Athlete Sportsmanship program, implemented in conjunction with the National Federation of State High School Associations, rewards student-athletes participating in basketball at more than 24,000 high schools in the United States and Canada. Each participating high school receives posters featuring the fundamentals of sportsmanship, along with certificates to be awarded to one male and one female basketball player, and one female and one male

(continued)

(continued) basketball coach, who display sportsmanship throughout the season. Each NBA team also honors a male and a female basketball player, and a male and a female coach, at a special ceremony at an NBA game during April. The NBA and WNBA Sportsmanship Awards, given annually at the conclusion of each regular season, recognize players who embody the spirit of sportsmanship. The leagues make donations on behalf of the winners and finalists to the high schools of their choice, and feature the winners in a PSA on sportsmanship.

NBA Reading Initiative and Reading Is Fundamental

The NBA promotes the importance of youth literacy and reading through a comprehensive reading initiative. The NBA and its teams recognize March as NBA Reading Month by holding "Reading Time-Outs"; organizing reading incentive programs and book drives; and distributing books to children at schools, libraries, and youth organizations in team markets and at the NBA Store in New York City, home of the league office. Additionally, the NBA produces and airs PSAs that emphasize the fun and fundamentals of reading. The NBA Reading Initiative supports the efforts of Reading Is Fundamental, the leading nonprofit children's literacy organization in the United States. (Note: in March, 2001, the NBA announced a formal partnership with Reading Is Fundamental and the creation of the NBA-sponsored Read to Achieve program.)

Prevent Child Abuse America

The NBA is a longtime supporter of Prevent Child Abuse America. Each year during the month of April, which is Child Abuse Prevention Month, the NBA produces a PSA that aims to bring attention to child abuse prevention.

King Holiday (January) and Black History Month (February)

Each year the NBA honors the work and legacy of Dr. Martin Luther King Jr. (in January) and the contributions of African Americans during Black History Month (February). To generate awareness about African-American accomplishments, the NBA has produced and aired PSAs that highlight Dr. King, as well as the achievements of author Langston Hughes, activist Rosa Parks, U.S. Supreme Court Justice Thurgood Marshall, inventor Garrett Morgan, inventor Lewis Latimer, and surgeon Daniel Hale Williams. The spots have featured prominent African-American players and coaches such as Grant Hill and Lenny Wilkens. For these efforts, the NBA received the 1998 Martin Luther King Jr. Federal Holiday Commission's "Making of the King Holiday Award," presented annually by Coretta Scott King to those who have made outstanding contributions to the growth, development, and spirit of the King holiday.

The league celebrated Black History Month in February 1999 by hosting a forum series on African-American contributions to professional basketball. The series of three forums featured NBA legends, including Earl Lloyd, the first African American to play in the NBA; and three of the 50 greatest players in the NBA, Isiah Thomas, Nate "Tiny" Archibald, and Earl "The Pearl" Monroe. Each forum covered one of three topics: the history of African Americans in professional basketball, how African Americans have changed the way the game is played, and the future of professional basketball.

Gallaudet University

Because sport plays such an important role in motivating individuals to reach their full potential in life, the NBA is proud to support Gallaudet University in Washington, D.C., the world's only four-year liberal arts university for students who are deaf or hard of hearing. Working in conjunction with Gallaudet University, the NBA helps organize the Gallaudet Congressional Basketball Classic, a fun-filled basketball game pitting Democrat and Republican members of Congress against each other. Since 1993, the Classic has raised more than $350,000 for Gallaudet programs serving people who are deaf or hard of hearing, from infants to senior citizens.

Thurgood Marshall Scholarship Fund

The Thurgood Marshall Scholarship Fund was established in 1987 by the National Association of State Universities and Land Grant Colleges with support from the NBA and other corporate sponsors. More than 220 students have achieved a quality education through scholarships provided by the fund. In honor of the civil rights leader and Supreme Court justice, the Fund is a national organization that awards four-year merit scholarships to students attending 38 historically black colleges and universities.[4]

Team- and Player-Based Initiatives

All of the programs described in the preceding paragraphs are league initiatives of the NBA. Their effectiveness, in large measure, stems from the involvement and support of the 29 teams and respective players. There are a variety of ways for the teams to implement the NBA Reading Initiative, for example. The Denver Nuggets have enlisted the aid of a corporate partner, Lucent Technologies, to assist them in their efforts. The Denver Nuggets' Read Team is an incentive program that encourages second- and third-grade students in the six-county Denver metropolitan area to read for 20 minutes per day for at least 20 days in two consecutive months. In its first year, more than 10,000 students participated in the program. The number of students who completed their reading goal nearly doubled in the second month of the program. Incentives include team merchandise, game tickets, and player appearances. The 1999-2000 season, the third year of the program, included visits to classrooms by Nuggets players. More than 200 classrooms are on the Read Team roster.[5]

League-based community initiatives depend on the member teams and their players for the actual implementation of the concepts. As is apparent in the Denver Nuggets' program, the teams may elect to bring in a sponsor to help with the costs or other aspects of the program. Lucent Technologies could be involved in this program in several ways and for several reasons (see chapter 8, "Sport Sponsorship"). Lucent could be purchasing the incentives (tickets, merchandise) given away in the program, providing books for the program, providing volunteers to read and assist with assemblies, and so forth. It would be safe to assume that Lucent believes in **cause marketing**—an affiliation with a nonprofit group or organization (in this case the literacy groups) to advance a particular cause or issue and contribute to the achievement of the goals and mission associated with that cause (see p. 285 for more on cause marketing).

Teams can also elect to conduct the community relations programming and charitable efforts by establishing their own foundations. By establishing a foundation, teams utilize their corporate partners and ticket purchasing/exchange, fund-raising, and special events to generate a funding resource that serves to assist a wide variety of social, educational, and charitable organizations within their "community." One of the most successful foundation-based programs is the Orlando Magic Youth Foundation (OMYF). The OMYF is committed to helping all children in central Florida realize their full potentials, especially those at risk, by supporting programs and partnerships that empower families and change lives. The foundation was created in 1988 to raise funds, and perhaps more importantly, to raise community awareness to help combat the many physical, emotional, and social challenges facing the children of central Florida. Since its inception, the OMYF has affected the lives of more than 1 million children through a program that grants $1 million annually to children's charities throughout central Florida, and through providing nearly $2 million of in-kind support in donations of merchandise, personal appearances, and tickets.

As previously mentioned, players are the driving force in the implementation of the various league and team initiatives we are describing. Players can also create their own initiatives, which can serve a variety of purposes. As the most recognizable franchise product, players, and subsequently their community relations efforts, often attract significant local public interest and media coverage. Generally speaking, funds generated or funds donated to a particular cause will be matched by the player's team or an affiliated corporate sponsor. Programs can be statistically based; contributions based on the productivity of a player, touchdowns, home runs, points scored, sacks, and so forth can be easily understood and tabulated. For example, Pedro Martinez of the Boston Red Sox could initiate a program whereby his designated charity would receive $50 for every strikeout recorded during the 2001 season, or perhaps Ronald McDonald House would receive $1000 for every win recorded by Pedro during the 2001 season. While these types of programs have been very popular and highly visible, there are obvious downsides. The current trend in player mobility adversely affects the longevity of the commitment by the player and her affiliated sponsors. If a player who has been very active in the community and a valuable resource in generating funds and awareness for the charity becomes a free agent or is traded, a void can exist. Shaquille O'Neal's move from Orlando to Los Angeles has worked out on and off the court, but his absence in Orlando was felt off the court.

The following Practitioner's Perspective details the community initiatives of Alonzo Mourning of the Miami Heat.

PRACTITIONER'S PERSPECTIVE

Zo's Summer Groove: A Player-Based Initiative by Neal Bendeskey, Game Plan Inc.

When Ben Drexler received a phone call from a staff member of Zo's Summer Groove, the annual charity event hosted by NBA superstar Alonzo Mourning, he could hardly believe the message. On a whim, he had entered a fast-food restaurant's "King of the Court" promotion. Drexler's entry had been selected from thousands of others, and his grand prize was the dream of a lifetime. Ben would have the opportunity to play in a basketball game with Alonzo Mourning and other NBA stars during the Zo's Summer Groove All-Star Game.

There was only one problem. Drexler has cerebral palsy and has used a wheelchair since he was 6 years old. But that wasn't about to stop the 23-year-old broadcast journalism student. His spirit was undaunted and he was up for the challenge. "When I saw the display and entry forms in my neighborhood Burger King, I figured 'why not?'" Drexler said. "I'm a big sports fan and I've always wanted to do something like this. It is the thrill of a lifetime."

The highlight of Drexler's experience came when Mourning, two-time NBA Defensive Player of the Year and leader of the Miami Heat, summoned all of his NBA pals over to Ben's wheelchair as a capacity crowd at Miami's AmericanAirlines Arena quietly watched. In unison, seven basketball stars lifted the chair so that Ben could dunk the ball. When, for extra measure, he did a pull-up on the rim, the crowd erupted in applause.

Drexler's experience is microcosm and a textbook example of how a professional athlete can use a community relations program as a marketing tool to connect with the community where he lives and works.

As to Mourning, he created Zo's Summer Groove in 1997. In its four-year history, the charity event has raised more than $1.5 million for its two benefiting charities—the Children's Home Society and 100 Black Men of South Florida. Zo's Summer Groove Weekend includes a celebrity golf tournament, a concert, a dinner/auction, youth basketball clinics, leadership training for south Florida students, an outdoor block party, and the crown jewel—the All-Star Game.

"It's easy for an athlete to simply write a check to charity," Mourning said. "But I wanted to do something special . . . to let South Florida know that I want to give back to my community.

And I couldn't think of a better way to do it than having an event to benefit kids. They are our future, and need positive role models to help point them in the right direction in life."

Mourning and his marketing agency, Game Plan Inc., have generated support for these worthwhile objectives from Miami's corporate community—from high-visibility sponsors such as HBO, Carnival Cruise Lines, Lucent Technologies, Nike, Publix Supermarkets, Coca-Cola, Burger King, and Chevron. These corporate partners not only contribute funding, but also conduct retail-based promotions that extend the brand awareness of the event and enhance Mourning's community image.

While Mourning's primary objective in hosting the event and tirelessly promoting it is to help kids, Zo's Summer Groove has served to enhance his image throughout south Florida and in NBA circles. The event has evolved into a "happening" and generates immense print and electronic media coverage. All this presents a softer side of the man who is known for his intense and fierce competitiveness on the court. In his own humble way, Mourning shrugs off the attention. "This is not about me," he says. "It's about helping kids who are already at risk and putting programs in place in the schools to help them avoid being in that situation. What's most important to me is that I know we are making an impact."

Thus far we have overviewed the types of efforts associated with community relations programs and have examined league-, team-, foundation-, and player-initiated community relations programs. We have seen that initiatives vary widely and that there are different approaches for different initiatives. Now we'll examine the rationale behind community relations programs both in a social context and as a marketing tool.

The Social Context of Community Relations Programs

Why are community relations programs important to sport organizations in a social context? The following reasons are the most common and compelling reasons for implementing these programs. The reasons, identified through a review of mission and purpose or intent statements from a variety of sport organizations, include these:

- Demonstrate that we are a significant, committed member of our community
- Give back to the community
- Address problems and issues in our local community
- Draw attention and allocate resources to improving the quality of life in our community
- Show that this is not just where we play our games—this is *our home*
- Make a difference in people's lives
- Encourage youths and enhance and enrich their lives
- Fulfill our responsibility as high-profile members of the community to lead by example
- Improve the lives of families and children through a comprehensive program of education, sport, and health initiatives

Are there common elements among these reasons? In a word, yes. All the reasons have to do with connecting with the community, building relationships, and helping to address problems and issues of importance to "our" local community. Breaking this down might be a useful way to analyze the intent of community relations in a social context. *Connecting with the community* refers to attracting the attention and interest of the community. Sport organizations, because of their visibility and the place that sport occupies in our daily lives, are more top-of-mind than others and have the ability to cut through the clutter of communication messages that bombard us every day. (We must also point out that this ability to connect is the proverbial two-edged sword. Because of their high profile, sport organizations, especially the actions of their players, can also seem to disconnect.) Thus sport organizations have the ability to connect, but they need to do so in a meaningful way. This meaningful way is by moving the level of interaction from connection to a relationship. This relationship, according to Regis McKenna, should emphasize "interactivity, connectivity and creativity that will integrate the customer (in this case John Q. Public) into the company and create and sustain a relationship between the company and the customer."[6] What makes the relationship work is that it is beneficial in some way to all parties concerned. As the listing shows, improving the community, giving back, and making a difference are all indicative of a relationship that is rewarding to everyone. An examination of corporate rationale as related to community relations and philanthropic activities can help illustrate the importance and structure of such relationships.

Sport organizations can create ties to their communities by giving locals—like these high school marching bands and cheerleaders—the opportunity to perform at high-profile events.

Corporate Rationale for Becoming a Neighbor of Choice

Consider for a moment the following list of corporate setbacks or plan disruptions that affected the perception of a corporate entity as both a "neighbor" and a business:

- Walt Disney's being prevented from opening a theme park in Northern Virginia
- Halts or delays in Wal-Mart's efforts to open stores in Massachusetts, Vermont, and Virginia

- Abandonment of plans of the New England Patriots to build a football stadium in Boston
- Initial setbacks for the Pittsburgh Pirates and Pittsburgh Steelers in securing public funds for stadium projects
- The stopping of du Pont's titanium mining efforts in southeast Georgia[7]

These companies and sport organizations were stopped from pursuing their business goals—which once went largely unquestioned—because they were not involved in helping to shape and define public opinion but instead merely reacted to it.[8] Today, corporations and other entities dependent on the public's support must demonstrate their worthiness to be part of the community and to be viewed as a neighbor of choice.

According to Edmund Burke, there is a psychological contract between the community and the companies in that community:

> People want to live in communities that are clean, environmentally safe, friendly and cooperative. It is the place to raise families, to grow businesses, and to prosper and survive. People work together to achieve these ends that are shared in common. While these are aspirations and may not be fully achievable, there is the expectation that everyone is seeking to achieve them in common. There is a reciprocity of trust—a common basis, a common set of values, that joins people together to live the good life. It is the implicit expectations that communities and companies have for each other. There are recognized values that are held in common—a company needs to remain competitive and a community needs to be treated honestly and fairly—and there will be a mutual attempt to make each other successful in achieving these ends.[9]

The concept of "community" today is more complicated than it was in the past. Burke identifies six different types of communities (figure 10.1) with which companies or organizations may be involved:

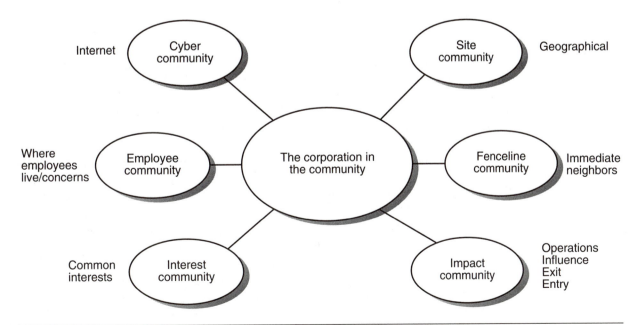

Figure 10.1 Corporations interact with communities in many different ways.

- *Site community.* The site community is defined by the geographical limitations of the city or town in which a company and/or any of its facilities are located. The **site community** enacts laws and regulations that determine how and where the company can operate. It imposes taxes and in exchange provides services such as fire and police. Sport organizations sometimes are assessed an amusement tax on each ticket sold, while other organizations are required to tax the income of visiting athletes, who are viewed as earning a portion of their income via their performance in a given city. In sport, the majority of community relations efforts are directed at the site community.

- *Employee community.* The **employee community** refers to those areas outside the site community where the employees may choose to live. In order to attract and retain employees, the corporation or organization needs to be concerned about the quality of life in any community where its employees may choose to live. To generate a favorable image in these communities, the employer is often involved in community relations or other philanthropic activities and encourages the employees residing in these communities to do likewise. In sport, these communities, since they may function as the player's home (at least during the season), may benefit from involvement of players as volunteers, spokespersons, or contributors or from other forms of player involvement and philanthropy.

- *Fenceline community.* A **fenceline community** is made up of the neighbors immediately surrounding the property of a company. The residents of a fenceline community are affected directly by the operations of the company: noise, parking, traffic, odors, crowd behavior, and other factors can affect the quality of life for fenceline neighbors. This is particularly true for sport organizations. Fenceline neighbors near sport facilities like Chicago's Wrigley Field or Boston's Fenway Park are often affected by the crowds attending sporting events at these stadiums, particularly by such factors as parking, pedestrian traffic, and lights for night games. Fenceline neighbors, or potential fenceline neighbors, can be extremely politically active in their support of or opposition to the construction of new or renovated sport facilities. A concerned group of potential neighbors and individuals who would have been displaced successfully prevented Springfield, Massachusetts, from constructing a new baseball stadium and attracting a tenant for that stadium in 1999.

- *Impact community.* Some business decisions or operations can affect a community even though the company is not located in that community. Communities in which this can occur are called **impact communities,** and there are four types. Communities that are affected by the operations of the company are called *operations impact communities.* Sometimes a company wants to influence certain segments of a community other than the one it is located in; these communities are called *influence impact communities.* Communities that a company is leaving for a new location are known as *existing impact communities.* Finally, communities in an area that a company is relocating to are called *entry impact communities.* These four types of impact areas are fairly common in the sport setting. For example, the athletic programs at the University of Massachusetts at Amherst are conducted in the town of Amherst. Yet it is the adjacent town of Hadley that must endure the traffic and snow removal problems associated with people traveling to and from the game. Hadley endures the operations impact, and as the University of Massachusetts is quick to point out, also enjoys the benefit of this traffic in terms of shopping, dining out, gasoline purchases, and so forth.

Influence impact, because of the very nature of sport franchises, is an integral part of all community relations programming in collegiate and professional sport franchises. As these types of sport organizations depend on attracting a significant portion of their audience from outside the site community, the influence impact community can be statewide or even regional, covering several states. This is particularly true in professional baseball, which may have minor league affiliates operating in other states and may attempt to attract these fans to the major league site as well. Influence impact may also be influenced by the radio network of the sport franchise. The late Bill Veeck is credited with recognizing the value of leaving the site community and traveling throughout the influence impact area to raise awareness and heighten interest in his product, professional baseball. Veeck referred to these activities in the impact influence community as safaris.[10]

Existing impact and entry impact are also common in sport given the relocation of franchises that began in 1958 when the Brooklyn Dodgers and New York Giants became the Los Angeles Dodgers and San Francisco Giants. It is essential for sport teams to keep up image and hope that fans will still support them after an announced move to a new market. In the fall of 1999, after the NBA's Vancouver Grizzlies were put up for sale, many speculated that the team might be sold and then moved. This possibility took on credibility when Robert Lurie submitted a bid to buy the franchise, after having previously purchased the St. Louis Blues of the NHL and their home, the Kiel Center. Vancouver stepped up both its marketing and community relations efforts to stem the tide of public skepticism and growing fear of an inevitable move. Lurie's bid was subsequently rejected by the NBA Board of Governors, which supported Commissioner Stern's belief that the franchise should be given another opportunity to prove its viability in Vancouver. (However, the 2000-2001 season was not very successful under new ownership and as of May 2001, the Vancouver Grizzlies had applied to the NBA Board of Governors for permission to relocate to Memphis, Tennessee.)

Given the revenue potential of a new market, entry impact is a sound business strategy. Wal-Mart has been particularly adept at entry strategy, launching community relations initiatives even before the store construction has begun. Support of community projects, youth sport teams, and educational programs are the most common approaches used in entry impact programs. Similar approaches have been used by the Nashville Predators (NHL) and the expansion edition of the NFL's Cleveland Browns, who combined community relations initiatives with ticket-selling and merchandising campaigns.

- *Cyber community.* The cyber community has recently emerged as one of the more intriguing types of communities for communication and community relations efforts. The **cyber community** is unique in that it has no geographic boundaries, has very diverse demographic populations and limited decision-making abilities, and has no identified leadership. Nevertheless, cyber communities are target audiences for community and corporate relations initiatives. Mike Gordon of the Pittsburgh Pirates (MLB) sends out an electronic newsletter weekly detailing all of the Pirates' community relations efforts for the upcoming week. Everyone who subscribes to the Pittsburgh Pirate e-mail service receives this update.

Cyber communities can also be used for cause-related activism. As environmentalists have been involved in spreading information about corporations and their record and practice relating to the environment, so too have sport enthusiasts. 1999's Team of the Century, a baseball promotion sponsored by MasterCard, was the target of sport enthusiasts with an agenda. The omission of Latino players from this team resulted in MasterCard executives being bombarded through the Internet by outraged fans who had been directed via various forms of electronic correspondence and given the executives' e-mail addresses. Jim Gray's interview and treatment of Pete Rose, associated with the same promotion, inspired a "fire Jim Gray" Web site and additional e-mail to NBA executives.

- *Common-interest communities.* These are also called functional communities because their membership comprises people with the same interest or function such as the environment, education, welfare, religion, or ethnicity. The purpose of a **common-interest community** is to bring together all of those who share an interest, develop plans that meet the needs of the common-interest community, and win support for the plans from the larger geographic community. In sport, a new stadium could be the common interest, and smaller subgroups interested in minority hiring practices, location, and funding might band together to generate information and action on the larger issue.[11]

We would point out that these communities are not exclusive of each other. For example, a common-interest community could contain fenceline community, cyber community, entry impact community, and on-site community members. Communities may also function independently or become interdependent on one another.

Each of these communities has expectations of the companies and organizations with which it interacts. Companies and organizations today also have expectations of themselves in relation to the community. As you would guess, providing employment opportunities and being environmentally responsible come first, but other expectations form the basis for the majority of community relations programs offered by professional sport franchises in North America, as follows:

- Keeping the community informed about current and future business plans and involving community representatives in decisions that can have an impact on the community
- Understanding and responding to the concerns and interests of the community
- Contributing to community charities and to the support of public agencies
- Being involved in improving public education as a partner and as a financial contributor
- Loaning executives to community agencies
- Encouraging and supporting employee volunteer programs
- Taking the lead in solving community problems[12]

PRACTITIONER'S PERSPECTIVE

An Oasis in the Desert: How the Phoenix Coyotes Meet and Exceed Community Expectations
by William Sutton

Let's take a look at the community relations activities of the Phoenix Coyotes of the NHL to illustrate how a well-integrated community relations program can meet community expectations.

The Los Arcos Arena Project

In 1999, Scottsdale voters approved a new home for the Coyotes. This new home involved the redevelopment of a shopping mall that had fallen on hard times and was no longer the attraction or the point of pride it had been in the past. The Coyotes worked with community members not only by keeping them informed about the project but also by soliciting their input about what the facility should contain and how it could benefit all of the citizens of Scottsdale. The result? A complex with a variety of restaurants, a multiplex cinema, new retail and shopping, a hotel and conference center, a public skating facility, a YMCA, and 14,000 *free* parking spaces as well as the state-of-the-art facility for the Coyotes. As everyone was informed about and vested in the community project, the Coyotes and their neighbors had found a project worthy of investment.[13]

Goals For Kids Foundation

The mission of the Phoenix Coyotes Goals for Kids Foundation was to work in conjunction with nonprofit organizations to enhance the quality of life for the children and adolescents in the state of Arizona. A nonprofit organization, Goals for Kids was formed to centralize the team's charity efforts and community relations endeavors (figure 10.2). Since 1996 (when the Coyotes came to Phoenix after relocating from Winnipeg), Goals for Kids raised over $1.5 million and provided funding to over 100 charities throughout Arizona, including Special Olympics Arizona, Valley Big Brothers/Big Sisters, Greater Phoenix Youth at Risk, and Association for Arizona Food Banks.[14]

Figure 10.2 Teams like the Phoenix Coyotes provide funding and other forms of support for a variety of charitable causes, like the former program Goals for Kids Foundation.

Reprinted, by permission, from The Phoenix Coyotes.

PRACTITIONER'S PERSPECTIVE

The Cox Communications Cool Coyotes Field Trip
by Bruce Bielenberg and Joe Levy, Phoenix Coyotes

As the 1998-1999 hockey season ended and plans were being formulated for the upcoming season, the Coyotes' staff began to address an ongoing complaint voiced by our season ticket holders. Why did we continue to include all of our preseason games in their season ticket packages (a common practice in the professional sport industry)?

Staff and Coyotes management decided to remove one of the preseason games from the package, thus saving the season ticket holders the cost of one game. But as the game was scheduled and would be played, what should be done to ensure attendance for that game?

Two factors came into play during our discussions. First, we wanted to find a way to position the game as a benefit for the community and to follow through with the mission of our Goals for Kids Foundation. Second, we needed to find a way to replace the revenue that would be lost with removal of the game from the season ticket package. The result was a promotion that was a win-win for the community, season ticket holders, and corporate partners.

On September 27, 1999, the Coyotes transformed their final preseason home game into a field trip for 16,210 fourth-, fifth-, and sixth-graders—free of charge. Ticket revenue was underwritten by corporate and individual sponsors, and the game and related activities became an educational tool. To accommodate the school schedule, the game time was scheduled for 11 A.M.

Each student received a workbook, and game-type educational lessons took place during breaks in the hockey game. Topics included geography, math, science, and English, all utilizing hockey facts, statistics, and facets. Overall the experience turned out to be great for everyone involved in creating the activity. Most of the students had never been to a hockey game before, so the Coyotes benefited from exposing a new generation of potential fans to their product. The Coyotes also benefited through the enormous goodwill and accompanying publicity resulting from the activity—the event was covered in *USA Today.*

Thus far in the chapter we have examined the approaches—league, team, foundation, and player—that are used to mount community relations initiatives. We have also looked at the various types of communities these efforts are targeted toward and the expectations of these communities. Let's now pull all this together and consider the role of community relations campaigns as they are conducted by professional sport franchises.

Community Relations Campaigns in Professional Sport Franchises

A sports team is a mirror image of the community it represents. Because of the ability to serve as a role model in that community, a sports team has an obligation to give back to the fans who embrace it. By allowing the true spirit of teamwork to resurface on the ice through our players, the Los Angeles Kings will strive to match that teamwork in the community. Through partnerships with committed organizations and individuals, the Kings Care Foundation will work to improve the health, education and social opportunities in the lives of our youth.[15]

This mission statement from the Los Angeles Kings' Kings Care Foundation is very similar to the mission statements you will find in the majority of team- and foundation-based community relations programs. It implies that an obligation exists—that the players have the ability to make contributions that will improve the quality of life of the various communities, that a partnering effort will take place, and that the activities and endeavors will make a difference.

But as we have mentioned, sport franchise community relations programs have generally been established for the purpose of achieving two business objectives. The first objective, as already discussed, is to demonstrate that the sport franchise is a good neighbor and that it is beneficial to the community. Secondly, the sport franchise uses the community relations program as a marketing communications vehicle, targeted at least in part toward the fans of tomorrow, the youth market. Clearly, the community relations program operates as a tactic designed to further, as well as complement, strategic marketing initiatives launched by franchise management.

As with many other businesses, owners of professional sport franchises have been the beneficiaries of attractive tax-relief benefits and long-term financial considerations from one or more governmental units. All too often these lucrative financial packages exceed those awarded to enterprises actively engaged in the production of goods and services that tend to yield greater local economic benefits. This imbalance of business-related incentives has the potential to alienate long-standing, influential members of the local business community from franchise management. Additionally, the construction of facilities housing these franchises—often a vehicle for urban development and thereby displacing small business owners, people who are homeless, and residents of low-cost housing—has a tendency to alienate a significant percentage of the consumer community. In such instances, community relations programs have emerged as a means for a franchise to combat these potential sources of ill will.

Community service-oriented programs that the franchise supports in order to demonstrate active corporate citizenship service are aimed fundamentally at altering or enhancing public perception while making it easier for people to understand the mission and intent of the professional sport franchise. These efforts are meant to portray the franchise as a *good neighbor* and are usually accomplished by a variety of programs designed to improve the quality of life within the urban (or suburban) community—as reflected in the mission statement of the NHL's Los Angeles Kings.

Specific programs such as the Recycling Program of the Atlanta Braves and the Sox Drive[16] of the Boston Red Sox are examples of franchise-managed cause-related marketing initiatives aimed at displaying a sense of social consciousness while at the same time meeting team marketing demands. In each case, the club demonstrates a social responsibility, acting as a collection point where full-paying customers can deposit recyclable items or clean socks for people who are homeless.

Most critical to the sport organization's launching a community service initiative, however, is the program's ability to merit mass media attention. Such recognition frequently translates to positive, image-enhancing organizational publicity, ultimately increasing consumer interest among current as well as potential paying customers and fellow corporate citizens. In fact, according to Breeding,[17] a sound community relations program may be the *only* positive story for a professional sport franchise when team performance is suffering.

Perhaps no community relations campaign better illustrates this than the NFL's association with the United Way. This program is managed through NFL Charities, which is funded by royalties generated from the sale of NFL-licensed products.[18] The intent of the campaign is that the generated revenues be channeled back into, and support programs within, NFL franchise markets. This "centrality of thought and purpose" affords the league, and ultimately each participating franchise, the opportunity to generate favorable press on a national level via messages carried on various national broadcasts (Monday Night Football), as well as in all major media markets throughout the United States.

While no one should discount the merits of these philanthropic endeavors, it would be naive not to recognize that the fundamental objective is to enhance league and, more specifically, team marketing operations. As a matter of fact, it is fair to argue that the development and implementation of community relations programs are fundamental to the marketing effectiveness of a professional sport organization. In addition to the ability to generate favorable media coverage, thus enhancing the image of the benefactor, a cause-related community relations campaign has significant appeal to team corporate sponsors, according to Carol Breeding, community relations director with the Atlanta Falcons.[19] The community relations campaign gives the sponsor an attractive tool for leveraging the team sponsorship while sharing the media spotlight and the reflected goodwill the campaign generates.

According to Sutton, McDonald, Milne, and Cimperman,[20] team-affiliated community service initiatives yield such business-related benefits as decreasing the price and team-performance sensitivity found in the marketplace. With the team marketing staff typically unable to control all elements contributing to these highly visible marketing attributes, proactive outreach activity acts as a camouflage vehicle.

Furthermore, a community relations campaign benefiting youth, tomorrow's fans, is essential to long-term team operational success. In fact, NFL Commissioner Paul Tagliabue has strongly encouraged franchise marketing personnel to actively support youth football through community outreach programs as a means of touching the lives of tomorrow's season ticket holders.[21] Furthermore, a cursory analysis of the community relations materials of major professional sport teams revealed that 75% of the targeted recipients were youths.

Structure of Urban Professional Sport Franchise Community Relations

Organizationally, as you would expect, the franchise community relations program is under the direction of a team marketing executive. While team-based community relations programs are funded and managed internally (with funding allocated as a percentage of overall revenue) a trend has emerged housing community relations within a foundation or similar philanthropic structure.

The primary function of a foundation such as the Orlando Magic Youth Foundation or the Kings Care Foundation is to subsidize a variety of existing projects managed by social welfare agencies. Thus the foundation functions as an enabler. Agencies seeking funding apply to the foundation, submitting formal proposals and budgets; the foundation typically selects the projects that demonstrate the greatest need, yield the greatest potential for impact, and place limited demand on existing resources.[22]

In other instances, though, the foundation may choose to function as the provider, creating programs and services that others do not offer and furnishing financial resources for staffing and program services. In either case, foundation-oriented activities rarely have direct commercial benefit—in this respect contrasting sharply to programs administered by the team. Most often, though, the community relations activity may have a predesigned business benefit that is implicit or apparent. So, you can be a good neighbor by being a smart businessperson.

Public Perception and Urban Professional Sport Franchise Community Relations

According to Ries and Trout,[23] "All that exists in the world of marketing are perceptions in the minds of the customer or prospect. The perception is the reality. Everything else is an illusion." Given that in the case of community relations programs, the customer or prospect is the general public, how are various community relations programs perceived? Are they perceived as important to the welfare and fabric of the inner-city community? Are they seen as part of the marketing communications mix utilized by the team to initiate the ultimate form of communication, a sale? Are they necessary? Are they recognizable?

With these critical questions in mind, researchers began a series of proprietary studies on behalf of four professional basketball franchises located in a variety of urban U.S. markets (Cleveland, Indianapolis, Orlando, and Philadelphia). Essentially, the research agenda was established to determine:

- The importance of community relations programs
- Levels of awareness and recognition of these programs
- Which professional team in the marketplace was perceived to offer the best community relations program
- Whether the most recognizable program was team based, league based, or player based

A total of 2500 individuals were surveyed in both urban and suburban locations, yielding a diverse yet representative sample (e.g., shopping malls, movie theaters) via a one-on-one 10- to 15-minute face-to-face interview. Following a brief introduction, survey team members asked respondents if they considered themselves to be a sport fans this was a means of targeting what was perceived to be the most knowledgeable sample. An affirmative response led the interviewer to the prescribed list of questions.

Using a 6-point Likert scale, where 1 equaled not at all important and 6 equaled extremely important, respondents were initially asked, *How important do you feel it is for a professional sports franchise to be involved in cause-related community-based activities?* As you might expect, respondents indicated that it was extremely important for a professional sport franchise to be actively engaged in the local community as evidenced by the mean score for this question (5.54). Anecdotal commentary provided by respondents indicated that this rating reflected expectations of any community corporate citizen.

Then respondents were asked to provide their perception of the professional basketball franchise within their local urban market: *On a scale from 1 (not at all involved) to 6 (extremely involved) how involved do you feel that Franchise X is in the local community?* The mean score for this question varied significantly from market to market, as revealed in table 10.1.

The dramatic variance was very likely caused by the inclusion of Orlando, which is home to only one major professional sport franchise, whereas the remaining three cities are home to multiple sport franchises. We might hypothesize that because Orlando is "the only show in town," the team and its players and programs receive a substantially higher proportion of media attention and coverage, thus increasing awareness and affecting perception within the community.

Next was an unaided-recall question: *Could you please name one of Franchise X's local community relations programs or causes?* Any response associated with the league, team, or players was recorded for analytical purposes. The results proved to be extremely telling—unfortunately, revealing significant ignorance among respondents about

Table 10.1 **Mean Scores for Actual Franchise Involvement in the Local Community**

Teams	Score
Cleveland	3.87
Indianapolis	4.56
Orlando	4.76
Philadelphia	2.74

1 = not at all involved; 6 = extremely involved

local team-administered community relations activities. Initially, less than half (39%) of all respondents were able to correctly identify any community relations initiative associated with the NBA, let alone the "hometown" franchise for which the study was being conducted. In other words, almost two-thirds of the respondents, all indicating that they considered themselves to be sport fans, failed to recall any program administered by the league, team, or a participating player.

Another finding, as evidenced in table 10.2, was that any community relations activity or program, whether offered by a league, team, or player, is, in the mind of the consumer, attributable to the team. Therefore, the team is clearly a beneficiary of the efforts initiated by the league and/or individual players, which lead to the positioning of the team as a good neighbor and concerned citizen.

Lastly, respondents indicating familiarity with the community relations initiatives of at least one local professional sport franchise were asked, *Which local franchise do you feel manages the best community outreach/relations program?* As you might imagine, the responses varied significantly, with the Magic (NBA) the team of choice in Orlando, the Pacers (NBA) in Indianapolis, the Indians (MLB) in Cleveland, and the Eagles (NFL) in Philadelphia. However, no team approached the level of recognition for

Table 10.2 **Identification of Franchise Community Relations Programs**

	Cleveland	Indianapolis	Orlando	Philadelphia
Correctly identified a community relations program offered in the market	23.6%	52.2%	57.2%	23.3%
First unaided response was a team program	57.5%	51.8%	55.8%	42.4%
First unaided response was a league program	10.0%	23.4%	22.1%	20.1%
First unaided response was a player program	32.5%	24.8%	22.1%	33.5%

operating the "best" program that the Orlando Magic attained. Approximately three-quarters (68%) of those queried in the Orlando market indicated that the Magic managed the best community relations program. No other franchise exceeded a 40% response rate.

When people were asked why they selected this team, the most common response was "they are always in the media"—clearly demonstrating that the respondent's perception of "the best" was significantly influenced by the media's receptivity to and presentation of the activity. Only very infrequently did respondents say that the determining factor was a specific civic cause or the resources generated or provided because of the franchise's support. Disappointingly, a limited number (<5%) of all respondents mentioned direct interaction or affiliation with any of the community outreach initiatives of the professional sport franchises included in the analysis.

Further investigation revealed that the higher-scoring teams (Orlando and Indianapolis) had similar market conditions and operational characteristics that very likely favorably affected the public's familiarity with franchise cause-related initiatives. As we noted earlier with respect to Orlando, the professional sport competitive landscape in each of these higher-recall markets was less cluttered when the data were collected than Cleveland and Philadelphia. Additionally, the community relations department at each of these franchises tended to demonstrate more focus in that they had a limited number of programs in operation. As reflected in the Orlando Magic Foundation mission statement, these franchises appeared to concentrate on 10 or fewer programs, each tailored to a targeted market (e.g., youth). In each case, the issue of clutter arises with an inherently competitive landscape or an excessive team-administered campaign agenda, distorting the recognition of franchise community-based initiatives.

Lastly, the foundation structure that was unique to Orlando appeared to act as an icon for respondent association. Respondents tended to indicate familiarity with the Orlando Magic Foundation and then to identify a program administered by the foundation. The research team's interpretation was that this "clearinghouse" process facilitated respondents' recall of franchise-administered community relations initiatives within the Orlando market.

Establishing Effective Franchise Community Relations Programs in Urban Settings

The results of this investigation suggest the following three criteria for recognition as an effective professional sport franchise community relations program by the consuming public: limited or focused (themed) project involvement, foundation structure, and ultimately the stimulation of significant media attention. Unfortunately, in the minds of the consumers, effectiveness was not determined by the specific cause or the amount of money generated or donated, but rather by the media's acknowledgment of the activity. The recommendation that follows from this is that urban sport franchise community relations divisions adopt a theme-oriented, foundation-based approach rather than a team-centered technique, with the aim of achieving the following benefits:

- The occasion for enhanced communication between the team (through the foundation) and the community (through its residents and agencies)
- The opportunity to react to issues and concerns that might prove more timely than agendas and programs created in past years
- The opportunity to involve residents and community agencies in decision-making and resource allocation as applicable to their community

- The long-term possibility of helping community agencies and organizations become more self-sufficient

- The appeal to corporate sponsors and area businesses to align themselves with community interests that may relate more closely to their own organizational needs and desires

- The possibility that increased interaction and better communication between the team and the community may lead to increased interest in and support of the team through the purchasing of tickets, merchandise, and so on

Given this list of possible benefits, the foundation-based approach also offers a number of ideal communication relations tactics:

- A board composed of management personnel from the team, representatives of community agencies (YMCAs, churches, coalitions, etc.), at-large residents of the community, teachers and school representatives, personnel from the police department and the judicial system, delegates from various area businesses (chamber of commerce), and civic club members

- A committee system to make recommendations to the board based on the needs and desires of the community and to present the case for an impartial decision

- A procedure to consider a variety of opportunities for involvement and the choice to fully fund some programs while providing challenge grants to others, encouraging them to learn how to solicit other funds and work to become self-sustaining

- The ability to serve programs that have traditionally been the target of sport franchise community relations programs, at-risk youth, while at the same time supporting early childhood programs that may in the long run reduce the number of youths who are at risk

- A vehicle through which the team can become much more fully integrated into the community and through which it can participate, via the foundation, in a variety of social and political forums

- Consideration of meaningful efforts by the franchise in the areas of job training, hiring, and utilization of community resources

- A consistent, year-round approach with stable and long-term resources that has the ability to make a real difference in the lives of the inner-city community

Current community relations programs provide much-appreciated opportunities but to a limited number of individuals or groups. For such a program to be truly effective, the community itself must be involved in goal setting and program planning and delivery. The best way to accomplish this is through the creation of a foundation/community-based approach to community relations programming. As Neil Austrian of NFL Properties stated, "It is the responsibility of NFL clubs to be actively involved members of our communities, to be corporate citizens. We can't just be takers. We must give something back."[24] Foundation/community-based community relations programming allows the sport organization to be more than just a source of funds to particular social service agencies; it permits the sport organization to have relationships with a variety of social service, educational, and cause-related organizations. This approach, much like that of traditional charitable foundations, allows organizations to apply to the sport-based foundation for funding and other forms of assistance (memorabilia items for auctions, player appearances, volunteers, etc.). For example, the OMYF, the foundation-based community relations arm of the Orlando Magic, conducts a variety of fund-raising activities throughout the year.

Social service and educational institutions that serve primarily youth can apply to the OMYF for assistance, and the OMYF can give assistance based on the merits of that request on a one-time basis, annually, or however it chooses. The OMYF has a foundation board composed of members of the community who may have some familiarity with the social service system and can provide valuable insight into the decision-making process.

Therefore, if professional franchises are truly involved, they will be partners with the local community. A true partnership will entail shared decision-making, two-way communication, and a vested interest in the well-being of each party. This partnership and its resources can then work with the residents of the community to make it a better place to work and live.

Obviously, there is an expectation that a professional sport franchise will establish a strong presence in the local community via educational and philanthropic outreach activities, and that the effectiveness of a community relations campaign is often linked to the breadth of the public relations agenda. Thus, professional sport franchises need to proactively develop and implement well-defined and focused long-term public relations initiatives aimed at enhancing the quality of life for the residents.

We have examined the concept of community relations as a marketing tool for sport organizations. In considering the concept of cause marketing, which perhaps is better termed "cause branding," we turn our attention to the potential sponsors of those programs—national and local corporations and businesses. We will examine their rationale and business motivation for becoming involved in community relations-type programming and other sponsorship activities.

Cause Marketing and Branding

Earlier we mentioned cause marketing as an effective approach to community relations programming. Here we consider the ways in which programs that are strategic in their type and scope of initiatives can yield a substantial return on investment. Through such programs, the concept of cause marketing has really evolved into **cause branding,** a strategic, stakeholder-based approach to integrating social issues into business strategy, brand equity, and organizational identity.[25]

The concept of cause marketing originated and became common practice when executives discovered that cause-related promotions influenced consumer purchasing decisions. The 1984 American Express campaign, which enabled customers to donate a few cents to restore the Statue of Liberty every time they used the card, is recognized as the impetus for establishing cause marketing programs, which have evolved into the cause branding efforts discussed in this section. In the rosters of sponsors involved in sport sponsorship activities, the names of companies such as Ford, General Motors, Home Depot, McDonald's, and Wal-Mart are fairly common from market to market. These companies have demonstrated a belief that *doing the right thing* in their communities is integral to their business success. Thus they have built customer and community service deep into their corporate cultures.[26] The programs selected by these industry leaders are important to the communities in which they operate, and make sound business sense as well. For example, McDonald's creation and support of the Ronald McDonald House Charities program is compatible with its business mission of attracting families to its restaurants. Families are the operative target market both for business growth and charitable activities. These types of activities are also attractive for sport organizations and players for the purposes of creating strategic alliances. Cam Neeley, former Boston Bruins hockey player, is actively involved in providing an alliance with the Bruins to help promote charitable activities, and serves as a

a

b

© Jim Baron/The Image Finders

(a) Wal-Mart and *(b)* McDonald's community relations programs are important aspects of their business success.

spokesperson and focal point for publicizing the cause as well as the two key facilitators, McDonald's and the Boston Bruins.

How do consumers feel about these activities, and can the activities really affect the business fortunes of companies? Consider the following findings from the 1999 *Cone/Roper Cause-Related Trends Report:*

- 83% of Americans have a more positive image of companies that support a cause they care about than of companies that do not support a cause

- 66% of Americans feel that cause programs are an acceptable business practice

- 63% of Americans feel that cause marketing programs should be a standard business practice

- 65% of Americans report that they would be likely to switch brands or retailers to one associated with a good cause, when price and quality are equal

- 87% of employees of companies with cause programs feel a strong sense of loyalty to the company versus 67% of those employed in companies without a cause association[27]

These statistics make it clear that the majority of the populace perceive cause branding activities not only as a good idea, but also as an expected outcome and essential element of sound business practices.

Some of the implementation vehicles for these cause branding activities, which can involve several partners, are quite creative. For example, Valvoline has established "Caring Hands," a program that raises charitable dollars through fund-raising activities at selected NASCAR races and in the past two years has raised $481,905. What is interesting is that although the funds are generated in conjunction with NASCAR events, they are distributed on a much broader basis. For example, at a Pittsburgh Pirate baseball game in June 2000, Valvoline presented a check for $4000 to the Big Brothers and Big Sisters Chapter of Greater Pittsburgh. While this money was generated by NASCAR activities, the Pittsburgh donation was related to Valvoline's sponsorship of the Pittsburgh Pirates; and the contribution amount was part of a formula, $10 donated for every double hit by a Pirate player during the 2000 baseball season.[28]

Corporate marketing departments wrote checks for $640 million to U.S. charities in 1999. This is in addition to soft contributions such as value-in-kind, services, and promotional support. In describing the impact of this support, Mark Feldman, vice president of Boston-based Cone, Inc., stated, "Cause association can be a very powerful business tool. It can forge, build and enhance consumer and business to business relationships. It also speaks to shareholders, analysts, potential business partners and many other constituencies, especially if it is integrated into a marketing program."[29]

PRACTITIONER'S PERSPECTIVE

Cause Marketing: A Direct Connect to the Customers
by Maria Vugrin, Cone, Inc.

In 1999, corporations paid over $630 million to nonprofit organizations for the rights to feature the charities in cause-related advertising, programs, and promotions. This represents a 400% increase in spending since 1990. It is becoming clear that the integration of social issues and business practices was not just a passing fad of the 1990s, but rather the beginning of a fundamental shift in how the world's leading companies are using cause associations to position their organizations and brands for the future. But what is fueling this increase, and how does it affect the sport community?

In a marketplace increasingly saturated with brands, companies are finding it harder to "out-innovate" their competitors through traditional marketing and advertising tactics, and thus have begun aligning with causes and nonprofits to develop an emotional connection with consumers and to differentiate their brands. According to the 1999 *Cone/Roper Cause-Related Trends Report,* American consumers and employees solidly and consistently support cause-related activities, and companies see benefits to their brand and organization's reputation, image, and bottom line.

The world of sport sponsorship has also become cluttered as an increasing number of corporations are realizing the value of tapping into the connection vast numbers of consumers have with sport leagues, events, and athletes. So it is no surprise that companies are beginning to integrate cause marketing into their sport sponsorships as an additional tactic to further differentiate them from their competitors. Cause programs in the sport arena fall along a spectrum that ranges from philanthropy to promotion to marketing and finally to branding.

Philanthropy programs primarily involve an in-kind product or financial donation, as is the case with New Balance's sponsorship of the American Red Cross team in the Boston Marathon. Companies often donate in order to "give back" to their communities and to gain a reputation as a good corporate citizen. As a running team sponsor, New Balance Athletic Shoe donated $15,000 to the Red Cross in 2000 and pledged an additional gift for 2001. The Red Cross applied this and other similar donations to its local humanitarian programs and services throughout the Massachusetts Bay area. Through this donation, New Balance was able to show its commitment to giving back to the neighborhoods in which it does business and to increase goodwill toward the company.

Cause promotions involve more than a company donation—they also engage consumers. They are short-term tactics designed to increase sales, of which a portion are then donated to a nonprofit or cause. The promotions appeal to the consumer as an easy way to "make a difference" or support a cause, often through an everyday purchase. For example, in 1998 General Mills unveiled three special edition Wheaties boxes featuring legendary athletes and a new program to support the Buoniconti Fund to Cure Paralysis. That year, during October and

(continued)

(continued)　November, General Mills donated 10 cents to the Miami Project to Cure Paralysis for every box of Wheaties, Honey Frosted Wheaties, or Crispy Wheaties 'n Raisins sold. This promotion successfully utilized the combined emotional appeal of the cause and the celebrity athletes.

Cause marketing programs use a combination of tactics, including philanthropy, promotions, volunteerism, and public awareness initiatives. They demand that the corporation make a deeper commitment to the cause and have a greater involvement in the program than just a fiscal relationship. One of the oldest cause marketing programs in the American sport world is the partnership between the NFL and United Way. This partnership began in 1973 when the NFL saw the value of addressing community problems and social issues through one organization rather than randomly through multiple sponsorships with independent nonprofit groups. Partnership activities range from the NFL's donating television airtime during games to promote the United Way to volunteer activities on the part of NFL athletes and team representatives through league programs in their communities. The partnership allowed the NFL to focus its giving in order to make a deeper and more lasting impact on issues that were important to its athletes, members, and viewers.

At the far end of the spectrum is cause branding, a business strategy that integrates a social issue or cause into brand equity and organizational identity to achieve significant bottom-line impacts. Cause branding programs are long term, and they affect a wider variety of stakeholders, including consumers, employees, retailers, suppliers, public officials, and communities. One difference in relation to cause marketing campaigns is that cause branding initiatives weave a company's brand persona into the program. Nike's P.L.A.Y. (Participate in the Lives of America's Youth) is a strong example of a cause branding initiative. Nike launched the initiative in 1994 with the goal of helping underserved kids build confidence and develop life skills through sport and recreation, inspirational coaches and activities, and safe places to play. Nike also worked with the Boys & Girls Clubs of America to develop and implement Nike-branded educational sport programs such as Nike University, Nike Swoosh Club, Nike Sports Leadership Camps, Nike Girls Sports, Nike Games, and P.L.A.Y. Daily Challenges. Nike utilizes multiple communication vehicles, such as marketing, public relations, advertising, and nonprofit partners, to increase the awareness and effectiveness of its programs and thus enhance its brand equity.

As corporations and sport organizations have become increasingly sophisticated in aligning with causes, they have begun to recognize the power of the Internet to increase awareness and deepen the effectiveness of cause-related sport programs. For example, Yahoo! sponsored and developed Web sites for the Mark McGwire Foundation for Children, a child abuse awareness organization, and for Touch'em All Foundation, an initiative cofounded by Garth Brooks and involving MLB players to help children in need. Both foundations benefit from Yahoo!'s ability to utilize the World Wide Web to educate and involve people everywhere.

When implemented correctly and with commitment, cause programs are a win-win for all involved. The nonprofit and sport organizations receive increased financial support, and consumer awareness is heightened through the marketing and merchandising efforts of the corporation/league. The corporations and leagues enjoy a buoyed reputation and often increased financial success. In the future, as more organizations realize success through their cause involvements, we can expect see an increase in the number and depth of cause branded sport programs.

Starting a Community Relations Program

In this chapter you have seen a number of examples of effective community relations programs, as well as examples of some established efforts that use community relations programming in a true marketing context. But how do you begin creating a community relations program or establishing an athlete in a community relations program? James Masteralexis, Esq., principal in the DiaMMond Management Group, explains the process as it relates to Peter Bergeron, a rookie with the Montreal Expos in the following Practitioner's Perspective.

PRACTITIONER'S PERSPECTIVE

Positioning a Young or Emerging Athlete
by James T. Masteralexis, Esq.

Positioning a young or emerging professional athlete in his hometown or local market is valuable for several reasons. First, it allows the athlete to connect and develop a bond with his community at a grassroots level. The athlete can create an association with a favorite local organization or worthy local charity or cause. Charitable work builds goodwill with the community and fosters positive name recognition and association for the athlete. This goodwill and association with a charity or cause can translate into endorsement opportunities later on in the athlete's career.

Second, in many respects, a local positioning campaign is excellent practice and preparation for future promotional activities and prospective regional and national advertising campaigns and activities. By beginning at a smaller, local level, the athlete learns firsthand about the intricacies of community relations activities and the promotional efforts, such as sponsorship, associated with those activities. The athlete develops communication skills as well as an appreciation of his role and obligations as a visible spokesperson for both the charity or cause and the sponsor of the program.

D.A.R.E. is an example of an organization that can benefit from the community relations efforts of sport organizations and players.

An athlete must truly desire to invest the time and energy in a local promotional campaign because it lacks the visibility and impact of a national campaign. Montreal Expos rookie outfielder Peter Bergeron was highly motivated and actually was the driving force behind his own local charitable efforts. While still playing in the minor leagues, Peter determined that he wanted to give back to his local community (Greenfield, Massachusetts) by hosting a charitable fund-raiser and baseball clinic for the Drug Abuse Resistance Education (D.A.R.E) conducted by the Greenfield Police Department. As a grade school student, Peter and his classmates had been taught the dangers of drug and alcohol abuse by D.A.R.E officers, and Peter believed that D.A.R.E had an important message that he could help promote and assist.

(continued)　　When Peter asked his agents, the DiaMMond Management Group, to help him support his favorite charity with a baseball clinic fund-raiser, we were glad to help. After securing a local radio station and newspaper as sponsors who would promote the event, we created a logo that conveyed the charitable nature of the event while also depicting the sponsors involved in promoting and producing the event.

Peter, because of his stature in the community and association with a worthwhile charity and cause, was able to assist us in securing a number of local sponsors to help underwrite the cost of the event and also to provide equipment and awards for the participants. The event was attended by more than 200 children and was highly successful. Interestingly enough, Peter's energetic work and the reaction to his event led to a local car dealership's offering him an endorsement deal.

In many respects, a local promotional campaign is similar to a local political campaign. The starting point is the home base (hometown) of the athlete, and from that point efforts are expanded regionally. If the athlete becomes more visible on and off the field, this "sphere of influence" can continue to grow.

Athletes can elect to create meaningful community relations programs in their hometowns as Peter Bergeron did, or on a larger scale as with the hospital building that Dikembe Mutombo of the Philadelphia 76ers has initiated in his homeland. Others, like former Pittsburgh Steeler and NFL Hall of Famer Lynn Swann, choose to initiate and support activities in their "adopted hometowns" where they lived and achieved their professional success. Regardless of where, athletes and their agents need to make a concerted effort to "give something back" to the community, however they choose to identify and define that community.

Postgame Wrap-Up

Improving the quality of life and making a difference in the target community constitute the most common goal of community relations programs in general. These programs can also make a difference in improving the perception of the sport organization in the eyes of the community, and ultimately increasing interest in and support for the sport organization in that target community.

One shortcoming common among sport organizations, teams, and even individual athletes is a lack of marketing leverage from these activities. Community relations programs are a valuable marketing tool that can be used to position or reposition a league, team, or individual athlete. Sport organizations must do a better job of capitalizing, in a promotional context, on the goodwill and exposure created through these activities.

As the price of attending sporting events continues to rise and the salaries of professional athletes continue to reach heights beyond the imagination of the average ticket holder, there must be a concentrated effort to give something back and relate to the constituency that buys tickets, watches on television, visits Web sites, and buys merchandise. Sport organizations, teams, and athletes must create programs to reach their communities that have meaning for those communities. There has to be a connection that is seen and felt to be relevant by the residents.

There are a number of ways to forge a connection. One way is through identification with and support of a cause. Causes focused on literacy, school violence, staying in school, and breast cancer are examples of causes that sport organizations have identified as worthy targets to address and affect through financial commitments and other types of activities. Connections can also be created through the visibility and diversity of foundations. Foundations can be used as a focal point for all of the activities of a sport organization. Funding can come from auctions, memorabilia sales, appearances, player fines, and so forth. Foundations can also connect to the community on a variety of levels because they are often used to disseminate funds to a broad range of projects, in contrast to the more sharply focused efforts associated with cause branding.

Regardless of the activities selected or the methodology employed to conduct the specific "connecting" activities, community relations programming is an essential part of the promotion mix. Community relations can improve image, position or reposition the sport entity, and demonstrate good citizenship, among other effects. Regardless of the primary audience for the community relations programming or the specific delivery system, community relations activities offer a leverageable asset that is an integral part of the promotion mix.

Discussion Items

1. If you were involved in selecting a community relations initiative for a professional or collegiate team based in a large city, what might you choose and why?

2. Cause-related branding can be a very effective tool in helping create relationships between the sport organization and its community. Conversely, do you feel that association with a controversial cause, value, or lifestyle can be detrimental to relationship building with the community?

3. In March 2001, the NBA announced that Reading Is Fundamental would become the national platform for its community relations initiatives. Why is this an appropriate activity for the NBA? Do you feel that it is the most appropriate platform for a professional sport league? Why or why not?

Learning Enrichment Activities

1. Examine the community relations efforts of your university athletic program or a professional sport franchise in your market. Is there a clearly defined goal for this community relations effort? If so, what is it? Do you feel that this message is being conveyed throughout the marketplace? If not, what actions should be undertaken to disseminate the message?

2. Visit the home page of each of five different sport organizations. Are there distinct links that discuss the organization's community relations projects? Do these links adequately convey what the organization is doing and why? If you were responsible for using the Internet to disseminate information and inform visitors to your team site about your social responsibility and citizenship, how would you elect to utilize the Web site?

3. The NFL is clearly associated and identified with United Way Charities. What types of charitable efforts are the following leagues or teams associated with?
   a. National Hockey League
   b. Women's National Basketball Association
   c. Ladies Professional Golf Association
   d. Major League Soccer
   e. Los Angeles Dodgers
   f. Phoenix Suns
   g. New York Liberty

4. Home Depot is a corporation with a very positive reputation and record of corporate giving and support. Home Depot is also active as a corporate partner with NASCAR. Investigate the relationship between NASCAR and Home Depot and explain how these parties are improving the quality of life in their community.

5. Identify three examples of cause branding types of activities associated with sport. Which of the activities you selected is the most effective? Why is that particular activity and association effective?

Atmospherics As a Sport Promotion Tool

chapter objectives

1. Understand how atmospherics assume significant importance as a promotional tool, particularly within the sport industry where the core product is often simultaneously produced and consumed

2. Understand and be able to apply the five-step atmospheric management process

3. Understand how the sport promotion specialist can use atmospherics effectively to produce specific cognitive and emotional effects on the target market

4. Understand how the use of interior as well as exterior design features can affect the sport atmosphere and influence consumption

5. Understand tools necessary for properly coordinating all sport atmosphere elements

Pregame Introductions

In supporting the case for a downtown ballpark in Colorado Springs, Colorado, one sport journalist wrote, "It should be clear to anyone . . . that the more tranquil conditions downtown (closer to the mountains), combined with the advanced architecture and amenities, would create a much improved game-day atmosphere."[1] Ah, the atmosphere. If you're a promotion specialist for a sport team, event, or the like, yours is the challenge of providing the very amenities referred to by this author and of creating an atmosphere attractive to an audience.

Several decades ago psychologists began studying the effects of environment on human behavior. Shortly thereafter, marketers joined in, with Kotler spearheading the topic in coining the term *atmospherics* to describe the intentional control and structuring of marketing-based environmental cues. Kotler has defined atmospherics as "the designing of buying and consuming environments in a manner calculated to produce specific cognitive and/or emotional effects on the target market."[2] Therefore, a discussion of atmospherics need not address critical issues related to place or point of distribution such as drawing radius, location, and parking. Instead, this chapter focuses on the manipulation of internal as well as external attributes of the physical setting in order to facilitate buyer interest and responsiveness. Many might consider this the collective entertainment value of the consumption experience, which is critical to attracting, influencing, and sustaining patronage in what Wolf refers to as today's "entertainment economy."[3]

What Is Meant by Atmospherics?

Atmospherics are of greatest importance in situations in which purchasers come to the organization's physical plant and come into contact with the personnel, for several reasons. Whether through intention or by default, the presentation of the personnel and the physical setting emit cues about the organization that are very telling. Secondly, atmospherics are useful as a device for establishing a distinctive character for an organization in situations in which most competing organizations are hard to differentiate. Thirdly, atmospherics are relevant when it is desirable to attune an organization to a distinctive class of consumers. These cues lead to inferences about the organization and its concern for the client, who carefully processes this information.

You can argue, then, that atmospherics assume the greatest importance as a promotional tool particularly in spectator sport, where the core product is simultaneously produced and consumed and is thus inconsistent, unpredictable, and essentially out of the control of the sport promotion specialist. Thus greater emphasis is warranted on atmospheric components over which the sport promotion specialist can exercise greater levels of control, such as the consumption environment.[4] Westerbeek and Shilbury argue for increasing the focus on the place element of the sport marketing mix, as elements of sport product's point of production largely determine fundamental marketing and promotional strategy decisions.[5]

In fact, it appears that among the most influential factors in an individual's becoming a dedicated professional sport team fan is the desire to "be a part of the game-day atmosphere."[6] Moreover, the results of a study involving British football fans showed that the production environment was more important to the fanatic supporter than to the occasional spectator.[7]

Positive atmospheric conditions provide a controllable consumption incentive (e.g., attendance) that can overcome a weak core product, as evidenced by the Baltimore Orioles and Chicago Cubs. While finishing near the bottom of their division, the Orioles continue to draw 88% of capacity in their relatively new stadium, Oriole Ball Park at Camden Yards, partly because of its invigorating environment, set against the Chesapeake Bay. The ballpark is commonly recognized as the benchmark of modern baseball park design with its nostalgic character and abundance of amenities. On the other hand, Wrigley Field, home of the Cubs, oozes with atmosphere that includes the Bleacher Bums, outfield wall vines, and the traditional singing during the seventh-inning stretch, causing even less-than-passionate Cubs fans to long to be at a game. In fact, the ambience of Wrigley extends beyond the ballpark to include the surrounding sidewalks and rooftop parties, all viewed by the club as part of the game-day atmosphere.

But the notion of atmospheric management is not limited to spectator sport environments, as athletic apparel retail outlets and sport grills worldwide strive to lure patrons with environmentally driven gimmicks such as indoor activity areas (e.g., basketball goals) and 24-hour sport television broadcasts. In fact, according to Shimp and DeLozier, all retail outlets, which in the case of sport include arenas, stadiums, ballparks, and fitness centers and the like, project a certain personality, or image, to consumers. A venue's image comprises many dimensions, each interacting with the others to influence the perception various customer groups hold of the venue.[8]

Therefore, sport businesses must direct considerable attention to ways in which the atmosphere of their consumption environment can promote the desired relationship with clientele. All too often, when a clear understanding of the critical issues is lacking, the importance of atmospheric considerations gives way to functional considerations, ultimately inhibiting presentation of the consumption environment.

Take Me Out to the Theme Park, I Mean Ballpark

According to Michael Hallmark of NBBJ Sports, "just as the movie industry reinvented itself with new multiplex theaters, new sport venues will have to be exciting, equaling the most spectacular theme parks, in order to draw families to these unique destinations of fun, civic pride and comfort."[9] If you are a sport promotion specialist, here is your greatest challenge, competing with other entertainment venues in the minds of sport consumers.

Atmospheric Management

Atmospheric management entails the following five-step process:

- Step 1: Defining the desired market and effects
- Step 2: Developing an attractive and meaningful theme
- Step 3: Specifying pertinent elements of the physical setting that are to carry the intended cognitions and effects to the target audience

- Step 4: Selecting specific sensory elements that convey the desired effects
- Step 5: Coordinating the production

Step 1: Defining the Desired Market and Effect

Amenities provide each environment a differentiation or positioning strategy that should be designed to attract and accommodate a targeted audience or consumer base. Atmospheric elements can be tailored to a defined market. Sport promoters attempting to lure families tend to provide atmospheric elements attractive to children, as well as family seating and picnic areas. USA Track & Field, for example, implemented the Adidas Youth Cheering Section in order to attract more youths to the U.S. Open Track & Field Championships. Similarly, the NHL's Phoenix Coyotes targeted young adults in converting an unused seating area into a section with a party-like atmosphere, with a little help from the team's flagship radio station, KDKB-FM. Fans gain access to this section, called the Doghouse, by using a password announced on KDKB's morning program. During intermissions, Doghouse patrons are treated to rock band concerts scheduled by the radio station.[10]

If your job is to promote sport, you'll do well to familiarize yourself with the specific values of your consumer base with respect to atmospherics. Researchers have investigated the preferences of various consumer groups in this regard. A study of females between 18 and 29 years of age revealed a keen interest among this group in issues associated with atmospheric conditions, leading the authors to recommend that sport businesses targeting this market (female Generation Xers) stress atmospheric elements within their product delivery. For instance, a female within this market will probably find a fitness or exercise center with a racquetball court and juice bar more enticing then a bare-bones facility.[11] Appropriate music at beach volleyball games and at the Gravity Games or X Games has a similar impact on the allure of the event to members of this generation.

Golf industry research has revealed differing perspectives on the importance of course atmospheric conditions. A survey of private golf club users indicated that atmospheric elements such as design and layout were of great interest.[12] Public golf course users, on the other hand, identified such aspects to be of little value; instead elements relating to access, including the price of greens fees, were of primary interest.[13]

Perhaps your greatest challenge in relation to atmospherics is to balance the interests of a new generation of sport consumers who, as illustrated by the study of female Generation Xers seek nonstop entertainment, with the interests of the traditional sport consumer market, who typically seek sport in a purer sense, absent bells and whistles. However, if only the traditionalist or purist attended sporting events, sport—particularly at the high-performance level—would die. In order to attract the entertainment-seeking patron, Spoelstra advocates that sport create an aura of fun.[14]

In an effort to provide a more enjoyable atmosphere in new Comerica Park in Detroit, Tigers' owner Michael Ilitch spent millions of dollars on special effects, such as a huge fountain at the edge of center field with a dancing lighted water display that can be choreographed to music—not to mention a Ferris wheel, a tiger carousel, special lighting effects, ornamental tigers decorating the scoreboard and entrance gates, statues, and specially made Pewabic tiles in baseball themes. Ilitch is aware that some traditionalists and baseball purists won't be as excited about all this, but they can access the ballpark without having to meander through the extras. There is a clear path for the traditionalists; the "fun stuff" is off to the sides. "We've thought that through carefully. We want to make the traditionalists happy, too," said Ilitch.[15]

If a sport facility's perceived image and the sport consumer's self-image are not congruent, favorable consumption behavior is rather unlikely.[16] Therefore, fundamental to effective atmospheric management is familiarity with personal characteristics and interests of the sport business's targeted consumer groups. Armed with consumer demographic and psychographic data, sport promotion specialists can more easily design and implement atmospheric effects tailored to meet consumer demands and stimulate buyer behavior. For instance, music by the Beach Boys during play stoppage or intermission would probably be of little appeal to fans at the Extreme Games, who reflect a demographic profile more interested in alternative rock. Likewise, these fans may be less concerned about spacious seating, leg room, and convenience than patrons at an NBA game, who reflect a more upscale demographic profile.

Step 2: Developing an Atmospheric Theme

Once you have identified audience characteristics, Gilmore suggests developing and employing an atmospheric theme in order to convey a sense of consistency to the consumer while also enriching the consumption experience.[17] The thematic presentation may also be inspired by the following:

- The sport business's key consumer groups
- The organization's philosophy and mission
- Cultural features of the marketplace
- The calendar, including anniversaries, holidays, and the like
- Milestones that may include player or performance achievements or attendance records
- Elements within the sport business's promotional campaign
- Other available resources such as celebrity appearances, opponents, and sponsor agreements

The sport promotion specialist should meet with members of the promotional staff and brainstorm on ideas that feed into an atmospheric theme. While a professional sport franchise may initiate a consistent season-long promotional theme supported by a catchy advertising slogan (e.g., "We're Gonna Rock the House!" or "The Silver Anniversary Season"), which in turn influences atmospheric planning, the team may also employ a series of rotational themes based on the day or night of the week, the opponent, holidays or celebrations, team and player milestones, a sponsor's involvement (see example below), and other ideas. While a long-term atmospheric theme

Blue Jackets Go Interactive

The Columbus Blue Jackets, an expansion NHL franchise, are in the final stages of developing themed interactive areas on Nationwide Arena's main concourse, which has been divided into quadrants and named after the team's Championship Partners. Attendees will be able to walk along the Pepsi Parkway, Bud Terrace, GM Drive, Bank One Lane, and Ohio Health Place. The interactive zones are included in the sponsors' packages, and each sponsor has the opportunity to develop its own interactive theme to fit with its core business. For Ohio Health, for example, a section could be devoted to health issues. A muscular skeleton could be displayed with hockey pads and equipment, showing why the equipment is necessary and how it functions. There might also be an interactive piece to test a goalie's "reaction" to hockey shots. Pepsi may have a zone where all activities will be kid oriented. There will also be a play area for kids within a scaled-down model home. At the end of the season, the model home as well as other merchandise will be given away to a lucky fan.

reinforces the consistency demanded of an integrated marketing communications plan, but a rotational theme or occasional alterations tend to spike consumer interest. Whether used on a short- or a long-term basis, the atmospheric theme should be abundantly apparent to event attendees and supported by venue decorations, information sources, promotional integration, and event staff attire.

Step 3: Specifying the Elements of the Physical Setting That Are to Carry the Intended Cognitions and Effects

The elements of the **physical setting** may include the exterior structure, special displays, interior design, and even the dress and actions of the organization's personnel. Success at this stage may require a unique blend of skills in such areas as architecture, interior design, window dressing, and wardrobe design.

Exterior Structure

The exterior of a facility is like the packaging on a product. A venue's facade communicates considerable information to the consumer, such as the type and caliber of product (service) sold within. In real estate the impression the façade makes is known as curb appeal. Components that make up the architecture and exterior design of a venue are the physical size, the shape, the storefront, and the lighting. Physical size can communicate strength, power, and security.[18] Thus domed arenas in Houston, New Orleans, Tampa, Atlanta, East Rutherford, San Antonio, Calgary, Detroit, Syracuse, Seattle, Indianapolis, and Minneapolis have attracted attention, sport teams, and events to the community. Annually, the University of Michigan and the University of Tennessee wage battle over who possesses the largest football stadium, with each institution's facility accommodating over 100,000 spectators, thus demonstrating a sense of power and strength in numbers of fans as well as team performance.

It would appear that the size of the stadium creates an image of power on the field. For many generations of British soccer fans, the Twin Towers of Wembley Stadium in London represented all that was good about English soccer. The final of the FA Challenge Cup, an annual knockout, season-long competition, was played there. Reaching Wembley and playing in the Cup Final was the pinnacle of many players' careers.

A venue's shape can also serve to stimulate interest and conversation. The unique shape of the aforementioned domes has enabled these facilities to represent tourist attractions for the community as well as icons for publicity-generating mega-sporting events. Additionally, a sport venue such as the Pyramid in Memphis has become well known because of its unique structure and shape.

The Look, Feel, and Taste of San Diego

Major League Baseball's San Diego Padres have prepared plans for an eight-acre park near their proposed downtown ballpark that will feature a sand volleyball court and lawn amphitheater. According to Padre executives, the park has been designed to look, feel, and even taste like San Diego. On game days, Padres ticket holders will be able to stroll through the park area, lined with restaurants and retail shops. Up to 3000 park-goers will be able to buy $5 park passes and watch the Padres from lawn chairs, picnic tables, and blankets in the park, which will also feature a large color video screen for showing the game. The Padres' bullpen will be just beyond the fence in left center field, and the park will have an autograph alley where fans can get a close view of warm-ups and seek autographs. There will also be a kids' entertainment zone with batting cages and pitching radar guns. On non-game days, the park will be open for public use.[19]

The venue's storefront serves as its permanent advertisement, providing information to consumers and conveying a distinct impression of the venue. Entrances should be wide and inviting, alerting consumers that they are welcome within (figure 11.1).

The use of outside lighting contributes significantly to a venue's beauty and image. While lighting serves an important function in providing safety and security for patrons, proper lighting and signage can also contribute much in the way of aesthetics. Lighting should complement a venue's architecture and clarify a venue's form and texture. Outside lighting can create a specific buying atmosphere by telling prospective consumers that they are entering an elegant place, a fun place, a homey place, an exciting place, a secure place, and so on that a developer or retailer may think are conducive to selling goods.

Figure 11.1   The Autozone Park entrance is a good example of an inviting entrance.

Special Displays

As an atmospheric-type promotion, point-of-purchase and point-of-sale displays, consisting of eye-catching exhibits intended to lure the consumer to the product or merchandise, are commonly found in the retail industry. Today's sport promoter has redefined the point-of-sale display to include fireworks, interactive games and contests, virtual reality experiences, and other forms of pageantry, each intending similarly to attract the consumer to the core product.

A number of sport organizations have gone so far as to produce elaborate internal and external auxiliary activities as a means of generating attention and enhancing the event's atmospheric presence and attendance experience. Special informational and interactive displays are commonplace at sporting events today. The NCAA, for instance, has developed two such displays, the NCAA Welcome Center and Hoop City, primarily as a means of enhancing consumer familiarity with the association through information dissemination, and secondarily to provide a championship-related entertainment component.

The NCAA Welcome Center, constructed on-site at various NCAA championships, comprises a series of displays that provide spectators with information on the association, its corporate partners, and the host community, as well as a variety of enjoyable interactive games. In addition, Hoop City, a more elaborate off-site event held in conjunction with the Men's and Women's Final Four, is open to the public and provides a host of participatory and merchandising opportunities ranging from interactive games, contests, and activities to pep rallies and celebrity appearances. The following Practitioner's Perspective provides further details on the NCAA Welcome Center.

PRACTITIONER'S PERSPECTIVE

NCAA Welcome Centers Enhance Championship Atmosphere
by John L. Johnson, Director Promotions and Special Events, NCAA

NCAA Welcome Centers launched operation during 1997-1998 at selected championships with the mission to improve the public's perception of the NCAA, express the importance of athletics and education, and improve the general public's understanding of how the Association functions.

The NCAA Welcome Center concept arose from on-site research conducted on behalf of the NCAA that revealed that attendees at NCAA championships were searching for information about the NCAA and how it functions. The NCAA staff administering the championships did not have many opportunities to interact with the general public. To address this, an internal NCAA staff project team was formed to move the concept to action and the following objectives were established in October 1996:

- To enhance the public's perception of the NCAA
- To enhance the image of the championship event and build awareness for all championships
- To improve the public's and student-athletes' understandings of intercollegiate athletics and the role the NCAA plays
- To create added value for corporate sponsors and licensing programs
- To create grassroots relationships with the general public and future student-athletes

During 1997-1998, NCAA Welcome Centers debuted at 5 championships; this number increased to 9 during 1998-2000; and a 10th championship, women's hockey, was added in 2000-2001. As of 2000-2001, all 10 NCAA Welcome Centers are at the following Division I championship events:

- Men's and Women's Frozen Four (ice hockey)
- Men's and Women's College World Series (baseball and softball)
- Women's volleyball
- Men's lacrosse
- Men's and Women's College Cup (soccer)
- Wrestling
- Women's gymnastics

As the NCAA strives to enhance the student-athlete experience by increasing attendance at the championship events, the NCAA Welcome Center objectives have evolved to include the following:

- To continue to enhance the image of the championship events and build awareness
- To continue to improve the public's and student-athletes' understandings of intercollegiate athletics and the role the NCAA plays
- To create added value for the corporate partner and licensing programs
- To build grassroots relationships with the general public and future student-athletes
- To make the NCAA Welcome Center a "destination" not only to educate but to entertain the customers
- To have the NCAA Welcome Center serve as an attendance draw—something that can be pre-promoted and will help increase event attendance

The NCAA Welcome Center includes video and photo displays that portray the more than 80 NCAA championships that are conducted each year. Informational brochures covering such topics as scholarship opportunities, eligibility requirements, the NCAA Foundation, and the Hall of Champions are also made available to those visiting the Welcome Center. Fans also may register to win tickets to the next year's championships as well as other championship-related items (e.g., official baseball or softball). The database is used to identify the championship fan for a given sport as well as provide a direct mailing list to help promote future NCAA championships.

An example of a welcome center at the 2000 NCAA Wrestling Championships.

Today, one of the primary missions of the NCAA Welcome Center is to help enhance a patron's NCAA championship experience in a more interactive way. The Welcome Center concept is moving from simply building awareness and education to helping entertain and build hands-on relationships with fans. Early efforts to further the relationship include providing more event-specific championship materials (e.g., additional photos, videos, and information on specific championships) as well as providing official equipment suppliers access to the NCAA Welcome Center to display their products.

This broadening of the mission is one of the first steps in developing a new promotional model for NCAA championships that is designed to increase attendance. Future plans include transitioning the NCAA Welcome Centers into interactive fan festivals that celebrate the journey of the student-athlete, entertain and educate patrons, and become an integral part of a championship event.

As revealed in the Practitioner's Perspective, an on-site display can serve to achieve a number of promotional objectives. Take, for instance, the NBA Jam Session and MLB FanFest, each a part of the respective league's All-Star Weekend festivities, featuring sport-specific electronic and high-tech interactive attractions that bear the names of corporate sponsors.

Be a Part of the Action

The NBA Jam Session features a variety of attractions meant to give fans the feeling of being a part of the NBA.[20] Jam Session attendees can don an NBA team replica jersey and test their skills in a variety of basketball activities ranging from three-point shooting contests to speed dribbling. Fans also have the opportunity to assess their ability as play-by-play announcers and to interact with current as well as former players.

Lastly, auxiliary activities such as these elaborate atmospheric displays also serve to extend the presence of the sporting event within the host community, thereby enhancing awareness and interest among a key consumer group, those unable to attend a Final Four or All-Star Game. With attendance figures surpassing 100,000, these enticing atmospheric attractions can be viewed as a type of point-of-purchase display affording a large volume of consumers a "product sampling" of the NBA, MLB, and NCAA entertainment experiences.

Racetrack Attractions

Greg Penske, an International Speedway board member, predicts that in order for racetracks to garner and then sustain the fan's interest, key attractions such as popular cartoon characters, rides, movie sound stages, and adventure rides, as well as interactive displays featuring virtual reality racing centers where guests can race against one another or against one of the drivers, will have to be commonplace in the not-too-distant future.[21]

Interior Design Features

The sport promotion specialist for the time being must assume the role of interior decorator, analyzing such features of the production environment as color schemes, fixtures and lighting, electronic elements, and dress codes. At this stage the fundamental task is to establish an ambience reflective of the desired consumer behavior.

Color scheme is among the prime factors affecting buyer behavior. Colors have different emotional qualities: for example, hot colors such as red, orange, and peach affect the autonomic nervous system, increasing blood circulation, heart rate, muscular activity, and perhaps most importantly sociability. Through the ages people have associated colors with their physical environment. Colors can also creatively alter the physical characteristics of a venue. Cool tones (e.g., blues) give the appearance of additional spaciousness, while soft colors can project a pleasant atmosphere that reflects the venue's friendliness and concern for the customer.[22] In addition to using colors to convey a particular mood, the interior decor will very likely be influenced by the team's color scheme.

Augusta National Golf Club and its management of the atmosphere of the Masters—the most famous golf tournament in the world—is an excellent example of the management of atmospherics and ambiance. From the complimentary pairing sheets and spectator booklets to the subdued green hues of scoreboards and concession stands, everything is focused on creating an ambience that golfers and spectators will enjoy. So that everything blends together, even the thrash containers and the sandwich wrappings are colored green.

Fixtures and lighting can communicate elegance, traditionalism, conservatism, and a host of other characteristics. Racquet and golf clubs typically use a dark wood trim along with dark wood furnishings to evoke a sense of elegance and exclusivity.[23] Similar trim fixtures were used in the FedEx Cabana, positioned on the fairway of the 18th hole at the FedEx St. Jude Golf Classic, to communicate a sense of dignity and gracefulness to invited guests.

On the other hand, interior lighting has several obvious functional as well as promotional features. Within indoor venues, consumers must have ample illumination in order to see elements of importance including seat location and distributed literature (e.g., souvenir program). Lighting should be coordinated with color schemes and venue design to create the intended atmosphere. Lights that are too intense can create consumer discomfort and irritation. Proper lighting intensity, direction, and color should be used to contribute to a venue's desired image.

Sport facilities worldwide have added electronic features in order to enhance the atmospheric presentation and elevate consumer entertainment. One of the most prominent fixtures within most sport venues, if not the most prominent, is the scoreboard, particularly in indoor arenas where the scoreboard serves more as an attractive chandelier. However, modern state-of-the-art scoreboards, perhaps more appropriately labeled "entertainment boards," provide more than team scores and game time, contributing significantly to the event atmosphere. For instance, the $5 million scoreboard at American Airlines Arena in Miami, complete with high-resolution video screens, is programmed to shoot fireworks and respond to crowd noise with strobe light displays and color changes, each providing behavioral stimuli.[24] Alternatively, such electronic entertainment centers administer competitive games (e.g., dot races), display live and replay footage, and run sponsor commercial spots. Critical to the effectiveness of this key atmospheric fixture is its maximal functionality, necessitating extensive training for all operating personnel.

© Larry Inman

It's important for spectators to be able to identify staff members. Hats, shirts, or other uniform pieces make staff members stand out.

While large-screen video display panels have become standard as a way to entertain and inform the audience en masse, modern technology affords facility managers an opportunity to deliver similar entertainment functions on a more personalized basis. ChoiceSeats (produced by Williams Cos Inc.), which are essentially computer panels mounted on seat armrests, allow spectators to view recorded game highlights, scan statistical updates, and order food and beverages.[25] While this type of technology is intended to intensify the spectator sport experience through added entertainment features and increased informational access, at a unit price of $1500 it may be some time before such devices become standard fixtures in sporting venues.[26]

Depending on the nature of the core business, the sport property should have a uniform dress code and either request staff members to dress accordingly or provide them with the clothing. Uniform dress, common in sport retail (e.g., Athlete's Foot and

Foot Locker), supports the atmospheric theme while also serving to identify the employees. Encouraging staff to adjust dress according to rotational themes (e.g., holidays and celebrations) instills a valuable sense of involvement, facilitating internal enthusiasm for the themed occasion. When the Gaelic Athletic Association redeveloped its headquarters, Croke Park in Dublin, it took a highly creative and effective step to secure staff that would reflect the appropriate ambience and image. The association contracted with Aer Lingus, the Irish national airline, to have the Aer Lingus ground crew provide ushering and information services in the new facility. The ground crew, well dressed, well manicured, and well trained in catering to the needs of clients, provided excellent service and effectively projected the desired image.

Physical Design Principles

Adherence to several basic physical design principles will also significantly enhance the fundamental atmospheric conditions. These principles include furnishing positive **cues,** reducing or eliminating negative cues, and merchandising the themed experience.[27]

It is important that a venue's atmospherics provide positive cues. Upon entering a sport facility the typical consumer, whether novice or veteran, will automatically begin a search for cues that will establish a level of comfort and sense of belonging. As the adage goes, "First impressions are lasting impressions." So it is critical for sport promotion specialists to use mechanisms that communicate as well as reinforce the anticipated signals.

Encounters with contact personnel such as parking attendants are the first opportunity for event, facility, and team promoters to convey a favorable "first" impression. In preparation for the opening of Comerica Park in Detroit, extra security officers and 150 greeters were dispersed around the stadium to aid patrons and ensure ease of entry and a positive first impression of the facility.

Most sport fans would agree that nothing is worse than a long, boring walk to the stadium. During this "anticipatory stage," patrons should encounter "intermittent stimuli" that build excitement and anxiety much like a roller-coaster ride.[28] Strategic placement of street vendors and entertainers, sponsor displays, and event personnel provides positive cues that the event patron is approaching an entertaining atmosphere.

Symbols such as flags, banners, and pennants can evoke emotional response and arousal among patrons. Within a team setting, these items are used to involve the supporting fan through their representation of the philosophy, value, and accomplishments of the organization.[29] These items can also function to "intimidate" opponents and their supporters. Placing the items in locations where spectators notice them upon entry will stimulate the appropriate response. For instance, scattered throughout the outer concourse of Busch Stadium in St. Louis, home to MLB's Cardinals, are banners depicting significant accomplishments, such as play-off and World Series victories and achievement of team and league records, of teams that once performed within (figure 11.2). Similarly, the museum at Barcelona Football Club's stadium, "Nou Camp," runs

Figure 11.2 Banners at Busch Stadium in St. Louis remind spectators of great moments in Cardinal history.

a continuous video of Ronald Koeman's winning goal in the European Cup champi-onship and also displays the cup itself, reminding fans of the glorious moment.[30]

Symbolism can also be conveyed through event, game, or even team-related **rituals** and traditions. Member institutions of the Southeastern Conference have established a number of traditions aimed at enhancing game atmosphere. For instance, approxi-mately an hour prior to kickoff at a University of Tennessee home football game, tens of thousands of fans line the street leading to Neyland Stadium to await the parade of team symbols into the stadium. The oncoming procession of flag-waving cheer-leaders and spirit squad members, as well as the marching band (which blasts an unending tune called "Rocky Top") signifies to the UT supporters and others in attendance, awestruck by the sight of such pageantry, that the battle is about to begin. The emotionally charged audience is thus well prepared to engage in enthusiastic support of the team. However, of greatest interest is the promotional merit of such activities that in and of themselves emerge as an atmospheric effect attractive to patrons. On occasion the team may lose, yet the pregame ritual remains consistent.

Similarly, fans of the University of Mississippi gather in "The Grove" (an area that links the campus and the football stadium) well before kickoff to express support for the football team as it parades through on its way to the field in preparation for the ensuing game. The Grove has emerged as an auxiliary atmospheric attraction complete with barbecue pits and pep rallies and other staged entertainment. These pregame product extensions serve as positive cues that enhance the game atmosphere and overall attendance experience.

Far too frequently, sport promotion specialists fail to play a prominent role in recognizing and initiating potential ritualistic patron behaviors, valuable to ensuring a pleasurable attendance atmosphere. Use of atmospheric resources such as enter-tainment boards, public address systems, and cheerleaders can perpetuate ritualistic behaviors. Think about the obnoxious cheer raised up by Denver Bronco spectators at a signal from the public address system following an opponent's miscue (e.g., missed field goal)—or about how various collegiate basketball crowds remain standing following player introductions until the home team scores its first bucket. Sport in particular is rife with built-in ritualistic opportunities (air ball, strikeout, touchdown, goal, the seventh-inning stretch), providing ample foundation for atmo-spheric enjoyment and enhancement.

Just as important as furnishing positive cues is eliminating negative cues. A sport promotion specialist needs to be diligent about removing such cues from the con-sumption environment. Undeniably the most profound negative cue—one that speaks volumes about the organization and significantly affects its image—is trash. All staff members must assume responsibility for ensuring that the environment is kept clean. In order to ensure the "clean" image expected by event attendees, the PGA TOUR's FedEx St. Jude Golf Classic annually employs a local high school athletic team to maintain litter-free grounds during tournament week.

The sport promotion specialist in collaboration with venue security and operations personnel is charged with ensuring patron safety as well as comfort. As an example, in an effort to create a family-friendly atmosphere, the Buffalo Bills promised an all-out blitz against disruptive fans whose drinking, smoking, fighting, swearing, urinating, stripping, and even fornicating had turned some fans and their families against attending games. The newly renovated stadium will use surveillance cam-eras, guest services booths for fans filing complaints, and on-site facilities for booking and locking up those arrested.[31] It is unfortunate that such measures must be taken at sporting events to ensure attendees' safety and well-being. However, the adoption of a proactive plan such as this will discourage potentially unruly patrons from misbehaving as well as provide attendees a feeling of security, and subsequently help achieve the desired atmosphere. Sport promotion specialists might consider proactively having stadium or arena staff attend the alcohol management programs offered by Miller Brewing Company or Anheuser Busch. Both programs help personnel manage the distribution of alcohol and the unruly behavior that may accompany overzealous imbibing.

Another frequently encountered negative cue at sporting events is *long lines*— lines to enter the venue, lines for concessions, lines for the restroom, and so on. Often this is a result of poor planning. Too frequently you hear the comment, "We never expected a crowd this size." Sport promotion specialists must diligently monitor ticket sales, as well as crowd behavior and composition, in order to minimize if not eliminate this common negative. On a broader scale, they must carefully monitor market conditions, as the rapid growth of the female market warrants additional amenities (restrooms). Comerica Park, the Detroit Tigers' new home, features more than 250 restroom stalls for women, far exceeding the average for facilities of similar size.[32]

Although facility size can represent power, strength, and security, it can also present a negative atmospheric cue to the sport consumer. Too often the philosophy of "bigger is better" has backfired and led to negative perceptions regarding the host facility and event or team tenant. An event staged in a facility that is too large often appears to have no atmosphere unless measures are taken to reduce the impact of unfilled seats and echoing acoustics—an issue confronting a number of college teams and Major League Soccer, WNBA, and NBA franchises. As a means of addressing this situation, the University of Memphis Lady Tiger basketball team opts to play its home games in the Roane Fieldhouse, a quaint 3000-seat on-campus arena, as opposed to the 21,000-seat Pyramid, home to the men's basketball team. The change in venue enables the team to create an exhilarating "packed-house" atmosphere and distinct home court advantage.

Additionally, some sport organizations ask patrons not planning to use their seats at a given game to provide advance notification, thus giving those in attendance an opportunity for on-the-spot seat upgrades (e.g., stadium upper bowl to lower bowl). Such programs stand not only to enhance the game atmosphere through crowd consolidation and socialization, but also to improve the attendance experience and service perception of the upgraded patron. Such patrons, following this valuable product sampling opportunity, may consider purchasing an upgraded ticket package next season.

New Name, New Image for Comiskey?

Local Chicago companies, including Motorola and Arthur Andersen, are being wooed by the White Sox, who are looking for a corporate partner to rename Comiskey Park and make it more fan friendly. The White Sox want a marketing partner to bring "some sizzle to the antiseptic" taxpayer-financed stadium that opened in 1991 and quickly fell from fan favor. The team is particularly interested in technology companies. The partner would help pay for an array of physical changes, from a new roof over the vertigo-inducing upper deck to a home run porch in left or right field.[33]

Posting or distributing facility layout maps, of the kind commonly found in shopping malls, can alleviate uncertainty particularly among inexperienced patrons. In fact, Brindley and Thorogood suggest the use of maps, signs, informational leaflets, color-coding for access areas, help desks, and uniformed staff for novice attendees at horse racing events[34], a suggestion applicable to all sport venues. These maps, which provide an ideal sponsorship platform, should identify all seating sections, restrooms, entries and exits, sponsor displays, any other points of interest, and concession and merchandise outlets.

To a certain degree, downtime is a challenge in all sports. Team sports such as soccer, basketball, and football have the ideal entertainment break in the form of half-time. In fact, Spoelstra notes that professional basketball averages about 82 minutes of downtime per game![35] But this pales in comparison to what happens in sporting activities such as track, swimming, and gymnastics, with organizers having to take special care to keep the crowd entertained and informed during the natural breaks often required for equipment adjustments or resting periods. As a means of entertaining fans attending the NCAA Women's Gymnastics Championship during rotational downtime, a professional gymnastics entertainer performs a variety of antics on the various pieces of apparatus. The performance entertains the audience during what can be a rather tedious period, thereby eliminating the negativity often associated with the activity's natural downtime.

Frequent breaks also offer spectators opportunities to engage in casual interaction with one another, which sport promotion specialists can instigate. To this end the public address announcer can introduce trivia games pitting rows and sections against one another, for example, or simply provide topics of conversation (e.g., news topics, business topics involving team or event corporate sponsors) during downtime.

Many facility, event, and team managers have found an atmospheric gold mine in a typical eyesore and potential atmospheric inhibitor, unused physical space, and thus eliminated a perception of the facility as cavernous while also providing a promotional benefit to the tenant, spectator, and quite frequently a sponsor. For instance, Norwest Bank, a subsidiary of Wells Fargo Bank, agreed to assume title sponsorship of the Fun Zone at Sioux Falls Stadium in Sioux Falls, South Dakota. Occupying previously unused facility space, the Norwest Fun Zone will provide kids a six-hole miniature golf course, inflatable jump facility, video games, and specialty playground equipment. Clowns, face painters, and caricaturists will be present on game days.[36] Similarly, the previously mentioned party-like Phoenix Coyotes' Dog-house is actually a converted obstructed-view seating area.[37]

Interactive Atmospherics-Linked Merchandising

A truly integrated atmospheric effect will spawn or include merchandising opportunities for the patron. This type of patron participatory action enriches the patrons' involvement in the effect, thereby increasing their affiliation or bond with the sport organization. Fan-adorning merchandise bearing the event or team symbol automatically establishes a bond or foundation of association. Interactive atmospherics-linked merchandising allows the sport organization to elevate the level of involvement among participating patrons. A common ritual in basketball arenas worldwide has fans attempting to distract an opposing free throw shooter by waving such objects as home team-colored pom-poms or towels provided by a sponsor. This type of interactive atmospheric merchandising gives the sport promotion specialist an opportunity to link event, sponsor, and patron; other benefits are that it gives the patron a means of direct involvement with the action on the court and also a means of reliving the experience again and again, thus serving as a post-experience reflection tactic as called for by O'Sullivan and Spangler.[38]

Collegiate Atmospheric Traditions

College football fans in Mississippi were stripped of their atmospherics-linked merchandise rituals when the Southeastern Conference ruled that Mississippi State fans could no longer bring cowbells to league games because the associated behavior was viewed as too obnoxious for opposing teams and their fans. Similarly, Ole Miss Rebel fans were banned from entering their home stadium with Confederate flags because the flag sticks were deemed a threat to patron safety, not to mention that the flag was offensive to a large proportion of visiting fans. But Northwestern University in Evanston, Illinois, was able to turn tailgating, an atmospheric element found at most college football games, into an ideal sponsorship platform. The American Tailgater Company became a sponsor of the athletic department, with a prime interest in selling tailgating merchandise to Northwestern football fans, while the university saw an opportunity to service patrons as well as a sponsor. American Tailgater was given exclusive access to the parking lot for product displays during Northwestern football home games.[39]

That the use of interactive atmospheric merchandising should enhance sales of logoed products would seem obvious. Thus if you are a sport promotion specialist, you should be on the lookout for opportunities to create links between logoed merchandise, atmospheric effects, consumer behavior, and sponsors where appropriate.

Step 4: Selecting Specific Sensory Elements That Convey the Desired Effects

According to Gilmore, effective atmospheric effects ensure utilization of all five **sensory elements.** Thus, proper atmospheric management necessitates adoption of activities that provide patrons with pleasurable sights, sounds, tastes, smells, and touches. In the design of atmospheric effects, visual elements should focus on color, brightness, size, and shapes, while aural elements must address volume and pitch. Olfactory elements, often used within the retail industry to alter consumers' moods and buying behavior, include scent as well as freshness, whereas tactile elements may focus on temperature.[40]

However, as the following examples show, few atmospheric elements operate in isolation. For instance, the roar of the crowd and the band's playing of the team fight song combine with the smell of fresh popcorn and hot dogs to define a sport event atmosphere.

The Sound of Music

Sound effects are among the most popular means of enhancing atmosphere in venues. In sport, this is typically done through the use of music, cheers, and occasionally piped-in crowd noise.

According to Wascovich, a good selection of music (figure 11.3) acts as a way of exciting spectators, enhancing downtime, and motivating a home team.[41] In fact, music has become such an integral part of any sporting event that arenas must install sound systems with the right blend of high-tech components such as "reverberation time," "ambient noise levels," and "sound levels."[42]

While music is typically viewed as an entertainment supplement, it also adds a cognitive component to the experience.[43] Music provides for a personal experience, one that evokes emotion and typically relates to celebration and joy. School or team

Song	Artist	Typically when played
We Will Rock You	Queen	Get crowd participation
Twist and Shout	Beatles	Get crowd participation
Minnie the Moocher	Cab Calloway	General crowd participation song
Shout	Otis Day & the Nights	Athlete/team does something exciting
I Feel Good	James Brown	Athlete/team does something exciting
I'm So Excited	Pointer Sisters	Athlete/team does something exciting
Start Me Up	Rolling Stones	Beginning of game
Everybody Have Fun Tonight	Wang Chung	Beginning of game
Let's Go	Wang Chung	Beginning of game
Nothin's Gonna Stop Us Now	Jefferson Starship	Coming Back
Wild Thing	Joan Jett	Coming Back
Don't Worry, Be Happy	Bobby McFerrin	If team loses
Dancing on the Ceiling	Lionel Ritchie	If team wins
Celebration	Pointer Sisters	If team wins
Victory	The Jacksons	If team wins
Na, Na, Hey, Hey, Good-bye	The Nylons	Player gets ejected or penalized; end of game when you know you've won
Happy Trails	Gene Autry	Player gets ejected or penalized
Havin' a Party	Southside Johnny	Winning but haven't won yet
Phantom of the Opera	Soundtrack	Introductions

Figure 11.3   Music, such as the songs listed here, is one way to give spectators a chance to be a part of the sporting event.
Reprinted, by permission, from T. L. Wascovich, 1993, *The sports marketing guide* (Cleveland, OH: Points Ahead, Inc.), 190.

fight songs, "Take Me Out to the Ball Game," and performances of the national anthem all mean something special to each listener. Music can be used to form cultural bonds among patrons,[44] thus accentuating the need for all sport organizations—teams and others—to have an organizational theme song. Undoubtedly, many graduates of Notre Dame, the University of Southern California, and the University of Michigan recall memorable moments at football games when they hear the school fight song. Team songs are common among school-supported teams and international sport clubs, although few American professional sport teams have commissioned the drafting of a team song that could be used not only for atmospheric effects but as a way of generating additional publicity.

The Dogs Were Out in 2000

Throughout 2000, sport arenas across America introduced players, teams, and mascots to the pop tune "Who Let the Dogs Out?" Performance of this infectious song depends on audience participation, in much the same way predecessors such as the Village People's hit "YMCA" and Sister Sledge's "We Are Family" did. According to the song's producer, working to ensure that the song was played on public address systems in stadiums around the country was the primary tactic used to promote the song.[45]

Music is also used as a form of communication, and many events associated with a sporting contest lend themselves to musical illustration as well as celebration or reaction among patrons. For instance, anyone attending an MLB or NHL game is familiar with the organ player's signaling the crowd to encourage the team by yelling "Charge!" Fans attending NBA arenas continent-wide are cued to stand and support the home team following a huge comeback when they hear Gary Glitter's "Rock 'n Roll Part II" (which, by the way, is significantly more popular now than it was when first released in the early 1970s!).

Outside of North America, much of the music at sporting events is in the form of singing by the fans themselves. In many arenas, fans sing in a form of community ritual, creating a spine-tingling atmosphere. The 20,000 fans on the Kop at Liverpool FC's grounds at Anfield, singing "You'll Never Walk Alone," is a wonderful example. Similarly, if you go to Welsh rugby internationals at the Millennium Stadium in Cardiff, you'll hear beautiful singing, in the great tradition of Welsh community and choral singing, when the fans sing "Hen Wlad fy Nhadau," or "Cwm Rhondda," in perfect harmony. The traveling hordes of Irish soccer and rugby fans who launch into the "The Fields of Athenry" or "Molly Malone" and the Australian fans who sing "Waltzing Matilda" create an atmosphere in arenas and stadiums that contributes significantly to the event. While the core product is important, the community singing is vital to its presentation.

Such singing is not confined to supporters of the home team. Fans traveling to away games often become the object of derisive singing, particularly when the home team is on top. This can lead in certain circumstances to antisocial activities among the fans, particularly those involved in long-standing local rivalries. Many of the songs used have been adapted from their original form and infused with local nuances.

In the United States, the national anthem informs the audience that the game is about to begin. In fact, according to Joe Price, a professor of religious studies at Whittier College, the game begins with the singing of the national anthem as this music represents the invocation or the call to worship. It lends a kind of civic framework and governmental sanction and respect to the game.[46] Furthermore, a selected theme song may alert patrons that the team is about to be introduced, whereas the playing of "Three Blind Mice" communicates the opinion that the referees have made a poor call. Fans, good and bad singers alike, often join in singing this song, which again acts as a catalyst for personal involvement and bonding among those sharing a viewpoint.

As a sport promotion specialist you must think carefully about how the music is to be performed. For performance accuracy, some might lean toward a selection of prerecorded tapes, as is the case in most national anthem performances at the Super Bowl and other major sporting events. However, the benefits derived from live musical performances can range from increased entertainment value to increased promotional value.

Research conducted by the NBA's Cleveland Cavs showed that the use of quality national anthem performers was of great importance to ticket plan holders and actually added perceived value to the attendance experience. This suggests that great effort should be extended to minimize error. The Chicago Cubs decided to discontinue using famous personalities more interested in plugging a product, movie, or TV show and instead to have local "celebrities" sing "Take Me Out to the Ball Game" during the seventh-inning stretch at Wrigley Field. But Chicago Cubs Manager of Entertainment and Special Projects Mary Therese Kraft said that guidelines would be established, as giving a live mike to anyone could cause problems, especially since Cubs games are televised all over the world. It is advisable to ask all performers under consideration to supply a tape before booking; a tape can serve as a screening device as well as backup should the performer or microphone fail.[47]

A live performance of the national anthem or any other designated music may also render a publicity opportunity. Such was the case when Faith Hill performed the national anthem at Super Bowl XXXIV[48] and Roseanne Barr sang the national anthem at a San Diego Padres game in the mid-1990s.

Moreover, a live band performance not only enhances auditory sensory activity but also taps visual and emotional elements. For instance, the uniform of a team band member is a symbolic representation of the team, as is the ritualistic nature of the band's performance (e.g., marching in and leading the team to battle; team *fight* song). The drum major's extravagant uniform, the cheerleaders, and the color guard further enhance the event's pageantry and visual stimulation. Again, these visual and auditory props provide valuable cues to the audience during the course of a sporting event: it's time to help the team, it's time to celebrate, and so on.

The provision of such cues, however, is rare outside of North America. Some sport organizations may even look unfavorably at the use of auditory or visual stimuli by the organization while the game is taking place. Fans tend to take their cues from the action on the field, and as they are well versed in the intricacies of the game, they respond unprompted to the game events.

Although not commonly used in sport venues, piped-in crowd noise serves frequently as background for a game broadcast, highlights, and pre- and postgame as a way of enhancing the realism of the presentation of the content. Unfortunately, VilCom, radio broadcast-rights holder for University of North Carolina men's basketball, was heavily criticized by listeners as well as media ethics experts for piping in crowd noise during Tar Heel games.[49] According to VilCom President Jim Heaver, the use of a production element such as sound effects to enhance transmission of a game broadcast is nothing new. Undoubtedly the primary intent was to provide the listener with an enhanced atmosphere, one that more closely resembled the environment of the arena.

Get a Whiff of This!

Smell is perhaps the most challenging sense impression to replicate, but one of the easiest to stimulate. In fact, DigiScents offers a computerized device that releases a variety of scents on demand. While Friedman suggests that arena concourse signage can be configured with this scent-emitting device to trigger consumer reaction,[50] other sport-related applications appear relevant as well.

For instance, arena concessionaires may employ such a device to trigger event patron taste buds, whereas indoor activity areas may use it to replicate outdoor conditions. Think about an indoor climbing wall or driving range that has the fresh smell of a pine forest, or a NASCAR-licensed video game that occasionally emits a smell resembling that of fumes from a competitor. In all cases, consumer behavior would be affected by the replication of relevant scents.

A Touching Situation

The interactive games and virtual reality experiences mentioned earlier have been designed and included in atmospheric special displays with the intent of giving consumers an opportunity to engage in the *feel* of the actual activity. Displays of authentic gear used by former as well as current athletes, commonly found at MLB's FanFest or the NBA's Jam Session, provide consumers with a real feel for the game. Additionally, in an effort to enhance the atmosphere of televised sport by allowing the viewer to feel like a part of the action, the XFL installed helmet-cams, huddle-cams, and a variety of other devices designed for close-to-the-action exposure.

Similarly, sporting good retail outlets have installed courts, tracks, and training equipment to give customers a chance to test the feel of various products. This is true in golf stores also, where consumers can often test a club and even have their swing scrutinized by an in-house professional to ensure that they are making a suitable purchase. Such product-sampling atmospherics not only assure the consumer of a proper fit and feel but also significantly enhance the buying experience.

The Total Sensory Package

NASCAR intends to offer Web patrons the most realistic user atmosphere possible. The auto racing circuit touts cutting-edge features designed to make Web site visitors feel as though they are at the race. While Quokka Sports Vice President of Entertainment Richard O'Connell says that features such as smell may never be an exact replication, he believes that the NASCAR site provides users considerable control over what they see and hear.

In-Arena Advertising Enhances Atmospherics

Shannon and Turley contend that in-arena advertising warrants consideration as an atmospheric component, as such communication influences the internal effects of a facility and is also a way to give audience members cues regarding purchase intentions. In fact, their research indicates that in-arena advertising is most effective when it provides cues about products that are available on-site or are integrated into the event (concessions, merchandise, specialty stands).[51] The sport promotion specialist can send influential behavioral cues alerting auditory as well as visual sensory elements through public address announcements, signage, souvenir program advertisements, and product display boards.[52] Strategic placement of food and beverage stations will transmit olfactory cues equivalent to the most powerful advertising messages.

Integrating a Supporting Cast

According to Gilmore, experiences are enhanced when services are used as the stage, goods are used as the props, and emotion is used as the catalyst to engage consumers in a personal manner that creates a memorable experience.[53] Therefore, the emotion of a particular moment, which may be a scoring play, a defined time interval (seventh-inning stretch), or a victory celebration, coupled with the emotional musical reinforcement, brings the experience to a crescendo—the ultimate objective of atmospheric management. Furthermore, Melnick contends that atmospherics are designed to allow the spectators to engage in a variety of events without fully participating in the actual action.[54] This would account for active participation in cheering the home team or jeering the referee, the opposing team, or the opponent's supporters. These events draw the spectator into the experience of the event through active participation in entertainment activities,[55] and indeed community events.

Thus, a supporting cast is critical to engaging consumers personally as called for by Gilmore and Melnick. This supporting cast within a team sport environment may include mascot, cheerleaders, band, spirit squad or dance team, and entertainers, as well as the ushers, vendors, public address announcer, and of course the athletes. Each of these parties assumes a defined role in the production process, with the sport promotion specialist as the director or conductor.

Unfortunately, these key performers are quite frequently far too detached from the immediate audience and thus fail to establish rapport, in turn failing to actively involve the spectator. For instance, why are members of the critically important spirit team (cheerleaders, mascot, etc.) at a football game nowhere but on the field? Why are vendors not encouraged or trained to add a little personality to their service? Why do public address announcers typically limit their messages to reporting a score or entering a player's uniform number? Are these "performers" forbidden to interact with spectators? Not only would such behavior enhance the personal contact with consumers, but it would also elevate their level of involvement and thus add to the game atmosphere.

Vendors are a key part of the ball-park atmosphere. They should be encouraged to interact with the crowd to help create a more memorable event.

As discussed in chapter 1, Martin emphasizes that management must take an active role in facilitating such interactions while instilling in sport organization *contact* personnel the following service-oriented traits and behaviors:[56]

• *Be courteous.* Personal behaviors most desired among sport consumers include simple cordial acts such as a greeting or a thank-you.

• *Be proactive.* Initiating personal interaction with audience members should be considered a fundamental responsibility of all staff members.

• *Establish rapport.* Service providers should become familiar with the customer's favorite players and other personal information relevant to ensuring social bonding. According to Martin, once rapport is established, customer encounters tend to be positive and criticisms constructive.[57]

• *Plan extra-transactional encounters.* All promotional unit employees should be trained and encouraged to initiate nontransactional encounters, such as a friendly conversation between an account representative and a ticket plan holder or between a media promotions specialist and a sports editor. Those seeking to develop social and business relationships frequently discuss sport to establish shared values or to define patterns of interaction.[58] Therefore, sport organization contact personnel are well equipped with ready-made content for extra-transactional discussions using team, event, facility, or player developments as key conversation catalysts.

Undoubtedly, training is the key to effective supporting cast performance. It is management's obligation to provide supporting cast members with the preparation they need in order to serve and interact with customers effectively. Martin suggests the following four-step training process:[59]

- Step 1. Develop and distribute a manual that outlines the value of supporting cast members and their impact on the atmospheric conditions.
- Step 2. Encourage supporting cast members to conduct mystery-patron audits of competitors or other businesses.
- Step 3. Meet periodically with supporting cast members collectively, as well as individually when necessary, to discuss and resolve issues as they arise.
- Step 4. Use apprenticeships to assist new supporting cast members in adapting to the interactive culture of the organization. Working alongside seasoned service provision veterans will help new hires more fully appreciate the organization's commitment to quality service and also better grasp the nature of their responsibilities.

Specific Supporting Cast Members

A great many individuals are involved in the atmospheric production during a sporting event, as well as within a sport retail outlet. Team mascots, spirit squad members, and dance team members, as well as merchandise and concession vendors, ushers, the athletes, and audience members (who play perhaps the most critical role in creating an enjoyable atmosphere) should be considered members of the production's supporting cast. For without good "performances" from each of these groups, the atmosphere is likely to become stale.

Mascots

"Mascoting," a North American phenomenon, has only recently been professionalized—but this has happened for good reason. A skillful mascot is invaluable to a sport organization. The mascot is a reflection of the organization and must act accordingly; if the organization wishes to reflect a bold, aggressive image, then the mascot is encouraged to act similarly. But the mascot's actions should also be in keeping with its nature—if the mascot is a dog, it should lick hands. The sport also dictates the mascot's personality, with hockey and football mascots insinuating more aggressive behavior than those in other sports.[60] All in all, mascots bear significant responsibility in coordinating and controlling the atmosphere. Before they perform, mascots should work diligently with the sport promotion specialist and other members of the supporting cast in an effort to carefully choreograph activities aimed at provoking audience involvement throughout the event.

Vendors

Food and beverage and merchandise vendors also play an important role as atmospheric production supporting cast members. Charismatic vendors displaying unique skills or equipment serve as atmospheric enhancement tools. For instance, some professional sport facilities have equipped vendors with the Hot Dog Launcher, which can deliver a hot dog, with mustard and ketchup, to a fan 300 feet away, providing unique entertainment for the recipient as well as onlookers.[61]

Announcers

Within a sporting event, the public address announcer should be viewed more as a master of ceremonies or ringleader than a play-by-play reporter. Dave Penzer from

Mascots are an invaluable part of the sporting experience. Whether entertaining the crowd inside or outside the arena, they need to uphold the organization's image.

World Championship Wrestling is considered the dean of professional wrestling ring announcers because of his interaction with fans and enthusiastic personality.[62] The sport event public address announcer is the conductor of the performance of all other supporting cast members, including the athletes, while also directing the audience's attention to key incidents that occur and triggering reactive behaviors. Even track and field producers have begun to hire entertaining announcers equipped with a handheld microphone and a sense of humor to interview athletes immediately after races and to roam the stadium talking to fans.

Providing the public address announcer with a script of cues along with an atmospheric operations itinerary is a basic responsibility of the sport promotion specialist. However, the style in which the script is delivered—which dramatically affects atmospheric effectiveness—rests entirely in the hands, or more appropriately in the voice and personality, of the announcer. Obviously, then, the organization works diligently to hire an announcer who not only possesses a great voice but also has the ability to establish a sound rapport with the audience.

Scheduled Performers

Certainly, invited performers (entertainers, former players, etc.) assume a vital role as short-term supporting cast members. When screening and selecting entertainment acts and special guest performers, it is advisable for the sport promotion specialist to seek individuals who have an established reputation for interacting with the audience. A sport-specific entertainment act such as the Famous Chicken delights the audience with humorous antics ranging from mimicking opposing players and umpires to dancing with his band of chicks. Because of the success of sport entertainment acts such as the Famous Chicken, who started out as the San Diego Chicken, mascot for MLB's Padres, a vaudeville-type cottage industry of performers has evolved.[63]

Such performances also lend themselves to additional promotional efforts such as publicity and personal contact. For example, in addition to sustaining the extravagant event atmosphere at Super Bowl XXXIV, Tina Turner's pregame performance was parlayed into a series of personal contact opportunities with players and special guests, as well as a publicity-generating tool.[64]

Star Searching

The Cubs chose to use local celebrities, including police officers and teachers, to sing "Take Me Out to the Ball Game" during the atmospherics-driven seventh-inning stretch at Wrigley Field for the 2000 season. It's the Cubs' way of answering critics who complained that what had started as a touching tribute to Harry Caray soon turned into a forum for celebrities to push a product, movie, or TV show.

Athletes

The athletes, of course, are key members of the supporting cast. While their skillful performance serves as a main attraction, the athletes should also be integrated into atmospherics-oriented activities. For example, athlete introductions involving music and lighting are a part of all NBA games. Prior to the championship matches at the NCAA Wrestling Championships, all national place winners are paraded onto the mat, one weight classification at a time, in a display of Olympic-style pageantry. In an effort to enhance contact with spectators, Arena Football League 2 (afl2) players are required to stay on the field for 30 minutes following each game. Players are expected to mingle with the crowd and sign autographs.

Past Athletes

The stars of previous years can also add atmosphere to major events. Presenting winning teams or individual athletes of years past is a way of emphasizing the history of an event. It is important to be careful not to ruin an athlete's history or memory in the eyes of the fans by having her perform on such occasions. Video board displays of best performances would suffice. It would seem that players of a quarter-century ago are the most appropriate for such occasions. They may have not aged as much as older stars, and some fans' memories of their performances are still fresh. Using players who are much older entails a risk of reminding fans of their own mortality.

Audience Members

And of course the fans themselves should be recognized and included as key supporting cast members. Supplying event patrons with roles to play elevates the level of direct engagement in

Team history displays are important parts of the sporting event as they remind patrons of why they support the team.

the activity, typically making the experience more memorable. Sport promotion specialists should learn how to spot dedicated fans longing for "leadership" who can be mobilized into action when necessary (e.g., for leading cheers or the wave). Establishing personal relationships with these patrons and rewarding "leadership" qualities are sure to encourage repeat behavior.

It is not unusual for dignitaries to be formally introduced to the players on the field at major world events. Typically they are introduced to the athletes by the team captain before the playing of the national anthem. While these guests would never be asked to lead the fans in support activities, their presence lends a certain sense of gravitas, however fleeting, to sport events. President Nelson Mandela's presence in 1995 at the World Rugby Cup final in Ellis Park, Johannesburg, was considered a momentous occasion. Rugby in South Africa was a sport of the ruling whites and by extension the sport of apartheid. President Mandela wore a Springbok shirt when presenting the World Cup trophy to Francois Pienaar, South Africa's captain. The wearing of the shirt was viewed, by some enthusiastic observers, as a graphic symbol of the "One nation, one team" theme of the tournament.

The wave is a great crowd interaction tool.

In order to ensure responsive behavior on the part of the crowd to overtures from the supporting cast, it is at times advisable for sport promotion specialists to "plant" additional atmospheric support cast members within the audience. These "hired hands," strategically placed, are expected to participate in a highly visible way in cheers and other fan participatory activities as a means of exerting *peer pressure* on fellow spectators to respond similarly. Essentially, these key cast members are attempting to instill long-term behavioral patterns and thus establish promotional rituals or traditions where none currently exist.

According to Melnick, spectators do not attend sporting events solely for entertainment purposes but also to encounter a satisfying social atmosphere. It would seem that sport venues are among the most legitimate types of location for casual social interaction, as patrons understand, and also often expect, that fellow spectators (who typically share a common interest such as support of team, love of sport) will welcome personal interaction. This common bond provides opportunity to use sports talk as a form of *icebreaker*. Therefore, it becomes management's job to proactively stimulate conversation among spectators using the ready-made content and connections. Melnick's suggestions include architectural conduciveness, internal "connection" promotions, and external "connection" promotions.[65]

Architectural conduciveness Future sport facility seating should be constructed with the idea of stimulating interaction among spectators. Swivel chairs, rows configured in a sawtooth pattern, and grouped seating arrangements are just a few of

Howdy Neighbor!

Joe Spears, a senior vice president at Hellmuth, Obata, & Kassabaum, the stadium construction company that came up with the notion of luxury suites, predicts that a trend in the future will involve breaking up large stadium upper decks into smaller, more identifiable blocks, or **"neighborhoods,"** each with its own distinct feel.[66] This "regionalization" of stadium seating is intended to reduce the inhibitors and develop a comfort zone aimed at stimulating interaction among event audience members.

the possibilities that facility designers may want to consider as ways of stimulating personal interaction among spectators.

Internal "connection" promotions Management can assume an active role in facilitating interaction among spectators by conducting activities and contests that encourage spectator collaboration. The awarding of prizes to trivia game participants, members of rows and sections with perfect attendance records, and the winning section in a noise-volume competition is just one example of what can be done to inspire sociability among large groups of spectators. In an effort to provoke one-to-one personal contact, several minor league baseball teams have hosted a number of interactive activities such as blind-date night, in which males and females are seated in alternating fashion in a special section.

External "connection" promotions Management can also play host to pre- and postgame parties (e.g., tailgating) that enable patrons to interact and celebrate together. Activities similar to those just mentioned can help encourage personal interaction among attendees.

Facilitation of patron-to-patron interaction is by no means limited to relations between one ticket buyer and another. Sport promotion specialists should help to bring about interaction among as many patrons as possible in order to maximize personal communication and facilitate social networking. For example, the Fort Wayne Fury of the Continental Basketball Association will pair a season ticket holder with a representative from another company that sponsors the Fury if so requested and if acceptable to the second party. The team will arrange for an informal introduction at a Fury game, and the parties will be able to sit together in the arena or meet in a private conference room.[67] Networking facilitation such as this illustrates the value of an atmosphere, such as a sporting event, conducive to social interaction. In fact, according to Kahle and Elton, the sport setting facilitates a comfortable blend of sports talk and business talk, allowing for the development of role and stylistic interaction before the parties get down to business transactions with important consequences.[68]

Step 5: Coordinating the Production

As we have seen throughout the chapter, atmospheric coordination requires careful organization and execution. The responsibilities associated with managing atmospheric conditions typically fall on the shoulders of those in the game operations unit in a sport team or event setting. More and more titles such as entertainment coordinator, special projects manager, and game presentation specialist, are becoming commonplace, with these individuals responsible for atmospheric enhancement programs. These creative individuals should possess skills in event planning and management, interior design, and technology.

The following tasks are critical to effective execution of atmospheric management:

- *Developing a checklist and itinerary of all staged activities.* The checklist allows the atmospheric manager to be certain that all preparatory tasks are completed and resources are available, including staff, supporting cast members, and performers (figure 11.4). The itinerary serves as a production script to ensure a fluid sequence of planned activities (figure 11.5).[69]

Item			Person responsible
____ Stock loge/skybox			_____
-Programs	-Beer/Pop		
-Premium item	-Host/Hostess		
-Food			
____ Prepare pressroom			_____
-Programs	-Beverages		
-Food	-Doorperson		
-Premium item			
____ Obtain autograph programs for sponsor promotion			_____
____ Provide programs to:	Visitors	Owners	_____
	Team	Public relations	
	Referees	Media	
____ Check walkie-talkies (indicate who gets them)			_____
____ Prepare itinerary			
____ Prepare public address announcements			_____
____ Announcer—go over game presentation			
____ Venue crew—go over music/game presentation			_____
____ Check scoreboard			
-Sponsors	-Special promotions	-VIPs	
____ Special VIP club setup			_____
____ Player warm-ups—on and off field on time			_____
____ National anthem—meet and put in place to perform			_____
____ Color guard—meet and put in place to perform			_____
____ First ball—meet and advise of procedure			_____
____ Introduction props (if any)—prepare			_____
____ Player introductions—conduct on time			_____
____ Spotlights—where and when to pan			_____
____ Quarter breaks—prepare contestants			_____
-Sponsor			
-Contestants			
____ Media, VIP list for proper admittance to venue			_____
____ Ball boy/ball girl/mascot coordination—meet and advise			_____

Figure 11.4 Sample game operations checklist.

Reprinted, by permission, from T. L. Wascovich, 1993, *The sports marketing guide* (Cleveland, OH: Points Ahead, Inc.), 185-186.

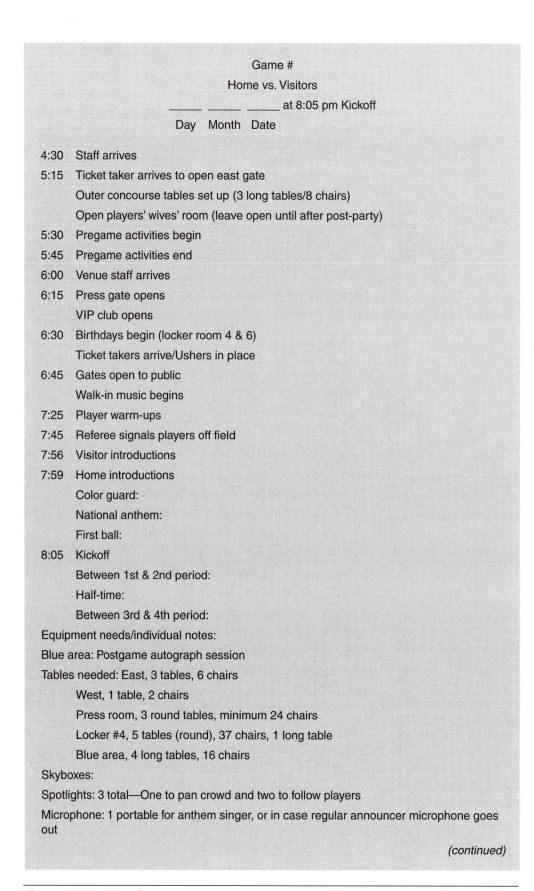

Game #

Home vs. Visitors

_____ _____ _____ at 8:05 pm Kickoff

Day   Month   Date

4:30   Staff arrives

5:15   Ticket taker arrives to open east gate

Outer concourse tables set up (3 long tables/8 chairs)

Open players' wives' room (leave open until after post-party)

5:30   Pregame activities begin

5:45   Pregame activities end

6:00   Venue staff arrives

6:15   Press gate opens

VIP club opens

6:30   Birthdays begin (locker room 4 & 6)

Ticket takers arrive/Ushers in place

6:45   Gates open to public

Walk-in music begins

7:25   Player warm-ups

7:45   Referee signals players off field

7:56   Visitor introductions

7:59   Home introductions

Color guard:

National anthem:

First ball:

8:05   Kickoff

Between 1st & 2nd period:

Half-time:

Between 3rd & 4th period:

Equipment needs/individual notes:

Blue area: Postgame autograph session

Tables needed: East, 3 tables, 6 chairs

West, 1 table, 2 chairs

Press room, 3 round tables, minimum 24 chairs

Locker #4, 5 tables (round), 37 chairs, 1 long table

Blue area, 4 long tables, 16 chairs

Skyboxes:

Spotlights: 3 total—One to pan crowd and two to follow players

Microphone: 1 portable for anthem singer, or in case regular announcer microphone goes out

(continued)

Figure 11.5   Sample game itinerary.

Also a part of the game itinerary are the following:

1. Home and visiting team rosters—depending on the time allowed, you may want to briefly say something about several players. Example:

   "He scored the game-winning goal last night, forward #12 ...!"

2. Special welcomes to: VIPs, groups, etc.

3. Any birthdays or special occasions being celebrated.

4. Public address announcements (see following for examples). These announcements are contingent upon league rules governing game operations.

   These must be organized in order of production during your game presentation.

Figure 11.5 Sample game itinerary.

Reprinted, by permission, from T. L. Wascovich, 1993, *The sports marketing guide* (Cleveland, OH: Points Ahead, Inc.), 191-192.

Read at the beginning of the game

____Coming up between the 1st and 2nd quarter it's the (client name) contest! If you have the autograph of _____ on the (client) ad, you're our first contestant. Please report to the sales tables five (5) minutes before the 1st quarter ends. If you are under 18, you must be accompanied by an adult or legal guardian.

During the contest—1st & 2nd/3rd & 4th

____It's now time for the (client name) contest! Our contestant is _____ from _____. _____ has two chances to score; if he/she does, he/she will receive two free tickets to the final (team) regular-season game and qualify for the (grand prize) courtesy of (client).

____**(If the contestant makes it)** Congratulations, _____. You've just won two tickets to the last (team) game of the regular season and a chance to win the (grand prize) from (client).

____**(If the contestant doesn't make it)** Ooooh! Nice try, _____. Thanks for participating in the (client name) contest.

Figure 11.6 Sample public address announcements for atmospheric contests.

Reprinted, by permission, from T. L. Wascovich, 1993, *The sports marketing guide* (Cleveland, OH: Points Ahead, Inc.), 196.

• *Drafting a script of all scoreboard and public address announcements* (figure 11.6). A script should alert all parties to who is supposed to announce what and when (detail is of the essence), the timing of public address announcements, and the timing of musical selections. This script, which should be carefully proofread for spelling and grammatical errors, should indicate points of emphasis in special type (e.g., bold font) for messages to be presented orally, as elements from this script will typically serve as cues for all performing cast members.

• *Employing an internal direct communication system (e.g., walkie-talkie).* Constant correspondence is of the essence when one is attempting to sequence activities effectively. The sport promotion specialist, assuming the role of command central, prompts all supporting cast members, in the same way a television program director works with actors. Communication failures or omissions typically result in errors (missed cues, improper sequencing), which may eventually become damaging to the sport organization's integrity and to satisfaction levels of the consumers.

Although the preceding list has appeared to boil down effective atmospheric management to three simple steps, you probably realize that effectively producing an enjoyable and stimulating atmosphere is a massive undertaking, demanding sound organizational and communication skills. It is the sport promotion specialist's responsibility to ensure that all elements of the production process have been adequately prepared, as the margin for error, and the tolerance of error among the participating parties and the onlookers, is quite small.

Postgame Wrap-Up

Atmospherics are defined as the designing of buying and consuming environments so as to produce specific cognitive and/or emotional effects on the target market; they are of greatest importance in situations in which purchasers come into direct contact with the organization's physical plant and personnel. Atmospherics assume considerable significance as a promotional tool particularly within the sport industry, where the core product is often simultaneously produced and consumed and thus is an inconsistent and unpredictable product essentially out of the control of the sport promotion specialist. Atmospheric management entails a five-step process of (1) defining the desired market and effects, (2) developing an atmospheric theme, (3) specifying the elements of the physical setting that are to carry the intended cognitions and effects to the target audience, (4) considering and selecting among specific sensory elements that convey the desired effects, and (5) coordinating the production process.

Discussion Items

1. What role should the sport promotion specialist play in screening and selecting members of the atmospheric supporting cast?
2. What atmospheric enhancements do you see emerging in the future?
3. What sensory element do you think is most influential with respect to sporting event atmospheric conditions? Why?
4. How frequently do you find that your consumption behavior is influenced by atmospheric conditions? In sport participation? Spectator sport? Sport retail?

Learning Enrichment Activities

1. Visit a sport business or event and retain a log of all positive and negative cues observed or encountered. Which list contains more items? Which items have the greatest influence on your impression of the business or event?
2. For a hypothetical business or event of your choice, construct a list of at least two effects that are used to address each sensory element.
3. Construct a plan for enhancing the atmosphere of a track meet to be held in order to provide international athletes a warm-up for the Olympic Games. The event is to be scheduled in a metropolitan area of your choice, but within close proximity of the next Summer Olympic Games.

The Role of Technology in Sport Promotion and Sales

"More of today's marketing is moving from the market-place into cyberspace." Phillip Kotler[1]

chapter objectives

1. Appreciate the evolving importance of the World Wide Web in the promotion of sport

2. Understand the importance of Web site content and the constant need to refresh and update site content

3. Appreciate the importance of privacy to many users of the World Wide Web

4. Discover how a number of well-known sport franchises have embraced the Web as a means of connecting with their fans and also adding to their income streams

5. Understand the possibilities of developing focused one-on-one marketing by individualizing site content delivery

key terms

sticky	lifetime value
personalization	first-call resolution
cookies	outer rim markets

Pregame Introductions

You might be forgiven if you wonder whether the Web entertainment revolution ended before it even began. A legion of online companies that once seemed to herald a new era in entertainment have crashed and burned as the first bloom wore off the Internet revolution. It seemed as if the attempt to convert the Web into the next big medium for movies, television, shows, music, or original Internet creations was doomed to failure. Amid such devastation we need to realize that some of the stuff actually works and that it is going to get better.[2] One of the areas of entertainment where it works is sport. Sport is not created for the Web—rather the sport industry, correctly, views the Web as an ancillary means of distribution. How best to maximize that distribution is the question facing the sport promotion specialist. The following Practitioner's Perspective offers some valuable insight.

PRACTITIONER'S PERSPECTIVE

Technology in Action
by Gordon Kaye, Senior Manager, Team Technology, Team Marketing and Business Operations, National Basketball Association

Professional sport organizations continue to face increased competition for the entertainment dollar *and* shifting trends in American leisure spending and interest. Teams are now, more than ever, seeking to capitalize on new and emerging technologies as a means to maximize overall organizational performance (on and off the field), efficiency, and profitability. With regard to tickets sales specifically, rapidly evolving technology and the evolution of the Internet and e-mail provide the "modernizing" sport industry with the tools to improve the *accessibility* and *distribution* of tickets as well as increased *personalization* of the team-customer interaction.

Making Tickets More Accessible: Selling Tickets on the Internet

In the "good old days" of professional sport, tickets were sold only through the box office and ticket windows at the venue. Teams kept track of tickets manually, printing tickets for the *entire season* at the beginning of the season and sorting each game's available tickets by hand. As computers became more prominent and accessible, teams capitalized on new distribution channels. Companies like Ticketmaster, Telecharge, and Ticketron made tickets accessible over the phone or through retail outlets.

Although phone and outlet sales made tickets easier to obtain, there were still some major drawbacks. Team information was difficult to obtain, as customer service representatives sold a wide variety of events and often did not have proper training. Long hold times—and even longer lines at outlets—often had customers waiting for prolonged periods to obtain tickets. In addition, excessive service fees, which are necessary to pay for the cost of the phone centers and outlets, often made that channel of distribution expensive for price-sensitive customers. Until recently, technology did not always permit phone centers and outlets real-time access to inventory, and this often caused conflicts and problems.

In its infancy, the Internet was viewed by many professional sport teams solely as a *promotional tool* to distribute information. With over 200 million homes worldwide connected to the Internet (it is estimated that approximately 55% of these, or 110 million homes, are in the United States),[3] teams are now beginning to identify opportunities to make the Internet, and their Web sites, a *transactional tool.* In its essence, the Internet serves as a relatively simple and cost-effective means of reaching more prospective customers and allowing them to make transactions in a comfortable and hassle-free environment. In its relatively short life, the Internet has grown from a tool to distribute information to a transactional site capable of generating significant additional revenue for teams through ticket sales.

As the Internet continues to reach deep into people's lives worldwide, teams and ticket providers will develop new and innovative technologies to make tickets more easily accessible over the Internet. Ticketmaster, for example, has developed technology to allow Internet ticket buyers the added convenience of printing tickets from a home computer. Customers will also be able to add value (concessions, merchandise) to their tickets from their home computers; making the transaction process easier in this way will increase revenue for teams. Furthermore, the Internet will play an important role in the development of the "paperless ticket."

Using Technology to Personalize Interaction

As much as technology permits teams to *broaden* the accessibility of information, it also provides a vehicle for organizations to better facilitate a more personal—and one-to-one—interaction with their fans. New technologies allow sport organizations to personalize interaction by increasing the amount of information collected and delivering that information in a more efficient and cost-effective manner. Organizations can then use that data to personalize the interaction between the fan and the team.

As one example of how technology allows teams to personalize their interaction, e-mail systems now allow teams to send specific, targeted e-mails to large lists of users in one simple keystroke. Programs like MailKing and POPMail identify users based on a set of demographics and targeted segments of the fan base. Figure 12.1 shows an e-mail message that is sent to over 1 million people but is personalized to each user based on that user's request for particular information.

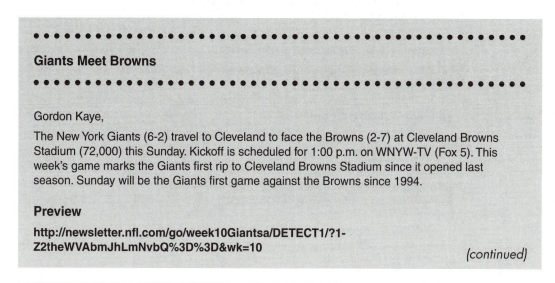

Giants Meet Browns

Gordon Kaye,

The New York Giants (6-2) travel to Cleveland to face the Browns (2-7) at Cleveland Browns Stadium (72,000) this Sunday. Kickoff is scheduled for 1:00 p.m. on WNYW-TV (Fox 5). This week's game marks the Giants first rip to Cleveland Browns Stadium since it opened last season. Sunday will be the Giants first game against the Browns since 1994.

Preview

http://newsletter.nfl.com/go/week10Giantsa/DETECT1/?1-Z2theWVAbmJhLmNvbQ%3D%3D&wk=10

(continued)

Figure 12.1 A personalized e-mail gives the user only the information he is interested in.

Michael Eisen's First-Half Awards

http://newsletter.nfl.com/go/week10Giantsa/DETECT2/?2-
Z2theWVAbmJhLmNvbQ%3D%3D&wk=10

Send Giants to the Pro Bowl

http://newsletter.nfl.com/go/week10Giantsa/DETECT3/?3-
Z2theWVAbmJhLmNvbQ%3D%3D&wk=10

Inteview with Coach Fassel

http://newsletter.nfl.com/go/week10Giantsa/DETECT4/?4-
Z2theWVAbmJhLmNvbQ%3D%3D&wk=10

• •

NFL Shop on NFL.com

• •

NFL SHOP MID-SEASON SALE! Limited Time Offer . . .

Have you heard about NFL Shop's Mid-Season Sale? Buy Now. Quantities Limited. NFL SHOP has the best prices of the season—today through 11/6

Be the first to show off your Giants gear without paying full price!!! It's easy, simply log on to NFL Shop now to purchase your Giants gear.

http://newsletter.nfl.com/go/week10Giantsa/DETECT5/?5-
Z2theWVAbmJhLmNvbQ%3D%3D&wk=10

• •

NFL.com

• •

Week 10 In The NFL

The NFL season is halfway home and the playoff races are beginning to heat up. Follow every play throughout Week 10 with GameDay Live and track your favorite players while games are in progress with PlayerTracker.

http://newsletter.nfl.com/go/week10Giantsa/DETECT6/?6-
Z2theWVAbmJhLmNvbQ%3D%3D&wk=10

http://newsletter.nfl.com/go/week10Giantsa/DETECT7/?7-
Z2theWVAbmJhLmNvbQ%3D%3D&wk=10

NFL.com's Game Scout

Want to find out how Lions RB James Stewart will do against the stingy Dolphins defense Sunday? Check out NFL.com's Game Scout, which uses stats and charts to delve into the weekend's biggest games.

http://newsletter.nfl.com/go/week10Giantsa/DETECT8/?8-
Z2theWVAbmJhLmNvbQ%3D%3D&wk=10

Figure 12.1 *(continued)*

Fantasy on NFL.com

Edge NFL Matchup co-hosts Ron Jaworski and Ron Hoge let fans in on their fantasy picks each week, while NFL.com's fantasy gurus, including Gil Brandt, share their top tips and pointers.

http://newsletter.nfl.com/go/week10Giantsa/DETECT9/?9-Z2theWVAbmJhLmNvbQ%3D%3D&wk=10

Live Radio Coverage

Plus, NFL.com is your home for live radio coverage of Sunday's action. Coverage begins Sunday morning with pregame shows from across the country.

http://newsletter.nfl.com/go/week10Giantsa/DETECT10/?10-Z2theWVAbmJhLmNvbQ%3D%3D&wk=10

Keep Your NFL.com Newsletter Profile Current

If you would like to adjust your personal NFL. com Newsletter profile, simply click on the following link.

http://newsletter.nfl.com/profile/Z2theWVAbmJhLmNvbQ%3D%3D&wk=10/

Forward This Message To Your Friends and Family!

http://f2f.ed4.net/f2f?NTU%3D+gkaye@nba.com

If you wish to unsubscribe from NFL.com's Newsletter, simply reply to this e-mail message with the word "UNSUB" at the top of your reply.

Figure 12.1 *(continued)*

Reprinted, by permission, from National Football League Properties. © National Football League Properties.

In this particular case, the user (Gordon Kaye) requested information about the New York Giants, the NFL Store, Fantasy Football, and NFL Internet Radio coverage. With one simple keystroke, the organization (in this case, the NFL) was able to personalize a specific targeted e-mail to that user based on a specific information request. On the "back end," teams can also track the user's interaction with that e-mail (e.g., whether the user clicked through from the links) to further improve their interaction with that customer in the future.

Recently, advancements in rich media delivery and compression have opened the door for teams to deliver similar targeted e-mails using streaming or compressed audio and video. Companies like RadicalMail and eCommercial deliver personalized, rich media content to large user lists. Much like text e-mail systems, rich media mass e-mail systems provide tools to track the user's interaction with the program.

There are literally thousands of other ways that teams can use technology to improve their one-on-one interaction with their fans: bar coding, fan loyalty programs, Internet data capture, targeted e-mail programs, wireless data delivery, and the Web are just some of the tools that are at our disposal at this time. And, because of how quickly the world of technology changes, we are confident that in the coming months there will be thousands more.

Technology is not the enemy!

The Internet and Sport Promotion

While the World Wide Web (WWW) is a client server application that provides a graphic user interface for information and interactive communication, sport promotion specialists should view it as a means of marketing communication that can be used to add customer value. That said, it is also a rapidly expanding form of communication that is expected to continue to grow exponentially. International Data Corporation expects that the Internet economy will reach $1 trillion by 2001, while Forrester Research suggests that online worldwide advertising will reach $33 billion by 2004.[4] The U.S. Internet population, which was 6 million households in 1994, is expected to reach 60 million households by 2002, while total U.S. purchasing on the Web is expected to reach $1.4 trillion by 2004.[5]

Just as sport drove the sales of radios and televisions in another era, some of the busiest sites on the Internet are sport related. Full-service sport sites such as ESPN's Sport Zone, CBS SportsLine (and its European subsidiary Sports.com), and CNN/SI provide news of scores and features to millions of fans daily.[6] Their popularity can be gauged from the fact that the three sites had a total of more than 12 million unique visitors during the month of May 2000 and that in February 2001, ESPN.com alone had 6.1 million individual visitors.[7] Underlying the growth of this medium of communication are a number of powerful phenomena:

- Digitalization, which consists of converting text, data, sound, and images into a stream of "bits" that can be dispatched at high speed.

- Higher-speed Internet connections that enable larger programs, or data-intensive services, to be delivered with acceptable download time. While dial-up modem connections to the Internet are reaching their technological speed limits for telephone connections, megabit-per-second Internet connection technologies, such as cable modems and digital subscriber link (DSL), are growing rapidly.

- Connectivity, which involves building networks, expresses the fact that much of the world's business is conducted over networks connecting people and companies. Allied to connectivity is the "always-connected" paradigm. Except for corporate users who are currently "always connected," most sport fans who access the WWW from home still dial in via an Internet service provider (ISP) and disconnect at the end of the session. This "sometimes-connected" mode makes economic sense when the user pays for Internet connection by the hour. However, within the technology alternatives for high-speed access, "always connected" does not carry a significant additional cost beyond the technology required for the high-speed connection, and this is reflected in the unlimited-use pricing of high-speed access.[8] "Always connected" presents new opportunities for sport promotion specialists to "push" information to sport fans when new information corresponds to the fan's interests. The "always-connected" paradigm opens a powerful technology door to Web integration of the various entertainment services that are entering the home.

Several aspects of the convergence of high-speed access, interconnection of Web site/databases, and "always connected" are evident in the merging simultaneous delivery of sport on television and the Web. Since 1996 the Hughes Electronics Corporation has been demonstrating the interconnection of the entertainment and Web technology through the interface between DirecTV and Direct.[9] The DirecPC and DirecTV systems permit the sport fan to click on a hyperlink displayed during a television program or commercial and have the PC hyperlink to the related Web site.[10] Use of this technology allows a fan to click the hyperlink for a batter at the plate, which causes the PC to hyperlink to a Web site with that player's statistics or asks the audience to predict the next pitch, with prizes for the most successful fans. In the case of satellite entertainment distribution, all the technology exists to allow the PC to control the TV, that is, if the PC is "always connected."

Web Content

While using the WWW to connect to customers, the sport promotion specialist must realize the importance of content that the organization puts on its Web site. Don't be distracted by technology. The promise of technology advances such as the evolution of broadband may seem alluring, but what will draw people to a site is the content that is there. It is content in the form of updated results and scores that draws people continually back to ESPN.com. Although the possibility of hearing an interview or viewing a particular play from a variety of different angles may be attractive to sport promotion specialists, it is the content that continues to drive people to the ESPN site. Sport organizations have many ways of creating content that will ensure that consumers return to their sites frequently. We need to understand that one of the reasons many online entertainment businesses failed was the difficulty of creating original content for the Web. Sport organizations do not have this problem. The content has already been created, and the Web as an ancillary form of distribution can be a powerful and effective way to deliver that content directly to the consumer.[11]

Insight into and access to the sport organization are critical elements in the creation of such content. The Cincinnati Bengals were the last major league team in North America to create an official team Web site. However, when they eventually created the site, they hired a beat writer from the local newspaper, the *Cincinnati Inquirer*, to provide the type of insightful commentary that they hope will make their site a first stop for news on the organization. That strategy, and the reasoning behind it, are sound. Public relations releases that organizations distribute are helpful, and better than what most fans or consumers would get from other sources. Access to the inner workings of the Bengals gives their Web site visitors a unique perspective on the organization (**www.cincinnatibengals.com/**).[12] Fans have many sources of information to choose from; but the Bengals' intent in adopting this approach is that the site will be the definitive source for team news, information, insight, and commentary. While this strategy will give Bengal fans a particular view of their organization, the team will probably not go as far as the 2000 Union des Associations Européennes de Football (UEFA) Cup champions, Galatasaray of Istanbul, who not only provide perspective on the management of the club, but also provide information on the social lives of their better known players (**www.galatasaray.org.tr/**).

Migala suggests that a sport promotion specialist consider the following "5 Cs" when creating content that will be attractive and "sticky" to fans.[13] (**"Sticky"** is a measure of the "time per person" that is spent on a site and is used to describe how well a site retains visitors. The better the content of a site, the longer the visits will be, or the stickier the site.)

Change
Choice
Community
Cool
Customize

• *Change.* Teams should view their Web site content as a news source and not simply as a brochure for their team. To that end, teams should be prepared to change the content of their site very frequently. The NHL site (**www.nhl.com/**) uses beat writers to cover the league, thus providing content that is constantly updated as stories develop. Migala suggests that as a result of this strategy, over 70% of the site's 345,000 average daily visitors frequent the site at least six times a week.[13]

• *Choice.* Although the Internet is expanding at an ever-increasing pace, we need to recognize that a significant portion of users do not yet have the capability of downloading video files or large complex graphics. This leads to slow-loading pages for the majority of people who connect to the Internet at lower speeds. A solution to this dilemma, without causing users to become frustrated by a sport organization's Web site offerings, is to offer the choice of a separate broadband connection that allows fans to connect to a multimedia experience.

• *Community.* The online community of a team should be provided innovative forums for communication and fan commerce, such as the New York Giants offer with their Global Fan Registry (**www.giants.com/registration.asp**). Loosely defined, a community is a group of people who have a common interest or purpose. In this case it is the New York Giants. Thus the community of a rugby club discussing representative team selection has the common interest of seeing how many, if any, of their club may have been selected.

• *Cool.* With such competition in the sport marketplace, the sport promotion specialist should recognize the importance of innovative features on the site. The PGA TOUR showed live video feed from the tee box of the treacherous 17th hole during the 2000 U.S. Open at Pebble Beach, California. Viewers got to see the exact magnificent but daunting view that each golfer had as he played what is arguably one of the more difficult holes in all of golf. The feature drew 5 million viewers.

• *Customize.* While sport organizations may have realized the value of direct e-mail communication, little has been done, suggests Migala, to customize the experience of the fan when she signs on to a site.[13] Customizing could include, for instance, finding out who the fan's favorite player is and ensuring that the fan is directed to an area of a site containing material about that player. Or, if a visitor is more interested in underage competition than, say, senior or adult-level competition, he could be directed upon arrival at the site to these areas.

The 5 Cs—Change, Choice, Community, Cool, and Customize—should be the mantra of sport promotion specialists developing and managing a presence on the Web. This will bring fans to the site continually, whereas failure to recognize the importance of each of the Cs will inevitably lessen the lure of the site.

Fan Interaction

Giving fans the opportunity to interact, via chat rooms, with players, coaches, and management is another means of creating interesting content. This exploits the two-way nature of the Internet and is a means of differentiating the medium from traditional media available to sport promotion specialists such as magazines, newspapers, and game programs, each of which is a one-way medium. The Washington Capitals regularly have management and players chat with fans (**www. washingtoncaps.com/interact/chat_schedule.cfm**). It is through these interactions that deeper and more long-lasting relationships with fans are created and nurtured. These opportunities to interact with team members and management help make a Web site "sticky."

Creating the opportunity for the fans to interact with the organization on a regular basis, as Adams suggests, allows the fans to congregate and to create communities at the official Web site of the organization rather than at another site.[14] Where the fans congregate in an online community is critical, because it is to that site that fans will turn for information, where they will shop and "click" with sponsors. Rivals.com, for instance, has created a very large network of sport team communities, which provide the fans with ample opportunities, outside official Web sites, to gather news, interact with each other, and voice their opinions about their particular team or sport (**www.rivals.com**). Since Rivals.com was launched in August 1999, it has been the number-one sport news site on the Internet in stickiness according to Nielsen/ NetRatings.[15] Visits by fans to "unofficial sites" are opportunities lost to sport organizations, not only for communicating directly on a one-to-one basis with consumers, but also for merchandising, ticketing, and community events.

While chat rooms and message boards are vital staples of a sport organization's attempt to create virtual communities, Liberman suggests that the sport promotion specialist can attract further fan interest by allowing the fan to become an integral part of the site.[16] This may occur in a number of ways.

- Select a quote of the day—whether it is witty, morbid, intelligent, or outlandish, the sport promotion specialist could place it prominently on the site with the fan's name and hometown.

- Encourage fans to record their own play-by-play and make it the "Fan Call of the Week."

- Allow testimonials to products sold via the organization's e-commerce site.[17]

Although the work involved in creating these opportunities may be significant, the fan has already done much of the work; and each contribution, at the very least, is an another address for the database, for an individual who has a significant interest in the sport organization.

A critical element of any cyber-promotion strategy is that an organization's site must be updated constantly. Allowing information to get old is a significant reason why individuals will not return to a site. If results or league standings are included on a site they must be updated in a timely manner. "In a timely manner" in today's world of immediate information means instantaneously. Updating the site to show the result of a collegiate game when a team returns to campus or when the sport promotion specialist has access to the campus computer network is too late. As soon as the final whistle is blown, the results should be appearing on the athletic department Web site. If they are not, people will go to other sites looking for the score and updates. Traffic diverted to another site is a lost opportunity.

One of the dilemmas facing a sport promotion specialist in attracting fans to contribute to message boards and chat rooms is how to ensure that postings do not create a poor impression of the organization. Monitoring chat rooms and message boards becomes necessary because no sport organization can afford to have offensive material posted on its site. Not monitoring chat rooms gives ample opportunity for individuals to disparage an organization, not merely by making negative comments about a player or team but by doing so in a vile and offensive manner. Allowing such commentary on a Web site flies in the face of logic because a message board is as much a part of the marketing communication mix as any other medium, and to allow it to create a negative impression of the organization is undoubtedly unwise. On the other hand, to expect that fans will not on occasion post offensive material is pollyannaic. As the Web site is owned by the organization, any message that the organization objects to can be removed. Liberman suggests that such monitoring may give the impression of heavy-handedness or even paranoia, but the benefits to the organization of removing inappropriate or derogatory material far outweigh the risk of a public relations fiasco.[18]

Chat rooms and message boards on a Web site are two significant means of interactivity between a sport organization and its fans. Milne and McDonald report that the dimensions of interactivity and functionality were the two most important factors identified by users in an evaluation of the Web sites of major league teams in North America.[19] This suggests that the opportunity for the sport fan to interact with a sport organization, as well as the structure of the Web site (speed, ease of exploration, information), is a particularly important aspect of Web site management that a sport promotion specialist has to be concerned about.

The interactivity with fans is one feature of the Web presence of the San Francisco Giants. As an organization, the Giants have embraced their Web presence, not only as an important medium of communication but also as a means of generating income from their e-commerce activities. Adams suggests that by investing in programs such as movable cameras, fan loyalty programs, video highlights, fan polls, and chat rooms, they will increase the long-term value of the site.[20] Certainly their initial experience of using the Web site as a means of informing their fans about Pacific Bell Park appears to justify their investment. Nearly 50% of all single game tickets for Giants home games have been bought online, while 15% of their 30,000 season tickets were handled online. Charter seat licenses were also available online, and the Giants found that the team's chances of making a sale were 50% higher if the fan had researched the licenses through the Web, rather than through a random phone call.[21] Not only did the site create income for the organization, but it also cut the Giants' advertising costs. Chief Operating Officer Larry Baer indicated that the Giants did not take out full-page ads in the local press as in the past, and that "the Web saved hundreds of thousands of dollars in advertising."[22]

© Shelby Thorner/Newsport

The Giant's use of the Web is a sales mechanism that drives fans to Pacific Bell Park.

Personalization

The technology of the Internet is facilitating a shift from a mass marketing to a one-to-one relationship marketing paradigm. One of the unique benefits of a cyber-

Mass marketing	One-to-one marketing
Average customer	Individual customer
Customer anonymity	Customer profile
Standard product	Customized market offering
Mass production	Customized production
Mass distribution	Individualized distribution
Mass promotion	Individualized incentives
One-way message	Two-way message
Economies of scale	Economies of scope
Share of market	Share of customer
All customers	Profitable customers
Customer attraction	Customer retention

Figure 12.2 Mass marketing versus one-to-one marketing techniques.

Reprinted from THE ONE TO ONE FUTURE by Don Peppers and Martha Rogers, Ph.D, copyright © 1993 by Don Peppers and Martha Rogers, Ph.D. Used by permission of Doubleday, a division of Random House, Inc.

promotion strategy is the ability to practice such one-to-one marketing in a meaningful way. This strategy is grounded in the idea of establishing a learning relationship with each customer,[23] or **personalization.** As each interaction takes place, the organization learns more about the consumers. As sport organizations learn more about their individual fans they can customize their product, offer, message, shipment method, and payment method to maximize consumer appeal. The success of one-to-one marketing hinges on what a sport organization knows about each of its fans, not what it knows about all of them. On this point, Peppers and Rogers have identified the main differences between mass marketing and one-to-one marketing,[24] which are outlined in figure 12.2.

Knowing fans well enough to customize services individually encompasses the answers to four questions:

- Who are the customers?
- Can they be differentiated?
- Can they be meaningfully interacted with?
- Can the organization's product and services be customized to fit each individual customer's need?[25]

Identification

Through a well-managed Web presence, a sport organization can readily identify each individual visitor to its site. This may be achieved through self-identification, such as completion of an online questionnaire by the fan on his first visit to the site. Fans provide a login name and a password, and each time they return they identify themselves to the site by using the name and password. However, such a process can be tedious and often lengthy. An alternative is the use of **"cookies"** or "browser cookies," which allow a Web site to identify each visitor without the visitor's having to log in each time. Thus sites are able to welcome an individual fan on a return visit by the name provided on the first visit. Amazon.com, for instance, uses cookies to greet users by name on their return visits.

Cookies are small data files that are placed on a user's hard drive when the user visits and logs on to a Web site for the first time. Data from the cookie file are accessed by the Web site when the user revisits the site or certain pages in it. A database on the user can be compiled, enabling the Web site to assess, for instance, how much time elapsed between visits; whether the user looked at the same pages, in the same order; what advertising the user was exposed to; and what advertising she reacted to by clicking through to the site of the advertising organization. Shopping sites can also use cookies to keep track of the contents of a shopping basket or a mailing address. People should recognize that cookies are merely plain text and cannot extract information from a user's machine and secretly transfer it to a Web server.[26]

Simply identifying the individual fan is not enough if an organization wishes to be able to market to fans on an individual basis. It is critical to know the fans in as much detail as is relevant to the sport organization—not just their addressable characteristics, but their preferences and habits also. Neither is it enough to know them from a single transaction; the organization must learn about them over time, recognizing that they have a **lifetime value.**

Differentiation

Can sport organization customers be differentiated? Customers are different in two principal ways: they represent different levels of value, and they have different needs.[27] Different levels of association with an organization can, for instance, identify sport fans. Fans can be categorized on the basis of whether they are season ticket holders, flex plan holders, or single game purchasers. Cross-referencing a database of season ticket sales and Web server logs will readily identify season ticket holders who regularly visit a sport organization Web site. Identifying customers will help to focus efforts so as to gain the most advantage with the most valuable customers. A sport promotion specialist will then be able to tailor the sport organization's response to each fan in order to reflect that customer's value and needs. For example, a sport organization might want to pursue season ticket holders who have not renewed and make them an offer that will entice them to consider a flex plan as distinct from a full-season ticket plan. There may be high-value customers who have complained about the organization or its services in the last year. It is essential for the organization to monitor its service closely and to seek regularly the fan's view of the service quality.

A service that a sport organization may consider offering through its Web presence is prefilling of data, which is a prerequisite for other services such as one-click ordering and automatic replenishment. When fans communicate with the sport organization, their list of preferences—which they have identified over time as important to them—are immediately taken into consideration in fulfilling their needs. For instance, a golf tee time or a court booking would fall into a particular time frame, followed by a preferred meal or snack in the sport club's dining room. Or say a customer has purchased a pair of sneakers at a Web sporting goods store. The next time that individual visits the site to purchase a pair of sneakers, all he is asked to select is color and style preferences. The other relevant information (shipping address, payment information, etc.) is already available to the retailer as a result of previous interaction with the consumer.

Interaction

Critical to any one-to-one marketing program are the effectiveness and cost-efficiency of customer interaction. Across interactive media, a sport promotion specialist should choose effectiveness, not cost-efficiency, because the latter may lead to a lowering of effectiveness. Sport promotion specialists should also recognize that strategic valuation insight comes only from the fans, as only they can reveal to the organization the future marketing opportunities, and that this information is obtainable only in a direct interaction with the fans.

Every time a customer accesses the organization Web site it should be more convenient for that fan to do so. In that regard, "1:1 micromarketing" should pick up where the last visit left off. When interacting with the fan, the organization should not ask for all relevant information at once, and a fan should expect not to be asked for information more than once by any unit of an organization.

Related to this principle was the dilemma facing soccer's Glasgow Rangers of the Scottish Premier League (**www.rangers.co.uk/home.htm**). Ticket holder information was scattered across 14 separate databases, and the team had 24 different telephone numbers (for ticket sales, merchandise, loyalty clubs, events, catering, etc.), making it impossible to disseminate information across the club easily. "Simplify, simplify," became the mantra of club management because they understood that in the competitive environment, which exists for fans' free time and disposable income, cradle-to-grave relationships were needed to secure fans' patronage.[28]

The 24 phone numbers were reduced to 5, while the newly established contact center was integrated with the club's Web site to allow for a more seamless customer experience and to enable the club to gather more information from fans. Rangers found that the single contact point, coupled with the complete view of the customer, allowed them to pin down cross-selling opportunities precisely. Revenue for the first six months of the project was reported to have been 3% higher than forecasts, and the level of **first-call resolution** soared from 5% to 60%.[28]

As a sport promotion specialist you should take the view that whenever and however a fan interacts with the sport organization you have a chance to get a better fix on *that* fan's particular, individual needs. Needs specification, in most situations, is inherently an iterative function. You should think of it as ratcheting up the learning curve on an individual customer's personal set of tastes, preferences, and desires.

Customizing

In customizing the sport organization's offerings to fans, sport promotion specialists must adapt their behavior to meet the customer's individually expressed needs. Information for the high-value customers should be personalized, perhaps via a dedicated area of the organization home page or at least through personalized e-mail. What such customization does is to expand the sport arena beyond the physical confines of the building, particularly when you use high-speed connections that are capable of delivering video. Then you are able to send particular plays, or particular views of favorite players whom fans have previously identified as important to them.

By tracking fan usage, an organization can give real-time feedback of what interests a fan's peer group, as Amazon.com does when it indicates that people who have purchased a particular item also purchased certain other items. Remembering an individual customer's preferences is also possible on a site, enabling the site to lead the user to specific databases.

Organizations also have the ability to push information to fans who may be considered less valuable to them. This is what Glasgow Celtic, the principal rivals of Glasgow Rangers, do via e-mail to their registered fans. Each press statement released by the club is sent via their Web site to subscribers.

It's a good thing for consumers to want different things from a sport organization so that the value of the organization in their lives can be increased. By using technology such as browser cookies, sport marketers have the capabilities to identify fans and thus begin to satisfy their individual needs, which is, after all, at the heart of the marketing function.

Permission Marketing

Many marketing activities, including direct mail and telemarketing, can be described as interruption marketing. Permission marketing (introduced in chapter 5) as applied to the Internet and e-commerce offers the customer an opportunity to volunteer to accept marketing communications. The concept of giving permission suggests that consumers will pay more attention to the message because they have "volunteered" to receive it and, in some cases, because they been given incentives for receiving it.

Permission marketing has been characterized as anticipated, personal, and relevant.[29] It is anticipated because customers look forward to hearing from the marketer, personal because there is a connection to the receiver, and relevant because the message is about something the prospect is interested in. Amazon.com is a leader in permission marketing. A recipient who logs on can communicate with the organization about what she is interested in—this is a subtle database-marketing enrollment.

Past purchasers are welcomed back and acknowledged by name. In addition to being recognized, the database selling approach is employed. Amazon.com characterizes consumers by their listening, reading, or viewing habits and interests. The company offers recommendations based upon past purchases and inquiries and can offer to send an e-mail (which the customer has agreed to receive) when a preferred author or artist has a new release. They also give incentives by offering electronic coupons or actual coupons enclosed with shipments of products or services. The receiver looks forward to receiving the messages because they are anticipated as being relevant and personal.

This same technique can be very effective in the sport industry. Visitors to team or league Web sites can be provided with the opportunity to subscribe to ticket, merchandise, venue, and player information, as well as to other offers and information. Because they have given their permission, visitors are more likely to download the information, read it, and accept and respond to it. It is estimated that permission-based marketing efforts are read by as many as 70% of the recipients.[30] Imagine if only half of those individuals actually purchased the product or service!

In the sport industry, new Internet products, such as e-commercials, are finding support because of their capabilities and results. Through e-commercials you can add video clips to an e-mail message that can be read without having to utilize special software or download additional programming. This would allow an organization like The Fédération Internationale de Football Association (FiFa) to select highlights from the careers of their Footballers of the 20th Century, such as Michelle Akers and Pele, and combine them with a message, perhaps related to the sale of USA or Brazilian team merchandise. E-commercials and their companion e-prospector can also monitor the success of those e-mails by identifying who has downloaded the message, what they read, if the message was passed on, and so forth. While there are still permission marketing and privacy issues to be worked out, this may be the future of electronic direct mail in the sport industry.

Privacy

By using browser cookies on a Web site, a sport organization can identify and track a fan's interaction with the site. This ability has become a concern for many Web users, and particularly for privacy advocates, who fear that Web sites will connect Web behavior with identifiable characteristics (name, address, phone number, e-mail address). Although such concerns are very legitimate, a means of overcoming the concern is to have a clearly stated privacy policy. This would indicate that the sport organization uses cookies but that their use is limited to functions within the organization Web site. Stating that you do not connect information gathered on a site with that of other organizations, or that you do not pass any specific information to third parties, should ameliorate many of the concerns of visitors to a sport organization site. The San Francisco Giants' site includes a statement of their privacy policy, which is available at **www.sfgiants.com/home/privacy.cfm**.

Tracking Web Use

Failure to indicate to Web users that you are tracking their use of a Web site is a dereliction of duty to them as consumers. Even if one considers the information collected on a sport organization Web site to be rather innocuous, a sport organization must recognize, and be concerned about, the ongoing debate about privacy on the Web.

Extending the Boundaries of the Stadium

By virtue of its global reach, the Internet offers the opportunity for extending the boundaries of a sport arena far beyond the immediate geographical area of a sport organization's traditional market. The concept of extending the reach of a sport organization has been enthusiastically embraced by the most valuable sport franchise in the world, Manchester United Football Club (**www.manutd.com/**). The organization has approximately 40,000 season ticket holders and regularly makes 12,000 tickets available to nonseason ticket holders. However, in order to attain a match ticket one must be a member of the club, and the way to do this is to join one the supporters' clubs, which are located in 24 countries around the world. The match tickets are then distributed through the supporters' clubs. We can recognize the potential of such a distribution system within the context of the concept of **"outer rim markets."**[31] Having supporters travel from outside a team's immediate market area to a home game from time to time significantly enhances the opportunities for sales in areas such as merchandise, souvenirs, media material, visits to the club museum, tours of the stadium and practice facilities, and the club restaurant. It is easy to appreciate the strategy in which teams focus on outer rim markets, with various units of the sport organization catering to every aspect of the fan's visit, including a stay at a club hotel, as at Chelsea Village in London (**www.chelseavillage.co.uk/ fr_village.htm**). Such strategy has the potential to enhance a sport organization's bottom line significantly. Organizations should embrace the idea of extending the boundaries of the stadium, and use of Web sites as a source of information is a method of doing this.

Nor should such strategy be confined to in-season trips to games. As sport arenas have developed and become major tourist attractions in recent years, there would appear to be significant potential for year-round "pilgrimages" by dedicated fans to arenas and stadiums. Such potential is best indicated by Manchester United and its use of the term "Theatre of Dreams" to characterize the stadium at Old Trafford, Manchester. Similarly, the Gaelic Athletic Association at its headquarters in Croke Park, Dublin, has created a museum that is not only a review of the games of hurling and Gaelic football, but also a valuable social history of modern Ireland. The museum has become an important place to visit for Gaelic games fans throughout the year, as well as a significant destination for international tourists attracted by the location of the museum, its striking layout, and its insightful view of modern Irish history.

Manchester United is also using the Internet as a strategy to build its brand on a global scale. The organization's Web site is designed and managed by Trans World International, U.K., the media arm of International Management Group (best known by its initials, IMG). While Fletcher Research reports that only 25% of British Web users go to sport sites,[32] the Manutd.com site receives 8 million hits a month.[33] A significant portion of the hits come from club supporters located in Southeast Asia.[34] A number of market analysts suggest that it has tremendous potential to contribute financially to the club once the Premier League allows the individual clubs to show their own games on their own channels. The Web site then becomes the delivery mechanism to fans not based in the United Kingdom.[35]

As you might expect from a site with such a large number of visitors, Manutd.com offers attractive content to those dedicated to the team. It provides reports, fan forums, contests, live radio broadcasts, game trackers, and information for subscribing to MUTV, the club's own TV station.

There are other ways to move the boundaries of the stadium outward. An extension of the typical services provided by sport organization Web sites is a link from Manutd.com to Eurobet, an Internet gambling site operated by Coral, one of the leading bookmakers in the United Kingdom. Not only is Manchester United promoting the Eurobet site and link, but the team is benefiting financially from the connection in that it will retain a portion of the revenues derived from people who started out on the Manutd.com site and who place bets with Eurobet.[36] As Southeast Asia is one of the biggest gaming markets in the world, the Eurobet link provides not only a service to fans who live in that part of the world but also perhaps an opportunity for the fans to contribute to the well-being of the club by gambling via the site.

By creating an interactive, "sticky" Web presence, sport organizations have an opportunity to service fans well beyond the limits of their traditional market areas. Not only can the Web site contribute to cultivating long-term relationships with fans, but organizations can also use the Web site to add to their income streams, much as Manchester United and the San Francisco Giants have done.

Ticketing

As the technology that allows for the printing of event tickets develops and becomes more sophisticated, the provision of tickets via a sport organization Web site is an area of sport promotion that will continue to grow. Jupiter Communications projects that by the year 2003, out of an estimated $3 billion that will be spent on sporting goods, apparel, and tickets on the Web, $1 billion will be spent on tickets. While many teams currently use the service of ticketing behemoth Ticketmaster, some are realizing significantly more profits from selling tickets on their own sites. The more successful teams have software that allows the fan to pick her own seat and get a view of the field or arena from that particular seat. Both the Oakland A's and the San Francisco Giants use Tickets.com to market their tickets online. Tickets.com reports that it sold over 1.3 million tickets during the first quarter of 2000, representing over $35.2 million in gross sales transactions from both sport and non-sport events.

Harris Sports Poll eSports Report indicates that 25% of die-hard NASCAR fans, 25% of die-hard NBA fans, and 12% of die-hard NHL fans have purchased tickets through sport Web sites. But this phenomenon is not confined to those characterized as die-hard fans, as a significant number of people who are classified as casual fans have purchased tickets via the Web: 18% of casual NASCAR fans, 17% of casual NBA fans, and 12% of casual NHL fans report purchasing tickets from a Web site.[37]

The online ticket-buying trend is likely to continue to grow as Web access develops and as the confidence of the sport fan about conducting commercial transactions over the Web increases. Reducing the cost to fans will lure them to a Web site as a source of tickets. There are a number of ways to do this. One is to reduce the price of tickets that are ordered over the Web versus those accessed in a traditional box office exchange. Friedman believes that there "is a mindset that almost anything can be bought for less money on the web" but that this may not be a good strategy, particularly for organizations who may have a traditional market that does not have ready access to the Web.[38] Such a strategy may cause a negative reaction among those who do not have ready access to the Web and may be seen as favoring a technological elite among the fans.

Loyalty Cards

Fans who purchase e-tickets can be rewarded in other ways, though. They can be rewarded with points on fan loyalty cards in programs such as the Compadres Club of the San Diego Padres (**www.padres.com/fanfare/compadres.html**) or the Frequent A's Fancard (**www.oaklandathletics.com/index2.html**). They can also be rewarded with organization merchandise for purchasing a certain number of tickets online. As with other aspects of rewards for frequent fans, sport promotion specialists are limited only by their imagination when it comes to e-tickets.

Loyalty cards allow the sport promotion specialist to compile significant data on fans by tracking their activity and thus be able to service and market to them more efficiently. By tracking such activity as attendance, merchandise sales, concession spending, parking value, and ticket resale, the organization begins to create a composite picture of the fan based on a host of minor and simple details. A sport promotion specialist needs to recognize that if total involvement is important, strict attention must be paid to all the minor details. The position should be one of striving to link together all aspects of a customer's interactions with the organization.[39]

Not only is this effective in servicing the fan as a client, but it also allows the organization to create robust, quantifiable data, which will assist in securing sport marketing relationships. Through use of such data, sport promotion specialists increase their ability to maintain long-term relationships with marketing partners. As corporate marketers need to justify their expenditures, they will possess valuable information from the sport organization that will help them serve as a partner of the sport organization, not merely as a subsidizer or sponsor.

Virtual Advertising

Since its debut in major league American sport in 1998, virtual advertising has become very much mainstream and offers the sport promotion specialist a number of opportunities—opportunities such as adding to an organization's commercial inventory and, by extension, to revenue streams; enhancing telecast advertising options; or adding creative insertions to generate greater spectator appreciation of an event. The technology can creatively and effectively insert signage behind, underneath, or above the athletes while they are in action during a telecast. The live audience in the arena has no idea that this is happening, and it does not interfere in any way with the competitors. The technology allows the organization to add a virtual first-down line during NFL games or a virtual 10-meter line in free kick situations in soccer games; it can identify track athletes or swimmers by inserting the flags of their respective nations on the track or on the surface of the water. All this makes critical events much easier for fans to view and understand.

Although the option of devising specific means of enhancing the event for telecast spectators is alluring, for many sport organizations there is a greater attraction in adding to the advertising inventory of the organization. The insertion of an advertisement in the center circle of a soccer field while the game is in progress may seem anathema to the soccer purist, but given the correct circumstances, the possibility exists. A more realistic option is to create virtual perimeter advertising boards along the side of the playing field in rugby, behind the goalposts in soccer, or behind the batter's box in baseball. The ability to change the advertising throughout the event telecast is attractive and alluring for both the sponsor and the sponsee. One advantage of virtual advertising is that, as Wertheim said, it is "zapper proof."[40] Wertheim suggests that because people are becoming more prone to changing channels, the effectiveness of the traditional 30-second commercial is decreasing; but because a virtual advertisement stays in place through the game's prime moments, the maximum number of viewers have the opportunity to see it. Also, according to Wertheim, studies have indicated that an on-field sign is more than twice as likely to be recalled as a 30-second advertisement.

The possibility of regionalizing advertising also exists. In a telecast of a cricket match between India and Pakistan, for instance, it would be possible to have perimeter advertising for Pakistani companies shown on the telecast of the game in

Pakistan while having advertisements for Indian companies shown on the telecast in India. This is what Symah Vision, a European-based company, did during a telecast of a Glasgow Rangers (Scotland) versus Parma (Italy) UEFA Cup game in 1998. Perimeter advertising featuring alternate corporate brand names was shown in Germany and Italy. The sport promotion specialist could sell the advertising space on a country-by-country, region-by-region, or even market-by-market basis, allowing sponsors to be very specific in their targeting.

Virtual advertising in the United States costs roughly the same as a 30-second commercial in a sport telecast. However, because the advertisement stays in place longer (e.g., for half an inning during a baseball game), is "virtually" part of the action, and remains on screen during critical moments, it can give greater value to advertisers.

Bar Coding

Bar coding is an effective way of linking many of a fan's interactions with a sport organization. A sport organization could begin by bar coding all tickets so that each ticket is scanned by a PDT (portable data terminal) laser scanner rather than being merely torn apart by ticket takers and placed in a receptacle. The data might then be transferred to the main computer system, and up-to-the-second viewing prompts that have been programmed in advance could signal that a particular customer, corporate partner, or VIP has entered the arena. If the organization identifies a particular reason to acknowledge the presence of the ticket holder (birthday, anniversary, first-time visitor), it can do so in various ways. For example, personnel can make a presentation as the individual approaches his seat, or a club representative can meet first-time arena visitors or the public address announcer can welcome them. Another way to use bar coding is to run reports at various times detailing every ticket scanned so that it becomes possible to track no-shows in each ticket category.[41]

Bar coding would not be a substitute for tickets; rather it would be an addition to the fan experience in that it provides the opportunity for personalization through the printing of individual ticket holders' names on their tickets. This would be consistent with the organization's branding position but would add significant value for the "giver and the receiver." The ticket becomes a powerful collector's item, particularly if the event is a world or national championship event such as the Olympic Games or Rugby's Super 12 Championship final, and it continues to be a sponsorship and promotional opportunity through the selling of the ticket back.[41]

For each season ticket, suite, or premium seat holder, a "smart" fan card such as the Frequent A's Fancard (**www.oaklandathletics.com/index2.html**) could be issued. The fan could simply present the card at the gate, have it scanned, and get into the arena. The card could also be used throughout the arena to purchase concessions or merchandise, visit a stadium restaurant or club, or enter promotions and sweepstakes. All of the transactions would be conducted via the fan's card with payment methods previously established, by credit card or automatic bank transfers, at the fan's discretion. Payments might be spread over a 12-month period, rather than over the course of a season, which would help with any problem related to high ticket prices and thus would be more highly personalized. Parking might also be an option on the fan card through the purchase of a bar-coded decal that would be attached to the windshield. The technology would give automatic access to parking areas and would also log the use of the space for particular games.[42]

Having various marketing partners offer benefits to cardholders would appear to be an appropriate extension of their use. Benefits could be whatever the sponsor wished to offer at a particular time and would be an opportunity to drive business to a corporate partner's locale.

As a final example of the use of bar coding, the sport organization could create an awards program, similar to the airlines' frequent flier programs, to reward use of the card. Each purchase could be rewarded with points that could be redeemed for prizes directly at the organization Web site. Premiums such as merchandise, apparel, travel, additional tickets, and everyday services of the organization's marketing partners could be awarded as amenities for using the fan's card.[43]

Webcasts

One of the current unanswered questions about the evolution of sport organization Web sites is whether sport fans will use their computers to view sport events. As technology improves, undoubtedly they will. Hiestand suggests that the economics of television-rights fees will for the foreseeable future prevent live webcasts of major sport events.[44] However, individual sport organizations that control the rights to their own games are currently exploring the capabilities of the technology.

Niche sports, which typically would not draw the interest of TV audiences in large enough numbers to justify live coverage, have in webcasting an opportunity to draw audiences to their events. The 2000 Paralympics in Sydney was one of the first major world sport events to experiment with live webcasting. There were 12 hours a day of live coverage for the duration of the games. This is in contrast to the coverage the Paralympics received in 1996, when they were televised in the United States for a mere 4 hours on CBS and for 9 hours on regional cable TV. Organizations wishing to promote sport events that will never make traditional TV can use webcasting to provide fans the opportunity to both listen to and watch a sport or event. The desire of sport sponsors to reach more specific target audiences associated with niche or

NBA.com TV Daily is a global video service showing updates and game highlights.

regional sports, such as lacrosse, will give sport organizations the opportunity to create sponsorship packages that will cover the costs of webcasting.

Glasgow Celtic used webcasting for a UEFA Cup match against AS La Jeunesse D'Esch in August 2000. The webcast was on the Celtic Web site (**www.celticfc.co.uk**) and was offered free of charge to about 15,000 users.[45] Although this initial experiment was free to Celtic fans, sport promotion specialists will undoubtedly recognize the potential of generating income from such webcasting.

English Premiership soccer teams appear to believe that the development of broadband technology will allow the webcasting of games of sufficiently high quality within the next few years. A number of teams—Liverpool, Chelsea, and Leicester City—have formed alliances with media companies that will allow the delivery of games via broadband technology. Liverpool has created a joint venture with Granada Media called Liverpool FC Broadband, which will offer clips of games and goals across all digital platforms once the next Premier League media contract comes into force in 2001-2002. The rationale behind the venture is the uniting of the content of the sport organization, Liverpool FC, and the technology of Granada Media. The intent of the venture is to appeal to Liverpool fans worldwide, who, through use of the portal, will create an added revenue stream for the sport organization.[46]

Many anticipate that once the latest contract for television rights to the English Premiership runs out, in 2004, individual clubs will attempt to retain the right to show pay-per-view games over the Internet. Analysts estimate that about 30% of U.S. Internet users will have broadband access by 2002, with European take-up not far behind. When pay-per-view games of sufficient quality are available on the Web, the benefits for clubs with strong global brands and a worldwide fan base, as well as their media partners, will be limitless.[47]

This scenario raises very interesting questions for leagues and their collective bargaining structure of media rights. With high-quality video streaming available to millions around the globe, the stakes will be so high that the allegiance of many clubs to the collective ethos of various leagues may come under severe strain.

Another development currently under way is wireless application protocol (WAP) technology. A likely consequence, it appears, is that many will be conducting e-business transactions on a mobile device by 2004. As mobile Internet penetration grows, so too will m-commerce (mobile phone commerce). Indeed, some suggest that m-commerce will far outstrip e-commerce in terms of the amount of commercial activity generated.[48]

Globally, mobile phone users outnumber desktop PCs. There are about 380 million mobile phone users, compared to 200 million PCs; and by 2003, the number of mobile phone users is expected to reach at least 1 billion, or one out of every six people on the planet. This is a huge user base, and mobile telephony creates a gigantic platform for communication, a platform that is growing exponentially.[49] If we consider the opportunity to access a sport organization's broadband Web site and view a game or highlights of an event via a WAP mobile phone, the opportunities for sport promotion specialists would appear to be unlimited.

Postgame Wrap-Up

Notwithstanding the implosion of many Web-based enterprises, the WWW is going to continue to grow in importance as a means of promotion. The critical point for sport promotion specialists to understand is that what is going to continuously draw people to an organization's site is content. Failure to maintain fresh, timely, well-delivered content will not make a site "sticky"; indeed it will make a site decidedly "unsticky" and incapable of attracting visits. This will reduce the organization's ability to create potential revenue streams.

The development of technology will allow promotion specialists to offer personalized products such as the proposed "MySportsCenter." This will be an online package of the day's sport highlights tailored to each user's interests and favorite team.[50] While such an idea may currently sound farfetched to those who promote sport, because ESPN.com is the standard by which sport sites are judged, ESPN.com's cutting-edge developments can be expected to migrate to other sites in the modern-day term for a New York minute, warp time.

Discussion Items

1. Discuss the importance of Migala's 5 Cs when one is developing a Web presence for a sport organization. Are there other items that might be added to these five?

2. Explain what significant advantage ESPN.com has over many other sport sites in terms of its ability to generate traffic.

3. What forms of technology, aside from those discussed in chapter 12, could be used by sport promotion specialists to promote their sport products?

Learning Enrichment Activities

1. Write a short essay on the issue of Web site privacy based on the privacy policy of the San Francisco Giants that you find at their Web site: **www.sfgiants.com/ home/privacy.cfm**.

2. Compare the Web presence of three major sport professional franchises from three different continents. What are the significant differences among the three?

3. Examine the Web presence of three voluntary sport organizations and observe how their Web use may differ from that of the professional franchises.

13

Managing Risk in Sport Promotion and Sales

Glenn Wong, Professor, Department of Sport Management, University of Massachusetts at Amherst

chapter objectives

1. Gain a basic knowledge of how the world of sport intersects with contract law, tort law, and intellectual property law

2. Gain insight into drafting contracts, protecting the organization against tort liability, and protecting the organization's copyrighted materials

3. Become familiar with the strategies for developing solid risk management programs

Pregame Introductions

It is important for sport promotion specialists to be aware of the legal implications of their actions in order to shield themselves and their organizations from liability that can result from promotional activities. It is of particular benefit for sport promotion specialists to have a sound working knowledge of contract law, tort law, and intellectual property law because they work within the boundaries of these laws every day.

For example, consider the following scenario in terms of *contract law.* It's the night before the big outdoor celebrity basketball tournament that you have spent the entire year planning. You are lying in bed, going over your mental checklist of items that have been taken care of. The courts have been laid out, the 3-point lines have been painted, and referees have been scheduled for every game. It seems as though everything is in place. However, haunting thoughts are running through your head—have you covered all of your bases? What if there is an exposed metal pole near a court that you did not account for? If someone in one of the games hustles after a ball that is going out of bounds, is unable to stop her momentum, and punctures a lung hitting the exposed pole, can you held be liable for the medical bills, pain, and suffering? You did make all of the participants sign a waiver and release of liability, but will this stand up in a court if they sue you?

Contract law and tort law might sometimes seem to overlap. But as a sport promotion specialist you might encounter *tort law* in certain types of situations. For example, say you have employed a mascot to entertain at your team's baseball games. The mascot is doing one of its typical zany tricks in the stands when it falls backward from one row to another and subsequently strikes a spectator in the back, causing severe spinal damage. Are you, as the representative of the baseball organization, liable for the actions of the mascot?

A sport promotion specialist is also likely to face *intellectual property* issues. As an example, suppose you have just started a Web site for your sport organization and have included a great deal of information and material that is not copyrighted. What do you do if someone is taking information off your site and using it for her own personal site? Do you have legal recourse against this individual if you did not give the person **consent** to use the information? How do you go about copyrighting information that is on your Web site?

These examples may sound farfetched, but the situations they illustrate are part of the reality of sport promotion. In this chapter we will consider the topics illustrated by these examples. For legal novices, each section begins with a brief introduction and then defines relevant legal principles to provide a basic knowledge of important terms. Each section presents actual cases and contracts from sport settings that apply specifically to the sport promotion specialist. It is vital to note that this chapter is not meant to provide legal advice, but rather to give an overview of some of the legal issues facing sport promotion specialists. Within an organizational setting, sport promotion specialists may end up working with in-house counsel, outside counsel, or both. But in all situations a basic knowledge of legal principles will prove beneficial.

Contracts

Drafting and reviewing contracts are a common part of the sport promotion specialist's job. Contracts come into play in dealings with a variety of parties, such as vendors, mascots, television or radio broadcast networks, officials, contest participants, venue owners and management, and insurance brokers.

Are Contracts Necessary?

Historically, many sport business contracts were oral rather than written. A handshake and someone's "word" were enough for management. As the revenues involved in sport have increased and disputes have arisen, however, the need for traditional written contracts has increased as well. The big business of modern sport requires that many agreements be finalized in writing so there are no ambiguities in the arrangement. For the sport promotion specialist, written contracts have several advantages. With a written contract, both parties can be more certain about the specific terms, so there is little room for disputes over the responsibilities of each person involved in the contract.

Although some contracts remain less formal, initiated by a handshake or a letter, the trend in sport is toward formal written contracts. Depending on the circumstances, a contract may be oral, informal, or formal. It is important to note, though, that although oral contracts are as enforceable as written contracts (in some cases), the lack of written material makes the existence of these contracts more difficult to prove. Therefore, when people enter into an unwritten contract, it is recommended that each side employ witnesses to verify the validity of the contract.

Despite the obvious advantages of employing contracts, there are also disadvantages to always requiring a contract in business. Drafting contracts and making sure that all pertinent information has been covered make for a time-consuming process, and enlisting the expertise of an attorney who can ensure that the contract is a sound document is an added cost. Also, some attorneys may not be familiar with the sport world. While conducting business with a large corporation, for example, you may be dealing with corporate attorneys who are not aware of some of the unique aspects of sport law. Any of these factors may increase the time it takes to finalize a written contract.

It is part of the sport promotion specialist's duties to consider the situation at hand, the industry practice, and costs and time frame, along with other factors, in deciding whether to use a written or an unwritten contract. But it is in everyone's best interest to make certain that a contract is formed.

Basic Legal Principles of Contract Law

To truly understand how contracts affect a sporting event, you must have a basic understanding of relevant legal principles in contract law. The following are some common terms that you should be familiar with when entering into contract negotiations:

• *Offer and acceptance.* These two terms are the building blocks of the contract. The offer is the promise that is made by one person to another, and the acceptance is the agreement by both parties to the terms of the contract.[1]

- *Legality.* For a contract to be enforceable it cannot violate public policy. For example, contracts cannot completely waive tort liability (to be discussed in the section on torts), and most contracts that violate statutes are not enforceable under the law. Examples of these contracts are gambling contracts, contracts with unlicensed professionals, and agreements made with loan sharks that violate laws regulating consumer credit transactions.[2]

- *Capacity.* This is the ability of a person to understand the nature and effect of his acts. The general rule for **capacity** is that anyone who has reached the age of 18 is considered capable enough to enter into a contract. Therefore, it is important in signing a contract to know that each party involved is of legal age or has a representative of legal age to sign the contract. Also, contracts entered into by people who are considered mentally incompetent are generally not enforceable. The same holds for people who are too incapacitated by drugs or alcohol to be able to understand the effects of their actions.[3]

- *The statute of frauds.* This statute requires that certain types of contracts be in writing. For example, contracts involving land interests such as mortgages and sales are subject to the statute of frauds and must be in writing. Also, it's important for sport promotion specialists to know that any contract that will not be fulfilled within a year after its making (e.g., game contracts, coaches' contracts) must be in writing as well.[4]

- *Breach of contract.* Breach of contract means the failure to perform the duty that is expressed in the contract. If a contract is totally breached by one party, then the wronged party has no obligation to fulfill the contract and should immediately seek legal remedy.[5]

Contract Questions and Problems for the Sport Promotion Specialist

Although part of the purpose of a contract is to reduce the possibility for disputes, there are many everyday situations in which sport promotion specialists may face contractual issues. The following sections deal with two types of situations that involve contracts—employment and promotional incentives.

Employment Contracts

In the course of their work, most sport promotion specialists employ people, whether temporary staff for one-day promotions, outside contractors or consultants to work on a day-by-day or project-by-project basis, or full-time sales staff. For the purposes of this chapter we'll focus on two types of hires—employees and independent contractors. We will also consider contract issues relating to the use of volunteers.

Employees   Employees under the direction of the sport promotion specialist might be a diverse group, including mascots, spirit group members, promotional assistants, and members of the sales staff. Sport promotion specialists should be aware of the special duties that arise within an employer-employee relationship. Regardless of the position of the employee, it is important to pay careful attention to the details of the person's employment contract.

For example, consider the details you would have to attend to in a contract with a mascot. Mascots are usually employees of an organization, and you must be aware of the issues that can arise if a mascot's contract is unclear and ambiguous. For example, can a team require a mascot to perform outside of the stadium or arena? Because of the promotional appeal of mascots and their role as ambassadors for teams, should they receive extra compensation for these appearances, or is this part of their contract?

Is the mascot permitted to accept invitations to perform at functions not sponsored by the organization? It is important to consider such questions when working with all types of employee contracts. It is these kinds of specific questions the contract must answer in order to head off difficult situations and protect the sport organization.

Independent contractors   If an organization is running one-time events such as one-day promotions, it will often employ hired talent. Whether it's the Famous Chicken, the Phillie Phanatic, or the singer of the national anthem, these people are likely to be considered **independent contractors** of the organization rather than employees. An independent contractor is someone who is hired by an employer but who is contracted to perform work according to his own way of doing things and is not subject to the control of the employer except in terms of the result of the work. Generally, an employer is not held liable for the actions of an independent contractor. Think back to the example earlier in the chapter of a mascot's accidentally injuring a spectator. If that mascot is not an employee, but an independent contractor brought in for one day, the organization that hired the mascot will most likely *not* be held liable for the mascot's actions. However, if the mascot is a full-time employee of the organization, the parent organization can be held liable for her actions through the doctrine of **vicarious liability.** This doctrine imposes liability for an act upon an individual who is not personally negligent but is held liable because of the relationship between the two parties.[6] The employer-employee relationship is an example of this type of relationship. Therefore, it is important that a contract make clear whether a person is an employee or an independent contractor. (This differentiation will be discussed further in the torts section of the chapter.) Figure 13.1 shows a portion of an endorsement contract between a coach and a head-wear company. Note clause 7.8, which explicitly states the relationship between the parties as that of employer and independent contractor (figure 13.1).[7]

Star players and entertainers may also be hired as independent contractors. At times sport promotion specialists are not able to control the actions of their star players or entertainers; it is not uncommon for top talent not to show up for an event. If your celebrity guest does not appear and the spectators want a refund, what recourse do you have?

Again, the answer comes back to the contract. Several different kinds of stipulations can be written into the contract between the organization and the hired talent to ensure the financial well-being of the organization in the case of a mass refund. First, sport promotion specialists can insist that entertainers remit a nonrefundable deposit to ensure that they will show up at the event. The deposit acts as a deterrent to cancellation. Another option is to insist that the talent be liable for any damages that the organization incurs such as money spent on advertising, tickets, and vending. A third option is to require the talent to post a performance bond, which ensures that the individual will arrive to perform. Some entertainers (especially more popular figures) may balk at any of these options, however. An alternative in this case is to take out insurance on the event; this protects the organization for everything from event cancellation caused by "acts of God" such as hurricanes to nonperformance of the talent.

Volunteers   Often organizations holding large events depend on a significant number of volunteers to ensure that an event runs smoothly. Taking on many volunteers, however, can pose an enormous risk to the organization. It is imperative for the sport promotion specialist to make sure that all volunteers sign a waiver and release of liability before they begin work. This waiver should protect the organization from any accident that may occur to the volunteer. **Waivers and releases of liability** may not always be upheld by the courts, however (this issue is discussed in the section on torts).

7. <u>MISCELLANEOUS PROVISIONS</u>:

7.1 <u>Termination</u>: This Agreement shall terminate on the earliest of the end of the Term as set forth herein; or the date the Coach ceases to be the Coach at the herein above-named school/college/university; or Company no longer manufactures the Endorsed Goods.

7.2 <u>Full Power</u>: Coach represents that he has the full right and power to enter into this Agreement and perform all obligations granted without violating the legal or equitable rights of any other person or party.

7.3 <u>Waiver</u>: The failure of any party hereto to exercise the rights granted it herein upon the occurrence of any of the contingencies set forth in this Agreement shall not in any event constitute a waiver of any such rights upon the occurrence of any additional such contingencies.

7.4 <u>Confidential Information</u>: Company may, from time to time, communicate to Coach certain information to enable Coach to effectively perform his services as provided herein. Coach shall treat all such information as confidential, whether or not so identified, and shall not disclose any part thereof without the prior written consent of Company. The foregoing obligations of this paragraph, however, shall not apply to any part of the information that: (i) has been disclosed in publicly available sources of information: (ii) is, through no fault of Coach, hereafter disclosed in publicly available source of information.

7.5 <u>Entire Understanding</u>: This Agreement constitutes the entire understanding between the parties hereto with respect to the subject matter of this Agreement and supersedes all prior agreements whether written or oral. No waiver, modification, or addition to this Agreement shall be valid unless made in writing and signed by the parties hereto.

7.6 <u>Law Governing</u>: This Agreement shall be governed by and construed in accordance with the laws of the State of Tennessee applicable to contracts entered into and preformed entirely therein and all parties agree and consent that jurisdiction and venue of all matters relating to this Agreement, except those commenced by third parties, shall be vested exclusively in the federal, state, and local courts of the State of Tennessee.

7.7 <u>Severability</u>: In the event any provisions of this Agreement is determined to be invalid by a court of competent jurisdiction, such determination shall in no way affect the validity of enforceability of any other provision herein.

7.8 <u>Independent Status</u>: This Agreement does not constitute and shall not be construed as constituting a partnership or joint venture, or an employee-employer relationship or one of principal and agent, it being understood that the parties are and shall remain independent contractors in all respects.

7.9 <u>Assignment</u>: Nothing herein shall prevent Coach from assigning the monetary benefits of this agreement as he may desire. Neither party may assign this Agreement without the prior written consent of the other party except that Company may assign same in the event of a consolidation or merger of Company into or with another person, firm, association or other form of business entity (collectively "person"), or reorganization of sale of all or Company to another person, provided such person assumes and agrees in writing to keep and perform all the obligations of Company hereunder, in which event Company shall be relieved of all such obligation.

7.10 <u>Headings</u>: Paragraph headings are used solely for convenience and are not intended nor in any sense are to be given any weight in the construction of this Agreement, i.e., construction is to be as if headings were not present.

7.11 <u>Counterparts</u>: This Agreement may be executed concurrently in one or more counterparts, each of which shall be an original, but all of which together shall constitute one and the same instrument. This Agreement shall not be binding upon Company until executed by authorized officer thereof.

Figure 13.1 The independent nature of the contracted relationship is described under "Miscellaneous Provisions" in this endorsement contract.

Reprinted, by permission, from M.J. Greenberg and J.T. Gray, *Miscellaneous provisions*, 1998, (Newark, NJ: Lexus Law Publishing), 448-449. Copyright © Lexis Nexis.

Therefore, you should not rely on only waivers and releases of liability, but should make sure that volunteers are properly trained; are assigned tasks commensurate with their skills, knowledge, and physical capabilities; and are properly supervised.

Are Advertisements Considered Contracts?

Apart from the clauses that can be included in a contract, the organization can protect itself in the case of a cancellation through the way it advertises. Advertisements must be worded so as not to leave the organization liable for damages if an event is canceled. All advertisements, whether on the radio, on television, or in print, should use the words "Scheduled to appear" rather than "Will appear." The first phrase enables the organization to declare that although the talent was scheduled to appear, there was never a guarantee.

Advertisements have generally not been viewed by the courts as an offer to enter into a contract, but it is still imperative that sport organizations protect themselves against liability that they may encounter as a consequence of an advertisement. Suppose, for example, that the Boston Red Sox decide to put on a promotion night at which they will give out free plush stuffed bears to the first 25,000 spectators to arrive at the game. The 25,001st person shows up, does not receive a stuffed bear, and demands one because he thought he was guaranteed a bear when he bought the ticket. The Red Sox are safe from litigation on a breach of contract claim, even if they advertised the giveaway. A giveaway is not considered a legal offer like one that is part of a standard contract, so the Red Sox are not forced to provide the spectator with the bear. Still, if only for public relations purposes, it would be advantageous for the Red Sox to specify in all of their advertisements that only 25,000 items are available, on a first-come, first-serve basis.

Contracts Should Be Airtight

Often, a contract stays in the file cabinet when things are going well. However, when things are not going well, or incidents occur, the contract is usually pulled out to be reexamined. Whether because a promotional item is of poor quality, because the talent doesn't show up, or even because a mascot isn't funny, people wish to be released from their contracts in many different types of situations. As a sport promotion specialist you must prepare all documents so that you are protected against people's attempts to break contracts. Broken contracts will undoubtedly cause a loss of profits for your organization.

The following case study provides an excellent example of why it is important to keep contracts airtight. The season ticket holder in this case wanted to be released from his club seat contract because of financial difficulties, among other reasons. The case study presents excerpts from an article dealing with this case to demonstrate the importance of a clear and complete contract.

CASE STUDY: PREMIUM SEATING

What does every stadium and arena built in the last 10 years have in common? Every one has some sort of premium or preferred seating. Premium seats may be in a luxury box or suite, or they may be located in a section that entitles ticket holders to receive amenities such as waiter service, special parking privileges, and access to special restaurants inside the facility.

Many facility owners and/or sports promotion specialists require premium-seat ticket holders to agree to a multi-year contract, with agreements made in writing in the form of a lengthy contract or license agreement. However, a number of luxury box or suite holders have

(continued)

(continued) tried to wriggle out of their agreements using a variety of arguments, while facility owners and operators in these circumstances have held fast in defense of the validity of such contracts. Most of these cases have been handled outside of the courts, and while some have been resolved by quiet compromise, others have seen facility owners and promoters take a hard stand. When they do, most suite holders throw in the towel, recognizing just how expensive it can be to fight a major corporation with deep pockets.

New Boston Garden Corporation (NBGC), which owns Boston's FleetCenter, recently came up against a fan who wouldn't back down. In what may be the first court ruling on premium-seat issues, two Massachusetts courts, in *New Boston Garden Corporation v. Baker* (Mass. Super.1999), upheld both the validity of the contract and NBGC's entire request for damages. If Gary K. Baker, the fan in question, had been successful with his arguments, there would have been the potential for diminishing this important income stream.

Club Seat holders are required to sign a "Club Seat License Agreement," an 18-page contract. Baker signed up for the required three-year package, agreeing to pay $18,000 per year, but stopped paying after the first year; he had marital problems, his son was diagnosed with cancer and the teams, especially the Celtics, were not championship contenders.

NBGC sued Baker for breach of contract. In filing a motion for summary judgment, NBGC essentially was requesting that the judge decide the case in favor of the corporation before a trial, since the evidence was so clearly in support of its position. Judge Fremont-Smith agreed and found that Baker had breached his contract with NBGC.

As oftentimes happens, a person who wants to get out of a contract will attack the validity of the contract. In this case, the court found that NBGC met all four requirements to establish a breach-of-contract claim:

1. An agreement was made between NBGC and the fan that was supported by valuable consideration (in other words, Baker received the seat license in exchange for money);

2. NBGC has been ready, willing, and able to perform (NBGC lived up to its end of the contract);

3. The fan's breach prevented NBGC from performing (Baker did not hold up his end); and

4. NBGC was damaged as a result.

This case is an important one for sport promotion specialists, and facility owners, operators, and developers. Fans who are sometimes caught up in their enthusiasm for a team must realize that they are entering into a hefty financial commitment, and a contract that the courts may uphold. Fans should also realize that these contracts make no representations or warranties that the team (or teams) will be of championship quality, exciting, or even fun to watch. The drafters of the documents must realize that their contracts are likely to be challenged, and that the contracts must withstand any and all legal challenges. The fan in this case made many interesting and creative arguments challenging the validity of NBGC's contract, and one can expect a jury to be predisposed to give a fan (and not the corporation that drafts the contract) the benefit of the doubt in any matters of ambiguity.[8]

Reprinted, by permission, from G. Wong, 2000, "Sit down strike: The validity of an arena's club seat license agreement is upheld," *Athletic Business* 24 (1):22.

As you can see from this case study, it is critical that sport promotion specialists consider all probabilities when they are drafting a contract. People often want to be let out of their contracts when the contracts are no longer convenient. Figure 13.2 presents excerpts from the actual licensing agreement between the club seat owner and the NBGC. Note the explicit mention of payment terms in sections 3.04 and 11.02.

CLUB SEAT LICENSE AGREEMENT

License Agreement (the "Agreement") made as of the date set forth on the Executive Summary attached hereto and made a part hereof by and between New Boston Garden Corporation (the "Owner") and American Specialty Underwriters ("Licensee").

Agreement

In consideration of the mutual promises, covenants and undertakings contained herein and for good and other valuable consideration, the receipt and sufficiency of which are hereby mutually acknowledged by the parties hereto, the Owner and the Licensee hereby agree as follows.

1. <u>License</u>. The Owner hereby grants the Licensee a license to use the Club Seats in the proposed New Boston Garden (the "Arena") designated on the Executive Summary and shown on the plan attached hereto as <u>Exhibit A</u>. The number of seats is set forth on the Executive Summary. The Owner in the exercise of its reasonable discretion may redesign or reconfigure the Arena or the Club Seats provided that the final location and design of the Club Seats are similar to that presently proposed.

2. <u>Term</u>. The term of the Agreement (the "Term") shall commence with the first Game or Event (as defined in Paragraph 4.03) following the issuance of a certificate of occupancy for the Arena and the substantial completion of the Owner's construction obligations under Section 8 hereof (the "Commencement Date"). The Term shall end after the last Game of Event (as defined in Paragraph 4.03) in the last year of the Agreement, as set forth on the Executive Summary. As used in this Agreement the term "License Year" means the twelve calendar months beginning on September 1 of a given calendar year and ending on the next August 31, which period is wholly or partially within the Term.

3. <u>Fees/Taxes/Payment</u>. The Licensee shall pay fees for the use of the Club Seats pursuant to this Agreement in accordance with this Section 3.

3.01 <u>Fees</u>. The Licensee shall pay fees in accordance with this Paragraph 3.01.

(a) The Licensee shall pay an annual fee (the "Annual Fee") for the use of the Club Seats, in the amount set forth in the Executive Summary and on <u>Exhibit B</u>. The Annual Fee shall be comprised of a Licensee Fee (as set forth on Exhibit B), a Base Club Seat Ticket Fee (as defined in Subparagraph 3.01(c)) and, if applicable, a Base Parking Fee (as defined in Section 7). The Annual Fee for each License Year shall be payable as set forth in the Executive Summary such that (i) the License Fee and the regular season portions of the Base Club Seat Ticket Fee and Base Parking Fee shall be paid on or before the first day of July immediately prior to such License Year and (ii) the playoff portions of the Base Club Seat Ticket Fee and Base Parking Fee shall be paid immediately upon invoicing by the Owner, but in any event not later than one month before the conclusion of the regular seasons of the respective teams for that License Year.

3.02 <u>Additional Taxes or Fees</u>. The Licensee shall pay, as an additional fee under this Agreement, any and all taxes or Fees or any fines and penalties assessed thereon for late payment, that may be assessed by any federal, state or local governmental authority with respect to this Agreement, admission to or the use of the Club Seats, any personal property of the Licensee located therein, any alteration or repair of the Club Seats, the licensing, use, or occupancy of the Club Seats, or the Security Deposit or the Annual Fee or the payment or receipt of either or both. The Licensee shall pay such taxes or fees in full within ten (10) days after receipt of the Owner's invoice thereof, if billed by Owner, or prior to delinquency, if billed directly by a governmental authority. Nothing contained in this Agreement shall require the Licensee to pay any franchise, corporate, estate, inheritance, successions, or transfer tax of the Owner, or any income, profits, or revenue tax or change upon the income of the Owner, or any real estate taxes and assessments on the Arena.

(continued)

Figure 13.2 Club seat license agreement for the FleetCenter in Boston (New Boston Garden Corporation).

3.03 Security Deposit. Upon execution of this Agreement the Licensee has paid a security deposit (the "Security Deposit") in the amount set forth on the Executive Summary. At the end of the Term the Security Deposit will be returned to the Licensee less the cost of any damage to the Club Seat or the Preferred Seating Area, reasonable wear and tear excepted. If this Agreement is terminated by the Owner due to a default by the Licensee, the Owner shall be under no obligation to refund the Security Deposit, but may retain it against damages incurred by the Owner as the result of such default and termination.

3.04 Payment. All charges and amounts to be paid to the Owner pursuant to this Agreement, including but not limited to the changes and amounts set forth in this Section (collectively, the "Fees"), shall be paid as provided in this Agreement, without deduction, offset, prior notice or demand. The Fees shall be paid to the Owner at the address of the Owner's representative set forth on the Executive Summary or at such other place or to such other person as the Owner may from time to time designate by notice given in accordance with this Agreement. All payments shall be in lawful money of the United States of America in immediately available funds or check drawn on a bank located within the continental United States.

11.02 Events of Default. The occurrence of any of the following events shall constitute a "default" by the Licensee: the failure to pay any Fees or other sums when due and payable hereunder, if the failure shall continue for ten (10) days after written notice thereof; the failure to comply with or perform under any of the other provisions hereof, including the provisions of the Club Seat Regulations, if such failure is not cured within thirty (30) days after notice by the Owner to the Licensee, or if such cure cannot reasonably be accomplished within thirty (30) days, such longer period as shall be reasonably necessary and continuously prosecutes the same to completion; if the Licensee seeks relief voluntarily or is subjected involuntarily to relief under any federal or state law for the benefit of creditors such as debt adjustments, liquidation, winding up, dissolution, reorganization or bankruptcy; or as a custodian (as defined in 11 U.S.C. Section 101), receiver or liquidator takes charge of any of the Licensee's property, whether by judicial appointment, agreement or operation of law.

Figure 13.2 *(continued)*

Reprinted, by permission, from the New Boston Garden Corporation.

Contracts Involved in Incentives

As discussed in chapter 3, the use of incentives to drive fans to sporting events is a recent trend in sport promotion. The prizes for winners of contests involving such feats as half-court shots, field goals, or long-range putts, for example, are usually large. Many sport promotion specialists take out an insurance policy for these types of events so that if someone wins, the prize money will not have to come directly from the organization's pocket. Instead, if the prize is $1 million, for example, the sport organization may choose to take out an insurance policy that costs only $10,000. An example of this type of insurance coverage is found in figure 13.3. While the coverage relates to a charity golf tournament, the basic elements are the same. Coverage rates are based on the contest participants and degree of difficulty (e.g., yardage).

With contracts relating to large prize incentives, the sport promotion specialist must pay special attention to all the contract language and be certain that she has carefully reviewed even the most minute details. It is critical that these types of contracts state explicitly how the contest will be run. If any ambiguity exists about how a contest is run, the organization leaves itself open to having the insurance company refuse to pay the claim. Another critical element in promotional contracts is a clause involving exclusion. For example, in a half-court shot contest, this clause should state that participants cannot have ever participated in college or professional

ACECO HOLE-IN-ONE INSURANCE PROGRAM

1655 Lafayette Street, Suite 200 Denver, Colorado 80218 Phone: (888) 422-3264 Fax: (303) 322-0557

July 26, 2000

Gossett Volkswagen
1901 Covington Pike
Memphis, TN 38128

<u>Important Information Concerning Your Insured Golf Tournament</u>

Dear Customer:

Thank you for doing business with us. We hope your golf tournament is a huge success. Please read the following Confirmation of Coverage very carefully. You must make certain that the golf tournament complies with all of our terms and conditions to avoid any problems in the event a hole-in-one should occur.

Below are a few things you can do to help avoid problems:

1. POSITIONING OF TEE BLOCKS: Call the golf course pro or director of golf to make sure the pro shop and maintenance crew understands where the tee blocks are to be positioned at the target and bonus holes. Sometimes the course will be shortened for tournaments to help speed up play. This can cause problems if the hole-in-one target and/or bonus holes are inadvertently shortened.

2. WITNESS REQUIREMENTS: It is your responsibility to provide two (2) non-playing adults to supervise the target hole(s) if the prize value is greater than $25,000. One (1) non-playing witness is required if the prize value is less than, or equal to, $25,000. No non-playing witnesses are required at the bonus hole(s); however, other players in the group will be considered witnesses. If you fail to provide witnesses where required, this contract instantly becomes null and void. Make sure that the witnesses are stationed in a position to see both the tee area and the base of the pin. This is especially important when the green is elevated. In the event of a hole-in-one, witnesses will be asked by our claims adjuster to describe the entire shot. The club pro should be able to help position the witnesses.

3. REPORTING OF CLAIMS: In the event of a claim, we must be notified no later than the next business day after the tournament. You agree to cooperate fully with us (or an appointed claims adjuster, as the case may be) while investigating the claim. You agree to provide us with the following documentation as may be requested:

   Target Hole: Signed scorecard, tournament pairing sheet, witness account, and newspaper clipping (when available).

   Bonus Hole: Signed scorecard and witness account of other player(s).

4. PREMIUM ADJUSTMENTS: The Premium charged is based on the yardage of the hole, number of attempts, and the prize value. Changes in any of these may affect your premium and should be reported to us prior to the tournament.

Thanks again for your business. A pre-printed tournament application is attached to simplify your next event. Please feel free to contact us at the number above should you have any questions regarding your insurance coverage.

Page 1 of 2

(continued)

Figure 13.3 Insurance coverage is commonly used to guard against loss resulting from promotion contests.

ACECO HOLE-IN-ONE INSURANCE PROGRAM

1655 Lafayette Street, Suite 200 Denver, Colorado 80218 Phone: (888) 422-3264 Fax: (303) 322-0557

Confirmation of Coverage

We are in receipt of your signed quote sheet. Thank you very much for your support of the ACECO hole-in-one insurance program. This document confirms insurance coverage for your tournament. If you would like to receive a copy of your insurance policy or if you have any questions regarding the confirmation of coverage, please contact us at the telephone number above.

Insured: Gossett Volkswagen   Policy #: H1AHO11469

Contact: _____ Phone: _____ Fax: _____

Tournament Name: Powertel AxA Liberty Bowl Golf Classic

Tournament Date(s): 8/1/00   Rain Date(s) (if any): n/a

Golf Course: Colonial Golf Course/South Course   City/State: TN

Attempts: Amateur 280   Pro 0

Target Hole # 5   Yardage: Men 165   Women 140   Pro _____   Prize Value: $19,500

Bonus Hole # _____ Yardage: Men _____ Women _____ Pro _____ Prize: _____

Bonus Hole # _____ Yardage: Men _____ Women _____ Pro _____ Prize: _____

Bonus Hole # _____ Yardage: Men _____ Women _____ Pro _____ Prize: _____

Basic Premium: $ 580

Bonus Premium: $ 0

Signage $ 0

Shipping $ 0

TOTAL DUE $ 580   *If paying by check, please make check payable to ACECO.*

Sign Order Confirmation

Target Hole Signage   Bonus Hole Signage

18" × 24" Magnetic   _____   Caribbean Cruise   _____

18" × 24" Caroplast   _____   Las Vegas Getaway   _____

24" × 48" Coroplast   _____   PING Irons   _____

                                             $500 Golf Shop Credit _____

                                             $500 Cash   _____

You should expect your signs to be delivered on or about _____

We have sent your signs to : _____

_____

_____

July 26, 2000   *Page 2 of 2*

Figure 13.3   *(continued)*

ACECO

1655 Lafayette Street, Suite 200 Denver, Colorado 80218 Phone: (888) 422-3264 Fax: (303) 322-0557

HOLE-IN-ONE AGREEMENT

PAYMENT: Premium must be postmarked to ACECO no later than the date of the event unless other billing arrangements have been made. Credit cards are accepted.

CONFIRMATION: ACECO'S CONFIRMATION OF COVERAGE will be sent via fax.

INSURED: Entity offering the hole-in-one prize. INSURED is reimbursed the PRIZE VALUE in the event of a winner. INSURED agrees to comply fully with all terms and conditions as detailed in this HOLE-IN-ONE AGREEMENT.

PRIZE VALUE: The stated PRIZE VALUE is the amount ACECO agrees to reimburse the INSURED in U.S. dollars in the event of a hole-in-one. The INSURED may include appropriate taxes and licensing fees if any. ACECO encourages INSUREDS to keep the PRIZE VALUE as close to actual cost as possible.

TARGET HOLE: Only one TARGET HOLE will be designated for each CONFIRMATION OF COVERAGE issued for each TOURNAMENT. The TARGET HOLE must be a par three hole on a regulation golf course. Constructed holes, temporary greens or modified par fours and par fives are not eligible for reimbursement unless so approved by ACECO in writing prior to the TOURNAMENT. Only one pre-designated cup may be used as the TARGET HOLE.

WITNESSES: It is the sole responsibility of the INSURED to provide two (2) non-playing adult WITNESSES, age 18 or older, to supervise the TARGET HOLE if the PRIZE VALUE is greater than $25,000. One (1) WITNESS is required if the PRIZE VALUE is less than, or equal to, $25,000. The WITNESS, or WITNESSES, must be in position to see both the teeing area and the base of the pin. In the event of a winner, each WITNESS will be asked to describe the entire SHOT. Bonus Prize holes do not require a WITNESS.

YARDAGE: United States Golf Association (USGA) permanent YARDAGE markers will be considered official YARDAGE at the TARGET HOLE for premium rating purposes. TOURNAMENT tee blocks are not to be moved closer to the TARGET HOLE than the permanent YARDAGE markers. Neither TARGET HOLE nor BONUS HOLE YARDAGES are to be less than 130 yards for men and 110 yards for women. At no time shall tee blocks be shorter than the yardage stated on the CONFIRMATION OF COVERAGE.

ATTEMPTS: An ATTEMPT is defined as a "stroke" by the USGA. Only one ATTEMPT per player per TARGET HOLE is permitted unless confirmed in writing by ACECO. No practice ATTEMPTS. "Mulligans" or substituted ATTEMPTS for other players are permitted. ATTEMPTS shall not exceed the number as stated on the INSURANCE POLICY. The number of ATTEMPTS may be adjusted up to the last business day before the TOURNAMENT. Under no circumstances will the number of ATTEMPTS be adjusted downward after conclusion of the TOURNAMENT.

ELIGIBILITY: To be eligible for reimbursement, a hole-in-one, (Ace), must occur by an officially registered TOURNAMENT contestant during a regulation round of golf.

MULTIPLE HOLES-IN-ONE: In the event multiple holes-in-one should occur at the designated TARGET HOLE, ACECO agrees to reimburse each hole-in-one that occurs, without limit.

CLAIM NOTIFICATION: In the event of a claim, ACECO must be notified no later than the next business day after the TOURNAMENT. The INSURED agrees to provide ACECO with appropriate documentation as may be requested. INSURED agrees to cooperate fully with ACECO or an appointed claims adjuster, as the case may be, while investigating the claim.

DISPUTED CLAIMS: In the event ACECO determines that a violation, or violations, of the INSURANCE POLICY occurred, the INSURED will have ample opportunity to respond before ACECO denies a claim. An arbitration committee of INSUREDS will review all circumstances and findings. It is important that each INSURED agree to abide by the ruling of the arbitration committee.

WEATHER: In the event a TOURNAMENT is canceled due to weather, ACECO agrees to reimburse the INSURED the premium or change the TOURNAMENT to another date without charge or penalty. ACECO must be notified via fax immediately if the TOURNAMENT DATE has been changed. Signage costs and shipping expenses will be absorbed by the Insured.

Figure 13.3 *(continued)*

Reprinted, by permission, from ACECO Hole-In-One Insurance.

basketball; or, if the contest is a 50-foot putt for $1 million, that the contestant cannot be a professional golfer.

Tort Liability

Sport promotion specialists are by no means immune to the impact of tort liability. When an individual has event management and game-day operations responsibilities, as well as supervisory capacity over mascots, cheerleaders, and other employees, he encounters potential tort law cases on a regular basis. In this section we consider various ways in which tort liability can affect the sport promotion specialist, as well as steps that can be taken to reduce, if not eliminate, liability.

Basic Legal Principles of Tort Law

As with contract law, it is important for sport promotion specialists to understand certain legal principles of tort law. The following are some basic terms relevant to tort liability:

- *Tort.* A tort is a private or civil wrong or injury, *other* than a breach of contract, suffered by an individual as the result of another person's conduct. Intentional acts to harm and the failure to exercise reasonable care are associated with tort law. However, most accidental acts are not usually considered to be torts unless one party can be considered negligent.[9]

- *Negligence.* This unintentional tort focuses on an individual's conduct or action. Negligent conduct is defined as that which falls below the standard established by the law for the protection of others against an unreasonably great risk of harm. Determining whether a person's actions constitute **negligence,** and proving that the person has actually been negligent, constitute a very complicated legal process.[10]

- *Assault and battery.* These are two common intentional torts whose meanings depend on whether the case is being tried in civil or criminal court. For the purposes of this chapter we focus on cases that occur in civil court. The major difference between the two torts relates to physical contact; in order for a crime to constitute battery, actual touching between the two parties must occur. With these torts, as with many intentional torts, it is not necessary for harm to have been done in order for the plaintiff to collect damages. The fact that a person has done and has intended to perform an action is sufficient to result in damages. The amount of damages collected generally depends on the amount of harm to the individual.[11]

- *Consent.* Consent is the voluntary yielding of one's will to another. It is an act of reason that is performed by an individual of mental capacity. Consent is an especially important concept for sport promotion specialists who use waivers and releases of liability.[12]

- *Privilege.* This is a limited benefit enjoyed by an individual or class that extends beyond the common advantages of other citizens. Acting in self-defense and defending one's own property are examples of situations in which privilege may be applicable.[13]

- *Immunity.* Immunity is a condition that protects against a tort action. This is a much debated area of the law that protects certain people or groups from negligence liability. Governmental agencies and representatives may claim that they are immune from negligence liability by employing the doctrine of sovereign immunity. Also, in some states, husbands engaging in acts against their wives, and parents disciplining their children, may be immune from being charged with an intentional tort.[14]

- *Reckless misconduct.* In its severity, the tort of reckless misconduct falls between assault and battery on the one hand and negligence on the other hand. In this tort there is intent on the part of the defendant to commit an act, but there is no intent to harm the plaintiff by the act. This type of tort is common in sport settings.[15]

- *Reasonable person standard.* This is the standard of care that most people are held accountable for in negligence cases. An individual is expected to exercise a reasonable degree of care when dealing with another person. However, if the individual possesses superior knowledge or skills, for example if she is a physician, then the person is held to the same degree of care as would be reasonable within their field of medicine.[16]

- *Standard of care for children.* Children are not held to the same standard as adults in negligence cases. Instead, they are held to the standard of care for children within their same age group.[17]

- *Contributory negligence.* Contributory negligence is an act of the *plaintiff* that amounts to a lack of ordinary care and contributes to the cause of the person's own injury. Defendants use this defense in negligence cases when they think that the plaintiff was acting recklessly when he was harmed.[18]

- *Comparative negligence.* This type of negligence refers to situations in which both the plaintiff and the defendant are negligent. The court seeks to divide the responsibility between the two parties. The judge or jury decides what percentage of the responsibility lies with each party, and damages are then awarded pro rata (proportionately).[19]

- *Assumption of risk.* This is an important term that all sport promotion specialists should understand. It signifies that a person has given consent to what would normally be an unpermitted, potentially injury-causing action. Frequently assumption of risk comes into the courts when one party is suing another over an injury that occurred during a game.[20]

- *Vicarious liability.* A person can be held liable for the negligent actions of another person depending on the relationship between them. For example, if employees are negligent in their actions, their company can be held liable as well. That is why, as was mentioned in the context of contracts, it is imperative to distinguish whether or not a person is an employee or an independent contractor.[21]

- *Waivers and releases of liability.* These are documents that are quite often used in a sport setting. Waivers and releases of liability are types of contracts that alter ordinary negligence principles of tort law. Waivers generally are attempts to release one party from liability for that party's own negligence.[22]

Tort Questions and Problems for the Sport Promotion Specialist

When dealing with various types of sport promotions, you as a sport promotion specialist must look to protect yourself from any tort liability. To be able to shield yourself, you should become familiar with scenarios in which you can be vulnerable to tort liability. Negligence is a tort that is often used to implicate sport organizations, and sport promotion specialists must know how to protect themselves from negligence liability. They should also be aware of the legal defenses available to them if, despite all precautions, they are accused of negligence.[23]

The most important concept to understand is that a risk management program should be in place from the beginning of any event. Whether for a single event or an entire season of games, sport promotion specialists need to have a **risk management** program in effect that will provide contingency plans for almost any possible scenario.

Am I Liable If Someone in the Stands Is Hit by a Ball?

In the case of *Lowe v. California League of Professional Baseball et al.* (1997)[24], a baseball organization was found liable when a fan was struck by a foul ball. However, the key element in this case was that the plaintiff was distracted by the team mascot immediately before he was hit. If the plaintiff, Lowe, had not been distracted by the mascot, could the team still have been found negligent? The answer to this question is generally no, but there are a limited number of exceptions.

The case of *Yates v. Chicago National League Ball Club, Inc.* (1992)[25] concerned a minor, Delbert Yates Jr., who was hit in the face by a foul ball at a Chicago Cubs game in 1983. As a result of the impact of the ball, Yates was taken to the hospital, underwent surgery on his face, and remained hospitalized for five days. At 90 days after surgery he continued to have headaches, and he seemed to be very socially withdrawn as compared to before the incident. The Yateses decided to sue the Cubs organization for negligence.

The Cubs alleged that Yates or his father or mother, who were at the game with him, should have been aware that the seat was not protected by the protective screen that stands behind home plate. When Yates Sr. had purchased his tickets he had requested tickets behind home plate, under the assumption that these seats would be protected by the screen. Yates alleged that the Cubs had failed to provide adequate screening behind home plate to ensure the safety of his family, and that the Cubs had failed to warn him so as to enable him to avoid the harm. The case was decided for the Yateses on both the trial and appellate court levels on the basis that the Cubs may not have provided an adequate amount of screening in the home plate area.

What does this case mean for you if you are a sport promotion specialist? It does *not* mean that you will definitely be held negligent for injuries that occur within your venue. Instead, it means that you must be careful to ensure the safety of spectators as part of your risk management program. Protective fences or netting should be sufficient to ensure that anyone who otherwise could be in immediate peril is always safe. Also, at least once a game, the public address announcer should alert the crowd that they should be ready at all times for errant throws, hits, passes, and so on that could land in the stands. The way to avoid incidents like the one in the preceding case is to make sure that all measures are taken to provide a safe environment for your spectators.

Am I Liable for Performance-Related Injuries?

One trend in sport marketing is to hire entertainers or daredevils to excite the crowd during pregame or half-time performances. Many of these programs have a very high risk factor. Whether it's someone parachuting into the stadium or someone in a gorilla suit flying down an aisle in a sled, these are acts that can render the organization susceptible to tort liability. Sport promotion specialists should be aware that a category of activities that can generally be labeled "dangerous activities" when booking these high-risk activities for an event.

As mentioned earlier, contracts must distinguish clearly between employees and independent contractors. At no time is this more applicable than when you are dealing with dangerous, high-risk stunts. When you hire entertainment to perform high-risk acts, it is crucial to sign the individual as an independent contractor. For example, you might want to hire a daredevil motorcycle act to appear at half-time in a football game. It is essential to have the performer sign a contract specifying that she is in no way considered to be an employee of the organization. Then if the daredevil were to injure someone in the crowd during a stunt, the organization usually could not be held liable. As noted in the discussion of contracts, employers may be held vicariously liable for the actions of employees, but generally not the actions of independent contractors.

However, the fact that the act is contracted independently does not mean that the organization is completely absolved from liability. If a spectator is injured by an act of an independent contractor, there are still two ways in which legal action could be brought against the organization. First, the injured person may claim that the sport promotion specialist was negligent in not conducting an adequate background check of the act. The sport promotion specialist should make sure that acts have not had prior problems such as causing injuries to spectators. Also, any act should have the proper amount of experience before being signed to perform. Don't hire a trapeze artist who hasn't been on the high wire many, many times!

Sport promotion specialists may also be held liable for the actions of an entertainer who injures a spectator when he should have foreseen the danger. Therefore, if a promotion specialist uses poor judgment and decides that a promotion is safe when it is not, he could be held liable for negligence.

There are ways in which you as a sport promotion specialist can protect yourself from liability when hiring an independent contractor. First, you can require all acts to have a personal insurance policy. If the entertainer is covered by insurance, the chances are decreased that the sport organization will have to pay damages if anyone is injured during the show (see figure 13.3 for an example insurance policy). Secondly, you should require that entertainers sign a waiver and release of liability. If an entertainer does so, it will be difficult for the individual to bring any legal action against the sport organization if she is injured (waivers and releases of liability are covered extensively later in this section).

Am I Responsible for Participants in Promotional Contests?

A recent trend in sport marketing is to conduct zany promotions during games to attract the attention of the crowd. However, the crazier these promotions become, the higher the risk for the participants. For example, promotions such as "dizzy bat races" and contests in which participants catch pop-ups from a pitching machine are common at baseball games. If participants are injured during such promotions, it is possible for the sport organization to be held liable. Therefore, if a promotion requires any physical activity, participants should be notified, and people with certain medical conditions (back or neck injuries, pregnancy, etc.) should not be allowed to participate. The sport promotion specialist should also outline any risks associated with these events to ensure that all participants are eligible and willing to participate.

How Can a Sport Promotion Specialist Affect Crowd Control?

Although the job of a sport promotion specialist usually seems removed from the issue of crowd security, certain promotions can have a tremendous impact on the crowd. Here we consider two different ways in which the sport promotion specialist can maintain control over the actions of a crowd during a game.

You might decide that you are going to send giveaway items into the stands. A recent trend in sport promotions has been to use large slingshots to shoot prizes deep into the upper decks. There are two things to be cautious about if you are performing this particular promotion. First, to avoid a lawsuit alleging that someone was injured by the projectile giveaway, the prizes should not be heavy or hard objects. Second, the prize sent into the stands should *not* be something of great value. If you send a valuable prize into the stands and cause a melee with people trampling each other to get to the prize, and a spectator is injured, the organization could be possibly be liable for the injuries. A parallel situation exists in intercollegiate and professional football.

Launching giveaway items into the audience can be exciting, but it also can lead to risks.

These organizations must make sure that kicked footballs do not enter the stands because of the possibility of injuries when people run after the ball. For example, in the case of *Hayden v. University of Notre Dame* (1999)[26], the University of Notre Dame was found liable for the injuries of a spectator who was injured during a scramble for a football when a field goal went over the protective netting into the stands.

The second way in which a sport promotion specialist can affect crowd control also relates to giveaway items. Often when the home team is not doing well or the visiting team is particularly unpopular with the hometown fans, items that were giveaways before the game turn into dangerous projectiles later in the game. The sport promotion specialist must make sure that all giveaways handed out at games are not sharp or hard enough to injure players if a spectator decides to throw the item onto the playing surface. In situations involving giveaway items, it is best to err on the side of caution, because it is impossible to predict when fans will decide to take out their frustrations on the players. As a safer alternative, the sport promotion specialist may choose to give out the promotional items as the fans are leaving the venue.

Is My Organization Responsible for Events That Happen Outside of the Game?

At many large sporting events, the festivities occurring outside of the venue can be just as entertaining and boisterous as the event going on inside. Inherent dangers exist when a large number of people are tailgating at a sporting event (figure 13.4). People tend to become intoxicated, and innocent persons may be put in dangerous situations due to fights and the like. As a sport promotion specialist, you have a duty to provide a safe environment to anyone who is at the event. If you do not uphold this duty, you can be found negligent in your duty and found guilty in court. In the case of *Bearman v. University of Notre Dame* (1983)[27], for example, the plaintiff sued Notre Dame for injuries she suffered as she was leaving a Notre Dame home football game. Someone who had been fighting fell onto her leg and broke it. She claimed that the school had "a duty to protect her from injury caused by the acts of other persons on the premises."

Although the defendants argued that they could not be held liable for the actions of this third party, they were ultimately unsuccessful. The court decided that because Notre Dame was aware of the drinking that occurs while people are tailgating, the school was also aware that the area might be unsafe at times. Therefore, Notre Dame did not exercise its duty to take care of its patrons and was found guilty.

Figure 13.4 Even at tailgating events, the sport promotions specialist must make sure all consumers are safe.

This case demonstrates that sport promotion specialists must make sure that all of their grounds are completely safe at all times. Adequate security should be provided at all events, especially in areas where dangerous activities are more likely to take place, such as at tailgates. A related issue that is more directly applicable to the sport promotion specialist's job is how to promote an event. The common phrase in marketing is "Promote the event, not the game." However, if the event you are promoting is a tailgate, for example, where you know there will be considerable drinking, you may be liable for accidents that occur at that event. Sport promotion specialists should make sure that they do not promote an event that they know could be dangerous. At the least, they are better advised to emphasize the camraderie, the atmosphere, and the food, and so on—not the alcoholic beverages.

Am I Liable for the Actions of My Mascot?

In general, mascots are an excellent marketing tool for sport teams; they engage younger fans in the game, excite the crowd during lulls in the action, provide comic relief in what might otherwise be a dismal contest, and also create excellent brand awareness. However, employing a mascot can lead to liability concerns. In the paragraphs to follow, we look at several scenarios that demonstrate how a mascot can become a liability for an organization, and how sport promotion specialists should attempt to protect themselves from this liability through preparation and training.

What If a Person in the Crowd Does Not Want to Participate?

Time-outs and other breaks in the action of a game are usually the times when mascots show off their comedic abilities and perform physical stunts. Often the mascot selects fans out of the crowd to participate. Usually fans are willing to participate because they feel they will be looked at as a "downer" if they don't, or some people just enjoy the fact that the crowd is looking at them. Whatever the reason, mascots generally do not have much trouble enlisting volunteers to participate in their acts. But there are exceptions, and mascots must be careful about whom they pick out of a crowd.

In the case of *Gil de Rebello v. The Miami Heat, et al.* (1998), "Burnie," the mascot of the Miami Heat, injured a woman he took out of the crowd to participate in an activity during a time-out. Burnie is considered an employee of the team, and therefore the team was held liable for his actions. Burnie, whose real name is Wes Lockard, was also a defendant in the suit; but the plaintiff, de Rebello, knew that if she wanted to receive major compensation for damages she would have to sue the Heat organization as well.

At the beginning of the time-out, Lockard went over to de Rebello, who was sitting in complimentary front row tickets, and grabbed her by the hand. She resisted and loudly told him that she did not want to participate in the routine. Lockard persisted, and proceeded to tug on her left arm with both of his hands in an attempt to get her to cooperate. Mascots are generally used to the type of reaction de Rebello displayed, because many people are reluctant to go out in front of the crowd until they are prodded by the people they are sitting with. de Rebello's purse strap got caught on the back of her seat and provided extra resistance to Lockard's pulling. Eventually, he pulled so forcefully that de Rebello's purse strap broke and she surged forward, falling to the floor. Lockard took this sudden movement as a sign that she wanted to participate, and proceeded to pull her to center court by pulling on her arm. When he finally realized that de Rebello did not want to participate he let up, but not until they had reached center court. de Rebello was very upset by the incident and left the game before it ended. She felt as though she had been humiliated in front of the entire crowd.

de Rebello was diagnosed with posttraumatic tendinitis in her left shoulder due to the incident and was not able to perform actions such as lifting heavy objects. She also consulted a psychologist because she felt that the incident had had "a profoundly negative effect on her mental and emotional well-being." She felt that her privacy and dignity had been injured by the accident and she avoided large gatherings afterward. She took pain medication for her shoulder and anti-anxiety medicine for her mental health. de Rebello was ultimately awarded $50,000 in damages from the Heat for her injuries, both mental and physical.[28]

This case demonstrates how cautious a mascot must be when choosing people from the crowd. It also suggests how important it is for the sport promotion specialist to monitor the actions of mascots—because not only the mascot, but also the organization, may eventually be held liable. There are ways to try to avoid situations such as this.

First, the sport promotion specialist can conduct training sessions for all mascots (figure 13.5). Training sessions need to cover which stunts should include fans and which should not, when certain actions are permissible, and, most importantly, how mascots should deal with people in the crowd who may not want to participate in a routine. If mascots know that they should never use physical force to compel people to leave their seats, situations like the de Rebello case will not occur. The second way to avoid these kinds of incidents is to pick people out of the crowd well in advance of the time they will participate. If there is a schedule of the mascot's activities, the sport promotion specialist can hand-select people for various routines as they walk into the event or as they take their seats. The mascot then either will or

Figure 13.5 Proper mascot training will minimize potential risk.

will not have the spectator's consent to participate. Sport promotion specialists should even consider requiring fans to sign a waiver and release of liability if they want to participate in any kind of routine. This should ensure that the organization is not held liable for any injuries.

When Can My Mascot Perform Routines?

Because of the nature of their profession, mascots tend to draw a great deal of attention to themselves. This is not generally a problem unless the mascot distracts spectators to the extent that they are not paying attention to the game. A mascot must know when play is occurring and also when it is and is not acceptable to be performing routines. Another legal case demonstrates the importance of making mascots aware of the potential risks they pose.

The case of *Lowe v. California League of Professional Baseball et al.* (1997) was brought by a man who was hit by a foul ball at a time, according to his testimony, when he was distracted by the home team mascot. "Tremor," the mascot of the Rancho Cucamonga Quakes of Class A baseball, is a 7-foot-tall caricature whose costume includes a large tail.

In the situation that led to the case, Tremor, while performing a routine in the left field stands, was behind Lowe in an aisle and was inadvertently touching Lowe with his protruding tail. Lowe's attention was distracted away from the action of the game. While paying attention to Tremor, Lowe was struck by a foul ball before he could react and suffered serious injuries as a result. On the trial court level, the baseball team was able to convince the court that Lowe had assumed the risk of being hit by a foul ball by his attendance at the game. However, the appeals court disagreed and stated that the team had a *duty not to increase* the inherent risks for spectators at baseball games beyond what was normally expected. The question was whether or not actions of the mascot that occurred while the game was in progress constituted a breach of the team's duty to the spectator. The court decided that the team had a duty to protect the fans from injury and had failed in this duty.

This case brings up two issues relating to mascots that sport promotion specialists should be aware of. The first is that sport promotion specialists need to run a risk management program with their mascots so that mascots are properly trained and are aware of safety issues. The training should make clear that all mascot antics should occur during breaks in the action, and not while the game is in progress. Also, despite the nature of their job, mascots should attempt not to draw any undue attention toward themselves while play is occurring. Secondly, the sport promotion specialist must ensure that a mascot's suit is manageable for the person who is wearing it. A person of small stature wearing a suit that is too tall may lose awareness of his surroundings, and incidents like the one in the Lowe case can result.[29]

Will a Waiver and Release of Liability Be Upheld by the Courts?

Many sport administrators use waivers and releases of liability to ensure that they are not liable for accidents that may occur during their events. Whether or not a waiver and release of liability will be upheld within the court system depends on many factors. Although some waivers and releases of liability are upheld in court, many are not. The following are reasons a waiver and release of liability may *not* be upheld in court:

- *The person signing the waiver did not have time to read it.* The individual who signs the waiver must have ample opportunity to read the terms of the contract. If an individual is rushed by the receiver of the waiver and is not allowed to read the entire document, the waiver generally is unenforceable.

- *The information in the waiver is difficult to see.* The important terms of the document must not be hidden in the fine print; all information must be conspicuous to the reader.

- *The person is forced to sign the waiver.* The signing of the document must result from a bargaining process that is free and open. In general, if one party is forced to sign a waiver, it is held not to be enforceable.

- *The language of the waiver is not clear.* The language must be clear, precise, and specific. The waiver must spell out who is free from liability and under what circumstances this party will not be found negligent.

- *The waiver concerns intentional misconduct.* A waiver and release of liability is not enforceable if it allows one party to commit intentional or reckless misconduct that could injure the other party. Only liability for negligent actions can be waived.

- *The person who signs the waiver is not competent.* Waivers are generally held to be invalid if they are signed by a minor or by someone who does not have the capacity to sign the document.

If a competent adult signs a waiver and release of liability, and none of these transgressions occur, a waiver and release of liability is generally upheld unless it violates public policy. Sport promotion specialists must make an educated assessment of whether or not the waiver and release of liability will be upheld in their particular situation. To do so they need to know what makes a waiver valid or invalid. Drafting a readable and complete waiver and release of liability is also critical.

To illustrate how the court decides whether or not a waiver and release of liability should be upheld, we look next at a case in which a waiver and release of liability was *not* upheld.

CASE STUDY: WAIVER AND RELEASE OF LIABILITY NOT UPHELD

In *Leon v. Family Fitness Center* (1998), the plaintiff, Carlos A. Leon, charged the Family Fitness Center with negligence. Leon had been sitting on a bench in the sauna in the fitness center when the bench collapsed beneath him, causing him to fall and suffer personal injuries. On the trial court level, the defendants, Family Fitness Center, were granted summary judgment, which means that the trial court did not believe that Leon had enough evidence to win a case. Leon appealed the trial court decision and was successful.

Leon had signed a document entitled "Club Membership Agreement (Retail Installment Contract)" and was a member of the club. The document was one page, and contained the following clause:

> Buyer is aware that participation in a sport or physical exercise may result in accidents or injury, and Buyer assumes the risk connected with the participation in sport or exercise and represents that Member is in good health and suffers from no physical impairment which would limit the use of FFC's facilities. Buyer specifically agrees that FFC, its officers, employees and agents shall not be liable for any claim, demand, cause of action of any kind whatsoever for, or on account of death, personal injury, property damage or loss of any kind resulting from or related to Member's use of the facilities or participation in any sport, exercise or activity within or without the club's premises, and Buyer agrees to hold FFC harmless from same.[30]

The court held that this waiver and release of liability should not be upheld for a number of reasons. First, the title of the document, "Club Membership Agreement (Retail Installment Contract)," did not relay to the reader that the document included a waiver and release of liability. Also, there was no language in the waiver to notify the reader that Family Fitness would not be liable for claims based on its own negligence. The court held that the language of the waiver was "fatally ambiguous." The court believed that an individual who entered into this agreement could be expected to waive any hazard known to relate to the use of fitness facilities—for example, use of a treadmill, which could lead to spraining an ankle. However, Leon could not have been expected to foresee that he would be injured by simply reclining on a sauna bench.

The final lines of the appeals court judgment are ones that all sport promotion specialists should take heed of:

> Reading the entire document leads to the inescapable conclusion the release does not clearly, explicitly, and comprehensibly set forth to an ordinary person untrained in the law, such as Leon, that the intent and effect of the document is to release claims for his own personal injuries resulting from the enterprise's own negligent acts, regardless [of] whether related to the sports or exercise activities it marketed.[31]

This case demonstrates two important points. First, sport promotion specialists must make sure that all waivers and releases of liability that their organization uses are sound. This means that the language is clear, specific, and unambiguous while still comprehensible to the ordinary reader. Secondly, sport promotion specialists should conduct routine checks of all equipment and other objects in all their facilitates to make sure that facilities are safe.[32]

The next case is one in which a waiver and release of liability *was upheld* for the defendant. It is important to note how this waiver and release of liability was written, as well as how it was presented to the participant to sign.

CASE STUDY: WAIVER AND RELEASE OF LIABILITY UPHELD

In the case of *Reed v. University of North Dakota, et al.* (1999), the plaintiff, Jace Reed, was a scholarship hockey player for the University of North Dakota (UND). As part of a preseason hockey conditioning program, Reed participated in a 10-kilometer charity road race sponsored by the North Dakota Association for the Disabled (NDAD). Reed became extremely dehydrated during the race and suffered major damages to his kidney and liver, which necessitated one kidney and two liver transplants. These transplants resulted in substantial medical expenses for Reed.

Reed sued all of the UND coaches, the athletic trainer, and the NDAD. The form that Reed signed contained the following statement:

(continued)

(continued)   I am entering this event at my own risk and assume all responsibility for injuries I may incur as a direct or indirect result of my participation. For myself and my heirs, I agree not to hold the participating sponsors and their directors, employees, and/or agents responsible for any claims. I also give permission for the free use of my name and/or picture in a broadcast, telecast, or other account of this event.[33]

Reed asserted that the release was ambiguous—in particular, that the phrases "participating sponsors" and "for injuries I may incur as a result of my participation" were vague and ambiguous. The court disagreed with Reed, stating that under the language of the release, Reed *had* assumed all responsibility for injuries that occurred as an indirect result of his participation in the race, and that he had agreed to pardon NDAD from any responsibility for his claims. Reed was ultimately unsuccessful because the waiver and release of liability was written in such a way that NDAD could not possibly be held liable for his injuries due to participation in the race. This case differs from the fitness center case in one significant way. That the bench in the sauna broke was not a foreseeable result of becoming a member of a health club. However, experiencing dehydration during the running of a road race is considered an occurrence that a reasonable person could foresee.

Reed's case illustrates the reasons that lead to the upholding of a waiver and release of liability in court. The language in the document was clear, unambiguous, and understandable to an ordinary person—it was not "legalese." The form was presented to Reed before he entered the race, and he was provided ample opportunity to read it.[34]

There have been a multitude of cases in sport in which the validity of waivers and releases of liability has come into question. Decisions have differed from sport to sport and from state to state. As you have seen, many factors enter into a court's decision whether or not to uphold a waiver and release of liability. It is incumbent on promotion specialists to draft waivers and releases of liability that are likely to be upheld. Sport managers should be prepared with a waiver that covers all aspects of their event.[35] Figure 13.6 shows a sample waiver that can provide a framework for this type of document.

What Role Does Insurance Play in Tort Liability?

Since all sport events do not have the same budget, it is not possible for organizers of all events to buy insurance that can absolve them from paying costs if they are found guilty of negligence or other applicable torts. However, insurance can play an important role in an overall risk management plan.

To reduce the liability of the organization, sport promotion specialists have two different approaches to the issue of insurance. First, you can buy insurance for an event. Many different types of insurance are available, from event cancellation to catastrophic injury insurance. Second, you should make certain that the companies you work with have liability insurance as well. Therefore it is in your best interest to require an insurance binder from all parties you conduct business with. An insurance binder is a guarantee that the insurance policy is in effect.

How Can a Sport Promotion Specialist Conduct an Effective Risk Management Program?

It is imperative to have an effective risk management program for a sport event. The amount of litigation involving sport-related injuries has increased greatly in recent years, and the best way to avoid losing a lawsuit is to have in place a risk management plan that covers all possible aspects of an event. The purpose of this section is not to

PUBLICITY WAIVER AND GENERAL RELEASE

This form must be completed by the participant prior to participation.

Publicity Release

In consideration of being allowed to participate in the [INSERT NAME OF PROMOTION] (hereafter referred to as "Promotion"), the undersigned grants [INSERT TEAM NAME] (hereinafter referred to as "Team") [INSERT SPONSOR NAME] (hereinafter referred to as "Sponsor") the National Basketball Association and its member teams, NBA Properties, Inc. and their owners, parents, subsidiaries, affiliates, licensees, employees and agents (hereinafter collectively referred to as the NBA) the non-revocable rights to:

1. Record, edit, use and re-use worldwide in perpetuity on standard or non-standard television, home video, print and electronic media, and in any other means of distribution, publication or exhibition whether now known or hereinafter created, the acts, pictures, poses, performances, statements and sound materials of myself on film, videotape, audio-tape and/or as otherwise telecast or recorded by or on behalf of Team, Sponsor and/or NBA for use by it and any of its partners' production or publication, including but not limited to for use in the programs and materials (hereinafter collectively referred to as "the Materials"); and

2. Use my name, voice, likeness, statements, actions and biographical data in connection with the production, publicity, advertising, promotion, exhibition or other exploitation or use of any of the Materials.

I hereby release Team, Sponsor and NBA from any claims or liabilities of any kind arising out of or in connection with the making or the use of the Materials or the use of my name, voice, likeness or biography.

I understand that I am to receive no compensation in connection with any use of the Materials.

I hold Team, Sponsor and NBA harmless from any liability arising out of or in connection with my statements and actions on the Materials.

General Release

In consideration of being allowed to participate in the Promotion, the undersigned: (a) acknowledge and fully understand that the participant will be engaging in activities that involve risks of injury which might result from not only the participant's actions, inactions or negligence, but might result from the actions or negligence of others, the conditions of the premises or of any equipment used and that there may be other risks not known or not reasonably foreseeable at this time; (b) assume all the aforementioned risks; and (c) release, waive, discharge, defend, indemnify and hold harmless the Team, Sponsor and NBA (collectively, "Released Parties"), each present and former officer, governor and member of the Released Parties, and the subsidiaries, affiliates, predecessors, assigns, present and former officers, owners, shareholders, directors, agents and employees of each and every one of the aforesaid entities and persons, sponsors, advertisers and owners and lessees of premises used to conduct the Promotion, from any and all liability to the undersigned, his or her heirs and next of kin for any and all claims, demands, losses or damages on account of any injury or loss in any way related to the Promotion or the participant's participation therein, including physical injury (and death) and damage to property, caused or alleged to be caused in whole or in part by any released party or otherwise.

Please print:

_____   _____
Last Name   First Name

_____
Address

_____   _____   _____
City   State   Zip

_____   _____
Phone   Date of Birth

_____   _____
Signature of Participant   Date

_____   _____
Signature of Parent / Guardian   Date

Figure 13.6 Waivers do insulate the sport organization from potential risk.

"The NBA and individual NBA member team identifications are trademarks and copyrighted designs, and/or other forms of intellectual property, that are the exclusive property of NBA Properties, Inc. and the respective NBA member teams. © 2002 NBA Properties, Inc. All rights reserved."

cover all elements of a risk management program, but rather to present a framework that indicates what a risk management plan should include.[36]

Developing a risk management program involves several steps. The first step is to set up a risk management group or committee. Second, the people in this group should identify all possible risks for the event. They should plan for all areas of the event, from the maintenance of the facility to the safety of the participants. This group should conduct regular safety checks of the premises and should draft a manual that outlines the procedures for dealing with any accident that may occur on the grounds.

After the risk management group members have explored all possible risks relating to the event, conducted thorough inspections of the grounds, and written the risk management policy, they should begin to implement the plan. An effective risk management plan includes, but is not limited to, regular safety checks, an efficient method for reporting accidents, the drafting of valid waivers and releases of liability, and procedures for every type of emergency that could occur. All employees should be aware of the risk management procedures and should have information about whom to contact when an emergency arises.

Sport promotion specialists should protect themselves from liability by having a sound risk management plan, waivers and releases of liability, and liability insurance. However, if they do not have the means to implement an insurance policy, it is still crucial to assemble and execute the most comprehensive risk management plan possible.

Intellectual Property

The area of law known as intellectual property can affect the sport promotion specialist in many different ways. There are three main areas within intellectual property law: **trademarks, copyrights,** and patents. In the area of sport promotion, patents are of little consequence because they relate to intangible assets, such as ideas and formulas; therefore our focus is on trademark law and copyright law. As discussed in chapter 9, trademark items are a critical source of revenue for an organization, and the sport promotion specialist must be aware of all of the trademarks that the team possesses. And as suggested by the example at the beginning of this chapter, the issues surrounding copyrighted material, such as information appearing on a Web site, are also crucial.

Terms Relevant to Intellectual Property

It is important that principles of intellectual property law are understood in order to be able to work with these concepts in a sport context. The following terms are fundamental to intellectual property law:

• *Trademark.* A trademark is a word, symbol, or device used by a manufacturer or merchant to identify its goods and distinguish them from those manufactured or sold by others.[37]

• *Trademark infringement.* This means the reproduction, counterfeiting, copying, or imitation, in commerce, of a registered trademark.[38]

• *Copyright.* Copyrights are a means of protecting any form of written or artistic expression. They can protect items such as books, pictorials, graphic and sculptural works, music, photographs, movies, and computer programs. The owner of a copyright can block the unauthorized copying or public performance of the copyrighted work.[39]

- *Fair use.* This is a doctrine that allows copyrighted works to be used without the permission of the copyright owner. The fair use doctrine can be employed only in certain situations such as criticism, news reporting, teaching, and scholarship or research.[40]

- *Likelihood of confusion.* For a party to be successful in a trademark infringement case, the party must show "likelihood of confusion," which means that the average customer would not be able to distinguish one company's mark from another's. It also must be proven that the infringer intended to confuse the consumer by using the mark. Likelihood of confusion is difficult to prove because the amount of confusion caused by marks can vary from person to person.[41]

- *Patent.* A patent is a document issued by the federal government that grants its owner a legally enforceable right to exclude others from practicing the invention described and claimed in the document.[42]

- *Ambush marketing.* Ambush marketing refers to intentional efforts of a company to weaken or ambush the official association that a competitor has with a sport organization as a result of the payment of sponsorship fees.[43]

Find Out What Is Protected

As outlined in chapter 9, a sport promotion specialist needs to conduct a review of the logos, names, and even the nicknames that the organization owns. In the NFL, for example, teams are encouraged by the league to register their team logos, names, helmet designs, uniforms, and so on to avoid leaving their marks unprotected. Finding out what items your organization has protected, as well as doing an inventory of items that may need protection, is a vital first step in dealing with the sport organization's intellectual property.

Teams that want to change their marks and/or names must deal with two procedural issues. First, the team has to register the mark and/or name to make sure that it is not being used, and cannot be used, by anyone else. Second, the sport organization must ensure that this change is acceptable to the league the organization belongs to. Minor league baseball teams are an excellent example of organizations that use their marks well. Many teams have created unique marks, often by altering existing parent club marks, that set them apart from other teams.[44]

Trademark Law

What if you go through an inventory of all of the marks that you believe your organization possesses, and realize that you have not protected any of these marks from trademark infringement? The possibility exists that you will have a "common-law" right to the mark, which means that because the organization has been using the mark for a long period of time, it has control over the mark. However, if other organizations have used the mark and you have not protected it from use by other parties, you may actually have lost your right to it. If you have not lost the right to the mark, you may still be able to protect it by going through the registration process.

What Is the Registration Process?

If you believe that your organization has a valuable unregistered mark, you should register it. The first step is to contact the United States Patent and Trademark Office and attempt to register the mark. If the mark has not been registered by another party, your attempt to register it will probably succeed. The registration for a mark is good for 20 years, and at the end of 20 years the registration can be renewed. In order to maintain rights to a mark, however, it is vital to use and protect the mark. If a person has registered a mark and does not use it for a long period of time or has not protected it from infringement, it is possible for someone else to use the mark without being penalized.

Trademarks can also be registered on the state level, although state trademark registration, depending on the individual state, generally offers less protection than federal registration. In general, it is rarely beneficial to register a mark on the state level if the mark is already federally protected. However, state registration can prove beneficial in protecting a mark before federal registration has been approved. An individual interested in obtaining state trademark protection or desiring information should contact the trademark department within the state government. State registrations generally run for 5- to 10-year periods and are renewable.

International intellectual property law is a highly complicated and problematic issue. The World Intellectual Property Organization handles disputes that may arise over the ownership and usage of marks around the world. The governing document for this organization is the World Intellectual Property Copyright Treaty, which has been signed by a large number of countries. However, countries that did not ratify this treaty are not subject to its guidelines. Although registering marks internationally is beneficial, it is vital to note that the international protection of intellectual property is not always clear-cut; often it is difficult to determine whether a particular country is subject to a treaty and what countries' laws are applicable in certain situations. The sport promotion specialist should consult legal counsel before attempting to register any mark internationally.[45]

As mentioned previously, it is not entirely necessary for an organization to register all of its marks with the government. A company that uses certain marks but does not officially register them can legally be considered the owner of the marks under the common-law system in the United States. The company can still guard against trademark infringement and protect the marks, but will have to demonstrate a continuing and consistent use of the mark in order to prove its common-law ownership. Although not mandatory, federal and/or state registration of marks provides the sport promotion specialist with a much stronger claim of ownership of a mark and protects against potential infringement.[46]

How Do You Protect a Trademark?

There are two basic ways of protecting a trademark:

- Using the trademark
- Making sure that no one else uses the mark

An organization must use a trademark that it has registered. That is, an organization cannot simply register any type of trademark that it wants, not use it, and then attempt to penalize anyone who wants to employ the mark. Someone who has a registered mark and does not use it is considered to have abandoned the mark, and will most likely not be successful in receiving damages if this mark is infringed on.

The second way to protect a trademark is by policing against infringement. Because of the popularity of apparel, souvenirs, and other items bearing sport logos, sport promotion specialists may find numerous parties attempting to infringe on their marks and must be on the lookout at all times for unauthorized use of these marks. Once a sport organization finds an infringement, it should immediately demand that the activity stop. First the organization should send letters demanding that the illegal production end. If the infringement continues, the organization should send a court order to cease and desist the illegal production to the infringing company. If the illegal production does not stop, the organization should pursue legal remedies to stop the company from producing the unlicensed merchandise and should send a court order. If an organization does not police unlicensed use of its marks, a court may rule that the organization has abandoned its right to the marks.[47]

Licensing of Your Marks

The ability to license the use of a sport organization's logos and name is a valuable right that sport promotion specialists receive when they register and protect their organization's marks. Once a mark is registered it can be licensed for a fee to other businesses that may have an interest in using the mark.

Licensing arrangements are usually made between the sport organization and a company interested in producing souvenirs and other products that bear the marks of the organization. For example, producers of seat cushions that are used for sporting events want to increase the marketability of their product. They believe that the marketability will be enhanced through use of the name or symbol of a recognizable sport organization. Therefore, the seat cushion producer attempts to enter into a licensing agreement with a sport organization in order to be granted the right to use the organization's marks. However, the sport organization must make sure that it has the right to license out its marks in a given situation. There are certain situations in which a conference, league, properties division, or organization (e.g., NCAA) might have the right to license the marks.

You, Your Organization, and Your Marks

If you are a promotion specialist for a college athletic program or for a team in a professional sport league, you must research what licensing rights you possess. In many cases, some licensing rights that a college athletic program would normally possess are given up to the conference it belongs to. For example, in the NCAA, a sport promotion specialist who is attempting to license the organization's marks may have to go through three different governing bodies. First it is necessary to ensure that a proposed mark is satisfactory to the college or university itself. In the era of political correctness, some mascots have been judged to be offensive and have been removed from use. Second, it may be necessary to deal with the conference to which the college or university belongs. Depending on how centralized the power is within the conference, this governing body will have to approve the mark. Finally, the NCAA, the governing body for the majority of U.S. intercollegiate athletics, will have to give approval to the mark. Only when approval has been obtained from all three of these entities can a mark be registered.

On the professional level, teams often give up some of their licensing rights to the league that they belong to for leaguewide products such as video games, T-shirts, and collectibles. In MLB, for example, Major League Baseball Properties is in charge of all of the merchandising, marketing, and licensing for all the major league teams. The marks of one team are not more valuable than those of any other, according to MLB Properties. Therefore, each team shares in the revenue from trademark licensing no matter how much money its marks bring to the total amount. More popular teams, such as the New York Yankees, have not viewed this arrangement as being fair for them because they sell more licensed apparel than most other teams. The Yankees have even made attempts to circumvent the system by signing exclusive deals with athletic apparel companies. Similar structures exist in other major professional sport leagues, although each league has its own unique licensing system. Generally, a team is subject to the restrictions put in place by the league or conference. However, clever sport promotion specialists have been able to circumvent some of these regulations by finding loopholes, such as the ability to allow a company to become the official sponsor of their venue even though the company is not an official sponsor of the entire league.[48]

Advantages and Disadvantages of Group Licensing

Group licensing is a term that should be familiar to sport promotion specialists. Within a group licensing program, a large number of colleges or universities relinquish their individual licensing rights in order to enter into agreement with a licensing company. That licensing company will then produce numerous types of souvenirs and other products that are each emblazoned with the logo of one of the schools. The schools receive a cut of the profits from the licensing company and do not have to undertake the task of manufacturing the products. If your organization is part of a group licensing program, there are inherent opportunities as well as difficulties. Universities can find it quite difficult to police their marks, that is, to make sure that no one is using their marks without their consent, because there are not enough people in a university athletic department to take care of this problem. But universities that are part of a group licensing program do not have to police their own marks; the licensing company does this for them. The second advantage of a group licensing program is that individual schools do not have to deal with individual vendors. If you are a sport promotion specialist for a university, you may have 100 different logoed items, and it is not feasible for you to negotiate contracts with 100 different vendors. If you are part of a group licensing program, however, the licensing company can negotiate one contract on your behalf (as well as for all the other schools in the group).

However, there are also disadvantages to group licensing. For example, each university must pay the licensing company a certain amount of money on each item sold. Therefore the university loses a percentage of what it would have earned if it had done the licensing on its own. The major disadvantage to group licensing programs, though, is that the organization rarely has control over what items its logos are used on. For example, a university may not want to be associated with products such as alcoholic beverages, cigarette lighters, toilet seat covers, or birth control items. But unless the contract contains certain stipulations, the university does not have much to say about whom the licensing companies decide to contract with. So, there are positive and negative aspects to a group licensing program. Sport promotion specialists need to make the decision on the basis of what they believe is most advantageous for their athletic department and the university.

Using the Mark of an Association

A sport association, league, or conference, such as the NCAA, MLB, or the Big Ten Conference, has certain marks that are protected. For example, all of the marks of the NCAA are valuable, and the organization takes great pains to protect them. Moreover, the marks of the NCAA extend far beyond simply their logos. The NCAA uses logos on its apparel and merchandise, but the most valuable marks that the NCAA possesses are the marks used for its championship events. The NCAA defines its championship events by using phrases such as the "Frozen Four" for the men's as well as the women's national hockey championship. The NCAA is able to register this term and therefore can license it out to people who want to use it to promote their own products. The NCAA is an example of an organization that maximizes its revenues by making sure that it has registered all potential marks.

Another type of licensing agreement between a sport organization and a company is the "official sponsor agreement," which differs from a complete licensing agreement. In this type of arrangement, a company will pay the NCAA, for example, a fee so that the company can use the NCAA logo in a promotional display. A motor oil company may want to use the NCAA logo because it is running a sweepstakes with a trip to the Final Four as the grand prize. The difference between this type of licensing agreement and those already discussed is that the NCAA logo is not part of the primary product but instead is being used to help sales.

Parent Organizations and Their Subsidiaries

Professional sport teams are usually just one organization within a much larger league. However, both the team and the parent organization—the league—have marks that are registered. Therefore the question arises whether or not teams and leagues have the right to use each other's marks freely. In the typical relationship between teams and leagues, the league holds the right to use any of the marks that the team possesses, but the teams are not necessarily able to use the marks of the leagues freely. This top-down relationship gives the leagues leverage when they are negotiating licensing agreements with companies.

Problems and Issues of Ambush Marketing

Ambush marketing, a topic originally addressed in chapter 8, is defined as "the intentional efforts of a company to weaken, or ambush a competitor's official association with a sport organization which was acquired through the payment of sponsorship fees."[49] There are several different ambush marketing scenarios. In one situation, a company is an official sponsor of an event, and another company, in an attempt to "ambush" the official sponsor, becomes a sponsor of a contest surrounding the event. In another situation, a company uses a logo or symbol that is similar to the logo of an official sponsor in order to create confusion among customers. In ambush marketing cases that have been tried, the standard that the plaintiff has been held to is "likelihood of confusion." If the official sponsoring organization is able to convince the court that the average customer is likely to be confused about which company is the official sponsor of the event, or about which company owns which logo, then the plaintiff—the official sponsor—will most likely succeed.

In another example of ambush marketing, a company buys advertising directly outside of the venue for an event sponsored by a competitor. For example, if a competing office supply store were to set up a gigantic billboard on the street leading up to the Staples Center in Los Angeles, this could be considered ambush marketing. Finally, a company may buy advertising on a television show that is sponsored by its main competitor. All of these forms of ambush marketing attempt to weaken the effect of an official sponsorship without spending exorbitant amounts of money.

"Ambush marketing" is more a promotion term than a legal term. If a situation seems to involve ambush marketing, the sport organization must determine whether there are any legal improprieties by checking to see if any violations of its contract with the official sponsor have occurred. The parties should check to see if the contract was an exclusive or nonexclusive sponsorship arrangement. If the two parties had an exclusive arrangement, the sport promotion specialist may go after the company involved in the ambush with the appropriate legal theory. For example, that company may be sued for a trademark violation if it is illegally using the marks of a sport organization in its advertisements. This relatively new area of litigation should be watched carefully for court decisions, which may affect the legal "dos and don'ts" of ambush marketing.[50]

Copyright Law

Now that we have discussed trademark law and how it affects sport promotion specialists, we will turn to copyright law. We consider five areas in which copyright law and sport intersect:

Original music

Trading cards

Telecast and radio broadcast rights

Media guides and programs

Copyrighted material

Original Music

Many colleges and universities, as well as professional sport teams, have fight songs or theme songs connected with their teams. What should sport promotion specialists do if their organization composes an original song for the team? The answer is to attempt to have the song copyrighted so that the organization can receive royalty fees any time the song is played at another venue. Organizations and individuals must protect a song against illicit copying; otherwise they may lose the rights to it. The case of *Maxwell v. Veeck* (1997) is an example. A songwriter, James Albion, wrote a fight song for the Fort Myers Miracle, a minor league baseball club, and granted the club an exclusive license to the song in exchange for two things: (1) production fees and (2) credit for having written the song any time the song was played at games. The Miracle did not give Albion credit each time they played the song at games, even when Albion was present. However, Albion never requested that the Miracle discontinue their use of the song. Eventually Albion sued the team for breach of copyright, but he was unsuccessful because he had not protected his song and therefore had lost any rights to it. It essential for organizations, if they do create songs, to make sure that other parties do not infringe on the copyrights.[51]

Trading Cards

Trading cards are a multibillion-dollar industry, and it is understandable that a sport promotion specialist would want to exploit this avenue as much as possible. However, professional sport teams on the major league level are not permitted to produce their own trading cards. Instead, the rights to decide who manufactures the cards belong to the league and the players' association, and the individual teams are generally kept out of this area. On the minor league level, though, some teams own the rights to make their own trading cards. The arrangement concerning trading cards depends on the agreement between the teams, the league, and the players' association.[52]

Telecast and Radio Broadcast Rights

When you watch a game on television or listen on the radio, you'll usually hear an announcer say, "This broadcast cannot be reproduced or retransmitted without the express written consent of . . . ." The broadcast of that game is a copyrightable work and should not be copied and reused without the consent of the organization that holds the copyright. If an organization does not copyright a broadcast, then any party can rebroadcast part or all of the event without fear of penalty.[53]

On the other hand, usually there are not restrictions on the use of highlights of games by sport news shows. Sport news networks do not have trouble receiving permission to rebroadcast highlights because the promotional value of being on television outweighs any revenues that a team might obtain by charging the networks fees for the highlights.[54]

Media Guides and Programs

Media guides and game programs are original works and thus should be copyrighted like any other original work (figure 13.7). The San Antonio Spurs used the following language to copyright their 1999-2000 media guide:

> The information in this publication was compiled by the San Antonio
> Spurs and is provided as a courtesy to our fans and the media and may be

used only for personal and editorial purposes. Any commercial use of this information is prohibited without the prior written consent of the San Antonio Spurs. All NBA and team insignia depicted in this guide are the property of NBA Properties, Inc., and the respective teams and may not be reproduced for commercial purposes without the prior written consent of NBA Properties, Inc.[55]

As you can see, it is imperative that the language within the media guide or program explicitly state that the information is copyrighted and cannot be reproduced without the consent of the proper authorities. The paragraph containing this type of material should be placed in a conspicuous location in the media guide. This will leave people no excuse for illicit use of any of the information or marks in the guide.

Copyrighted Material

Often during games, especially during time-outs or at emotional points in a game, a sport promotion specialist will want to use music or movie clips to increase the crowd's involvement in the event. If you want to use such material, you might have to pay a fee because it is copyrighted. It is in your best interest to attempt to contact the owner of the material to obtain written permission. Although companies do not always charge fees for use of material, it remains important to find out whether they do or not.

Figure 13.7 Souvenir programs generally contain copyrighted material.

Reprinted, by permission, from the United States Racquetball Association.

Legal Advisement and Representation

As discussed earlier, and as should be obvious from the discussions of contracts, tort liability, and intellectual property, in some situations it is necessary for a sport promotion specialist to seek legal assistance. While many sport organizations choose to employ in-house counsel, others have found it highly beneficial, as illustrated in the following Practitioner's Perspective, to secure the services of legal counsel external to the organization.

PRACTITIONER'S PERSPECTIVE

Seeking Counsel
by Richard Ensor, Commissioner, Metro Atlantic Athletic Conference, Attorney

In the area of the law, the sport promotion specialist should not necessarily undertake all of the organization's legal issues. Instead, he must understand when it is appropriate to contact legal counsel and when issues can be resolved without the aid and added cost of legal services. At the least, a sport promotion specialist should be aware of how he would go about obtaining the assistance of legal counsel on behalf of the sport organization. There are three possible avenues for enlisting the services of legal counsel. The situation faced by a promotion specialist will vary depending on the composition and/or resources of the organization.

In the first situation, the organization that the sport promotion specialist works for has its own legal counsel working in the same building. For example, the Fleet Center in Boston employs full-time legal counsel to handle any problems that may arise within the building. The "in-house counsel" can deal with matters ranging from contracts for sponsors to suits filed by someone who fell on a wet floor in the building.

In-house counsel, however, may not always be the most qualified to handle particular problems. Therefore, even if an organization employs in-house counsel, these people may call on other lawyers who have expertise in a particular area. For example, in-house counsel may enlist the services of a lawyer whose practice focuses on defending companies against cases involving the Americans with Disabilities Act. If the in-house counsel does not have a solid knowledge of this legislation, it is in the best interests of the organization to enlist the services of an attorney who can develop a proper defense. The NCAA, for example, uses a combination of in-house staff counsel and outside counsel for many of its cases.

The second situation that a sport promotion specialist may face occurs when she works within a large corporation or conglomerate. These types of organizations may employ a team of attorneys for the entire corporation. For example, if a promotion specialist for the Los Angeles Dodgers is seeking legal counsel, he may utilize the services of a lawyer who works for the parent company, the Fox Corporation, and not solely for the Dodgers.

There are advantages and disadvantages in dealing with "corporate counsel." Because of the size of these companies, the sport promotion specialist in this setting will have available the resources of an entire team of attorneys, each of whom specializes in a particular area of the law. However, when one is dealing with lawyers who are not familiar with the peculiarities of law and sport, problems can arise. Therefore, it is in the sport promotion specialist's best interests to present the issue to the corporate attorney very thoroughly and specifically.

The third situation that a sport promotion specialist may encounter is the availability of "outside counsel" only. This situation is actually common in the sport world, usually either because the organization does not employ any in-house counsel, or because the in-house counsel is not qualified to handle a particular problem.

The MAAC (Metro Atlantic Athletic Conference), like most major intercollegiate athletic conferences, employs outside counsel. On the level of professional sport, many teams in MLB, for example, call on the services of attorneys who are especially skilled in the area of salary arbitration. Instead of attempting to handle the cases itself, the team hires an attorney on a temporary basis to handle salary arbitration cases. The organization is able to defer to the skill of an attorney whose practice deals primarily with arbitration cases. Another situation in which the use of outside counsel makes sense was referred to earlier—when cases involve the Americans with Disabilities Act. It is not logical for in-house counsel to work on a case involving this legislation when an attorney with this specialty is available. Another area of the law that calls for increased specialization is intellectual property law. It is becoming more common for organizations to hire outside counsel with expertise in this area.

As you can see from the Practitioner's Perspective, the specifics of each situation dictate whether it is best for a sport organization to use in-house or specialist legal advice. The decision is heavily influenced by the legal issues and potential challenges as well as available organizational resources.

Postgame Wrap-Up

Sport and the law can intersect on any level of athletic participation, from recreational intramural competition to the highest levels of international competition. The sport promotion specialist must be aware of the many ways in which the law can become a prominent part of her daily routine.

The importance of drafting comprehensive and unambiguous contracts cannot be emphasized enough. An airtight contract can protect an organization from liability in numerous ways. Sport promotion specialists should not only review new and existing contracts, but also employ the services of a lawyer specializing in contracts to ensure that their contracts are comprehensive, thorough, and without error.

Sport promotion specialists must be constantly aware of the risks associated with any event they are conducting. With an effective risk management plan, an organization can avoid incidents that might land them in court. Training programs for employees, especially mascots, are vital in creating a solid risk management program and avoiding costly court proceedings. As a sport promotion specialist you must be aware at all times of any situations that could lead to tort liability and must work to resolve these problems before incidents occur.

Intellectual property is an area of the law that is continually expanding. With the introduction of new technologies, copyright and trademark infringement is becoming more frequent. Sport promotion specialists should be sure to register all existing marks and symbols that an organization possesses, register any new ones that an organization creates, and diligently protect registered marks from infringement by unauthorized users. A comprehensive plan for registering, licensing, and protecting all marks should be created to guide the organization.

Discussion Items

1. Compose a list of the various practices with whom a sport promotion specialist may enter into a contract. For each, consider whether the individual will be hired as an independent contractor or as an employee. Are there advantages or disadvantages to each arrangement?

2. Talk about the various clauses that should be included in a contract used for promotions involving large prizes. What characteristics should prohibit people from participating in these promotional contests?

3. What topics should a sport promotion specialist include in the training for a mascot?

4. Discuss why a waiver and release of liability may or may not be upheld in a court.

5. Outline at least five components that an effective risk management program should include.

6. Make a list of the various items that an organization can have trademarked.

7. Discuss the advantages and disadvantages of entering into a group licensing program.

Learning Enrichment Activities

1. Attend a sporting event and watch all the event promotions, identifying any risk management suggestions that you would make to the organization. Be sure to assess fan contests, mascot activities, and promotional content.

2. Attend a sporting event or watch a major event on television. Attempt to identify a company or companies that is using ambush marketing techniques and discuss with classmates efforts that should be made to address such tactics.

3. Attend a sporting event and look at the souvenirs and apparel being sold in a store outside the stadium or arena, those being sold inside of the building, and those being sold by vendors on the street. For each location and for the various items, check to see whether there is evidence that the items are properly licensed (where applicable).

Aftermarketing: Developing Relationships and Creating Lifetime Value With Customer Service

chapter objectives

1. Understand the importance of service and follow-up care in relation to the success of future selling efforts

2. Comprehend the significance and applicability of the lifetime value concept to the sales process

3. Identify the key components of an effective customer service program

4. Appreciate the role that data-based marketing and technological advances can play in creating more effective customer service programs and practices

5. Recognize the importance of experiential and entertainment factors as they relate to the product or service being sold

<table>
<tr><td rowspan="4">key terms</td><td>aftermarketing</td><td>customer service</td></tr>
<tr><td>relationship marketing</td><td>Nordstrom rules</td></tr>
<tr><td>frequent fan program</td><td>lifetime value</td></tr>
<tr><td>Four Ps</td><td>experiences</td></tr>
</table>

Pregame Introductions

As we have stated throughout this book, customers always have a choice. They can elect to purchase the services or products of Company A or can choose Company B or a number of other providers. Because so much choice is available to the customers, businesses face endless challenges to the loyalty of their customer base. To combat that threat, companies, and sport organizations in particular, must become better marketers. What that means, in the words of Regis McKenna, is "marketing that finds a way to integrate the customer into the company, to create and sustain a relationship between the customer and the company."[1]

In this chapter we discuss many of the components of **aftermarketing**—the process of providing continuing satisfaction and reinforcement to individuals who are past or current customers, which will in turn create lasting relationships with all customers.[2] These activities include, but are not limited to, communications programs, frequent purchaser programs, customer acknowledgement and recognition efforts, and service quality and retention initiatives. In short, these are activities designed to increase and improve communication, strengthen and enhance relationships, and convey to consumers that they are valuable to the organization. The activity must be sincere and must be designed to help nurture a long-term, mutually rewarding, and satisfying relationship between the consumer and the organization.

Defining Relationships

Relationship marketing, ever since the term was introduced in 1983, has been among the most desired outcomes of all marketing efforts in a variety of industry segments.[3] However, given the unique nature of sport, where demand can fluctuate widely and there is a dependency on pre-selling the product,[4] relationship marketing is even more critical to the success of the sport organization (figure 14.1). For example, the NFL's Green Bay Packers function in the smallest market of any professional sport franchise in the United States. Although they benefit from revenue sharing, they still must effectively sell all of their tickets, rent all of their luxury suites, and sell their entire advertising inventory every year. They are able to do so because of the long-term relationships they have established not only in Green Bay, but also throughout the state of Wisconsin and in the upper Midwest. Regardless of how the Packers perform or are expected to perform, those tickets, suites, and ad spaces must be sold.

As we have entered a new millennium, relationship marketing has continued to evolve in concept and increase in importance. More and more emphasis has been placed on the importance of customer retention and on increasing the breadth and depth of that existing relationship. In this chapter we use Gordon's definition of relationship marketing and apply it to the sport context to illustrate how essential this concept is in our customer interactions. According to Gordon, "relationship marketing is the ongoing process of identifying and creating new value with individual

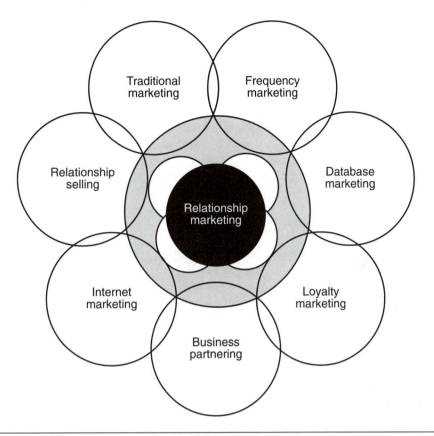

Figure 14.1   Relationship marketing involves interacting with many different areas.

customers and then sharing the benefits from this over a lifetime of association."[5] This definition implies that new value will be created and shared between the customer and the organization. More importantly, it recognizes the fact that consumers not only are the purchasers, but also play a role in defining the value they want—*thus value is created with customers, not for them.* The definition also recognizes the lifetime value of the customer (discussed later in this chapter) and reflects the idea that this process is continuous and cooperative—operating in real time. This approach to relationship marketing suggests a number of steps, identified by Gordon, that are integral to the process. Next we examine each of these steps and illustrate their applicability to the sport setting.

Step 1: Using Technology to Communicate With and Serve Individual Customers (or Customer Groups)

Sport organizations can provide individual customers, or logical groups of customers (such as suite holders, season ticket holders, partial plan purchasers, sponsors, corporate partners, and donors), the value each wants by using technology appropriately and integrating technology throughout the organization in all business communication interactions. How do we find out what value they want? The answer is very simple—ask them!

Amazon.com is an effective e-tailer because of its use of technology and permission marketing to further engage its customers in a real-time marketing environment. If you are a return visitor with a purchasing history, you are given the option of viewing recommendations for books, music selections, or electronic products on the basis of previous purchases. Amazon gives you continued opportunities to narrow down recommendations by asking you if you already own any of the recommended products and if so, whether or not you liked them. Among other options, you can register for automatic e-mails when *your* preferred authors or musicians bring out new releases, and can suggest new authors or books on the basis of the subject matter of books you have previously purchased. The key is well-managed customer information used in a way that the customer feels is helpful and valuable and not intrusive.

Sport has lagged behind other businesses noticeably in both the development and the acceptance of relationship marketing, as well as in the use of technology to communicate with and better serve its clientele. **Frequent fan programs** (modeled on frequent flier programs) were not initiated until 1996 when the San Diego Padres started their Frequent Friars Club. These types of programs use bar code technology to track fan attendance, reward frequent attendees with coupons on-site, and monitor accounts with regard to cumulative points that can be used for prizes based on the number of games attended.[6] Enhancements such as adding concession merchandise and purchases from local corporate partners are under consideration at the time of this writing. (For additional information on this topic see the Practitioner's Perspective by Gordon Kaye later in this chapter.)

Ticketing is poised to become a leading, if not *the* leading, online sport commerce item.[7] If people

College World Series Rewards

Rewards Enrollment Form

1999-00 Southwestern Bell Spurs Rewards Scoreboard

10 *Points* – FREE beef chalupa
20 *Points* – FREE 98/99 Championship Book "One For San Antonio"
30 *Points* – Buy One Game Ticket – Get One FREE and FREE basket of Mama's Famous Fried Mushrooms
40 *Points* – FREE Whataburger
50 *Points* – FREE Chicken Sandwich combo
60 *Points* – FREE 98/99 Championship Lapel Pin
100 *Points* – FREE Dove Bar
130 *Points* – FREE Player Poster
170 *Points* – Commemorative 99/00 Spurs Yearbook
200 *Points* – FREE $25 Gift Certificate for any flight on Southwest Airlines
240 *Points* – Two FREE Tickets to an upcoming game & Dinner for Two
280 *Points* – Invitation to an Exclusive Spurs Practice
320 *Points* – FREE Tim Duncan Commemorative Pin & Buy one Dinner and get One FREE.
370 *Points* – Commemorative Photo with Championship Trophy
410 *Points* – Autographed Photo of a Spurs Player
440 *Points* – Exclusive Perfect Attendance Pullover Jacket

Get Your Spurs Rewards Card Today!

Earn exclusive rewards and valuable discounts just by attending Spurs home games.

Here's how to join:

1. Fill out the enclosed *Southwestern Bell Spurs Rewards Enrollment Form.*

2. Turn in a completed enrollment form and receive your FREE Southwestern Bell Spurs Rewards card immediately.

3. Swipe your Southwestern Bell Spurs Rewards Card at any kiosk to receive 10 points at each home game, which instantly add up to exclusive and valuable rewards.

4. Answer the on screen questions at the kiosks to receive your personal discount coupon(s) with exclusive savings from selected sponsors.

5. Bring your Southwestern Bell Spurs Rewards card to every home game and watch your points add up for great rewards. *(See 1999-00 Southwestern Bell Spurs Rewards Scoreboard on back of brochure)*

Reward programs, like the ones offered by the Spurs and the NCAA College World Series, create incentives for fans.
Reprinted with permission of the NCAA®. Reprinted, by permission, from the San Antonio Spurs.

can print tickets at home, and the box office can re-create unused tickets for either resale or redistribution, this would represent one of the values that ticket holders have demanded—because it provides flexibility and ensures that tickets can be used. "Smart" tickets—tickets encoded with an additional value for food and beverage, parking, and other supplemental purchases—also provide the corporate account holder an important value: the convenience of being able to ensure that corporate guests have the entire hospitality package taken care of whether or not they are accompanied by the host. Both of these concepts should become reality and begin to be common practice sometime in 2001. (For additional examples of the use of technology in communicating with and serving customers, see chapter 12.)

Step 2: Growing Through Scope and Partnering

In attempting to serve customers as they want to be served, sport organizations may find they have to do things they have not done before and may need to expand the scope of their products and services. According to Blanchard and Bowles, providing customers with what they want must be compatible with what the organization wants[8]—implying that the organization cannot be all things to all people. If the organization has determined that what the customer wants is reasonable and within the scope of reality, the organization may have to form nontraditional alliances and partnerships in order to serve the customers better or more completely.

In the past, in both professional and collegiate sport, ticket sales and ticket distribution were areas identified by consumers as needing improvement. When ticket activities were expanded to include advance game and season ticket sales, mail order sales, telephone sales, group sales, and the use of independent agents and consignment selling, traditional team structures were unable to adequately service demand.[9] As doing this in-house proved to be impractical, these organizations needed to find an outside source with whom to partner for service delivery expansion, as well as fiscal margins and return on investment. Enter Ticketron in 1968, which was followed by Ticketmaster, which acquired Ticketron in 1991. This partnership has resulted in Ticketmaster's partnering with the majority of professional sport franchises for phone and Internet ticket sales.

Step 3: Rethinking the Four Ps

Marketers have long discussed the concept of the **Four Ps:** product, price, promotion, and place. But often the discussion focuses exclusively, or at least heavily, on the organization or its products and/or services. A more effective way of viewing the Four Ps, at least in relation to sales and promotional activities, is from an orientation that is more consumer or service based. This should provide some insight into how to better plan our products and services and position them more appropriately to the consumer.

Product

In relationship marketing, the product is not developed in isolation from the consumer, but in conjunction with the consumer, whose input, feedback, and testing reactions are solicited. While sport has traditionally been better than other industries about using customer feedback and input to design and develop products, there have been exceptions. The concept of the club seat—a premium seat at a premium price—was developed to create a product targeted at the corporate client who was not able to sit in locations close to the playing surface because of lack of inventory. The premise was to take a seat further away from the playing surface and add a level of services and amenities that would compensate for the location and justify a steep price tag.

Initially the amenities were cell phone service, fax delivery, meeting space, and other heavily business-oriented services along with in-seat waitperson service. The reaction was very mixed and sales lagged, and organizations conducted focus group research to determine why the seats were difficult to sell. Teams learned that recreating the business environment at the sport facility was detrimental—if people were coming to the arena to work, why purchase tickets at all? Feedback from the target market, which could have been obtained as the concept was being developed, has resulted in the creation of lounge areas, in-seat computer screens that provide replays as well as statistics and updates from other games,[10] complimentary memberships in golf clubs, extra game tickets for employees, and so forth. Developing a product or determining how a product should be packaged should ideally involve the ultimate end user—the purchaser.

Price

In relationship marketing, the price varies according to the preferences and dictates of the customer, with the value varying commensurately. The price then combines the features and services the customer wants and the costs associated with delivering such flexibility and options. Spectator sport affords this type of relationship pricing. Prices in a stadium or arena vary according to proximity from the playing surface, the amenities (if any) associated with a particular class of seating, and the number of games if the purchase involves a ticket plan. The customer makes her selection based on which purchase options are the most appealing. In most instances customers consider cost versus location, but in others they consider cost versus amenities or services. In any case, it is consumers, on the basis of their relationship with the sport organization, who have helped create the variations in product pricing and the "bells and whistles" that can be customized for the product.

© Jim Baron/The Image Finders

For these Cleveland fans, low ticket prices may be more important than proximity to the action.

Promotion

Traditional marketing has been mass oriented in its promotional communication, with the ultimate message one of asking the consumer to make a purchase. In relationship marketing, the consumers have significant input into not only how they will receive the message, but also how often they receive it, what the content should be, and ultimately how they respond and react to the message. Consumer input gained through relationship marketing practices can define the promotional offer, as well as the frequency and restrictions of the offer.

Promotional activities can also be created because of the relationship between a sport organization and a corporate marketing partner. Such was the case in 1996, when MLB's Pittsburgh Pirates, because of their relationship with Giant Eagle, a grocery chain, worked to create a promotion targeted at both the customer bases. The promotion centered on the Giant Eagle Advantage Card, a preferred shopping card entitling the bearer to discounts on food items at Giant Eagle grocery stores. The creation was the Giant Eagle Advantage Card Night, which extended the discount to selected Pirate games on one Wednesday night per month from May through September. Reaction to the promotion and feedback from the fans resulted in several other co-promotions using the Giant Eagle Advantage Card.[11]

Placement and Distribution

Traditional marketing sees distribution as the channel that takes the product from the producer to the consumer. Traditional businesses such as airlines attempt to influence distribution choice through incentivization—extra membership miles for booking a ticket online or special e-saver fares. Some banks, in an effort to "force" consumers to utilize ATMs for transactions other than just cash withdrawals, are considering charging fees for all teller transactions that could also be accomplished at the ATM. Relationship marketing, on the other hand, considers distribution from the perspective of the customer, who decides where, how, and when to buy the combination of products and services that make up the vendor's offering. Thus distribution is viewed as more of a process than simply a channel.

Sport utilizes a variety of channels to distribute its respective products, and when viewed in the aggregate, it is clear that the distribution system is a process that affords the consumer a variety of options based on price, access, and convenience in relation to obtaining the product. Customers can make ticket purchases on the Internet, through Ticketmaster, by calling a personal account representative at the organization, by going to the ticket window, or through the mail. Consumers determine the distribution channel that best fits their needs or lifestyle.

Step 4: Creating the Position of Relationship Manager

It has been commonplace for businesses, and many sport organizations, to employ an individual who is responsible for managing the relationships between the organization and the consumer base. These individuals are employed under a variety of titles—customer service manager, retention specialist, membership coordinator, and so forth. Regardless of the exact title, these people are responsible for maintaining the relationship with the customer. In maintaining this relationship, the role of the relationship manager may include the following:

- Serving as the point of contact between the organization and the consumer
- Listening to consumers and integrating their suggestions into the business

- Helping create value for the consumer with regard to the product or service, promotional activities, distribution process, or other considerations
- Integrating technology to facilitate better communication and delivery

Mary Ann Kellerman is director of customer relations for the Cleveland Cavs. In her role in the Cavs' efforts in relationship marketing, she coordinates personal account representatives who work with sales personnel to service accounts and ultimately renew ticket plans. According to Kellerman, "Our goal is to meet and exceed our guests' expectations and create lasting memories while providing exceptional value. We accomplish this through research programs that establish forums for our guests to provide feedback regarding their satisfaction and perceptions."[12]

In examining these few tenets of relationship marketing,[13] we will deal specifically with elements such as customer service and communication strategies that are core elements in relationship marketing.

Defining Customer Service

In examining the concept of customer service, we should first look at the industry leader in customer service (or guest relations), Disney. Years and years of interaction, testing, and other such activities have resulted in what Disney calls the Magic Marketing Formula. The Disney Magic Marketing Formula is "Ask the guests what they want, then give it to them." Let's examine this formula by considering one component at a time.

The simplest way to analyze the term "guests" is to apply it to your own personal situation. Think of customers as guests in your house. When entertaining guests in your home, you make certain assumptions. First, you assume that the guests may be unfamiliar with your house—they may need to ask where they should park, where

Because of Disney's renowned customer service and guest relations, consumers know they'll enjoy the same courtesy at the Disney Quest store in Chicago as they do at DisneyWorld in Orlando.

the bathroom is, and so forth. In customer service, similarly, we assume that guests will need some type of assistance to enjoy their visit. Secondly, we assume that if everything goes well during their visit, they will want to return. Third, it is likely that at some point, our guests might voice a special need or concern, which will need to be addressed immediately. In the Disney vernacular, this is turning lemons into lemonade. So an effective sport organization needs to become an effective host, establish a guest relations program, monitor satisfaction through research and regular communication with the guests, and provide a delivery system that effectively incorporates all of these elements.

So how do we define **customer service?** Customer service begins with the philosophy that everyone is part of the company. After all, this is the perception of the customer, and the perception of the customer is the marketing reality for the sport organization. It follows that, if you work for the company you are a part of it, so every problem or issue a customer has is relevant to you. You then function as a problem solver to turn the lemons into lemonade—making an unpleasant experience better. The final element of effective customer service is establishing regular communication forums and programs to work with customers not only to solve problems, but also to make proactive efforts to prevent problems.

Designing an Effective Customer Relations and Servicing Program

To design an effective customer relations and servicing program, sport organizations must bear in mind a series of rules and philosophies and apply them. This section explains these steps and describes and illustrates each element in detail.

Rule 1: Know Your Customers

To develop a truly effective customer relations and servicing program, it is essential that we *know* the customers for whom the program is designed. Knowing them means understanding their psychographic and lifestyle patterns, identifying them geographically and demographically, and understanding their usage and interest levels in the products and services that we offer. To obtain this information in order to develop an effective customer service program, the organization needs to ask the following series of questions:

- Who are my consumers—past, present, and future—in terms of both demographics (age, gender, income, etc.) and psychographics (lifestyles, attitudes, opinions)?
- Where do my current and potential consumers reside? Where do they work? How do they travel from their home or place of business to the places where they consume the sport product?
- How and why did they become involved with the sport product?
- Has their involvement or consumption of the sport product changed?[14]
- Are there related products or services that may be of interest to the consumer?
- Is the consumer aware of these related products or services?
- Are we, the organization, aware of the level of commitment or the feelings of the consumer toward the organization?

Surveys, newsletters, Internet messages and chat rooms, face-to-face meetings, luncheons, and other special activities are all common ways for sport organizations to communicate with, interact with, and learn about their customers. Communication should mean a two-way exchange of information. Don't just provide the customers the opportunity to answer your questions; provide them with a forum to ask questions or simply state their own views and preferences.

Rule 2: Determine Your Organizational Vision of Great Customer Relations and Service

Blanchard and Bowles, authors of *Raving Fans,* state that unless you have your own vision of what you hope to do, you cannot understand fully what the customers may ask for.[15] You must know what you want your organization to become and the organizational resource limits (fiscal, space, human, timing) that will affect your vision for customer service. For example, an immediate-response mechanism to handle and resolve all customer complaints might be the vision—but the practical implementation of that vision, which is affected by resource allocation and availability, might have to be that all customer complaints will be resolved within three to five business days.

This vision of what you want customer service to become must also take into account the organizational culture and structure, as well as the "visions" of other departmental units that may be affected by the ramifications of your "vision." For example, one of the most common problems facing all sport organizations that sell tickets is the fact that the primary reason for nonrenewal of ticket plans is the number of games in the plan for which tickets went unused. This is a consistent threat to marketing departments that may have a vision of renewal rates of 90% or more. To combat the "unused ticket factor," marketing personnel have developed exchange dates—preselected games for which tickets are available to the purchaser in exchange for unused tickets from past games. While this is a simple idea on the surface, the marketing vision of customer service—providing incentives for unused tickets—may conflict with the task of the box office manager, who must consider how this vision affects existing policies and day-to-day operations. In other words, the "you" in "knowing what you want" might involve a number of other people throughout the organization; and what you want, your original concept, might require input from others and modifications.

Rule 3: Determine What Your Customer Wants and Determine the Compatibility With Your Vision

Simply, ask your customers what they want, and figure out if it is something that is compatible with your vision and thus something you can deliver. We have already pointed to the Disney philosophy of asking customers what they want and then delivering it. In some cases this is relatively easy. In others, the customer's vision and your vision might need to be altered, and a modified vision that is a compromise of sorts may be the outcome. In still others, the customer's vision may be so far beyond the realm of what you as an organization can provide that that customer may have to look elsewhere in order for the vision to be fulfilled. Are we ignoring these customers? No, we are simply stating that our place of business and our business goals are not the best for them. We are employing the age-old axiom—we cannot be all things to all people.

For example, your customers may say to you, I would like a ticket plan where I can pick the games I want to attend and only purchase those games. For some organizations this may be fine. Organizations may offer weekend plans and even plans allowing fans to purchase tickets for a 10-game plan and to select the 10 games. Other organizations fear that the sale of such plans might cannibalize the sale of all-

Sport fans and beer often go hand in hand.

© Newsport Photography

inclusive plans, or may not want to deal with the logistical problem of permitting fans to select the games in their plans. It is strictly a decision that either falls within the vision of what an organization wants to be in terms of customer service or falls outside of that vision.

What makes sense to one organization might not make sense to another because of their visions of serving the customer. Let's think about the case of the Texas Motor Speedway (TMS) in Denton County, Texas. A referendum was passed that would enable the TMS to sell beer, but a companion ordinance stated that if TMS sold beer, then the TMS fans could not bring their own beer to the track—something that was currently permitted. After extensive polling and research, it was determined that 73% of the TMS customers preferred that the TMS not sell beer. TMS Vice President and General Manager Eddie Gossage abided by their wishes and wrote off an estimated $3 million annually in beer revenue.[16] Gossage's vision of retaining fans and not wishing to alienate people is supported by his organization, but may not have been within the organizational vision of other similar venues. In this case the vision of what the organization wanted and the vision of what the customer wanted were compatible, and thus the vision was deliverable. Perhaps in another organization, the vision of $3 million in revenue would have altered the customer service vision.

Rule 4: Design an Effective System to Deliver the Vision

Knowing your customers, knowing what you want, and knowing what the customer wants are all keys steps; but having all of this information without an effective delivery system can render the organization ineffective when it comes to customer service.

In sport settings, the most common forms of delivery system employ two elements: personal account representatives and a guest relations program. Personal account representatives provide personal and ongoing service to the organization's best customers—season ticket holders or volume purchasers. In the case of season ticket holders, personal account representatives are instructed to initiate contact a minimum of three times during the year. The three recommended contact times are before the season, during the season, and after the season. This is the minimum number of expected contacts. The representative can initiate other contacts to inform the season ticket holder of special offerings or opportunities, upcoming events, or programs. For example, if an attractive opponent is coming to town, say the Los Angeles Lakers, a personal account representative could contact the season ticket holder to ask whether he needs additional tickets. Conversely, season ticket holders can feel free to contact their personal account representatives at any time to provide assistance, information, and so forth. The personal account representative functions to provide a consistent and familiar point of contact and assistance between the organization and its best customers.

Guest relations programs are on-site customer care programs located at the sporting venue. The intent of these programs is to assist the casual or occasional fan who has not established a relationship with the sport organization. As mentioned

Guest relations personnel help guests feel comfortable on-site.

earlier, "guests" coming to the venue for the first time may need help in becoming more familiar with the sporting venue and the surrounding area. Guest relations personnel function as hosts and problem solvers, dealing with a wide array of situations—from unruly fans, to lost children, to lost or duplicate tickets, to medical emergencies. Their role is to minimize problems and maximize enjoyment. They accomplish this by being highly visible and accessible and providing on-site solutions to problems as they arise. The following are descriptors for an effective customer service delivery system:

- Visible—customers should know where to seek assistance and problem resolution
- Responsive—problems and questions need to be resolved in a timely fashion
- Consistent—problems and issues need to be resolved on a consistent basis for all fans
- Proactive—communication between the organization and its customers should work to identify concerns before they become problems
- Empathetic—the organization must be able to identify with customers and relate to their feelings and issues
- Reassuring—customers should feel that the organization has heard them, and that the contact person was knowledgeable and had the skills and support to provide a resolution
- Visionary—those working in customer service should be able to see how problem resolution and customer satisfaction can lead to a long-term relationship

Rule 5: Choose the Right People to Implement and Manage the Delivery System

As quality parts are essential to ensure that a car runs properly and that it can take us to our destination, so too are quality people essential to ensure that our customer service program leads to long-term relationships. Customer service personnel must be selected carefully. They must have exceptional listening skills, must be knowledgeable about the organization, and must demonstrate interest, patience, and empathy.

Anderson and Zemke have identified the 10 Deadly Sins of Customer Service, all of which can be controlled by the attitude and interactions of the customer service personnel:

- *I don't know.* Customers expect you to be knowledgeable about the organization and its products/services—if you are not, they will find another organization that is.

- *I don't care.* Customers want you to care about serving them. When your attitude, conversation, or appearance makes it clear that you would rather be doing something else, they'll find themselves wishing the same thing.

- *I can't be bothered.* Actions speak louder than words—if customers feels that they are not your immediate priority, they will find someone who can convey to them their importance.

- *I don't like you.* The more hostile, aggressive, or obnoxious the customer service person is, the more memorable the experience is for the customer—for all the wrong reasons.

- *I know it all.* When you jump in with a solution or comment before the customer has finished explaining his problem or question, you are implying you know it all. Knowledge is a tool to help serve customers better, not to beat them into submission or intimidate them.

- *You don't know anything.* As trite as the saying is, it is true: there are no dumb questions, only dumb answers. When you rudely or insensitively cut off, put down, or demean customers for having an inaccurate or confused idea about your product or service or what you can do for them, you are holding the door open for them to leave and find another organization that can better appreciate them for who they are.

- *We don't want your kind here.* Prejudice, like customers, comes in all sizes, colors, ages, educational levels, dress, appearances, and so on. Do you treat customers who show up in suits better than those in shorts with tattoos and body piercings? Your attitude may convey your innermost feelings and biases to the customer, who may feel free to leave and find another organization that might be more accepting.

- *Don't come back.* The purpose of serving customers well is to convince them to come back again and again. The easiest way to discourage that is to make it clear in words or actions that they're an inconvenience in your day and that they are unwelcome.

- *I'm right and you're wrong.* One of the easiest traps to fall into is arguing with a customer over something that really is more a point of personal pique or pride than professional service. Customers are not always right, but it doesn't cost you anything to give them the benefit of the doubt.

- *Hurry up and wait.* Time is a critical concern for everyone. Respect your customers' time and you'll find they will respect you in return.[17]

Perhaps the best example of the match between an effective delivery system and the people who implement and manage that delivery system is Nordstrom, the Seattle-based retailer. Widely acclaimed and recognized as America's number-one customer service company, Nordstrom provides an exceptional model of customer service that should be emulated throughout the sport industry. On orientation day, each new Nordstrom employee receives a copy of the employee handbook, which is a 5- by 8-inch gray card with the following message:

Welcome to Nordstrom

We're glad to have you with our company. Our number one goal is to provide outstanding customer service. Set both your personal and professional goals high. We have great confidence in your ability to reach them.

Nordstrom Rules:

Rule #1: Use your good judgment in all situations. There will be no other rules. Please feel free to ask your department manager, sales manager, or divisional manager any question at any time.[18]

Simply stated, Nordstrom has given every employee the responsibility and ability to do virtually whatever it takes to satisfy the customer. Nordstrom gives its employees the freedom to make decisions, and Nordstrom management is willing to live with those decisions. Because the company has the faith and trust in its frontline people to push decision-making down to the sales floor, the Nordstrom shopping experience is as close to working with the owner of a small business as a customer can get in a large store.[19] By empowering employees, Nordstrom has made those employees feel vested in the company and actually feel as though they *are* the company, which comes through to the customer in all of their interactions.

CASE STUDY: LISTEN, PROBE, SOLVE

We have examined the core rationale and approach for effective customer service. Now we look at a sport case scenario that employs a three-step model for dealing with a customer complaint. We think this three-step model—Listen, Probe, Solve[20]—can serve as a basis for all sport organizations in their customer services approaches.

Wendy is a sponsorship salesperson for the Gotham City Bats, a professional baseball franchise. She is calling on Alfred Chang, owner of an automobile dealership who was a corporate partner of the Bats during their first year of play this past season. Wendy is attempting to renew, and perhaps upsell, Mr. Chang into a larger sponsor package for the upcoming year.

Step One: Listen to Find the Problem

The importance of listening to find the problem cannot be overstated. In a problem-solving situation, you are listening for two reasons: (1) to allow the customer to vent and express her frustration and (2) to find the *real* problem, which may be obvious but sometimes isn't. For example, listen to what Mr. Chang has to say to Wendy regarding his sponsorship renewal:

"I am not interested in renewing my current sponsorship package because there were elements in the package that I did not use. There were 1000 tickets in addition to my four season tickets included in my package, and look in my desk—they are still here—what was I supposed to do with them?"

At this point Wendy knows that Mr. Chang is not happy with his purchase from last year, and that a renewal is in doubt and possibly out of the question. Was Mr. Chang upset with the sponsorship package or just dissatisfied with the tickets that were part of the package because they went unused? Wendy needs to have more information from Mr. Chang before she can determine the best course of action. Therefore Wendy employs the tactics described in Step Two.

Step Two: Probe for Understanding and Confirmation

Customers, particularly when they are upset, don't always explain everything clearly or completely. Ask questions about anything that you may not understand, need clarified, or need additional details about. Then when you have identified the problem and clearly understand it, restate it back to the customer. Wendy's initial response to Mr. Chang probes to determine the core of the problem.

"I'm sorry that you were unable to use the tickets in your sponsorship, Mr. Chang. Were the tickets the only problem area of your sponsorship package? How did you feel about the signage and exposure you received through your stadium sign and television advertisements on our game broadcasts?"

Mr. Chang responds:

"The sign and advertising were fine, but the tickets went unused. The salesperson told me to use them to run promotions or give them to my employees. My employees used the four season tickets because the location was good. They had no interest in sitting in the outfield, where the 1000 tickets were located. Even though they were passes good for any game, I couldn't use them."

At this point Wendy has determined that Mr. Chang is unhappy with the 1000 general admission passes he was given as part of his sponsorship package. Mr. Chang has indicated that the other elements were satisfactory and were utilized. Wendy now needs to identify some possible alternatives and implement a solution that will satisfy Mr. Chang so that he wants to renew the current package or at least get one of comparable value.

Step Three: Find and Implement Solutions

If the problem is one you have encountered before, you may already know the best solution. In this case, Wendy can use the "feel, felt, found" approach:

"Mr. Chang, I understand how you feel. We have had cases in the past where sponsors have felt the same way about elements in their packages. We've found that _____ solves the problem."

In the event the solution is less obvious, Wendy may choose to present several options and ask for Mr. Chang's preference:

"Mr. Chang, there are several possibilities that we can consider to make this sponsorship package work better for you next year. We could drop the additional tickets from your package, or I can include those same 1000 ticket passes at no cost to you and help you design an effective test-drive promotion to utilize those passes. Which option do you feel is best for you?"

By involving Mr. Chang in generating the solution to his problem, Wendy is not only building a relationship with Mr. Chang, but also conveying to him that she is interested in his business and in satisfying his needs. The key is to prove that this interest is genuine, and Wendy does this by living up to her commitment if Mr. Chang chooses the second option.

Customer Service and Relationships With Lifetime Value

As we said previously, the goal of effective customer service is to build, fix, and strengthen relationships with customers so that the relationships not only last over time but also grow and expand. Shani and Calasani describe this process as "an integrated effort to identify, maintain and build a network with individual consumers and to continuously strengthen the network for the mutual benefit of both parties, through interactive, individualized and value added contracts over a long period of time."[21] In sport, according to McDonald and Milne,[22] these efforts require an organization to implement the following four steps:

- *Build a customer database.* According to Jackson and Wang,[23] database marketing is extremely versatile and can be utilized in a wide variety of ways. McDonald[24] identifies three applications for database marketing in the professional sport industry: (1) segmenting customers with high current and future value to the organization, (2) providing a vehicle for targeting communication efforts to the organization's best customers, and (3) personalizing customer service efforts related to customer value. The customer database should include basic information such as names, addresses, telephone numbers, and fax and e-mail information. It should also include product information relating to the style and model of the purchase or the seat location and number of tickets and the like. Additionally, it should include such specific personal data as birth dates for all household members; alma mater; preferred radio station; favorite retailer, Web site, restaurant; preferred recreational activities and vacation destination. This will permit the organization to customize activities to the individual based on his personal preferences and interests.

- *Collect customer-level data.* Periodic surveys either on-site, through the mail, or via the Internet are excellent ways to capture meaningful data about the customers in your database. Frequent fan programs and bar-coded tickets also can add valuable information to the database with regard to customer usage patterns and frequency, type of purchases, and so on.

• *Differentiate your customers.* Customers should be segmented based on measurements of lifetime value and relationship strength. Means and style of communication with customers should vary depending on how they have responded to past offers, length of the relationship, level of purchase, and other such information. Access to special events and rewards can be the basis for the segmentation, and these same rewards and special activities can be used to increase consumer interaction and investment with the sport organization.

• *Develop innovative programs.* Applications of the database to enhance and measure relationships with customers are limitless. The most valuable members could be provided with special benefits and privileges. Customers and their family members can receive special offers or incentives, or merely recognition on their birthdays or anniversaries related to the relationship with the organization.

The San Diego Padres' Compadres Club is an excellent illustration of the program we have just examined. The Compadres Club was the first frequent fan program established in sport. It was intended as an incentive-related program that rewarded fans for their attendance and associated spending at Padres games. The more games attended and the more money spent at concession and merchandise stands, the higher the level of benefits the Compadres Club member received. Prospective members complete a lifestyle survey, which also functions as the application and is the initial entry into the database. Information is added to the database through additional surveys and as the patron swipes the bar-coded membership card when attending a game or making a purchase. The information is then utilized to develop targeted offers and incentives to Compadres Club members based on their level of involvement.[25]

PRACTITIONER'S PERSPECTIVE

Customers As Assets—the Core of Lifetime Value
by Gordon Kaye, Senior Manager, Team Marketing and Business Operations, National Basketball Association

When examining the potential **lifetime value** of a customer, it is apparent that the customer is more than just a customer; a customer is an asset that must be valued by the organization. In the communications industry, telephone subscribers, magazine subscribers, and cable television subscribers are all viewed as assets when the net value of the organization is determined. If a cable television company is sold, the subscribers are viewed as assets and are accorded a value for the terms of the sales agreement. The sport organization has not been so practical in its assessment of resources. When sport organizations fail to view their customers in terms of their potential lifetime value to the organization, both their sales strategies and customer service strategies are questionable in terms of overall effectiveness, especially in relation to retention.

For example, let's examine the potential value of a season ticket holder for the Gotham Bats professional basketball franchise. Let us make the following assumptions:

• The average per-game ticket price for season tickets is $46.00.
• The ticket plan contains 43 games.
• Each season ticket account contains 2.5 tickets.

- Each game attended produces additional revenue of $30 per account in concession and parking spending.
- This results in *average annual expenditure of $6235.00.*
- Assume that prices across the board increase 5% annually.
- Assume that the retention or renewal rate for season ticket holders is 90%.
- After 10 years, our hypothetical ticket holder will have spent *$88,579.73.*
- After 20 years, our hypothetical ticket holder will have spent *$222,711.01.*

Although this does not deduct the costs associated with maintaining the relationship, neither does it reflect other potential revenue opportunities from upgrading the ticket type, increasing the number of tickets per account, play-off tickets, and incremental sales gained from word-of-mouth referral by a satisfied customer.[26] Nonetheless, these figures do indicate that if we viewed our customers as assets with long-term value, perhaps our sales strategies and retention and servicing strategies would be radically different.

NASCAR is an excellent example of an organization that has integrated the concept of lifetime value in all of its marketing and sales philosophies. NASCAR and its marketing partners integrate their marketing efforts to constantly introduce new ideas, products, and services to create not just customers but loyal lifetime customers. NASCAR has become very adept at targeting the mass market and at the same time giving individual attention to each fan.[27] Simply stated, NASCAR values every one of its customers for her current involvement and potential long-term value.

Putting Your Brand on Customer Service—Establishing a Trademark

In this chapter we have discussed NASCAR and Nordstrom as examples of the many companies and organizations that have distinguished themselves in some aspect of customer service and customer relationships. All these companies have established an identity and are distinctive in the eyes of their respective target markets. Having an identity or trademark is essential in a world where customer loyalty is a difficult yet attainable goal. There are many different ways to establish a trademark. For any organization, but particularly those involved in a high degree of repeat business like sport organizations, the trademark should reflect the personality of the organization, the wants and needs of the customers, and the nature of the service the organization provides. Anderson and Zemke suggest five ways to establish a trademark in customer service:[28]

- *Be reliable.* Doing what you say you are going to do every time is a terrific trademark. Reliability is basic to trust, which is the foundation for any lasting relationship. For example, if you guarantee that every season ticket holder will receive every promotional giveaway item during the course of the season, regardless of whether or not she attended those particular games, you must make sure that you have done exactly that for every item from the course of the year—not some or most, but all.

- *Call customers by name.* People love to hear their own names and to receive mail that has been personalized. Our experience as consultants indicates that long-term customers such as season ticket holders are immediately turned off when they receive mail from the sport organization addressed to "Dear Season Ticket Holder." Given our example of the potential lifetime value of such account holders, why would we ever send them any correspondence that is not personalized and tailored to them?

- *Spell the customer's (and the company's) name correctly.* Spelling names correctly demonstrates both common courtesy and professional care. Employees communicating with customers must take the time to know their customers—is Kelly a Ms. or a Mr.? At one time there was a sport marketing agency called DelWilber + Associates, and the CEO's name was Del Wilber. Each week, the human resource department received numerous letters addressed to Del Wilbur or Dell Wilber, many of them accompanied by resumes from college students. Needless to say, those letters usually went unanswered. Take the time to be professional, accurate, and courteous, and your customers will do the same.

- *Recognize your repeat customers.* Programs such as the San Diego Padres Compadres reward repeat customers, and our illustration of lifetime value provides a rationale for that reward system. An accurate, well-maintained database provides a record-keeping mechanism that can not only monitor usage and deliver rewards but also provide anecdotal information on purchasing patterns and enable us to recognize our repeat customers in upcoming communication activities. Amazon.com's personalized welcome message greets me every time I log on. Its recommendations feature, tailored to my past purchasing activities, is an effective way of demonstrating a familiarity with me and my interests; it is a service that can be interpreted as demonstrating an interest in my preferences and aggressively attempting to increase my lifetime value through suggested new purchases.

- *Know your products and more.* You are responsible for being the complete authority on all information about your products and services. Customers look for you to know more than they do. You can distinguish yourself (and the reputation of the organization) by answering questions for your customers when you know the answers and finding out the answers when you don't. Customers tend to have more trust in, hence more loyalty to, organizations that are knowledgeable and helpful. Ticketmaster is the industry giant (almost without competition) in the sale of sporting event tickets by phone and online. A customer calling Ticketmaster expects Ticketmaster to be knowledgeable about not only the event that is being sold, but also about the teams or the performer, the venue, and the market surrounding the venue. This is difficult when the phone rooms are not located in the customer's market and the customer has questions related to the locality. To provide better service, Ticketmaster helped establish Citysearch online, a Web site that provides valuable information about what to do and where to go in the local markets. While phone room personnel might not have the answers a caller is seeking, they have a resource to help answer commonly asked questions from out-of-town callers.

Customer Expectations in the New Millennium

This chapter has examined relationship marketing, customer service, and lifetime value. This discussion is rather traditional in form and is based on examples from current industry leaders in these areas. Perhaps we should give some attention to the expectations of today's (and tomorrow's) consumers with respect to how they view the industry. This will serve as a useful and thought-provoking guide for practitioners and scholars alike for viewing the current state of the art of customer relations and considering what is important to today's consumer. These perspectives will also help us in planning new strategies and tactics and making alterations and modifications accordingly.

What Do Consumers Expect?

There are two components of customer expectations in relation to service. The first component has to do with the level of performance expectance, and the second relates to the certainty of receiving that level of service. As previously discussed, how effectively these expectations are met helps to establish the customer service trademark of the organization. Expectations are influenced by prior experience[29] and also by such word-of-mouth sources such as reputation and endorsement. Advertising and other promotional media can also influence the perception of consumers and thus their expectations. Boston's Fenway Park, home of the Boston Red Sox, bills itself as Friendly Fenway Park—raising the consumer's expectation of the organization's commitment to hospitality management and guest relations.

What if the product or service is relatively unknown, untried, unpublicized, and unfamiliar to the consumer? Does the fact that there is no prior experience or word of mouth mean that there are no expectations? Quite the contrary—as there is no basis for the expectations, the consumer's hopes and perceptions might lead to an unrealistic expectation based solely on his own desires and imagination. In some cases, the product or service may be less rewarding or even anticlimactic because of the consumer's subjective imagination and the expectations that are the product of that imagination. Take, for example, the emergence during the last decade of gourmet coffee shops such as Starbucks. According to Sergio Zyman, these stores have been successful because they have created an image and expectation in the mind of the consumer that overcame more than 100 years of past practice and expectation. "Starbuck's through its advertising, its stores, its chirpy but professional young workers, its lattes, capuccinos, dark wooden counters and fresh roasted distribution system, has told me that good coffee doesn't come in vacuum-packed cans. Starbucks has taught me to expect better."[30]

In a sporting context, these same types of changes have taken place in the venues we patronize as fans. The multipurpose venues constructed in the late 1960s and early 1970s are being bulldozed after a life span of less than 30 years to make way for the

Starbuck's has redefined American's coffee expectations.

new sport-specific venues that we have come to expect as better serving our needs. The Camden Yards model, a retro park with modern amenities and services, has become the model for customer service and satisfaction.

Season ticket purchases, particularly those for new leagues such as the WNBA and the Women's United Soccer Association, have a significant defection rate—nonrenewals in the second and even third years of the purchase. The reason is partly expectations—realistic or not—that are not met, and partly also the reality of customers' not using the product (not attending as many games) to the extent that they expected to.

In short, our expectations of what is good and what isn't are changing rapidly and are influenced by both seen forces and unseen forces such as our imaginations.

What Today's Consumer Is Searching For

Time is arguably the most critical factor when people are making a decision about leisure activities. You don't really pay for things with money; you pay for them with time.[31] Thus consumers are looking for relationships with organizations worthy of their most valuable investment, their time. Organizations that can demonstrate to consumers that they are worth that investment will be successful and will endure and prosper. Those that can't will be left behind by the consumers in their search for the next great thing.

So what are consumers looking for from their relationships with sport organizations? They are looking for basically two things as a return on their investment of time. Consumers are looking to be entertained and they are looking for an experience. An examination of each of these areas should provide some insight into the behavior of today's consumers and what they are looking for in terms of service and long-term relationships.

Entertainment

Entertainment or, as Michael Wolf calls it, the E-Factor, is increasingly playing a fundamental role in determining which stores we shop at, what airline we fly, what restaurant we choose to go to, what clothes we wear, which pots we cook with, which computer we use, which Web sites we visit. The relative scarcity of free time and the necessity to plan for it have the effect of upping the ante for each entertainment decision. Not only is a bad movie perceived as a waste of time; it also represents a major opportunity lost in terms of other fun or entertainment one might have had.[32] Our scarcity of time also has led us to combine entertainment with day-to-day work and living requirements so that we can hope to get more bang for our "time dollars." Thus we have seen theme restaurants to entertain us while we eat, laundromats that are combined with bars, coffee shops with online computer terminals, and on and on. Restaurants such as the ESPN Zones are really entertainment centers that offer video games, batting cages, race car and skiing simulators, and a fantastic viewing experience, including the opportunity to watch live television programming. Shopping is another example of the integration of entertainment with daily-life chores. Seattle-based retailer, Recreational Equipment, Inc., is an excellent example of blending shopping and entertainment to create a memorable and repeatable shopping trip. Recreational Equipment's flagship store is more than 100,000 square feet in size and contains a 65-foot rock-climbing wall, a 35-foot waterfall, an indoor rain room for testing waterproof gear, and a 470-foot biking and hiking trail for testing equipment and footwear. This store has become one of Seattle's top tourist attractions, visited by more than 1.5 million visitors annually.[33] We are not asking to be entertained; we are demanding to be entertained—and if we are not entertained and do not enjoy our experience, we will search elsewhere until our needs have been met.

The Experiential Element

Experiences involve entertainment at the core of their respective products, but combine service and interaction to create something that is memorable and has value. As previously mentioned, people scrutinize their spending of money and time for goods and services to make way for more memorable and more highly valued experiences. Companies and organizations stage an experience when they engage customers in a memorable way.[34] Companies and organizations must redesign and/or reposition their goods and services in such a way that they experimentalize them. For example, Rawlings Sporting Goods of St. Louis has introduced a baseball that makes playing catch more engaging and hence an experience. This "radar ball" contains a microchip that digitally displays, after each toss, how fast the ball was thrown. Consumers pay about six times the cost of a regular baseball for the radar ball, which retails for more than $30, because it engages them. With radar guns costing around $1000, the radar ball makes it affordable for you to know your throwing velocity. It also uses technology to create a richer experience for the participants, who need each other to fully maximize the benefits of playing with the radar ball. Thanks to Rawlings, right now in some backyard, some child is asking, "Hey Dad, how fast was that one?"[35]

Tying Customer Service, Long-Term Relationships, and Lifetime Value to Entertainment and Experimentalization

Adding entertainment and creating experiences change the level and amount of interaction between the customer and the personnel of the company or organization. These personnel, regardless of their primary duties and job titles, all function as experience stagers and entertainment providers working to engage the customer and provide a memorable and pleasurable experience. Figure 14.2 depicts the "worth" elements of an experience.[36] If the experience is worth remembering, repeating, recommending, planning for, and committing resources to, it will lead to a long-term relationship between the consumer and the organization and increased lifetime value.

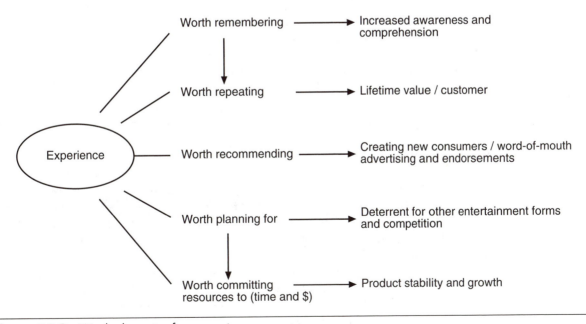

Figure 14.2 Worth elements of an experience.

Disney is well known for creating experiences that not only have worth value but also provide the spectrum of experiences—esthetic, escapist, educational, and entertaining. Club Disney is a new play-site experience for children 10 and under. At Club Disney, adults and children pay to play in any of nine play modules. The company designed each module to fulfill a pledge posted near the entrance: "Our mission is to create a place in the community where children and their grown-ups have fun and bond with each other through enriching activities and imaginative play."[37] Club Disney succeeds because of the worth dimensions, the trademark Disney image, Disney's guest services program and event stagers, and the fact that the customers are engaged in creating a memorable experience facilitated by Disney personnel.

Creating and staging an experience constitute an essential element in sport-related venues and programming because this facet, more than any other, sets up in the mind of the consumer the need or desire to return for another similar, yet different, experience. Given that there are 81 home games for an MLB team and 41 for an NBA basketball team, and that venues such as Disneyworld, Six Flags, and the Mall of America are destinations that depend on repeat business and new business created by word of mouth, isn't the need to create an experience a critical strategic decision?

Postgame Wrap-Up

Customer retention (as discussed in this chapter and chapter 5) is one of the cornerstones of a successful business. Today's consumer is always searching for *"the next new thing"* or *"the next great thing."* How will this affect your business? Will everyone come once and then go searching for something else, or will people come time after time, creating a relationship with you and your organization? The key to retaining customers and achieving a valuable lifetime relationship with your clientele is to offer products and services of such quality and presentation that you are creating "raving fans." Raving fans, as defined by Ken Blanchard and Sheldon Bowles in their seminal work *Raving Fans,* are loyal patrons and ambassadors of your business.

In sport, creating raving fans is even more essential because of the dependency on the customer to repeat the purchase. Major League Baseball has 81 home games. Top Flite is one of more than a dozen golf ball manufacturers. A number of shoe manufacturers produce running shoes. The point is to remember that consumers have a choice: if your organization is not meeting their needs, they'll find an organization that will.

Customers should be viewed as organizational assets. They need to be managed, developed, and cared for, in the hopes that like assets such as stocks and bonds, they appreciate and grow in value. A ticket purchaser must be viewed as someone who can continue to purchase tickets for years to come. The purchaser of a pair of running shoes will need replacement pairs. The organization must do everything in its power to maintain organizational or brand loyalty and to develop a relationship with the customer that is mutually satisfying and rewarding for all parties concerned.

We are entering the era of the consumer in terms of sport and entertainment options. Sport organizations need to realize that because consumers have a choice, the organizations must work hard to create value, satisfaction, and enjoyment for consumers with regard to their purchases. They must convey to the consumer that he is valued by the organization. Communication needs to be regular, and two way, providing consumers with a forum to convey to the organization what they are looking for in the relationship. Communicating and listening to the consumer are the duties of everyone in the organization, because everyone works in the customer service and satisfaction department.

Discussion Items

1. Discuss how frequent fan programs and similar activities made possible by technology can improve customer satisfaction and lead to relationship building of a long-term nature.

2. Think of all of the transactions (purchases, attendance at events, and so forth) that you have been a part of. Are you a "raving fan" of any of the providers of these goods, services, or experiences? What has made you a raving fan or prevented you from becoming one?

3. Choose your favorite provider of the transactions discussed in your previous answer. If you were to continue your current level of purchasing with this provider, how much would you spend in one year? How much in 10 years? How much over a 30-year period? Do you feel that this provider acknowledges your revenue potential as part of your current relationship? If not, what types of improvements would you suggest to the provider that might not only lead to retaining you as a customer but also encourage you to increase the volume of your business?

Learning Enrichment Activities

1. In conjunction with the athletic department on your campus, arrange an opportunity to attend an athletic event for the purpose of talking to the attendees. Write an interview script containing three to five questions about the customers' experience and about what could be done to enhance their experience and encourage them to attend more often.

2. Review publications such as *Street & Smith's SportsBusiness Journal, Team Marketing Report, Wall Street Journal,* and *Business Week.* Identify organizations that are attempting to create "raving fans." What do these organizations have in common in their approaches?

3. List and discuss the five most memorable sporting/entertainment experiences you have had in the past five years. What are the common elements that made these experiences memorable to you?

4. Imagine that you are interviewing for the newly created position of vice president of imagineering with the Gotham Bats, a professional baseball team. You are asked your opinion on experimentalization—attempting to do things in new ways to provide a motivation for increasing purchasing behavior. What types of experimentalization can you envision that could positively affect the fans' experience at a baseball game?

5. Attend a sport or entertainment event of your choosing. After attending, analyze the event in terms of the worth dimensions associated with an event or activity that serve to promote that activity internally and externally in the future.

APPENDIX A

The following appendix is the Redbirds FansFirst plan.

Redbirds

FansFirst Plan 2001

Goal: The FansFirst plan will establish a clear and effective means by which the Memphis Redbirds will become the area's standard for customer and employee service.

This goal will be achieved by:

1. Clearly defining and understanding our Service Theme.
2. Hiring, training and retaining the best employees and empowering them to effectively deal with customers.
3. Clearly defining the roles of our employees and demonstrating how these roles figure into our FansFirst plan.
4. Consistently exceeding each fan's expectations of customer service with our individualized FansFirst approach.
5. Regularly assessing and monitoring our FansFirst plan in order to maintain and actively improve our customer service.
6. Fostering and maintaining a creative, rewarding and open work climate that will lead directly to improvement of our service.

Reprinted, by permission, from the Memphis Redbirds.

Redbirds

Service Theme:
"We use the great game of baseball to provide
fun and entertainment for fans of all ages."

Understanding our Service Theme:

- "We"—*every* Redbirds representative is included in this pronoun. We all have a responsibility to provide our fans with the quality service they deserve.
- "use the great game of baseball"—in other words, baseball is our vehicle. The game is at the core of everything we do.
- "to provide fun and entertainment"—the atmosphere at the ballpark is fun and entertaining when all elements of our operation are working together. Just think about Rockey, double plays, the post-game bands, the boardwalk games, home runs, BBQ and so much more!
- "for fans of all ages." —we have something for everyone. From the die-hard baseball fan to the casual observer and from grandparents to grandchildren, we can give them a quality Redbirds experience.

Reprinted, by permission, from the Memphis Redbirds.

Redbirds

We will hire, train and retain the best, most customer-friendly employees and empower them to effectively deal with our fans.

- ◆ We will establish and maintain a high standard for our hiring practices.
- ◆ All employees will undergo orientation sessions to learn and understand our approach to customer service.
- ◆ All employees will be provided with all appropriate team information through outlets such as the pre-game/post-game meetings and the Redbirds Review.
- ◆ All employees will be given the freedom to bring their own personality and charisma to our FansFirst approach. This in turn will keep our customer service fresh and genuine.
- ◆ All employees will understand the existing channels of communication in order to report and react to fan suggestions and concerns in the appropriate manner.

Reprinted, by permission, from the Memphis Redbirds.

Redbirds

We will clearly define the roles of all departments/employees and demonstrate exactly how each of these roles figures into our FansFirst plan.

- Accounting
- Backstop Baseball Emporium (retail store)
- Community Relations
- Development
- Marketing
- Media Relations
- Operations
- Ovations Food Service
- Promotions
- Sales
- Boardwalk Staff
- Concessions Staff
- Press Box Staff
- Retail Representatives
- Security
- Suite Hosts
- Ticket Sellers
- Ticket Takers
- Ushers
- Volunteer Groups

Reprinted, by permission, from the Memphis Redbirds.

Redbirds

We will consistently exceed each fan's expectation of customer service with our personalized FansFirst approach.

Every fan deserves, and can expect, the following:
- A personal welcome upon entering the ballpark
- A knowledgeable staff
- An accessible staff
- An "aggressively friendly" staff
- A familiar staff
- A quality choice of souvenirs and apparel
- A quality choice of concessions
- A fun, family-oriented ballpark
- A safe ballpark
- A clean ballpark
- An answer to every question
- An opportunity to offer suggestions
- A personal "thank you" upon leaving the ballpark
- A seamless Redbirds experience
- The game of baseball, pure & simple

Reprinted, by permission, from the Memphis Redbirds.

Redbirds

We will regularly assess and monitor our FansFirst plan in order to maintain and actively improve our customer service.

- FansFirst forms will be made available each game and will allow fans to rate our service and offer suggestions.
- During 18 pre-selected dates (once per four game series), a staff member will ask fans a series of prescribed questions. For example, a typical question would be "how could we improve your Redbirds experience?"
- The FansFirst information center will work to be prepared with every potential answer for fans on game day.
- Every fan suggestion or comment will be channeled through a central clearinghouse in order to insure consistency and continuity in response.
- In order to gather input from employees, suggestion forms will be made available in the Game Day Staff room.
- All the information discussed above will be collected and distributed through monthly FansFirst reports. These reports will be given to our Directors and Managers who will, in turn, communicate the appropriate suggestions and comments to all employees.

Reprinted, by permission, from the Memphis Redbirds.

Redbirds

We will foster and maintain an open, rewarding and creative work climate.

♦ The Redbirds organization will operate with the understanding that "good treatment of workers results in similar treatment of customers." Therefore, all employees will receive the same individualized attention that we provide our fans.

♦ We will create opportunities to allow full-time staff and Game Day staff the chance to get to know one another. These functions will serve to reinforce the fact that everyone is working toward a common goal in serving our fans.

♦ All employees will be eligible to win the monthly "Outstanding Customer Service Award." Winners will receive a plaque and gift certificate to the Redbirds Store.

♦ All employees will receive a FansFirst pin to wear with their uniform. The pin will serve as a constant reminder of our Redbirds value system and will become an award of merit. All employees will be eligible to earn progressive honors in the form of red, silver and gold FansFirst pins.

♦ Those individuals in management positions should make themselves readily available for employee comments and suggestions on a regular basis.

Reprinted, by permission, from the Memphis Redbirds.

APPENDIX B

The following appendix is the policy and screening procedures for those parties requesting credentials for the Women's Final Four from the NCAA.

P.O. Box 6222

Indianapolis, Indiana

46206-6222

Telephone 317/917-6222

Shipping/Overnight Address:

1802 Alonzo Watford Sr. Drive

Indianapolis, Indiana 46202

www.ncaa.org

MEMORANDUM

January 11, 2001

TO: Sports Editors, Sports Directors.

From: Scottie Rodgers
Assistant Director of the Division I Women's Basketball Championship, Media.

Subject: 2001 Women's Final Four Credential Application.

I have enclosed an application form for working press credentials to the 2001 Women's Final Four, which will be played at the Savvis Center in St. Louis, Missouri. Note that no applications will be accepted after March 1.

Credentials for <u>all other rounds</u> of the tournament must be requested from the media coordinators at the site. A list of the regional media coordinators and sites is on page six of the application form. <u>Please make a copy of this list for your files</u>. Media coordinators for the first- and second-rounds will not be determined until after the bracket announcement on Sunday, March 11.

Please alert your staff that the NCAA Division I Women's Basketball Committee chair Maryalyce Jeremiah, senior associate director of athletics at California State University-Fullerton, will participate in two telephonic press conferences prior to the tournament. The first teleconference will begin at 2:30 p.m. Eastern time, Tuesday, March 6, and the confirmation code is **432542**. The second teleconference will be at 7:15 p.m. Eastern time, Sunday, March 11, and the confirmation code is **625430**. Please advise your representatives to call **913/981-5509** about five minutes before each call is scheduled to begin.

Thank you for promptly returning the application form to me. Please contact me at 317/917-6539 should you have any questions about the Women's Basketball Championship.

SFR:bra

Enclosure

cc: NCAA Division I Women's Basketball Committee
Selected NCAA Staff Members

Equal Opportunity/

Affirmative Action

Employer

National Collegiate Athletic Association

An association of 1,200 colleges, universities and conferences serving the student-athlete

"Reprinted with the permission of the NCAA. All rights reserved. 2001."

2001 NCAA WOMEN'S FINAL FOUR
MEDIA CREDENTIAL APPLICATION

DEADLINE IS MARCH 1
PLEASE RETURN PROMPTLY

SAVVIS CENTER
ST. LOUIS, MARCH 30 & APRIL 1

This credential application is for the WOMEN'S FINAL FOUR only.

All media outlets planning coverage of the 2001 NCAA Women's Final Four should read these instructions carefully and complete the enclosed form. The application does not guarantee that credentials requested will be issued. If you have any questions or need assistance, please contact Scottie Rodgers, Assistant Director of the Division I Women's Basketball Championship, Media, at 317/917-6222, ext. 6539.

1. CREDENTIALS

Please direct requests for working-media credentials for first- and second-round and regional games to the host media coordinator at each site. Please see the directory included in this document for a listing the regional media coordinators. Media coordinators for the first and second rounds will not be known until the bracket is announced on Sunday, March 11.

The official credential application form shall be used to request Women's Final Four credentials. Thursday, March 1, is the deadline for submitting applications, which will be considered in the order that they are received. Meeting the deadline does not guarantee any media agency a credential or a seat since space for the priorities listed in the criteria herein may be assigned before March 1. Please apply for credentials only for individuals who will staff the Women's Final Four regardless of the four teams participating.

Return to: Scottie Rodgers
NCAA
P.O. Box 6222
Indianapolis, Indiana 46206-6222
Office: 317/917-6222, ext. 6539
Fax: 317/917-6826
e-mail: srodgers@ncaa.org

"Reprinted with the permission of the NCAA. All rights reserved. 2001."

All Women's Final Four credentials shall be claimed beginning at 4 p.m. Wednesday, March 28, at the Marriott Pavilion Hotel (Senator Room). **Individuals claiming credentials shall present photo identification.** An individual wishing to claim more than one credential shall make advance arrangements with the NCAA.

2. MEDIA HOTEL ACCOMMODATIONS

The media hotel for the Women's Final Four is the Marriott Pavilion ($118 per night, plus tax). **There is a three-night minimum stay. Each individual will be charged for three nights, even if the person elects to depart early.**

A valid credit card and the individual's signature is required to guarantee all reservations and to confirm use of the card for payment of charges. The hotel is authorized to debit against the card on or any time after Friday, March 23, or the date the reservation begins, if earlier. The hotel may check the card to ensure that it is valid before that date.

Once a credential confirmation letter has been issued by the NCAA, any changes to your original request must be made in writing to Bernadette Ramsey at the NCAA national office (phone: 317/917-6222, ext. 6549; e-mail: bramsey@ncaa.org) as soon as possible if a press agency desires to reassign the individual staffing the Women's Final Four or change hotel arrival plans.

Beginning Sunday, March 25, Ms. Ramsey will be at the Marriott Pavilion (314/421-1776) in St. Louis.

3. TELEPHONE SERVICE

A telephone order form will be sent with the credential confirmation letter.
The NCAA will provide a limited number of telephones in the media work room at the arena. The only way to ensure that you will have access to a telephone for your exclusive use is to order one when you receive the order form with your confirmation.

4. TRANSPORTATION

Complimentary shuttle transportation will be provided by the NCAA and the St. Louis Organizing Committee to and from the St. Louis airport. The NCAA and SLOC will also provide shuttle transportation to and from the Marriott Pavilion to the Savvis Center. Transportation passes will be mailed with the credential confirmation letters.

5. TELEPHONIC NEWS CONFERENCES

The NCAA will schedule two telephonic news conferences in conjunction with the 2001 Division I Women's Basketball Championship.

Maryalyce Jeremiah, senior associate director of athletics at California State University, Fullerton and chair of the Division I Women's Basketball Committee, will be featured on the calls, scheduled for Tuesday, March 6 and Sunday, March 11.

More information on these calls will be made available once the arrangements are finalized.

6. CREDENTIALS CRITERIA FOR DOMESTIC MEDIA AGENCIES

A. Print, Radio, Television

The NCAA Division I Women's Basketball Committee has reiterated its opposition to all sports wagering and encourages the media to assist in the education of the public with regard to the hazards of sports wagering.

Requests for working-media credentials for first and second rounds and regionals shall be directed to the host media coordinator. Requests for the Women's Final Four shall be directed to the NCAA national office.

A "press agency" for purposes of these criteria shall mean a daily or weekly publication, cable system, radio or television station and network requiring immediate news coverage. "Immediate news coverage" for purposes of these criteria shall mean the editorial, audio and/or visual deadline for the tournament action being documented occurs no later than 48 hours after the competition at the site has been completed.

Separate publications sharing common ownership may not be combined for purposes of meeting circulation or other criteria. A credential may be issued only to an authorized full-time, salaried representative of, or a representative who regularly and customarily performs services for, such an entity. Credentials are not transferable.

Credentials distributed to a participating institution may be utilized only by student-athletes, full-time staff members of the institution or others designated by the chief executive officer.

"Reprinted with the permission of the NCAA. All rights reserved. 2001."

Any press agency that has been certified for Women's Final Four credentials shall receive a first- and second-round and/or regional credential upon request.

A press agency or television or radio station in the immediate geographic area and/or locale of a participating or host institution that has staffed its games on a regular basis throughout the season and does not otherwise meet the established criteria may be designated by the participating or host institution as "minority media enterprises." A "minority media enterprise" shall mean a business enterprise involved in the dissemination of sports news to individuals socially or economically disadvantaged from cultural, racial or chronic-economic circumstances or other similar circumstances or other similar cause. Such persons include, but are not limited to, African-Americans, Puerto Ricans, Spanish-speaking Americans and American Indians.

NCAA policy prohibits the issuance of media credentials to representatives of any organization that regularly publishes or otherwise promotes the advertising of "tout sheets" or "tip sheets," or other advertising designed to encourage gambling on college sports events.

Subject to limitations of space, credentials at all sites shall be assigned in accordance with the following priorities:

Print

Separate publications sharing common ownership may not be combined for purposes of meeting circulation or other criteria. A credential may be issued only to an authorized full-time, salaried representative of, or a representative who regularly and customarily performs services for such an entity. Credentials are not transferable.

1. A news agency, regardless of circulation or television homes, in the geographic area and/or locale of a participating institution that has staffed at least 90 percent of its home games throughout the season. This includes newspapers or other periodicals specifically designed to cover the activities and events of a single institution. (Note: Organizations affiliated with institutions are referenced in No. 2 above.)

2. A news agency, regardless of circulation or television homes, that has staffed at least 90 percent of the home games of the host institution throughout the season.

3. Any press agency with a minimum daily circulation of 60,000 to 99,999 shall be accredited for one working press credential. Other press agencies may receive more than one credential according to the following circulation requirements:

   > 100,000 - 249,999 — one seat, one limited access
   > 250,000 - 349,999 — two seats, one limited access
   > 350,000 - 449,999 — three seats, one limited access
   > 450,000 - 649,999 — four seats, one limited access
   > 650,000 - 999,999 — five seats, two limited access
   > 1 million and above — six seats, two limited access

   (Note: A limited access credential will only be used at the Women's Final Four. It only permits access to the working press room, locker rooms and interview room. A hotel room may not be available for an individual who receives a limited access credential.)

4. The Associated Press and the primary newspaper(s) that provide daily coverage for the host and participating institutions each may receive a maximum of eight seats and two restricted credentials at the Women's Final Four.

5. A national weekly publication that has a circulation between 500,000 and three million and a national monthly publication with a circulation between 750,000 and three million each may receive two seats and two limited access credentials. Publications that have a minimum circulation of three million may receive a maximum of four seats and two limited access credentials. A weekly that does not meet this criteria or the criteria required of governing media agencies of the host and participating teams does not qualify for credentials.

6. The media coordinator may authorize a media agency to receive a credential for a "special need."

   a. A specialty publication that is distributed nationally on a regular basis during the basketball season is a media agency that may have a "special need" and may receive one seat in the overflow press section if space is available.

   b. A "special need" entity that normally provides specific services for a media agency (e.g., scores) shall not receive credentials if many of its clients have been accredited to staff the event.

   A "special need" entity shall be limited to one credential.

"Reprinted with the permission of the NCAA. All rights reserved. 2001."

7.   At the media coordinator's discretion, one credential may be issued to a reporter representing the "news side" of the major newspaper of the participating and/or host institution.

Television

1.   Television stations from the locale of the tournament site may be represented by two crews if it is representing multiple, regularly scheduled news programs. A crew is defined to include one talent, one cameraperson and one audio technician or one producer. One limited access credential may be provided to a network, cable system or station for a technician who is responsible for maintenance of the satellite truck that may be parked at the arena.

2.   Television stations from the locale of the participating institutions may be represented by one crew per station. A crew is defined to include one talent, one cameraperson and one audio technician or one producer. One limited access credential may be provided to a network, cable system or station for a technician who is responsible for maintenance of the satellite truck that may be parked at the arena.

3.   A national television network, which may include separate requests from the sports, news, entertainment and affiliate division, or cable system that originates a daily sports news program, may be represented by one crew (Example: CBS News Path, CBS World News, CBS News, CBS This Morning, NBC News Channel, NBC Nightside, NBC World News, NBC Today Show, Good Morning America, ABC Weekend News, ABC World News Tonight, ABC News One, ESPN, CNN, and FOX). A crew is defined to include one talent, one cameraperson, one audio technician and one audio technician or one producer. One limited access credential may be provided to a network, cable system or station for a technician who is responsible for maintenance of the satellite truck that may be parked at the arena.

4.   A television station in a market area estimated to have represented a minimum of one million U.S. television households the previous year by the A.C. Nielsen Company may be represented by one crew. A crew is defined to include one talent, one photographer and one audio technician or one producer. One limited access credential may be provided to a network, cable system or station for a technician who is responsible for maintenance of the satellite truck that may be parked at the arena.

5.   Credentials may be authorized to the following news services: NPI (one seat, one video), Conus Communications (one seat, two video), SNS Sports Newsatellite (one seat, two video), National Sports and Entertainment (one seat, one video) and Christian Broadcasting Network (one seat, one video).

Radio

1.   One credential may be assigned to the following radio networks: AP, ABC, CBS, ESPN Radio, One-on-One Sports Radio, USA Radio Network, Premier Prime Sports Radio, Global Sports Network, Mutual Broadcasting, NBC, American Urban, Echlin Sports Service, National Public Voice of America, Sports Byline USA or UPI Audio.

2.   One credential may be assigned to a radio station in a market area representing at least one million radio homes that regularly (10 or more) originates college basketball games and a daily "sports talk" program.

3.   Each radio station that has purchased live broadcasting rights is limited to the number of individuals required to originate 90 percent of its games during the regular season, up to a maximum of four credentials.

Agencies Not Eligible

1.   Representatives staffing Web sites, specialty publications (including books and magazines), services (computer on-lines and scores), other college newspapers or magazines, professional basketball teams and telephone reporting services shall not be accredited for credentials.

2.   A press credential may not be authorized to a media representative or an individual normally identified as a media representative for the primary purpose of authoring a book about a coach, student-athlete or participating institution.

"Reprinted with the permission of the NCAA. All rights reserved. 2001."

3. Television shows produced by a syndicator or independent producer for or by a head basketball coach of a participating or host institution, public television stations, syndicated television or cable programmers will not be accredited for working press or photography credentials.

B. Print Photographers

Sports editors shall request all photography credentials. Most media agencies will be limited to one credential.

"Immediate news coverage" for purposes of these criteria shall mean the editorial, audio and/or visual deadline for the tournament action being documented occurs no later than 48 hours after the competition at that site has been completed.

Any photographer approved to work in the official photographers' boxes at the ends of the floor must secure an armband from the media coordinator.

Subject to limitations of space, photography credentials shall be assigned to agencies requiring immediate news coverage in accordance with the following priorities:

1. Two photographers, certified by the director of athletics or designated representative of each participating and host institution, who will be the sole representatives of all media organizations affiliated with such institutions and all media organizations whose coverage primarily is directed to any such institution and its activities.

2. The primary press agencies at the competition site that have staffed at least 90 percent of the home games of the host institution or conference may receive a maximum of three (two floor) credentials.

3. The Associated Press may receive four (three floor level) credentials. Sports Illustrated magazine and USA Today each may receive three (two floor level) credentials. The Sporting News magazine, Reuters and Knight-Ridder may receive two (one floor level) credentials. All Sport photo may receive one credential.

4. A participating institution may identify four credentials for media agencies that do not meet the minimum daily or weekly circulation requirements. These agencies shall be certified by the director of athletics or designated representative of the participating and/or host institution to have staffed at least 90 percent of its home games throughout the season and each of its games in the championship.

5. A press agency with a minimum daily circulation of 350,000, a weekly circulation to 500,000, or a monthly circulation of one million may receive one credential.

6. A "special need" publication shall not receive a photography credential.

7. CREDENTIAL CRITERIA FOR INTERNATIONAL MEDIA AGENCIES (Women's Final Four Only)

When space is available, credentials will be issued to a full-time, salaried employee, or a representative who regularly and customarily performs services, for:

a. A newspaper that has a minimum circulation of five percent of the total population of the country;

b. A specialty publication that has a minimum circulation of one percent of the total population of the country;

c. The official publication of the country's basketball federation;

d. A television station that has a signal reaching 25 percent of the homes in the country and has purchased the rights through Trans World International.

e. Each of the two largest sports networks in the country, and

f. A photography position for the respective media agency above.

"Reprinted with the permission of the NCAA. All rights reserved. 2001."

2001 DIVISION I WOMEN'S BASKETBALL CHAMPIONSHIP
Regional Media Coordinators

EAST
Michelle Chini
Coordinator of Media Relations
Duquesne University
600 Forbes Avenue
Pittsburgh, Pennsylvania 15282
Office: 412/396-6560
Fax: 412/396-6210
E-Mail: chini@mail.cc.duq.edu
Web site:
   www.godukes.duq.edu

MIDEAST
Tammy Wilson
Assistant Director of Media Relations
Southeastern Conference
2201 Richard Arrington Boulevard North
Birmingham, Alabama 35203-1103
Office: 205/458-3010
Fax: 205/458-3030
E-Mail: twilson@sec.org
Web site:
   www.secsports.com

MIDWEST
Colleen Krueger
Associate Sports Information Director
University of Colorado
Fieldhouse Annex 50
Boulder, Colorado 80303
Office: 303/492-5890
Fax: 303/492-3811
E-Mail: colleen.krueger@colorado.edu
Web site:
   www.cu-sports.com

WEST
Jason Krump
Assistant Sports Information Director
Washington State University
Bohler Addition 195
Pullman, Washington 99164-1602
Office: 509/335-0269
Fax: 509/335-0267
E-Mail: jkrump@wsu.edu
Web site:
   www.spokanehoops.com
and
   www.wsucougars.com

NOTE: Media coordinators for the first and second rounds will not be known until the bracket is announced Sunday, March 11.

"Reprinted with the permission of the NCAA. All rights reserved. 2001."

2001 NCAA® WOMEN'S FINAL FOUR®
MEDIA CREDENTIAL APPLICATION

DEADLINE IS MARCH 1

Apply for working media credentials to the 2001 NCAA Women's Final Four only if you will attend regardless of which teams advance to St. Louis. If you plan to cover the Women's Final Four ONLY if the team you regularly cover reaches the Women's Final Four, **DO NOT** fill out this form. You may obtain your credential(s) through that team's sports information director.

Media Agency _____

Sports Editor/ Director Making Request _____

Address _____

City/State/Zip _____

Telephone(_____)_____Fax (_____) _____

E-mail _____

Only a limited number of seats will be available at courtside. Seats will be assigned per the priority established by the sports editor/director. Please list names in order of priority.

Print Media

Daily Circulation _____

Priority	Seat	Limited access	Still photographer	Still photo tech/editor
1. _____	_____	_____	_____	_____
2. _____	_____	_____	_____	_____
3. _____	_____	_____	_____	_____
4. _____	_____	_____	_____	_____

Electronic Media

Number of TV Homes in your DMA _____

Priority	Radio	TV talent	TV photographer	TV tech
1. _____	_____	_____	_____	_____
2. _____	_____	_____	_____	_____
3. _____	_____	_____	_____	_____
4. _____	_____	_____	_____	_____

PLEASE RETURN THIS FORM IMMEDIATELY TO SCOTTIE RODGERS VIA MAIL (NCAA P.O. BOX 6222, INDIANAPOLIS, INDIANA 46206-6222) OR FAX (317/917-6826).

Check if no hotel is needed through the NCAA _____
If hotel is needed through the NCAA, fill out the accompanying request form.

Detach on perforation

"Reprinted with the permission of the NCAA. All rights reserved. 2001."

2001 NCAA® WOMEN'S FINAL FOUR®
HOTEL REQUEST FORM

<u>DEADLINE IS MARCH 1</u>
CONFIRMATION LETTERS WILL BE SENT AS SOON AS POSSIBLE AFTER MARCH 1

The media hotel for the 2001 NCAA Women's Final Four is the Marriott Pavilion ($118 per night, plus tax). There is a three-night minimum stay. Each individual will be charged for three nights, even if the person elects to depart early.

Should an agency elect NOT to staff the Women's Final Four and need to cancel its hotel room, it should contact Bernadette Ramsey (phone: 317/917-6222, ext. 6549; e-mail: bramsey@ncaa.org) no later than Tuesday, March 27.

Please indicate your room preference below (smoking (S) or non-smoking (NS); single (SGL) or double/double (D/D)). Single rooms may not be available for all media representatives. The NCAA cannot guarantee a hotel room for every media representative.

Media Agency _____

Sports Editor/Director Making Request _____

Name	Arrive	Depart	Arrival Time	Room Type (S or NS/ SGL or D/D)	Individuals Sharing
1. _____	_____	_____	_____	_____	_____
2. _____	_____	_____	_____	_____	_____
3. _____	_____	_____	_____	_____	_____
4. _____	_____	_____	_____	_____	_____
5. _____	_____	_____	_____	_____	_____
6. _____	_____	_____	_____	_____	_____

Credit Card Information

A VALID CREDIT CARD IS REQUIRED TO GUARANTEE RESERVATIONS

"I hereby authorize the hotel to use this credit card information for payment of charges incurred as noted above."

Sign: _____ Date: _____

Credit Card Type (Please circle one): American Express • Mastercard • VISA • Discover • Diners Club

Credit Card Number _____ Expiration Date _____

Cardholder's Name as Printed on Card _____

PLEASE RETURN THIS FORM <u>IMMEDIATELY</u> TO SCOTTIE RODGERS VIA MAIL (NCAA, P.O. BOX 6222, INDIANAPOLIS, INDIANA 46206-6222) OR FAX (317/917-6826).

NCAA 15392-10/00

"Reprinted with the permission of the NCAA. All rights reserved. 2001."

ENDNOTES

Chapter 1

1. Broughton, D., Lee, J., and Nethery, R. (1999). The question: How big is the U.S. sports industry? *Street & Smith's SportsBusiness Journal* 2(35): 23-29.

2. Kotler, P. (1975). *Marketing for non-profit organizations.* Englewood Cliffs, NJ: Prentice Hall, 5.

3. Mullin, B.J., Hardy, S., and Sutton, W.A. (2000). *Sport marketing.* 2nd ed. Champaign, IL: Human Kinetics, 9.

4. Meenaghan, T., and O'Sullivan, P. (1999). Playpower-sports meets marketing. *European Journal of Marketing* 33(3/4): 241-249.

5. Shaaf, P. (1994). *Sports marketing.* Amherst, NY: Prometheus Books, 22.

6. Wascovich, T.R. (1993). *The sport marketing guide.* Cleveland: PointsAhead, 4.

7. Kotler, P. (1975). *Marketing for non-profit organizations.*

8. Shimp, T.A., and DeLozier, M.W. (1986). *Promotion management and marketing communications.* Chicago: Dryden Press.

9. Mullin, B.J., Hardy, S., and Sutton, W.A. (2000). *Sport marketing.*

10. Kotler, P. (1975). *Marketing for non-profit organizations.*

11. Capulsky, R.J., and Wolf, J.M. (1991). Relationship marketing: Positioning for the future. *Journal of Business Strategy* (July/August): 16-26.

12. Gordon, M.E., McKage, K., and Fox, M.A. (1998). Relationship marketing effectiveness: The role of involvement. *Psychology & Marketing* 15(5): 443-459.

13. Gordon, M.E., McKage, K., and Fox, M.A. (1998). Relationship marketing effectiveness: The role of involvement.

14. Shani, D. (1997). A framework for implementing relationship marketing in the sport industry. *Sport Marketing Quarterly* 6(2): 9-15.

15. Kotler, P. (1975). *Marketing for non-profit organizations.*

16. Martin, C. (1990). The employee/customer interface: An empirical investigation of employee behaviors and customer perceptions. *Journal of Sport Management* 4: 1-20.

17. Normann, R. (1984). *Service management: Strategy and leadership in service business.* Chichester: Wiley.

18. Martin, C. (1990). The employee/customer interface: An empirical investigation of employee behaviors and customer perceptions.

19. Martin, C. (1990). The employee/customer interface: An empirical investigation of employee behaviors and customer perceptions.

20. Martin, C. (1990). The employee/customer interface: An empirical investigation of employee behaviors and customer perceptions.

21. Kahle, L., and Elton, M. (1997). Sports talk and the development of marketing relationships. *Sport Marketing Quarterly* 6(2): 35-39.

22. Kahle, L., and Elton, M. (1997). Sports talk and the development of marketing relationships.

23. Smith, P.R. (1993). *Marketing communications: An integrated approach.* London: Kogan Page.

24. McDonald, M.A., and Milne, G.R. (1997). A conceptual framework for evaluating marketing relationships in professional sport franchises. *Sport Marketing Quarterly* 6(2): 27-32.

25. Higgins, S.H., and Martin, J.H. (1996). Managing sport innovations: A diffusion theory perspective. *Sport Marketing Quarterly* 5(1): 43-48.

26. Capodagli, B., and Jackson, L. (1999). *The Disney way.* New York: McGraw-Hill.

27. Bennett, R. (1997). Anger, catharsis, and purchasing behavior following aggressive customer complaints. *Journal of Consumer Marketing* 14(2): 156-172.

28. Martin, C. (1990). The employee/customer interface: An empirical investigation of employee behaviors and customer perceptions.

29. Bennett, R. (1997). Anger, catharsis, and purchasing behavior following aggressive customer complaints.

30. Shimp, T.A., and DeLozier, M.W. (1986). *Promotion management and marketing communications.*

31. Kotler, P. (1975). Marketing for non-profit organizations.

32. Kuzma, J.R., Shanklin, W.L., and McCally, J.F. (1993). Number one principle for sporting events seeking corporate sponsors: Meet benefactor's objectives. *Sport Marketing Quarterly* 2(3): 27-32.

33. Kotler, P. (1975). Marketing for non-profit organizations.

34. Shimp, T.A., and DeLozier, M.W. (1986). *Promotion management and marketing communications.*

35. Mullin, B.J., Hardy, S., and Sutton, W.A. (2000). *Sport marketing.*

36. Wolf, M. (1998). The entertainment economy. New York: Random House.

37. 1999 State of the Industry Report. Sporting Goods Manufacturers Association.

38. Shaaf, P. (1994). *Sports marketing.*

39. Kuzma, J.R., Shanklin, W.L., and McCally, J.F. (1993). Number one principle for sporting events seeking corporate sponsors: Meet benefactor's objectives.

40. Meenaghan, T., and O'Sullivan, P. (1999). Playpower-sports meets marketing.

41. 1999 IEG, Inc. Chicago, IL.

42. Irwin, R.L., and Sutton, W.A. (1994). Sport sponsorship objectives: An analysis of the relative importance for major corporate sponsors. *European Journal of Sport Management* 1(2): 93-101.

43. Lieberman, D. (2000). Where will media's new king take us? *USA Today* (January 12): B1-2.

44. Duncan, T., and Caywood, C. (1996). The concept, process, and evolution of integrated marketing communication. In Thorson, E., and Moore, J., *Integrated communication: Synergy of persuasive voices* (Mahwah, NJ: Erlbaum), 13-34.

45. Lord, K.R., and Putrevu, S. (1998). Communicating in print: A comparison of consumer responses to different promotional formats. *Journal of Current Issues and Research in Advertising* 20(2): 1-18.

46. Bernstein, A. (1999). The Coca-Cola Co.'s six steps to sport marketing. *Street & Smith's SportsBusiness Journal* 1(39): 26.

47. Smolianov, P., and Shilbury, D. (1996). An investigation of sport marketing competencies. *Sport Marketing Quarterly* 5(4): 27-36.

48. Lainson, S. (1996). Sports as entertainment. *News You Can Use.* Issue 3:1.

49. Irwin, R.L., Zwick, D., and Sutton, W.A. (1999). Assessing organizational attributes contributing to marketing excellence in American professional sport franchises. *European Journal of Marketing* 3(33): 314-327.

50. Gladden, J.M., and Milne, G.R. (1999). Examining the importance of brand equity in professional sport. *Sport Marketing Quarterly* 8(1): 21-29.

51. Cawley, R. (1999). Get to work, then get a career. *Street & Smith's SportsBusiness Journal* 2(33; December 6-12): 21.

52. Bovinet, J.W. (1999). Customer communication in selected professional sports (MLB, NFL, NHL, NBA): A test. *Sport Marketing Quarterly* 8(3): 41-44.

Chapter 2

1. Shimp, T.A., and DeLozier, M.W. (1986). *Promotion management and marketing communications.* Chicago: Dryden Press.

2. Turco, D. (1996). Marketing to Generation X. *Sport Marketing Quarterly* 5(4): 19-24.

3. McCarthy, L. (1998). Marketing sport to Hispanic consumers. *Sport Marketing Quarterly* 7(4): 19-24.

4. Mullin, B.J., Hardy, S., and Sutton, W.A. (1993). *Sport marketing.* Champaign, IL: Human Kinetics.

5. Hiestand, M. (1999). Online leagues of their own: Internet provides fantasy groups ways to have fun by association. *USA Today* (October 6): 1C.

6. Eaton, B. (1997). Servicing the media as a sport consumer. Manuscript. University of Memphis, TN.

7. McDonald, M.A., Sutton, W.A., and Milne, G.R. (1995). TEAMQUAL: Measuring quality service in professional team sports. *Sport Marketing Quarterly* 4(2): 9-15.

8. Ries, A., and Trout, J. (1993). *The 22 immutable laws of marketing.* New York: Harper Business.

9. Lough, N., Irwin, R.L., and Short, G. (2000). Corporate sponsorship motives among North American companies: A contemporary analysis. *International Journal of Sport Management* 1(4): 283-295.

10. Lough, N., Irwin, R.L., and Short, G. (2000). Corporate sponsorship motives among North American companies: A contemporary analysis.

11. Bodley, H. (1999). *USA Today* (July 25): 5C.

12. Brindley, C., and Thorogood, R. (1998). Attracting the under-30's to U.K. horse racing events. *Sport Marketing Quarterly* 7(4): 25-34.

13. Smith, P.R. (1993). *Marketing communications: An integrated approach.* London: Kogan Page.

14. Bernstein, A. (1999). In search of the winning play. *Street & Smith's SportsBusiness Journal* (December 22-28): 23.

15. Lombardo, J. (1999). AFL leans on SFX to score $6M. *Street & Smith's SportsBusiness Journal* 2(24): 1, 59.

16. Smith, P.R. (1993). *Marketing communications: An integrated approach.*

17. Shilbury, D., Quick, S., and Westebeek, H. (1998). *Strategic sport marketing.* St. Leonards, Australia: Allen & Unwin.

18. Smith, P.R. (1993). *Marketing communications: An integrated approach.*

19. Lombardo, J. (1999). AFL leans on SFX to score $6M.

20. Smith, P.R. (1993). *Marketing communications: An integrated approach.*

21. Stotlar, D.K. (1993). *Successful sport marketing.* Madison, WI: Brown & Benchmark.

22. Howard, J.A., and Sheth, J.N. (1969). *The theory of buyer behavior.* New York: Wiley.

23. Mullin, B.J., Hardy, S., and Sutton, W.A. (1993). *Sport marketing.*

24. Irwin, R.L., and Sutton, W.A. (1994). Sport sponsorship objectives: An analysis of the relative importance for major corporate sponsors. *European Journal of Sport Management* 1(2): 93-101.

25. Higgins, S.H., and Martin, J.H. (1996). Managing sport innovations: A diffusion theory perspective. *Sport Marketing Quarterly* 5(1): 43-48.

26. Barrett, T. and Slack, T. (1999). An analysis of the influence of competitive and institutional pressures on corporate sponsorship decisions. *Journal of Sport Management* 13(2): 114-138.

27. O'Sullivan, E.L., and Spangler, K.J. (1998). *Experience marketing.* State College, PA: Venture.

28. Mullin, B.J., Hardy, S., and Sutton, W.A. (1993). *Sport marketing.*

Chapter 3

1. Kotler, P. (1975). *Marketing for non-profit organizations.* Englewood Cliffs, NJ: Prentice Hall.

2. Smith, P.R. (1993). *Marketing communications: An integrated approach.* London: Kogan Page.

3. McDonald, M., and Rascher, D. (2000). Does bat day make cents? The effect of promotions on the demand for Major League Baseball. *Journal of Sport Management* 14: 8-27.

4. Smith, P.R. (1993). *Marketing communications: An integrated approach.*

5. Cronan, C. (1999). Woeful Lightning takes hit after cutting comp tickets. *Sports Business Journal* 1(39): 6.

6. Mullin, B.J., Hardy, S., and Sutton, W.A. (2000). *Sport marketing.* 2nd ed. Champaign, IL: Human Kinetics.

7. Mawson, M.L., and Coan, E.E. (1994). Marketing techniques used by NBA franchises to promote home game attendance. *Sport Marketing Quarterly* 3(1): 37-45.

8. Spoelstra, J. (1997). *Ice to the Eskimos: How to sell a product nobody wants.* New York: Harper Business.

9. Brewington, P. (1999). Attendance up, losses continue. *USA Today* (July 16): 11C.

10. King, B. (1999). Teams line up for another Beanie Baby boost to their bottom line. *Street & Smith's SportsBusiness Journal* 1(50): 46.

11. Millennium fad: Pokemon hits sports as the latest hip giveaway. (1999). *Team Marketing Report* 12(3): 10.

12. Mullin, B.J., Hardy, S., and Sutton, W.A. (2000). *Sport marketing.*

13. McDonald, M., and Rascher, D. (2000). Does bat day make cents? The effect of promotions on the demand for Major League Baseball.

14. Boyd, T.C., and Krehbiel, T.C. (1999). The effect of promotion timing on Major League Baseball attendance. *Sport Marketing Quarterly* 8(4): 23-34.

15. Smith, D. (1999). "Genius with a racket" changed tennis' attitudes. *USA Today* (July 8): 8C.

16. Zhang, J.J., Smith, D.W., Pease, D.G., and Jambor, E.A. (1997). Negative influence of market competitors on the attendance of professional sport games: The case of a minor league hockey team. *Sport Marketing Quarterly* 6(3): 31-40.

17. Funk, D., Mahony, D., Gladden, J., Howard, D., Kahle, L., Madrigal, R., James, J., Nakazawa, M., and Trail, G. (1999). Understanding the sport spectator and sport fan: The three A's to allegiance. Fourteenth Annual North American Society for Sport Management Conference, Vancouver, British Columbia.

18. Mullin, B.J., Hardy, S., and Sutton, W.A. (2000). *Sport marketing.*

19. Suggs, W. (1998). Amateurs' legs power racing boom. *Sports Business Journal* 1(32): 19.

20. Newman, L. (2001). Happiness of fun runner wins road race. *Irish Times*, June 5. **http://scripts.ireland.com/search.**

21. Irwin, R.L., and Sutton, W.A. (1994). Sport sponsorship objectives: An analysis of the relative importance for major corporate sponsors. *European Journal of Sport Management* 1(2): 93-101.

22. Sandler, M.A. (1999). Sports commissions in the United States making communities better through sports. Manuscript.

23. Kuzma, J.R., Shanklin, W.L., and McCally, J.F. (1993). Number one principle for sporting event seeking corporate sponsors: Meet benefactor's objectives. *Sport Marketing Quarterly* 2(3): 27-32.

24. Mullin, B.J., Hardy, S., and Sutton, W.A. (2000). *Sport marketing.*

25. Irwin, R.L., Zwick, D., and Sutton, W.A. (1999). Assessing organizational attributes contributing to marketing excellence in American professional sport franchises. *Journal of Consumer Marketing* 16(6): 603-615.

26. Mawson, M.L., and Coan, E.E. (1994). Marketing techniques used by NBA franchises to promote home game attendance.

27. Spoelstra, J. (1997). *Ice to the Eskimos: How to sell a product nobody wants.*

28. Mullin, B.J., Hardy, S., and Sutton, W.A. (2000). *Sport marketing.*

29. Mullin, B.J., Hardy, S., and Sutton, W.A. (2000). *Sport marketing.*

30. Brindley, C., and Thorogood, R. (1998). Attracting the under-30's to U.K. horse racing events. *Sport Marketing Quarterly* 7(4): 25-34.

31. Melnick, M.J. (1993). Searching for sociability in the stands: A theory of sport spectating. *Journal of Sport Management* 7: 44-60.

32. Cowell, A. (1999). How Manchester United scores on its balance sheets. *Strategy & Business* 17: 79-81.

33. Shoham, A., and Kahle, L.R. (1996). Spectators, viewers, readers: Communication and consumption communities in sport marketing. *Sport Marketing Quarterly* 5(1): 11-19.

34. Rascher, D. (1999). The optimal distribution of talent in major league baseball. In *Sport economics: Current research,* ed. L. Hadly, E. Gustafson, and J. Fizel (Westport, CT: Praeger Press).

35. Armstrong, K.L. (1998). Ten strategies to employ when marketing sport to black consumers. *Sport Marketing Quarterly* 7(3): 11-18.

36. McCarthy, L. (1998). Marketing sport to Hispanic consumers. *Sport Marketing Quarterly* 7(4): 19-24.

37. Bradish, C. (1999). Cause marketing: An investigation of social marketing in sport. Fourteenth Annual North American Society for Sport Management Conference, Vancouver, British Columbia.

38. 2000 FedEx St. Jude patron analysis.(2000). Unpublished report.

39. Taylor, T., and Tooney, K. (1999). Sport, gender, and cultural diversity: Exploring the nexus. *Journal of Sport Management* 13(1): 1-17.

40. Funk, D., Mahony, D., Gladden, J., Howard, D., Kahle, L., Madrigal, R., James, J., Nakazawa, M., and Trail, G. (1999). Understanding the sport spectator and sport fan: The three A's to allegiance.

41. Wolf, M.J. (1999). *The entertainment economy.* Toronto: Times Books.

42. Hansen, H., and Gauthier, R. (1992). Marketing objectives of professional and university sport organizations. *Journal of Sport Management* 6(1): 27-37.

43. Fielding, L.W., Miller, L.K., and Brown, J.R. (1999). Harlem Globetrotters, Inc. *Journal of Sport Management* 13(1): 45-77.

44. Stotlar, D.K. (1995). Motives for attending sports grills. *Sport Marketing Quarterly* 4(3): 9-16.

45. Sutton, W.A. (1999). Techtainment. *Street & Smith's SportsBusiness Journal* 1(45): 10.

46. Lowy, J. (1999). Psychologists concerned about advertisers' pitches to children. *Commercial Appeal* (December 19): G1, G3.

47. Is that your final answer? "Millionaire" treads its way into sport promotions. (2000). *Team Marketing Report* 12(5): 4-5.

48. Kotler, P. (1975). Marketing for non-profit organizations.

49. Is the golf course the new "cool" hangout? (1999). *The Tournament Extra!* (June 11): 14, 26.

50. Horovitz, B. (1999). Marketers tap into loyalty of sports fans. *USA Today* (July 7): 1B.

51. Hofacre, S., and Burman, T.K. (1992). Demographic changes in the U.S. into the twenty-first century: Their impact on sport marketing. *Sport Marketing Quarterly* 1(1): 31-36.

52. Farrell, G. (1999). Marketers put a price on your life. *USA Today* (July 7): 3B.

53. Smith, P.R. (1993). *Marketing communications: An integrated approach.*

Chapter 4

1. Ries, A., and Trout, J. (1981). *Positioning: The battle for your mind.* New York: Warner Books, 3.

2. Trout, J., and Rifkin, S. (1996). *The new positioning: The latest on the world's #1 business strategy.* New York: McGraw-Hill, 3-4.

3. Aaker, D.A. (1991). *Managing brand equity.* New York: Free Press, 15.

4. Cox, J., and Stevens, H. (2000). *Selling the wheel.* New York: Simon & Schuster, 244.

5. Trout, J., and Rifkin, S. (1996). *The new positioning: The latest on the world's #1 business strategy,* 12.

6. Mullin, B., Hardy, S., and Sutton, W.A. (2000). *Sport marketing.* 2nd ed. Champaign, IL: Human Kinetics, 327.

7. Ries, A., and Trout, J. (1993). *The 22 immutable laws of marketing.* New York: Harper Business, 23.

8. Vitale, J. (1998). *There's a customer born every minute.* New York: Amacom, 82.

9. Cates, B. (1996). *Unlimited referrals.* Silver Spring, MD: Thunder Hill Press, 181.

10. Cates, B. (1996). *Unlimited referrals,* 17.

11. Compiled from Cates, B., 1996, *Unlimited referrals,* 241-248.

12. Sutton, W.A. (1999). Making sport marketing part of your corporate strategy. Presentation at Cleveland CAVS Sport Marketing Seminar, Cleveland, April 19.

13. Staying fresh: Tupperware parties boost WNBA season ticket packages. (2000). *Team Marketing Report* 12:(4; January): 3.

14. Brooks, C., and Harris, K. (1998). Celebrity endorsement: An overview of the key theoretical issues. *Sport Marketing Quarterly* 7(2): 34-44.

15. McCracken, G. (1999). Who is the celebrity endorser? Cultural foundations of the endorsement process. *Journal of Consumer Research* 19(December): 310-321.

16. Sugar, B. (1978). *Hit the sign and win a free suit of clothes from Harry Finklestein.* Chicago: Contemporary Books, 327-329.

17. Trout, J., and Rifkin, S. (1996). *The new positioning: The latest on the world's #1 business strategy,* 27.

18. Material for this section reprinted from Mullin, B., Hardy, S., & Sutton, W.A., 2000, *Sport marketing,* 191-192. Rayovac information originally cited from "Rayovac taps Michael Jordan to recharge battery brand," 1995, *Sports Marketing Letter* 7(4; April): 1, 3.

19. Information compiled from pages and links at **http://www.qscores.com/site/about.html**.

20. Meyers, B. (1998). Shoemakers giving sports stars the boot. *USA Today* (February 13): B1-2.

21. Mullen, L., and Burwell, B. (2000). Puma, Carter discussing new marriage. *Street & Smith's SportsBusiness Journal* 3(14; July 24-30): 1, 41.

22. Lombardo, J. (1999). Most advertisers Kerry on with Wood. *Street & Smith's SportsBusiness Journal* 1(49; March 29-April 4): 6.

23. Phillips, M. (1997). Taking stock: Top sports pros find a new way to score—getting equity stakes. *Wall Street Journal* (April 18): A1-A3.

24. Gellene, D. (1997). Outlived by fame and fortunes. *Los Angeles Times* (September 11): D4.

25. Wollenberg, S. (1997). Jackie Robinson a celebrity endorser again. *Marketing News* 31(9; April 28): 1.

26. Fisher, E. (2000). Stretching the corporate limits. *Washington Times* (July 28). **http://www.washtimes.com**.

27. Hagstrom, R.G. (1998). *The NASCAR way.* New York: Wiley, 57.

28. Hagstrom, R.G. (1998). *The NASCAR way,* 59.

29. Top ten sponsorship myths we wish would go away. (1995). *IEG Sponsorship Report* (January 16).

30. Rohm, A. (1997). The creation of consumer bonds within Reebok running. *Sport Marketing Quarterly* 6(2): 17-25.

31. McMillan, Z. (1999). Juniors, Bean learn at clinic. *Commercial Appeal* (June 9): D5.

32. Hagstrom, R.G. (1998). *The NASCAR way,* 8-10.

33. Crosset, T. (1995). Toward an understanding of on-site fan-athlete relations: A case study of the LPGA. *Sport Marketing Quarterly* 4(2): 31-38.

34. Brockington, L. (1999). SI for Kids plans tour to mark its birthday. *Street & Smith's SportsBusiness Journal* 1(33): 4.

35. Kahle, L., and Elton, M. (1997). Sports talk and the development of marketing relationships. *Sport Marketing Quarterly* 6(2): 35-39.

36. Martin, C. (1990). The employee/customer interface: An empirical investigation of employee behaviors and customer perceptions. *Journal of Sport Management* 4: 1-20.

37. Martin, C. (1990). The employee/customer interface: An empirical investigation of employee behaviors and customer perceptions.

Chapter 5

1. Mullin, B.J., Hardy, S., and Sutton, W.A. (2000). *Sport marketing.* 2nd ed. Champaign, IL: Human Kinetics, 222.

2. Zyman, S. (1999). *The end of marketing as we know it.* New York: Harper Collins, 4.

3. Material relating to figure 4.1 is derived from Mullin, B.J., Hardy, S., and Sutton, W.A., 2000, *Sport marketing,* 223.

4. Crosby, J.V. (1996). *Managing the big sale.* Lincolnwood, IL: NTC Business Books, 115.

5. McCormack, M. (1996). *On selling.* West Hollywood, CA: Dove Books, 7.

6. Honebein, P. (1997). *Strategies for effective customer education.* Lincolnwood, IL: NTC Business Books, 25.

7. Material for these first four items is derived from Mullin, B.J., Hardy, S., and Sutton, W.A., 2000, *Sport marketing,* 224.

8. Stephens, N.J. (1997). *Streetwise customer-focused selling.* Holbrook, MA: Adams Media Corporation, 11.

9. Stephens, N.J. (1997). *Streetwise customer-focused selling,* 25.

10. Sutton, W.A., Lachowetz, A., and Clark, J. (2000). Eduselling: The role of customer education in selling

to corporate clients in the sport industry. *International Journal of Sports Marketing & Sponsorship* 2(2; June/July): 145-158.

11. Crosby, V.J. (1996). *Managing the big sale*, 68.

12. Stephens, N.J. (1997). *Streetwise customer-focused selling*, 4.

13. McCormack, M. (1996). *On selling*, 9-10.

14. Sattler, T.P., and Doniek, C.A. (1995). Secrets of successful sales people. *Fitness Management* (January). Also created from Ziglar, Z., 1991, *Ziglar on selling*. Zig Ziglar Corporation. New York: Balantine Books.

15. Vavra, T.G. (1997). *Improving your measurement of customer satisfaction*. Milwaukee: ASQ Quality Press, 64-65.

16. Cannie, J.K. (1994). *Turning lost customers into gold*. New York: Amacom.

17. Figure 2.8 is reprinted from figure 10.3 in Mullin, B.J., Hardy, S., and Sutton, W.A., 2000, *Sport marketing*, 216.

18. Vitale, J. (1998). *There's a customer born every minute*. New York: Amacom, 59.

19. O'Dell, S.M., and Pajunen, J.A. (1997). *The butterfly customer*. Ontario, Canada: Wiley.

20. Mullin, B.J., Hardy, S., and Sutton, W.A. (2000). *Sport marketing*, 13-14.

21. Popcorn, F. (1991). *The Popcorn report: Faith Popcorn on the future of your company, your world, your life*. New York: Doubleday, Currency.

22. Cox, J., and Stevens, H. (2000). *Selling the wheel*. New York: Simon & Schuster, 192.

23. Ziccardi, D. (1997). *Masterminding the store*. New York: Wiley, 50.

24. Beemer, C.B. (1997). *Predatory marketing*. New York: Morrow, 111-112.

25. Mullin, B.J., Hardy, S., and Sutton, W.A. (2000). *Sport marketing*, 13-14.

26. Johnson, R.S. (1998). The Jordan effect. *Fortune* (June 22): 124-138.

27. Sutton, W.A., McDonald, M.A., Milne, G.R., and Cimperman, J. (1997). Creating and fostering fan identification in professional sports. *Sport Marketing Quarterly* 6(1): 15-22.

28. Bowman, D.P. (1998). *Presentations*. Holbrook, MA: Adams Media Corporation, 46.

29. Conversation with Chris Wright, senior vice president of marketing, Minnesota Timberwolves, June 12, 2000, Indianapolis.

30. This information was compiled from Dr. Sutton's visit to Pittsburgh and participation in a sales presentation by Vic Gregovits, vice president for marketing and broadcasting, Pittsburgh Pirates, July 2, 1999.

31. Jones, S.K. (1991). *Creative strategy in direct marketing*. Lincolnwood, IL: NTC, 104.

32. Mullin, B.J., Hardy, S., and Sutton, W.A. (2000). *Sport marketing*, 236.

33. Personal correspondence with Brenda Tinnen, senior vice president of marketing and sales, Phoenix Coyotes, August 14, 1998.

34. Mullin, B.J., Hardy, S., and Sutton, W.A. (2000). *Sport marketing*, 237-238.

35. Spoelstra, J. (1997). *Ice to the Eskimos: How to sell a product nobody wants*. New York: Harper Business, 173.

36. Phoenix Coyotes 1998-1999 annual report. (1999). Phoenix: Phoenix Coyotes. An earlier version of this material also appeared in Mullin, B.J., Hardy, S., and Sutton, W.A., 2000, *Sport marketing*, 239.

37. Stone, B., and Wyman, J. (1986). *Successful telemarketing: Opportunities and techniques for increasing sales and profits*. Lincolnwood, IL: NTC Business Books, 6.

38. Day, G.S. (1990). *Market driven strategy*. New York: Free Press, 234.

39. Mullin, B.J., Hardy, S., and Sutton, W.A. (2000). *Sport marketing*, 234.

40. Red Sox telephone ticket system dials up immediate sales results. (1998). *Team Marketing Report* 10(5; February): 3.

41. Reprinted from Mullin, B.J., Hardy, S., and Sutton, W.A., 2000, *Sport marketing*, 234-235.

42. Reprinted from Mullin, B.J., Hardy, S., and Sutton, W.A., 2000, *Sport marketing*, 235-236.

43. Bernstein, A. (1998). High-tech a (virtual) sign of the times. *Street & Smith's SportsBusiness Journal* 1(9; June 22-28): 24.

44. Breighner, B. (1995). *Face-to-face selling.* Indianapolis: Park Avenue, x.

45. McKenna, R. (1991). *Relationship marketing.* Reading, MA: Addison-Wesley, 4.

46. Gronroos, C. (1990). *Service management and marketing: Managing moments of truth in service competition.* New York: Lexington Books.

47. Burton, R., and Cornilles, R. (1998). Emerging ticket theory in team sport sales: Selling tickets in a more competitive arena. *Sport Marketing Quarterly* 7(2): 29-37.

48. Mullin, B.J., Hardy, S., and Sutton, W.A. (2000). *Sport marketing,* 241.

49. Mullin, B.J., Hardy, S., and Sutton, W.A. (2000). *Sport marketing,* 241.

50. This paragraph reprinted from Mullin, B.J., Hardy, S., and Sutton, W.A., 2000, *Sport marketing,* 242.

51. Spoelstra, J. (1997). *Ice to Eskimos: How to sell a product nobody wants,* 146-151.

52. Breighner, B. (1995). *Face-to-face selling,* 84-85.

53. Stephens, N.J. (1998). *Streetwise customer-focused selling,* 25.

54. Suggs, W. (1999). Firms look to college sports. *Street & Smith's SportsBusiness Journal* 2(13; July 19-25): 22.

55. McCarthy, L.M., and Irwin, R.L. (1998). Permanent seat licenses (PSLs) as an emerging source of revenue production. *Sport Marketing Quarterly* 7(3): 41.

56. Mullin, B.J., Hardy, S., and Sutton, W.A. (2000). *Sport marketing,* 254.

57. Bernstein, A. (1999). Hitting the mark: The buyer's mind. *Street & Smith's SportsBusiness Journal* 2(21; September 13-19): 23.

58. Hagan, A. (1999). Gatorade signs on as WNBA sponsor. WNBA press release (September 9).

59. Bernstein, A. (1999). Brand-building the name of the game. *Street & Smith's SportsBusiness Journal* 2(21; September 13-19): 27-30.

60. Carter, D.M. (1996). *Keeping score: An inside look at sport marketing.* Grants Pass, OR: Oasis Press, 198.

61. King, B. (1999). General Mills joins Petty team. *Street & Smith's SportsBusiness Journal* 2(22; September 20-26): 8.

62. Poole, M. (2000). Inside the deal. *Street & Smith's SportsBusiness Journal* 2(39; January 17-23): 14.

63. Russell, K. (1999). Kodak looks at big picture for Games. *Street & Smith's SportsBusiness Journal* 2(27; October 25-31): 29.

64. Carter, D.M. (1996). *Keeping score: An inside look at sport marketing,* 198.

65. Bernstein, A. (1999). Brand-building the name of the game.

66. Irwin, R.L., and Sutton, W.A. (1994). Sport sponsorship objectives: An analysis of their relative importance for major corporate sponsors. *European Journal for Sport Management* 1(2): 93-101.

67. Organizational style and structure has been modified and expanded from the earlier version that appeared in Mullin, B.J., Hardy, S., and Sutton, W.A., 2000, *Sport marketing,* 225.

68. Mielke, J. (1997). Specialization through departmentalization. *That's the Ticket* 1(1; May): 5.

69. Miller, L., Shaad, S., Burch, D., and Turner, R. (1999). *Sales success in sport marketing.* Wichita, KS: Events Unlimited, 155-167.

70. Rackham, N., and DeVincentis, J. (1999). *Rethinking the sales force.* New York: McGraw-Hill, 7.

71. Levitt, T. (1960). Marketing myopia. *Harvard Business Review* (July-August): 45-56.

72. Ries, A., and Trout, J. (1986). *Positioning: The battle for your mind.* New York: McGraw-Hill.

73. For an excellent discussion of the value of time, see Williams, P., 1995, *Go for the magic* (Nashville, TN: Nelson).

74. Huntsman, M., and Rose, D. (1999). Outsourcing college marketing: A growing trend. *Athletics Administration* 11(2; April): 9.

75. Zuffelato, S. (1999). Presentation to Sales and Promotional Management in Sport class, University of Massachusetts-Amherst, Amherst, March 24.

Chapter 6

1. Brockington, L. (1999). Personalities key in NBA's wide ranging ads. *Street & Smith's SportsBusiness Journal* (November 11): 5.

2. Kaufman, M. (1999). Lockout no big deal, absence of MJ is. *Street & Smith's SportsBusiness Journal* (November 1-7): 26.

3. This section was derived from Gladden, J.M., and McDonald, M.A., 1999, The brand management efforts of a niche specialist: New balance in the athletic footwear industry, *International Journal of Sports Marketing & Sponsorship* 1(2): 168-184.

4. Mullin, B.J., Hardy, S., and Sutton, W.A. (2000). *Sport marketing.* 2nd ed. Champaign, IL: Human Kinetics, 185.

5. Pride, W.M., and Ferrell, O.C. (1989). *Marketing: concepts and strategies.* Boston: Houghton Mifflin, 468.

6. Batra, R., Myers, J.G., and Aaker, D.A. (1996). *Advertising management.* 5th ed. Upper Saddle River, NJ: Prentice Hall, 3.

7. Batra, R., Myers, J.G., and Aaker, D.A. (1996). *Advertising management,* 3.

8. Wolf, M.J. (1999). *The entertainment economy.* New York: Times Books, 256.

9. Batra, R., Myers, J.G., and Aaker, D.A. (1996). *Advertising management,* 47.

10. Studies show different data on dot-coms' Super Bowl success. (2000). *Sports Business Daily* (February 3): 3.

11. Verducci, T. (1997). Quittin' time. *Sports Illustrated* (August 11): 30-35.

12. "Deferring" dreams: But will they pay off with interest? (2000). *Sports Business Daily* (February 23): 11.

13. Bhonslay, M. (1998). Avon races to cost-effective branding. *Street & Smith's SportsBusiness Journal* (September 13-19): 34.

14. Mullin, B.J., Hardy, S., and Sutton, W.A. (2000). *Sport marketing,* 184.

15. Schultz, D.E., and Barnes, B.E. (1999). *Strategic brand communication campaigns.* Lincolnwood, IL: NTC Business Books, 12.

16. Schultz, D.E., and Barnes, B.E. (1999). *Strategic brand communication campaigns,* 21.

17. Batra, R., Myers, J.G., and Aaker, D.A. (1996). *Advertising management,* 386.

18. Keller, K.L. (1998). *Strategic brand management.* Upper Saddle River, NJ: Prentice Hall, Inc.

19. Schultz, D.E., and Barnes, B.E. (1999). *Strategic brand communication campaigns,* 44.

20. Schoenfeld, B. (1998). How long can Sharks defy logic? *Street & Smith's SportsBusiness Journal* (December 14-20): 1, 49.

21. In fact, the development of the Sharks logo took one year and required 220 iterations. See Schoenfeld, B., 1998, How long can Sharks defy logic?

22. Levine turns to cyberspace for latest marketing endeavor. (1997). *Sports Business Daily* (January 17).

23. Levine turns to cyberspace for latest marketing endeavor. (1997). 63.

24. Bernstein, A. (1999). Marketer's aim: An NHL brand. *Street & Smith's SportsBusiness Journal* (October 4): 13.

25. Eisner, M. (1999). *Work in progress.* New York: Hyperion, 235.

26. For a more in-depth discussion of why brand management is suitable to the sport setting, see Gladden, J.M., Milne, G.R., and Sutton, W.A., 1998, A conceptual framework for evaluating brand equity in division I college athletics, *Journal of Sport Management* 12(1): 1-19.

27. Aaker, D.A. (1991). *Managing brand equity.* New York: Free Press, 173.

28. Batra, R., Myers, J.G., and Aaker, D.A. (1996). *Advertising management,* 100.

29. Russell, K. (1999). Key to winning: Put bodies in the seats. *Street & Smith's SportsBusiness Journal* (July 26-August 1): 29.

30. Zyman, S. (1999). *The end of marketing as we know it.* New York: Harper Business, 3.

31. Schultz, D.E., and Barnes, B.E. (1999). *Strategic brand communication campaigns,* 68.

32. Batra, R., Myers, J.G., and Aaker, D.A. (1996). *Advertising management,* 109.

33. Dallas' MLS Team sets up a Hispanic marketing group to Burn. (1997). *Sports Business Daily* (December 17): 8; Franchise notes. (1997). *Sports Business Daily* (December 12): 9.

34. Gladden, J.M., and McDonald, M.A. (1999). The brand management efforts of a niche specialist: New balance in the athletic footwear industry, 177-178.

35. Batra, R., Myers, J.G., and Aaker, D.A. (1996). *Advertising management,* 176.

36. Gladden, J.M., and McDonald, M.A. (1999). The brand management efforts of a niche specialist: New balance in the athletic footwear industry, 178.

37. Mullin, B.J., Hardy, S., and Sutton, W.A. (2000). *Sport marketing*.

38. Rofe, J. (2001). Baseball teams make pitches. *Street & Smith's SportsBusiness Journal* (April 16-22): 8.

39. Aaker, D.A. (1991). *Managing brand equity*, 109.

40. Aaker, D.A. (1991). *Managing brand equity*, 10-113.

41. Czerniawski, R.D., and Maloney, M.W. (1999). *Creating brand loyalty*. New York: American Management Association, 85.

42. Aaker, D.A., and Joachimstahler, E. (2000). *Brand leadership*. New York: Free Press, 50.

43. Keller, K.L. (1993). Conceptualizing, measuring and managing consumer-based brand equity. *Journal of Marketing* 57(1): 1-22.

44. Keller, K.L. (1993). Conceptualizing, measuring and managing consumer-based brand equity.

45. The discussion of brand association in sport is largely based on Gladden, J.M., and Funk, D.C., (2001), Developing an understanding of brand associations in team sport: Empirical evidence from consumers of professional sport, *Journal of Sport Management* 16(1).

46. Branvold, S.E., Pan, D.W., and Gabert, T.E. (1997). Effects of winning percentage and market size on attendance in minor league baseball. *Sport Marketing Quarterly* 6(4): 35-42; Porter, P.K., and Scully, G.W. (1982). Measuring managerial efficiency: The case of baseball. *Southern Economic Journal* 48(3): 642-650.

47. Mullin, B.J., Hardy, S., and Sutton, W.A. (2000). *Sport marketing*, 14.

48. NBA team marketing campaigns. (1999). Courtesy of NBA Entertainment.

49. Schofield, J.A. (1983). Performance and attendance at professional team sports. *Journal of Sport Behavior* 6(4): 197-206.

50. NBA team marketing campaigns. (1999).

51. Ostrowski, J. (1999). Marlins take marketing to the streets. *Street & Smith's SportsBusiness Journal* (May 10-16): 26.

52. Baker, M.S. (1998). Seahawks make strides despite team's stumble. *Street & Smith's SportsBusiness Journal* (January 18-24): 23.

53. NBA team marketing campaigns. (1999).

54. See Fournier, S., 1998, Consumers and their brands: Developing relationship theory in consumer research, *Journal of Consumer Research* 24(4): 343-373; and Garbarino, E., and Johnson, M.S., 1999, The different roles of satisfaction, trust, and commitment in customer relationships, *Journal of Marketing* 63(2): 70-87.

55. Mullen, L. (1998). Olympics "bruised" by allegations. *Street & Smith's SportsBusiness Journal* (December 21-27): 4.

56. Biehal, G.J., and Sheinan, D.A. (1998). Managing the brand in a corporate advertising environment: A decision-making framework for brand managers. *Journal of Advertising* 27(2): 99-110.

57. Schoenfeld, B. (1998). How long can Sharks defy logic?

58. Lombardo, J. (1998). Browns gear grabs green. *Street & Smith's SportsBusiness Journal* (December 7-13): 13.

59. Suggs, W. (1998). National powerhouse logos on wane. *Street & Smith's SportsBusiness Journal* (May 11-17): 14.

60. Rofe, J. (2001). Baseball teams make pitches.

61. NBA team marketing campaigns. (1999).

62. Hemmer, A. (1999). Reds' ad budget jumps. *Street & Smith's SportsBusiness Journal* (December 13): 6.

63. NBA team marketing campaigns. (1999).

64. Gladden, J.M., and Funk, D.C. (2001). Understanding brand loyalty in professional sport: Examining the link between brand associations and brand loyalty, *International Journal of Sports Marketing and Sponsorship* 3(1): 45-69.

65. For example, see Cialdini, R.B., Borden, R.J., Thorne, R.J., Walker, M.R., Freeman, S., and Sloan, L.R.,

1976, Basking in reflected glory: Three football field studies, *Journal of Personality and Social Psychology* 34: 366-375; and Sutton, W.A., McDonald, M.A., Milne, G.R., and Cimperman, J., 1997, Creating and fostering fan identification in professional sports, *Sport Marketing Quarterly* 6(1): 15-22.

66. Wernerfelt, B. (1990). Advertising content when brand choice is a signal. *Journal of Business* 63(1): 91-98.

67. Wakefield, K.L. (1995). The pervasive effects of social influence on sport event attendance. *Journal of Sport and Social Issues* 19(4): 335-351.

68. Holbrook, M.B. (1993). Nostalgia and consumption preferences: Some emerging patterns of consumer tastes. *Journal of Consumer Research* 20(2): 245-256.

69. Rofe, J. (2001). Baseball teams make pitches.

70. NBA team marketing campaigns. (1999).

71. Meyers, B. (1999). Businessman markets hockey team that doesn't exist—yet. *USA Today* (March 25): 1B-2B.

72. NBA team marketing campaigns. (1999).

73. Batra, R., Myers, J.G., and Aaker, D.A. (1996). *Advertising management*, 547.

74. Batra, R., Myers, J.G., and Aaker, D.A. (1996). *Advertising management*, 548-554.

75. Schultz, D.E., and Barnes, B.E. (1999). *Strategic brand communication campaigns*, 203.

76. Schultz, D.E., and Barnes, B.E. (1999). *Strategic brand communication campaigns*, 203.

77. Schultz, D.E., and Barnes, B.E. (1999). *Strategic brand communication campaigns*, 204.

78. Schultz, D.E., and Barnes, B.E. (1999). *Strategic brand communication campaigns*, 324.

79. Schultz, D.E., and Barnes, B.E. (1999). *Strategic brand communication campaigns*, 324.

80. Schultz, D.E., and Barnes, B.E. (1999). *Strategic brand communication campaigns*, 325.

81. Schultz, D.E., and Barnes, B.E. (1999). *Strategic brand communication campaigns*, 324.

82. Schultz, D.E., and Barnes, B.E. (1999). *Strategic brand communication campaigns*, 325.

83. Schultz, D.E., and Barnes, B.E. (1999). *Strategic brand communication campaigns*, 281.

84. Schultz, D.E., and Barnes, B.E. (1999). *Strategic brand communication campaigns*, 283.

85. Schultz, D.E., and Barnes, B.E. (1999). *Strategic brand communication campaigns*, 319.

86. Batra, R., Myers, J.G., and Aaker, D.A. (1996). *Advertising management*, 20.

87. Batra, R., Myers, J.G., and Aaker, D.A. (1996). *Advertising management*, 13.

Chapter 7

1. (2000). *Wall Street Journal* (February 2).

2. Lord, K.R., and Putrevu, S. (1998). Communicating in print: A comparison of consumer responses to different promotional formats. *Journal of Current Issues and Research in Advertising* 20(2): 1-18.

3. Mullin, B.J., Hardy, S., and Sutton, W.A. (2000). *Sport marketing.* 2nd ed. Champaign, IL: Human Kinetics.

4. Helitzer, M. (1995). *The dream job: Sport publicity, promotion, and marketing.* Athens, OH: University Sports Press.

5. Lord, K.R., and Putrevu, S. (1998). Communicating in print: A comparison of consumer responses to different promotional formats.

6. Hagstrom, R.G. (1998). *The NASCAR way.* New York: Wiley.

7. Helitzer, M. (1995). *The dream job: Sport publicity, promotion, and marketing.*

8. Langdon, J. (2000). A compilation of effective strategies to maximize media coverage of NCAA Division I athletic programs located in large metropolitan areas. Manuscript.

9. Pitts, B.G., and Stotlar, D.K. (1996). *Fundamentals of sport marketing.* Morgantown, WV: Fitness Information Technology.

10. Helitzer, M. (1995). *The dream job: Sport publicity, promotion, and marketing.*

11. Helitzer, M. (1995). *The dream job: Sport publicity, promotion, and marketing.*

12. Davis, H.M. (1998). Media relations. In *Principles and practice of sport management,* ed. L. Masteralexis, C.A. Barr, and M.A. Hums (Gaithersburg, MD: Aspen).

13. Davis, H.M. (1998). Media relations.

14. Lechner, T. (1995). A sight for sore eyes: Sports photography. In Helitzer, M., 1995, *The dream job: Sport publicity, promotion, and marketing.*

15. Childers, T.L., and Houston, M.J. (1984). Conditions for a picture-superiority effect on consumer memory. *Journal of Consumer Research* 11 (September): 643-654.

16. Lechner, T. (1995). A sight for sore eyes: Sports photography.

17. White, C. (1999). World Cup bug strikes the nation. *USA Today* (July 15): 16C.

18. Helitzer, M. (1995). *The dream job: Sport publicity, promotion, and marketing.*

19. Wade, D. (2000). Baseball media 101. *Commercial Appeal* (July 4): D1, D5.

20. Eaton, B. (1997). The media as a service customer. Manuscript.

21. (2000, February 4). *Sports Business Daily.*

22. For a thorough discussion of sport broadcasting see Shilbury, D., Quick, S., and Westerbeek, H., 1998, *Strategic sport marketing* (Sydney: Allen & Unwin).

23. Dupon, K.P. (2000). *Boston Globe* (June 6).

24. McCarthy, M. (2000). NBA chief shoots for the net. *USA Today* (January 21, 2000): B1-2.

25. Ashwell, T. (1998). Sports broadcasting. In *Principles and practice of sport management,* ed. L. Masteralexis, C.A. Barr, and M.A. Hums.

26. Phillies radio network tunes in to kids with hopes to attract listeners for life. (1998). *Team Marketing Report* (March): 9.

27. Davis, H.M. (1998). Media relations.

28. Senator's ad tactics boost program revenues and provide for increased regional marketing presence. (2000).

29. Shoham, A., and Kahle, L.R. (1996). Spectators, viewers, and readers: Communication and consumption communities in sport marketing. *Sport Marketing Quarterly* 5(1): 11-19.

30. Pitts, B.G., and Stotlar, D.K. (1996). *Fundamentals of sport marketing.*

31. Techsportlight. *Team Marketing Report* 12(2): 7.

32. Lord, K.R., and Putrevu, S. (1998). Communicating in print: A comparison of consumer responses to different promotional formats.

33. Senator's ad tactics boost program revenues and provide for increased regional marketing presence. (2000).

34. Ashwell, T. (1998). Sports broadcasting.

35. Bernstein, P. (2000). *Daily Variety.*

36. Davis, H.M. (1998). Media relations.

37. Davis, H.M. (1998). Media relations.

38. Eaton, B. (1997). The media as a service customer.

Chapter 8

1. Lewis, G.M. (1967). America's first intercollegiate sport: The regatta's from 1852 to 1875. *Research Quarterly* 38(4): 637-648.

2. Sugar, B. (1985). *Hit the sign and win a free suit of clothes from Harry Finklestein.* Chicago: Contemporary Books.

3. Ueborroth, P. (1985). *Made in America.* New York: Morrow.

4. 1999 sponsorship will grow 12 percent to $7.6 billion in North America. (1999). *IEG Newsletter* (January 18).

5. 1999 sponsorship will grow 12 percent to $7.6 billion in North America. (1999).

6. Howard, D., and Crompton, J. (1995). *Financing sport.* Morgantown, WV: Fitness Information Technology.

7. 2001 BCS FedEx customer/host analysis. Unpublished report. University of Memphis Bureau of Sport & Leisure Commerce.

8. Sears sponsor to sell new image. (1994). *IEG Sponsorship Report* 13(February 14): 1.

9. Gray, D.P. (1996). Sponsorship on campus. *Sport Marketing Quarterly* 5(2): 29-34.

10. McCauley, A., and Sutton, W.A. (1999). In search of a new defender: The threat of ambush marketing in the global sport arena. *International Journal of Sports Marketing & Sponsorship* 1(1): 64-86.

11. McCauley, A., and Sutton, W.A. (1999). In search of a new defender: The threat of ambush marketing in the global sport arena.

12. Irwin, R.L., and Assimakopoulos, M.K. (1992). An approach to the evaluation and selection of sport sponsorship proposals. *Sport Marketing Quarterly* 1(2): 43-51.

13. Rapp, S., and Collins, T.L. (1994). *Beyond maxi-marketing.* New York: McGraw-Hill.

14. Cornwell, B.T. (1995). Sponsorship-linked marketing development. *Sport Marketing Quarterly* 4(4): 13-24; p. 15.

15. Berrett, T., and Slack, T. (1999). An analysis of the influence of competitive and institutional pressures on corporate sponsorship decisions. *Journal of Sport Management* 13(2): 114-138.

16. Irwin, R.L., and Sutton, W.A. (1994). Sport sponsorship objectives: An analysis of their relative importance for major corporate sponsors. *European Journal of Sport Management* 1(2): 93-101.

17. Lough, N., Irwin, R.L., and Short, G. (2000). Corporate sponsorship motives among North American companies: A contemporary analysis. *International Journal of Sport Management* 1(4): 283-295.

18. Irwin, R.L., Cingiene, V., and Lough, N. (2001). Sport sponsorship in central Europe. Manuscript.

19. Howard, D., and Crompton, J. (1995). *Financing sport.*

20. Irwin, R.L., Assimakopoulos, M.K., and Sutton, W.A. (1994). A model for screening sport sponsorship opportunities. *Journal of Promotion Management* 2(3): 53-69.

21. Martin, J.H. (1994). Using a perceptual map of the consumer's sport schema to help make sponsorship decisions. *Sport Marketing Quarterly* 3(3): 27-33.

22. Irwin, R., and Mackin, R. (1999). FedEx FCS customer/host analysis. University of Memphis Bureau of Sport & Leisure Commerce.

23. Copeland, R., Frisby, W., and McCarville, R. (1996). Understanding the sport sponsorship process from a corporate perspective. *Journal of Sport Management* 10: 32-48.

24. Hagstrom, R. (1998). *The NASCAR way.* New York: Wiley.

25. Irwin, D. (1993). In search of sponsors. *Athletic Management* 5(3; May): 10-16.

26. Kuzma, J.R., Shanklin, W.L., and McCally, J.F. (1993). Number one principle for sporting event seeking corporate sponsors: Meet benefactor's objectives. *Sport Marketing Quarterly* 2(3): 27-32.

27. Irwin, R.L., and Sutton, W.A. (1995). Creating the ideal sponsorship arrangement. Proceedings from the Bi-Annual World Marketing Congress, Melbourne, Australia: Academy of Marketing Science.

28. Irwin, R.L., and Sutton, W.A. (1994). Sport sponsorship objectives: An analysis of their relative importance for major corporate sponsors.

29. Berrett, T., and Slack, T. (1999). An analysis of the influence of competitive and institutional pressures on corporate sponsorship decisions.

30. Irwin, R.L., Assimakopoulos, M.K., and Sutton, W.A. (1994). A model for screening sport sponsorship opportunities.

31. Arthur, D., Scott, D., and Woods, T. (1997). A conceptual model of the corporate decision-making process of sport sponsorship acquisition. *Journal of Sport Management* 11(3): 223-233.

32. Cornwell, B.T. (1995). Sponsorship-linked marketing development.

33. Arthur, D., Scott, D., Woods, T., and Booker, R. (1998). Sport sponsorship should…A process model for the effective implementation and management of sport sponsorship programs. *Sport Marketing Quarterly* 7(4): 49-61.

34. Cornwell, B.T. (1995). Sponsorship-linked marketing development.

35. Copeland, R., Frisby, W., and McCarville, R. (1996). Understanding the sport sponsorship process from a corporate perspective.

36. Arthur, D., Scott, D., Woods, T., and Booker, R. (1998). Sport sponsorship should…A process model for the effective implementation and management of sport sponsorship programs.

37. Copeland, R., Frisby, W., and McCarville, R. (1996). Understanding the sport sponsorship process from a corporate perspective.

38. Arthur, D., Scott, D., Woods, T., and Booker, R. (1998). Sport sponsorship should…A process model for the effective implementation and management of sport sponsorship programs.

39. Copeland, R., Frisby, W., and McCarville, R. (1996). Understanding the sport sponsorship process from a corporate perspective.

40. Copeland, R., Frisby, W., and McCarville, R. (1996). Understanding the sport sponsorship process from a corporate perspective.

41. Komoroski, L., and Biemond, H. (1996). Sponsor accountability: Designing and utilizing an evaluation system. *Sport Marketing Quarterly* 5(2): 35-39.

42. 1999 Southern Heritage Classic patron analysis. Unpublished report. University of Memphis Bureau of Sport & Leisure Commerce.

43. Pitts, B. (1998). An analysis of sponsorship recall during Gay Games IV. *Sport Marketing Quarterly* 7(4): 11-18.

44. Mullin, B., Hardy, S., and Sutton, W.A. (2000). *Sport marketing.* 2nd ed. Champaign, IL: Human Kinetics.

45. Stotlar, D.K. (1999). Sponsorship in North America: A survey of sport executives. *International Journal of Sports Marketing and Sponsorship* 1(1): 87-100.

46. White, A.B., and Irwin, R.L. (1996). Assessing a corporate partner program: A key to success. *Sport Marketing Quarterly* 5(2): 21-28.

47. Howard, D., and Crompton, J. (1995). *Financing sport.*

Chapter 9

1. Gareau, R. (1988). Corporate licensing—the world's fastest growing marketing discipline. *Trademark World* 14: 22-26.

2. A white paper: Sports licensed products. (1999). North Palm Beach, FL: Sporting Goods Manufacturers Association.

3. Shaaf, P. (1985). *Sports marketing.* Amherst, NY: Prometheus Books.

4. Moving the chains: XFL marketers explain what it will take for their league to be a success. (2000; November 1). *Team Marketing Report* 12(9): 8.

5. Mullin, B.J., Hardy, S., and Sutton, W.A. (2000). *Sport marketing.* 2nd ed. Champaign, IL: Human Kinetics.

6. ESPN Chilton sport poll. (1999; July 24). *Team Licensing Business* 9(6): 17.

7. A definitive chronicle: Sports licensed products. (1998). North Palm Beach, FL: Sporting Goods Manufacturers Association.

8. A white paper: Sports licensed products. (1999).

9. Rosenblatt, R. (1988). The profit motive. *Sports, Inc.* (December 5): 18-21.

10. A white paper: Sports licensed products. (1999).

11. Pittaway, B. (2000). Players to charge for TV goals. *The Observer* (January 16): C1.

12. A definitive chronicle: Sports licensed products. (1998).

13. Bernstein, A. (1999). New Starter runs into stop signs from the leagues. *Street & Smith's SportsBusiness Journal* 2(35): 15.

14. A white paper: Sports licensed products. (1999).

15. A definitive chronicle: Sports licensed products. (1998).

16. A white paper: Sports licensed products. (1999).

17. Lowy, J. (1999). Psychologists concerned about advertisers' pitches to children. *Commercial Appeal* (December 19): G1, G3.

18. Hagstrom, R.G. (1998). *The NASCAR way.* New York: Wiley.

19. Williams, P. (1999). Feel the glove? Rawlings licensee does, and makes it into luggage. *Street & Smith's SportsBusiness Journal* 2(35): 21.

20. A white paper: Sports licensed products. (1999).

21. Baghdikian, E. (1996). Building the sports organization's merchandise licensing program: The appropriateness, significance, and considerations. *Sport Marketing Quarterly* 5(1): 35-41.

22. Irwin, R.L., and Stotlar, D.K. (1993). Operational protocol analysis of sport and collegiate licensing programs. *Sport Marketing Quarterly* 2(1): 7-16.

23. Mazzeo, M.E., Cuneen, J., and Claussen, C.L. (1997). Determining the costs and forecasting profits for a multi-logoed collegiate memorabilia poster: A profitability study in new product development. *Sport Marketing Quarterly* 6(3): 41-47.

24. Shaaf, P. (1985). *Sports marketing.*

25. Gladden, J.M., and Milne, G.R. (1999). Examining the importance of brand equity in professional sport. *Sport Marketing Quarterly* 8(1): 21-29.

26. Shaaf, P. (1985). *Sports marketing.*

27. Schlossberg, H. (1997). *Sport marketing.* Malden, MA: Blackwell Business.

28. A white paper: Sports licensed products. (1999).

29. Schlossberg, H. (1997). *Sport marketing.*

30. Sandomir, R. (1999). Women's World Cup: Sales of merchandise just didn't take off. *New York Times* (July 13): D4.

31. The game: Extra innings: Women's World Cup. Women's World Cup projects royalties of $2.5 million based on retail sales of $50 million. *Brandweek* 40(21): 16.

32. Gaston, F.P. (1984). Administrative decision making: A study of collegiate trademark licensing programs. Unpublished doctoral dissertation, University of Alabama, Tuscaloosa.

33. Gladden, J.M., and Milne, G.R. (1999). Examining the importance of brand equity in professional sport.

34. McVoy, C. (1998). The SGB interview. *Sporting Goods Business* (June 10): 32-33.

35. A definitive chronicle: Sports licensed products. (1998).

36. A white paper: Sports licensed products. (1999).

37. A white paper: Sports licensed products. (1999).

38. A definitive chronicle: Sports licensed products. (1998).

39. Mazzeo, M.E., Cunnen, J., and Claussen, C.L. (1997). Determining the costs and forecasting profits for a multi-logoed collegiate memorabilia poster: A profitability study in new product development.

40. NCAA license agreement. (1999). Item 14, Marketing effort.

41. Irwin, R. (1991). A license to profit. *Athletic Management* (January 10): 18-21.

42. A white paper: Sports licensed products. (1999).

43. A definitive chronicle: Sports licensed products. (1998).

44. A definitive chronicle: Sports licensed products. (1998).

45. Souvenirs must be licensed. (1990). *Rocky Mountain News* (March 2): 19.

46. A white paper: Sports licensed products. (1999).

47. Meenaghan, T. and O'Sullivan, P. (1999). Play power—sports meets marketing. *European Journal of Marketing,* 33(3/4): 241-249.

48. Shaaf, P. (1985). *Sports marketing.*

49. A white paper: Sports licensed products. (1999).

50. Shaaf, P. (1985). *Sports marketing.*

51. A white paper: Sports licensed products. (1999).

52. 1999 state of the industry report. (1999). New York: Sporting Goods Manufacturers Association.

53. Bernstein, A. (2000). MJ-less NBA suffers on the shelves. *Street & Smith's SportsBusiness Journal* 2(36): 1, 43.

54. Rosenblatt, R. (1988). The profit motive.

55. A white paper: Sports licensed products. (1999).

56. Irwin, R.L. (1990). Development of a collegiate licensing administrative paradigm. Unpublished doctoral dissertation, University of Northern Colorado, Greeley.

57. Irwin, R.L., and Stotlar, D.K. (1993). Operational protocol analysis of sport and collegiate licensing programs.

58. National Football League Properties, Inc. Prospective licensee information package. National Football League Properties, Inc., 280 Park Avenue, New York, NY.

59. Harrison, T. (1985). Solutions to recurring errors in royalty payments. *The Licensing Book* 2(7): 10-12.

60. Irwin, R.L., and Stotlar, D.K. (1993). Operational protocol analysis of sport and collegiate licensing programs.

61. Shaaf, P. (1985). *Sports marketing*.

62. Mullin, B.J., Hardy, S., and Sutton, W.A. (2000). *Sport marketing*.

63. Lombardo, J. (2000). NFL: Technology on its way. *Street & Smith's SportsBusiness Journal* 2(36): 28.

64. VanMeter, D. (1994). Sale of licensed products and services. In Howard, D.R., and Crompton, J.L., *Financing sport* (Morgantown, WV: Fitness Information Technologies).

65. Titans fan learns the value of his slogan. (2001; April 13). *Mark's Sportslaw News.* **http://www.sportslawnews.com/flamepit.htm**.

66. Welch, W.M. (1999). Golf mecca tries to control name. *USA Today* (June 11): 3C.

67. Irwin, R.L. (1990). Development of a collegiate licensing administrative paradigm.

68. Gladden, J.M., and Milne, G.R. (1999). Examining the importance of brand equity in professional sport.

69. Irwin, R.L. (1990). Development of a collegiate licensing administrative paradigm.

70. Baghdikian, E. (1996). Building the sports organization's merchandise licensing program: The appropriateness, significance, and considerations.

Chapter 10

1. Matera, F.R., and Artigue, R.J. (2000). *Public relations campaigns and techniques: Building bridges into the 21st century*. Boston: Allyn & Bacon, 147.

2. Mullin, B., Hardy, S., and Sutton, W.A. (2000). *Sport marketing*. 2nd ed. Champaign, IL: Human Kinetics, 317.

3. Mullin, B., Hardy, S., and Sutton, W.A. (2000). *Sport marketing*, 320.

4. This material has been compiled from *NBA marketing reference guide, community relations* volume, 2000, 4-5.

5. *NBA marketing reference guide, community relations* volume. (2000). 28.

6. McKenna, R. (1991). *Relationship marketing: Successful strategies for the age of the consumer*. Reading, MA: Addison-Wesley, 4.

7. Burke, E.M. (1999). *Corporate community relations*. Westport, CT: Praeger, 3.

8. Burke, E.M. (1999). *Corporate community relations*.

9. Burke, E.M. (1999). *Corporate community relations*, 5.

10. Veeck, B., and Linn, E. (1962). Veeck: As in wreck. New York: Putnam's.

11. Material on the six communities is derived from information contained in Burke, E.M., 1999, *Corporate community relations*, 60-67.

12. Burke, E.M. (1999). *Corporate community relations*, 7-8.

13. Phoenix Coyotes 1998-1999 annual report. (1999). Phoenix: Phoenix Coyotes.

14. Phoenix Coyotes 1999-2000 yearbook. (2000). Phoenix: Phoenix Coyotes, 75.

15. Kings in the community [electronic media **www.lakings.com**]. (2000, June 19). Los Angeles Kings Community Relations, producer and distributor.

16. Red Sox in the community [electronic media, **www.bostonredsox.com**]. (2000, June 20). Boston Red Sox Community Relations, producer and distributor.

17. Breeding, C. (1996). Community relations in the NFL. Presented at the Fifth Annual Georgia Southern University Sport Management Conference, Statesboro, GA, February 22.

18. Irwin, R.L. (1996). Sport Licensing. In *The management of sport: Foundations and applications,* ed. B.K. Parkhouse (St. Louis: Mosby-Year Book).

19. Breeding, C. (1996). Community relations in the NFL.

20. Sutton, W.A., McDonald, M.A., Milne, G.R., and Cimperman, J. (1997). Creating and fostering fan identification in professional sports. *Sport Marketing Quarterly* 6 (1): 15-22.

21. Breeding, C. (1996). Community relations in the NFL.

22. Breeding, C. (1996). Community relations in the NFL.

23. Ries, A., and Trout, J. (1993). *The 22 immutable laws of marketing.* New York: Collins.

24. Lions den [electronic media **www.detroitlions.com**]. (1996, October 15). Detroit Lions Community Relations, producer and distributor.

25. Cone Communications, Inc. (1999). Cone/Roper cause-related trends report. Boston: Cone, Inc., 1.

26. Cone Communications, Inc. (1999). Cone/Roper cause-related trends report, 21.

27. Cone Communications, Inc. (1999). Cone/Roper cause-related trends report, 2-3.

28. Valvoline donates to local charity. (2000). *Street & Smith's SportsBusiness Journal* 3(10; June 26-July 2): 63.

29. Poole, M. (2000). Support for charities is solid marketing—and the right thing to do. *Street & Smith's SportsBusiness Journal* 3(10; June 26-July 2): 13.

Chapter 11

1. Routon, R. (1999). Maybe I'll see you all downtown. *Gazette* (March 31): SP1, SP3.

2. Kotler, P. (1975). *Marketing for non-profit organizations.* Englewood Cliffs, NJ: Prentice Hall.

3. Wolf, M.J. (1999). *The entertainment economy.* New York: Random House.

4. Mullin, B.J., Hardy, S., and Sutton, W.A. (2000). *Sport marketing.* 2nd ed. Champaign, IL: Human Kinetics.

5. Westerbeek, H.M., and Shilbury, D. (1999). Increasing the focus on "place" in the marketing mix for facility dependent sport services. *Sport Management Review* 2: 1-23.

6. Kolbe, R.H., and James, J.D. (2000). An identification and examination of influences that shape the creation of a professional team fan. *International Journal of Sports Marketing & Sponsorship* 2(1): 23-37.

7. Canter, D., Comber, M., and Uzzel, D.L. (1989). *Football in its place: An environmental psychology of football grounds.* London: Routledge.

8. Shimp, T.A., and DeLozier, M.W. (1986). *Promotion management and marketing communications.* Chicago: Dryden Press.

9. Building American pyramids. (1998, October 5). **http://www.sportstechmedia.com**.

10. *Team Marketing Report.* Coyotes target young adults. (1998, September): 5.

11. Shoham, A., Rose, G.M., Kropp, F., and Kahle, L.R. (1997). Generation X Women: A sports consumption community perspective. *Sport Marketing Quarterly* 6(4): 23-34.

12. University of Memphis. (1999). Golf Motives. Unpublished report.

13. Faircloth, J.B., Richard, M.D., and Richard, V.P. (1995). An analysis of choice intentions of public course golfers. *Sport Marketing Quarterly* 4(1): 13-21.

14. Spoelstra, J. (1991). *How to sell the last seat in the house.* Portland: SRO Partner.

15. Lam, P. (2000). *Detroit Free Press* (March 7).

16. Mullin, B.J., Hardy, S., and Sutton, W.A. (2000). *Sport marketing.*

17. Gilmore, J.H. (1998). Welcome to the experience economy. *Harvard Business Review* 76: 97-106.

18. Shimp, T.A., and DeLozier, M.W. (1986). *Promotion management and marketing communications.*

19. Kucher, K. (2000). *San Diego Union-Tribune* (January 28).

20. Mullin, L. (2000). Jam Session gets an NBA-owned home. *Street & Smith's SportBusiness Journal* (January 17-23): 13.

21. Penske, G. (1999). Track to riches: Offer fans more. *USA Today* (May 28): 14F.

22. Kotler, P. (1975). *Marketing for non-profit organizations.*

23. Mullin, B.J., Hardy, S., and Sutton, W.A. (2000). *Sport marketing.*

24. Lee, J. (1999). But is it art? *Street & Smith's SportBusiness Journal* (December 13-19): 4.

25. Davis, M. (1998). Old ball game has high-tech look. *Kansas City Star* (August 22): 1B, 10B.

26. Mullin, B.J., Hardy, S., and Sutton, W.A. (2000). *Sport marketing.*

27. Gilmore, J.H. (1998). Welcome to the experience economy.

28. O'Sullivan, E.L., and Spangler, K.J. (1998). *Experience marketing.* State College, Pa: Venture.

29. Cassirer, E. (1957). *The philosophy of symbolic forms,* vol. III: *The phenomenology of knowledge.* Forge Village, MA: Murray Printing.

30. Westerbeek, H.M., and Shilbury, D. (1999). Increasing the focus on "place" in the marketing mix for facility dependent sport services.

31. Herbeck, K., and Beebe, D. (1999). *Buffalo News* (August 22).

32. Lam, P. (2000). *Detroit Free Press.*

33. Borden, L. (2000). *Crain's Chicago Business* (March 7).

34. Brindley, and Thorogood. (1998). Attracting the under-30s to U.K. horse racing events. *Sport Marketing Quarterly* 7(4), 25-34..

35. Spoelstra, J. (1991). *How to sell the last seat in the house.*

36. Bank to add fun in South Dakota. (2000). *Stadium Insider* 1(16; March 6): 2.

37. *Team Marketing Report.* Coyotes target young adults. (1998, September): 5.

38. O'Sullivan, E.L., and Spangler, K.J. (1998). *Experience marketing.*

39. Tailgating catalog ignites first deal; looks to cook in NASCAR, NCAA, NFL. (1998). *Team Marketing Report* (August): 6.

40. Gilmore, J.H. (1998). Welcome to the experience economy.

41. Wascovich, T.R. (1993). *The sports marketing guide.* Cleveland: PointsAhead.

42. Mullin, B.J., Hardy, S., and Sutton, W.A. (2000). *Sport marketing.*

43. Arnheim, R. (1997). Schonberg's thought and the theory of music. *British Journal of Aesthetics* 37: 403-407.

44. Seeger, A. (1997). Traditional music in community life: Aspects of performance, recordings and preservation. *Cultural Survival Quarterly* 30: 20-28.

45. Brady, E. (2000). "Dogs out" at a park near you. *USA Today* (October 25): 3C.

46. Grossman, C.L. (2000). This Sunday, praise the Lord and pass the chips. *USA Today* (January 27): 9D.

47. Wascovich, T.R. (1993). *The sports marketing guide.*

48. Lieber, J. (2000). National anthem singer Hill can't hide allegiance to Titan. *USA Today* (January 31): 13C.

49. UNC broadcasts not as they seem. (1999). *Commercial Appeal* (February 2): D9.

50. Friedman, A. (2000). Change in concourse signs? You can smell it. *Street & Smith's SportBusiness Journal* (January 17-23): 15.

51. Shannon, J.R., and Turley, L.W. (1997). The influence of in-arena promotions on purchase behavior and purchase intentions. *Sport Marketing Quarterly* 6(4): 53-59.

52. Motsinger, S.E., Turner, E.T., and Evans, J.D. (1997). A comparison of food and beverage concession operations in three different types of North Carolina venues. *Sport Marketing Quarterly* 6(4): 43-52.

53. Gilmore, J.H. (1998). Welcome to the experience economy.

54. Melnick, M.J. (1993). Searching for sociability in the stands: A theory of sport spectating. *Journal of Sport Management* 7: 44-60.

55. Gilmore, J.H. (1998). Welcome to the experience economy.

56. Martin, C. (1990). The employee/customer interface: An empirical investigation of employee behaviors and customer perceptions. *Journal of Sport Management* 4: 1-20.

57. Martin, C. (1990). The employee/customer interface: An empirical investigation of employee behaviors and customer perceptions.

58. Kahle, L., and Elton, M. (1997). Sports talk and the development of marketing relationships. *Sport Marketing Quarterly* 6(2): 35-39.

59. Martin, C. (1990). The employee/customer interface: An empirical investigation of employee behaviors and customer perceptions.

60. Steward, M. (1999). Doggone it, Harvey's done. *Calgary Herald* (April 14): A-1.

61. Hiestand, M. (1999). Airborne hot-dogs taking off. *USA Today* (June 3): 2C.

62. Narvez, A. (1999). Ring announcer paid dues on the road. *Commercial Appeal* (November 27): D3.

63. Spoelstra, J. (1991). *How to sell the last seat in the house.*

64. Lieber, J. (2000). Turner belts out a new song with the same old intensity. *USA Today* (January 31): 13C.

65. Melnick, M.J. (1993). Searching for sociability in the stands: A theory of sport spectating.

66. Brady, E. (1999). Far-flung ideas put fan near action. *USA Today* (May 19): 7C.

67. Fort Wayne Fury creates business opportunities for ticket holders by setting tee times on the hardwood. (March, 2000). *Team Marketing Report* 12(3): 1, 3.

68. Kahle, L., and Elton, M. (1997). Sports talk and the development of marketing relationships.

69. Wascovich, T.R. (1993). *The sports marketing guide.*

Chapter 12

1. Kotler, P. (2001). *Principles of marketing.* 9th ed. Upper Saddle River, NJ: Prentice Hall.

2. Orwall, B. (2001). Thumbs up. *Wall Street Journal Reports. Entertainment and Technology* (March 26): R6.

3. *Screen Digest* [online]. (1999). **www.screendigest.com** (September).

4. Commerce.net. (2000). International Data Corporation. *Worldwide industry statistics* [online]. **www.commerce.net/research/stats/indust.html**.

5. Kotler, P. (2001). *Principles of marketing.*

6. Mullin, B., Hardy, S., and Sutton, W.A. (2000). *Sport marketing.* 2nd ed. Champaign, IL: Human Kinetics.

7. Beatty, S. (2001). Score! ESPN.com has a strong lead over its rivals. But the race is far from over. *Wall Street Journal Reports. Entertainment and Technology* (March 26): R9.

8. Keating, J. (1996). AT&T WorldNet high speed access strategy. Internal AT&T memorandum (August 19).

9. Dillon, J. (1996). DirectPC™, How turbo-Internet really works data sheet. Internal Hughes Network Systems document (February 28).

10. Hughes Electronics Corporation (1998). *DirectPC in Hughes Electronic Review* 1(2).

11. Orwall, B. (2001). Thumbs up. *Wall Street Journal Reports. Entertainment and Technology* (March 26): R6.

12. Liberman, N. (2000). Bengals turn to a real reporter, but will the truth hurt? *Street & Smith's SportsBusiness Journal* 3(4; May 15-21): 16.

13. Migala, D. (2000). Remember these 5 C's to make your content shine. *Street & Smith's SportsBusiness Journal* 3(13; July 17-23): 17.

14. Adams, H. (2000). Ignite Sports Media sees team Web sites as conduit for generating substantial revenue. *Street & Smith's SportsBusiness Journal* 2(52; April 17-30): 35-36.

15. Gould, B. and Gould, D. (2000). Rivals.com ranks as #1 site in stickiness for ten consecutive months. *Street & Smith's SportsBusiness Journal* 3(10; June 26-July 2): 39-40; Liberman, N. (2000). Sticky is sweet in Web world as sites try to keep users from straying. *Street & Smith's SportsBusiness Journal* 2 (37; January 3-9): 13.

16. Liberman, N. (2000). Beyond chat: Letting your visitors do the work that will draw traffic. *Street & Smith's SportsBusiness Journal* 3(10; June 26-July 2): 19.

17. Liberman, N. (2000). Beyond chat: Letting your visitors do the work that will draw traffic.

18. Liberman, N. (2000). If that message board is yours, learn from the Mets lesson: Monitor it. *Street & Smith's SportsBusiness Journal* 3(2; May 1-7): 16.

19. Milne, G., and McDonald, M. (1999). *Sport marketing: Managing the exchange process.* Sudbury, MA: Jones and Bartlett.

20. Adams, H. (2000). Ignite Sports Media sees team Web sites as conduit for generating substantial revenue. *Street & Smith's SportsBusiness Journal* 2(52): 35-36.

21. Sweet, D. (2000). The Web @ work/San Francisco Giants. *Wall Street Journal* (April 3): 10.

22. Sweet, D. (2000). The Web @ work/San Francisco Giants.

23. Pine, J.B., Peppers, D., and Rogers, M. (1995). Do you want to keep your customers forever? *Harvard Business Review* 73(2; March-April): 103-114.

24. Peppers, D., and Rogers, M. (1993). *The one to one future.* New York: Doubleday, Currency.

25. Peppers, D., Rogers, M., and Dorf, B. (1999). Is your company ready for one-to-one marketing? *Harvard Business Review* 77(1): 151-160.

26. Fleischman, G. (1999). Fresh from your browser's oven. *New York Times* (July 15).

27. Peppers, D., Rogers, M., and Dorf, B. (1999). Is your company ready for one-to-one marketing?

28. Inside 1to1. (2000, April 13). Glasgow Rangers score one to one. Peppers & Rogers, *Marketing 1 to 1, Inc.* [online]. **http://1to1.com/publications/inside1to1/il-041300/index.html**.

29. Godin, S. (1999). *Permission marketing.* New York: Simon and Schuster.

30. Godin, S. (1999). *Permission marketing.*

31. Mullin, B., Hardy, S., and Sutton, W.A. (2000). *Sport marketing.*

32. Fletcher Research (1999). Use of UK sports Internet sites. *Street & Smith's SportsBusiness Journal* 2(35; December 20-26): 31.

33. Garrahan, M. (2000). Internet slump hits Manchester United. *The Business of Sport. Financial Times* [online] (April 25). **www.ft.com/sport/bos/qa7fa.htm**.

34. Garrahan, M. (2000). Manchester United hits a billion. *The Business of Sport. Financial Times* [online] (March 8). **www.ft.com/sport/bos/q9ace.htm**; Stoddard, B. (2000). Managing change, managing sport or What do we do next coach. Keynote address to the Third International Sport Management Alliance Conference in conjunction with the 5th Annual Sport Management Association of Australia and New Zealand, Sydney, Australia, January.

35. Garrahan, M. (2000). Manchester United hits a billion.

36. Garrahan, M. (2000). Manchester United hits a billion.

37. Harris Sports Poll eSports Report. (2000). Reasons NASCAR fans visit sports Web sites. *Street & Smith's SportsBusiness Journal* 3(2; March): 17; Harris Sports Poll eSports Report. (2000). Reasons NBA fans visit sports Web sites. *Street & Smith's SportsBusiness Journal* 3(3; March): 19; Harris Sports Poll eSports Report. (2000). Reasons NHL fans visit sports Web sites. *Street & Smith's SportsBusiness Journal* 3(1; March): 17.

38. Friedman, A. (2000). Printing tickets from the Web will work only if priced properly. *Street & Smith's SportsBusiness Journal* 2(45; February 28-March 5): 15.

39. Zwartynski, M.A. (1998). Sports marketing and technology. Paper submitted to Dr. W.A. Sutton.

40. Wertheim, L.J. (1998). Now you see it. *Sports Illustrated* 89(8; August 24).

41. Zwartynski, M.A. (1998). Sports marketing and technology.

42. Zwartynski, M.A. (1998). Sports marketing and technology.

43. Zwartynski, M.A. (1998). Sports marketing and technology.

44. Hiestand, M. (2000). Paralympics on line to test live market. *USA Today* (July 25): C9.

45. Stuart, J. (2000). Glasgow Celtic takes a historic shot on the net. *Street & Smith's SportsBusiness Journal* 3(19; August 28-September 3): 35.

46. Financial Times Service. (2000). He turns, he shoots, he scores—on broadband. *Irish Times on the Web.* Finance section [online] (August 4). **http://scripts.ireland.com/search/highlight.plx?TextRes= Broadband%20and%20Soccer&Path=/newspaper/finance/2000/0804/persfin9.htm**.

47. Financial Times Service. (2000). He turns, he shoots, he scores—on broadband.

48. Guider, I. (2000). Ireland to cash in on mobile boom. *Sunday Times Business* (August 13).

49. Tull. (2000). Introduction to WAP [online]. **http://AYG.com/content.Po?name=wap/overview**.

50. Orwall (2001). Thumbs up.

Chapter 13

1. Wong, G.M. (1994). *Essentials of amateur sports law.* 2nd ed. Westport, CT: Praeger, 65-68.

2. Berry, R.C., and Wong, G.M. (1993). *Law and business of the sports industries.* Westport, CT: Praeger, 331.

3. Berry, R.C., and Wong, G.M. (1993). *Law and business of the sports industries,* 332.

4. Wong, G.M. (1994). *Essentials of amateur sports law.* 2nd ed., 73-74.

5. Berry, R.C., and Wong, G.M. (1993). *Law and business of the sports industries,* 333.

6. Wong, G.M. (1994). *Essentials of amateur sports law.* 2nd ed., 381.

7. Reprinted from Greenberg, M.J., 1993, *Sports law practice* (Charlottesville, VA: Michie).

8. Wong, G.M. (2000). Sit-down strike: The validity of an arena's club seat license agreement is upheld. *Athletic Business* 24(1): 22.

9. Wong, G.M. (1994). *Essentials of amateur sports law.* 2nd ed., 348-349.

10. Yasser, R., McCurdy, J.R., and Goplerud, C.P. (1997). *Sports law: Cases and materials.* 3rd ed. Cincinnati: Anderson, 675.

11. Wong, G.M. (1994). *Essentials of amateur sports law.* 2nd ed., 350-353.

12. Berry, R.C., and Wong, G.M. (1993). *Law and business of the sports industries,* 401-402.

13. Yasser, R., McCurdy, J.R., and Goplerud, C.P. (1997). *Sports law: Cases and materials,* 674.

14. Wong, G.M. (1994). *Essentials of amateur sports law.* 2nd ed., 356.

15. Berry, R.C., and Wong, G.M. (1993). *Law and business of the sports industries,* 404-405.

16. Wong, G.M. (1994). *Essentials of amateur sports law.* 2nd ed., 368-370.

17. Yasser, R., McCurdy, J.R., and Goplerud, C.P. (1997). *Sports law: Cases and materials,* 676.

18. Berry, R.C., and Wong, G.M. (1993). *Law and business of the sports industries,* 421.

19. Wong, G.M. (1994). *Essentials of amateur sports law.* 2nd ed., 374-375.

20. Wong, G.M. (1994). *Essentials of amateur sports law.* 2nd ed., 375-376.

21. Berry, R.C., and Wong, G.M. (1993). *Law and business of the sports industries,* 429.

22. Berry, R.C., and Wong, G.M. (1993). *Law and business of the sports industries,* 535-565.

23. For more cases involving negligence see Wong, G.M., 1994, *Essentials of amateur sports law,* 2nd ed., chapter 7, "Application of Tort Law."

24. *Lowe v. California League of Professional Baseball, et.al.,* 65 Cal. Rptr. 2d 105 (1997).

25. *Yates v. Chicago National League Ball Club, Inc.,* 595 N.E.2d 570 (1992).

26. *Hayden v. University of Notre Dame,* 716 N.E.2d 603 (1999).

27. *Bearman v. University of Notre Dame,* 453 N.E.2d 1196 (1983).

28. *Gil de Rebello v. The Miami Heat et. al.,* 137 F. 3d 56 (1998).

29. Another case in which a mascot was involved in tort liability was *Seidel v. Giles; Philadelphia Phillies,* Common Pleas Court 91-12-1807 Pa. (Nov. 1995).

30. *Leon v. Family Fitness Center,* 71 Cal Rptr. 2d 923 (1998).

31. *Leon v. Family Fitness Center,* 71 Cal Rptr. 2d 923 (1998).

32. The following are other cases in which a court has decided not to uphold a waiver and release of liability: *Brown v. Racquetball Centers, Inc.,* 534 A. 2d 842 Pa. Super. (1987); *Doyle v. Bowdoin College,* 403 A. 2d 1206 (1979); *Jeter v. Remelar, Inc.,* 1995, Fla. Jury Verdict Review and Analysis 5:7-8 (9), case no. 92-24725.

33. *Reed v. University of North Dakota,* 589 N.W. 2d 880 (1999).

34. The following are cases in which a court has upheld a valid waiver and release of liability: *Cabbage Patch Settlement House v. Wheatly,* 987 S.W. 2d 784 (1999); *Watts v. Country Cycle Club,* 655 N.Y.S. 2d 422 (1997); *Gara v. Woodbridge Tavern,* 568 N.W. 2d 138 (1997).

35. For more information on waivers and releases of liability see Cotten, Doyice, J. and Mary, B., 1997, *Legal aspects of waivers in sport, recreation and fitness activities* (Canton, OH: PRC).

36. For more detailed information on risk management plans, refer to Appenzeller, H., 1993, *Managing sports and risk management strategies* (Durham, NC: Carolina Press); Peterson, J.A., 1987, *Risk management for park, recreation, and leisure services* (Champaign, IL: Management Learning Laboratories); Sawyer, T.H., and Smith, O., 1999, *The management of clubs, recreation and sport* (Champaign, IL: Sagamore).

37. Wong, G.M. (1994). *Essentials of amateur sports law.* 2nd ed., 599.

38. Berry, R.C., and Wong, G.M. (1993). *Law and business of the sports industries,* 633.

39. Wong, G.M. *Essentials of amateur sports law.* 3rd ed. In press. Westport, CT: Praeger.

40. Wong, G.M. (1994). *Essentials of amateur sports law.* 3rd ed.

41. Berry, R.C., and Wong, G.M. (1993). *Law and business of the sports industries,* 630.

42. Wong, G.M. (1994). *Essentials of amateur sports law.* 3rd ed.

43. Wong, G.M. (1994). *Essentials of amateur sports law.* 2nd ed., 608-609.

44. Reprinted from "Minor League Preview 2000," 2000, *Baseball America* 20(8; April 17-30): 13.

45. For a case dealing with international intellectual property law, refer to *ISL Marketing and Federation Internationale de Football Association v. Nutt,* case no. D2000-0363, World Intellectual Property Organization Administrative Panel Decision, July 17, 2000.

46. For more information on common-law rights to a trademark refer to *White v. Board of Regents of the University of Nebraska at Lincoln,* 614 N.W. 2d 330 (2000).

47. See the following cases that deal with licensing arrangements for professional sport: *Gridiron.com, Inc. v. National Football League, Player's Association, Inc. et al.,* 106 F. Supp. 2d 1309 (2000); *Major League Baseball Player's Association v. Dad's Kid Corp.,* 806 F. Supp. 458 S.D.N.Y. (1992). See the following cases dealing with licensing arrangements for intercollegiate sports: *Texas A&M University System v. University Book Store, Inc.,* Court of Appeals for the Tenth Supreme Judicial District of Texas at Waco, no. 10-84-088 CV (1984) (unreported decision); *University of Pittsburgh v. Champion Products, Inc.,* 686 F. 2d 1040 3d Cir. (1982), Cert. Denied, 459 U.S. 1087 (1982).

48. For additional information on licensing and intellectual property in professional sport, see the following articles: CNNSI.com, 2001, Joining forces: Yankees, Manchester United announce joint marketing deal (February 6); ESPN.com, 2000, Court curtails Gridiron.com's activities (July 12).

49. Wong, G.M. (1994). *Essentials of amateur sports law.* 2nd ed., 608-609.

50. For a case that dealt with ambush marketing in sport see *National Hockey League, et al. v. Pepsi-Cola Canada Ltd.,* Supreme Court of British Columbia (Vancouver Registry), no. c902104 (1992).

51. For the full decision in the *Maxwell v. Veeck* case, visit the "Legal Research" section at Lexus-Nexus Academic Universe, and enter the citation information, *Maxwell v. Veeck,* 110 F.3d 749 (1997).

52. For more information on intellectual property issues and trading cards see the following cases: *Major League Baseball Properties, Inc. v. Pacific Trading Cards. Inc.,* 150 F. 3d 149 2d Cir. (1998); *Dream Team Collectibles, Inc. v. NBA Properties, Inc. et al.,* 958 F. Supp. 1401 E.D. Missouri (1997); *Cardtoons, L.C. v. Major League Baseball Player's Association,* 95 F. 3d 959 10th Cir. (1996).

53. For more information on sport broadcasts and the law, see a case dealing with real-time updates: *National Basketball Association, Inc. v. Motorola, Inc.,* 105 F. 3d 841 2d Cir. (1997); a case involving footage of a boxing match: *Monster Communications Inc. v. Turner Broadcasting System, Inc. et al.,* 935 F. Supp. 490 S.D.N.Y. (1996); an influential decision on who owns the rights to broadcasts in NCAA football: *NCAA v. Board of Regents of University of Oklahoma,* 468 U.S. 85 (1984).

54. For more information on the rebroadcast of copyrighted broadcasts for highlight purposes see the following case: *New Boston Television v. Entertainment Sports Programming Network, Inc.,* 1981 WL 1374, 81 D. Ma. (1981).

55. 1999-2000 San Antonio Spurs media guide. San Antonio: San Antonio Spurs.

Chapter 14

1. McKenna, R. (1991). *Relationship marketing.* Reading, MA: Addison-Wesley, 4.

2. Vavra, T. (1992). *Aftermarketing: How to keep customers through relationship marketing.* Burr Ridge, IL: Irwin, 22.

3. For an excellent theoretical examination of this topic see Berry, L.L., 1983, Relationship marketing, in *Emerging perspectives on services marketing,* ed. L. Berry, G.L. Shostack, and G. Upah (Chicago: American Marketing Association).

4. Mullin, B., Hardy, S., and Sutton, W.A. (2000). *Sport marketing.* 2nd ed. Champaign, IL: Human Kinetics, 13-14.

5. Gordon, I. (1998). *Relationship marketing.* Toronto: Wiley, 9.

6. For a comprehensive examination of this program see Mullin, B., Hardy, S., and Sutton, W.A., 2000, *Sport marketing*, 229-232.

7. Liberman, N. (2000). Report reveals where the money is online, plus other Web truths. *Street & Smith's SportsBusiness Journal* 2(48; March 20-26): 17.

8. Blanchard, K., and Bowles, S. (1993). *Raving fans*. New York: Morrow, 23-70.

9. Miller, L.K., and Fielding, L.W. (1997). Ticket distribution agencies and professional sport franchises: The successful partnership. *Sport Marketing Quarterly* 6(1): 48.

10. Frost, M. (2000). Choice seat presentation at the NBA 2000 Marketing Meetings, Denver, Colorado, March 13.

11. Brenner, S. (1997). Pursuing relationships in professional sport. *Sport Marketing Quarterly* 6(2): 33.

12. Mullin, B., Hardy, S., and Sutton, W.A. (2000). *Sport marketing*, 247-248.

13. The material in this section was based in part on the work of Gordon, I., 1998, *Relationship marketing*, 10-16.

14. Mullin, B., Hardy, S., and Sutton, W.A. (2000). *Sport marketing*, 44.

15. Blanchard, K., and Bowles, S. (1993). *Raving fans*, 52.

16. Poole, M. (2000). Some sports execs have their fingers firmly on their fans' pulse. *Street & Smith's SportsBusiness Journal* 3(8; June 12-18): 13.

17. Compiled from Anderson, K., and Zemke, R., 1991, *Delivering knock your socks off service* (New York: Amacom), 36-38.

18. Spector, R., and McCarthy, P.D. (1995). *The Nordstrom way*. New York: Wiley, 15-16.

19. Spector, R., and McCarthy, P.D. (1995). *The Nordstrom way*, 23.

20. Adapted from Anderson, K., and Zemke, R., 1991, *Delivering knock your socks off service*, 99-102.

21. Shani, D., and Calasani, S. (1992). Exploiting niches using relationship marketing. *Journal of Consumer Marketing* 9(3): 33-44.

22. McDonald, M.A., and Milne, G.R. (1997). A conceptual framework for evaluating marketing relationships in professional sport franchises. *Sport Marketing Quarterly* 6(2): 27-32.

23. Jackson, R., and Wang, P. (1994). *Strategic database marketing*. Lincolnwood, IL: NTC Business Books.

24. McDonald, M.A. (1996). Service quality and customer lifetime value in professional sport franchises. Unpublished doctoral dissertation, University of Massachusetts-Amherst, 44-45.

25. Sutton, W.A. (1997). SMQ profile/interview: Don Johnson. *Sport Marketing Quarterly* 6(2): 5-8.

26. For an excellent model that takes these factors into account see McDonald, M.A., 1996, Service quality and customer lifetime value in professional sport franchises.

27. Lapio, R. Jr., and Speter, K.M. (2000). NASCAR: A lesson in integrated and relationship marketing. *Sport Marketing Quarterly* 9(2): 85-95.

28. Adapted from Anderson, K., and Zemke, R., 1991, *Delivering knock your socks off service*, 126-128.

29. Vavra, T.G. (1997). *Improving your measurement of customer satisfaction*. Milwaukee: ASQ Quality Press.

30. Zyman, S. (1999). *The end of marketing as we know it*. New York: Harper Business, 79.

31. Williams, P. (1995). *Go for the magic*. Nashville: Nelson, 37.

32. Wolf, M. (1999). *The entertainment economy*. New York: Random House, 45.

33. Wolf, M. (1999). *The entertainment economy*, 63.

34. Pine, B.J., and Gilmore, J.H. (1999). *The experience economy*. Boston: Harvard Business School Press, 4.

35. Pine, B.J., and Gilmore, J.H. (1999). *The experience economy*, 16-17.

36. Hardy, S.H., and Sutton, W.A. (1999). The SMQ and the sport marketplace: Where we've been and where we're going. *Sport Marketing Quarterly* 8(4): 11.

37. Pine, B.J., and Gilmore, J.H. (1999). *The experience economy*, 41.

INDEX

Note: The italicized *f* and *t* refer to figures and tables, respectively.

Richard Irwin, EdD, joined the University of Memphis department of human movement sciences and education faculty as an associate professor in 1994. In addition to serving as coordinator for the Sport and Leisure Studies Unit (composed of the undergraduate sport and leisure studies and graduate sport and leisure commerce degree programs), Dr. Irwin is the director of the Bureau of Sport and Leisure Commerce at the University of Memphis. He has also served as the director of sales and marketing for the AXA Liberty Bowl, an annual college postseason football game, since 2000 as well as a member of the Memphis/Shelby County Sport Authority Board of Advisors since 1998. Along with coauthor William Sutton, Dr. Irwin served as coprincipal for Audience Analysts, a sport and event market research consultancy agency. Dr. Irwin has been a contributing author for several textbooks as well as the author of more than 50 articles while delivering presentations at international, national, regional, and state conferences.

William A. Sutton serves as vice president of Team Marketing Services, for the National Basketball Association (NBA) and holds an appointment as professor in the sports studies department at the University of Massachusetts at Amherst. Prior to assuming his present positions, Dr. Sutton was a principal in the consulting firm Audience Analysts and had worked for such clients as the NBA, NFL, NHL, Major League Baseball Properties, LPGA, NCAA, Hoop-It-Up, IBM, Mazda, and Sprint. He has also served as vice president for information services at Del Wilber + Associates, a sport and lifestyle marketing agency; as coordinator of the sport management program at The Ohio State University; and was a faculty member at Robert Morris College. A former president of the North American Society for Sport Management (NASSM), Dr. Sutton has also served as coeditor of *Sport Marketing Quarterly* and serves on the editorial board of the *Journal of Sports Marketing & Sponsorship.* Dr. Sutton is widely published in sport marketing and has made more than 100 national and international presentations. He is a coauthor of the text *Sport Marketing* (Human Kinetics, 2000). A graduate of Oklahoma State University (1972, 1980, 1983), he was named Sport Marketer of the Year in 1998 by the Cyber Journal of Sport Marketing. Dr. Sutton resides in Amherst, Massachusetts, and can be reached at **wsutton@nba.com**.

Larry M. McCarthy, PhD, was born in Cork, Ireland. He graduated from The Ohio State University in December 1993, with a PhD in sport management. He is an associate professor of management at the W. Paul Stillman School of Business at Seton Hall University where he teaches in the Center for Sport Management. Prior to that appointment, he was the Graduate Sport Management Program coordinator in the Department of Recreation and Sport Management at Georgia Southern University. He holds an MA from New York University (NYU) and a BEd from the National University of Ireland (NUI). His research interests focus on the activities of professional sport franchises, cross-cultural studies, and international sport management. He has published articles in national and international journals and has presented his research work at regional, national, and international conferences. He was appointed by the Atlanta Committee for the Olympic Games (ACOG) as an Olympic Envoy to the Olympic Council of Ireland for the Centennial Olympic Games.

You'll find
other outstanding
sport management resources at

www.humankinetics.com

In the U.S. call

1-800-747-4457

Australia 08 8277 1555
Canada 1-800-465-7301
Europe .... +44 (0) 113 278 1708
New Zealand 09-523-3462

HUMAN KINETICS
The Information Leader in Physical Activity
P.O. Box 5076 • Champaign, IL 61825-5076 USA

RECEIVED

– 8 JAN 2003

- - - - - - - - - - - - - - - -